INSIDERS' GUIDE® TO
SAVANNAH AND HILTON HEAD

Help Us Keep This Guide Up to Date

Every effort has been made by the authors and editors to make this guide as accurate and useful as possible. However, many things can change after a guide is published—establishments close, phone numbers change, hiking trails are rerouted, facilities come under new management, etc.

We would love to hear from you concerning your experiences with this guide and how you feel it could be improved and be kept up to date. While we may not be able to respond to all comments and suggestions, we'll take them to heart and we'll also make certain to share them with the authors. Please send your comments and suggestions to the following address:

The Globe Pequot Press
Reader Response/Editorial Department
P.O. Box 480
Guilford, CT 06437

Or you may e-mail us at:

editorial@globe-pequot.com

Thanks for your input, and happy travels!

Insiders' Guide®
to Savannah and
Hilton Head

FOURTH EDITION

By Rich Wittish and Betty Darby

INSIDERS'
►GUIDE®

Guilford, Connecticut
An imprint of The Globe Pequot Press

Copyright © 2002 by The Globe Pequot Press
Previous editions of this book were published by Falcon Publishing, Inc. in 1999 and 2000.

Cover by Wendell Metzen, Index Stock

Maps by Eric West

ISBN: 0-7627-1045-4

Manufactured in the United States of America
Fourth Edition/First Printing

Contents

Directory of Maps

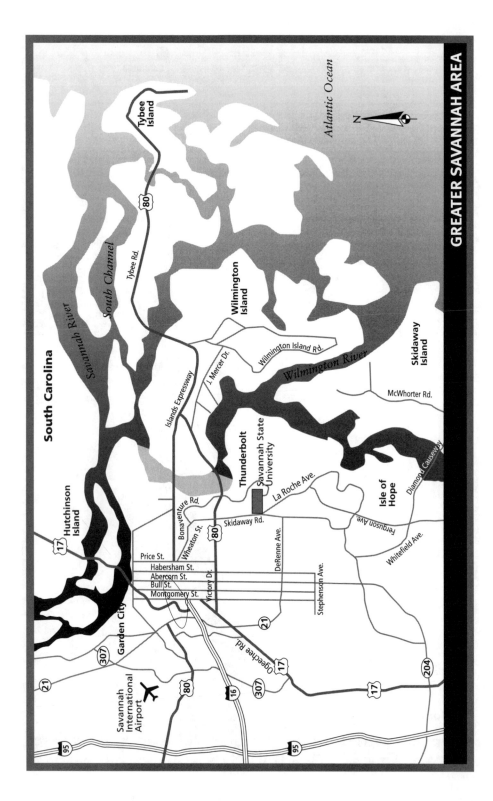

GREATER SAVANNAH AREA

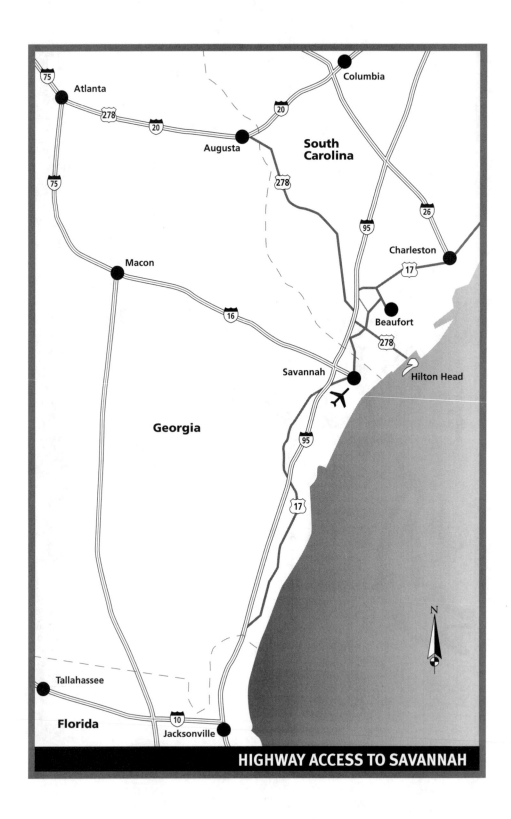

HIGHWAY ACCESS TO SAVANNAH

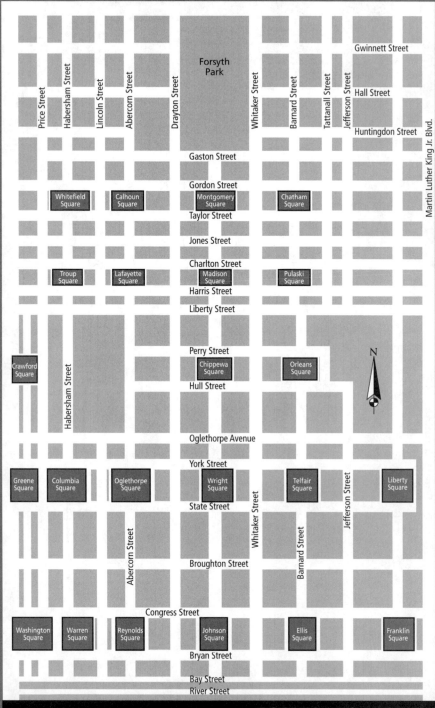

DOWNTOWN SAVANNAH

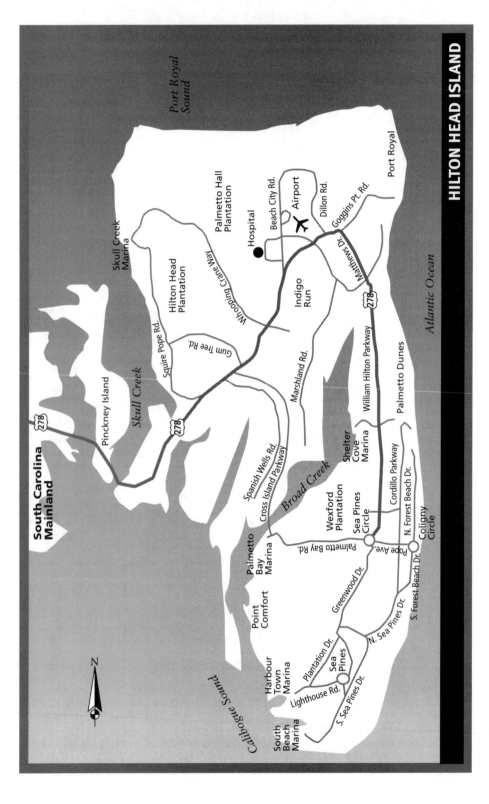

Preface

We're having a wonderful time in Savannah, and we're glad that you are coming to join us. That's not just a postcard cliche. Savannah calls herself the Hostess City, and a traditionally welcoming attitude toward visitors is part of that legacy.

Long before tourism was considered an industry, hospitality was regarded around Savannah as something akin to religion. If you aren't gracious to guests, you "don't know how to act" and are "an embarrassment to your mother"—two of the deadliest faults possible in the South's social self-portrait. So relax: You are about to tour a city composed of people who, by and large, do know how to act and who have very proud mothers.

With the fourth edition of this book, we hope to give you the flavor of a city we have come to love, along with all the facts and figures you need to get yourself housed, entertained, fed, and properly toured. No, we're not native Savannahians—that's a multigenerational thing—but between the two of us, we've logged more than forty-five years in our adopted city. Job commitments brought us here with no real avowed intention of remaining, but over the years we forgot to leave.

Savannah is that kind of place. You could build a case that Savannah is a living laboratory for demonstrating the relativity of time. Time does seem to move at a different clip here. Change takes place slowly and is accepted even more slowly. Maybe *languidly* is a better term than *slowly,* because it emphasizes that there is something deliberate and intentional about this pacing. Pick the right hour at one of the downtown squares, when the traffic is still, look around at the massive oaks and stately town homes, and you could easily erase 100, even 150 years off the calendar. Pick a marsh view at sunset, and you could erase a few thousand.

But don't get the impression we're a moldy, moss-draped museum, either. The corporate bigwigs and entertainment moguls of the day jet through the skies on corporate aircraft built here. The Port of Savannah is one of the nation's busiest, taking in goods from throughout the world. Baryshnikov danced here; Blues Traveler rocked here; our symphony puts on 300 performances in a season (we're fudging a little—that includes ensemble sessions, but you get the point). There's diversity in our universities and colleges. In short, Savannah has a place in the world's appointment books of today, not just in the history books.

Now, on to business. We've shared lots of things to do in these pages, based on years of entertaining visiting friends and relatives (and ourselves, too). We'll tell you how to chow down on some of the most delectable food imaginable and how to hole up in some of the most charming bed-and-breakfasts in the country. Parasailing, meeting alligators, retracing history, buying antiques, beach bumming, taking yourself out to the ol' ball game—we tell you where and how (and how much it costs) to tap into these activities.

Additionally, if you've fallen in love with Savannah long distance thanks to a certain best-selling book or any one of several popular movies, we've included some tips on how to arrange your own personal brush with *Midnight in the Garden of Good and Evil* or Savannah's film docket.

This is our fourth edition, newly updated and revised. The bulk of the changes are in predictable areas, as Savannah's restaurant, lodging, and nightlife scenes grow and change to accommodate her growing popularity. Revision and updating remains an ongoing process, to make sure that what you find within the pages of the guide you picked up last week accurately depicts the city you will find on your visit next week. You are invited to be part of this process. Comments, critiques, and suggestions are welcome, and they can be shared easily with us and our publishers, either online or on paper. (See How to Use This Book for details.)

Savannah gives herself lots of names, and others have added to the list: the Hostess City, the Coastal Empire, the Garden of Good and Evil, the Sovereign State of Chatham (Chatham County, that is), and so on. We firmly believe that, after your visit, you'll name her one of your favorite vacation destinations. We wager you'll be back. Like us, you may even forget to leave.

Acknowledgments

Writing a book of this scope involves obtaining a lot of help from a lot of people. With that in mind, I offer special thanks to the following: John Burke and Michael Richter, who provided valuable information and insights for the fishing and boating sections of the Parks and Recreation chapter; Becky Bowden, who helped me get started in the right direction when I began writing the Hilton Head chapter; Ron Perry, a Hilton Head Realtor who aided me in gathering data on the island's planned communities; journalist Richard Fogaley, who gave us much-needed advice concerning Savannah's restaurants; Phyl Gatlin, who provided photographs for the Close-Up in the Restaurants chapter; Preston Russell and Barbara Hines, authors of a splendid history of Savannah who graciously checked this book's History chapter for accuracy and content; Martha Giddens Nesbit, who allowed us to use a recipe from her *Savannah Collection* cookbook; and Cheryl Lauer, who lent her photographic skills to this endeavor along with encouraging words when they were needed.

Thanks also to many other folks who took time out of their busy schedules to talk with me or otherwise assist me. Among them are a horde of public relations and marketing specialists and other people who served as spokespersons for their respective businesses, agencies, and organizations. Those who were especially helpful were, from Savannah, Jenny Stacy of the Savannah Area Chamber of Commerce, John Howell of the Metropolitan Planning Commission, Lara Hadley of the City of Savannah's Cultural Affairs Department, Ed Poenicke of the Chatham County Extension Service, Gordon Varnedoe of the Savannah Waterfront Association, Sue Cole and Harris Lentini of Oatland Island Education Center, Elizabeth Stewart of Savannah Onstage, Henry Lewandoski of Chatham County Mosquito Control, Scott Smith of the Coastal Heritage Society, Dr. Carol Brown of the Dr. Martin Luther King Jr. Observance Day Association, Mike Beytagh of the St. Patrick's Day Parade Committee, Margie Richter of Discover Montessori School, Janice Lewis of Maggie's Morning School, Bonnie Eminger of the Child Care Licensing Section of the Georgia Department of Human Resources, Earl Etheridge of the City of Savannah's Department of Recreation Services, Vicki Blumberg and Anthony Russell of Chatham County's Department of Parks, Recreation and Cultural Affairs, Danny McConnell of the YMCA of Coastal Georgia, Pat Metz of the U.S. Fish and Wildlife Service, Chica Arndt of Wormsloe Historic Site, and Duane Harris, Stuart Stevens, and Terry West of the Coastal Resources Division of the Georgia Department of Natural Resources.

Special thanks also to Hilton Head islanders Amanda Loniero of the Hilton Head Chamber of Commerce, Carole Doremus of Sea Pines, Manny Peralta of the Spanish Wells Property Owners Association, and Ed Drane, Bud Culbertson, and Nan Johnson of the Town of Hilton Head Island. Many thanks to my editor, Erin Turner.

And thanks most of all to my wife, Linda, and daughter, Erica, for the love and support they gave me, particularly when the light at the end of the Insiders' Guide tunnel seemed somewhat dim.

—Rich Wittish

A massive project such as this can be daunting at best. Thanks to the help of dedicated professionals in the information field and ordinary Savannahians who were eager to share the good parts of our city, I was able to enjoy myself along the way.

Much of the information that goes into such a project comes by way of professional "question-answerers." Any well-run organization of any size has at least one individual or department, variously known as the public relations department, public affairs office, media contact, official spokesperson, and so on, whose job it is to field questions. Although it's their job to pass on information, they are to be commended for their cheerful attitude, enthusiasm about their mission, and attention to detail. One hesitates to start naming names in this category for fear of leaving someone out, so I'm intentionally keeping my list short here. The Savannah Police Department provided a solid briefing on alcohol regulations and their enforcement. Jay Self from the city's film office spared me time during a hectic premiere week. Everyone at Senior Citizens Inc. made a special effort to help me understand their many missions.

Writers take shameless advantage of their friends and family when working on such projects. My friends, acquaintances, and even coworkers no doubt tired of me constantly asking things like, "Yeah, but where else do you take visitors?" and "Where do you go at night when you don't go home?" I also leaned heavily on the expertise of friends. Cheryl Lauer took my photo and allowed herself be recruited as photo liaison for the first edition. Suzanne Aikens was a big help on musical questions, for example, and Midge Schildkraut filled me in on Savannah's Jewish community. My mother, Rosalyn Darby, let me drag her along on tours to get an outsider's viewpoint (although that didn't work too well, since she's been a regular visitor to the city for years). She even accompanied the small group I put together for my research mission to the drag show, and she says she had a nice time.

I shouldn't forget to give thanks to those who gave us something worth writing about. Savannah was planned, built, and preserved by visionaries, known and unknown, and populated in both the past and present by people interesting and hospitable enough to make it worth visiting (and living in). With that in mind, special thanks to anyone who preserved a building or defended a tree that a developer thought was inconveniently placed.

A closing word of thanks goes to Coleman Prophett, B. C. Akins, and Tommy Toles, the leaders of my first newsroom, who recognized the importance of teaching the trade to wet-behind-the-ears journalism students.

—Betty Darby

How to Use This Book

We hope you'll treat this book as you would a valued traveling companion, taking it with you wherever you go during your time in Savannah, Tybee Island, and Hilton Head and consulting it whenever you need help, advice, or answers to questions. Don't leave it home alone or in your hotel room; stick it in your travel bag, briefcase, or backpack so you'll have it handy when you need information on where to eat, shop, or spend the night.

We've organized this book so you can flip to whatever subjects interest you, while bypassing those that don't. Of course, it's our hope that eventually you'll take a look at every chapter, because each contains valuable information and tips. Even if you're not a history buff, for instance, it's probably a good idea to read the History chapter early in the game so that you can have an understanding of Savannah's past—a past that plays a vital role in its present and comes alive when you walk along the city's streets and through its magnificent squares.

For the most part, we've arranged the content of chapters geographically, then alphabetically within geographic sections. This was done in an effort to make restaurants, accommodations, attractions, and other points of interest as easy as possible to find. We've divided the local area into four sections; you'll find an explanation of the territory the sections cover in the Area Overview chapter, and you can see where they are by referring to the maps at the front of the book. Another good way to find specific topics of interest is by looking in the extensive index in the back of the book. You'll note that the area code for almost every phone number listed is 912 (843 in the case of places in South Carolina).

In addition to giving you a full rundown on the many topics you might expect to find in a guidebook, we've included a couple of chapters regarding subjects unique to Savannah. One chapter is entitled Savannah: Hollywood of the South and involves the phenomenon that is *Midnight in the Garden of Good and Evil*, the best-seller that has made the city a mecca for its readers. The other special chapter concerns Savannah's celebration of St. Patrick's Day, the city's favorite holiday.

We know that plenty of folks who make it to Savannah also have Hilton Head, South Carolina, on their travel itinerary. With this in mind, we have included a thorough chapter

Vine-draped steps mount to the parlor floor of an historic home downtown. PHOTO: BETTY DARBY

on Hilton Head, providing information on its history, accommodations, popular planned residential communities, restaurants and nightlife and, of course, golf and tennis. In turn, we have also devoted an entire chapter to another nearby destination that you may not be so familiar with—fun and quirky little Tybee Island.

We've done our darnedest to make this book as comprehensive and accurate as possible and to include the best that our area has to offer, and we've covered a lot of territory. Naturally, when you take on a project that's as massive and challenging as this one, you realize that omissions are inevitable and that most everyone has different tastes and opinions. If you discover a favorite restaurant, nightspot, shop, or other business that we've missed or something that's in error, please let us know so it can be added or corrected in future editions. We'll be updating, improving, and expanding our guide on a regular basis. Contact us with comments or suggestions online at www.insiders.com, or write us at:

Insiders' Guide to Savannah
The Globe Pequot Press
P.O. Box 480
Guilford, CT 06437

Area Overview

Head south to Savannah through South Carolina on U.S. Highway 17, and you find yourself on a two-lane road winding through marshland and passing by a few "gentlemen's clubs" that were video poker parlors and fireworks stands in their past lives. You're in the far reaches of the Lowcountry, and if you didn't know better, you'd swear you were in a desert... a desert where marsh grass stands in for sand. You're becoming convinced that you've driven all the way to Nowhere—that you've exiled yourself by automobile to the end of the world.

Then you round a bend of the highway, and suddenly you're staring at civilization in the form of the graceful towers of the Eugene Talmadge Memorial Bridge. Travel a bit farther, and you see the horizon to the left of the bridge filling with the low skyline of a city. In a few minutes, you leave South Carolina and the marsh behind and begin crossing the Savannah River into Georgia. On your left as you ascend the bridge is Hutchinson Island, where a recently built convention center and sixteen-story hotel herald the creation of a resort area. Cresting the crown of the bridge, you're 196 feet above the water and looking down and ahead toward your destination, the city of Savannah.

Glancing to your left, you see the golden dome of City Hall and a riverfront of brick cotton warehouses that have been converted into shops and restaurants. Beyond the waterfront, a canopy of trees stretches to the south, interrupted here and there by the spires of churches and the upper floors of a hotel, several office buildings, and an apartment complex or two. Off to your right, the river is bordered by manufacturing plants and the docks, warehouses, and towering cranes of the Georgia Ports Authority. Straight ahead is a network of roadways, with some of the thoroughfares leading to the Southside, where many Savannahians live and many more do their shopping.

This seagull's-eye view of the area gives you a pretty good idea of the lay of the land, and your tires haven't even settled on Georgia ground yet. As you read deeper into this chapter, we'll give you a more complete picture of the region, including brief looks at some places you can't readily see from the bridge—Savannah's inshore islands.

As we mentioned in our How to Use This Book chapter, we've arranged many of the chapters in this guide by geographic sections. The boundaries and makeup of those sections are discussed here. Before we get into that, however, let us toss your way some nice-to-know, getting-grounded information about the Savannah area.

Savannah Statistics

Savannah is the seat of government of Chatham County, one of the most populous counties in the largest state (in terms of area) east of the Mississippi River. Some 232,000 people live in Chatham, with 131,510 residing within Savannah's city limits. About a quarter of the county's 443 square miles are unincorporated, and there are also seven other municipalities within Chatham's borders: Bloomingdale, Garden City, Port Wentworth, Pooler, Thunderbolt, Vernonburg, and the city of Tybee Island.

The people who live here have a broad variety of backgrounds, jobs, and interests, which is what you might expect from a place that dates back to 1733 and serves as a port, a center of higher education, a tourist destination, a site for industrial plants, a home to the military, and a mecca

3

percentage of folks sixty-five and older increasing. The experts say this situation is the result of several factors, including a lower birth rate, the aging of the baby boomers, increased longevity due to medical advancements and healthier lifestyles, and the county's growing popularity as a retirement community.

The area's nonagricultural economy is diversified, with 30 percent of the workforce involved in services and healthcare, 26 percent in retailing and wholesaling, 15 percent in government, 13 percent in manufacturing, 7 percent in transportation and utilities, 6 percent in construction, and 3 percent in insurance, real estate, and financial services. Among the county's major employers are Memorial Health University Medical Center, St. Joseph's and Candler Hospitals, the Kroger supermarket chain, Gulfstream Aerospace Corporation, International Paper Company, Great Dane Trailers, Kerr-McGee, Hunter Army Airfield, the Savannah-Chatham County Board of Education and the governments of Georgia, Savannah, and the county. A trio of large-scale employers joined them recently: J. C. Bamford Excavators, which manufactures heavy construction equipment and hired 550 workers for a plant that opened here in February 2000; a Pitney Bowes customer service center that employs 300 people and began training workers in the summer of 1998; and the Lummus Corp., which makes cotton-ginning equipment, opened its plant here in January 1999 and has a workforce of 140.

According to the Georgia Department of Labor, a total of 140,000 people were employed in the Savannah area in December 2000, with the region's unemployment rate at 2.7 percent. Average weekly earnings in Chatham County in July 1999 were $786.83.

The Savannah area is blessed with a climate classified as semitropical. Average seasonal temperatures are 51 in winter, 66 in spring, 81 in summer, and 68 in autumn. From these figures, you can see that the best times to visit (as far as most

for artists and historic preservationists. Because of its history, diversity, and charms, Savannah is a melting pot: Grab a morning cup of coffee at the Express Cafe & Bakery on Barnard Street, and you could be standing in line with a college student who just blew in from the North or a society matron whose ancestors walked up the Savannah River bluff with Georgia's founder, James Edward Oglethorpe.

Chatham County's population is about 55 percent white, 40.5 percent African American, 2 percent Asian, and 2 percent Hispanic. The growth rate from 1990 through 2000 was 7 percent, and projections indicate the county will continue to grow until the year 2015 at an annual rate of from 0.7 percent to 1.5 percent, depending on which study you look at. Savannah's population is also getting older, with the percentage of people twenty-five and younger declining and the

Savannah's riverfront features a plaza and one-time cotton warehouses that have been converted into shops and restaurants. PHOTO: BETTY DARBY

folks are concerned) are the spring and fall. The days can get mighty hot and sticky during the summer—according to the Savannah Area Chamber of Commerce, the city on average experiences sixty-seven days each year when the mercury climbs higher than 90.

Winters are fairly mild, with the temperature dipping below freezing an average of (ironically) thirty-two days a year. We seldom see snow, and the descent of even a few flakes is cause for excitement. The average annual rainfall is 48.2 inches, and Mother Nature delivers some frog-choking downpours now and then, particularly during the summer in the afternoons. Because Savannah is in a low-lying area and much of the city's sewer system is antiquated, streets are prone to

flooding when tides are high—be careful if you're driving around and get caught in a sudden storm.

Being on the southeast coast, Savannah often finds itself threatened by hurricanes. In recent years, the city has been spared the destruction caused by major storms. Savannah had close calls from Hurricane Hugo in 1989, Bertha in 1996, and Floyd in 1999, but the last hurricane to hit here was David in 1979, when winds as strong as 90 MPH caused widespread power outages that lasted for several days.

That gives you the big picture. (For an at-a-glance version and a few extra facts, see the Vital Statistics page in this chapter.) Now let's look more closely at the four areas into which we've divided the county.

Here's Looking at You, Savannah

Historic Downtown

Our downtown area is bordered by the Savannah River on the north, East Broad Street on the east, Park Avenue on the south and Martin Luther King Jr. Boulevard on the west. Downtown Savannah is the section most visitors come to see. It's the oldest part of the city—Oglethorpe landed here when he arrived to found Georgia more than 260 years ago. The city squares he laid out—those green jewels in Savannah's crown—are still here.

This is the site of the Historic District, 2.5 square miles of beautifully restored homes and historic churches. It's an area that's been designated by the U.S. Department of the Interior as a National Historic Landmark. It's a place of monuments, shady sidewalks, and a cemetery that's a park. It's where art students sit on curbs while sketching old buildings, where the

Irish and others put themselves on parade on St. Patrick's Day, and where tourists look for places mentioned in the best-selling book, *Midnight in the Garden of Good and Evil*.

The downtown is also a place for fun, good eating, and shopping. River Street and City Market are here, with their stores and restaurants, and so is Broughton Street, which was once the city's main shopping district and is making a comeback after losing customers to the malls of the Southside (see our Shopping chapter). Downtown also hosts festivals, with many of Savannah's major annual events being held along the river, in City Market and at Forsyth Park, a lush green playground on Bull Street (see our Annual Events and Festivals chapter).

The downtown is the home of the city's financial district, Johnson Square, which is ringed by the main offices of several banks. There are also numerous museums and the Savannah College of Art and Design. SCAD is the largest school of its kind in the nation, and its 4,500 students bring much vitality and creativity to the area (see our Education and Arts and Culture chapters).

Interestingly enough, Savannah's downtown is not really "down," geographically speaking. If you look at a map of the city, you'll see that the Historic District is in the northern part of town. That's because Savannah got its start on a bluff on the south bank of the river, causing the heart of the city to be north of everything else. When you're in downtown Savannah, you can't go much farther north and still be in Georgia. Savannah has not grown in that direction, across the north channel of the Savannah River (which is known as the Back River), because what's over there is mostly marshland, and it's also South Carolina.

Having said that, we must mention that when you're downtown on River Street gazing across the south channel of the Savannah River, you're looking at Hutchinson Island, a part of Georgia that's being developed in a big way. An

companies. According to the Chamber of Commerce, tourists spent more than $1.17 billion here in 2000 (up from $587 million in 1993, the year before *Midnight* appeared in print), and tourism supported 19,150 jobs in 2000 (up from 16,603 in 1993).

The Westin opened in early December 1999. Other significant hotel projects completed in 1999 were the 68-room Marshall House on Broughton Street, a 42-room expansion of the River Street Inn on Bay Street, and a 24-room addition to The Mulberry Inn on Bay. Under construction early in 2001 were two hotels on Martin Luther King Jr. Boulevard, which appears to be undergoing a commercial rebirth. The new hotels are a five-story, 155-room Courtyard by Marriott at MLK and Liberty Street, and a six-story, 150-room Radisson at MLK and Bay Street.The Marriott opened in late July 2001, and the Radisson was scheduled to open in February 2002.

Because Savannah hasn't been able to expand much to the north, most early development was southward, and much recent growth has been to the east and west.

Islands

The growth eastward has occurred principally on Chatham County's inshore islands, referred to as such because they're not on the Atlantic Ocean. They're separated from the mainland and neighboring islands by salt marsh, rivers, and tidal creeks. The islands in our Islands area are those immediately east of Savannah—Oatland, Talahi, Whitemarsh, and Wilmington—and those southeast of the city—Dutch, Skidaway, and Isle of Hope. Because of its unique qualities and status as a destination for tourists, we have devoted a separate chapter to Tybee Island, which is also east of Savannah.

The residential development of the eastside islands took off in the late 1980s, and Whitemarsh Island (pronounced "WHIT-marsh") was the fastest-growing part of the county in 1996, with Wilmington Island not far behind. Growth slowed on Whitemarsh in 1997, with most of the island being built out, but residential

automobile racetrack opened there in the spring of 1997, the $98 million Savannah Harbor Resort complex is being created there, and the $83.5 million Savannah International Trade and Convention Center opened there in mid-2000.

A significant part of the Hutchinson Island resort complex is a 400-room, sixteen-story Westin hotel that's emblematic of the growth in tourism being experienced by the city. Fueled by the popularity of *Midnight* and by the aggressive marketing efforts of the Savannah Area Chamber of Commerce and individual components of the city's hospitality industry, that growth—from 3.73 million visitors in 1995 to 5.73 million in 2000—has caused an upsurge in hotel building and expansion, a blossoming of new restaurants and specialty shops, and a proliferation of tour

Savannah Vital Statistics

Nickname: Hostess City of the South

Mayor: Floyd Adams Jr.

Governor: Roy Barnes

Outlying counties: Effingham, Bryan, Liberty

Population: Savannah,131,510; Chatham County, 232,048; Georgia, 8.2 million

Area (sq. mi.): Savannah, 65.1

Average temperatures: July, 82; January, 49

Average annual precipitation: Rainfall, 48.2 inches; snowfall, less than one-half inch

Major universities: Armstrong Atlantic State University, Savannah State University, Savannah College of Art and Design

Important dates:

Feb. 12, 1733: Founded as capital of Georgia, the thirteenth colony

1734: Becomes first city in North America planned on a system of squares; also becomes site of first agricultural experimental garden in North America

1736: Becomes site of first Sunday school in America

Oct. 9, 1779: Colonial army suffers crushing defeat in attempt to retake city from British during Siege of Savannah.

1788: Becomes site of first African American Baptist congregation in United States

1793: Eli Whitney perfects cotton gin on a plantation just west of Savannah.

May 22, 1819: Serves as embarkation point for first steamship to cross Atlantic (SS *Savannah*)

April 19, 1862: Fort Pulaski, east of city, becomes site of first rifled cannon used in warfare.

Dec. 21, 1864: Confederate Savannah surrenders to Union forces led by General William T. Sherman at the conclusion of his March to the Sea.

1886: Opens first art museum (Telfair) in Southeast

1908, 1910, 1911: Hosts Grand Prix and Vanderbilt Cup auto racing

1911: Establishes first motorized fire department in United States

November 1955: Historic Savannah Foundation preservation group holds first general membership meeting.

July 22–Aug. 2, 1996: Hosts yachting events of Summer Olympic Games

Major area employers: Gulfstream Aerospace Corp. (4,800), Memorial Health University Medical Center (4,500), International Paper Co. (2,400), St. Joseph's/Candler Health System (3,700), Kroger supermarkets (796)

Famous sons and daughters:

Johnny Mercer, lyricist

Conrad Aiken, poet

Juliette Gordon Low, founder of the Girl Scouts

Clarence Thomas, Supreme Court justice

Major airports: Savannah International Airport

Major interstates: Interstate 95 (north-south), Interstate 16 (east-west)

Public transportation: Chatham Area Transit (CAT)

Military base: Hunter Army Airfield

Driving laws: Seat belts mandatory for occupants of the front seat of a vehicle and all occupants less than 18 years of age; safety restraining systems required for children less than 4 years old, but seat belts will suffice for those between 3 and 4. Maximum speed limit under normal conditions 55 MPH, 70 MPH on rural interstates, and 65 MPH on urban interstates. Speed limit decreases to 30 MPH in business and residential districts. Headlights required between the half hour after sunset and the half hour before sunrise and when raining.

Alcohol laws: Drinking by persons under 21 prohibited. Motorists 21 years and older considered under the influence of intoxicants when 0.08 grams or more by alcohol is present in the blood; for those younger than 21, the limit is 0.02 grams. Sunday sales of alcoholic beverages prohibited except in establishments that derive at least 50 percent of their food and beverage sales from the sale of prepared meals or foods. Sales of alcoholic beverages are prohibited between 2:55 A.M. on Sunday and 7 A.M. on Monday and between 3 A.M. and 7 A.M. other days.

Drinking on city streets prohibited except in the area bounded generally by the city limits on the north, West Boundary Street on the west, Jones Street on the south, and East Broad Street on the east. In this area, drinking from cans, bottles, or glasses is prohibited, and paper or plastic cups containing alcoholic beverages must not exceed sixteen fluid ounces in size.

Daily newspaper: *Savannah Morning News*

Sales tax: 6 percent (4 percent state, 2 percent local option) on the purchase of all goods and some services

Room tax: 6 percent

Information for tourists:

Savannah Area Chamber of Commerce
Savannah Convention & Visitors Bureau
101 E. Bay St., Savannah GA 31402
(912) 644–6449

This downtown fountain honors Savannah's German heritage. PHOTO: KYLE CASON

development continued on Wilmington, the fastest growing part of Chatham during 1998. Most of the building on these islands has been residential, although a large shopping center and three schools have been constructed on Whitemarsh in recent years.

Despite the buildup, the eastside islands retain a natural beauty and laid-back quality. You can still take an evening stroll on an island street, look up at a sky brilliant with stars, and listen to the plaintive calls of mourning doves and the chuck-will's-widow. For the most part, the eastside islands remain quiet havens where folks sit on their docks and watch the marsh turn from gold to green as the seasons change; where oaks festooned with Spanish moss bend over roadways to create cool, verdant tunnels; where you can hop in your car, drive around the corner, and enjoy a meal of fresh seafood.

Farther to the south, you'll find the gated residential enclave of Dutch Island; Skidaway Island, site of The Landings, a private community of upscale homes; and Isle of Hope, with its dignified old houses adorning secluded narrow streets. The Landings covers much of Skidaway Island with 3,250 beautifully landscaped dwellings, two deep-water marinas, six private 18-hole golf courses, a fitness center, four clubhouses, thirty-four tennis courts, and more than 40 miles of biking and nature trails. Isle of Hope is entirely residential except for the marina on Bluff Drive (see our Neighborhoods and Real Estate chapter). Bluff Drive is a lovely lane running alongside the Skidaway River, and it's our choice as the Savannah area's most picturesque street. The Isle is also the location of Wormsloe Historic Site, the place where one of Georgia's first settlers constructed a Colonial estate (see our Attractions chapter).

Southside/Midtown

Southside/Midtown is the vast area south of Historic Downtown. Note that the locals refer to the northern portion of this area as Midtown. Midtown starts in the vicinity of the southern end of Forsyth Park and runs south to DeRenne Avenue, although some folks might tell you that it extends all the way to Oglethorpe Mall. Most of Savannah's Victorian District and all of the South Victorian District are in Midtown. The districts are filled with Victorian-style frame houses and are on the National Register of Historic Places.

That distinction also applies to Ardsley Park and Chatham Crescent, two other areas in Midtown. Among the streets of Ardsley Park is one of Savannah's prettiest—oak- and azalea-lined Washington Avenue. At the eastern end of the avenue is Daffin Park, site of a lake and public tennis courts and athletic fields used by recreation league teams playing baseball, softball, football, and soccer. Daffin is also the stomping ground of professional athletes—the members of the city's minor-league baseball team, the Savannah Sand Gnats (see our Spectator Sports chapter). The Gnats play their home games at Grayson Stadium, which stands among the tall pines in the eastern portion of the park.

You'll find several shopping centers in Midtown, the main library (which has been renovated extensively and reopened in 1999), and much of Savannah's health-care community. Clustered just north of DeRenne Avenue, between Reynolds Street and the Truman Parkway, are numerous doctors' offices, pharmacies, medical laboratories, and two of the city's hospitals, Memorial Health University Medical Center and Candler Hospital (see our Healthcare chapter).

Once south of DeRenne, you are in the part of town most locals call the Southside. It's an area of subdivisions, churches,

The Savannah International Trade and Convention Center, which opened in mid-2000, enables the city to attract large-scale gatherings of business people. PHOTO: BETTY DARBY

Savannah's City Hall sports a real gold dome. PHOTO: KYLE CASON

recreational facilities, and commercial development. Savannah's main drag, Abercorn Street, turns into the area's primary retail strip here. We think of Abercorn south of DeRenne as the Land of a Thousand Curb Cuts. That's an exaggeration, but not much of one. The six-lane thoroughfare is nicked by the myriad entrances and exits to and from restaurants, motels, office complexes, convenience marts, both of Savannah's malls, auto dealerships, used-car lots, strip shopping centers, and megastores selling building materials, pet supplies, party goods, books, liquor, and office equipment. Interrupting this cascade of commercialism on Abercorn are St. Joseph's Hospital and the doctors' offices that have sprung up around it (see our Healthcare chapter) and the campus of Armstrong Atlantic State University. The area we've designated as the Southside is also home to several other institutions of higher education, including Savannah State University, Savannah Technical College, and South College (see our Education chapter).

Outdoor activities abound in the Southside. Just east and southeast of Oglethorpe Mall is Bacon Park, a city- and county-owned recreational complex consisting of softball diamonds, soccer fields, tennis courts, a public golf course, a stadium where high school football teams play, an aquatic center, and a lake surrounded by a walking/jogging track. This area is also the site of the Chatham County track and field complex inside T. A. Wright Stadium at Savannah State University. Among features of this world-class facility are an eight-lane track, a dual pole vault runway, a javelin runway, a steeplechase water jump, and shot put, discus, and hammer-throw circles.

The Southside past Oglethorpe Mall is where suburbia evolved in the 1950s and '60s, mainly in the sprawling subdivision of Windsor Forest. Residential growth has continued in recent years farther out Abercorn Street at Georgetown, one of the fastest growing areas in Chatham County in the '90s, and in the Henderson Golf

Insiders' Tip

The Savannah Area Chamber of Commerce, using information provided by Coldwell Banker, notes that the prices of homes in Savannah are lower than those in nearby large cities. The price of a 2,200-square-foot home in Savannah in the fall of 2000 was $145,250, less than prices for comparable homes in Columbia, South Carolina ($160,021); Charlotte, North Carolina ($182,178); Jacksonville, Florida ($201,873); and Atlanta, Georgia ($238,801). Prices in Savannah were much lower than those of Miami, Florida ($275,729); Chicago, Illinois ($438,212); and Stamford, Connecticut ($450,521). The homes cited are single-family dwellings with four bedrooms and two and one-half baths.

Club area (see our Neighborhoods and Real Estate chapter).

To the west of the residential and commercial development of the Southside is Hunter Army Airfield, a 5,400-acre military post and site of the army's longest runway. As of January 2001, a total of 4,637 soldiers and civilians were working at Hunter, the home of a Ranger battalion, units of the Third Infantry Division

Huge container cranes are part of the reason why Savannah is one of the most-visited ports on the East Coast. PHOTO: BETTY DARBY

(Mechanized), and a Coast Guard air station. The bulk of the division is based an hour away at Fort Stewart, the largest Army installation east of the Mississippi River. With its 11,000-foot runway, Hunter serves as a location from which troops and equipment of the Third can be deployed throughout the world.

Two of Chatham's municipalities are in Southside/Midtown: Thunderbolt, a quaint fishing village of 2,340 people living alongside the Wilmington River, and Vernonburg, a settlement of 138 souls who reside on a handful of streets leading to the banks of the Vernon River. South of Vernonburg are the rustic residential communities of Beaulieu and Coffee Bluff.

West Chatham

West Chatham is where folks roll up their sleeves and get to work. It's where much of the area's industry flexes its muscles. This is the home of the county's largest manufacturer, Gulfstream Aerospace Corporation, which employs 4,800 people and produces corporate jet aircraft. West Chatham is the site of the headquarters of the Georgia Ports Authority, which operates two deep-water terminals on the Savannah River. Most of the cargo handled on Savannah's docks is shipped in containers, and the city is one of the busiest container ports in the United States.

Many of the people who work at the port and the industries west of Savannah live in West Chatham's four municipalities. Of these, Garden City is the largest in terms of population—11,289 people call it home. Port Wentworth, the town closest to the river, has a population of 3,276, and Bloomingdale has 2,665 residents. Garden City and Bloomingdale grew considerably in 1998 when a majority of voters there opted for annexations that added about 7

A Gnasty Welcome to Savannah

"What just bit me?"

"What's that smell?"

Visitors to Savannah sometimes ask those questions even before inquiring about where to eat, what to visit, and how to find the Garden of Good and Evil.

The smell can hit you out on Interstate 16, a few miles before you get to town, and the biting can begin as soon as you leave the safety of your car. You might think those unseen forces making lunch of your bare forearm are a figment of your imagination, but they're not. They're sand flies. Savannahians call them sand gnats and sometimes refer to them as "no-see-ums."

A sand gnat feeds on a human by slashing skin with its teeth and drinking the pool of blood that forms. Sounds gross, but you can't see this carnage taking place because your average sand gnat is about a millimeter long—so tiny it can fly through a standard window screen without grazing its wing tips. What you might see, particularly if you are prone to allergies, are small welts appearing where gnats have feasted. Try not to scratch; if you leave the bumps alone, they will disappear in about an hour.

Incidentally, the gnats biting you are females. They need the protein in blood for laying eggs. Sand gnats breed in the mud of salt marshes and are most prevalent in the spring and fall, but a few days of temperatures in the sixties can bring them out at other times. Although some folks recommend dousing yourself with a certain brand-name skin softener as a defense against sand gnats, entomologists say you can best fight these bugs by applying insect repellent containing the chemical compound DEET and by wearing long clothing and hats.

Savannahians have a love-hate relationship with sand gnats. They detest the gnat as an insect but adore it as the mascot of the city's minor-league baseball team. The management and fans of the Savannah ball club chose the Sand Gnat nickname when the team became an affiliate of the Los Angeles Dodgers organization in 1996. (They've since become affiliated with the Texas Rangers.) Sand Gnat merchandise is so popular, it's a best-seller among fans of minor-league teams.

Not nearly as lovable as the baseball team's bug-eyed mascot is the rotten-egg, cabbage-being-cooked smell that periodically wafts over Savannah. The odor emanates from the industries lining the banks of the Savannah River. The dominant component of the smell is sulfur dioxide, a pungent gas released during the manufacture of paper. Industry officials say they have spent big bucks attempting to eliminate the smell, and they assure us they have lessened it. The smell persists, however, as do the sand gnats. Savannahians have learned to live with both, and you can too.

square miles to Garden City and more than 1,000 acres to Bloomingdale. Pooler, a town of 6,239, is one of the fastest-developing parts of the region. Another booming section of West Chatham is Southbridge, an upscale residential community just off Interstate 16 and south of Pooler. The sector encompassing Southbridge and the nearby Quacco Road area was the fastest growing portion of the county in 1997, according to the Metropolitan Planning Commission. About 500 families were living at Southbridge as of the fall of 1999, and the development was expected to top out at 1,400 residences (see our Neighborhoods and Real Estate chapter).

According to government planners, West Chatham will be a hotbed of residential development during this decade. Areas that are expected to boom with new homes are the Godley Tract in the northeastern part of West Chatham, the town of Pooler, and Berwick Plantation on U.S. 17.

West Chatham is also the location of Savannah International Airport, where a $68.5 million terminal was opened in 1994 (see our Getting Here, Getting Around chapter). Close by the airport are Cross-Roads Business Park, a state-of-the-art industrial park, and Crosswinds, a new golf course that's lighted for nighttime play.

Getting Here,
Getting Around

Georgia's first city sits near the mouth of the Savannah River, which forms the boundary between Georgia and South Carolina. Take the Talmadge Bridge over the Savannah River and by the time you're back over dry land, you're in another state. Head south for about two and a half hours, and you've gone from Georgia's northernmost coastal point to the Florida border—a pretty short stretch between states, considering Georgia is the largest state east of the Mississippi.

The first Europeans to get to Savannah arrived in sailing vessels. Gen. James Edward Oglethorpe, Georgia's founder, came in 1733 to settle the colony and establish, among other things, a thriving port. Today, however, it's mainly cargo that arrives by ship. Although the rankings may vary from day to day, The Port of Savannah is the tenth-largest container port in the United States, with about 2,000 ships making their way upriver every year to load or unload their goods. In 2001, the port crossed a significant milestone when it recorded its first year of handling over a million TEUs, the volume measurement used to calculate containerized freight. On a very rare occasion, you'll see a cruise ship that has docked in Savannah (an advocacy group is diligently advocating for expansion as a cruise destination), and the Intracoastal Waterway is traveled by private vessels, but most of our guests today come by plane, train, or—predominately—by car.

However they arrive, Savannah is pretty easy to get to. Two interstate highways pass right through: I-95, a continually busy superhighway that stretches from Florida to Maine, and I-16, a strictly instate interstate that connects Savannah to Macon (and I-75) with some 165 miles of the widest-open interstate (translation: dull and usually lightly traveled) you're likely to find in the East. Air travelers are going to find Savannah outfitted for them in a grand style, probably several cuts above what an experienced traveler would expect for a city this size. Savannah opened a new $68.5 million airport terminal in 1994. If you've ever navigated your way through big-city airports like those in Chicago or Atlanta, Savannah International Airport will be a nice change. Like that of its namesake city, the pace is a little slower and friendlier at our airport, and there are no football-field length corridors to run through in order to make your connections. On the other hand, it's attractive (well, as attractive as an airport can be), modern, and has all the relevant amenities.

Other transportation options include Amtrak and Greyhound, which make stops every day in Savannah.

Once you get here, there are several options to get you around, although the best way is still the oldest way—on foot, or as you might hear it called, "riding shank's mare." If you aren't interested in hoofing it, though, you'll find a well-developed system of taxis, a public bus system, a full array of rental car agencies, even "pedicabs," which are kind of a cross between a tricycle and a rickshaw, driven by strong-legged guides.

Overall, you should find Savannah to be a pretty friendly and easy place for traveling. You won't find elaborate freeway systems with HOV lanes or throngs of harried commuters rushing to catch their five o'clock train. Sorry, Savannah just isn't big enough for that stuff.

What we do have is a network of parkways that will take you around certain sections of the city. There are two-lane roads passing through beautiful marshes, and one-way streets designed to get you quickly from one place to another. And, of course, there are the squares—the very construction of which forces you to slow down . . . take your time . . . enjoy the scenery. This isn't to say we don't have congested streets and other roadways that seem more like speedways, especially in the commercial sections of the city. But big traffic jams are usually big news and might even make the morning paper the next day.

You may notice people also tend to move slower here, especially during the very hot and humid summer months. That doesn't always apply to driving, however, so don't dawdle if you've chosen the left lane of a busy street. And if you are lost, ask a local. More likely than not, they will be happy to get you headed in the right direction. Those of us who live or work in the Historic Downtown are particularly experienced at giving directions.

Having said all this, remember that Savannah is still a modern city, calling for the same commonsense security measures you need in any city. It may feel, particularly in the Historic Downtown, like a small town, but it isn't. Always use the same precautions you would in any city: Be aware of your surroundings, don't venture out alone at night, and keep your wallet or purse secure. There is street crime in Savannah and it has occasionally turned violent.

We have broken this chapter into two sections. Getting Here is just what you would expect: a look at the various modes of transportation to get you to Savannah. Getting Around helps you navigate once you've arrived. It includes a look at parking, public transportation, local roadways, and more.

Insiders' Tip

Always lock your car downtown, just as you probably do in your own hometown. That turns vehicles into ovens in the summer. Locals often keep a towel or pillowcase in the front seat to drape across the steering wheel when they park to spare themselves scorched fingers later. During the summer, give serious consideration to choosing the city's parking garages, which offer shade, over metered spaces in the sun.

Getting Here

By Air

Savannah International Airport
400 Airways Avenue
Savannah, GA
(912) 964-0514

The Savannah International Airport is about 10 miles north of Savannah. The exit number off I-95 is 104, although older signs and printed matter may still call it exit 18-A. (Georgia renumbered its interstate exists in early 2000 to reflect distance from starting points.) Delta (800-221-1212) and USAirways (800-428-4322) are the largest carriers and also have been with the airport the longest. The other airlines are smaller, discount carriers including AirTran (800-825-8538), Continental Express (800-525-0280), United Express, and the newest entry, Northwest, which inaugurated service to Detroit in fall of 2001. Nonstop flights are also available via various carriers to Atlanta, Charlotte, Newark, Cincinnati, Houston, Dallas/Fort Worth, and New York's La Guardia.

The lineup at the airport is frequently fluid—new airlines, a few dropouts, shifting around of the offerings. Your travel agent or your favorite airline will know the latest picture. The Airport Commission is on a constant mission to beef up the offerings. By the way, the airport offers a convenient service: Call the main number (912-964-0514), which you'll have difficulty finding in the phone book like everyone else because you'll look under Savannah Airport instead of Savannah International Airport, and the voice mail menu gives you submenus that take you directly to the various airlines or rental car companies.

Oh, and if you are wondering about the name, Savannah International Airport is correct, even though there are no international flights at the moment. A small airline did offer flights to the Bahamas briefly, but the "international" portion of the title derives from the availability of customs facilities—meaning the airport is ready for international flights as soon as an airline jumps in there. Actually, the name could include Hilton Head Island in its title, since surveys show about half of the passengers are on their way to Hilton Head Island or its vicinity (just check the number of golf bags on the luggage carousel if you doubt this).

Although the airline getting you here may change, one constant will be where you will arrive. In May 1994, Savannah opened a $68.5 million terminal with eight gates, restaurants, gift shops, ATM machines, a postal center, and other traveler amenities. When passengers arrive or depart, they walk through Savannah Square, a relaxing seating area patterned after Savannah's famous downtown squares. A new parking deck added some 1,000 parking spaces to the existing stock early in 2000. Other parking expansions to accommodate more rental cars and to improve security at the airport are in the works, but the administration has a history of clearly posting directions and options, so you'll be no more confused than the locals.

Private Plane Service

Signature Flight Support
1006 Bob Harmon Road
Savannah International Airport
Savannah, GA
(912) 964–1557

Signature Flight Support is open twenty-four hours a day, seven days a week. It offers tie-down service for single- and twin-engine planes, along with parking for jets. Fees depend on the aircraft, but if you purchase fuel, there is no charge. Repair service is available.

Savannah Aviation
Hangar Road
Savannah, GA
(912) 964–1022

Savannah Aviation is open Monday through Friday from 6 A.M. to 10 P.M. and from 7 A.M. to 9 P.M. on the weekends. Tie-down service is available. Fees vary depending on the aircraft and whether you get fuel. Repairs can be made to small planes.

Rental Cars

Passengers have a choice of several rental car agencies on the premises. Serving Savannah International are Alamo (912-964-7364), Avis (912-964-1781), Budget (912-964-4600), National (912-964-1771), Thrifty (912-966-2277), and Hertz (912-964-9595). Again, a reminder: The airport's main number (912-964-0514) includes a voice mail option that connects you directly to these rental agencies. These services also tend to be "fluid," so call ahead if you consider it particularly important that you deal with a specific car rental agency.

Chatham Area Transit buses cover much of the county. PHOTO: KYLE CASON

Taxi Service

The airport distributes a rate brochure (available either outside near all the cabs or inside near the baggage claim) that gives passengers an idea of what it will cost to take a taxi to local bed-and-breakfasts, hotels, motels, and inns. Typically, it costs around $21 to get to the Historic Downtown, $26 to reach Southside/Midtown, $6.50 to $10 to get to west Chatham County (where the airport is located), and about $40 for a ride to Tybee Island. Expect to pay about $50 for a taxi to Hilton Head Island. These rates are regulated by the Airport Commission and, of course, are subject to change.

Taxi service at the airport can be arranged by calling the taxi stand at (912) 964-8016, or by simply showing up at the cab stand curbside, which is clearly marked and impossible to miss. We've never seen the cab stand unattended. Low Country Adventures (800-845-5582) provides airport shuttle service to and from Hilton Head for $27 one way (see our Hilton Head chapter). Coastal Transportation Services (912-964-5999) offers shuttle service to surrounding Georgia areas (as far west as Statesboro, home of Georgia Southern University) and other areas at varying rates.

There is no scheduled provider of limousine service to and from the airport. However, there are several private limousine services in the city, and these are listed in this chapter. If you are interested in a ride from the airport, always inquire when calling as to whether the company has a permit to pick up at the airport.

By Train

Amtrak
2611 Seaboard Coastline Drive
Savannah, GA
(912) 234-2611

The Silver Meteor, Silver Star, and Silver Palm take turns coming into Savannah as part of their treks along the eastern seaboard. Savannah is in the New York–Miami Amtrak corridor, and travelers have a choice of six departure times each day. Note that there is no train service currently to Atlanta, an omission advo-

north toward New York and south to Miami. There are also westbound options. If you are coming to Savannah on Greyhound, you will disembark at the terminal on the far western reaches of Oglethorpe Avenue, one of the Historic Downtown's main thoroughfares. Head out the front door of the station and walk to your left along Oglethorpe—within a few blocks you will be in the heart of the Historic Downtown. If you arrive at night, use caution when walking, as you would in any city. The bus station's locale used to be on the fringes of the restored Historic District, but revitalization has moved into the area, and you'll find more foot traffic and less gritty surroundings. Taxi service is available at the bus terminal.

By Car

Savannah is reachable by car via two major interstates: I-95 from the north and south and I-16 running east and west. I-95 is the main artery along the eastern seaboard, stretching from Maine to the tip of Florida. It is especially busy in the Savannah area during spring, when snowbirds and spring-breakers are heading south for some winter relief. I-16 cuts an east-west path across middle Georgia before merging with Interstate 75, which takes you into Atlanta. The following information is a helpful rundown on how to get to the main geographical sections of the city from either of these interstates.

To Historic Downtown

The best option to get to the Historic Downtown is to use I-16 heading east. The interstate dead-ends near the western boundary of the Historic Downtown—the corner of Liberty and Montgomery Streets. If you are the independent sort, heading right or straight ahead will get you deeper into the Historic Downtown. Want to swing by the Savannah Visitors Center for a pit stop and reassurance first? Take a left onto Liberty Street, then your next right on Martin Luther King Jr. Boulevard, or take the Louisville Road

cacy groups periodically tackle. To check the schedule, Amtrak's reservation number is (800) 872-7245.

The Amtrak station is about 4 miles from the Historic Downtown. Heading west on I-16, take the Chatham Parkway exit. At the stop sign turn left, then take your first right. The station is open every day from 4:30 A.M. to noon and from 4:30 P.M. to midnight. Taxicabs are at the station when each train pulls in. Rental cars are not available at the station.

By Bus

Greyhound Bus Lines
610 W. Oglethorpe Avenue
Savannah, GA
(912) 232–2135

Savannah is on Greyhound Bus Lines' busiest eastern corridor—the stretch between New York City and Miami. Buses depart the city twenty-three times a day, seven days a week, with the most frequent departures, as would be expected, headed

exit, which is near the end of the interstate and has signs guiding you to the Visitors Center. You are now essentially a block from the traffic light where the interstate dumped you. The Visitors Center is on the western side of MLK, calling for a tricky left-hand turn into the parking lot. I-95 doesn't go directly into the city, so if you are traveling the north-south route, you'll need to take I-16 (the exit is clearly marked, although it features a wicked curve and tricky dual merge) for the final 10 miles or so.

To Islands

There are a couple of options to get you to Tybee or the eastern islands of Oatland, Talahi, Whitemarsh, and Wilmington. Take I-16 into the Historic Downtown area and get on any northbound street until you reach Bay Street. Continue east on Bay Street, which, in less than a mile, merges with President Street, then becomes President Street Extension. Follow the President Street Extension until it becomes Islands Expressway. In about 3 miles, it will merge with U.S. Highway 80, which is the main route to Tybee and the eastern islands.

A second option to get you to Tybee, along with the eastern and southeastern islands (Dutch and Isle of Hope), involves leaving I-16 at the 37th Street exit. Take 37th Street to Abercorn Street, take a right, then proceed to Victory Drive, where you will turn left (east). To reach Skidaway Island, take a right off Victory on Waters Avenue. To reach the southeastern islands, look for Skidaway Road off Victory Drive and take a right to get to Dutch Island and Isle of Hope. If you continue east on Victory, it will become U.S. 80, which will take you to the eastern islands and Tybee.

To Southside/Midtown

If you are staying near the Southside, you might want to consider exiting I-95 at Georgia Highway 204 in the southern reaches of the county, about 20 miles south of the Historic Downtown. Georgia 204 is also Abercorn Street, the main north-south thoroughfare running throughout the entire city. After exiting, head north. After about 3 miles you will enter the Southside—the city's main commercial district, with strip shopping centers, hotels, car dealerships, and Savannah's two malls.

Another option to get to the Southside or Midtown area: Take Lynes Parkway (I-516). After about 4 miles, it turns into DeRenne Avenue, a main east-west thoroughfare. Take a right onto Abercorn Street off DeRenne, and you are at the edge of the Southside. If you go left onto Abercorn, you will be heading to Midtown and, beyond that, the Historic Downtown.

Insiders' Tip

It rarely snows in Savannah, but every few years we get a slight dusting or maybe some ice on the roads. Watch out! Even if you are an experienced driver from northern climes, be forewarned: The city has no snow removal equipment, most drivers don't have tire chains, you can't get anywhere without crossing some form of bridge, and despite the fact that most Savannahians have no idea of how to drive in such conditions, a fair percentage will still pile into their cars to take in the novel sight of snow-draped palm trees.

The Talmadge Bridge spans the Savannah River, linking Savannah and Hutchinson Island.
PHOTO: KYLE CASON

To West Chatham

The West Chatham communities of Pooler, Bloomingdale, and Garden City are all accessible from I-16 via various marked exits. From I-95 you can also take the Pooler Parkway, which will connect you to U.S. 80 and take you through Bloomingdale, Pooler, and Garden City.

Getting Around

Once you have made it to Savannah, there are several ways you can navigate within the city—from public transportation to a comfortable pair of shoes. Following are some ideas for getting around and a few things to watch out for while traversing the town.

Hitting the Road

Historic Downtown

If it wasn't for the squares, Savannah's Historic Downtown would follow a fairly simple grid pattern. There are thirteen main north-south streets in the Historic Downtown, stretching from the northernmost point of the city—the Savannah River—south to Forsyth Park. These streets include (listed east to west) East Broad, Houston, Price, Habersham, Lincoln, Abercorn, Drayton, Bull, Whitaker, Barnard, Jefferson, Montgomery, and Martin Luther King Jr. Likewise, there are twenty-three main east-west streets, starting (for our purposes) at East Broad and ending at Martin Luther King (which was formerly known as West Broad). These main east-west roadways include River, Bay, Bryan, Congress, Broughton, State, York, Oglethorpe, Hull, Perry, Liberty, Harris, Charlton, Jones, Taylor, Gordon, Gaston, Huntingdon, Hall, Gwinnett, Bolton, Waldburg, and Park.

If our streets resemble a series of necklaces, then some of them are lucky enough to have pearls in the form of squares. In fact, six of the north-south streets—Montgomery, Barnard, Bull, Abercorn, Habersham, and Houston—have these jewels, making them the most beautiful streets in the Historic Downtown. Bull Street, however, commands center stage. Located in the center of the Historic Downtown and easy to spot because it begins at golden-domed City Hall, Bull Street offers some of the most notable squares in the city, including the one where Forrest Gump spent his time and where the main plot unfolds in *Midnight in the Garden of Good and Evil*.

It is crucial that you understand how to navigate around the squares while traveling in the Historic Downtown. Imagine heading north or south on one of the six streets with squares. Every couple of blocks you are going to run into one. They're beautiful but they slow you down—not necessarily a bad thing—but local commuters opt for the plainer, straighter one-way Whitaker Street to get out of town and the equally straight, plain and one-way Drayton Street to get in.

No, the squares aren't your standard traffic circles. There is only one lane, and traffic moves in a counterclockwise direction around a beautiful park filled with trees, benches, and in some instances, a monument or fountain. The traffic moves very slowly, so you have ample time to figure out where you would like to exit. When entering a square, always yield to any car making its way around the square—it has the right-of-way. Once the coast is clear, enter the square driving to your right. Because we have many visitors (and not a few locals) who don't understand that part about who has the right-of-way on the square, be cautious.

If you don't want to hit any squares, you can take a straight southbound route

through the Historic Downtown on either Price Street or Whitaker Street. Both run one way. Drayton Street, a one-way northern thoroughfare, will get you all the way to the Savannah River without being interrupted by squares. These aren't, however, the prettiest routes. Note that you also will run into squares when traveling east to west in the Historic Downtown. The majority of the east-west routes pass by to the north or south of the squares, but a few intersect them. Again, when approaching a square from the east or west, you must yield to any traffic that is already making its way around the square. Once traffic has cleared you enter the square by traveling to your right or going straight ahead. Liberty and Oglethorpe are the main east west streets without squares, and they feature broad, tree-lined center medians. Other squareless east-west routes include Jones, Gaston, Broughton (the downtown business district's "main street"), and Bay. All of this sounds com-

Insiders' Tip

If you are going to depend on parking meters, keep plenty of change handy. Meters in prime locations or offering the longest time span often take only quarters. None of them take pennies. By the way, the meter maids in Savannah haven't taken up working on weekends—at least not yet. Conversely, the ones at Tybee Island, our beach, are most vigilant on weekends.

plicated. It isn't, as you will see. Yield when entering a square, travel to the right—as is quite obvious—and you'll do fine.

Islands

The eastern islands, including White-marsh, Talahi, Oatland, and Wilmington, are directly off U.S. 80, which is also the only route to Tybee Island. It is a fairly wide, four-lane highway taking you through scenic marshlands before narrowing into a two-lane road as you near Tybee. Skidaway Road leads to Dutch Island and the Isle of Hope (but not, oddly enough, to Skidaway Island). Waters Avenue is the direct route to Skidaway Island. This well-marked, two-lane road is very busy and congested most times of the day. While driving on Skidaway, keep your eyes open for people turning on and off the road. (Please see our Tybee Island chapter for more information on getting around there.) Pay particular attention to speed limits in school zones.

Southside/Midtown

Abercorn Street is the main artery running through Savannah's Southside. It begins at the Savannah River in the Historic Downtown, and in its early stretches is a charming, square-filled route through the Historic Downtown. It continues south some 20 miles to I-95, picking up additional lanes and additional traffic. All the motels, hotels, shopping centers, car dealerships, and other businesses in the Southside are either right on Abercorn or on a street just off this main drag. The six-lane street is heavily traveled and usually very busy. Try to avoid Abercorn during morning and afternoon rush hours—typically 7:30 to 9 A.M. and 4 to 6 P.M. If you are a road-warrior veteran of a gridlocked metropolis, however, you might find our version of rush hour amusing.

DeRenne Avenue, which becomes I-516 at its western end, is the main Southside east-west route. You will find two of the city's hospitals off DeRenne (one just off, and the other a few blocks north on Waters Avenue), along with gas stations, shopping centers, banks, and several medical offices. This road also is heavily traveled and should be avoided during morning and afternoon rush hours.

Victory Drive (U.S. 80) is Midtown's main drag. It travels through residential neighborhoods and by shopping centers and Grayson Stadium, home of Savannah's minor-league baseball team, the Sand Gnats (see our Spectator Sports chapter). When traveling east, Victory Drive is the main route to Tybee and the eastern Islands.

Eisenhower Drive is another major east-west road that accesses Hunter Army Airfield to the west and Skidaway Road to the east. It parallels DeRenne and Victory.

West Chatham

Bay Street, which runs right in front of City Hall in the Historic Downtown, continues to West Chatham, eventually taking you to Garden City and Port Wentworth. George Washington Highway, which turns into Augusta Road, is also another main thoroughfare for this part of town. U.S. 80 runs through the area as well, taking motorists to Bloomingdale, Pooler, and Garden City.

Parking

When Oglethorpe designed the original city plan for Savannah, he didn't leave space for parking cars. That wasn't a problem at the time, but over the ensuing 270 years, it has caused some difficulties. You can find parking, generally, but it is not free, and it is often not as convenient as you would like in the Historic Downtown. We focus our parking information section on that part of town for a couple of reasons: It's the place most tourists want to roam, and it's the main area in the city where you have to pay to park. Venture outside the Historic Downtown to Southside/Midtown, Islands, or West Chatham, and you shouldn't have any trouble finding ample free parking. (An exception is Tybee Island, which is covered in a separate chapter.)

Despite the high volume of vehicles jostling for places in the Historic Downtown every day, a metered spot or one in a garage or parking lot usually is available. It's the daily downtown worker who finds parking an expensive nightmare, with meters vigilantly patrolled and waiting lists for monthly spaces in the city lots and prime private lots. As a visitor, you might not find a place right next to the square or shop you want to visit, but chances are good you will find one within comfortable walking distance. Be advised that it gets more crowded as you get closer to River Street—a main tourist hub overlooking the Savannah River. And remember that no matter how good the parking situation may be the rest of the year, it is going to be tough, if not altogether impossible, to get a spot near downtown on St. Patrick's Day. (See our St. Patrick's Day chapter for more information on the perils of parking during the city's big fest.)

Parking for the majority of the Historic Downtown area (and a little farther south) is metered, costing 50 cents an hour and up, depending on location. As we mention in other chapters, the downtown area is patrolled by vigilant parking enforcers who are out in force from 8 A.M. to 5 P.M., Monday through Friday. Leave your meter expired for even a minute or two, and chances are pretty good you are going to get a ticket. The damage will cost you anywhere from $8 for an expired meter to $50 for expired or missing state vehicle license tags. The majority of the tickets range between $8 and $15, and you have seven days to pay up. After that, an additional $8 is tacked on. Wait thirty days to pay and your $8 ticket suddenly costs you an additional $18. Parking meters are serious business in the city of Savannah, so take careful note of the time and carry change. Most merchants are friendly, but some are grouchy about making meter change.

Parking Services is going high-tech downtown, with the installation of two new varieties of meter beyond the traditional put-in-a-coin-and-turn-the-handle

Insiders' Tip

Lost in Historic Downtown? Can't remember where you parked your car or how to get back to your hotel? Look for somebody doling out parking tickets. Under the "Ask Me" program, parking enforcement attendants—the ones buzzing around in those little blue-and-white carts writing parking tickets—are trained to assist tourists in need. They can give directions, help point out the nearest bathroom, even use thier radios to track down misplaced cars.

versions. One requires parkers to walk to the middle of the block and buy a paper receipt from a machine, then return to the car and put it on the dashboard. Another version requires drivers to note the number of a parking space, walk to a midblock computer, and feed in coins. If all of this sounds likely to breed confusion, increase inconvenience, and enhance the chances you will get a parking ticket despite your efforts to comply—well, you are right.

Metered parking is scarcer than ever since security concerns prompted the lifting of curbside parking near federal buildings, so read on to learn about your parking garage options.

You won't find meters along Broughton Street, the main shopping district in the Historic Downtown that is experiencing a resurgence with new businesses, shops, and restaurants after years of decline. To help bring people into the area, the city allows free two-hour parking along Broughton Street (with a few spaces that allow only thirty minutes of parking). While there are no meters, you can be ticketed for exceeding the time limit—it is monitored.

City Parking Garages

The city has three public garages, where parking costs $1 for the first hour and 50 cents for each subsequent hour. (Rates usually go up in January.) At the State Street Parking Garage (at State and Abercorn Streets) and the Robinson Parking Garage (at Montgomery and York Streets), you can park all day for $4. Both are open weekdays from 6 A.M. to 9 P.M. Hourly rates are the same at the Bryan Street Parking Garage (Bryan and Abercorn Streets), but it costs $5 to park all day. The Bryan Street garage is open and staffed twenty-four hours a day, seven days a week. Note that the garages, particularly Bryan Street, often fill up during the business day.

City Parking Lots

The city operates a few public parking lots as well. Two are on River Street and cost $1 for the first hour, 50 cents per additional hour, or $5 for the day. For easy access to the lots, from Bay Street take the Abercorn, Lincoln, or Barnard Street ramps to River Street. From the Lincoln ramp, turn left to reach the lots. From the Abercorn or Barnard ramps, turn either way on River Street to reach a city lot.

The city also operates the Liberty Street lot at the corner of Liberty and Montgomery Streets on the western edge of the Historic Downtown. It's $2 per day to park there. And there is limited parking in the parking lot at the city's Civic Center, which is on Montgomery Street between Liberty and Oglethorpe Streets. If there isn't an event going on, it will only cost you $1 to park at the center for the entire day.

There are a handful of private parking garages and lots in town. Many cater strictly to local businesses and have lengthy waiting lists to get in.

The Savannah Visitors Center, which shares an entrance with the Savannah History Museum, is a starting point for many motor-coach tours. PHOTO: BETTY DARBY

Visitor Parking Day Passes

Here's a real bargain. To take the hassle out of feeding meters, the city offers a Visitor Parking Day Pass. The pass, which costs $5, is valid for forty-eight hours and allows visitors to park at any meter in the Historic Downtown, at time-controlled lots and parking spaces, in the three city parking garages, or at the city parking lot. The pass, which must be displayed on the driver's-side dash, is not valid in all the areas you would expect—private parking lots, hotel parking garages, sweeping zones, freight zones, bagged meters (meters that are covered to tell you that parking is not allowed temporarily), etc.

You can purchase a day pass or find out more information on parking at the Visitors Center or at the offices of City of Savannah Parking Services, 100 E. Bryan Street (912-651-6470). The pass comes with a map showing parking locations.

Public Transportation

Chatham Area Transit
900 E. Gwinnett Street
(912) 233–5767 (TDD)

If you hear someone say they are going to "catch a CAT," they are referring to a ride on Chatham County's public bus system. Chatham Area Transit (CAT) has a fleet of buses (easy to spot with the outstretched cats drawn on their sides) traveling on twenty-two routes throughout the county.

Realistically, visitors don't often use the public bus system, but there's no reason not to. You can get just about anywhere you want by catching a CAT, including the city's two malls, the Historic Downtown area, and the Islands (except Tybee). CAT buses do not, however, go to West Chatham. It costs 75 cents every time you board a bus, and there are no transfers. Children shorter than forty inches tall—the height of the fare box—get to ride free (limit two free children's fares per adult), and the fare for riders sixty-five and older and persons with disabilities is 37 cents each way. If you plan on doing a lot

of traveling around Savannah on CAT, there is a weekly Flash Pass—good for unlimited rides—available for $12.

CAT buses run each day from 6 A.M. to midnight. Bus stops are marked with bright orange signs throughout the city. There is no service on Thanksgiving, Christmas, or New Year's Day. CAT produces a comprehensive bus booklet, explaining everything from how to enter the bus to what routes will get you to different historic sites. The bus book, which also contains all the system's routes, can be found in area grocery stores, libraries, and malls, among other places.

One of the newest amenities added by CAT is a bike rack on the front of each bus, so bikers can catch a CAT, too. We've yet to see anyone actually use this rack, but it's nice to know it is there.

CAT also operates a paratransit van system for Americans with Disabilities Act (ADA)-eligible riders. ADA-eligible visitors are welcome to use the TELERIDE service. In order to use the door-to-door service, visitors must present an ID card from their hometown transit system that proves their eligibility. TELERIDE costs $1.20 each way. For more information, call (912) 354-6900. If you are in the Historic Downtown and want to purchase tokens, passes, or talk to someone about a route, stop in at CAT Central, 124 Bull Street, in the county's historic courthouse.

CAT Shuttle
Chatham Area Transit
900 E. Gwinnett Street
Savannah, GA
(912) 233–5767 (TDD)

Although the CAT shuttle is another service of the county's public transportation system, it rates a separate entry because it caters in large part to the thousands of tourists exploring Savannah's Historic Downtown. The shuttle—a modern pseudotrolley in dark green with gold trim—makes a continuous, wide loop through Historic Downtown, stopping along the way at the Visitor's Center, several hotels, City Market, River Street, and many historic points of interest. The shuttle stops are clearly marked with signs that have a map of the route and timetable. Fares have been changed repeatedly, but at the moment, they're free. All shuttles are wheelchair accessible. More information on the shuttle can be found by calling CAT or stopping by CAT Central, 124 Bull Street.

Taxis and Limousines

The best thing to do if you want taxi service in Savannah is to call the cab company directly. In theory, perhaps, you could hail a passing cab, but we've never seen it done—when we want a cab, we telephone and ask for one or go to the cab lineups outside major hotels and the airport. There are several companies in town, typically charging $1.20 to $1.30 per mile.

Limousine service also is available from a variety of local companies. Limos typically cost around $45 to $65 per hour, and some of the companies require a two-hour minimum. Advanced reservations are required to ensure prompt service.

Taxi services include Adam Cab Inc. (912-927-7466), Airport Taxi Service (912-269-5586), All American Cab (912-961-7433), Savannah Cab Company (912-236-2424), and Yellow Cab (912-236-1133).

For limousines, try A & E Luxury Limousine Service (912-354-2982), Low Country Adventures (912-966-2112, 800-845-5582), and Sherrie's Diamond's (912-355-8449).

Bicycles

At present, Savannah is not exactly a bike-friendly city. In fact, because of its age, layout, and other considerations, there are only a few bike paths in town. However, relief may soon be in sight. In 1997, voters passed a measure that would allow several million dollars to be used to construct a series of bike paths throughout the county. That construction is still well in the future, however, so don't count on it to help you out much on your trip. Mean-

while, wear a helmet, follow traffic laws, and be aware that most motorists here don't have regular experience in sharing the roadway with bikes.

For the most part, bikes are not serious commuting or traveling modes in Savannah, although the growing student population at Savannah College of Art and Design is upping the bike census. This is not to say you can't get around on a bike in Historic Downtown or a few other places—some people do. It is just not the preferred (or the safest) mode of transportation. In fact, there is one Historic Downtown road, Bay Street, that we recommend completely avoiding on your bike. Bay Street is a very narrow, heavily traveled road where bikers will find themselves competing for space with eighteen-wheelers. In the summer of 1999, the city banned bike riding through the downtown squares in the name of pedestrian safety, although the ban does not apply to kids on bikes.

The designated bike paths in the city include the following:

West to East Corridor: 52nd Street to Ward Street to LaRoche Avenue to the entrance of Savannah State University

North to South Corridor: Habersham Street to Stephenson Avenue to Hodgson Memorial Drive to Edgewater Drive to Hillyer Drive to Dyches Drive to Lorwood Drive to Tibet Avenue to Largo Drive to Windsor Road to Science Drive

McQueens Island Trail: 6 miles for hiking and biking between Bull River and Fort Pulaski along U.S. 80

McCorkle Trail: Wilmington Island at Charlie C. Brooks Park, 7001 Johnny Mercer Boulevard

Walking

The best way to enjoy Savannah's Historic Downtown is with a comfortable pair of shoes. *Walking Magazine* dubbed Savannah one of the Top 10 walking cities in the United States. To help find your way around on foot, we have included a walking tour in the Attractions chapter—that's

Steep stone stairs sweep down the bluff from Bay Street toward River Street. PHOTO: BETTY DARBY

a good place to start. Before you set out, however, here are a few tips, along with some rules of the walking road to make your trip a little easier.

Enjoy the Squares, Carefully

Historic Downtown is only about 2.5 square miles, so it is fairly easy to see the entire area on foot. Savannah's famed squares make the trip even easier because they are perfect for strolling. Besides spacious walkways, there are also many benches in case you need to take a rest between jaunts.

A word of caution: Pedestrians don't get the same respect here they get elsewhere. Do not assume traffic will stop when you step into a crosswalk, no matter how clearly it is marked. In fact, if you do see someone yield to a pedestrian, check the car as it passes—it probably has out-of-state license plates. And when you are driving, don't be surprised that pedestrians casually jaywalk here. We don't recommend it—we just point out that it happens.

Crossing Bay Street

Although the Historic Downtown is generally very pedestrian friendly, one area that isn't is Bay Street. This is the main street running east to west in front of City Hall. Many tourists encounter Bay Street, as it must be crossed to reach River Street, the tourist haven running along the Savannah River. As mentioned in our Bicycles section, Bay Street is a very busy, narrow four-lane road that serves as the main throughway for eighteen-wheeler traffic trying to make it to other areas in the city. Many visitors think they can beat the traffic on Bay Street, get halfway across, and find themselves stuck in the middle, dangerously close to traffic and unable to safely pass to the other side. After experimenting with several options, the city went with increasing the number of traditional traffic lights to get pedestrians across. Most have a button-activated pedestrian signal: Push it, wait (and wait), then move quite briskly across.

Getting to River Street

Savannah is built on a bluff overlooking the river, even though it probably looks flat to you. River Street runs along the Savannah River, which means it's lower than the rest of the city and can present a challenge to pedestrians. One of our favorite city projects of late was the 1998 installation of an elevator behind City Hall on Bay Street. The handicapped-accessible elevator whisks riders down to River Street, avoiding the stairs and the cobblestone streets on its way. The elevator is between City Hall (can't miss that giant gold dome) and the Hyatt Regency Savannah (which, bless it, is a giant modern fortress that sticks out like a sore thumb and can't be missed either). Part of the elevator project included the installation of a public rest room facility on the River Street level. We've stopped in periodically and been impressed with its upkeep. There's also a small information station with a friendly question-answerer, a brochure rack, and—most important in Savannah's climate—a water fountain. The more adventurous pedestrian might want to skip the elevator and hoof it to River Street. One option to get to River Street involves stairs. There is a hodgepodge of choices available—we prefer the wide, easily negotiated set that runs along the east (right-hand when you face the river) side of City Hall. All these stairs are old, and many aren't particularly easy to navigate, such as narrow slate steps curving along a stone wall with an aged metal railing. The steps tend to be beside the ramps that carry traffic to River Street. Be extremely careful, and if you want, walk down the ramps that cars use to get to the river.

Although you can avoid the tricky stairs this way, you won't avoid the cobblestone ramps, another potential pedestrian pitfall. The cobblestones are very beautiful and not as steep as the stairs, but beware walking on them with any type of heeled shoe. (Purists will point out that these are ballast stones, not proper cobblestones, but we figure a round, smooth rock is a round, smooth rock—whatever you call it.) These roads and ramps are uneven and difficult to walk on, even for people with the surest feet and flattest shoes. If you are not above sneaking, you can duck into the elevator at the Savannah Hyatt Regency for a ride down to River Street—but you can't take a ride up without a room key.

Quick Trips

Here are a few suggested routes that may save you some time and frustration when getting from a few popular point A's to point B's. Note that all these jaunts are in the fifteen-to-twenty-minute range.

Historic Downtown to Oglethorpe Mall—Option One: Take Whitaker Street south about 2 miles to Victory Drive. Turn left on Victory Drive, then right at the second light onto Abercorn Street. The mall is about 4 miles down Abercorn Street. Turn left into Oglethorpe on Mall Boulevard.

Option Two: Take Bay Street east. In less than 1 mile it runs into President Street Extension. From President Street Extension, take Truman Parkway. After a couple of miles, exit to the right on DeRenne Avenue (you can't miss it—that's as far as the parkway construction has gotten so far), then turn left onto Abercorn and look for Mall Boulevard after about 0.5 mile.

Historic Downtown to Savannah Mall: Take I-16 4 miles west to the Lynes Memorial Parkway exit and go south. After 2.5 miles on the Lynes Parkway, exit at the Southwest Bypass (also known as the Veterans Parkway) and continue 7.5 miles until it ends at Georgia 204. Turn left onto Georgia 204, which becomes Abercorn Street, and the mall will be some 3 miles ahead on your left.

Historic Downtown to Grayson Stadium: Take Bay Street east to President Street Extension, then take Truman Park-

Insiders' Tip

There are some disadvantages to being close to sea level. Drenching thunderstorms are frequent in the summer, and if an incoming or high tide has filled up the drainage ditches (we call them canals), the water won't run off. Street flooding results, and in some areas—including well-developed residential areas—the water gets high enough to disable cars. Wait really heavy storms out—the flooding is usually short-lived. Better to spend some extra time indoors than to risk getting stuck in rising waters.

way to Victory Drive. Head west on Victory after exiting, and the stadium will be on your left after about 1 mile.

Historic Downtown to Savannah International Airport: Take I-16 west to I-95 north. The airport is 14 miles away at exit 104 off I-95.

Historic Downtown to Amtrak Station: Go west on Liberty Street, which turns into Louisville Road after less than a mile. Take a left on Telfair Road, then a right on Seaboard Coastline Drive.

History

Perhaps no other city owes as much to one man as Savannah owes to James Edward Oglethorpe, the English soldier and politician who founded Georgia. Oglethorpe was the mastermind and driving force behind the development of the colony of Georgia, whose first city was Savannah. He selected the site of the city and christened it, giving it the same name as the river that flowed beside it. Oglethorpe supervised the first phase of the building of Savannah, and he nurtured the city during its infancy as a town. He defended it in its early years, militarily and financially.

More than that, Oglethorpe bestowed on Savannah a gift that has flourished throughout the decades and centuries since his passing. He designed and laid out the town and, in so doing, created the atmosphere that makes Savannah unique among cities. He left a legacy that has been admired and enjoyed by countless residents and visitors—a treasure that will be the pride of the city for as long as it stands.

Oglethorpe and His Idea

Oglethorpe was born into a family that had a long history of service to England. After serving in the British army and fighting the Turks as the aide-de-camp of an Austrian prince, Oglethorpe was elected to the lower house of Parliament in 1722 at the age of 25. He developed an interest in the misfortunes of the poor, in particular the plight of debtors who had been thrown into prison by creditors hoping the debtors' friends would secure their release by paying the debts. He worked for prison reform and attempted to find solutions to England's unemployment problems.

Together with John Perceval, another member of Parliament, Oglethorpe hatched the idea of giving people who were out of work a fresh start by transporting them to a new colony in America that would be located between Spanish Florida and the English colony of South Carolina. Oglethorpe and Perceval petitioned King George II for a charter, which the king signed on April 21, 1732. The deal was not one-sided: The crown was motivated by the prospect of having colonists raise produce and raw materials to ship to England while serving as a market for English goods. The idea of having the new colony act as a buffer between the Spanish in Florida and thriving South Carolina was not lost on the royals either. To top it all off, the colony was to be named Georgia in honor of the king.

The colony would be managed by Oglethorpe, Perceval, and nineteen other trustees, who would receive no pay and no land for their involvement. There were also rules for the colony: Slavery, lawyers, and "brandies and distilled liquors" (in particular rum) were prohibited, as were Catholics. In time, all would be allowed. Those who took advantage of the free passage to Georgia offered by the trustees agreed to remain in the colony for three years, and each received a town lot for a house and fifty acres to farm. A colonist would not own the acreage and could occupy it only as long as he farmed it properly. Grants of 500 acres were available to people who paid their way to the colony.

The trustees adopted as their motto the Latin phrase *Non Sibi Sed Allis* ("Not for themselves but others"). It appears on Georgia's original seal, which also bears a rendering of a silkworm crawling across a mulberry leaf; it was hoped that the colony would produce silk in abundance.

Before the English Came

Although Oglethorpe brought a European-style civilization to this land across the sea known as Georgia, he and his little band of settlers were very much the new kids on the block. According to Max E. White, author of *Georgia's Indian Heritage*, human beings had existed in Georgia many centuries before. White states that "the earliest evidence of man's presence in Georgia and the Southeast is in the form of fluted projectile points identical to or very similar to those found west of the Mississippi and dated to about 12,000 years ago." In addition to discovering such rudimentary tools as projectile points, modern man has found other evidence of the native peoples of Georgia—shell middens and ceremonial mounds. The middens are piles of refuse "composed primarily of mussel shells discarded by prehistoric diners." "Many times," says White, "people were buried in these shell heaps and utilitarian objects, such as bone awls, projectile points, etc., were often placed with them." The remnants of shell middens can be seen in the Savannah area at Skidaway Island State Park (see our Parks and Recreation chapter).

Although Oglethorpe and his Englishmen were the first Europeans to make a go of settling in southeast Georgia, others had visited before them. Spanish explorer Hernando de Soto passed through in 1539-40 during his trek across the southeastern United States. After de Soto's countrymen established a settlement at St. Augustine, Florida, in 1565, they built Catholic missions and churches on Georgia's sea islands, the last of which was closed in 1702. French explorer Jean Ribault—who started short-lived settlements at what are now Jacksonville, Florida, and Beaufort, South Carolina—sailed along the Georgia coast in 1562.

"Almost all of Georgia was forest-covered when the Europeans first appeared on the scene," says White. The Native Americans living there were, for the most part, members of the Creek and Cherokee nations, "practicing an economy based on agriculture, hunting, fishing, and gathering." Most were Indians belonging to the Creek Confederacy, and one of them—Tomo-chi-chi—would have a significant impact on the survival of Oglethorpe's new colony.

A Whole New World

Oglethorpe and his fellow trustees recruited 114 colonists comprising thirty-five families for the first voyage to Georgia and the task of starting a settlement there. Oglethorpe was the only trustee to make the trip. They left Gravesend, England, on November 17, 1732, aboard a 200-ton vessel named the *Anne* and arrived in what is now Charleston, South Carolina, on January 13, 1733. The settlers then made their way south down the South Carolina coast and, after transferring to smaller boats, landed in the new colony on February 1. That was the date of Georgia's founding according to the Julian calendar. When that calendar was abandoned in favor of the Gregorian calendar nineteen years later, the date became February 12—the day now celebrated as Georgia Day (see our Georgia Heritage Celebration entry in the Annual Events and Festivals chapter). Oglethorpe had gone ahead of the colonists several days before their landing and chose a site for the town of Savannah on a forty-foot-high bluff overlooking the Savannah River—Yamacraw Bluff. In a letter to the trustees explaining his choice of the site for a city, he stated that he "thought it healthy" and wrote, "The last and fullest consideration of the Healthfulness of the place was that an Indian nation, who knew the Nature of the Country, chose it for their Habitation."

The Indians were the one hundred-odd members of the Yamacraw tribe of the Lower Creek nation, led by an eighty-year-old chief named Tomo-chi-chi (meaning to "fly up"). The Yamacraws would prove friendly and helpful to the colonists—providing them with food, interceding with other tribes on their behalf, and aiding them in their struggle against the Spanish. The Yamacraws had come to the coast some eight years before the English, led there by Tomo-chi-chi from what is now west Georgia. Other new neighbors were the Musgroves—Mary, an Indian woman, and her husband John, who was white. The Musgroves ran a nearby trading post called Musgrove Cowpen, and they would serve as interpreters for the Europeans and the Native Americans.

Washington's guns, cannon on display on Bay Street near City Hall, are reminders of our first president's visit to Savannah in 1791. PHOTO: BETTY DARBY

Savannah's Priceless Jewels

The squares of Savannah lend the town a beauty and charm that's unique among American cities. But it's likely that James Edward Oglethorpe had defense as much as aesthetics in mind when he included the little parks in his plan for the city.

According to *Historic Savannah*, a survey of the city's buildings published by the Historic Savannah Foundation in 1979, "military considerations certainly played a major role" in the plan. The smallness of the squares and lots surrounding them "made the town more compact and easier to defend." The squares were also places where colonists living in the outposts could bring their families and livestock if attacked by Spaniards or Indians.

As conceived by Oglethorpe, the squares were at the center of the town's wards. Each ward had four "tythings," with each tything containing ten lots for houses. In a ward, the tythings were on the northern and southern sides of the square, with the eastern and western sides of the square set aside as trust lots for public buildings. Oglethorpe laid out six wards and their squares. Four of these squares—now named Johnson, Wright, Ellis, and Telfair—were laid out in 1733, with Johnson being the first. Later, Oglethorpe laid out Reynolds and Oglethorpe Squares.

Eventually, a total of twenty-four squares were created. Two of them, Elbert and Liberty, have been "lost" to progress—bisected by Montgomery Street, they now exist as half-squares, with one half still parklike and the other half covered by public buildings. A third square, Ellis, is completely covered by a public parking garage.

No one knows for sure what inspired Oglethorpe to design Savannah as he did. "Perhaps his interest in town planning grew out of his friendship with an English architect, Robert Castell," surmises *Historic Savannah*. "Perhaps, because of his previous military service under Prince Eugene of Savoy, Oglethorpe followed the traditions of old Roman military camps. And perhaps he may have seen and utilized a plan of Peking, originally printed in 1688 and reproduced years later."

Castell, who died in debtors' prison, a circumstance that might have prompted Oglethorpe's interest in prison reform, had published a book called *The Villas of the Ancients,* and Oglethorpe owned two copies. According to historian William Harden, the book was "richly illustrated, and containing matter certainly of interest, and very probably of utility to one who might have in view the founding of a town or planning the laying out of pleasure grounds." Whatever Oglethorpe's inspiration, it lives happily on in the form of Savannah's priceless jewels, her squares.

The following is a list of Savannah's squares, with brief explanations of who or what they are named for:

Calhoun Square—for John C. Calhoun, a South Carolinian considered to be the Old South's greatest spokesman in the U.S. Senate

Chatham Square—for William Pitt, English prime minister and the Earl of Chatham during the period when Georgia was a royal colony

Chippewa Square—for the Battle of Chippewa, an American victory in Canada during the War of 1812

Columbia Square—for the female personification of the United States

Crawford Square—for William Crawford, a Georgia governor and U.S. secretary of the treasury

Elbert Square—for Samuel Elbert, a patriot of the American Revolution and a Georgia governor

Ellis Square—for Sir Henry Ellis, Georgia's second royal governor

Franklin Square—for statesman and inventor Benjamin Franklin, who at one time was an agent for Georgia in London

Greene Square—for Gen. Nathanael Greene of Rhode Island, Revolutionary War hero and short-lived owner of a plantation west of Savannah

Johnson Square—for Robert Johnson, the royal governor of South Carolina who aided Oglethorpe in establishing the colony of Georgia

Lafayette Square—for the Marquis de Lafayette, the Frenchman who was an important ally of the United States during the Revolutionary War

Liberty Square—in recognition of the nation's freedom and independence and for the Sons of Liberty, a group of young men who fanned the flames of revolution during the late 1700s

Madison Square—for James Madison, fourth president of the United States

Monterey Square—for the Mexican city captured by U.S. forces during the war with Mexico

Oglethorpe Square—for James Edward Oglethorpe, founder of Georgia

Orleans Square—for the Battle of New Orleans, an American victory in the War of 1812

Pulaski Square—for Polish Count Casimir Pulaski, who fought on the American side during the Revolutionary War and was killed during the Siege of Savannah

Reynolds Square—for John Reynolds, Georgia's first royal governor

Telfair Square—for the Telfair family, whose members made important contributions to Georgia in the areas of politics, business, the arts, and philanthropy

Troup Square—for Georgia governor George Michael Troup, who was also a U.S. senator

Warren Square—for Gen. Joseph Warren, a hero of the Revolutionary War

Washington Square—for George Washington, first president of the United States

Whitefield Square—for George Whitefield, one of the founders of the Bethesda orphanage

Wright Square—for Sir James Wright, Georgia's third royal governor

The colonists spent their first night in their new home camped out in an area that is now the site of a small park at Bay and Whitaker Streets. In the following days and weeks, Oglethorpe and Col. William Bull of South Carolina laid out the new city, and the settlers set about clearing the pine woods on the bluff with the help of black slaves from the neighboring colony. They also began cultivating a ten-acre plot that would be known as Trustees Garden. On this parcel, at the present Bay and East Broad Streets, were planted fruit trees and the mulberry trees that were envisioned as the basis of Georgia's silk industry.

Things went well at the outset. By fall 1734, according to a letter from a South Carolina merchant who had visited the town, there were eighty houses and forty more being built. During Georgia's first decade, the trustees sent more than 2,000 settlers. Other new arrivals brought diversity to the colony. Among them was a boatload of Jews from Portugal who established a Jewish congregation, Mickve Israel. It was the third founded in America and continues today as the South's oldest. Another was a group of Germans, the Salzburgers, who settled 21 miles upriver from Savannah in what is now Effingham County. Their community of New Ebenezer prospered, and the house of worship they built in 1769 is the oldest standing church in Georgia.

Also during the colony's infancy, Savannah became the site of the oldest orphanage in American with a continuous existence: Bethesda Home for Boys. The orphanage's founders, George Whitefield and James Habersham, came to Georgia in 1738 at the request of two Anglican ministers, the Wesley brothers, Charles and John, the latter of whom preached in Savannah during the mid-1730s and went on to found the Methodist church. Bethesda was situated southeast of the town on the banks of the Moon River, with the foundation of the first building being laid in March 1740. It is still in operation, and visitors are welcome to tour the site, a museum, and a chapel (see our Attractions chapter).

Oglethorpe remained involved with the colony during its first ten years, and in July 1742, he led a contingent of soldiers and Indian allies in a battle that forever wrested control of the region from the Spanish in Florida. In the Battle of Bloody Marsh, his band of defenders surprised and defeated a numerically superior Spanish invasion force about 70 miles south of Savannah at St. Simons Island. The Spanish never attempted another invasion, and a peace treaty between Spain and England was signed in 1748.

Oglethorpe left Georgia on July 22, 1743, never to return. Even before his departure, Savannah began to decline as the population dwindled due to the hardships of bringing civilization to a wilderness: insects, alligators, extremes in the weather, difficulties in growing crops. The colony remained a trusteeship until 1752, when the trustees, burdened by financial problems and turnover in their ranks, relinquished their charter to the crown a year before it was to expire. As Preston Russell and Barbara Hines wrote in their

lyrical *Savannah: A History of Her People Since 1733*, "Non Sibi Sed Allis had fallen on its nose. The dream was long since dead, but Savannah was here to stay."

A Royal Comeback

Under control of the crown, Georgia's government changed from the benevolent dictatorship of the trustees to a more traditional setup headed by a governor and having an assembly of elected representatives. Under this arrangement, Georgia was upgraded from colony to province, with Savannah serving as the seat of government.

The first Royal Assembly met in Savannah in January 1755, and one of its first acts was to adopt a law allowing slavery. The first of Georgia's three royal governors, John Reynolds, began a two-and-a-half-year tenure in October 1754; he was succeeded by Henry Ellis, who gave way to James Wright in 1760. Wright, who ruled as governor until January 1776, was a godsend for Savannah's struggling economy. "In mere months, Wright led the youngest colony through stages of development that had required years in other colonies," states Edward Chan Sieg in his book *Eden on the Marsh: An Illustrated History of Savannah*. "Wright's administration was geared to accommodate the 'men of substance' who began to pour into Georgia from other colonies and from the plantations of the Indies. Aided by liberal credit policies and cheap labor, they transformed the coastal plains into the great plantations of legend. Wharf facilities and warehouses appeared on the bluff as shipping demands increased almost daily."

The major export was rice, the growing of which had been made possible by the repeal of the ban on slavery. The idea of making Savannah a silk-production center had flopped, apparently due to a combination of mismanagement and the silkworms' problems with the climate. By 1766, Wright was estimating that the province of Georgia was inhabited by as many as 10,000 whites and 7,800 black slaves—up from a total of 3,000 people nine years earlier—and that exports of rice had tripled over a six-year span.

The Great Rebellion

In the mid-1760s, many residents of England's American colonies reacted with outrage to what they deemed unfair taxation of imported items by the mother country. As the following decade unfolded, their dissatisfaction grew to the point that they sought independence from England.

The fervor for freedom took hold somewhat slowly in Savannah, but by mid-1774, it began to show itself in the actions of a group of dissidents called the Liberty Boys. Despite Governor Wright's efforts to stop them, they met several times to protest England's closing of the Boston Harbor as punishment for the Boston Tea Party. In January 1775, Noble Wimberly Jones, a Liberty Boy who had been speaker of the Royal Assembly, convened a meeting of Georgia's First Provincial Congress. Wright dissolved the body, but on July 4 a meeting of a second provincial congress was held, with the 102 delegates electing representatives to the colonies' Second Continental Congress.

In the interim, in May members of the Liberty Boys celebrated the opening shot of the American revolution by breaking into the city's munitions room, stealing 600 pounds of powder, and shipping it to Boston to be used in the fight against the British. The powder really hit the fan on January 18, 1776, when three British warships showed up off the coast of Savannah. The newly established provincial government placed Wright under house arrest, putting an end to British rule in Savannah for the time being. The

Insiders' Tip

The first African American church in America—the African Baptist Church—was established in Savannah in 1788 by a slave named Andrew Bryan. From its congregation evolved two churches still in existence: First African Baptist on Montgomery Street and First Bryan Baptist on Bryan Street.

An avenue of live oaks leads to Wormsloe Historic Site. PHOTO: KYLE CASON

governor later slipped away and escaped on an English vessel.

On August 10, Savannahians aching for freedom celebrated the signing of the Declaration of Independence, a document endorsed by three Georgians, George Walton of Savannah and Lyman Hall and Button Gwinnett of nearby St. John's Parish. The new state of Georgia elected Archibald Bulloch as governor and completed a constitution in February 1777. Bulloch died during his first year in office and was replaced by Gwinnett.

Savannah, being in an exposed position on the far southeastern reaches of the new United States, paid for its location on December 29, 1778, when 3,000 British troops commanded by Col. Archibald Campbell routed the city's 700 defenders. The enemy had landed below Savannah two days before and slipped behind American Gen. Robert Howe and his forces. The British sacked the city, and James Wright returned to take control of Savannah. He and a small redcoat garrison found themselves under siege in September 1779 by a force of Frenchmen, Irishmen, and volunteers from Haiti. They were joined by a contingent of American troops from South Carolina, and on October 9, the overall commander of the allied forces, French Count Charles Henri d'Estaing, ordered an attack on a defensive position southwest of the city in an area near the existing Savannah Visitors Center. The assault on this position, the Spring Hill redoubt, was, in the words of authors Russell and Hines, "a disaster, the bloodiest single hour in the entire Revolution."

"Through three valiant advances and the staggering retreat," they wrote, "French and Americans were slaughtered by land and naval artillery from Spring Hill redoubt and from... ships in the river." The defenders lost fifty-five men; the attackers suffered more than 1,000 casualties, including the deaths of two men later immortalized in monuments in Savannah's squares—Casimir Pulaski, a Polish count who had brought a group of lancers to the fray, and Sgt. William Jasper, who fell while attempting to save the flag of his South Carolina regiment. Savannah remained in possession of the British until after the climactic Battle of Yorktown. Wright and his compatriots evacuated the city several months after that American victory in Virginia, and American forces took control of the city on July 11, 1782.

The Antebellum Era

The Revolutionary War left Savannah a shambles, but the city recovered and prospered in the years between the end of that fight for freedom and an even grimmer struggle in the 1860s. Much of Savannah's prosperity in the years after the Revolution and before the American Civil War was due to a machine invented in 1793 on a plantation west of the city. While serving as a tutor at Mulberry Grove—a plantation owned by the widow of Revolutionary War Gen. Nathanael Greene—a Connecticut school teacher named Eli Whitney perfected the cotton gin, a device for removing the seeds from cotton bolls. The machine helped revolutionize the cotton-producing industry and, in so doing, reinforced the value of slavery in the agrarian South—a circumstance that would bring disaster to the region and Savannah.

But in the early 1800s, cotton brought wealth to the city's port. On the subject of the city's transformation, Russell and Hines wrote, "In 1790 cotton exports were one thousand bales; by 1820 they were ninety thousand bales a year. In 1794 Savannah's population was 2,000 with export revenues under $500,000. By 1819 she was America's sixteenth largest city with exports exceeding $14,000,000." As Savannah prospered, its residents built elegant homes and other imposing structures. Probably the most famed of the designers of these buildings was architect William Jay, who came to the city from England in 1818, stayed for seven years, and is responsible for existing masterpieces such as the Richardson-Owens-Thomas House, the Scarbrough House, and the Telfair Academy of Arts and Sciences (see our Attractions chapter).

Savannahians experienced some giddy high points during the years between the wars. Among the highest was the transat-

lantic voyage of the SS *Savannah*, a vessel that was bankrolled by local merchants and propelled by steam and sail. The ship left Savannah on May 22, 1819, and arrived in Liverpool, England, a record-breaking twenty-nine days and eleven hours later. On the return trip, the *Savannah* shattered that record by four days. A much more lasting achievement involving transportation occurred in 1847 when the

Colonial Cemetery is the final resting place of many early settlers. PHOTO: KYLE CASON

Central of Georgia Railroad was completed, with Savannah as its eastern termi-
nus. At that time, "Savannah reached its
antebellum zenith," stated author Edward
Chan Sieg.

"Now profits really soared and Savannah enjoyed a period of unprecedented
growth. In addition to cotton, other
sources of income were tobacco, rice, corn,
lumber, and naval store…. The population
tripled, the city limits were extended, gas
lighting made its appearance. Hospitals,
churches and orphanages grew in number
for blacks and whites as excess wealth permitted the emergence of the charity traditions which were Savannah's birthright."

Other highly memorable moments
occurred when two heroes of the revolution visited the city. In May 1791, while he
was serving as the first president of the
United States, George Washington came
to town for four days and attended

numerous get-togethers. One of these was a ball at which, according to William Harden's *A History of Savannah and South Georgia,* the Father of Our Country was "introduced to ninety-six elegantly dressed ladies." In appreciation of his stay, Washington presented the militiamen of the Chatham Artillery with two brass cannon used at Yorktown; they now occupy a spot on Bay Street just east of City Hall. The other visitor was Washington's French ally, the Marquis de Lafayette. He stopped over in March 1825 and was honored with a parade and many toasts.

Unfortunately, there were also some low points, including fires that destroyed large parts of the city in 1796 and 1820, deadly outbreaks of yellow fever in 1820 and 1854 (the epidemic of the former year killed 666), and a storm in 1804 that caused the drowning of more than one hundred slaves, submerged Hutchinson Island, and greatly damaged many of the area's plantations. But as bad as those occurrences were, they were almost insignificant when compared to a disaster that was yet to come.

The Worst Kind of War

Disputes between Northern and Southern states over slavery and states' rights boiled over in the mid-1800s with cata-clysmic results: the secession of Georgia and her Southern neighbors from the Union, the South's forming of a Confederacy, and the fighting of a war of the worst kind—a civil war. Although the war started in Charleston on April 16, 1861, when Confederate forces fired on and captured Fort Sumter, it was Savannah that, in the words of writers Russell and Hines, committed "the first belligerent act of the rebellious South."

Three months before Sumter, members of three militia outfits traveled by steamer from Savannah to Cockspur Island and seized Fort Pulaski, a large masonry edifice guarding the mouth of the Savannah River. Wrote Col. Charles H. Olmstead, who commanded the Confederates, "In due time Fort Pulaski was reached; its garrison, one elderly United States sergeant, made no defense, and the three companies of the First Volunteer Regiment marched in with drums beating and colors flying, and so for them a soldier's life began." Olmstead and others thought Fort Pulaski was impregnable. But fifteen months after its bloodless seizure, shells from rifled cannon emplaced on Tybee Island by Federal troops left the thick walls of the fort looking like Swiss cheese (see our Tybee Island chapter). After thirty hours of bombardment, Olmstead realized that holding the fort was impossible and surrendered it and its 385 defenders.

Following Pulaski's fall, the new occupants of the fort and their comrades in the Union navy began a blockade of Savannah. The city's exports of cotton and other goods were thus bottled up, and the residents spent most of the war enduring the hardships of the siege by sea and mourning the loss of relatives and loved ones who fell on faraway fields of fire. Among those who died were brothers Joseph C. and William N. Habersham, killed in fighting near Atlanta on the same day in July 1864.

Later that year came Union Gen. William T. Sherman's devastating March to the Sea across Georgia. The prize at the end of the trek was Savannah. Sherman took it on December 21, but not before a

Clad in Civil War regalia, members of the staff at Old Fort Jackson gaze at the Savannah River from the parapet of the structure, which was a key part of Confederate defenses south of the city.

battle at Fort McAllister south of Savannah near Richmond Hill (see our Daytrips chapter) and a skirmish at what would become the town of Pooler. The Union commander also allowed a force of 10,000 badly outnumbered Confederate defenders to slip out of the city and into South Carolina. In an oft-quoted telegram to President Abraham Lincoln that the commander in chief received on Christmas Eve, Sherman wrote, "I beg to present you as a Christmas Gift, the City of Savannah with 150 heavy guns and plenty of ammunition; and also about 25,000 bales of Cotton."

Savannah was out of the war, and its citizens settled in to cope with the city's occupation by Union troops. For the most part, it was a benign affair. "The occupation was a model of order, even occasional pleasantry, with both sides generally behaving like ladies and gentlemen," wrote Russell and Hines. Regardless of this, however, some of the women of the town refused to walk beneath the American flag.

Bouncing Back Again

Unlike some Southern cities, Savannah survived the Civil War without being decimated by shell fire or burned to the ground, although a fire that broke out a month after the city's surrender destroyed one hundred buildings. But the war took its toll, leaving the city bankrupt and its people in need of food. However, within a year of the end of hostilities, said Sieg in *Eden on the Marsh*, "Savannah was rolling again," a beneficiary of the rapid rebuilding of the South's railroads and a resurgence in cotton production. In Savannah, "exports for 1867 exceeded fifty million dollars," wrote Sieg. "The predictors of doom following the loss of slave labor were proved wrong as a rising market pushed cotton production to levels never realized" under slavery.

After the war, Savannah and the rest of the South entered into an eleven-year period of Reconstruction during which radical Northern politicians hoped to build a power base with the support of former slaves. Ultimately they failed, and slavery was replaced by a caste system and the creation of a so-called separate but equal society that was more separate than it was equal. In Savannah, "blacks entered a long period of assimilation," said Sieg. "As a result, they developed their own culture, built their own institutions, formed their own business associations, created their own art, music, and literature—and in the process, developed a black elite that led the march into the twentieth century." Among the institutions founded was the Georgia State Industrial College, which is now Savannah State University (see our Education and Child Care chapter).

Economically, the last quarter of the nineteenth century saw the rice plantations around Savannah go out of business, turpentine and rosin from Georgia's pine forests rival cotton as the city's chief export, and the port enhanced by the dredging of the Savannah River shipping channel to a depth of twenty-six feet from fourteen feet at the end of the war. There was also a spate of disasters during the last twenty-five years of the 1800s: Yellow fever killed more than 1,000 people in 1876, and the city was damaged by five significant fires, a tornado, two hurricanes, and an earthquake.

Racing into the Twentieth Century

Savannah focused international attention on itself early in the twentieth century by hosting Grand Prix and Vanderbilt Cup automobile racing in 1908, 1910, and 1911. During the first decade of the new century, the city expanded in other ways: A new City Hall was built, and much of the present-day skyline took shape. In the years that followed, Savannah began stretching southward from downtown with the creation of the city's first residential subdivision, Ardsley Park, after World War I (see our Neighborhoods and Real Estate chapter). In the black community, residents formed the

Negro Civic Improvement League to clean up overcrowded neighborhoods and started their own businesses, including the Wage Earners Savings Bank, which by 1915 covered a downtown block. (The bank building is now the site of the Ralph Mark Gilbert Civil Rights Museum, which you can learn about in our Attractions chapter.)

Not all was rosy, however. By the early 1920s cotton production in the South had fizzled out as laborers moved to the industrialized North and the boll weevil decimated Georgia's fields. Late in the decade came the Great Depression, and with it financial stagnation. During the 1930s, Savannah received an economic boost when the Union Bag and Paper Company set up shop just west of the city, bringing with it nearly 600 jobs and a payroll of $1 million. Union Bag, later known as Union Camp, was recently purchased by International Paper Company and is still one of the city's largest employers. The company helped end Savannah's hard times, as did another, more far-reaching event—World War II.

On the Home Front

Savannah contributed mightily to America's war effort. At the Southeastern Shipyard, some 15,000 workers built Liberty Ships. The city's little airport, Hunter Field, was appropriated by the military and turned into a huge air base. In 1943, it became a staging area for bomber aircraft and crews headed for duty in Europe; some 9,000 planes and 70,000 men were processed out of Hunter during the war.

With their airport gone, city officials began building another one in western Chatham County. It, too, was taken over by the government and became a training base for the crews of heavy bombers. Called Chatham Field, the base eventually became the site of Savannah International Airport. Hunter continues to be used by the military and is now known as Hunter Army Airfield.

"The war turned Savannah from a sleepy, traditional, backward-looking town on a muddy river into a full-fledged, twentieth-century American city," wrote Edward Chan Sieg. "Savannahians gave what they had to the war effort, burying another generation of their youth and generously entertaining the youth of other cities." Savannah boomed, what with the influx of workers who came from the countryside to build ships and the city's popularity with military personnel from nearby bases, including the Marine Corps basic training complex at Parris Island, South Carolina.

The boom ended when the war did. The shipyard closed and most of the troops went home. "What remained was a partially deserted, once-fashionable Historic District," said Sieg. "Savannah had moved south to low-roofed suburbs, abandoning hundreds of high-ceilinged townhouses to the dereliction of uncaring tenants, little or no maintenance, and, worst of all, unprofitable values. No wonder that the postwar business leaders reached the conclusion that if Savannah were to survive and flourish, the old city must make way for progress. But the preservationist attitude found its way into the lives of a handful of influential residents who became dedicated to the principle that demolition was not the only answer to decay."

Preserving the Past and Making Progress

Savannahians reacted with shame in 1946 when Great Britain's Lady Astor called the city "a beautiful lady with a dirty face." They were moved to action when the town's City Market on Ellis Square was demolished in 1954 and replaced with a parking garage. The following year, a group of seven women led by Anna C. Hunter chartered the Historic Savannah Foundation for the purpose of saving noteworthy structures from destruction. By the time of the foundation's first general membership meeting in November 1955, the organization had 700 members.

Its first project was saving the Isaiah Davenport House (see our Attractions chapter), and it was successfully followed by many others. Of the group's efforts, Russell and Hines wrote, "The foundation determined to reawaken interest in Savannah's heritage, to convince the public of the economic benefits of restoration, and to promote tourism.... During the next decade the foundation would deluge the city with a massive public relations campaign, arrange for a professional inventory of historic buildings, establish a revolving fund, and help establish a tourism and convention bureau within the Chamber of Commerce."

The group formulated a preservation plan that became a national model and the basis of the city's Historic Zoning Ordinance. By 1970, the foundation had saved more than 150 structures that were resold to individuals for restoration; the organization continues its efforts today from offices at 321 E. York Street.

In recent years, the Savannah College of Art and Design (SCAD)(see our Education and Child Care chapter) has stepped forward as a leader in historic preservation. Among the many buildings the college has restored to house classrooms and offices are former public school buildings, the old Chatham County Jail and portions of what was once the Central of Georgia Railroad complex. In the 1970s, the city government beautified River Street by creating Rousakis Plaza along the waterfront and started a revitalization of the Broughton Street shopping district that is a work in progress.

Since then, Savannahians have witnessed other progressive developments, including the construction of a new airport terminal, the replacement of the aging Talmadge Memorial Bridge, improvements and growth at the city's port facilities, and the construction of the Savannah International Trade and Convention Center on Hutchinson Island. In 1996, Savannah found itself back on the international stage it had trod during the time of the great auto races; this time, the city was hosting the yachting events of Atlanta's 1996 Summer Olympic Games. The opening and closing ceremonies of the games in Savannah were held at the eastern end of River Street, close to where James Edward Oglethorpe and his little band of colonists landed 263 years before.

Bed-and-Breakfast Inns

Savannah is perfect for romance. Scattered around the Historic Downtown are the city's "other" accommodations: bed-and-breakfasts, guest houses, and inns. From a single suite in a privately owned nineteenth century home to magnificently restored mansions, the city offers it all. Stay here and just outside your window you are apt to see horse-drawn carriages, magnolia trees in bloom, and parks perfect for strolling. Many times, you'll also spy a bride and groom coming up the stairs to enjoy their honeymoon.

There are between forty-five and fifty of these establishments to choose from, mostly in Historic Downtown, and the list continues to grow. According to local innkeepers, one of the latest trends in this niche of the hospitality industry is the upsurge of smaller establishments with fewer than five bedrooms. These take many forms, but generally it's a case of a homeowner deciding to convert a portion of a home into a bed-and-breakfast inn. There are more than twenty-five of these smaller establishments (more are coming), and they provide an interesting mix to the already established lot of bed-and-breakfast inns. In these home-based establishments, you may find yourself lodged in a restored carriage house or even occupying the full garden level of the owner's home. (A word of explanation is required: The lowest floor, or ground floor, is known as the garden level. In historic homes, the main entrance often is one the second floor, up a steep flight of steps, and that level is known as the parlor level.)

No matter which one you choose, there is one constant: Each establishment is as unique as its owner. There are lavish, sophisticated inns where sit-down breakfasts are served every morning promptly between 8 and 10 A.M. in a meticulously restored parlor, and there are relaxed and comfortable places where you may feel compelled to take off your shoes and prop your feet up on the slightly worn couch.

The decor can be just as diverse. Maybe you will find a beautiful courtyard with fountains and wrought-iron furniture just right for quiet conversations . . . perhaps there will be marble fireplaces, whirlpool tubs, and eighteenth-century antiques. Many bed-and-breakfast inns boast "Savannah Colors," a group of fifty-six historically accurate colors discovered by a local artist who went around scraping the newer paint off historic buildings and crawling through attics to uncover the hues Savannahians used to color their lives in earlier times. In these places, the restorations are so exacting you may feel transported back to another era. Some hosts won't be happy until you are dripping with Southern hospitality. One innkeeper told us she wanted her guests to feel like they had just visited one of their best Southern friends. But if privacy is what you are looking for, that can be found too. Check into a few bed-and-breakfasts in town, and you might not see the owners for the entire visit.

Another great reason to choose these accommodations is that no matter where you stay, one of the most beautifully preserved historic areas in the entire country awaits just outside your doorstep. All of Savannah's bed-and-breakfasts, guest houses, and inns put you within comfortable walking distance of museum houses, squares, historic churches, monuments, art galleries, coffee shops, and restaurants. If you choose, you can park your car and not move it for your entire stay. (See our Tybee Island chapter for separate options there.)

Although owners may call their establishment a bed-and-breakfast, an inn, or a guest house, in many cases the terms are interchangeable. In fact, the most popular term to describe any of these types of establishments in Savannah seems to be *inn*. However, you may find everything from a one-room inn to a thirty-two-room inn.

Whatever the title, guests can expect to find the amenities expected in finer accommodations, including air-conditioning and private baths. Most accept major credit cards, and a few allow pets. Because of the age and historic value of the properties, many of these lodging options, especially guest houses and smaller bed-and-breakfasts, no longer allow smoking inside. Even those that do allow smoking often restrict it to balconies or courtyards. Many have limited or no wheelchair access, since they are in old mansions. If stairs are a challenge for you, check out the situation by asking when you make reservations. Some inns don't allow young children, and although this may sound harsh to parents at first brush, we'll point out that the B&B experience isn't likely to appeal to kids anyway. Unless otherwise noted, assume that the listed establishments accept major credit cards and do not allow pets. Our listings will point out which accommodations do not allow children. Still, we suggest calling ahead to check on these details if they are a vital part of your travel plans. After all, you'll need to call ahead for reservations anyway—they're not just recommended, they're essential.

And one note on parking: Parking is at a premium in the Historic Downtown. Most of the area, including residential neighborhoods, has metered parking that is patrolled by very vigilant enforcers. Leave your meter expired for even a few minutes, and you are going to be ticketed. Do not make the mistake of thinking that because you have out-of-town license plates you will get a courtesy reminder—that doesn't happen here any longer. It is important to inquire about the parking situation when you call to find out about your accommodations.

Finally, because of the limited number of rooms available and the popularity of Savannah, innkeepers suggest making reservations at least one month in advance. At some places, you may find six weeks is needed. The spring months (anywhere from mid-February through April in Savannah, depending on a year's given conditions) and fall are particularly busy ones for the B&B scene, so book as soon as possible. Choice weekends, including those featuring key Historic Downtown tours of homes or gardens, book up very quickly. To help with your reservations, there are several private reservation services in town, each having access to a portion of the market. Remember, these services only have a set number of bed-and-breakfast inns as clients. When making reservations, you may want to check with more than one reservation service to get a good idea of what is available. Two of these services are RSVP Bed and Breakfast Reservation Service of Savannah

Insiders' Tip

Don't forget about St. Patrick's Day. This is the busiest day of the entire year. If you are hoping to stay on or near the parade route, reservations should be made many months in advance. Some prime spots are booked a year ahead of time. And remember, if you like to party long and loud, you'll have plenty of company in Savannah for St. Paddy's—but you won't fit in with the B&B crowd. Do them—and yourself—a favor and check out more conventional accommodations. You'll find them listed in our Hotels and Motels chapter.

(912–232–7787, 800–729–7787) and Savannah Historic Inns & Guest Houses Reservation Service (912–233–7666, 800–262–4667). The Savannah Area Convention & Visitors Bureau also offers its own reservation service at (877) SAVANNAH.

The following bed-and-breakfast listings are arranged in alphabetical order, and prices are indicated by the dollar-sign code explained in the Price Code featured below. You'll see a range of prices for some of these listings. Due to the wide variety of room options at some bed-and-breakfasts, it is not uncommon for one inn to offer both lower-priced accommodations and luxurious, upscale suites. Be specific when calling for details.

These entries are not meant to be an all-inclusive list of city inns. Instead, we hope to give a good sampling of the variety of special bed-and-breakfast inns doing business in Savannah. If you don't find something that sounds appealing in the following listings, refer again to the reservations services mentioned above. Chances are there are a few newcomers who cropped up between the researching of this book and your reading of it.

Price-Code Key

The dollar signs indicate the average cost for a one-night stay for two adults, not including taxes, gratuities, or add-on amenities. Most establishments charge from $10 to $25 extra for additional guests. Please inquire about the additional fee when you call for reservations. Again, remember that reservations are essential. If you are on a really tight travel budget, chances are B&Bs aren't the accommodations for you—amenities and atmosphere come with a price tag.

$ . . . . $99 and lower
$$ . . . . $100 to $150
$$$ . . . . $151 to $200
$$$$ . . . . $201 to $250
$$$$$ . . . . more than $251

Azalea Inn
217 E. Huntingdon Street
Savannah, GA
(912) 236–2707, (800) 582–3823
$$$

This cheery yellow Victorian is a comfortable, welcoming place with period charm but appealing informality. Owners John McAvoy and Jessie Balentine are the innkeepers at this seven-room inn on the outer fringe of the Historic District.

The Azalea is decorated in an array of flowery colors and textures, with comfortable green chairs inviting you to perch in the parlors. Guest rooms are furnished with four-poster beds and armoires. Many of the suites have fireplaces equipped with gas logs. Some have balconies. In the dining room, you'll find an elaborate mural, a legacy from previous owners who called it "historical and hysterical." It depicts famous scenes and people from history, but look closely and you will find contemporary figures there, along with visual puns like generals in bunny slippers.

The inn is not wheelchair accessible, and smoking is only allowed outside.

The Ballastone
14 E. Oglethorpe Avenue
Savannah, GA
(912) 236–1484, (800) 822–4553
$$$$–$$$$$

The Ballastone is a magnificently restored, four-story 1838 mansion just off Bull Street, one of the historic area's main thoroughfares. Arriving guests will notice the beautiful Queen Anne staircase in the entryway and the warm, lavishly decorated parlor off to the right. Ceiling fans, rice poster and canopy beds, marble-topped tables, and fireplaces are some of the things you might find in one of the eighteen individually decorated rooms. All are lavishly appointed and meticulously kept.

The Victoria Room, decorated in rich yellows, reds, and greens, has a massive king bed and whirlpool tub, while the Gazebo Room has deep greens and two queen beds. Besides the wonderful surroundings, guests enjoy afternoon Victorian tea along with evening hors d'oeuvres. There is a terry cloth robe waiting in the bathroom and nightly turndown service with chocolates and cordials. On weekday mornings, you can choose to have continental breakfast in your room, the parlor, or outside in the courtyard. On Saturdays and Sundays, guests are treated to a full breakfast at their choice of location. Children sixteen years of age and older are welcome at The Ballastone. The inn has been recommended by *Brides, Glamour, Gourmet,* and *Condé Nast Traveler.* This is one of the inns which more closely resembles a small European hotel than a mom-and-pop bed-and-breakfast.

Bed and Breakfast Inn
117 W. Gordon Street
Savannah, GA
(912) 238–0518
$$–$$$

This charming and well-established bed-and-breakfast was an early comer to the scene. The circa-1853 Federal rowhouse on Gordon Row adjoins innkeeper Bob McAllister's home in one of the most attractive areas of the Historic Downtown. McAllister's a well-known host on the local scene, and his hospitality shows in the B&B's operation.

Rooms are furnished in a mixture of antiques and reproductions. (The innkeeper maintains antique chairs shouldn't be subjected to daily use, and guests shouldn't be subjected to antique chairs.) You'll love details such as pocket doors on the parlor level. Renovation has given the building a spacious deck overlooking a beautiful courtyard. The garden suites are prime rooms, complete with full kitchens and living and dining areas. You really won't need that kitchen, though. We can vouch for the freshly cooked breakfast, complete with a talented chef whose repertoire includes wonderful biscuits. If you can get a room over St. Patrick's Day—regular returnees fill most of them—you're in for a real treat, as the breakfast party here is a favorite stopping-off point as locals (including many parade participants) head in for the festivities.

Broughton Street Bed & Breakfast
511 E. Broughton Street
Savannah, GA
(912) 232–6633, (877) 232–6633
$$$–$$$$

Staying at the Broughton Street Bed & Breakfast is like having your own private town house in the heart of Savannah's Historic Downtown. The inn offers two rooms at the quiet end of Broughton Street, essentially downtown Savannah's "Main Street," which is in the midst of a resurgence

Savannah's bed-and-breakfast inns welcome guests with warm Southern hospitality. PHOTO: PHYL M. GATLIN

after years of decline. A new option for guests is the inn's adjacent cottage, a small two-story structure. The master bedroom in the main building includes a four-poster bed, working fireplace, spacious bay window overlooking the street, and a small whirlpool bath and shower combination. The other bedroom has a queen bed with a view of the small rear courtyard.

Besides their private quarters, guests get the run of the house, which includes a library with a huge, inviting leather couch and fireplace. There is a main parlor and dining room perfect for relaxing. All the rooms are nicely decorated with antiques. Wine and hors d'oeuvres are served in the evening. The inn is not wheelchair accessible. Children twelve and older are welcome.

This inn, housed in a circa-1883 town house, was remodeled beginning in 1993. The owners subsequently operated it as a bed-and-breakfast until selling it in the spring of 2000. At the time of the sale, the furnishings were sold as well, but the new owners have outfitted it with a new supply of antiques and reproductions, and the resulting decor provides guests with the same kind of elegant ambience.

Claudia's Manor
101 East 35th Street
Savannah, GA
(912) 233–2379
$$–$$$

Claudia's Manor is several blocks deep into the Victorian District, housed in a circa-1915 Spanish-style mansion and its carriage house. Here, you'll find four rooms, one equipped with a Jacuzzi, and three suites. Among the suites you'll find the View of Africa, where the decor draws on traditional African artwork and other ethnic elements. Another suite offers the View of the Orient, repeating the ethnic theme with an Asian approach. This B&B is farther away from the main Historic District than the others—definitely too far for any but the most athletic to consider walking distance to such places as River Street. However, it is among our more affordable entries, while still offering the amenities one would expect.

Colonial Park Inn
220 E. Liberty Street
Savannah, GA
(912) 232–3622, (800) 799–3622
$$$

Spend some time with innkeepers Alice and Bob Clark, and you get the idea that they like what they do. Since 1995, the Clarks have been inviting people into their Liberty Street home/inn to stay in their guest suites. They have gotten to know some of their guests so well they keep in contact with them, and the Clarks have even received gifts—including a cherub that graces the courtyard—from satisfied customers. "It feels like we are getting paid for having friends come and stay," says Alice.

The Colonial Park Inn is a comfortable, private alternative to some of the more formal inns in town. There are two complete, private entrance suites, including a ground-floor apartment and carriage house. Decorated in soft colors, such as lavenders and pinks, the rooms offer many of the things needed for a comfortable stay.

The Garden Suite has two bedrooms: one with twin brass beds, the other with a double bed. There is also a nicely decorated living room with fireplace and a cozy full kitchen. The suite looks out into the garden. Behind the main house is the Carriage House Suite, a small, private accommodation with a king bed that can be converted to two twins. Decorated in soothing blues and pinks, it also has a small kitchen and a shower. Children over twelve are welcome at Colonial Park Inn.

Columbia Square Inn
125 Habersham Street
Savannah, GA
(912) 236–0444
www.columbiasquareinn.com
$$

There are two things you notice when entering the Columbia Square Inn: the wonderful, wide heart-pine floorboards and the white walls. Although some innkeepers prefer lavish draperies and

Insiders' Tip

Reservations are a must, but while you are making them, be sure to check with the innkeepers on their cancellation policy. Some inns charge if you cancel, on the grounds that they turned away other reservations.

antiques to match, proprietor Barbara Wall's tastes are understated and elegant. There is no clutter here. The floors are nearly uncovered as are the windows, which reveal a view of the fountain in the center of Columbia Square and a magnificent magnolia tree reaching to the top of the home.

All rooms in the home, which the Walls restored several years ago (they occupy the ground floor), are spacious and decorated in the same manner. A leather settee or chair is neatly arranged in front of the fireplace along with a sofa to form a comfortable sitting area in each room. There are four-poster beds and armoires, and one of the rooms has an extra bedroom and a small veranda filled with gigantic ferns. Wall likes to give her guests their space, so everything they might need, from an ironing board to a cold drink, can be found in the rooms. There are small refrigerators, coffeemakers, and microwaves in each. She has found, however, that one of the most popular items she supplies are the Band Aids—to take care of those blisters that come from all that exploring. Continental breakfast is served in the rooms, but guests are welcome to spend their time in the other parts of the inn, including the parlor and dining room. Wall says that guests are delighted and surprised by the quiet conditions at her inn, which is, after all, situated in a prime location.

East Bay Inn
225 E. Bay Street
Savannah, GA
(912) 238–1225, (800) 500–1225
$$–$$$

If you are looking for the charm and ambience of a larger inn for a more moderate price, try the East Bay Inn. Located along bustling Bay Street, it features twenty-eight rooms, each with eighteenth-century furnishings, hardwood floors, four-poster rice beds, high ceilings, and large beautiful windows. Some of the rooms have exposed brick walls that add to the charm. All are very nicely done and meticulously kept. You will feel comfortable whether here on business or for a romantic getaway.

Although one of the larger accommodations in this category, East Bay Inn still has an intimate feeling. Continental breakfast is served every morning in a small cafe that was formerly a bar. It features pretty tables for two covered in white linen. Evening cordials are presented in the lobby, which is decorated in deep greens and reds. Two rooms at the inn are set aside for pet owners; the pet fee is nonrefundable. The inn is not wheelchair accessible.

Another nice addition to the inn's offerings is Skyler's Restaurant. Located in the basement, with exposed brick walls and a huge, beautiful fireplace, Skyler's is a popular choice among locals, especially during the lunch hour. The menu is eclectic, offering items from fresh chow mein to chicken hoagies and crab cakes. You can't beat the teriyaki chicken Caesar salad! (Read more about it in our Restaurants chapter.)

Eliza Thompson House
5 W. Jones Street
Savannah, GA
(912) 236–3620, (800) 348–9378
$$$

This gorgeous inn was an early arrival on the B&B scene, but it underwent a major redecoration and upgrading a few years ago as it changed hands. It fills two buildings. (There are twelve rooms in the main circa-1847 house and thirteen in the courtyard addition or carriage house.) The Eliza Thompson House is run with the efficiency and style of a small European hotel, but it still ranks as a bed-and-breakfast because of its emphasis on personal amenities. It changed hands in 2001, becoming part of an eclectic Savannah-based chain.

Jones Street is a brick street in the residential portion of the Historic Downtown, almost completely canopied by the trees that line either side. Your views are either of this street or the meticulously maintained courtyard, which is equipped with a beautiful fountain complete with original iron sculpture. Guests can breakfast here or, on those rare occasions when the weather does not permit (we do have winter here, such as it is), in a glass-walled alcove overlooking it. Wine and cheese are served in the parlor in the late afternoons, and there's dessert and coffee in the evenings.

The East Bay Inn houses a popular restaurant, Skyler's, in its basement. PHOTO: BETTY DARBY

Rooms differ dramatically in style, although they are all traditionally furnished with antiques. You'll find a fabric-draped ceiling in one, a canopied bed in another. Look for the sumptuous imported bed linens throughout. Wheelchair-accessible (with a bit of effort) suites are available.

Foley House Inn
14 W. Hull Street
Savannah, GA
(912) 232–6622, (800) 647–3708
$$$

When you first walk inside this 1896 brick home, you are struck by the rich burgundy and blue colors blanketing the walls and floors. The sumptuous design and detail extend throughout the parlor and all of the nineteen individually styled rooms. Look out your window at Foley House Inn, and you will see beautiful Chippewa Square. Historic First Baptist Church is across the street and a statue of Gen. James Edward

Oglethorpe, the founder of Georgia, stands in the center of the square. (He's facing south, brandishing a sword to keep the Spanish colonists in Florida, which was part of the Georgia colony's early mission.)

When asked what makes her inn distinctive, owner Inge Svensson Moore replies simply, "I am European." The influence is evident. As *National Geographic Traveler* put it, "Moore has successfully fused continental with Southern." She and her inn even made the cover of a prominent British travel magazine in the spring of 1999. In one suite decorated in deep pink, there is a canopied bed, two fireplaces, and a lovely bay window. In another, the walls are painted rich yellow, and red draperies hang in the sitting area situated by the bay window. They also frame the bed. A large, ornate armoire with his-and-her mirrored closets fills one wall.

All the rooms include fireplaces, and many have whirlpool baths. Tea and hors d'oeuvres are served each afternoon in the parlor, and guests can choose to have their continental breakfast there, in the small courtyard, or in their rooms. Evening cordials are also featured, as is concierge service for making all your dining and exploring reservations. Note that the inn is not conveniently wheelchair accessible.

The Gastonian
220 E. Gaston Street
Savannah, GA
(912) 232–2869, (800) 322–6603
$$$$–$$$$$

Everything about The Gastonian makes you want to come in and relax, from the magnificent verandas taking up one side of the house to the beautifully landscaped courtyard and warm rooms. Little details sometimes make the biggest impressions, and that is what you notice at The Gastonian. Come back from dinner, and you will find pralines on your pillow, the fireplace going (when the weather's right), and soft music playing on the radio. There is a concierge who is friendly and ready to make all your reservations, from dinner to horse-drawn carriage tours. The inn is actually two historic, wonderfully preserved mansions next to each other along Gaston Street. It is in a residential neighborhood, just a short walk from one of Savannah's most beautiful parks— Forsyth.

Georgian and Regency period antiques fill the main parlors, while all of the eighteen rooms are styled individually. Each has a working fireplace, high ceilings, wooden floors, and Persian rugs, and is named for a noted Savannahian. In the Mary Hilyer Room, you will find a beautiful antique quilt with green and red flowers covering one wall. There is a whirlpool bath with a basket of Caswell Massey soaps and lotions nearby and a wonderful stained-glass window. French doors take you out to the veranda, where a wicker lounge chair awaits. Newlyweds often come to The Gastonian to have their pictures taken in the beautiful courtyard.

Insiders' Tip

Did you enjoy your romantic bed-and-breakfast stay? Hang on to those business cards! Weekends at these plush homes-away-from-home are a popular and different gift for newlyweds and others who are celebrating. Of course, the price may make such a gift more feasible as a group offering from the office or a gang of friends.

There is also a sundeck with a hot tub—a perfect spot for enjoying continental breakfast. This inn has served as a temporary home for some of Savannah's visiting movie stars when the city was serving as a filming location.

Granite Steps
126 E. Gaston Street
Savannah, GA
(912) 233–5380
$$$$–$$$$$

The family behind Granite Steps, a luxury circa-1881 mansion restored as a bed-and-breakfast, is involved in luxury resorts in Atlanta, California, and Scotland. This mansion, named for the grand sweeping entrance stairway, was chosen for filming in scenes from the movie *Midnight in the Garden of Good and Evil*.

The building here is imposing, but the inn is also intimate, with two large rooms and three suites. Expect the full array of amenities, along with full breakfast, afternoon tea and coffee, and evening hors d'oeuvres.

The Hamilton-Turner Inn
330 Abercorn Street
Savannah, GA
(912) 233–1833, (888) 448–8849
$$$–$$$$

This circa-1873 mansion is so Victorian in architecture that it is really over the top. It has gone through many variations lately, and until recently one of its roles was as a rental party venue with a gift shop of *Midnight in the Garden of Good and Evil* merchandise—capitalizing on the fact that the book's "Mandy" character once owned it and lived here. Charlie and Sue Strickland transformed the four-story structure to its former glamour and opened the inn in mid-1998.

There are fourteen bedrooms furnished largely in antiques and a separate courtroom whose suite is the size of a house. The location, literally smack in the middle of the Historic District, is a selling point here.

Ivy Inne
505 E. President Street
Savannah, GA
(912) 236–1122, (800) 489–8182
$$–$$$

You will discover privacy, space, comfort, and a very good value at the Ivy Inne. The inn consists of a single suite, the entire ground floor of the innkeeper's home, and includes a private entrance, living room, bedroom, kitchen, and breakfast room. Staying here is like having your own apartment in Savannah's Historic Downtown. The living area is comfortably appointed with a sleigh bed, couch, and brick fireplace. Just off the living room is the bedroom, where you will find another brick fireplace and a queen bed. Small, arched doorways bring you into the full kitchen. The little breakfast room is full of windows and overlooks the side yard. This light, airy, and inviting space is the perfect spot to enjoy breakfast, which you fix yourself from the fully stocked and equipped kitchen. Children are welcome, and there's no additional charge for children under the age of six. You will find useful things such as an ironing board and umbrella in the hall closet. The inn is not wheelchair accessible.

Joan's on Jones
17 W. Jones Street
Savannah, GA
(912) 234–3863, (800) 407–3863
$$$

Joan's on Jones is one of the most established of the smaller bed-and-breakfast inns in Savannah. Innkeepers Joan and Gary Levy have been welcoming guests to their Jones Street home since 1990. (That's a long time in the history of a relatively recent trend.) The experience has taught them many things, Joan says, including the ability to sense who wants attention and who wants to be left alone. Whichever you need, the Joneses are ready to satisfy.

The inn features two suites, both with private entrances and ample room. It is another establishment where you'll feel as if you have your own apartment in the heart of the city. This particular apartment is in a restored 1883 Victorian town house on one of the city's most scenic streets. The Jones Street Suite is painted a rich terra-cotta that Joan discovered in a local historic home and reproduced in her own. It is formally decorated and has pretty stained-glass windows and two fireplaces. Over one fireplace is a collection of old letters and other correspondence found behind the mantel during the restoration process. Reading lamps are over the bed for convenience, and there is a small kitchenette. The Garden Suite—just off a back courtyard that is perfect for relaxing with its lounge garden chairs—has a huge, brick cooking hearth, queen iron bed, and exposed brick walls. There is also a full kitchen. This suite is less formal but more intimate and romantic.

When we first visited, one of the producers from the movie *Midnight in the Garden of Good and Evil* was staying for an extended visit. When you arrive at Joan's on Jones, you will find a bottle of wine waiting for you. Well-behaved dogs are

Many Savannah mansions have found a second life as bed-and-breakfast establishments, such as the Hamilton-Turner House. PHOTO: BETTY DARBY

allowed in the back suite for a nonrefundable fee. Continental breakfast is served each morning, and if you are really hungry, one of the most popular Southern restaurants in the city, Mrs. Wilkes', is just down the brick-paved street (see our Restaurants chapter) and serves a much less crowded breakfast than its popular lunch.

The Kehoe House
123 Habersham Street
Savannah, GA
(912) 232–1020, (800) 820–1020
$$$$–$$$$$

Listed on the National Register of Historic Places, The Kehoe House is a brick Victorian mansion overlooking the fountain in Columbia Square. Everything about this sophisticated, European-style inn—one of Consul Courts offerings—is grand and opulent, from the beautiful, leaded-glass doors and the chandeliers dripping from the ceiling to the massive table that seats ten in the double parlor.

Each of the fifteen spacious rooms is furnished separately with armoires, deco-

rative fireplaces, and elegant antiques. Some of the rooms peer out into a nice side courtyard or have verandas for enjoying the cool breezes. English afternoon tea is served every day at 4 P.M., and guests enjoy a full breakfast in the parlor. Children older than twelve are welcome at The Kehoe House.

Magnolia Place Inn
503 Whitaker Street
Savannah, GA
(912) 236–7674, (800) 238–7674
www.magnoliaplaceinn.com
$$$$–$$$$$

The Magnolia Place Inn merits its name: two magnificent examples of that signature Southern tree flank its wide, sweeping front staircase. It is across from Forsyth Park, Savannah's answer to Central Park, complete with an enormous Victorian fountain.

In this circa-1878 mansion, you'll find fifteen grandly furnished rooms and two suites. The inn recently has begun to capitalize on its history as the birthplace of Pulitzer Prize–winning poet Conrad Aiken.

Magnolia Place Inn is the birthplace of poet Conrad Aiken. PHOTO: COURTESY OF MAGNOLIA PLACE INN

The entire operation is pitched toward catching that *Gone With the Wind* persona, complete with antique furnishings and, in most rooms, fireplaces. Many rooms feature Jacuzzis, and all have at least queen-size beds.

Temper your romantic stay with history lessons. The various rooms are named for figures from Savannah's history (you'll spot that those names are also on Savannah's famous squares).

Save some film—the commanding entrance demands a photo. In fact, people are always double-parking on the busy one-way street outside (Whitaker Street is definitely one of our main drags) and hopping out to shoot it. And there's an impressive butterfly collection in the parlor.

The Manor House
201 W. Liberty Street
Savannah, GA
(912) 233–9597, (800) 462–3595
$$$

If you are looking for a little more space, The Manor House offers five lavishly decorated suites that feature a master bedroom and parlor. Some of the suites even have kitchens. The Manor House was built as a private residence in the 1830s, and some of the suites include huge whirlpool baths and lovely verandas perfect for relaxing with a book or pleasant conversation. The gigantic pocket doors slip into the wall, separating the master bedroom and parlor to provide privacy when needed.

The Twelve Oaks Suite, decorated in rich reds and greens, has a fireplace, a queen sofa bed, and a bench for two at the foot of the regular queen bed—the perfect spot for enjoying your continental breakfast. Terry cloth robes are provided, and this suite also features a huge whirlpool bath for soaking. Guests at The Manor House, which is across the street from the Civic Center, will be treated to nightly turndown service featuring brandy and chocolates and a continental breakfast each morning, served in their room or the main parlor. It's so romantic and inviting, you may forget about the beautiful city just outside your doorstep. The Manor House is not wheelchair accessible. Children older than twelve are welcome. You can also bring your pet.

912 Barnard
912 Barnard Street
Savannah, GA
(912) 234–9121
www.912barnard.com
$–$$

One of the few bed-and-breakfast establishments in Savannah's Victorian District, 912 Barnard is on the fringe of the Historic Downtown area. This section of the city is filled with large, elaborate, and beautiful (or formerly beautiful) Victorian homes and is one Savannah's most active areas of restoration. On some blocks, you will find boarded-up homes in desperate need of rescuing, while others are well on their way to being revitalized.

There are only a handful of guest rooms at 912 Barnard, which is on a block where lots of restoration has taken place and is ongoing. This is one of the more affordable bed-and-breakfasts, but note that it does not accept credit cards. This nice Victorian rowhouse is small, relaxed, and laid back. There is a sit-down breakfast every morning in the dining room, where you will find the table decorated with a lace tablecloth and pretty antique china. The adjoining parlor, also decorated in antiques, is light, airy, and very relaxing with several beautiful windows to bring in the surrounding trees.

The Charleston Room, one of the guest accommodations, features a huge, wonderful bay window, a queen-size Charleston rice bed, sitting area, and fireplace. In the less-sedate Miami Room, you will find hubcaps from a 1972 Cadillac Seville lining one wall. The art deco–inspired room also has a private balcony, and if you look closely, you might find a pink flamingo or two. This B&B bills itself as catering to the gay and lesbian community.

The Old Georgian Inn
212 W. Hall Street
Savannah, GA
(912) 236–2911, (800) 835–6831
$$–$$$$

On the outer reaches of the Historic District, in a neighborhood being revitalized, this circa-1890 mansion was rescued from dilapidation and put into service as a bed-and-breakfast in 1996. Previous visitors may know it as the Grande Toots Inn, but owner Maisha Evans—new innkeeper as of March 2000—has made some changes, including giving it a more conservative title and upgrading the furnishings. A few blocks away from Forsyth Park, this grand mansion features an Italian marble floor, leaded-glass doors, and handsome wallpapers. One of the most striking things about the inn—something that separates it from many others—is that many of the wood surfaces were left unpainted, revealing wonderfully rich and warm browns throughout the house.

Besides the parlor, small dining room, and large dining room (set up with intimate tables for two), guests have a choice of five different accommodations in a variety of styles and price ranges. The top of the line is the Azalea Room, which is spacious, light, and airy and includes a fireplace, Colonial queen bed with white coverlets, and couch. The bath is full of windows and equipped with a whirlpool bath. A smaller option is the Camellia Room, which also has a fireplace and patchwork quilt for linens. It shares a hall bath with another smaller room. In all, between the main house and the carriage house to the rear, there are four rooms for guests.

A continental-plus breakfast is served daily, along with a full Southern breakfast on weekends, when Evans also serves liqueurs. Turndown service is provided.

Insiders' Tip

The bed-and-breakfast industry is a very fluid one. Even established, experienced, and successful innkeepers can simply tire of the business and decide to redesign that extra space as guest rooms for visiting grandchildren. Conversely, couples fixing up a roomy house may launch a bed-and-breakfast rather spontaneously to help pay off that renovation loan. Policies change too—one bad experience with a St. Bernard and an establishment that welcomed pets changes its mind. Our point here is that it's best to call ahead for reservations and confirmation of those essential travel details, like whether your cat is welcome.

Hotels and Motels

As you might have noticed while reading the Area Overview chapter, Savannah is a city of great diversity, and that characteristic holds true when it comes to the accommodations it offers its visitors. Savannah has several hotels that are large and contemporary, and others that are medium-size and quaint. It has motels that are moderately priced but comfortable, and others where, for a few dollars more, you'll be awash in amenities. Many of the hotels and motels offer suites in addition to rooms with the standard two double beds or one king-size bed, and a couple of establishments have nothing but suites.

For visitors seeking more of a personal touch, there are numerous bed-and-breakfast inns scattered throughout Historic Downtown; so many, in fact, we've devoted a separate chapter to them (see our Bed-and-Breakfast Inns chapter). Most of the hotels and motels described here are situated in one of two locations: on or very near Bay Street in Historic Downtown or on or just off Abercorn Street near Oglethorpe Mall in the Midtown area. There are several motels in three other nearby locales: on or near the beach at Tybee Island, which is about 25 minutes from downtown Savannah; in the Southside on Abercorn between Oglethorpe Mall and Savannah Mall; and out on Interstate 95, 10 or more miles from the heart of the city.

The motels at the beach are discussed in the Tybee Island chapter of this book. The accommodations between the malls and out on I–95 represent several major chains and should offer no surprises, but we recommend that, if your destination is Savannah and not the House of the Mouse or some other touristy spot in Florida, you stay closer to our city and soak up some of the atmosphere of our historic old town.

You can be in the midst of that atmosphere by taking a room at a hotel or motel in the downtown area. In most cases, you'll pay accordingly for the location, but you can find some values if you're not too picky about the view from your room and the extras you receive.

Another cost-saving option is to stay at lodgings in the Midtown area. You'll be out of the mainstream of tourism but not by much—the motels and inns in Midtown are only 5 miles from Bay Street, which is about twelve to fifteen minutes traveling time if you avoid rush-hour traffic. Although most of these establishments are geared toward people on business trips, the innkeepers are more than happy to have tourists stay with them. Another reason to take a room in Midtown is that parking will be free. That's not necessarily the case if you stay in Historic Downtown, and we've indicated in our listings if and what you'll have to pay to park at a hotel or motel there.

All of the hotels and motels described in this chapter accept major credit cards and have rooms accessible to the handicapped. Almost all have nonsmoking rooms, and most do not allow pets; if a hotel or motel does not have nonsmoking rooms or does accept pets, that information is included in our listing for the establishment.

You can expect that all accommodations will have color cable TV. If you're looking for premium channels, a phone call might be in order.

In season generally runs from mid-March through October. Some establishments decrease their rates during the hot summer months, and others jack them up on weekends, so you should call in advance to ascertain how much you'll have to spend. If you're planning to stay here on St. Patrick's Day weekend, expect to fork out considerably more than you would at any other time of year and make reservations months in advance. (See our St. Patrick's Day chapter for more information.)

Price-Code Key

Each entry includes a symbol denoting a price range for the average one-night stay, in-season, for two adults. Note that these prices do not include tax, gratuities, and add-on amenities such as premium movie channels or room service. Here's the code:

$ .... $85 or lower
$$ .... $86 to $125
$$$ .... $126 to $170
$$$$ .... $171 and higher

Historic Downtown

Best Western Historic District
412 W. Bay Street
Savannah, GA
(912) 233–1011
www.bestwestern.com
$$$

Once you arrive at the Best Western Historic District, you can park your car and leave it for the rest of your stay, according to the folks who run the 142-room motel. The Best Western fronts on Bay Street, and the motel's rear building is on the western end of River Street, placing the three-story establishment about a block from the shops and restaurants along the river and in City Market (see our Attractions chapter). It's also within walking distance of much of the Historic District. If you want to do your sight-seeing while riding, hop on a tour bus or trolley at the motel's front door.

The Best Western—where a top-to-bottom renovation was completed in early 1999—offers guests deluxe, complimentary continental breakfasts from 6:30 until 9:30 A.M., and there's a fenced-in pool for swimming and sunning on the River Street side of the property. Eighty-seven of the rooms have two full-size beds, and the rest have kings. Parking is free at this motel, which has been accommodating visitors to Savannah since the early 1970s.

Insiders' Tip

When you visit Savannah, you're staying in "the most beautiful city in North America," according to *Le Monde*, one of the leading newspapers of Paris, France. *Conde Nast Traveler* magazine reader polls named Savannah one of the Top 10 U.S. cities to visit from 1994 through 1997.

Courtyard by Marriott
Savannah-Historic District
415 W. Liberty Street
Savannah, GA
(912) 790–8287, (800) 321–2211
www.courtyard.com
$$$

The five-story Courtyard opened in late July 2001, adding 147 guest rooms and 9 suites to Savannah's inventory of overnight accommodations. The suites and eighty-six of the guest rooms offer king-size beds, with nine of the rooms featuring spa-type bathrooms complete with whirlpool tubs. The other rooms have double queen-size beds.

The new Courtyard, with a decor that's traditionally Southern in style, covers an entire block bounded by Martin Luther King Jr. Boulevard and Liberty, Montgomery, and Harris Streets. The main entrance is on Liberty, making the front door a short walk from the Savannah Visitors Center. The hotel's spacious courtyard—a lushly landscaped spot that creates an oasis in the heart of the downtown area—faces Harris Street and is also the site of a heated outdoor pool. Guests can relax here or at the hotel's spa, an exercise facility that includes a large whirlpool.

The Courtyard Cafe, which is in the northwest corner of the ground floor, is a roomy restaurant with plenty of windows to give diners a view of what's happening on Liberty Street and MLK. The Cafe serves breakfast and dinner seven days a week, and Camellia's Lounge is the setting for afternoon teas from 3 to 6 P.M. Thursday through Sunday. Valet parking in the hotel's underground garage or on two surface lots is available for $10 a day.

Days Inn-Days Suites
Historic Riverfront
201 W. Bay Street
Savannah, GA
(912) 236–4440
www.aladv.com/disv
$$$

When you stay at this Days Inn, you're a block from two of Savannah's meccas for tourists: River Street to the north and City Market to the south. This three-story brick hotel is built right on the sidewalk of Bay Street, and if you take a suite, you'll be staying in a building that dates to 1851 and was once the home of the Bargain Corner, a grocery store that was a local landmark. The fifty-seven suites have high-ceilinged bedrooms with queen-size beds, kitchens with full-size refrigerators, and living-dining rooms with pullout sleeper sofas. Including the suites, there are a total of 253 rooms, all of which are entered from interior hallways secured by a coded access system. There's an outdoor pool and the Daybreak restaurant, which serves breakfast, lunch, and dinner. Parking is complimentary in a secured garage adjacent to the motel.

Hampton Inn Savannah
Historic District
201 E. Bay Street
Savannah, GA
(912) 231–9700, (800) HAMPTON

www.hotelsavannah.com
$$$

The Hampton Inn opened in January 1997, but the eight-story hotel fits right in with the city's Historic District. The stucco, brick, and ironwork of the exterior has the look of old Savannah. So does the lobby with its authentic gray bricks that were found on the site during construction, heart-pine floors from an old mill in central Georgia, antique and traditional furniture, Persian rugs, and dark wood bar from England, purchased at a local antique store. The regal way to stay at this Hampton is in a king special: a corner room with windows on two walls, a king-size bed, and a pull-out love seat, wet bar, refrigerator, microwave, and videocassette recorder. The hotel has eight of these rooms, but you might need to make reservations early to get one.

The Hampton is at Bay and Abercorn Streets, 1 block south of River Street. Check out the glorious view of the Savannah River, the Eugene Talmadge Memorial Bridge, and Historic Downtown from the rooftop pool, but wear shades on a sunny day—it's bright up there. The hotel offers a complimentary, deluxe continental breakfast each day from 6 until 11 A.M. The hotel has 1,000 square feet of meeting space with limited food service, and catering by outside sources is allowed. You can park in the hotel's underground garage for $8 a day, and if it's full, the fee will get you a spot at the city-owned garage across Abercorn.

Hilton Savannah DeSoto
15 E. Liberty Street
Savannah, GA
(912) 232–9000, (800) 426–8483
www.savannahdesoto.hilton.com
$$$$

The Hilton projects an aura that's both classical and rich: The lobby, hallways, and rooms are adorned with white columns, dark wood paneling, and burgundy and forest-green furnishings. The fifteen-story hotel stands in the midst of the Historic District, and the views from rooms on the upper floors are spectacular. The concierge floor—the 13th, numbered as such by hotel officials apparently unconcerned with superstition—offers what staff members call the "skyline view." You'll pay extra to stay there, but you'll get the view, a room featuring deluxe amenities such as the Hilton's trademark terry cloth bathrobes and the use of a private lounge serving continental breakfasts in the morning and drinks and hors d'oeuvres in the evening. Step out on the balcony of the lounge and enjoy a panoramic look at the graceful Eugene Talmadge Memorial Bridge and Savannah's riverfront. If you really want to stay in style, request a "corner king"—a room with a king-size bed, balcony, two large corner windows, and a bathroom equipped with a double vanity. You can dine on the premises at the first-floor Magnolia Restaurant, which serves breakfast, lunch, and dinner Southern style,

and you can unwind at the Lion's Den lounge, where the bar brings back memories of TV's *Cheers* and the library is stocked with real books.

The hotel pool is on a second-floor deck that can accommodate outdoor gatherings of as many as 150 people. The Hilton has 19,000 square feet of space for meetings and other functions that can accommodate up to 550 people for a banquet; the Harborview Room, whose fifteenth-floor location makes it the highest meeting room in the city; and a 5,408-square-foot ballroom with eighteen-foot ceilings and elaborate crystal chandeliers. Also available for get-togethers is an atrium on the hotel's ground floor.

The Hilton was built in 1968 on the site of the DeSoto Hotel, which was constructed in 1890 and was a Savannah landmark for decades. A sitting room off the lobby of the Hilton affords guests a glimpse of the old hotel—the walls are

Insiders' Tip

As best we can determine, Savannah's first hotel was a place called the Mansion House on Bay Street. While poking around the Georgia Historical Society, we found an article from a *Savannah News-Press* magazine of 1969 stating the city's "earliest inns were the Mansion House, City Hotel and the Screven (House), all of them operating about the middle of the last century." Englishman John Lambert, writing in his *Travels through Lower Canada and the United States,* published in 1810, said he stayed in March 1808 at "the hotel of Colonel Shelman," a house "fitted up with separate sleeping rooms." Lambert indicated the hotel was the only establishment of its kind in Savannah. A blurb in the *Patriot and Commercial Advertiser* newspaper of June 1, 1807, refers to the arrival of General Moreau at the Mansion House hotel, leading us to believe the places where the general and Lambert stayed were one and the same.

covered with memorabilia, including framed banquet programs from visits by several U.S. presidents. Covered, secured parking is available for $7 a day, and valet service is $10.

Hyatt Regency Savannah
2 W. Bay Street
Savannah, GA
(912) 238–1234, (800) 233–1234
www.savannah-online.com/hyatt
$$$$

You can't sleep where James Edward Oglethorpe laid his head while founding Georgia in 1733, but you can get darn close by bedding down at the Hyatt Regency Savannah. The spot where Oglethorpe pitched his tent is in the small park on Bay Street in front of the 347-room hotel. But that's not the main attraction of the Hyatt Regency—the hotel's drawing card is its location overlooking River Street and the Savannah River. The hotel is built over the brick street, creating a tunnel for automobile traffic.

This location places guests in the midst of Savannah's waterfront shops and festivals and affords terrific views of the river and the ships plying it. You'll pay extra for a room on the river, but where else can you get accommodations with a "Ships Passing Light" that activates when a huge oceangoing vessel glides by your window? On the fourth of the hotel's seven floors, you're at eye level with the decks of freighters and other ships as they make their way in or out of port. There are also great views of River Street and/or the river from the Hyatt's second-floor sundeck, various meeting rooms, a glassed-in restaurant aptly called the Windows, and an adjoining lounge named MD's. Speaking of glassed-in, that's a perfect description of the hotel's Harborside Center, an 11,000-square-foot gathering place on River Street offering floor-to-ceiling views. The Hyatt has a total of 28,000 square feet of meeting space, including an 8,000-square-foot ballroom and a banquet room.

The hotel lobby is an atrium with the aura of a rain forest. Palm trees and bird-of-paradise plants adorn the floor of this open space, which stretches seven floors to the ceiling, and bright green philodendrons cascade from the balconies of interior rooms. The atrium is also the headquarters of a concierge who can schedule tours of the city and help plan your stay, and you can board tour buses at the front door of the hotel. The Hyatt accommodates fitness buffs with an exercise room and a heated indoor pool. If you're arriving in style, there's a helicopter pad on the roof. Valet parking is $14 per day.

The Marshall House
123 E. Broughton Street
Savannah, GA
(912) 644–7896, (800) 589–6304
www.coastalhotel.com/georgia/savannah/
marshallhouse
$$$$

The Marshall House has the distinction of being one of Savannah's newest—and oldest—hotels. The sixty-eight-room luxury boutique hotel opened its doors August 1, 1999, after an extensive renovation. The hotel occupies the building that housed the original Marshall House, which was built in 1851 and closed in 1957 after a 147-year run during which it was also a hospital for Union soldiers.

The new Marshall House combines its historic past with sophisticated features and amenities that include Café M, a ninety-seat glass-roofed courtyard restaurant. Rooms offer fireplaces, pine floors, minibars, CD players, velour robes, and bathrooms with pedestal sinks. Also available are a 275-square-foot boardroom, a fully equipped business center, and a 1,200-square-foot meeting room for corporate and social functions. The hotel is also the site of Chadwick's, an eighty-seat jazz lounge.

Adding to the flavor of the hotel are historical memorabilia and locally produced artwork that tell the history of The Marshall House and of Savannah.

Guests are provided with workout privileges at the Downtown Athletic Club. The hotel is pet friendly and accommodates each canine visitor with a "Pooch Pack" containing a packet of dog food, a bowl, and a small toy. Valet parking is $10 a day, with self-parking in a garage behind the hotel costing $7 a day.

The Mulberry Inn
601 E. Bay Street
Savannah, GA
(912) 238–1200, (800) HOLIDAY
www.savannahhotel.com
$$$$

The Mulberry aims for a classic Savannah look and hits the mark. Traditional furnishings, oil paintings, polished hardwood floors, and chandeliers grace the lobby, and antique furniture is sprinkled throughout the hallways and sitting areas. Reproductions of antiques and burgundy and forest-green furnishings carry out the theme in the 145 rooms, 25 of which are suites. Twenty-three of the rooms were added in 1999. The two- and three-story establishment—a Holiday Inn historic hotel and the recipient of the Bass Hotels and Resorts' Hotel of the Year award—surrounds a tree-shaded brick courtyard adorned with wrought-iron tables and chairs. Then there's the name of the inn, which refers to the mulberry trees planted by Georgia's colonists in an attempt to raise silkworms. The trees grew on a site that is now Trustee's Garden, across East Broad Street from the hotel.

Want more history? The Mulberry's got it. The two-story portion of the inn housing the lobby was built as a cotton warehouse and livery stable in the mid-1800s, then was converted to a Coca-Cola bottling plant in the early 1900s. The building was transformed into an inn and expanded in the 1980s. The front desk occupies the spot where the bottling machinery did its work, and there are photos on one of the walls of the lobby to prove it. The Mulberry's elegant Cafe Courtyard serves breakfast, lunch, and dinner, and the inn presents a complimentary tea each afternoon from 4 until 6 P.M. Hot and iced tea, coffee, and dessert treats are available for guests, and a pianist provides background music. Other amenities include concierge and bellman services, a secured outdoor pool, a hot tub, an exercise center, and Sgt. Jasper's Tavern, a full-service lounge. The hotel has three meeting rooms, with the largest accommodating 125 people theater style. The inn also offers full banquet and catering services. Parking at a garage across a side street is $8 per day.

Planters Inn
29 Abercorn Street
Savannah, GA
(912) 232–5678, (800) 554–1187
www.plantersinnsavannah.com
$$$

Built in 1912 as the John Wesley Hotel, the Planters Inn has been thoroughly remodeled but retains the elegance and charm of the early days of the twentieth century. The hotel's high ceilings, four-poster beds, lavish draperies, and antique furniture give you the feeling you've stepped back in time, but the friendly staff and the services they provide will make you aware you're very much in the present. Among the extras are nightly turndown service, complimentary continental breakfasts served in the hospitality room from 7 to 10:30 A.M., and complimentary "afternoon wine" provided in the lobby from 6 to 7 P.M. every day but Sunday. Parking is available at a neighboring garage for $6.95 per day.

The seven-floor hotel is on the site of a three-story residence built in 1812 as one of two twin houses. The other house still stands next door to the hotel. The exquisite lobby of the Planters Inn is part of the original house, which mirrored the one built beside it. If you decide to stay at this hotel, ask about a room with a fireplace (there are three on the seventh floor), a balcony (there are four), or a view of Reynolds Square, the little park in front of Planters Inn. The centerpiece of the square is a statue of John Wesley, the founder of Methodism for whom the hotel was originally named.

A four-poster and fireplace make for a romantic weekend getaway at the Planters Inn.

Quality Inn Heart of Savannah
300 W. Bay Street
Savannah, GA
(912) 236–6321, (800) 228–5151
$$$

One of the operators of the Quality Inn Heart of Savannah likes to say that the tourist hot spots of River Street and City Market grew up around this motel on Bay Street. The Quality Inn opened in 1963, long before those two nearby areas became popular with visitors. The two-story, fifty-two-room motel continues to provide guests with friendly service and well-maintained accommodations. Rooms with two double beds or queen beds are available. There's no pool, but a complimentary continental breakfast is available in the lobby from 7 until 10 A.M. each day, and pets are accepted free of charge. Tour buses stop at the front door, and the folks who man the front desk will help you make arrangements.

River Street Inn
115 E. Bay Street
Savannah, GA
(912) 234–6400
www.riverstreetinn.com
$$$$

Guests of this inn experience a historic atmosphere in the midst of the activity of River Street. The rooms of this hotel occupy the top three floors of a renovated five-story cotton warehouse on the Savannah River. The main entrance to the inn and its "parkside" rooms look out on Bay Street. Thirty-two of the inn's eighty-six rooms face the river, and several of these have small French balconies you can step out onto for a grand view of the street and the waterway.

Each of the inn's rooms is different; there are various decors featuring a mixture of authentic period antiques and reproductions, including four-poster and canopy beds. Hardwood floors, area rugs, and polished brass bathroom fixtures complete the elegant look of old-time Savannah. The lower floors of the structure housing the River Street Inn were built in 1817 to store cotton for export, and the top three floors were added in 1853. The inn was opened in 1987.

Guests receive complimentary newspapers in the morning, use of the nearby Downtown Athletic Club, and homemade chocolates before retiring in the evening, and there's a wine reception in the afternoon. The inn can accommodate small meetings and conferences, with seating for fifteen in its Board Room and for forty in its Meeting Room. Although there's no swimming pool, there's a rooftop cabana with hot tub for sunning and relaxing. Parking is $4 per day.

Savannah Marriott Riverfront
100 General McIntosh Boulevard
Savannah, GA
(912) 233–7722, (800) 228–9290
www.marriotthotels.com/SAVRF/
$$$$

When we think of the Savannah Marriott Riverfront, the word *spacious* leaps to mind. The atrium at the heart of the hotel has 7,000 square feet of carpeted space that can easily accommodate themed events and trade shows attended by as many as 500 people. A total of 140 rooms on the seven upper floors of the hotel open onto balconies with views of the atrium, the north side of which looks out on the Savannah River through expansive, floor-to-ceiling panes of glass. The hotel's 15,000-square-foot ballroom is the second largest in the city, and there are an additional 15,000 square feet of meeting space in the form of conference rooms and boardrooms.

Among the hotel's forty-six suites are ten deluxe models, each containing 1,430 square feet of space. The Marriott's two restaurants—T.G.I. Friday's and River's Edge—seat 250 and 106, respectively. You get the picture—everywhere you look, there are scads of space. The real lure of the Marriott, though, is its location on the Savannah River and the riverwalk at the eastern end of River Street. A total of 109 of the hotel's 383 rooms face the water, and for $20 to $35 extra, you can be, as the Marriott folks say, "perched on the river" with a knockout view of passing ships. Special accommodations include rooms on the concierge floor and deluxe suites with walk-around wet bars, glass-topped dining tables, and large bathrooms featuring double vanities. Guests staying on the private, keyed concierge floor (the eighth) enjoy complimentary continental breakfasts, hors d'oeuvres in late afternoon, and dessert buffet at night, Sunday night through Friday morning.

There are two pools—one outside and the other in the atrium—and fitness and whirlpool rooms just off the atrium. You can get breakfast and a great view of the river at the River's Edge, lunch and dinner at Friday's, and room service from 6:30 A.M. until midnight. If you'd like a tour of the city, you can make arrangements at the trolley desk in the lobby. Guests who are delegates to meetings at the Savannah International Trade and Convention Center will find a shuttle service at the Waving Girl Landing boat dock adjacent to the hotel; the shuttle will take them across the Savannah River to the Trade Center and back.

Parking in one of the hotel's 620 spaces is $7 a day. The hotel, which opened in 1992 as a Radisson and was converted to a Marriott in 1994, hosted 750 athletes, trainers, and coaches while serving as the Olympic village for yachting events in 1996.

The Westin Savannah Harbor Resort & Spa
One Resort Drive
Savannah, GA
(912) 201–2000
www.westinsavannah.com
$$$$

The city's largest luxury hotel, the Westin rises majestically above the Hutchinson Island waterfront across the Savannah River from the Historic Downtown. The sixteen-story, 400-room hotel and its

Luxury on a grand scale is the theme at the Westin Savannah Harbor Resort. PHOTO: COURTESY OF THE WESTIN SAVANNAH HARBOR RESORT

riverside neighbor, the Savannah International Trade & Convention Center, are the focal points of the island's Savannah Harbor development—the centerpieces of what is seen as the creation of a "second city" just north of Savannah's downtown area.

Built at a cost of $103 million and incorporating the features of local Regency-style landmarks in its architecture, the Westin opened in December 1999. The lobby and other public areas exude the atmosphere found in the city's fine old homes—high ceilings, hardwood floors, elaborate sconces, and walls painted in pastels. Adding to the ambience are many paintings and photographs by regional artists. The Savannah look is carried through the guest rooms, each of which features the Westin's "Heavenly Bed," an extremely comfortable innovation consisting of a pillowtop mattress set, a down blanket, three sheets, a comforter, a duvet coverlet, and five pillows. The fifty-five rooms and suites on the hotel's club level—the top two floors—have balconies providing marvelous views, and guests staying at these lofty heights have access to a concierge lounge.

Speaking of lounges, the hotel has one that celebrates the work of one of Savannah's favorite sons, beloved lyricist Johnny Mercer. Named Midnight Sun after one of Mercer's songs, this elegantly clubby bar overlooks the river and specializes in drinks also named for Mercer tunes, such as "Blues in the Night." The Westin's restaurant, Aqua Star, can seat 145 and provides second-floor views of Savannah while serving a breakfast buffet each morning, a lunch buffet Monday through Saturday, brunch on Sunday, and dinner each evening. For special gatherings, there's a private dining room in the southeastern corner of the second floor, situated so it looks out on the river and the marina just east of the hotel. The Westin offers almost 20,000 square feet of meeting space that includes 11,500 square feet in the plush Grand Ballroom and 3,400 square feet in the first-floor Harbor Ballroom.

What really sets the Westin apart from other Savannah accommodations are the amenities available through the hotel's affiliation with the nearby Club at Savannah Harbor, which features an eighteen-hole golf course designed by Robert Cupp and Sam Snead and a one-of-a-kind Greenbrier Spa. The par 72 course—managed by Troon Golf—plays more than 7,000 yards from its championship tees, and its clubhouse complex is the site of a pro shop, an exercise facility, a heated pool, four Har-Tru tennis courts, and the aforementioned spa. The Spa is patterned after the spa at the famed Greenbrier resort in White Sulphur Springs, West Virginia, and is the first off-site facility to be licensed by the resort. The Spa has 14 massage rooms, 2 steam rooms, 2 saunas, 2 Swiss shower rooms, 4 treatment rooms for sulfur and mud baths or body wraps, and a manicure and pedicure room.

Another unique feature of the hotel is Camp Harbor Light, the Westin's children's program. The camp is for kids ages four to twelve. It provides daily activities for children such as scavenger hunts, arts and crafts, bingo alongside the hotel's heated riverside pool, and ice-cream sundae socials. The fee for the full-day program is $50 for one child and $35 for an additional child in the same family; half-day fees are $40 and $25.

Valet parking at the hotel is $13 per day. If you stay at the Westin, you won't necessarily have to drive into town to see the sights. Although the Historic Downtown is across the river from the hotel, it's only a few minutes away by water taxi.

Southside/Midtown

Best Western Central
45 Eisenhower Drive
Savannah, GA
(912) 355-1000, (800) 528-1234
$

This motel at Eisenhower Drive and Abercorn Street, near one of the main entrances to Hunter Army Airfield, is part

Sumptuous lobbies at the Westin Savannah Harbor Resort offer a refuge after a day of sight-seeing.

PHOTO: COURTESY OF THE WESTIN SAVANNAH HARBOR RESORT

of the nationwide chain but has some distinctive touches that give it a local flavor. An arbor draped with star jasmine adorns the pool area, which is set in a large grassy strip crowned by a huge oak tree. The two-story motel has eighty-seven rooms with two double beds and forty-two rooms with king-size beds. A complimentary continental breakfast is available from 6 to 10 A.M. each day in an area off the lobby that doubles as meeting room for as many as fifty people seated theater style. There's an upstairs meeting room that can accommodate seventy-five. Also upstairs is a piano bar that opened in March 2001; it's open Monday through Saturday, with live entertainment Tuesday through Saturday starting at 8 P.M. Small pets are allowed at the motel for a $15 fee.

Clubhouse Inn of Savannah
6800 Abercorn Street
Savannah, GA
(912) 356–1234, (800) 258–2466
www.clubhouseinn.com
$$

The folks at the Clubhouse Inn strive to create a "home away from home" atmosphere at their spacious motel on Abercorn Street. They serve a complimentary buffet each morning that gives guests the opportunity to enjoy a full breakfast in a glassed-in dining room looking out on the pool and patio. In the evenings from 5 until 7 P.M., the manager hosts a reception where each guest can have up to two complimentary mixed drinks. The two-story inn, part of a small chain of motels scattered throughout the United States, has 138 interior rooms that include 16 suites. Each suite has a bedroom with king-size, queen-size or double beds and a sitting area/kitchen with a wet bar. Other rooms have either kings or doubles.

Country Inn & Suites by Carlson
7576 White Bluff Road
(912) 692–0404, (800) 456–4000
www.countryinns.com
$$

This sixty-two-room hotel brings a bit of the country to the hubbub of the

Oglethorpe Mall area. You'll get a cozy feeling while lounging in the lobby, which has a fireplace, hardwood floor, Oriental carpet, and overstuffed chairs and couches, or while bedding down in the guest rooms and suites, featuring fluffy comforters, wreaths, and swags.

Guest rooms offer two queen-size beds or a king size, and there are three types of suites: the country suite, which has a bedroom with two queens and a king and a living room with a sleeper sofa; the celebration suite, whose expanded living and bedroom area includes a king-size bed, whirlpool bath, and wet bar; and the home "suite" home, which has a kitchen, living room, and two bedrooms, one with a king and one with two queens. All suites come equipped with microwaves and refrigerators. A particularly attractive feature of the Country Inn is its spacious indoor pool area, where you'll find a kidney-shaped pool, a whirlpool, and plenty of space for relaxing. The inn also offers a fitness room, a meeting room that accommodates eighteen people, and a dining area where complimentary continental breakfasts are available from 6 to 9:30 A.M. There's also a social hour here from 5 to 7 P.M. Monday through Thursday at which complimentary beer, wine, and light snacks are served.

Courtyard by Marriott
6703 Abercorn Street
Savannah, GA
(912) 354-7878, (800) 321-2211
www.marriott.com
$$

Savannah's Courtyard by Marriott stands between two of the city's busiest thoroughfares, Abercorn Street and White Bluff Road, but the three-story motel's beautifully landscaped grounds will give you a feeling of being away from the madding crowd. The centerpiece of the motel is the tree-filled courtyard with its quaint gazebo and swimming pool. Just off the pool is an enclosed whirlpool surrounded by lots of space for lounging, and there's a fitness room near the lobby that sports state-of-the-art exercise equipment. The Courtyard's large dining area is open for breakfast (with a full meal priced at $7.95 and continental servings available) and for light dinners Monday through Friday. There are 144 interior rooms including 12 suites, all of which have sleeper sofas. Rooms on the upper floors open onto balconies. There are two meeting rooms, each of which can accommodate twenty-four people seated at tables.

Fairfield Inn by Marriott
2 Lee Boulevard
Savannah, GA
(912) 353-7100, (800) 228-2800
www.fairfield.com/savfi
$

The three-story Fairfield Inn, one of Marriott's economy motels, gives guests several options involving rooms. The first floor has "drive-up" rooms accessible

Insiders' Tip

The Old Town Trolley swings by twelve motels on the Southside each morning around 9 A.M. to pick up people who want to take tours of Savannah's Historic District. The trolley makes a return trip at 3 P.M. If your motel isn't a regular stop, ask the desk clerk to call Old Town and have them come by and get you. Tour fees range from $18 to $22 for adults and are $9 for children ages 4 to 12 and free for kids younger than 4.

from the parking lot, the second floor has rooms with secured balconies, and the third floor has rooms entered from interior hallways. Guests use key cards to activate the elevator to the second and third floors. The inn, which underwent a renovation completed in 2001, has rooms with king-size and two double beds. The Fairfield, on Lee Boulevard between Abercorn Street and White Bluff Road, offers complimentary continental breakfast from 6 until 9 A.M. on weekdays and 7 to 10 A.M. on weekends, and there's free coffee in the lobby around the clock. If you're seeking some exercise, try the outdoor pool or drive the short distance to the Family Center YMCA on Habersham Street. Your visit there is free when you show your Fairfield entry pass.

Hampton Inn Midtown
201 Stephenson Avenue
Savannah, GA
(912) 355–4100, (800) 426–7866
www.hiltonhotels.com
$

This Hampton Inn is just off the beaten path of Abercorn Street and, like the motels nearby, is close to Oglethorpe Mall and the stores and offices that surround it. The Hampton is where Habersham Street dead-ends into Stephenson Avenue, which is about a block from the Family Center YMCA, where you can show your motel key card and gain access to the Y's extensive fitness facilities. If you'd like to do some swimming, take a dip in the motel's kidney-shaped pool at the rear of the property far from passing traffic.

The Hampton was built in the mid-1980s but underwent a $900,000 renovation in the summer of 1997 that refurbished the motel's 129 rooms (single king-bed and two double-bed options are available). The two-building, two-story motel offers complimentary continental breakfast for guests from 6 until 10 A.M. in a dining area off the lobby, and punch and cookies are set out for snacking from 10 A.M. until 6 P.M.

Holiday Inn Midtown
7100 Abercorn Street
Savannah, GA
(912) 352–7100, (800) 255–8268
www.hometown.aol.com/HtmlSalesDep
$$

As its name implies, this 171-room Holiday Inn stands smack dab in the middle of town. The 2 two-story wings of the motel flank a courtyard that includes a spacious pool area set among oleanders and magnolias. Some rooms have king-size beds, others have two doubles, and all were completely renovated as part of a process that was finished in March 2000. The Marketplace restaurant serves breakfast and dinner, and Mulligan's, a 110-seat lounge, is geared for the after-work and after-date crowd. The Holiday Inn Midtown has a fitness room and offers same-day dry cleaning service. Kids twelve and younger stay and eat free. The motel's several meeting rooms can accommodate up to 300 people.

Homewood Suites Hotel
5820 White Bluff Road
Savannah, GA
(912) 353–8500
www.homewoodsuites.com/hws/savannah
$$

The largest all-suite establishment in Savannah offers guests free local telephone calls and an Executive Center for business travelers. The Executive Center sports a typewriter, computer, and printer, and you can arrange to send and receive faxes at the front desk.

The 106 suites are configured as either one-bedroom "Homewood" suites, the hotel's most popular offerings; as master suites, which have fireplaces; or as two-bedroom, two-bath suites. Each suite features a fully equipped kitchen with two-burner stove, microwave, and full-size refrigerator; a sleeper sofa; and telephone with voice mail.

Leave a grocery list at the front desk, and your shopping will be done for you and charged to your room. In addition to the three-story building and 2 two-story buildings housing the suites, there is a spacious lodge that can accommodate fifty people for the hotel's complimentary, deluxe continental breakfasts and evening socials. The socials, held from 5 until 7 P.M. each day, offer guests beer, wine, soft drinks, and snacks, such as pizza, tacos, and Buffalo wings. A pool and whirlpool are situated just outside the lodge, and there is a court nearby where you can play basketball, tennis, or volleyball. If you need to burn off more energy, try the fitness room off the lobby in the lodge. The hotel also has two meeting rooms, one for up to fifty people and the other for ten, and an on-site laundry facility. Guests wishing to cookout will find two grills for their use under the huge oak tree that graces the property.

La Quinta Inn
6805 Abercorn Street
Savannah, GA
(912) 355-3004, (800) 531-5900
www.laquinta.com
$

With its red-tile roofs and stucco exterior, the motel has the distinctive Southwestern appearance of all La Quinta Inns and espouses the chain's credo of providing spacious, comfortable rooms and "100 percent guest satisfaction." The two-story motel has 154 rooms including two suites and rooms with kings and doubles housed in two buildings that ramble over nicely landscaped grounds between Abercorn and White Bluff Road. The La Quinta opened on Abercorn in the late 1970s, but the rooms look new because of a remodeling completed in the summer of 2001. The outdoor pool is tucked in a secluded nook set way back off the street, and there is HBO on the tube. A complimentary continental breakfast is available each morning in an area off the lobby. La Quinta accepts small pets.

Masters Inn Suites
7110 Hodgson Memorial Drive
Savannah, GA
(912) 354-8560, (800) 344-4378
www.mastersinn-savannah.com
$

Although Masters Inn Suites is near Oglethorpe Mall and nestled amid the shopping centers and office parks of the Southside, this three-story hotel looks and feels as if it belongs in downtown— downtown New Orleans, that is. The hotel is built around an atrium decorated with palm trees, exotic plants, a gurgling fountain, and intricate black ironwork.

The French Quarter theme surfaces in the sitting rooms of the hotel's fifty-one suites with their wrought-iron tables and chairs. Each sitting room also contains a sofa, coffee table, easy chairs, and a small refrigerator, a microwave oven, and a coffeemaker. Six luxury suites have larger sitting rooms, king-size beds, and whirlpool bathtubs. All rooms are entered from the interior of the hotel. Guests can exercise in the outdoor pool at the rear of the hotel or in the fully equipped fitness room. Afterward, you can relax in the hotel's combination whirlpool bath-steam room. Many of the guests are business people, and there is a conference room seating forty-five.

Residence Inn by Marriott
5710 White Bluff Road
Savannah, GA
(912) 356-3266, (800) 331-3131
$$

This Residence Inn has sixty-six one- and two-bedroom and studio suites under one roof. All suites have kitchens, and each of the two-bedroom accommodations has two full bathrooms, three televisions, and a wood-burning fireplace. Kitchens are equipped with ovens, stoves, and dishwashers, and the staff of the inn will do your grocery shopping for you. Just leave your shopping list at the front desk, and the groceries will be charged to your bill and deposited in your room by 6 P.M. Copies of *USA Today,* the *Savannah Morning News,* and the *Wall Street Journal* newspapers are free, as are deluxe continental breakfasts served in the Gatehouse sitting area. The Gatehouse is also the scene of social hours held from 5 to 7 P.M. Monday through Thursday—complimentary appetizers, beer, wine, and other beverages are served, and guests attending these gatherings snack on such goodies as hot chicken wings, nachos, lasagna, and black beans and rice. For those seeking recreation, you can enjoy an indoor pool and whirlpool, an exercise room, and an outdoor court for tennis, basketball, or volleyball. Pets are welcome, but there is a $100 nonrefundable cleaning fee.

Restaurants

Historic Downtown

Islands

Southside/Midtown

West Chatham

Your taste buds will be glad you came to Savannah—but your waistline might not. The city offers a quantity and variety of restaurants completely out of proportion to its size. The recipe just adds up: Take plenty of fresh shrimp, crab, and fish from local waters, mix in the cultural contacts that go with more than 250 years as a seaport, consider the long growing season and the agricultural tradition of the South in general, then flavor with a generous helping of legendary Southern hospitality. The result is scores of restaurants serving just about every type of food imaginable.

The setting improves the flavor of food, as any good hostess will tell you. Savannah's restaurants serve their guests in unique settings that include the stone-walled halls of former cotton warehouses on the riverfront, balconies overlooking breathtaking marshes, historic mansions with antique furnishings, and unpretentious little places nestled under towering oaks.

Remember the scene in the movie *Forrest Gump* in which the character Bubba launched into an extensive list of ways to prepare shrimp? Well, in Savannah you'll find at least that many ways of serving this local favorite. If your day takes you out to Tybee Island, you're likely to spot shrimp boats, often working surprisingly close to the beach. And if your meal involves shrimp, you are about to discover what an amazing difference real freshness—as opposed to being iced down and flown inland—can make in its flavor.

With a little pushing and shoving, you can put Savannah's restaurants into four main categories: seafood, soul food or regional cooking, ethnic, and a sprinkling of haute cuisine. Some, of course, will defy labeling, and others will boast a menu that has a grip on more than one category.

We make no claims to offer a complete and comprehensive restaurant listing here. Instead, we've singled out places we like to go, places our friends talk about, and places that have been fixtures for Savannah travelers for years. We've tried to make sure that we included something for every pocketbook, as well as something for every taste.

We've assigned price codes to help you anticipate in advance what you'll find in the price column of the menu. Remember, though, that these are guidelines only. Your selections could easily bump the meal up or down by at least a category. That said, we add that we find the cost of eating out in Savannah compares favorably with the cost of similar meals in other cities.

Because we've left many of the desirable parts of a special meal out of our calculations—things like the perfect wine to complement a complex seafood dish or a sherry-flavored Savannah trifle as dessert—you'll want to use these prices as general guidelines only.

You'll also note that we haven't included chain restaurants, except in a very few exceptions where location or other circumstances make them especially significant. Savannah boasts a wide range of such chains, with many fine examples among them, but we feel our readers will already know what to expect from these restaurants. You'll find these listed in the Yellow Pages of your telephone directory.

City ordinances require restaurants to provide nonsmoking sections, and you'll find some restaurants restrict smoking entirely. We've noted these and have pointed out some special provisions made for smokers.

Parking in the Historic Downtown is always an adventure, so give yourself plenty of time to find a space, particularly if you have dinner reservations. Restaurants outside the downtown area generally have plenty of nearby parking.

If your travels take you to nearby Tybee Island or Hilton Head, South Carolina, note that restaurants in those two locales (a smattering of eateries in Tybee, more than two dozen outstanding dining spots in Hilton Head) are discussed in the individual chapters that cover those two island destinations.

Price-Code Key

Here is our price chart, based on dinner for two, minus beverages (alcoholic or otherwise), appetizer, dessert, tax, and tip.

$	$15 and lower
$$	$16 to $20
$$$	$21 to $50
$$$$	$51 and higher

Historic Downtown

The Cafe at City Market
224 W. St. Julian Street
Savannah, GA
(912) 236–7133
$$$

Dine indoors at this restaurant in the eastern part of City Market, and you'll experience the atmosphere of a big-city bistro during the 1930s, '40s and '50s, with recorded music to match (Sinatra is a favorite in the evenings). Dine outdoors, and you'll be sitting under an awning on an open-air deck "watching the world go by," as owner and chef Matt Maher puts it. At either location, you choose from a menu that's somewhat international in content and contains an item or two you've probably never encountered before, such as these lunchtime sandwiches: grilled cheese with artichoke hearts, mushrooms, and prosciutto ham, and pan-fried crab cake. Also featured on the lunch menu is the Southern pecan chicken salad.

The dinner menu offers specialties such as salmon Oscar and rib-eye steak flamed with Irish whiskey. There's room for sixty-five diners inside and forty-five on the deck; you can smoke outside or in the bar but not in the main dining room. Maher, who opened the cafe in 1991, recommends making reservations for dinner on weekends during the spring and summer.

Cafe Metropole
108 Martin Luther King Jr. Boulevard
Savannah, GA
(912) 236–1211
$$ lunch, $$–$$$ dinner

An old bus depot has been converted—with minimal renovation—into a delightful restaurant. The food is as trendy as the nondecor decor: sandwiches and salads and a small but constantly changing variety of other dishes, all capitalizing on fresh ingredients and attractive presentation. On weekend nights, there's live music and dancing (although they dropped the swing night when other places started hosting similar events). There's brunch on Sundays. We're not sure how this place will handle cold weather, but the rolled-up bus bay doors and fans kept it plenty nice in summer (even for us air-conditioning fiends).

Casbah Moroccan Restaurant
118 E. Broughton Street
Savannah, GA
(912) 234–6168
$$$

Dinner at the Casbah turns into an evening-long event in which the food—which is very good—is only a part. Proprietor Sami Samir has recreated a bit of the atmosphere of Morocco in what started out as an abandoned storefront on the city's main shopping street.

The decor is now lush, dark, and romantic, with hassocks and other plush upholstered seating, floor-to-ceiling drapes, and a balcony from which the belly dancer descends. Guests are escorted to their seats, where a waiter opens and closes the meal by washing their hands from a decorative pitcher filled with rose water. The dancer comes on for short intervals throughout the evening, and the performances we've witnessed were interesting, entertaining, and quite decorous. The menu is heavily weighted with dishes like lamb cooked in honey and almonds, but even the less-adventurous palate will find an option here. Many dishes are variations on kebabs, in lamb, beef, or chicken (we opted for the dish featuring all three). For the appetizer course, we had a salad sampler, which features six different salads or relishes. The choices are not what we call light eating, but the meal is sedately paced, meaning you may still be able to manage, or at least share, a dessert. The staff is attentive, well versed on the dishes and customs, and experienced at putting guests at ease in unfamiliar surroundings. If the dancing is important to your evening, please check when making reservations to be sure you haven't selected one of the occasional dates when there is no dancer. A wine list is available. Reservations are strongly recommended. Allow plenty of time—at least a couple of hours. Dress ranges from dressy casual to business attire, but women may feel more comfortable in pants, given the seating arrangements. There is a smoking section, but we've seen smokers asked to refrain when the place is crowded, so ask in advance if this is important to your evening. Open for dinner 5:30 to 10:30 P.M.; closed Mondays.

Clary's Cafe
404 Abercorn Street
Savannah, GA
(912) 233-0402
4430 Habersham Street
Savannah, GA
(912) 351-0302
$$

Visitors to Savannah know the original Clary's as the place where characters from

Insiders' Tip

In a rush for lunch? Whip into Tanner's sandwich shop at 21 E. Broughton Street and grab a couple of chili dogs and the orangiest orange drink you'll ever taste or see—a mixture of fresh and frozen orange juices, water, a little salt, and plenty of sugar. Tanner's, in business since 1942, is on the south side of Broughton near the corner of Drayton Street, and it's open in the morning and afternoon Monday through Saturday.

Midnight in the Garden of Good and Evil congregated, but this cafe at Jones and Abercorn Streets was, as owner Michael Faber puts it, "famous before The Book." Clary's opened in 1903 and, as a pharmacy and soda fountain, has been a hangout of Savannahians throughout its existence. Faber bought it in February 1994, during the week that *Midnight* hit the bookstores, and he renovated the building and converted the pharmacy into dining space. He's made the most of the restaurant's connection to the book, with touches such as a stained-glass window depicting the Bird Girl and the *Midnight in the Garden* T-shirts worn by employees. (For much more on the phenomenon du jour, see our Savannah: Hollywood of the South chapter.)

As stated earlier, however, there's more to Clary's than its association with the

Clary's was featured prominently in John Berendt's best-seller about Savannah. PHOTO: BETTY DARBY

best-selling book. The Midtown restaurant has extensive menus for breakfast, lunch, and dinner, and the downtown Clary's serves breakfast and lunch, each offering food that Faber says is made from scratch each day, including the four different soups. Among the breakfast specialties are the malted waffles and pancakes made with a special flour brought in from Michigan; for lunch, there are a variety of salads, burgers, sandwiches, and those aforementioned soups; and in the evening, featured items are the seafood pot pie, the fillet of red snapper served on a seasoned oak plank, the old-fashioned pot roast, and the Triple Peaks salad, which has scoops of tuna, chicken, and shrimp salads on fresh greens and pasta salad. Leading the list of appetizers are the crab cakes and fried green tomatoes a la Clary's. Faber, who was in the restaurant business in Chicago for thirty-five years before moving to Savannah in 1988, opened a second Clary's in Midtown in September 1998. The newest Clary's, at Habersham and 61st Streets, exudes the charm of the original, right down to the old-fashioned marble

soda fountain and the leaded-glass windows. The menu at the Midtown location is the same as that of the downtown eatery, and there are 300 free parking spaces adjacent to the Habersham Street site.

The Cotton Exchange
201 E. River Street
Savannah, GA
(912) 232-7088
$$$

The oldest restaurant on River Street, The Cotton Exchange serves lunch and dinner in what was once a cotton warehouse built in 1799. The Exchange opened in 1971 and for a time offered mainly sandwiches, but the restaurant later expanded into the dinner market. Among the standouts on the dinner menu are the shish-kebab dishes and the seafood platters. The folks at The Exchange haven't forgotten how to make outstanding sandwiches, in particular their Reubens and our favorite, a chargrilled hamburger they call the Congress. With your sandwich, you get a choice of a side dish, and we recommend the zesty German potato salad.

The Exchange occupies two rooms—one's a full bar where you can eat and which is the only smoking area.

Debi's Restaurant
10 W. State Street
Savannah, GA
(912) 236–3516
$

Professional people flock to Debi's at lunchtime for the salads and specials, the latter of which change daily and consist of a meat and two vegetables (the meat selections on a recent visit were chopped steak, corned beef, fried chicken, and sausage with peppers and onions). Service is fast and friendly at this restaurant on State Street between Whitaker and Bull Streets.

Debi's opened in 1992 in what had been a men's clothing store, but owner Debi Christiansen and members of her family have been in the restaurant business in Savannah for twenty-five years. (Her mom runs Mary's Seafood and Steakhouse on the Southside.) Debi's seats 130, has a full bar, and also serves breakfast. A note for movie buffs: Debi's is the restaurant where Forrest Gump's girlfriend Jenny waitressed while living in Savannah.

The Express Cafe
39 Barnard Street
Savannah, GA
(912) 233–4683
$$

This popular breakfast and lunch spot has a European air. We've never had anything here that wasn't good, and we've worked our way through the menu over the years: quiche, stuffed croissants, soup in bread bowls, sandwiches loaded with fresh vegetables, fresh baguettes, and so on. The desserts are special things as well. The Express opens at 7 A.M. weekdays and 8 A.M. weekends, closing at midafternoon. It's closed Monday and Tuesday.

45 South at the Pirates' House
20 East Broad Street
Savannah, GA
(912) 233–1881
$$$$

The contemporary continental cuisine and elegant clubby ambience of 45 South make it an ideal spot for celebrating special occasions and for entertaining guests. This restaurant on East Broad near Bay Street is relatively small (about seventy seats), but it provides Savannahians with a taste of "big-city dining," says manager Bobby Erb. The food is American with French influences. Among the entrees are grilled ahi tuna with spinach, breast of duck with ginger beets, sliced breast of pheasant with wild mushrooms, and rack of Cervena venison.

Appetizers are priced around $10 and include the sautéed lump crab cakes with shrimp, endive, radicchio, and sauce remoulade and the tempura of eggplant with grilled tomato, baked goat cheese, and a red pepper coulis. The wine list offers 220 selections.

The jewel-tone surroundings—emerald green and ruby—are rich but not overstated: Soft lighting, fresh-cut orchids on tables, and high-back, upholstered chairs combine to create a comfortable atmosphere. Forty-five South was established on the Southside in 1984 by restaurateur Sandy Hollinger. He relocated it downtown to quarters that were once part of The Pirates' House after he purchased that well-known restaurant in 1988. Forty-five South is open only for dinner and closed on Sundays; reservations are strongly suggested, as is the wearing of jackets by male guests. Valet parking is available.

Garibaldi's Cafe
315 W. Congress Street
Savannah, GA
(912) 232–7118
$$$

A varied and sophisticated menu of continental dishes awaits at this small, attractive restaurant that is part of a small chain (there's another one in Charleston, South Carolina). Dinner is served nightly, and there's a full bar and extensive wine selections. Try the whole scored flounder in apricot sauce. Pasta dishes are staples, and there are always interesting seafood selections along with decadent desserts.

Reservations are available, and dress is business attire on up.

Good Eats
606 Abercorn Street
Savannah, GA
(912) 447–5444
$$

This restaurant is a pleasant surprise, offering weekday lunch and Friday and Saturday dinner in a small dining room decorated with contemporary primitive paintings. The emphasis here is on fresh and organic food, and vegetarians will find they have options. Our recommendation? Even though it sounds pedestrian and less glamorous than other menu entries, go for the chicken salad in whatever form it is being served that day. Good Eats bakes its own bread, by the way. And even though we usually are purists when it comes to sweet tea (a beverage held in religious regard around here), Good Eats experiments successfully with it, the latest incarnation being iced Earl Grey.

Huey's
115 E. River Street
Savannah, GA
(912) 234–7385
$$$

Huey's brings the Big Easy to Savannah with its New Orleans–style cuisine. Huey's, with floor-to-ceiling windows right on the sidewalk, also offers a great view of the Savannah River, a circumstance that makes a breakfast of café au lait and beignets something special. For those unfamiliar with "N'awlins," as Huey's owner Bill Hall refers to his Louisiana hometown, beignets (pronounced "ben-yeas") are delectable French doughnuts.

Huey's also has some specialties for breakfast eaters with heartier appetites, including eggs Benedict and eggs sardou, the latter consisting of a bed of creamed spinach with artichoke hearts on a toasted English muffin with two poached eggs topped with hollandaise sauce.

For lunch and dinner, there are such dishes as red beans and rice served with andouille sausage, and muffuletta, a sandwich made with freshly baked bread, Genoa salami, cappicola ham, provolone cheese, and an olive dressing. The food is zesty but moderately spiced; if you want more zip, there's Tabasco sauce on your table.

Huey's has seating for seventy in its streetside dining room and for twenty in the adjacent patio bar. Smoking is allowed in the patio area but not the dining room. The restaurant has been in business on River Street since 1987.

Il Pasticcio
2 E. Broughton Street
Savannah, GA
(912) 231–8888
$$$

You'd never guess this large, upscale bastion of fine Italian cuisine once was a low-end department store. They're proud of their wines, and the dinner-only menu is creative and extensive, with ambience to spare. Consider this one on the dressy side, with reservations recommended.

The Lady and Sons
311 W. Congress Street
Savannah, GA
(912) 233–2600
$$

There's a menu at this Southern specialty restaurant, but unless you're going to be here long enough to return repeatedly, skip it and go directly to the buffet. This is the slow-cooked, perfectly seasoned stuff that Southerners consider real home cooking. Fried chicken, squash casserole, seasoned greens, "hoecakes" (ask, if you don't know), cheese biscuits—you get the picture. If you are going the menu route, we recommend crab cakes. Lunch is served daily, and dinner is available on Thursday, Friday, and Saturday.

Mrs. Wilkes'
107 W. Jones Street
Savannah, GA
(912) 232–5997
$$, no credit cards

Lunch at Mrs. Wilkes' is served beginning at 11 A.M., but the line of customers starts forming well before then on the shady sidewalk alongside Jones Street. The line usually moves at a fairly rapid clip, but Mrs. Wilkes says folks have told her of waiting for two hours to get in the door of her establishment, which is on the garden floor of a three-story house. "They said it was worth the wait," says Mrs. Wilkes, whose first name is Sema. It's worth the wait because dining at Mrs. Wilkes' is about more than eating lunch; it's about having a unique experience.

At 11, after the first group of diners has filed in and taken their places around the seven 10-seat tables in the two low-ceilinged dining rooms, Mrs. Wilkes rings a little bell and says grace. Then members of her family and staff place heaping platters and bowls of Southern-style food on the tables, serving it country style. Chatting with newly made acquaintances at your table, you dig in and pass around the platters and bowls (sometimes as many as eighteen of them). After you've finished eating, you help clear your table, taking your dishes and silverware to the rear of the room. As you're leaving, a new group of ten diners is admitted to take their seats at your table.

At our most recent visit to Mrs. Wilkes', the tables were loaded with fried chicken, barbecue chicken, beef stew, sausage, baked ham, collard greens, snap beans, black-eyed peas, squash, rice and gravy, okra and tomatoes, mashed potatoes, candied yams, pickled beets, apple salad, and macaroni salad.

The menu is changed on a daily basis, "because some people eat here every day," says Mrs. Wilkes. However, you'll always be served beef stew, baked ham, and fried chicken, the last being a specialty of the house. When asked about her fried chicken by Bryant Gumbel during an interview on NBC television's *Today* show, Mrs. Wilkes said, "If the Colonel's was as good, he'd be a general."

Mrs. Wilkes got started in the food service business in 1943 when her husband's job brought him to Savannah from the central Georgia town of Vidalia. L. H. Wilkes took a room at a boardinghouse in the building where Mrs. Wilkes' is now. Mrs. Wilkes would visit L. H. on weekends, got to know the owner of the boardinghouse and eventually began helping her out by cooking for the boarders. The Wilkeses raised a family in Savannah and in 1965 bought the boardinghouse, which they restored and converted into apartments. Mrs. Wilkes also cooked and served meals, first for her neighbors, then for visitors; word of the quality of her food and her down-home hospitality spread, to the extent that *Condé Nast Traveler* magazine in 1990 named her place one of the fifty most distinguished restaurants in the United States.

Lunch at Mrs. Wilkes' is $12, and you can eat breakfast there for $5. The dining rooms are open Monday through Friday. Mrs. Wilkes doesn't take credit cards but says she will accept a check "if it's good." Smoking is prohibited.

Nita's Place
129 E. Broughton Street
Savannah, GA
(912) 238–8233
$$

Definitive soul food is what you will find at Nita's Place. This down-home and unpretentious restaurant has acquired a reputation far bigger than its little hole-in-the-wall location in the heart of downtown would lead you to believe. Dig in to the slow-cooked, superbly seasoned vegetables and meats that distinguish classic African American cooking. The menu varies daily, but look for favorites like squash casserole and macaroni and cheese.

Nita's has moved from its original tiny spot around the corner to Broughton Street, where the still-small quarters were once part of a dime store. Relocation is a dangerous business for a restaurant, but Nita's food seems to have traveled well.

**The Olde Pink House
Restaurant & Planters Tavern
23 Abercorn Street
Savannah, GA
(912) 232–4286
$$$**

Experience Savannah as it was in post-Colonial days by dining at the Georgian-style mansion that is The Olde Pink House. This is the only restaurant in Savannah lodged in a historically significant house—a structure built in the late 1700s for wealthy merchant James Habersham Jr. and expanded in the early 1800s when it was the Planters' Bank, the first such establishment in Georgia. Known also as the Habersham House, the building, on the northwest corner of Abercorn and Bryan Streets, has a pink exterior because it was constructed of bricks made from red clay and covered with white stucco; the red bled through the stucco, coloring it pink, and the structure has been painted that hue ever since. A tearoom was opened in the house in the

1930s, and it has been a restaurant for the past fifty years.

The Olde Pink House serves regional cuisine in seven elegant dining rooms occupying the upper two floors of the building, which has a basement housing the Planters Tavern. Examples of this type of cooking are the sautéed shrimp with country ham and grits cake, she-crab soup laced with sherry, Caesar salad with corn bread oysters, crispy scored flounder with apricot shallot sauce, and grilled pork tenderloin crusted with almonds and molasses.

Before dining, you might want to walk downstairs to the tavern and relax with a drink while sitting in front one of the large brick fireplaces on either end of the room, which was originally the house's kitchen. Take a good look around and you'll notice a metal door that once was part of a bank vault; it now leads to the restaurant's wine cellar. Other points of interest within the house are the oil painting of residents of old Savannah and

This historic mansion now houses The Olde Pink House restaurant. PHOTO: KYLE CASON

notable Americans such as George Washington, a display featuring Habersham's somewhat gaudy shoe and knee buckles, and the staircase winding from the first floor to the second.

The Olde Pink House is open for candlelight dinners seven days a week, and jazz pianist Gail Thurmond performs in the tavern every evening. The bar is also the only place where smoking is allowed. Reservations are definitely recommended. If you're interested in dining in the restaurant's most romantic spot, ask for a table by a window in the second-floor Office Room—it has a view of picturesque Reynolds Square.

Olympia Cafe
5 E. River Street
Savannah, GA
(912) 233-3131
$$$

This authentic Greek restaurant is a welcome respite from the glare and bustle of River Street. Brick walls and flooring, lots of plants, and soft lighting add to the atmosphere, but that's all incidental to the food. Favorites here include red snapper Aegean, served with tomato sauce, spices, and feta cheese. Lamb chops marinated in olive oil and herbs before chargrilling are another favorite. Spanakopita is one of those dishes by which a Greek restaurant is measured, and you'll find this version of the flavored spinach pastry measures up well. On the lighter and less-expensive side of the menu, you can choose gyro sandwiches and chicken kebobs. On our last visit, we particularly enjoyed the Greek antipasto tray, even though we never quite figured out what some of the items on it were. Beverage selections include Greek coffee, and there is a full bar. Dress is generally nice and casual, but kick it up a notch for weekend dinners, when reservations are recommended. Don't be confused when you arrive—Olympia Cafe also operates a quick-and-casual takeout place on one side and a thirty-five-flavor ice cream parlor on the other.

Insiders' Tip

If you decide to get a take-out meal along River Street (or anywhere else near the water), resist the urge to share it with that single begging seagull that will invariably show up. Otherwise, hordes of its friends will arrive, and you will have no peace.

The Pirates' House Restaurant
20 East Broad Street
Savannah, GA
(912) 233-5757
$$$

This restaurant is a local institution. Locals have been coming here, and steering tourists here, for decades. The restaurant wanders from room to room, each of which is atmospheric (haunted, in fact, by some accounts). These quarters are Savannah's link to Robert Louis Stevenson's classic *Treasure Island*. When you have children in your party, it's hard to find a classy restaurant that accommodates younger patrons. The Pirates' House does this quite well, without damaging arrangements for adults out for a dress-up dinner. The menu is varied and includes lots of seafood. Locals head for the lunch buffet and always remember the fried chicken. The dessert menu is vast and intimidating: We suggest you consider dining here and skipping dessert, then making a return trip for dessert only before you leave Savannah. Nice casual will do for dress, but brush up a little bit for dinner. There's full bar service. The restaurant also has a gift shop.

Regional Cuisine Offers a Taste of Savannah

When you're in Savannah, you might run across some cuisine you're not likely to find in other parts of the country. Two examples, the Lowcountry shrimp boil and the oyster roast, combine food with other elements you might have noticed being mentioned throughout this book: Savannahians' love of getting together and their fondness for being outdoors.

You can order Lowcountry boil in a restaurant, and the same goes for oysters, but perhaps the best way to experience them is by attending an outdoor party at which they are the featured components. Lowcountry boil—also known as Frogmore stew because it supposedly originated in Frogmore, South Carolina, which is about ninety minutes northeast of Savannah—consists of smoked sausage, corn on the cob, and shrimp all boiled together in a large pot. Some cooks add other ingredients, with new potatoes seeming to be the most popular.

Oysters served at an oyster roast are roasted on a big piece of tin or steel that's supported by cinder blocks. A red-hot fire is built under the sheet of metal, and the oysters are placed on it and covered with wet cloth—burlap sacks do nicely. The oysters will steam open in about twenty minutes, and they're ready to eat. Special oyster knives are used to help dig the oysters out of their shells, and it's a good idea to wear gloves to prevent being cut by the oyster's tough exterior.

We think the best way to enjoy a Lowcountry boil or oyster roast is by standing around on a crisp day in autumn, chatting with friends, and diving into a pile of oysters or a big heap of sausage, shrimp, and corn that's been dumped on a table covered with newspaper. It doesn't hurt, by the way, if there's a keg of beer handy.

Among other foods associated with this area are Savannah red rice, a dessert called trifle, and a cookie known as the benne wafer. The benne wafer has a taste all its own because it's made with benne seeds, which is what folks in the Lowcountry call sesame seeds. Trifle, a gift of the English colonists to Savannah, consists of pound cake that's been sprinkled with sherry, layered with custard, and topped with

Cooks at an oyster roast pour a batch of oysters onto a table as a hungry guest waits to dig in.
PHOTO: PHYL M. GATLIN

whipped cream. Savannah red rice goes great with fried chicken and seafood. The following is a recipe for this distinctly local dish provided by Martha Giddens Nesbit, who edited and wrote much of the food section of Savannah's daily newspaper for more than a decade and is the author of the *Savannah Collection* and *Savannah Entertains* cookbooks.

In her recipe, which serves four people, Martha uses four slices of bacon that have been fried crisp, crumbled, and reserved, one chopped onion, one chopped celery stalk, a cup of raw rice, one 16-ounce can of tomatoes, three-quarters of a cup of water, a teaspoon of salt, and a quarter-teaspoon of cayenne pepper.

Fry the chopped onion and celery in bacon fat, then remove some of the fat, if desired, and add the rice, tomatoes, water, salt, and pepper. Combine the ingredients and transfer them to a one-and-one-half-quart baking dish. Bake at 350 degrees for twenty minutes or until the rice is soft but not dry. Stir in the reserved bacon and serve hot or at room temperature.

Something else you're likely to encounter during mealtimes in Savannah is sweetened iced tea, which we call just plain ol' "sweet tea." Savannahians drink it year-round, and here's a good way to make a gallon-size pitcherful: Place three family-size tea bags in the basket of your automatic coffeemaker and brew up a full coffeepot of tea. Put about a cup of sugar in the pitcher and pour the hot tea on top. Stir it up and add a full coffeepot of water and stir again. When it cools, you've got sweet tea.

Ray's Famous Cafe
146 Montgomery Street
Savannah, GA
(912) 232–4155
$

What makes Ray's Famous Cafe famous? Well, it's the clientele, much of which consists of members of the local courthouse crowd. You can see many of the town's attorneys, judges, and politicians here, either in the flesh or represented in the more than one hundred caricatures that line the walls of the little cafe, which is on Montgomery Street just north of Oglethorpe Avenue and almost directly across from the Chatham County Courthouse. When owner Ray Hord opened this restaurant in 1991, he called it the Uptown Country Cafe, but soon decided the name wasn't very catchy; so he changed it, and also altered the atmosphere of the place by asking *Savannah Morning News* political cartoonist Mark Streeter to drop by and make sketches of customers. And that's how Ray's Famous Cafe got to be famous. Although the caricatures have made Ray's an "in" place at which to eat lunch and breakfast, they're not the only things that bring people back. There are also the quality and variety of the home cooking and the promptness with which it's delivered. Ray's offers specials each day, with two meats and usually eight vegetables being featured, and a standard menu that is, says Hord, "so vast that a guy who works downtown can eat here several times a week and still get something different every time." Among the favorites of regulars are the baked and fried chicken, the chicken and dumplings, and the country steak. Ray's is open Monday through Friday. Credit cards are not accepted, but out-of-town checks are.

The Riverhouse Restaurant
125 W. River Street
Savannah, GA
(912) 234–1900
$$$

The Riverhouse and its bakery occupy four bays of an old cotton warehouse near the west end of River Street, and the bricks and thick wooden beams of the building lend charm to the upscale but casual atmosphere. Operated by the Harris family, which established it in 1982, The Riverhouse specializes in fresh seafood. Featured dishes include the grouper Florentine, which is served atop angel-hair pasta, and salmon Anna Marie, in which the fish is encrusted in potato and onion and served with red-pepper and lemon-butter sauces. Among the appetizers are the seafood strudel—a light pastry filled with spinach, feta cheese, shrimp, and crabmeat—and shrimp served on grits with a tasso gravy. The restaurant serves lunch and dinner, and "dessert only" customers are welcome any time in the bakery.

The Shrimp Factory
313 E. River Street
Savannah, GA
(912) 236-4229
$$$

This restaurant near the eastern end of River Street offers what owner Cheryl Harris Power likes to call "fine casual dining," meaning the atmosphere is relaxed but replete with special touches such as the salad being tossed tableside. The Shrimp Factory prides itself on its seafood, steaks, and chicken dishes, and as might be expected, you can find shrimp served "in so many ways" here—fried, with crab au gratin, with chicken jambalaya, with sausage Creole, and as shrimp scampi. Pecan pie is a specialty of the house, as is the pine bark stew, which is best described as a "Southern bouilla-baisse."

The restaurant occupies the bottom floor of a warehouse built in the 1820s for storing cotton, resin, and other products, and the building's heart-pine ceiling beams and rafters and brick walls give the Shrimp Factory a rustic feel. The restaurant has been in existence since 1977, and it's open seven days a week for lunch and dinner.

606 East Cafe
319 W. Congress Street
Savannah, GA
(912) 233–2887
$$

Good American food in a fun and funky setting is what you can expect here. Among other aspects of the far-out, anything-goes decor, you might find a basket of windup toys on your table and lingerie hanging from a line overhead. Choose from various burgers (plain to boursin burger and back), lasagna, a dozen-plus sandwiches including meat loaf, and more. Lunch and dinner are served seven days a week. A full bar is available, and there's outdoor seating when weather permits (it usually does).

Six Pence Pub
245 Bull Street
Savannah, GA
(912) 233–3156
$

A restaurant serving lunch and dinner daily, the Six Pence takes on the more convivial atmosphere of a pub as the evening unfolds. What you'll find here is what you might expect from a pub in Great Britain in terms of food and cozy atmosphere. Six Pence offers specials each day, with patrons having a particular liking for the shepherd's pie, the meat loaf and mashed potatoes, the French onion and potato soups, and a meat pie made with mushrooms, peas and carrots, and beef that's been marinated in beer.

Most of the memorabilia adorning the walls and bar is authentic—from the Toby mugs to the coronation collectibles dating to 1898 to the pub signs, some of which are more than 200 years old. Be sure to look for the ship's bell that's a replica of the one on the *Titanic* and was a souvenir gift from that ill-fated vessel's maiden voyage. Also search out the handwritten, hand-painted proclamations presented to King George VI in 1937.

The pub also has its own ghost, a fellow who reportedly hangs out in the basement and has a penchant for turning faucets and light fixtures on and off. Nicknamed "Larry" by former Six Pence owner Wendy Snowden, this apparition has the appearance of a young man from the late 1800s.

Skyler's
225 E. Bay Street
Savannah, GA
(912) 232–3955
$$$

The co-owners of Skyler's—Nguyen Nguyet and Charles Coolidge—like to say their restaurant is "where East meets West." Nguyen, who's better known to patrons and friends as Miss Moon, is a former resident of Vietnam, and Charles is a native of Atlanta; they worked together as chefs at the Hyatt hotel here and developed a cooking style that Coolidge deems a "fusion of Asian-Continental cuisine with coastal dishes." They took that style with them when they left the hotel and opened the original Skyler's on State Street in 1990. The restaurant quickly outgrew that location, and Miss Moon and Coolidge moved it in 1993 to the cellar of the East Bay Inn, where there was more room and the ambience of a one-time cotton warehouse—brick floors and walls and a ceiling dominated by thick wooden beams. Skyler's specializes in crab cakes, roast pork, teriyaki chicken, and Caesar salad and seats its customers in Windsor chairs that make eating here an extremely comfortable experience. The main dining room accommodates seventy people, and there's a banquet room with seating for sixty. Access to the restaurant is through the lobby of the East Bay Inn. Skyler's is open for lunch on weekdays and serves dinner on Wednesday, Thursday, Friday, and Saturday.

Soho South Cafe
12 W. Liberty Street
Savannah, GA
(912) 233–1633
$$–$$$

What a place: a combination restaurant and art gallery in the minimally renovated lofty space once occupied by a garage. It's worth the trip just to look around, but the food could stand on its own anywhere. Soho South (which you will also hear called Soho Savannah, even though that isn't the official name) serves a sophisticated but affordable lunch and does dinner on Friday and Saturday nights. Your table might be from a patio suite or a circa-1950s dinette set. The quiche is the best available in Savannah and sells out early at lunch. Salads, soups, portabello mushroom burgers—we've never been disappointed here. Save room for the decadent desserts, which include a berry trifle-thing that's hard to resist. The clientele tends to be the local ladies-who-lunch crowd, with the occasional business lunch thrown in, and more and more tourists are getting steered here. This place has experimented with dinner before, but at the moment it's strictly lunch. Before you leave, swing by the rest room—even if you don't need the facilities, the decor is worth checking out.

Spanky's Pizza Gallery & Saloon
317 E. River Street
Savannah, GA
(912) 236–3009
308 Mall Way
Savannah, GA
(912) 355–3383
200 Governor Treutlen Road
Pooler, GA
(912) 748–8188
1605 Strand
Tybee Island, GA
(912) 786–5520
$$

Ansley Williams, Alben Yarbrough, and Dusty Yarbrough opened the first Spanky's on River Street in 1976, intending to bring pizza to the area. They also served burgers and chicken sandwiches at the restaurant, which is housed in what had been a cotton warehouse. According to Williams, the chicken breasts used for the sandwiches were too large for the buns on which they were served, so the restaurateurs

Elegant banquet facilities are available at local resorts such as the Westin Savannah Harbor Resort.
PHOTO: COURTESY OF THE WESTIN SAVANNAH HARBOR RESORT

sliced off the excess chicken and, not wanting to be wasteful, battered and fried the strips of meat and sold them as "chicken fingers." Their concoction was a hit with locals and has become a mainstay of eateries throughout southeast Georgia. The success of the River Street location led to the opening of Spanky's restaurants in other parts of the state and locally on the Southside near Oglethorpe Mall, in Pooler, and on Tybee Island (that one's called Spanky's Beachside). Williams and the Yarbroughs eventually went their separate ways, with Williams retaining ownership of the Spanky's on River Street and the Yarbroughs remaining involved with the others.

Although the Spanky's restaurants have different owners, the menus are basically the same, with the chicken fingers, pizza, and burgers still featured. Another favorite of veteran customers are Spanky's Spuds, which are circular-sliced potatoes that are battered and fried. The restaurants are open daily for lunch and dinner.

Typhoon
8 E. Broughton Street
Savannah, GA
(912) 232–0755, (912) 232–0756
$$–$$$

Typhoon blew into Savannah in mid-August 1998 and swept Savannahians away with its Malaysian-Chinese cuisine. Dishes such as curry chicken, kung pau calamari, and five-spice crispy duck have given locals a new and more appreciative perspective on Asian food. The decor of this restaurant on Broughton near Bull Street is also unique, incorporating lots of bamboo and rattan to achieve a natural look (notice that even the columns supporting the ceiling are scribed with a bamboo motif). Typhoon serves lunch Monday through Friday and dinner daily. Beer is available, as are wines from an ever-expanding list of selections. The management suggests that you make reservations on weekends.

Vinnie Van GoGo
317 W. Bryan Street
Savannah, GA
(912) 233–6394
$$

Vinnie's serves pizza with real character—thin crust with fresh ingredients, including options like spinach, artichoke, and broccoli, for dinner only. Experiment with pesto instead of regular sauce. A regular fourteen-inch pie is $9 to start, plus $1.50 for each ingredient. Dine in the cramped interior or at outside tables overlooking City Market (semienclosed when it's cold). Pizza is available by the slice, and one of those with the excellent spinach salad is an ample meal. Our personal favorite among the pizzas is feta, sun-dried tomato, and black olive. Beer is available. Get the wine list: Cork and screw-top are your options. Your most casual duds are probably too dressy for Vinnie's, but the food's tops.

Walls' Barbecue
515 E. York Lane
Savannah, GA
(912) 232–9754
$

Ninety-five percent of the barbecue pork, barbecue chicken, deviled crabs, and other food sold at Walls' is taken out by customers. Walls' is essentially a building with a kitchen and counter on York Lane, which runs from Price to Houston Streets between York Street and Oglethorpe Avenue. If you want to eat in, there are three tables where you can sit. Walls' also offers fried fish, fried chicken, spare ribs, and vegetable plates, and all the dinners come with red rice, potato salad, and a vegetable.

Margaret T. Weston, who has owned Walls' since 1979, says the business was started in the mid-1960s by her parents, Richard and Janie Walls, in a building in back of their cottage on York Street. "My daddy had a wood yard and he got tired of chopping wood, but he wanted security for my mother and me—he wanted us to be able to take care of ourselves." So Richard Walls started his barbecue business, choosing it, says Mrs. Weston with a smile, "because it was something he could get out of." Soon after the business opened, Walls began driving a taxicab, leaving Mrs. Walls and her daughter to do the cooking, and cook they have, much to the delight of Savannahians who love barbecue. Walls' is open for lunch and early dinner Thursday through Saturday.

Windows
2 W. Bay Street
Savannah, GA
(912) 944–3620
$$$

Windows is aptly named. At this restaurant, four floors above River Street in the Hyatt Regency Hotel, the windows run from the floor practically to the ceiling, giving diners spectacular views of the Savannah River and the graceful Eugene Talmadge Bridge. Windows serves breakfast, lunch, and dinner 365 days a year. It's a popular spot for weekday business lunches because of the self-service salad bar and the pasta bar, where cooks prepare pasta dishes to the specifications of customers. Also popular at lunchtime are dishes from the wok, either vegetarian or featuring chicken and scallops, shrimp and scallops, or Hunan pork and shrimp. The breakfast menu offers a full range of standard items, and the dinner menu changes seasonally. Drinks are available, made at the bar at adjacent M.D.'s lounge (see our Nightlife chapter). Reservations aren't required, but by making one, you'll enhance your chances of getting one of the eleven window tables.

Islands

Desposito's Seafood
Macceo Drive
Thunderbolt, GA
(912) 897–9963
$

On evenings when the weather's nice, Desposito's owner David Boone and his mom, Walton, open the windows of the enclosed porch of this little cinder-block and wood eatery at Thunderbolt. You can sit out there at tables covered with newspaper and eat boiled shrimp, crab legs, and steamed oysters as the breeze from the nearby Wilmington River wafts through the place.

Desposito's—which Walton Boone bought in late 1982 and David took over in December 1996 when she "retired" (she still works part-time)—also serves deviled crab; homemade chili, pecan pie, and potato salad; and the Lowcountry basket, which is filled with shrimp, corn on the cob, sausage, and the aforementioned potato salad. In addition to the porch, there's a dining room, and a bar that serves beer and wine and has one of those old-fashioned bowling machines. Desposito's is open for dinner daily and lunch on Friday, Saturday, and Sunday. MasterCard and Visa only are accepted. It's on the eastern side of the Wilmington River and north of U.S. Highway 80.

Little Saigon
4700-F U.S. Highway 80
Savannah, GA
(912) 897–1559
$

Savannah has a great many Asian restaurants, many of them quite acceptable but generally all tending to seem the same. Little Saigon is the happiest of exceptions. It evolved from an earlier Vietnamese/Chinese restaurant, and now serves Thai—the trendiest part of its menu—and Vietnamese, which to our way of thinking is a subtler and tastier side of the menu. This family-owned restaurant is one of those places you would never wind up at if a local didn't steer you that way. Little Saigon is in a nondescript strip shopping center, four lanes across from a Wal-Mart on the highway leading to the beach. Forget the unpromising-sounding location, because the offerings inside the sparkling clean restaurant are plenty promising. On the Thai options, diners can choose from a spiciness index of mild, medium, hot, and "Thai hot." (We love hot food, but we've found that "medium" works just fine for us here—the staff gives solid guidance on the heat factor.) The menu has the classic Pahd Thai and a variety of curries. Our favorites, however, are among the simplest of the Vietnamese offerings: summer rolls, which are fresh chopped vegetables and shrimp (among other things) wrapped in rice paper, and the Vietnamese pork chop, which is grilled and seasoned and served sliced over jasmine rice.

Snappers Seafood Restaurant
104 Bryan Woods Road
Savannah, GA
(912) 897–6101
$$$

Set in a wooded area on the marsh that borders Turner Creek, Snappers has specialized in seafood since its opening in 1987. Shrimp accounts for 40 percent of sales at this restaurant on Whitemarsh Island, and flounder, trout, and mahimahi are also big sellers.

In recent years, however, the management began to change the menu a bit by placing more of an emphasis on serving certified Angus steaks, pasta dishes, and seafood with which many coastal Georgians are not accustomed, such as mussels, calamari, and clams. A trend toward offering more grilled and steamed seafood—as opposed to fried—is also in evidence. Whatever your selection, it will be accompanied by complimentary bowls of a Snappers standby—sweet, bite-size hush puppies. We dare you to eat just one! Snappers occupies a site that reportedly was once a cotton patch owned by Nicholas Turnbull, reputedly the island's first Scottish settler, and the restaurant has honored him with its Highlander Pie, which is filled with ground beef and spices and served with mashed potatoes.

Snappers Seafood Restaurant sits just south of busy U.S. Highway 80, but diners feel as though they're in a secluded spot because the surrounding forest serves as a buffer to the noise of traffic, and floor-to-ceiling windows provide soothing views of the woods and the adjacent marsh. The restaurant's Ossabaw and Wassaw dining rooms are named for nearby islands, as is an alcove that seats eighteen and is popular with small groups. The alcove is called, appropriately enough, Little Tybee.

Teeple's Seafood Restaurant
2917 River Drive
Thunderbolt, GA
(912) 354–1157
$$$

"Don't come if you're in a hurry," says owner Mildred Teeple Hill of her restaurant on the bluff overlooking the Wilmington River, an eatery where all the food is "cooked to order." Teeple's has been a fixture on River Drive since 1975, when Mildred's brother, Charlie, opened the restaurant next door to its present location. According to the Teeples, theirs is the first restaurant in the area to feature tables with holes cut in the middle into which you shove your oyster and crab shells and shrimp peelings. Mildred says her father, Charles, came up with that idea for keeping tables clean and even built the restaurant's first furniture, some of which is still in use. As you might have guessed by now, Teeple's specializes in serving blue crabs, oysters, and shrimp cooked Lowcountry style, but steaks, chicken fingers, sandwiches, and other types of seafood are also available. Whatever your meal, the folks here expect you to take all the time you want to enjoy it; if business slows down, you might even be paid a visit by Mildred or one of her staff, eager to find out where you're from and to chat for awhile. If you're fortunate enough to find Mildred at your table, ask here about life in Thunderbolt and the way things used to be when it was a thriving fishing community; she was born in the little riverside town and has lived there for more than fifty years, and she'll be happy to give you the details. Teeple's serves dinner daily and lunch on weekends.

Williams Seafood Restaurant
8010 Tybee Road
Savannah, GA
(912) 897–2219
$$$

Members of the Williams family have been providing Savannahians with seafood since 1936, when Tom Williams began selling the fish and crabs he caught while tending the bridge over the Bull River on the road to Tybee Island. Tom's wife, Leila, developed a special recipe for deviled crab, and sales to motorists headed to and from the beach boomed. The Williamses opened a roadside stand and eventually a restaurant near the bridge. On the site of that original spot is the existing Williams Seafood Restaurant, and it's operated by a third generation of the Williams family.

The deviled crab is still on the menu. Other favorites of the families who have made Williams a regular part of their lives through the years are the shrimp and flounder. This large, unpretentious-looking restaurant seats upwards of 500 people and also serves steak, hamburger, and chicken. Beer and wine are available, as are catering and banquet facilities. The restaurant is open for lunch and dinner.

Williams is just off U.S. 80 at the western end of the newest bridge over the Bull River. Remnants of the bridge Tom Williams once tended can be seen nearby.

Southside/Midtown

Barnes Restaurant
5320 Waters Avenue
Savannah, GA
(912) 354–8745
4685 U.S. Highway 80 E.
Savannah, GA
(912) 898–0220
10201 Abercorn Street
Savannah, GA
(912) 961–6767
Ga. Highway 21
Rincon, GA
(912) 826–7440
$$

The folks at the four Barnes restaurants pride themselves on the fact that everything from the barbecue sauce to the potato salad to the sweet iced tea is homemade. The sauce on Barnes's chopped pork and sliced beef barbecue is made according to a recipe developed by restaurant founder Nesbert Barnes and perfected over the years by his son, Hugh; it's spread on meat that's slow-cooked at low temperatures over oak and hickory wood. There's a step-by-step guide for making the tea, and an employee specifically designated to perform the task; if the tea maker is not present on a given day, the manager gets the job.

When Barnes opened in 1975, just south of where the existing building stands on Waters Avenue at 68th Street, it filled only take-out orders. A dining room was added three years later, and the existing restaurant opened in summer 1993. The island restaurant went into operation two years afterward and the Abercorn site opened in mid-July 2000. The restaurant in Rincon, which is in Effingham County just west of the Chatham County line, was added in October 2000.

Today families, business people, and retirees flock to Barnes for the barbecue and the tea. Chicken fingers, ribs, shrimp salad, and onion rings are other big sellers at all four locations. Barnes serves lunch and dinner, and you're likely to encounter a line of customers waiting at the Waters Avenue restaurant if you get there around noon. Don't be discouraged; the line moves fast and the Lowcountry/Southern-style food is worth waiting for.

Bella's Italian Cafe
4420 Habersham Street
Savannah, GA
(912) 354–4005
$$$

Located on Habersham Street between 60th and 61st Streets, Bella's is "where Savannah eats Italian," according to owner Joyce Shanks. She claims the manicotti at Bella's is the best south of Brooklyn, and she ought to know. She grew up in that New York borough, learning to cook manicotti and other Italian dishes in the kitchen of her grandmother, Bella. Joyce's manicotti is stuffed with a mixture of three cheeses, baked in marinara sauce, and topped with bubbling cheese. Her chicken Parmesan—a double chicken breast deep-fried in bread crumbs and baked with marinara and melted cheeses—is another popular entree, but we could make a meal of just Bella's breadsticks—yeast dough that's deep fried, tastes like doughnuts, and is served with marinara and herb butter.

Bella's, which has been at its existing site in Habersham Village shopping center since 1993 after a four-year stint at Savannah Mall, can accommodate sixty diners in cozy, family-oriented surroundings. The restaurant serves dinner seven days a week and lunch on weekdays. Beer and wine are available. Bella's doesn't take reservations, and it's a good idea to arrive early if you're dining on a weekend. There are only a few parking spaces in front of the restaurant but plenty of spots in the lot at the corner of Habersham and 61st. Bella's accepts major credit cards with the exception of Discover.

Carey Hilliard's Restaurant
3316 Skidaway Road
Savannah, GA
(912) 354-7240
8410 Waters Avenue
Savannah, GA
(912) 355-2468
514 U.S. Highway 80
Garden City, GA
(912) 964-5671
5350 GA Highway 21
Garden City, GA
(912) 963-0060
11111 Abercorn Street
Savannah, GA
(912) 925-3225
$

That there are five Carey Hilliard's in Savannah should tell you something about the popularity of these restaurants, which provide casual dining in an atmosphere geared toward families. Founder Carey Hilliard opened his first establishment in

> ## Insiders' Tip
> Perhaps the influx of thousands of college students has something to do with it, but area restaurants are now more likely to offer vegetarian, and even vegan, options on their menus. But if the menu doesn't actually use the word *vegetarian*, you might want to ask—Southern cooks traditionally use "side meat" such as salt pork or ham hocks as seasoning in vegetables.

1960 on Skidaway Road in what had been an A&W Root Beer stand. The drive-in, curb-service feature was retained, and all five restaurants offer it today. Order from your car, and you receive many of the amenities you would by dining inside, including china plates and silverware.

Barbecue has always been, and still is, a big seller at Carey Hilliard's, which serves lunch and dinner, but seafood dishes account for about half the orders these days. Among the favorites of customers are the fried shrimp, oysters, and deviled crabs. Seating at the restaurants averages 250. Beer and wine are available.

Elizabeth on Thirty-Seventh Street
105 E. 37th Street
Savannah, GA
(912) 236-5547
$$$$

This is where national food writers dine when they come to town. It's also where locals celebrate and entertain to impress. Chef/owner Elizabeth Terry is pretty

Sophisticated food in elegant surroundings, like at Elizabeth on 37th, is one wonderful option for dining out in Savannah. PHOTO: COURTESY OF ELIZABETH ON 37TH

much considered the queen of local haute cuisine, and she produces a Southern regional menu that is hard to characterize, but sophisticated and appealing. (In other words, don't look for the overcooked or fried, flat qualities some folks consider regional cooking.) It makes the best of local offerings, but that does not mean you are faced with seafood selections only. Dress up and dig in for dinner only. Reservations are strongly recommended.

Hirano's Restaurant
4426 Habersham Street
Savannah, GA
(912) 353-8337
13015 Abercorn Street
Savannah, GA
(912) 961-0770
U.S. Highway 80
Savannah, GA
(912) 898-3880
$$

Japanese cuisine became a major hit in Savannah with the opening of this small storefront restaurant on Habersham Street. Folks stand in line for a chance to order simple, fresh food from a limited menu. Large servings and reasonable prices are hallmarks here. The teriyaki chicken, served with rice and salad, runs less than $5, so if you pick your items carefully, this can be a budget meal as well as a real treat. Combination plates carry higher prices.

The food is prepared at open griddles behind the counter—this is not one of the showy knife-twirling restaurants. If you are eager to get started at the Habersham site, opt for a seat at the counter overlooking the cooking. Those seats come open more quickly than the small stock of tables. The Habersham location has a separate sushi bar, but call ahead if you are interested—it tends to keep shorter hours. All the Hirano's serve a delicious California roll of avocado and cooked crab rolled in rice for those who are wary of traditional sushi. The recent opening of a third Hirano's shows just how popular it is. The new one is on Whitemarsh Island on U.S. 80 near the suburban islands area.

Johnny Harris Restaurant
1651 E. Victory Drive
Savannah, GA
(912) 354-7810
$$$

Stepping into the main dining room at Johnny Harris is like fox-trotting back into the late 1930s and the '40s, when this establishment was an elegant supper club on the outskirts of Savannah. The bandstand that occupied the middle of the floor is gone, but the room retains the charm of that bygone era. Remaining from those good old days are the dark wood paneling of the Old English decor and a thirty-foot-high ceiling adorned for a starry, night-sky effect.

You can also still slip into one of the booths lining the perimeter of the oval-shaped room and place an order by pushing a service button that illuminates a green light overhead.

The restaurant has been a favorite of Savannahians for decades, and many patrons bring their grandchildren and great-grandchildren so they can experience the atmosphere, service, and food—in particular the barbecue, fried chicken, prime rib, and crabmeat au gratin (meat of the crab's claw folded in a cream sauce and baked with two cheeses). Johnny Harris is the oldest restaurant in Savannah and one of the oldest in Georgia, but you'll notice it's not in the Historic Downtown. It's in Midtown, on Victory Drive just east of Bee Road. That intersection is where the original restaurant was built in 1924 by a Southerner from out of town named Johnny Harris; the original wooden building was torn down, and the brick structure that houses the existing restaurant was built in 1936. Johnny Harris died in 1942, and the restaurant has been run by the Donaldson family of Savannah ever since.

Johnny Harris has seating under one roof for 275 people in the main room, the adjacent cafe area, a lounge with a full-service bar, and a banquet room that can accommodate up to sixty. Smoking is allowed in the cafe area and lounge but prohibited in the main room, where live dinner music is provided on Friday nights and dancing to tunes of the '40s, '50s, and '60s is featured on Saturday nights. Hearkening back to the restaurant's earlier days, the management requires that male dancers wear coats. Johnny Harris serves lunch and dinner Monday though Saturday and takes but does not require reservations.

If you get the chance, stroll through the restaurant's back hallways and take a gander at the more than sixty framed menus hanging on the walls. They bear the autographs of well-known entertainers, politicians, and sports figures who have eaten at Johnny Harris. The first to scribble his signature was the late comedian Red Skelton; among the most recent was actor and filmmaker Clint Eastwood. You might also consider purchasing some of the restaurant's barbecue sauce to take home with you. It's bottled hot and sold at Johnny Harris and other outlets in Georgia, South Carolina, and Florida, and it is shipped worldwide via mail order.

Larry's Restaurant
3000 Skidaway Road
Savannah, GA
(912) 355–8272
$

Eat your vegetables at Larry's. You'll select three when you order an entree from the luncheon menu, which changes daily. (For information on what's cooking, call the menu line at 912-355-5821.) Among the favorite choices are the sweet-potato soufflé, the squash casserole, and the turnip greens, and they go just fine with the fried chicken, beef stew, or chicken and dumplings. There's plenty more to choose from at this eatery, which has been serving breakfast and lunch on Skidaway Road a couple of blocks south of Victory Drive since 1981.

Larry's is a hangout of locals—one of those places where the parking lot is usually filled with vehicles (many of them pickup trucks), and the waitresses call customers by name. The food and atmosphere aren't fancy, but the homestyle grub is good, plentiful, and inexpensive, and the air hums with the conversation of folks talking with longtime cronies or renewing old acquaintances. Larry's, which seats 150, is closed on weekends.

Mary's Seafood and Steakhouse
10002 Abercorn Street
Savannah, GA
(912) 927–1300
$$$

After many years of serving customers from a location on Largo Drive, Mary's moved to new quarters on Abercorn Street in November 1998. Fried and broiled seafood platters, crab legs, stuffed flounder, filet mignon, and the queen-size prime rib grab the spotlight at this restaurant, which has three dining rooms and a bar, all decorated in the style of an English pub. The filet mignon and the New York strip steak are served on a hot lava stone that continues to cook the meat after it is brought to your table, and you can ask for other dishes to be served on the "hot rock." The Southside restaurant, owned by Mary Buckley since 1988, offers dinner seven days a week.

Orleans Brick Oven
108 Mall Boulevard
Savannah, GA
(912) 691–0006
$$

Orleans Brick Oven specializes in gourmet pizzas and pasta, making it a popular lunch and dinner spot for business people and shoppers at nearby Oglethorpe Mall. The pizzas, featuring the restaurant's honey herb crust, are baked in a wood-fired brick oven and are available with a wide variety of toppings—everything from artichokes, chicken, and sun-dried tomatoes to Creole crawfish and tasso with andouille sausage. The Brick Oven offers sixteen different pasta dishes, including Orleans shrimp jambalaya over fettucini and marsala marinara chicken over linguine. The management strives to create the ambience of old New Orleans with a courtyard look that incorporates lots of wrought iron, plants, and murals depicting the French Quarter. Orleans Brick Oven, which opened in December 1996, serves dinner seven days a week and lunch Monday through Saturday. It's across from the Belk department store end of the mall.

Rancho Allegre
44 Posey Street
Savannah, GA
(912) 691–0110
$$

Rancho Allegre is our nominee for Savannah's biggest culinary surprise. After all, who would expect to find a restaurant tucked away just off Abercorn Street near the eastern end of the Hunter Army Airfield runway, amid auto repair shops and wholesale houses—one that serves Cuban cuisine, no less. But there it is, occupying what was once a residence before the commercialization spawned by nearby Oglethorpe Mall caught up with it. This rancho serves a variety of exotic-sounding dishes featuring chicken, beef, pork, and seafood, such as pollo a la Juliana (pepper chicken strips), ropa vieja (shredded beef slowly cooked in Creole sauce), masas de cerdo fritas (fried pork chunks), and camarones al ajilio (garlic shrimp). Most entries are accompanied by rice, beans, and sweet plantains. We're betting this is also one of few places in town where you can get Cuban coffee, flan, and fried yuca. The Rancho Allegre serves lunch and dinner Monday through Saturday. Posey Street, by the way, runs between Abercorn and White Bluff Road and is just south of Eisenhower Drive.

Semolina
Twelve Oaks Shopping Center,
5500 Abercorn Street
Savannah, GA
(912) 353–9335
$$

Semolina specializes in pasta, but it's not an Italian restaurant. The main dishes served at this eatery in Twelve Oaks Shopping Center (on Abercorn Street just south of DeRenne Avenue) are international in flavor, meaning they combine pasta with fare from several cultures. Two of the favorites of Semolina fans are chicken cordon bleu pasta and chicken enchilada pasta, in which rigatoni is adorned with chicken, onions, green peppers, and black beans sautéed in a tortilla cheese sauce. Appetizers also have an international flair. There's baked feta cheese and marinara sauce, and shrimp Napoleon: shrimp, Gouda cheese, and tasso layered between rounds of eggplant and smothered in a spicy cream sauce. The crowd-pleaser dessert is bread pudding made with apples and cinnamon and served hot; one order is big enough for two diners.

Semolina has seating for 102 in booths or tables in an upbeat atmosphere featuring sponge-painted walls and oversized strands of linguine (they're rubber) and huge vegetables (they're papier-mâché) hanging from the ceiling. Semolina—one of a chain of twenty-one restaurants in Georgia, Florida, North Carolina, and Louisiana—serves lunch and dinner. Smoking is not allowed.

Toucan Cafe
531 Stephenson Avenue
Savannah, GA
(912) 352–2233
$$$

Nestled in the woods off Stephenson Avenue, the Toucan Cafe combines eclectic food, an interior that pulsates with the high-impact colors of the tropics, and an exterior that has a classic Mediterranean look. The cuisine reflects the influences of several exotic cultures—Jamaican jerk chicken and Jamaican jerk talapia, both of which are served with black beans, rice, and pineapple salsa; Thai chicken and eggplant and Thai shrimp and eggplant, both of which are served in a mild green curry coconut sauce with bell peppers and onions over rice, and Hellenic stuffed chicken, made with spinach and feta cheese, served over rice, and topped with Greek-style baby peas. Those are just a few of the dishes offered by owners Steve and Nancy Magulias who, in late 1998, moved the cafe to newly built quarters on Stephenson from a small storefront in nearby Eisenhower Plaza where the Toucan had been located since 1994.

The Toucan Cafe serves dinner Monday through Saturday and lunch Monday through Friday; reservations aren't required but will be accepted for parties of six or more. Smoking is prohibited.

Tubby's Tank House
2909 River Drive
Thunderbolt, GA
(912) 354–9040
115 E. River Street
Savannah, GA
(912) 233–0770
$$$

Tubby's specializes in fresh seafood, much of it caught by part-owner Stan "Tubby" Strickland, a sport fisherman with a knack for hauling in mahimahi, grouper, tuna, and wahoo. In fact, says fellow owner Ansley Williams, Tubby's is a seafood restaurant because of Strickland's ability as an angler. Williams says that in 1994 when he, Strickland, and managing partner Ray Clark decided to start a new restaurant, they settled on opening a seafood place because Strickland "was catching so much fish we needed a place to distribute it." The result was Tubby's, a rustic-looking restaurant perched on the bluff at Thunderbolt.

In addition to the aforementioned sports fish, Tubby's serves shrimp, scallops, oysters, and Tubby's Tank Out, a seafood platter that, according to Williams, "is more than one human can eat." Burgers, chicken fingers, and a variety of salads are available for those not inclined toward eating fish.

Another feature of Tubby's is its splendid view of the Intracoastal Waterway, which, in these parts, is the Wilmington River. When the weather's nice, the best seats for a look at the water are outdoors on Tubby's wide porch or on the rooftop deck. Tubby's serves lunch and dinner seven days a week, hosts oyster roasts on Thursday nights during the winter and Thursday sunset parties in the summer, and offers dancing in the back room on Thursday, Friday, and Saturday nights. A second Tubby's opened on River Street in February 1998. The menu at the downtown restaurant is similar to that of the original establishment, and the River Street location is also open for lunch and dinner each day of the week. Live entertainment is provided at night.

Wang's II Chinese Restaurant
7601 Waters Avenue
Savannah, GA
(912) 355–0321
$$

Wang's II offers Hunan and Szechuan cuisine for lunch and dinner seven days a week. Some of the dishes on the extensive menu are spicier than others, but they're designated as such and can be cooked to suit your taste. All the food at this restaurant on Waters Avenue between Eisenhower Drive and Mall Boulevard is monosodium glutamate–free, according to the management. Among the more popular dishes are the crispy fish; sauteed string beans with chicken, beef, shrimp, or roast pork; and General Tso's chicken, which consists of chunks of chicken in a spicy brown sauce.

Wang's II, which opened in 1991, has a full bar and seating for 150 in an elegant dining room featuring black lacquer chairs and glass-topped tables. The restaurant does not take Discover, and reservations are recommended on Friday and Saturday nights. In case you're wondering, there's no Wang's I.

Yanni's
11211 Abercorn Street
Savannah, GA
(912) 925–6814
$$$

Yanni Andronikos is a jeweler by trade, so his restaurant is a labor of love that he likes to call "an extension of my living room." Andronikos's longtime dream of operating a restaurant was realized in mid-October 2000 when he opened Yanni's on Abercorn just east of Largo Drive. Yanni's specializes in dishes featuring fresh fish and offers lots of traditional Greek fare, with Andronikos using the best recipes he's found in regions of Greece that concentrate on specific types of food, such as lamb chops from Crete, eggplant salad from northern Greece, and gyros from Athens. The restaurant serves lunch and dinner daily in a cozy dining room adorned with seascape murals, trellised grape leaves, and tiny white lights.

West Chatham

Love's Seafood Restaurant
6817 Basin Road
Savannah, GA
(912) 925–3616
$$$

Love's is in southwest Chatham County 14 miles from the Historic Downtown,

Great views, such as those from the Westin Savannah Harbor Resort, are often a part of the Savannah dining experience. PHOTO: COURTESY OF THE WESTIN SAVANNAH HARBOR RESORT

but city dwellers are more than happy to make the ride to this restaurant on the banks of the serene Ogeechee River. A major reason for the pilgrimages is Love's fried catfish, 90 percent of it caught in the river and all of it battered with a fine cracker meal that makes it so light it seems to float off the plate. Besides, says Fulton Love, who runs the restaurant with his wife Donna, you can get there from downtown in fifteen minutes if you take Interstate 16, Interstate 95 and Georgia Highway 204 to U.S. Highway 17 and the Chatham-Bryan county line.

The restaurant is where the U.S. 17 bridge crosses the river, and has been there since 1949, when it was started as a fishing camp by Fulton's folks, O. F. and Thelma. If you've watched the movie *Forrest Gump*—and who hasn't?—you've seen the bridge and the restaurant in the scene where Forrest and his girlfriend part company. You can see the beautiful Ogeechee from about 250 of the 304 seats at Love's, but the best views are from the porch, which seats 50 and is a nonsmoking area.

Love's serves steak and chicken fingers in an atmosphere that's rustic but upscale; however, the main draws here are the catfish and seafood, in particular the fried shrimp, shrimp and red snapper stuffed with crabmeat, and the seafood fettucini. Beer, wine, and mixed drinks are available.

Love's, which serves about 600 pounds of catfish a week and is probably the oldest catfish restaurant in Georgia, takes reservations for parties of twelve or more. It's open Tuesday through Saturday for dinner and Sunday for lunch and dinner; it's closed on Mondays when the owners are, as they put it, "Gone fishing."

Lovezzola's Pizza Restaurant
320 U.S. Highway 80 E.
Pooler, GA
(912) 748–6414
$$

Pizza fans, rejoice! There is real pizza, as opposed to the franchise mass-production type, south of the Mason-Dixon Line. Paul Lovezzola has been hand throwing the dough for New York–style pizza at his restaurant for the past nineteen years. This transplanted New Yorker hasn't lost his accent or his taste for slow-cooked sauces and individually prepared pizzas in those years.

Sit in his casual, family-style dining room at a table with red-and-white checked plastic tablecloths, and he'll point out his ancestral hometown on the map of Italy featured on the placemats. He serves up his pizza with the usual selection of toppings and offers pasta dishes, submarine sandwiches, and a salad bar as well.

His regulars include not only travelers along I-95 (he's just off exit 104) and expatriate Northerners, but also a solid group of Southern converts who have been won over to the concept of pizza as a real food.

Pooler is one of Chatham County's municipalities on its western side, easy to find because it is close to the interstate and worth the drive for a taste of what pizza was before it became fast food. Take-outs are available, as is delivery in a limited area that includes the motels clustered around the Pooler exit off I-95.

Nightlife

Bars
Billiards
Coffeehouses
Movies

After a day spent beaching, boating, shopping, eating, fishing, touring, visiting museums, checking out aged graveyards, and getting acclimated to the local heat and humidity, what do you do when the sun goes down? After an especially active tourist day, many folks would just opt to turn in early. Don't worry, though: You'll recover before your stay is over, and you'll want to sample Savannah's nightlife.

Savannah's traditional nightlife is an at-home thing. We have perfected the art of hospitality and party-giving here, and the night's best food, drink, and entertainment is probably being served and going on in someone's backyard, on their dock, or in their living room. If you have friends, family, or savvy business acquaintances in town, chances are good you'll get a chance to see what we mean.

That doesn't mean you're out of luck if you don't have an invitation, however. Savannah has plenty of nightspots to entertain guests, and locals turn out too when they're tired of the homegrown party thing. The bar and entertainment scene falls into three general categories: River Street, a restored area along the Savannah River that was refurbished with just this sort of thing in mind; City Market, a restored quadrant of the Historic Downtown that's heavy on clubs and bars as well as shops; and a variety of watering holes and entertainment sites scattered along routes to the south of the city (the Southside, in local parlance).

If you don't have something very specific in mind (say, jazz or a sports bar), our advice is to follow your ear, literally. Visitors will fare better on River Street and in City Market, where there are lots of nightspots clustered together. You can follow the music you hear spilling out the doors and wander conveniently from site to site. We're not scoffing at the Southside offerings: It's just that the nightspots there are more scattered, making it harder for someone unfamiliar with the terrain to get around.

Which brings us to the question of alcohol and the law. Savannah's folklore stresses the city's hard-drinking reputation, with tales that the town was never dry, even during Prohibition (which lingered long in Georgia, where some counties are still dry). You'll probably get tired of locals telling you the favorite question posed to a newcomer is, "What do you drink?"

Believe all this if you want to, but don't base your actions on it. Local law enforcement aggressively pursues alcohol offenses. Drivers can face charges with a blood-alcohol level of .08 percent, and unless you have a medical lab in your backseat, don't try to guess how many drinks it takes an individual to reach that level. Remember that the law prohibits open containers with alcohol in vehicles.

The law provides "zero tolerance" for alcohol levels in those younger than the legal drinking age of twenty-one. In addition to drunken driving laws that the Georgia General Assembly has tightened up in recent years, however, Savannah offers its own, city-specific reasons for designating a nondrinking driver, calling a cab, or drinking near where you are staying. Most of our tourist nightspots are in an area of narrow, often one-way, streets. Also, streets throughout the city tend to be lined with trees—either unyielding live oaks of massive girth or palm trees that are easily uprooted or snapped by collisions.

Don't be surprised (or flattered) to find yourself carded in many drinking establishments. Savannah has a large college and military population, and many soldiers and students are not of legal drinking age. With their licenses at stake, bars and restaurants tend to be thorough on the question of age. Although bars can stay open until 3 A.M., many of them pack it in early on slow nights, especially through the week.

Also note that city ordinances prohibit open bottles or cans on the street, but (as of this writing) if you want to wander out of a River Street watering hole or a City Market club, most places are glad to provide you with a plastic or foam cup. This practice, pretty unusual based on our experience with other cities, is under hostile scrutiny from Savannah City Council, however, so check with your bartender before you wander out with a cup of beer in case things have changed. (Remember, this go-cup leniency is in the city of Savannah, not the other municipalities.)

We've spent a lot of space covering alcohol, but we don't mean to give you the impression that all nightlife has to do with booze. We've included coffeehouses, which are growing in popularity, as well as movies and other activities. Also, Savannah is home to an active Alcoholics Anonymous family: If you want to catch a meeting and talk firsthand about alcohol-free nightlife in Savannah, call (912) 354-0993 for the extensive schedule.

The bars listed here are a sampling, but we think we've included at least something for everyone.

Bars

Churchill's Pub
9 Drayton Street
Savannah, GA
(912) 232-8501

Churchill's serves both lunch and dinner, and in fact has both an extensive seating section and a long menu. But the bar is the attraction here: long, ornate, wooden—it looks like Doc Holiday (who originally hailed from Georgia) would be at home leaning against it. There's no music or dancing, just food and alcohol. Winston Churchill's mug adorns the sign outside, and it seems we're always seeing a group of British tourists posing for snapshots beneath it.

Coach's Corner
3016 E. Victory Drive
Savannah, GA
(912) 352-2933

The sports bar has become an American institution. Coach's Corner is a good example. More televised sports than you thought the airwaves could provide are on the multiple TV sets here. There's a full bar, but beer's the main drink of choice. A limited food menu is available. Dress is casual, needless to say. Come by the Victory Drive site—it's in Thunderbolt, on the way to and from the beach—during October of a good season for the Atlanta Braves, and you can catch a giant motorized tomahawk chopping away, backed up by an occasional live chopper.

Kevin Barry's Irish Pub
117 W. River Street
Savannah, GA
(912) 233-9626

Savannah prides itself on its Irish heritage, not just during the elaborate St. Patrick's Day observance, but year-round. Just check out this pub. The stone-walled setting is dark and atmospheric, brightened considerably by a constantly changing program of authentic Irish performers (Wednesday through Sunday nights). Count on acceptable food, standard drinks, and an impressive collection of bottled and draft beers and ales. There's even a small gift shop for Irish goods. Brush up on your Irish history (and learn who the real Kevin Barry was) by reading the captions to the framed photos of figures who were either historic freedom fighters or long-dead terrorists, depending on your outlook.

Malone's Food and Spirits
27 Barnard Street
Savannah, GA
(912) 234-3059

This large nightspot and restaurant anchors a corner of City Market. Inside, there's a little bit of everything over a lot of floor space: sports on TV, pool tables, food, and drink. There are even outside tables, and live bands often perform outside on weekends. It's a mixture of a young night-out crowd and older after-work folks. Lunch and dinner are served.

M.D.'s Lounge
2 W. Bay Street
Savannah, GA
(912) 238-1234

Before or after a nice dinner at one of the classier River Street restaurants, you may not be in the mood to nightcap it at one of the street's sing-along suds pubs. M.D.'s is a nice alternative—a dressier

place for a drink. The decor is upscale and subtle, the drinks are fine, and there's usually an inoffensive and unobtrusive musical lounge act. The whole thing would fall into the "very nice but forgettable" category if not for the view. This bar is inside the Hyatt Regency Savannah (see our Hotels and Motels chapter) and has glass walls overlooking the Savannah River (literally—this portion of the hotel overhangs River Street). If you are lucky (or determined enough to stay put for awhile), you'll get to see one of the giant container ships headed to or from the port upriver. Granted, you can see them from the street too, but from M.D.'s vantage point, you're more on eye level with the oceangoing giants.

Midnight Sun
Westin Savannah Harbor Resort
1 Resort Drive
Savannah, GA
(912) 201-2000

The Midnight Sun is the bar inside Savannah's new Westin Savannah Harbor Resort, and it was designed with both local color and the view in mind. From within this clublike atmosphere, you can look out on both the hotel pool and the Savannah River, with River Street and Savannah's skyline beyond it. The name comes from a song by Savannah's favorite son, lyricist Johnny Mercer. So do the names of many of the drinks, and if the song title comes with a color, you'll find the drink color coordinated. (See what we mean by local color?) They even dub the martinis here "Mercertinis." The bar is open to the general public, not just hotel guests, and it adds another dimension to a River Street outing to take the ferry (currently $3 round-trip) across to enjoy the ambience and view Savannah from an angle few but sailors have enjoyed until recently.

Moon River Brew Pub
21 W. Bay Street
Savannah, GA
(912) 447-0943

This brewpub is Savannah's only on-

Irish musicians regularly perform at Kevin Barry's on River Street, a popular nightspot. PHOTO: BETTY DARBY

with the beer and the booze. We have friends who swear by this place, and you can't say it doesn't have plenty of atmosphere: Christmas decorations that never come down, a stuffed crow (at least we hope it's stuffed—maybe it's just dead), a rogue's gallery of politician's photos, and a soft-focus nude painting about which any of the regulars is willing to tell you lies. Drinks are cheap, the air is thick, and there's a sign above the bar reading TIPPING IS NOT A CITY IN CHINA.

Stogies Cigar Bar
112 W. Congress Street
Savannah, GA
(912) 233-4277

Stogies' circa-1820s building is furnished with sofas and oversized chairs designed for long, comfortable conversations and long, comfortable smokes. There's a walk-in humidor and a pool table upstairs. The bar stocks liquor, cognacs, ports, and wines, and the new focus is on the art of the martini. It caters to an older, more sophisticated crowd. Light, recorded background jazz doesn't drown out conversation. Although you don't have to be dressed to the hilt, you'll feel more comfortable in your town-and-country casuals or business attire here.

Savannah Smiles
314 Williamson Street
Savannah, GA
(912) 527-6453

Savannah Smiles brought something different to the Savannah night scene. It features "dueling pianos" in an audience participation format that is a mix of rock 'n' roll standards and light comedy (with food and drink in addition, of course). You can catch the dueling pianos from 8 P.M. to 2 A.M. Wednesday through Saturday, as well as 5:30 to 7 P.M. Sunday. The bar hours are more liberal: 5:30 P.M. to 3 A.M. (2 A.M. on Sunday). It's closed Monday and Tuesday. Finding it can be a bit of a challenge—Savannah Smiles is sandwiched between West Bay Street and River

premises microbrewery. We debated whether to list this one as a restaurant or a nightspot. On the one hand, they serve both lunch and dinner, and it's a lot more serious than typical bar munchies—oysters with pecan pesto and chicken walnut enchiladas, for example. On the other hand, if made-on-the-premises beer is its reason for being, it's a nightspot, eh? Whichever side of the debate you agree with, know that you can get nine different fresh microbrews here in Imperial pints and half pints ($4 and $2.50, respectively). We like the idea of the sampler, which includes four-ounce tasters of all six varieties for $4.50. Hours are 11 A.M. to 11 P.M., (except they don't close until 1 A.M. on weekend nights) and 10 P.M. on Sundays. The daily happy hour is 4 to 7 P.M.

Pinkie Master's Lounge
318 Drayton Street
Savannah, GA
(912) 238-0447

This modest neighborhood watering hole is legendary in Savannah as a political bar. Journalists once plied local sources with alcohol here; Jimmy Carter (yes, that Jimmy Carter) once gave a speech standing on the bar. What you'll find today is a small bar where regulars talk back to the television set. There's an eclectic jukebox, darts, and a few game machines, along

This slightly scruffy but popular downtown bar, Pinkie Masters, is patronized mainly by locals and holds a particular mystique for journalists. PHOTO: BETTY DARBY

Street, sort of behind the Quality Inn, and chances are you won't be able to find a local who ever heard of Williamson Street.

Wet Willie's
101 E. River Street
Savannah, GA
(912) 233–5650

This high-volume River Street bar caters to younger drinkers. The drinks are frozen concoctions with names like the infamous spring break potion, Sex on the Beach. Beware! Grain alcohol gives a single drink here the punch of at least two conventional alcoholic beverages. There's a light food menu, a small dance floor, and lots of loud recorded music.

The Zoo
121 W. Congress Street
Savannah, GA
(912) 236–6266

This dance club caters to the young crowd (eighteen-year-olds are admitted, although you must be the legal drinking age of twenty-one to imbibe) with a series of themed dance nights (hip-hop, swing, etc.). They also periodically stage specialty acts, like Jello wrestling or swimsuit modeling promotions. The latest version, staged in February, was the "Earliest Tan Line" com-

petition. The Zoo, a multifloored establishment, is currently open Wednesday through Saturday nights, but the schedule is a little fluid with the seasons.

Billiards

B&B Billiards
411 W. Congress Street
Savannah, GA
(912) 233–7116

On the fringe of City Market, this is a popular spot to shoot some pool and hang out with friends. Look for a mix of students, middle-aged locals, and the occasional tourist.

Green Room Billiards
1100 Eisenhower Drive
(912) 351–9026

This suburban pool parlor is also a bar and restaurant, and its location next to a shopping center multiplex makes it a good place to kill time before or after a movie. If you want to do any serious playing on weekends, arrive before 9 P.M.—that's when the wait for tables (there's seventeen of them) starts to mount up. Open from 1 P.M. to 2 A.M. Sunday through Thursday and 1 P.M. through 3 A.M. weekends.

Coffeehouses

The coffeehouse boom has just hit Savannah, and new venues seem to be springing up overnight. Here's one to get you going. Starbucks is located downtown at Broughton and Bull Streets (as well as in suburban shopping centers); we figure you know what to expect there.

Gallery Espresso
6 E. Liberty Street
Savannah, GA
(912) 233–5348

This is one of the city's first (and our personal favorite) on the coffeehouse scene. Coffee, both plain and in its multiple new forms, is augmented by a limited menu of baked goods. There's an occasional poetry reading or casual performance. The walls are home to displays by local artists, and there have been some really appealing exhibits shown here. It's usually open until 1 A.M.

Movies

Savannah has typical movie offerings for a city its size, nothing more and nothing less. The blockbusters and major releases open here the same weekends they open everywhere else, but you may have to wait longer (or even until video) to catch, say, the Sundance winners or other nonmainstream fare. The 1998 opening of a pair of massive, competing multiplexes boasting stadium seating and luxe concession stands hasn't changed that.

Savannah has forty-eight movie screens scattered among five multiplexes and one small two-screen independent. If that sounds like a lot of screens, don't get excited: Duplication eats up a lot of them. The daily newspaper has showtimes, but we've saved ourselves disappointment more than once by calling the recorded message to double-check. You'll find those numbers in the listings that follow. *Diversions*, the entertainment section that appears in Friday's *Morning News* and is distributed free throughout the week at various restaurants and nightspots, contains a good little sketch map to help locate the theaters, all of which are outside the Historic Downtown. Ticket prices don't vary by more than a quarter or so—expect to pay in the range of $6.50 for a prime-time adult ticket. Child, senior, and matinee tickets are available at discounts. Theaters offer same-day advance purchase options, and the newer ones even let you buy a day ahead and with credit cards. The addition of new multiplexes—literally next door to one another and behind Savannah Mall, just across the street from its parking lot— has shaken up Savannah's movie scene. Both include stadium seating, meaning

Insiders' Tip

Planning on catching a popular movie on a weekend night? Swing by the theater during the day and get your same-day tickets in advance to ensure you won't be disappointed. All the local theaters have this service.

auditorium seating which is pitched so that you can see over the person in front of you. They've also upscaled their amenities and gussied up the snack bars.

Carmike Cinema 10
(10 screens)
511 Stephenson Avenue
Savannah, GA
(912) 353–8683

Eisenhower Cinemas
(6 screens)
1100 Eisenhower Drive
Savannah, GA
(912) 352–3533

Regal Cinemas Savannah 10
(10 screens)
1132 Shawnee Avenue
Savannah, GA
(912) 927–7700

Victory Square Cinemas
(9 screens)
3001 Skidaway Road
Savannah, GA
(912) 355–0110

Westside Cinemas
(2 screens)
403 Highway 80
Garden City, GA
(912) 966–9101

Club One and Lady Chablis: Anything but a Drag

In a city as inherently conservative as Savannah, you wouldn't expect tourism and the gay nightlife scene to intersect. You would be wrong.

Club One Jefferson has been the most prominent social setting, under various names, for Savannah's out-of-the-closet gay community since the 1980s. Its dance and performance scene had attracted occasional bolder and curious straights, but for the most part, Club One was a world unto itself.

The Lady Chablis changed all that.

The flamboyant drag queen (is there any other kind?) caught the eye of author John Berendt when he was writing the book that would become the phenomenal best-seller *Midnight in the Garden of Good and Evil*. The self-titled "Grand Empress of Savannah" is featured prominently therein. That alone was enough to make the performer famous, but then she went on to play herself in the movie version.

As the cult following for The Book grew, its readers flocked to Savannah. They wanted to gawk at The Book's houses, tour The Book's cemetery, and buy The Book trinkets. Most particularly, they wanted to get a look at The Lady Chablis.

And that presented the folks at Club One with a dilemma: How could they tap into that market without scaring the tourists back to Peoria, while at the same time keeping the flood of Book fanciers from displacing their regular clientele? Fortunately, they've come up with a smooth compromise. When Chablis is in town, they put on an earlier, somewhat tamer version of

Club One Jefferson frequently features the Lady Chablis.
PHOTO: BETTY DARBY

her show, reserving the stronger material for the later shows. It works well: Tourists get a sample of the strong stuff without a full dose, and the regular customers do not find their entertainment diluted, since the club's gay scene doesn't get moving until later anyway. Actually, the crowd has changed since this phenomenon began, and you're likely to find a mix of gays and young straights at the bar and on the dance floor.

Don't misinterpret us here. Even though the early show (8:30 P.M. is early) is milder, it isn't mild. If you don't understand what a drag show is or are not at peace with the concept, don't go. Don't go if you can't take earthy language. Skip it if you feel too nervous, although we went to the early show with a group of friends (first-timers all) and didn't feel uncomfortable at all once we got there.

You can't take it for granted that you'll see Chablis. She no longer lives in Savannah, although she was booked at least once a month in Savannah throughout 2001. Call the club at (912) 232–0200 to find out who's on the schedule for the week. You'll usually get a recorded message, and the phone menu includes directions from various parts of town.

The show bar is upstairs, and it's perfectly adequate but not particularly luxurious. It's also small. There are small tables on the front and along the sides and several rows of seats. Don't fret if you don't get a front seat—the place is small enough for you to see from all angles. In fact, if you're male, don't sit down front at all, unless you're willing to be flirted with by the performers. You'll have to fetch your own drinks from the bar on the upstairs level. Check the speaker location before you sit down: The room is small, but the speakers are big.

A drag show consists of female impersonators in drop-dead glamorous gowns and jewelry, dancing and lip-synching to recorded music. The show we caught featured one performer who was convincing as a beautiful woman, one performer who was convincing as an attractive woman who was trying very hard, one performer who was convincing as a homely but brave woman, and two others who were pretty unconvincing. The Lady Chablis emcees when she is there and performs several numbers. She also explains to the audience that they can come down front and tip performers if they wish. Bring folding money if you want to try that and don't worry: For the early show at least, it's a modest hand-to-hand exchange instead of the risque version you probably imagined (besides, the performers are wearing more clothes than the audience).

At the conclusion of the early show, Chablis comes back out to sign autographs, so bring your copy of The Book or Chablis' own book, *Hiding My Candy*.

Club One Jefferson has shows every weekend. They only stage the 8:30 P.M. show when Chablis performs. Other performers vary, but drag shows are staples, along with the occasional beauty pageant or striptease act. Normal cover is $6 to $10. Chablis tickets are now going for $25 a show, but be aware ticket prices will vary with the act. Again, check that surprisingly clear and helpful telephone message referred to earlier.

Elsewhere in Club One Jefferson, you'll find a video bar with what the management describes as the largest video wall in the Southeast, full restaurant service, and a full bar. Dance music downstairs is Top 40, while the main level has techno and house music.

Pretty much anything goes by way of dress, but it's predominately casual. The club takes major credit cards and has an ATM on site. Club One's at 1 Jefferson Street, just off Bay Street at the edge of City Market. It's rare in that it is open seven days a week. Hours are 5 P.M. to 3 A.M., closing an hour earlier on Sunday.

Wynnsong 11
(11 screens)
1150 Shawnee Street
Savannah, GA
(912) 920–1227

There are a few other movie options, but they will require some checking on your part and some luck as far as scheduling. The Lucas Theatre, a restored movie palace in the Historic District that primarily hosts touring shows and concerts, periodically runs movies, usually on a theme: holiday movies, for example, or movies made in Savannah. Savannah College of Art and Design, better known locally as SCAD, operates Trustees Theatre on Broughton Street and occasionally shows movies which have become campus standards or are film show entries. SCAD also hosts an annual film festival in that theater, showcasing some genuinely avant-garde stuff.

Shopping

Someday an enterprising psychology student is going to conduct ground-breaking research and discover what we already know: When you are traveling for pleasure, your hold on your purse strings is looser. Admit it! You'd never consider buying goofy-shaped mugs or snide T-shirts at home, at least not at full price. Ah, but when vacationing, that's a different story.

First of all, there are all those obligatory gifts—something for the neighbor who is feeding the dog, something for the grandkids or the grandparents, some kind of group offering for the office crowd. More important, however, are the travel gifts you buy yourself. These are things you would love under any circumstances: an attractive print, an antique armoire, the perfect addition to a prized collection. These things take on added significance when they remind us of a special trip, and we're more likely to treat ourselves to something we really want when we're shopping with the laid-back attitude of the vacationer.

So, if shopping is part of your vacation behavior, Savannah is your kind of vacation destination. Savannah is the regional shopping center for a large chunk of southeast Georgia; many people (outside of Brunswick, that is) consider it the only real metropolitan area until you get to Jacksonville, Florida (two and a half hours down Interstate 95), or in-state Macon (three hours west on Interstate 16).

With all this retail territory to cover, it stands to reason we had to be selective about what we included in this chapter. We'd like to share with you the rhyme and reason of what we left in and what we left out. First of all, we figured travelers don't need a comprehensive list of grocery stores and shoe shops. No, we're not implying that you should travel hungry and barefoot, but because we know you are basically eating in restaurants and dragging your wardrobe around with you in a heavy suitcase, we left these and similar fundamental things out. We also skipped most of the chain stores: We don't mean to slight anybody, but our Wal-Marts probably look just like your Wal-Marts, and your hotel concierge or bed-and-breakfast host can point you in the right direction if you need one.

Instead, we've tried to concentrate on the needs of recreational shoppers while still steering the retail-impaired to the places where travelers are most likely to get the things they need. We concentrated on including shops that stock items of local or regional interest. Then we added places that struck us as unusual or interesting. Next, we included places where we like to browse and buy for ourselves.

About Locations

Before launching into our own category-by-category rundown of stores, we thought we would review the major shopping locations with you and provide a few pointers along the way.

River Street

River Street is literally along the Savannah River. It is reached by street ramps that lead down from the bluff-level Bay Street. In between these two levels is Factors' Walk. River Street is a major part of Savannah's tourist scene, and you'll find it is a prominent player for restaurants, nightlife, and annual events. But don't forget shopping! This restored waterfront strip features a steady progression of shops all along its length, beginning at the west end across from a small power plant (whose smokestacks make handy landmarks) and extending eastward many blocks until you reach the *Waving Girl* statue that is a local riverfront landmark. Factors' Walk, which parallels River Street halfway up the bluff, also features shops, although more widely scattered.

Parking is scarce. There are a few small private lots, where you pay as you enter. There's limited street-side parking on the various streets leading to River Street. Lots of motorists park illegally along River Street itself, but it's a bad idea—the city periodically cracks down on the long-winked-at. Use of the railroad track running down the middle of River Street was discontinued in early 1999, but even so, it seems unwise to park anywhere near a railroad track.

We always opt to park at the Bay Street level and hike down, avoiding driving on tricky cobblestones. If you follow our example, however, watch your step and wear appropriate footwear: The stairs (located in each block) are steep and irregular, and once you get to the cobblestones, you'll find them as hard to walk on as they are to drive over. The going is much smoother once you get to the River Street level. The addition of a public elevator, tucked away between Savannah City Hall and the eastern side of the Hyatt Regency Savannah, has made life a lot simpler in this regard and, as a bonus, you'll find well-maintained public rest rooms in the small building at the River Street foot of the elevator.

Don't expect much in the way of bargains on River Street: These shopkeepers saw you and your credit cards coming a mile away, and just as in any touristy area in any city, you'll find few discounts. Still, River Street offers a great variety, mingling local and regional goods, Savannah-themed merchandise imported from elsewhere and generic trinkets and gifts. Even if you don't buy, you'll enjoy looking at goods that range from the genuinely artistic to the genuinely tacky (such as doormats bedecked with Confederate flags and the slogan "Yankee Go Home," which a shopkeeper assured us sell well to Northern visitors).

City Market

This restored area in the commercial section of the Historic Downtown runs from Barnard Street to Montgomery Street, north of Broughton Street. The complex is made up of nightclubs, restaurants, art galleries, and shops. The stores here tend to be more thematic—cat motif merchandise, New Age, outdoor furniture and gifts, and so on—than their cousins a few blocks away on River Street.

Broughton Street and Historic Downtown Areas

Broughton Street was where Savannah shopped before malls seized control of the retail world. It suffered the same fate as Main Streets all across America but has begun a comeback as a home to restaurants, college activities, and trendy shopping, including a slew of antique dealers. In fact, some of the very best recreational shopping in the city is to be done on Broughton Street. New upscale offerings stand side by side with the small low-end shops that kept the street going in its hard-luck days, things like wig shops and cut-price clothing shops. You'll also find two of Savannah's retail grand dames still in place. When other stores abandoned the main drag for suburban malls, Globe Shoe Company (17 E. Broughton St.) and Levy Jewelers (101 E. Broughton St.) dug in. These stores are where Old Savannah bought her shoes for debutante parties and her bridal silver, and while both stores now have other locations as well, they never closed their doors on Broughton.

You'll find plenty of intriguing stores scattered throughout the Historic Downtown. One eye-catching congregation clusters at the intersection of Bull and Liberty Streets near the Hilton Savannah DeSoto Hotel. The intersection of Jones and Whitaker Streets forms the nucleus for another appealing set of shops that mostly specializes in arts and collectibles. They call themselves, collectively, the Walk on Whitaker, and capitalize on their close proximity to both Mrs. Wilkes' eatery (see Restaurants) and Monterey Square (see Savannah: Hollywood of the South chapter). You'll also find individual shops, especially antique shops, sprinkled throughout the Historic Downtown.

Looking back over all these areas, here's how we'd put it in perspective: River Street is long on local color and has lots of shops cheek by jowl, where you can walk out one door and in the next. There's a variety of merchandise aimed at all age levels and the compact location makes it easy to keep groups—be they children or merely hard-to-herd adults—together. Broughton Street's offerings aren't as likely to appeal much to children and are more widely spaced, but the merchandise is actually several cuts better, and oddly enough, the prices are more reasonable. City Market falls between these two descriptions, and you can stop by the other Historic District shops as you make your way around the city on tours, and so on.

Malls and Shopping Centers

Savannah has two malls, both south of downtown in a heavily trafficked area of suburban and chain-store development. There are various ways to get to them, but the most direct route and the one hardest to get lost on (although it's also the most crowded and traffic-light plagued) is straight out Abercorn Street from town. About 6 miles from the Historic Downtown, you'll spot Oglethorpe Mall on your left (you really can't miss it). Another couple of miles south, and you'll spot Savannah Mall on the right.

As for that ubiquitous American retail staple, the strip shopping center, Savannah has its share scattered mainly in the Southside/Midtown area. Because you know what to expect in most of these—a grocery store, major discount retailer, chain or local drug store, etc.—we have left them out as a rule. However, the Habersham Shopping Center, with its handful of very interesting shops, merits a special mention. We have included it here.

Oglethorpe Mall
7804 Abercorn Street
Savannah, GA
(912) 354-7038
Oglethorpe Mall is the city's original mall, with Sears, JCPenney, Belk, and Rich's (a Southern unit of the famous Atlanta department store) as its anchors. There are 140 specialty stores here, mostly on a single story, although some of the anchors have a second level. There's ample parking, but the multilevel parking deck comes in handy around the holidays and when it rains. You'll find a predictable array of stores inside (The Gap, Victoria's Secret, CD stores, etc.), along with a few restaurants and food-court

Insiders' Tip
Combine shopping with the national pastime. The Savannah Sand Gnats organization, the local minor league baseball team currently associated with the Texas Rangers, sells a variety of caps, shirts, and so forth with the team's attractive (but pesky) logo.

Shopkeepers on River Street work hard to have appealing entrances. PHOTO: BETTY DARBY

outlets. Barnes and Noble opened here in 2000, and its daily 9 A.M. to 11 P.M. hours—complete with coffeeshop—have made this an unlikely but popular late night adult hangout. Over the course of its thirty-something years, the mall has rebuilt itself repeatedly, and the latest project under way is the renovation of the food courts.

If you are traveling with kids who are young (or look young), you need to be aware of mall policies requiring adult supervision of anyone age sixteen or younger during most weekend business hours. From 4 to 9 P.M. on Fridays, 1 to 9 P.M. on Saturdays, and noon to 6 P.M. on Sundays, those younger than seventeen must be accompanied by a parent or guardian at least twenty-one years old. Anyone twenty-one or younger will be asked for ID, with mall management considering driver's licenses, official state ID cards, college student ID cards, passports or visas, and mall employee IDs as acceptable identification.

Savannah Mall
14045 Abercorn Street
Savannah, GA
(912) 927–7467

The city's newest mall, which opened in 1990, is anchored by three large chain department stores, and offers 120 specialty stores on two stories. When you hear locals talk about "the new mall," this is the one they mean. Again, the collection of stores is fairly standard, including Abercrombie & Fitch, The Disney Store, Foot Locker, Champ's Sports, Victoria's Secret, Banana Republic, a Hallmark shop, etc. You'll find Waldenbooks here, too. There's a large food court, several full-service restaurants, and a large carousel that periodically offers rides for tickets (prices vary with promotions) or in exchange for points earned by purchases.

Habersham Shopping Center
Habersham Street at 60th to 63rd Streets

This small strip shopping center runs along both sides of Habersham Street, from just after its intersection with 60th Street to 63rd Street. It appears modest at first glance—a small grocery store, an Eckerds, a dry cleaner, and other businesses clearly set up to serve the surrounding established neighborhood—but look closer and you'll find some interesting specialty shops. They include Hannah Banana Books; Punch and Judy, a children's store; and Merry Times, a card and gift shop. We like the Fresh Flower Market, styled after European flower markets. Other entries include a bakery and some nifty restaurants (which we cover in our Restaurants section).

Shopping Savannah

Anything south of, say, DeRenne Avenue is dubbed the Southside by Savannahians. This is where you'll find the strip malls, discount houses, shopping centers, megastores, etc. The Savannah Festival Factory Outlet Center, a typical example of this new kind of strip mall, is at the far southern edge of the city, where Abercorn is better known as Georgia Highway 204 and passes under Interstate 95. This outlet center includes a Springmaid/Wamsutta factory store, Bugle Boy, and Bass Shoes, among many others.

East and west of Savannah, you'll find mainly grocery stores and other retail outlets in support of the suburban residential development there, with a few interesting shops thrown in and a large spate of beach-oriented shops at the end of the road on Tybee Island. (Check our Tybee chapter for more on shopping there.)

Now that we've roughly covered the general shopping areas, let's get more specific. We've divided our featured stores into categories. Join us on a quick shopping trip.

Antiques

In this section, we cover a sampling of both high-end and low-end antique dealers. Serious collectors with serious budgets should seek out the upscale places; collectors and browsers will have better luck in the more mainstream, less expensive stores.

Abercorn Antique Village
201 E. 37th Street
Savannah, GA
(912) 233-0064
This rambling yellow Victorian home houses collections from fifty-plus dealers. Look for French country furniture, statuary, oil paintings, crystal, jewelry, and so on. This is a good browsing location with a wide price range—stuff for the serious collector and less-pricey offerings as well.

Insiders' Tip

Sales taxes in Georgia vary by county, ranging from a minimum of 4 percent (the state's share) to as much as 7 percent, depending on local voter willingness to up the ante. In Chatham County (which includes Savannah and Tybee Island), it's 6 percent. Because the state exempts its share of the sales tax on groceries, expect to pay only the local sales tax on these. Also, state law exempts Bibles from sales tax, although you'll find many bookstore clerks are unaware of this.

Alexandra's Antique Gallery
320 W. Broughton Street
Savannah, GA
(912) 233–3999

This conglomeration of some seventy antique dealers in a single four-story building offers something for everyone, be it high-end furniture or browsers' plunder. Don't be put off by the humble exterior or intimidated by the size: There's an elevator to help you along. We stop by periodically, sometimes finding treasures and sometimes coming up empty.

On previous trips, we found the basement stocked with furniture and fixtures salvaged from an old shoe store. Later finds have included baby-boomer era toys, kitchenware from the 1920s, and curious stuff like hand-shaped lasts for making gloves. The first floor sports some Victorian furniture (although the main stock is goods other than furniture), with cookbooks, other books, glassware, collectible toys, old panoramic photos, quilts, and china spread out over the other floors. One section of the first floor contains new gift merchandise, and there are several Savannah-themed items in stock. The arrangement calls for leisurely browsing. This is one place you can bring a nonantiquing friend or spouse with you without feeling guilty or pressured; there's enough variety and sheer oddity among the displays to keep just about any adult entertained. Only the bravest would consider bringing a child into this environment, however.

The Attic
224 W. Bay Street
Savannah, GA
(912) 236–4879

Looking for antique fishing lures? Good examples can fetch $65 and up, and you'll find them among some of the other sports antiques here, along with fencing masks and old skis. It's an eclectic stock of mainly American antiques and collectibles—furniture, jewelry, glassware. It's not what you would call high end, but it's fun. The location itself is of interest to fans of *Midnight in the Garden of Good and Evil*, since it was the location of the financially ill-fated Emma's, a piano bar that is featured in that best-seller.

A cluster of interesting shops stretches along Whitaker Street from Jones to Taylor Streets. PHOTO: BETTY DARBY

Fran Campbell Antiques and Interiors Inc.
305 E. 38th Street
Savannah, GA
(912) 238–5400

This shop specializes in upscale eighteenth- and nineteenth-century English and American furniture, Chinese export porcelain, antique accessories, and objets d'art. Design services are available.

Capra Capra Antiques
319 Abercorn Street
Savannah, GA
(912) 236–9004

Located directly across from the front door of the Cathedral of St. John the Baptist, this could well be the most elegant and beautiful antique shop in Savannah. The 1888 building has been carefully restored, and it houses high-end antiques in room settings that show them to great advantage. Specialties include Biedermeier pieces and Russian art and antiques, including the occasional Faberge and Bolin piece. Other offerings are neoclassical pieces, Chinese porcelain and bronzes from the eighteenth and nineteenth centuries, ivory from Japan and China during those same time periods, as many as 200 clocks, and a limited number of modern sculptures and contemporary artworks to demonstrate how quality from different styles and periods can work together.

Cobb's Galleries Inc.
122 E. 37th Street
Savannah, GA
(912) 234–1582

This popular antique shop keeps outgrowing its quarters. It is now located in a Victorian mansion at the corner of 37th and Abercorn Streets, the supposedly haunted Krouskoff House. That's appropriate, because owner Al Cobb wrote a book about a supposedly haunted bed that wreaked havoc in his household; you can buy a copy in the shop. Most of the stock is more conventional: an extensive collection of art pottery, about a thousand cookbooks, sports memorabilia, collectible liquor decanters, what have you. What's surprising about this shop is the sheer volume.

Pierce Antiques
101 W. Jones Street
Savannah, GA
(912) 238–3525

Pierce Antiques handles what owner Tom Pierce calls midrange antiques, primarily primitive Americana and fine English pieces. Tom retired from a corporate career in Maine, and contacts there ensure his shop tends to have a selection of pieces from Maine. He also tries to keep on hand a small collection of stuffed animals, children's pieces, and toy tea sets. On our visit, the stock included a good supply of textiles and, holding pride of place in the center of the store, an impressive Scandinavian china service. Shipping can be arranged.

Savannah Galleries
30 E. Bryan Street
Savannah, GA
(912) 232–1234

Here you'll find 10,000 square feet of high-end antique English, French, and American furniture, silver, porcelain, and Oriental rugs. Pieces range from elegant marquetry to rustic painted pine pieces.

Design services are available as are search services, and the staff will assist in building collections. Cleaning, repair, and appraisal of antique and modern Oriental rugs are also available. The owners, native Savannahians, have restored many fine old homes and are familiar with the furnishings such projects require. This establishment has been in operation since the 1960s and is experienced in shipping its merchandise.

Southern Antiques and Interiors Inc.
28 Abercorn Street
Savannah, GA
(912) 236–5080

This shop offers 12,000 square feet of high-end furniture, mostly English and Continental pieces from the eighteenth and nineteenth centuries. Reproductions are also available, usually made to order in the English workshops with which the firm has a relationship. Southern Antiques specializes in larger pieces and has both case goods and soft (upholstered) furniture. The store carries about $1 million in inventory and is experienced in shipping because the bulk of its business involves out-of-town customers. Custom constructions can be designed to fit specific spaces, and the time frame for custom work is less than that for placing special orders with commercial manufacturers.

When It Was a Game
107 W. Congress Street
Savannah, GA
(912) 201–0012
www.WhenItWasAGame.net

This sports memorabilia shop is geared toward serious collectors of sporting antiques, mainly from the 1920s and 1930s, but it includes a few gift items and contemporary prints. If two stores make a chain, then this is a chain—the original store is still in business on nearby Hilton Head Island. The Savannah store, which opened in 2001, is near Congress Street's corner with Whitaker Street—appropriately enough, in one of the areas that was used for the period golf movie *The Legend of Bagger Vance*. The store is closed on Monday and open Tuesday through Saturday and on Sunday afternoons.

Bookstores

The Book Lady
17 W. York Street
Savannah, GA
(912) 233–3628

Used and rare books are what you will find at The Book Lady, a quaint bookstore near the post office on York Street. Owner Anita Raskin has filled her store with hundreds of previously owned books. Besides art, architecture, religion, fiction, and the usual fare, you will also find sections called Pretty Books and Nice Old Books among the lot. There are also several local titles on Savannah and the area. For that hard-to-find book, Anita offers a search service.

Books-A-Million
8108 Abercorn Street
Savannah, GA
(912) 925–8112

This national retail chain offers thousands of titles, with deep discounts on best-sellers. The selection of magazines is among the most extensive in the city, along with the largest selection of out-of-town Sunday papers (several days delayed, however). The local and regional section includes an extensive collection of Southern titles. The store also offers children's books, gifts, cards, and gift wrap. Grab one of the free book newsletters and settle in at the in-store coffee shop.

E. Shaver Bookseller
326 Bull Street
Savannah, GA
(912) 234–7257

Book lovers will delight in this independent bookstore, which occupies the ground floor of the Shavers' Historic District home. The shop has become a fixture for both downtown residents and tourists. An impressive array of hardcover and paperback books is available, and the knowledgeable staff offers solid advice.

Local titles are well represented. The shop also offers an efficient book search service for older titles. A whole room is devoted to children's titles. Limited gift offerings include museum-style notecards, tote bags, and appointment calendars. This is what bookstores were before there were megachains.

Ex Libris
228 Martin Luther King Jr. Boulevard
Savannah, GA
(912) 238–2427

Ex Libris is part coffeehouse, part bookstore, and part gift shop, all put together by the Savannah College of Art and Design. The shop is on the western edge of the Historic Downtown and may be a

Relax while you choose a book at Ex Libris bookstore. PHOTO: THE SAVANNAH COLLEGE OF ART AND DESIGN

little out of your way, but it's worth the trip. After browsing through art books, posters, framed art, and many other eclectic and fun items you most likely won't find anywhere else in Savannah, you can sit and relax on the gigantic leather sofa and simply enjoy the beautifully restored building. A magnificent stairway takes up the center of the building and is the focal point of the room, along with "pillars" made out of hundreds of old books. The

store is especially beautiful during the Christmas season, when the college opens its holiday shop and offers decorations and other festive items.

Hannah Banana Books
4515 Habersham Street
Savannah, GA
(912) 353-7447

This friendly independent offers a wide range of hardcovers and paperbacks, including a substantial selection by Savannah and Georgia authors. Inventory also includes children's books, and the store offers special orders. There's also a stock of attractive and original cards and a handful of other gifts, mainly book related. The store plays frequent host to book signings by local authors. (By the way, the shopkeeper named it for her dog.)

Media Play
11701 Abercorn Street
Savannah, GA
(912) 925–9201

OK, OK, so this isn't exactly a bookstore. The national chain is divided among books, tapes and CDs, videos, and computer software. We're calling it a bookstore because books are what we buy here. There's a reasonably good magazine collection, deep discounts on best-sellers, and a schedule of special events for readers.

Candy

When we travel and need a gift for a hostess, or when we want to send a present with regional flavor (pun intended), we often opt for pralines. No one can claim these superrich candies (made of sugar, butter, cream, and pecans) are good for you, but at $11.95 to $12.95 per pound, your purse will probably stop you before you do yourself too much harm. You can find them made and sold in two shops on River Street. Although the shops would scream to hear it, we can't taste any difference.

River Street Sweets
13 E. River Street
Savannah, GA
(912) 234–4608

Pralines are made right here, in full view, and there's usually someone near the door to offer you a sample. Display cases showcase other store specialties: confections of chocolate and nuts, spiced pecans, divinity, etc. There's a wide array of gift baskets and special packaging and an efficient shipping service.

Savannah Candy Kitchen
225 E. River Street
Savannah, GA
(912) 233–8411

Kids of all ages will run rampant in this large candy store, which fills several rooms. In addition to pralines and other store-made specialties, you'll also find gourmet jelly beans and a staggering selection of other mass-produced candy—the kinds you remember from childhood and assumed no one sold any more. Choose from a wide selection of decorative tins to fill with goodies. Again, this store offers gift shipping.

Clothing

Alberts
213 Julian Street
Savannah, GA
(912) 236–8070

We're talking sleek, modern, ultratrendy clothing in lines that include BCBG, Max Studio, and French Connection. On our last visit, we spotted a short white cotton shift with a line of beige embroidery at the hem, $118, and short-sleeve cotton blouses at $90. They also have an extensive line of beauty/bath products, like sea salt soak.

Chutzpah & Panache
251 Bull Street
Savannah, GA
(912) 234–5007

Chutzpah & Panache is a charming boutique in the heart of the Historic Downtown. Fine woven and hand-printed women's dresses, blouses, pants, and scarves are the stock in trade. The clothes are flowing, pretty, and very comfortable.

Gaucho
18 E. Broughton Street
Savannah, GA
(912) 234–7414
250 Bull Street
Savannah, GA
(912) 232–7414

When browsing through either location of Gaucho, you might be reminded of those who believe you can never be too rich or too thin. The selection is wider here than at Albert's, although if you like one shop you should definitely check out the other as well.

Gaucho had a wide selection of hats and accessories on our last visit, along with hand-painted blouses and, in the back, shoes. It's worth stopping by just to see the restoration at the Broughton Street site, especially the dressing room area.

Jezebel
25 E. River Street
Savannah, GA
(912) 236–4333
Twelve Oaks Shopping Center
5500 Abercorn Street
Savannah, GA
(912) 354–8889

This upscale ladies' clothing boutique features casual and formal clothing for the Southern woman. Comfortable linen pants, dresses, and shirts perfect for weathering 90-degree temperatures are Jezebel hallmarks. Brands include Flax and Cut Loose, among others. Long flowing dresses, pants, and shirts with pretty prints are included in the mix, along with extravagant costume jewelry, shoes, hats, and more.

Profiles Ladies' Accessories and Gifts
215 W. River Street
Savannah, GA
(912) 233–3892

This elegant accessories shop will make lovers of better costume jewelry drool. The store designs and manufactures its own line of earrings and other pieces, so you may recognize the name from shopping elsewhere. A wide range of handbags, scarves, belts, and gloves is also offered, along with gift items like lovely glass ornaments and perfume bottles. The costume jewelry is of good quality in a wide variety of styles, from fun to dramatic.

Dime Stores

Mack's 5 and 10 Cent Store
Medical Arts Shopping Center
4800 Waters Avenue
Savannah, GA
(912) 354–3025

You'll think this store is a time machine. This classic dime store opened in 1946 and moved to its present location in 1962, where not much has changed since. Although this is a fun store for browsing, it has a practical side too because, crammed into a tiny space, it somehow manages to have everything. When we needed pinwheels for a photo assignment, we knew, without question, we could find them here. People come here for stuff they still want but can't find elsewhere—things like hair nets, soft peppermint sticks, or flyswatters with wire mesh flaps. There are all sorts of housewares, along with plastic flowers, inexpensive toys, greeting cards, embroidered hankies, and cardboard cutouts for elementary school bulletin boards.

Contemporary merchandise isn't ignored. You can find toys here for children in Memorial Health University Medical

Insiders' Tip

Roadside produce stands as well as regular grocery stores are good places to pick up Vidalia onions. These famous mild, sweet onions are grown only in and around nearby Vidalia and have acquired a dedicated national following of gourmets.

Center across the street. By the way, Mack's can still legitimately call itself a five-and-dime: Look hard enough, and you can still find items for these prices. We spotted tiny plastic boats for a dime and plastic rings and individual candies for a nickel.

Gifts and Fun Shops

Arts & Crafts Emporium of Savannah
234 Bull Street
Savannah, GA
(912) 238–0003

Hundreds of artisans from around the country rent spaces, ranging from large areas to small shelves, to show their wares in this gigantic arts-and-crafts store. Wander around and some of the thousands of items you will encounter could include Christmas decorations, original watercolor paintings, jewelry, handmade children's dresses, pottery, dolls, small furniture, and much more. Although the work carried is by no means all done by locals, Savannah painters and potters are well represented. Look for the reproductions of old photos of Savannah to get an idea of what we've lost as well as what we've preserved.

Baskets, Bears & T's . . . Oh, My!
305 E. River Street
Savannah, GA
(912) 232–4546

The title of this cozy shop pretty well describes the stock. The collection of stuffed animals includes both collectors' treasures and high-quality children's toys. Look for brands like Ty, Russ, Boyd's Bears, Enesco, and other, smaller lines. Upstairs you'll find 2,500 square feet devoted to baskets of every imaginable shape, size, and material. T-shirts include both Savannah-themed versions and witty (but not vulgar) novelty shirts. Other stock includes dolls (such as the Susan Wakeen line), books of local interest, and plenty of furniture perfect for toys. Other gift and novelty items are scattered in among it all—items owner/manager Carol Devine describes as "silly stuff...things that strike me at the moment."

Not everyone can shop 'till they drop, even on River Street with its many stores and boutiques.
PHOTO: PHYL M. GATLIN

Byrd Cookie Company and Gourmet Marketplace
6700 Waters Avenue
Savannah, GA
(912) 355–1716

You can buy these well-known local cookies all over town, but the advantage of choosing them from this shop is that you can sample the wide range of flavors here:

Key Lime Coolers, Benne Bits, raspberry, butter cookies, and so on. They're sold in decorative tins ($6.95 each) that are excellent choices for those obligation gifts. One is sufficient for a solid token gift, or you can assemble a collection if you need something more impressive. A locally popular favorite is the benne wafer, a subtly sweet concoction made of unhulled sesame seeds. If you show up during a production run, you can even watch the manufacturing process through a glass window. In addition to Byrd Cookies and the Seckinger-Lee line of cookies and snacks that Byrd also produces, this shop features an array of clever gifts (most with a culinary theme), a selection of other gourmet food items, and fresh flowers. Note that it is closed on Saturday but open on Sunday. Shipping is available.

Callaway Gardens Country Store
301 E. River Street
Savannah, GA
(912) 236–4055

Everything you might expect to discover in a country store can be found at Callaway Gardens. This large shop on the eastern end of River Street sells hard candy, several brands of jewelry, Mary Engelbreit books, cards, and writing paper. The store also features gourmet food items like muscadine preserves, speckled heart grits, handmade candy, and other Southern delicacies, including Vidalia onion jelly and hot sauce.

The Cat House
310 W. St. Julian Street
Savannah, GA
(912) 236–2287

Cat lovers shouldn't miss this City Market store. Owner Janet Waters advertises that her shop is full of "Feline Fancies for Feline Fanciers." Adorned with pictures of Julian and other felines owned by Waters, the shop features fuzzy stuffed cats, along with cat greeting cards, figurines, toys, books, and more. For those having problems with a finicky cat, you can find books

with advice on how to better understand and take care of your feline friends.

Charlotte's Corner
1 W. Liberty Street
Savannah, GA
(912) 233–8061

This eclectic gift shop offers a little bit of everything, spread out over four rooms. There are lots of shirts—T-shirts, tank tops, sleep shirts, sweatshirts. Fancy children's clothing featuring appliques and smocking—the things that grandparents buy—are well represented in the stock. A line of fun clothes for adults is included, and there are plenty of toys. Woven afghans are offered in various motifs, including local ones. In addition to a line of *Midnight in the Garden of Good and Evil* merchandise, there are local souvenirs including other Savannah books, ornaments, and prints by local artists.

A Fine Choice
20 W. State Street
Savannah, GA
(912) 650–1845

Owner Sherry Georges has packed a lot of varied gift merchandise into a small space, and she's hit upon a supply that isn't replicated all over town. It's also well organized for such a small shop with so much in it—pigs on these shelves, cats here, dragons there, paperweights here. We priced a set of three wise monkeys at $34 a set. The store also has a line of paperweights featuring Mount St. Helen's ashes. It also stocks unusual jewelry and a line of greeting cards.

Gypsy Moth
311 W. St. Julian Street
Savannah, GA
(912) 232–6800

This City Market gift shop gained lots of attention when a local politician denounced it as demonic. Turns out he'd misinterpreted the Third World folk art it stocks, which includes some pretty graphic renditions of Christian martyrdom, Mexican Day of the Dead items, and the like. We've bought *molas,* the reverse-applique fabric art produced by Central American Indians, here. Lately, the stock is increasingly devoted to clothing, some of it vintage, mainly for the young, thin, and trendy. There's always something unusual on the shelves.

Harry Barker
411 E. Liberty Street
Savannah, GA
(912) 527–2700
www.harrybarker.com

Luxury items for dogs? It had to happen. This thriving little specialty store sells by Web and by mail, but its retail incarnation is in the midst of Savannah's historic district, in one of the more residential parts. Harry Barker is the name of owner Carol Perkins's dog, but the dog was named for the store, not vice versa. The stock includes upscale dog bowls, elegant dog beds, canine wardrobes, and gourmet doggy treats.

Midnight Star Pottery
32 Barnard Street
Savannah, GA
(912) 236–3473

This store is actually a pottery-painting studio where the customers pick out pieces of pottery, then go to work painting a one-of-a-kind creation. There are hundreds of pieces of pottery to choose from, including tiles, bowls, goblets, and vases. Many people make an outing to Midnight Star Pottery an event for family gatherings, wedding showers, or birthday parties. If you are a repeat visitor, note that this shop has moved a block or so from its original location.

Nellie's Nook
19 E. River Street
Savannah, GA
(912) 233–5401

This shop focuses mainly on major collectible lines, including what it calls the largest collection of Sheila pieces in the country. The Sheila line is made up of shal-

low, three-dimensional wooden representations of historic buildings, presented in limited editions. The collection includes several Savannah buildings, including Savannah City Hall. Other stock includes Boyd's Bears, Harmony Kingdom figurines, the All God's Children figurines, Fenton Glass, Sandicast Dogs, the Herd line of elephant sculptures, Barlow knives and related faux scrimshaw jewelry from that company, Coca-Cola collectibles, and other specific collections. The store handles mail orders as well.

Sails & Rails
423 E. River Street
Savannah, GA
(912) 232–7201

It's hard to miss Sails and Rails on East River Street. It's the shop with the brightly displayed kites, flags, and windsocks blowing outside. This unique shop includes dozens of kites, along with flags from around the world and decorative ones for your front porch. Windsocks—ranging from those with pictures of snowmen on them to others shaped like whales—are also for sale, along with things for toy train enthusiasts.

True Grits
107 E. River Street
Savannah, GA
(912) 234–8006

This novel gift shop comes in two separate and distinct parts, one a basic gift shop and the other specializing in nautical and Civil War items.

On the gifty side, choose from 250 different varieties of hot sauce, each label claiming to be deadlier than the other. You'll also see plenty of shirts, toys, mugs, and plates with Savannah scenes. In the newer portion of the shop(s), you'll find items with nautical themes: lighthouse figurines and lighthouse needlework kits; large, realistic wooden ship models; tables made from hatch covers or using four-bladed brass props as bases; and antique telescopes. Civil War merchandise includes replica swords and hats, many history

Home and Food

Anatolia
7 W. York Street
Savannah, GA
(912) 447–5006

This shop has a wide selection in a narrow range of product types: heavy, rustic pine furniture made in Europe of salvaged wood; Turkish-made pottery that's old but short of antique; and a large array of new and old Turkish rugs.

Among the more unique items are "mountain benches," low benches with clusters of branches serving as legs and Turkish carpeting as upholstery. They're made in New York, and one will set you back $395. You can also choose from many pieces of unusual luggage. Picture a Gladstone bag or portmanteau made of carpet material with leather straps, fittings, and closures. You guessed it! It's a carpetbag, a modern reproduction of the Reconstruction-era icon, and you can leave Savannah with your own for between $210 and $275.

books, and three different versions of Civil War–themed chess sets. (One set features President and Mrs. Lincoln and CSA President and Mrs. Jefferson Davis as the respective kings and queens, and William T. Sherman and Robert E. Lee in the role of bishops.)

Wild Birds Unlimited
Medical Arts Shopping Center
4821 Waters Avenue
Savannah, GA
(912) 692–0060

Bird enthusiasts can stock up on birdseed, feeders, houses, binoculars, toys, gifts, and CDs here. This shop is geared to those who want to watch birds in the wild (including their own backyards), so it doesn't handle pet bird supplies. Some of the feeders and birdhouses double as lawn sculptures, including ornate, copper-roofed models. You'll also find a small stock of educational toys, and such unique items as hummingbird feeders and houses especially designed for butterflies and bats.

Chili Chompers
30 Barnard Street
Savannah, GA
(912) 234–1932

You can't miss Chili Chompers. The eye-catching window displays are usually full of everything a salsa-loving, chili-eating, spicy food–craving addict can't live without. This unique boutique, which includes gifts and food, touts itself as "The Cool Store with the HOT Stuff." Inside you will find all things Tabasco—from a plain old bottle of the stuff to Tabasco posters, earrings, neckties, and even boxer shorts. Don't miss the salsa-tasting bar, where you can try (if you dare!) before you buy.

Eclectibles!
10 W. Broughton Street
Savannah, GA
(912) 443–9292

Owner Kim Miltenberger-Thurman describes the stock of her home, garden, and gift shop as "fun, whimsical and fitting with any decor." We found stock that ranged from comical garden sculpture on stakes in the $32–$36 range to large serving trays with hand-painted olive motifs at $72, and some large cloisonne bells whose price we were afraid to check for fear we would end up buying them. Days and hours of operation are a bit erratic here.

Edison Lighting
407 Whitaker Street
Savannah, GA
(912) 447–1008

This lighting showroom specializes in antique reproduction lighting. The shop works with interior designers and architects, but it also serves those who are shopping on their own. Both interior and exterior lighting fixtures are available. When we visited, the lamps in stock included brass, ceramic, and iron examples.

Kitchen Kaboodle
28 Drayton Street
Savannah, GA
(912) 238–3474

Take your kitchen seriously? Looking for a gift for someone who does? Check this place out. You'll find gadgets, neat kitchen decor, even gardener's gifts. It's heavier on the gift angle than the gourmet angle, but a fun place to browse. This shop recently relocated to larger quarters on the ground floor of the Planters Inn, a few blocks away from its original City Market location.

Marco Polo Trading Company
38 Barnard Street
Savannah, GA
(912) 234–4164

Indiana Jones would have been right at home here. The stock of furnishings and accessories is largely hand-selected by the owners on trips to Indonesia. It's heavy on teak—a teak bathmat for $35, a hand-carved teak bed for $2,800.

Other items we spotted on a recent visit included brightly colored woven mats described as perfect for beach use, old-fashioned photo albums with black pages,

and so forth. They carry the Shabby Chic line of slipcovered furniture. The shop is both large and crowded and merits leisurely browsing.

The Market at Jones and Whitaker
401 Whitaker Street
Savannah, GA
(912) 231–1006

Patterned after a French market, this eclectic shop on a strategically located corner offers a bit of everything. There's hand-painted furniture, candles, gifts, cookbooks, even a corner devoted especially to pet presents and treats. The stock also includes lines of specialty foods, breads, cheeses, coffees, even a small collection of sandwiches prepared elsewhere. You can snap up the ingredients for a European-style picnic here and then head out to one of the squares for the perfect setting. Gift wrap and shipping services are available.

One Fish, Two Fish
405 Whitaker Street
Savannah, GA
(912) 447–4600

This tiny shop features cottage furniture, gifts, and what owner Jennifer Beaufait calls "garden fancies." On our visit, the stock included artisan's work on wooden furniture and a selection of pottery, including examples from St. Simons Island farther down the coast. Prices are moderate, with plenty of gift items in the $20–$30 range.

Peanut Shop of Savannah
407 E. River Street
Savannah, GA
(912) 232–8612

Peanut brittle, roasted peanuts, and plain ol' peanuts, along with hard candy and Key lime jelly, are just some of the many things you will find inside the Peanut Shop. If you aren't sure what kind of peanuts you want, don't worry, there are usually several samples out so you can try before you buy.

Savannah Hardscapes
513 W. Jones Street
Savannah, GA
(912) 443–9000

This shop takes a little effort to find—it's west of Martin Luther King Boulevard, a couple of blocks farther west than most tourist-oriented development on Jones—but it can be a rewarding experience. Come inside the old brick-walled structure and hear twenty or so different kinds of fountains at work, and you'll see what we mean. We still have a little trouble grasping what "hardscapes" means, but the stock is a vibrant mix of garden furnishings and decor with pieces that could work both inside and out. Fountains on display include spooky pyramids with realistic ground fog effects, life-size metal sculptures of children, and classic standing cranes, along with an assortment of small spouting frogs and crabs. On our last trip, we spotted a birdbath featuring small alligators crawling into the basin. A burnished metal rocking chair proved to be surprisingly comfortable, despite the construction material and its $1,150 price tag. There were expensive sculptured trellises and gates, and inexpensive tabletop gargoyles and candleholders. An adjoining room holds a large collection of large pottery and terra-cotta figures. Across the street, there's an open yard with the stock of stepping stones, garden rocks, and so on, including some unusual plants, replicas of Easter Island statues, and concrete bulldogs.

Walsh Mountain Ironworks
417 Whitaker Street
Savannah, GA
(912) 239–9818

This shop features the wrought-iron works of Canadian Greg Walsh. Items range from $19 candlesticks to an iron four-poster bed for $1,000. There's a mixture of indoor and outdoor pieces, including a garden trellis and gate. A limited supply of other gift/decorating items not of Walsh's manufacture is included, leaning toward either the Gothic or the Victo-rian. The shop has a catalog and will ship purchases.

Willows
101 W. Broughton Street
Savannah, GA
(912) 233–0780

This upscale boutique features home decor and some furnishing. Bamboo, wicker, and other modern furniture, along with pottery, cotton, and linen duvet covers, rugs, and sheer window coverings are just some of the many items you will enjoy browsing through. Favorite finds have included metallic insect sculptures that double as fun jewelry—and have freaked out a few nervous folks!

New Age

Moon Dance
306 W. St. Julian Street
Savannah, GA
(912) 236–9003

This City Market shop carries books with mystical, women's, and New Age themes, along with music, herbs, crystals, incense, and gifts. It's also a center for classes, lectures, and service sessions by various New Age practitioners.

Thrifts and Flea Markets

This kind of shopping isn't for everyone, just the most dedicated bargain hunters. If you don't mind rolling up your sleeves, these places can be real treasure troves. Of course, you'll occasionally come away empty-handed, but if you are into the thrill of the chase, you won't mind a bit.

Goodwill Industries
2123 E. Victory Drive
Savannah, GA
(912) 352–2413
7220 Sallie Mood Drive
Savannah, GA
(912) 354–7423

Chances are your community has these stores, with donated goods refurbished, sorted, and stocked by the disabled. But you should definitely check ours out: With our large military and college populations (which tend to be mobile), Savannah's Goodwills see lots of merchandise turnover. We have friends who have furnished entire beach houses with stuff from these stores. The Sallie Mood Drive location is the best place for furniture: It's in the back, behind swinging doors and easy to miss if you aren't specifically looking for it. We've bought three-drawer pine dressers rescued from dormitories for $35, current hardback best-sellers for $2, glass ice buckets from the 1950s for $4, and so on. There are actually four locations, but these are the only two we've had much luck in.

Keller's Flea Market
5901 Ogeechee Road
Savannah, GA
(912) 927-4848

Ever wonder where people buy velvet wall-hangings depicting the Last Supper, wild stallions, and dogs playing poker? We've found them here ($10 each). In fact, if you go often enough and search diligently, we're convinced you can find just about anything in one of the 400-plus booths. Some are just tables under shed roofs; others are enclosed ministores. Don't expect anything fancy—this is the base of the food chain of retail shopping. Still, we've made some real finds here and had fun people watching.

Among the booths you'll find the equivalent of yard sales, estate sales, and salvage sales. Some have new merchandise, including designer label stuff that doesn't appear very convincing and pure junk that isn't masquerading as anything else. Handcrafters, small-scale importers, and collectors set up here. Go early on Saturday, and you'll see the antique dealers scouting for stuff they'll clean up (and mark up) for their own shops. Our finds here have included an IBM Selectric typewriter for $35 (in need of some repair, but still worth it), used books, carved onyx parrots, and a

Insiders' Tip
If you've got military privileges, you'll find a PX and commissary at Hunter Army Airfield in Savannah.

possibly authentic (but probably not) poster from the 1955 World Series.

Other merchandise on a typical weekend includes fresh produce, houseplants and plants for landscaping, sports cards, T-shirts, and bumper stickers with politically incorrect slogans.

One section features exotic birds, reptiles, puppies, and chickens, but real animal lovers should give that section a wide berth. The market is open Saturday and Sunday. Ogeechee Road is also U.S. Highway 17, and the market is in the county's far southern section. About 2 miles past Savannah Mall, you'll spot the exit for U.S. Highway 17. Take the exit, turn left at the end of the ramp, and you'll soon see the market on your left. Dress casually or you'll look like an idiot.

Tobacco

The Tinder Box
244 Bull Street
Savannah, GA
(912) 232-2650

This smoking specialty shop stocks tobacco in all its forms, and chances are you don't realize how many forms that is. There are between 180 and 200 different types of cigars in stock at any given time, along with thirty blends of pipe tobacco (including their own custom blend). Cigarettes include imported Dunhills, Export A (Canadian), and the American-made, additive-free Nat Sherman cigarettes in various sizes and shapes. The inventory even includes Indonesian clove cigarettes and Darsham Bidis, which is Indian tobacco wrapped in eucalyptus and flavored with strawberry or vanilla.

The Tinder Box has accessories that include elegant lighters, cutters, punches, clippers, and humidors in fine wood (the most expensive currently in stock is $1,250). They also stock books and magazines for cigar and pipe enthusiasts.

The most distinguishing feature at The Tinder Box, however, is the lounge, a small comfortable room at the rear of the store with leather sofas and big-screen TV. Here customers from Savannah's business district (and tourists, of course) can relax with their smokes. Individual locker-size humidors with full temperature and humidity control are available for rental to house customers' personal tobacco collections.

The shop is part of a franchised chain of tobacco shops.

Verdery's Lamps and Ye Ole Tobacco Shop
130 East Bay
Savannah, GA
(912) 236–1178
280 Eisenhower Drive
Savannah, GA
(912) 691–0807

Lamps and tobacco might sound like a strange combination, but the way the shopkeepers see it, it gives them something for both male and female shoppers. The Bay Street store relocated in 1998 from the store's longtime site on River Street. On the lighting side, they offer custom lamps and shades, along with repairs and restorative work. For tobacco enthusiasts, there's a walk-in humidor with more than 100 brands and 200 sizes of cigars, ranging in price from 65 cents to $29.95 each. The pipe tobacco selection includes Verdery's own custom blends. In addition to the usual line of American cigarette brands, they have imported Dunhills, Gauloises,

and others, along with clove cigarettes and additive-free versions. The store also stocks pipes and leather goods for smokers.

Toys

Enchantments
3 W. Perry Street
Savannah, GA
(912) 651–9035

This is a shop for indulgent grandparents and adults who aren't afraid to admit they still like toys. The Steiff line of German teddy bears and other animals is the star of the show, but there are also other lines of quality stuffed animals for both collector and child, including many which are not in the stratospheric price range.

Toy Smart
309 Eisenhower Drive
Savannah, GA
(912) 351–6060
2 N. Lincoln Street, off River Street
Savannah, GA
(912) 651–8888

Tired of violent-themed, over-advertised plastic toys? If so, this set of local toy stores is for you. We don't mean to imply that all the stock here is made by elves at the North Pole, but it is less schlocky than your run-of-the-mill toys. You'll find appealing educational toys (that don't come across as homework on the make), high-quality stuffed animals, Madame Alexander dolls, Thomas the Tank Engine merchandise, and other items geared toward children whose parents pay close attention to what goes into the toy box. The Eisenhower Drive store (a few blocks east and north of Oglethorpe Mall) is roomier and better for browsing; the River Street store is smaller and crowded but features a small toy museum that will prompt aging baby boomers to remember, "I used to have one of those."

Attractions

Savannah is perfect for strolling, and we thought this chapter would be the perfect place to provide you with a little direction. With most of the city's best-known attractions in the Historic Downtown, a walking tour seemed in order to give your personal trek some guidance.

Here's the format: We provide detailed listings of many of the popular historic sites downtown, and in between we give explicit directions (in italics) on how to get from one location to the next. The tour takes in a little more than 2.5 miles; how long it takes depends on how fast you walk and whether you decide to take a detour or two and further explore some sites. We heartily encourage you to do so.

You will find many benches for leisurely breaks along the way. If you get hungry or have an urge to do some browsing, you will be passing by many restaurants and specialty shops. (If you stumble on a place that catches your fancy and is not listed in this chapter, chances are you can find out more about it in our Restaurants or Shopping chapters.) For another great dining option, pack a picnic before setting out. Each square you encounter—and we will cover ten—is perfect for relaxing near the magnolia trees while enjoying a good sandwich. If you've brought the dog along for a romp, be aware that the city has both leash laws and scoop laws.

We offer a basic map at the front of this book. If you need a further visual aid, several good maps of the Historic Downtown are available in shops around town and typically cost less than $5. The Savannah Visitors Center, located in the 300 block of Martin Luther King Jr. Boulevard near its intersection with Liberty Street, or the Chamber of Commerce offices at Drayton and Bay Streets (912-644-6400) also provide a visitors' guide that has a great map.

Following our Insiders' Historic Downtown tour, we provide information on other guided touring options in the city, plus a variety of other interesting attractions to explore both in Savannah's downtown and the outlying areas: the Islands, Southside, and West Chatham.

Doing the Historic Downtown

Whether you are coming to the Historic Downtown from the Talmadge Bridge or you're already there and wandering around on foot, you can't miss the gold dome on top of City Hall. Because of this, we decided to start our tour at this landmark on Bay Street and the northern tip of Bull Street. So look up (or down, depending on your vantage point), and when you spot the gold dome, head in that direction. Once you arrive, don't be shy—wander inside for a quick look around. You will be glad you did, and the office workers don't mind a bit.

City Hall
Bay and Bull Streets
Savannah, GA
(912) 651–6410, (912) 236–7284

Local architect Hyman Wallace Witcover designed and built City Hall in 1905 for an estimated $205,167. This price was to include statues of chariots and horses on top of the structure, but budget constraints prevented them from being built. The exterior is composed of several materials,

The U.S. Customs building turns an imposing face on Bay Street. PHOTO: BETTY DARBY

United States Custom House
1 E. Bay Street
Savannah, GA

The magnificent columns in front of the Custom House each weigh fifteen tons. Across the street are cannon presented to the Chatham Artillery in 1791 by George Washington.

In 1972, the structure was designated a historic custom house by the U.S. commissioner of customs. As you walk by, notice the wonderful ironwork fencing that not only decorates the building, but also guards it. It is just one of many fine examples of wrought iron you will notice throughout your walking tour. Although it is a landmark, it's also the working home of the Customs office, busy tracking the business of Savannah's port.

Continue south on Bull Street in the direction of Johnson Square.

Johnson Square
Bull Street, between Bryan and Congress Streets

This is Savannah's first square. It is named for Robert Johnson, the governor of South Carolina who helped the Georgia colony get established. During the early days of the colony, this was the center of activity for the city. In the center is a monument to Revolutionary War hero Gen. Nathanael Greene, who died in 1786; his grave is here as well. Today, the square is the center of banking in Savannah. Stand in the middle and you will be surrounded by several banks. If you need to pick up some cash, this is a good spot to find an ATM. This is also a popular square for downtown workers to lunch in,

---

including rough-hewn granite blocks, colored limestone, and polished granite. The dome, rising seventy feet, was originally copper. However, in 1987 a local philanthropist donated $240,000 to the city, allowing the dome to be gilded with thin layers of 23-karat gold leaf. The gold was applied to the dome, cupola, and clock hands. Usually, most of the faces of the clock have the right time—but if your group is splitting up to tour, don't depend on it for your rendezvous time!

Inside the foyer you will find a lovely and intricate mosaic on the floor. Look up in the foyer, and you will see more detailed tiles. Go farther into the rotunda and look up for a pretty, circular view all the way up to the fourth floor and the stained glass in the dome. The original building directory is also in the rotunda on a giant tablet. Today, Savannah city offices are located throughout the community, but the second floor of City Hall is much like it was when the building was originally built. It still houses the mayor's office, clerk of council offices, and the council chambers. The stern and imposing council chambers have stood in for courtrooms in a couple of Hollywood productions, even.

After leaving City Hall, head south on Bull Street. Look to your left while crossing Bay Street. The huge building on the corner opposite City Hall is the United States Custom House.

Insiders' Tip

If you're venturing south of the Historic Downtown to do some sight-seeing, be sure to take a drive down portions of two streets in Midtown—Victory Drive between Abercorn Street and Waters Avenue, and Washington Avenue between Bull Street and Waters. You'll see stately homes set amid huge, graceful oak trees, and if you hit it just right during the springtime, medians and yards bursting with the color of azaleas in bloom. Palm trees were first planted along Victory Drive in 1906 when it was called Estill Avenue, and this thoroughfare—which starts at Ogeechee Road, runs to the Wilmington River, and continues to Tybee Island as U.S. 80—was once reputed to be the longest avenue of palms in the nation. When Estill Avenue was widened and extended in 1922, it was renamed Victory Drive in honor of the Americans who fought and died in World War I.

Christ Episcopal Church
28 Bull Street
Savannah, GA
(912) 232-8230

Christ Church is known as Georgia's Mother Church. It was founded in 1733, on the exact spot where the first Christian religious service in Georgia was held. The present church replaced two churches that were destroyed. In 1735, John Wesley, the founder of Methodism, served as pastor here and founded what is believed to be the world's first Protestant Sunday school.

Also interesting: Christ Church has one of the rarest church bells in the entire country. It is known as a Revere Bell and was created by Paul Revere and Sons, the company owned by the noted "British are coming" patriot. It is one of about 130 Revere bells, the majority of which are found in New England states; only a handful made it to the South. The bell in the tower is actually the third Revere Bell the church has owned. The first, purchased in 1816 for $716, cracked during shipment. The second cracked the second Sunday it rang. The third bell, as they say, was the charm. The church didn't have any significant problems with the third bell until 1995, when repairs needed to be made to the apparatus holding the bell. After a two-year repair job, the bell was rung again in early November 1997.

Continue heading south on Bull Street, crossing Congress Street and proceeding to Broughton Street. This is Savannah's original business district, and after decades of decline, it is becoming a shining example of what urban redevelopment can do. Look east and west to see many trendy shops and a restaurant selection that ranges from Malaysian to Moroccan to Japanese (not to mention a good ol' hot dog place as well). Take a detour if you are hungry. If not, continue south on Bull Street to Wright Square, the second square on our trip.

Wright Square
Bull Street, between State and York Streets

Wright Square is named for Sir James Wright, the last royal governor of Georgia. The monument in the center is for William Washington Gordon, one of the founders of the Central of Georgia Railroad. (The railroad's offices used to be about a block away; you will pass the site on this walking tour.) The large boulder, taken from Stone Mountain near Atlanta, marks the grave of Tomo-chi-chi, the Yamacraw Indian chief who was instrumental in helping the founders get established in their new colony.

Taking up the entire western side of the square is the federal courthouse. Made of Georgia marble, its architecture is a conglomeration of many styles: Spanish, French, Italian Renaissance, and Romanesque among them. On the eastern side of the square, you'll see the old Chatham County Courthouse, a light-colored brick building designed in 1889 by noted Boston architect William G. Preston. It now houses county offices. On the same side as the courthouse is Lutheran Church of the Ascension.

Lutheran Church of the Ascension
21 E. State Street
Savannah, GA
(912) 232–4151

Massive red doors lead into Lutheran Church of the Ascension, formed in 1741 by German settlers. The present church was built between 1875 and 1879 and was designed by George B. Clarke, using Norman and Gothic styles. One of the church's most striking features is the Ascension Window, depicting the Ascension of the Lord.

Continue heading south on Bull Street. On the northeastern corner of Bull and Oglethorpe Streets is the Juliette Gordon Low Center.

Juliette Gordon Low Center
142 Bull Street
Savannah, GA
(912) 233–4501

The Juliette Gordon Low Center gives visitors an authentic glimpse of what life was like in the 1800s for one of Savannah's most prominent families—one that just happened to include Juliette Gordon Low, founder of the Girl Scouts.

But the Low Center isn't just about the Girl Scouts. This beautifully restored home, Savannah's first National Historic Landmark, is full of the Gordon's original belongings—from Georgian Revival chairs in the dining room to a painting of Niagara Falls by moonlight, a souvenir the Gordons bought some years after their honeymoon. When entering the main hallway, you will immediately notice the beautiful winding staircase with a rose-colored bull's-eye glass window in the background; it was installed in 1886 to give more light in the stairway. In the library is a brass chandelier original to the home. The south parlor, decorated in striking yellow, red, and green, has a pier mirror installed in 1884.

Construction on the home began in 1818 in the newly fashionable English Regency style. William Washington Gordon and his wife, Sarah, were the first of four generations of the Gordon family to live in the home. William Gordon served as mayor of Savannah and is credited as a founder of the Central of Georgia Railroad. The house was eventually inherited by William Washington Gordon II and his wife, Eleanor Kinzie Gordon, the parents of Juliette Gordon. Juliette spent her childhood here.

After passing through another generation of Gordons, the house in 1953 was threatened with demolition. A concerned group of local Girl Scouts, including youngsters and adults, appealed to the national organization to save the birthplace of their founder, and the building was purchased by the Girl Scouts. It was restored and opened to the public three years later. Today, thousands of Girl Scouts from around the world make the pilgrimage to Savannah to visit the home of the group's cherished founder. The house is open from 10 A.M. to 4 P.M. Monday through Saturday (except Wednesday) and from 12:30 to 4:30 P.M. on Sundays. Cost is $6 for adults and $5 for students ages 6 to 18.

Continuing south on Bull Street, you will pass the offices for the local school district on the left, housed in a rambling brick building that once housed a school and still sports nice frescoes above its entrances, and Independent Presbyterian Church on the right.

Independent Presbyterian Church
25 W. Oglethorpe Avenue
Savannah, GA
(912) 236–3346

This church was founded in 1755 and is considered one of the most important Federal-style churches in the country. The original was designed by John Holden Greene of Rhode Island. It burned in 1889. The current building has an elevated mahogany pulpit, and the four Corinthian columns of the sanctuary were made from a single tree trunk that was carefully selected through exhaustive searches in the South. Woodrow Wilson married Ellen Axson, granddaughter of the church's pastor, here.

Continue south to Chippewa Square.

Chippewa Square
Bull Street, between Perry and Hull Streets

Gen. James Oglethorpe is immortalized in bronze in the center of this square. First Baptist Church, organized in 1800, is on the northwestern corner of the square. Across the park on the northeastern corner is the Savannah Theater, which hosts many locally produced shows throughout the year.

For movie buffs, this is the square where Forrest Gump sat waiting for the bus. The bench was placed on the far northern tip of the square. Next time you see the film, notice that traffic in the

square is moving in the wrong direction! The beautiful building on the southwest corner is known as the Philbrick-Eastman House and is a fine example of Greek Revival architecture. It served as home for many prominent families; today, it houses a law firm. It was also a location for the movie *Now and Then*, which starred Demi Moore, Rita Wilson, and Melanie Griffith, among others.

While walking south through the square, look to your left along W. Perry Street, and you will notice a row of magnificently restored private homes, among the many you will see on your trip today. You are getting into the more residential portion of the Historic District.

Continue south on Bull Street. After crossing Perry Street, notice a dolphin downspout on the home to your right. These interesting adornments to lovely houses are a common sight throughout Savannah.

There are several boutiques, a coffee shop, and a few lunch spots in this area. Duck into Arts & Crafts Emporium of Savannah, Gaucho, Chutzpah & Panache and look for buys. (Check the Shopping and Restaurants chapters for more information.) Farther down Liberty Street is the Hilton Savannah DeSoto, built on the site of the DeSoto Hotel, which was razed in 1966. Next is Madison Square.

Madison Square
Bull Street, between Harris and Charlton Streets

Madison Square is named for James Madison, the fourth U.S. president. When entering Madison Square, you will notice the Sorrel-Weed House on the northwest corner of the square. It was completed in 1841 and is an example of Greek Revival architecture. In 1997, the home was purchased and underwent an extensive $2 million renovation that restored it to its original condition. This renovation included painting the home its supposedly original bright orange color, which did not please neighbors and members of a local historic review committee. However, the homeowner won out, as you will see when walking by.

On the northeastern corner is E. Shaver Bookseller, a popular locally owned bookstore. If you need a break, this could be a good place to take it. On the southeastern edge of the square is a gigantic redbrick building that was the former Savannah Volunteer Guards Armory. This structure and the large building across the street on the southwest corner of the square—the old Scottish Rite Temple—are owned by the Savannah College of Art and Design. The armory was the first building the art school founders purchased when they came to town in the late 1970s. At the time, there was an old greasy spoon inside, so complete renovation was needed. It was the first in a long list of buildings purchased and restored by the school; you'll find them throughout the Historic Downtown. Today, the armory houses classrooms and Exhibit A, an art gallery that features artwork by students and professors and, at times, work by famous artists. It is free and open to the public. (For more information on the Savannah College of Art and Design, see our Education and Child Care chapter.)

Look to the northwest corner of the square. The Gothic brick mansion is the Green-Meldrim House.

Green-Meldrim House
1 W. Macon Street
Savannah, GA
(912) 233-3845

Built in 1853 by architect-builder John S. Norris for a wealthy cotton merchant, the Green-Meldrim House is best known as being headquarters for Gen. William T. Sherman, who gave the city of Savannah to President Lincoln as a Christmas present. The famous telegram to Lincoln, dated December 22, 1864, reads, "I beg to present to you as a Christmas Gift, the City of Savannah with 150 heavy guns and plenty of ammunition; and also about 25,000 bales of Cotton."

Today, the home serves as a parish house and is owned by its neighbor, St. John's Church. When you walk by, notice the beautiful and elaborate ironwork and the oriel windows that give light from three sides. Inside are American black walnut wooden floors, elaborate moldings, marble mantels, and other original adornments. The home is open for tours from 10 A.M. to 4 P.M. on Tuesday, Thursday, and Friday and 10 A.M. to 1 P.M. Saturday. Admission is $5 for adults and $3 for students.

Continuing south on Bull Street, you will pass Jones Street, considered one of Savannah's most picturesque roadways. Notice the brick streets and wonderfully restored homes. It is well worth a short detour. It is also home to one of Savannah's most noted restaurants, Mrs. Wilkes', which is known for its Southern fare (see our Restaurants chapter). Next is Monterey Square.

Monterey Square
Bull Street, between Taylor and Gordon Streets

This is the final square on Bull Street. Its name commemorates the Battle of Monterey in the Mexican War. The square was laid out in 1847. In the center is a monument honoring Casimir Pulaski, a Polish nobleman who was killed during the American Revolution. He may or may not be buried under the monument that honors him; historians disagree. The monument was rededicated in 2001 after a restoration period of several years that saw its foundation standing empty.

During filming of the movie *Midnight in the Garden of Good and Evil,* set designers brought in their own monument. Now, when you see Monterey Square on the big screen, you'll know the monument is not the original. The square contains other significant sites used in the movie, including the home where the book's main plot unfolds, the Mercer-Wilder House, commonly known as Mercer House, which is on the western edge of the square.

Mercer House
429 Bull Street
Savannah, GA

Cited by Historic Savannah Foundation as nationally significant for its architectural style, this home was designed by

John S. Norris and completed in 1871. The striking ironwork—including cast-iron window pediments, eight cast-iron balconies, and the sidewalk fence—is one of the house's signature features. The house was named for Confederate Gen. Hugh Mercer, songwriter Johnny Mercer's great-grandfather, but General Mercer sold the house. He never lived there nor did any member of the Mercer family.

In 1970, after the house was neglected and empty for many years, Jim Williams, the antique dealer and central character in *Midnight in the Garden of Good and Evil*, finished a complete restoration of the home. Today, the private home is owned by Dorothy Kingery, sister of the late Williams. It is not open to the public. It went on the market in 1999 for $8.9 million.

Looking past Mercer House, on the southwest corner of the square, you will notice rowhouses along Gordon Street. One of these homes—7 W. Gordon Street—has also had a brush with celebrity. If you are a fan of the PBS show This Old House, *you may be familiar with the renovation that took place here in 1996 at the home of Mills and Marianne Fleming. For several months, Norm Abram, Steve Thomas, and the rest of the crew from the popular PBS series were in town helping restore the 1884 home, which made headlines when it was built for being one of the first homes in the city to have indoor plumbing. Across the square from Mercer House, on the eastern side of the square, is Temple Mickve Israel.*

Temple Mickve Israel
20 E. Gordon Street
Savannah, GA
(912) 233–1547

Temple Mickve Israel began with a group of Spanish Portuguese Jews who came to Savannah in 1733, just five months after the founding of the colony. It is the site of the first Jewish congregation in the South and the third in the entire United States. It is also the only Gothic synagogue in the country. The temple was designed by Henry G. Harrison and houses the oldest Torah in America. There are also hundreds of documents, historical books, and letters from Presidents Washington, Jefferson, and Madison in the museum adjoining the temple. Free tours of the sanctuary and museum take place Monday through Friday from 10 A.M. to noon and 2 to 4 P.M.

Continuing south on Bull Street, you will pass the George Armstrong House on the northwest corner of Bull and Gaston Streets. This massive building, constructed in 1920, was given to the city in 1935 and converted into Armstrong Junior College, predecessor of Armstrong Atlantic University, which subsequently moved to Savannah's Southside. (For more on Armstrong Atlantic, see our Education and Child Care chapter.) Today it houses a law firm.

Across the street, on the northeast corner of Bull and Gaston Streets is the Oglethorpe Club, one of Savannah's most elite and private clubs. Straight ahead is Forsyth Park.

Forsyth Park
Bull Street, between Gaston Street and Park Avenue

This thirty-acre park filled with azaleas, magnolia trees, walkways, park benches, and more is one of Savannah's most beautiful spots. If you are in need of a break during the walking tour, don't miss a stroll through Forsyth Park; in fact, we suggest a picnic. The park was laid out in 1851. One of its most recognizable and often photographed features is the white fountain near the center. Visit on the weekend, and you might see a bride and groom getting pictures taken beside the ornate swans and other creatures in the fountain.

The monument in the center of the park was erected by the United Daughters of the Confederacy and honors those killed during the Civil War. The park is also home to a Fragrant Garden for the Blind and is surrounded by beautiful and elaborately restored homes, many of which are Victorian in style. Across from the northwestern corner of the park is the Georgia Historical Society. (For much more on Forsyth Park, see our Parks and Recreation chapter.)

Georgia Historical Society
501 Whitaker Street
Savannah, GA
(912) 651–2128

Dr. William Bacon Stevens, a physician who later became the Episcopal Bishop of Pennsylvania, and attorney I. K. Tefft are generally credited with organizing the Savannah-based Georgia Historical Society. The pair were soon joined by Dr. Richard D. Arnold, a founder of the American Medical Association. In 1839, the group incorporated one of the country's oldest (and the Southeast's first) historical societies.

Nearly 160 years later, the realization of their efforts can easily be seen in thousands of historic documents, artifacts, newspapers, and other source materials documenting Georgia's past. Visitors to the society will find everything in its massive archives, from copies of letters Gen. James Edward Oglethorpe wrote to the Trustees of the Colony to the grapeshot that killed Casimir Pulaski and was extracted from the Polish war hero's leg. There are minutes from the first Georgia Medical Society meeting, held in Savannah in 1804; photographs from the now-defunct YWCA; and family letters such as the one written by Garnett Andrews about the cotton gin Eli Whitney had invented.

The society also publishes, in cooperation with the University of Georgia, the highly acclaimed *Georgia Historical Quarterly*, a collection of scholarly articles. Entry to the Georgia Historical Society is free. The building is open to the public from 10 A.M. to 5 P.M. Tuesday through Friday and 9 A.M. to 3 P.M. on Saturday.

This is the midpoint of the walking tour. We will travel north for the next portion of the tour, heading back in the direction of City Hall, where we started. Continue 1 block east on Gaston Street, crossing Drayton Street. Check out the many beautifully restored homes. Head north by turning left on Abercorn and stay on this street until you reach Calhoun Square.

Calhoun Square
Abercorn Street, between Taylor and
Gordon Streets

The first of the Abercorn Street squares on our tour was named for John Calhoun, a South Carolina statesman. It was laid out in 1851. When entering the square, you can't help but notice Wesley Monumental Methodist Church on the southwestern corner of the square. This Gothic Revival church was built as a memorial to John and Charles Wesley, founders of the Methodist movement. The sanctuary was built between 1876 and 1890. It features a Wesley Window opposite the pulpit, which contains the busts of the men for whom the church was named.

On the southeastern edge of the square is the Massie Heritage Interpretation Center.

Massie Heritage Interpretation Center
207 E. Gordon Street
Savannah, GA
(912) 651–7380

Honored as Georgia's oldest school in continuous operation, the Massie Heritage Interpretation Center is also the only remaining original building from Georgia's oldest chartered school system. The Greek Revival structure is listed on the National Register of Historic Places. It was completed in 1856 and is known for its gable roof, wood cupola, and cornice, among other features. Today, an enrichment program is offered to increase student understanding of Savannah's historic and architectural heritage. The center is open to the public from 9 A.M. to 4 P.M. Monday through Friday. It's free, but a donation is requested.

Continue north on Abercorn Street. On your way, you will pass Clary's Cafe, a must for fans of The Book. It's the spot where Luther Driggers, the man rumored to have enough poison to kill the entire city, often hung out. You will also pass Jones Street before entering Lafayette Square.

Lafayette Square
Abercorn Street, between Harris and Charlton Streets

This square, which was laid out in 1837, was named for Marquis de Lafayette, who visited Savannah in 1825. There are several significant buildings on this square, but when you enter it you can't help but notice the Cathedral of St. John the Baptist, located near the northeast corner.

Cathedral of St. John the Baptist
223 East Harris Street
Savannah, GA
(912) 233–4709

This magnificent Gothic cathedral with its twin spires is one of Savannah's most noted landmarks. It is also the oldest Roman Catholic church in Georgia and the seat of the Diocese of Savannah. The parish organized in the late 1700s and erected its first church on Liberty Square. It wasn't until 1876 that the cathedral was built; tragically, it was destroyed by fire twenty years later.

When the cathedral was rebuilt, the original designs were used. One of the cathedral's most striking features is its stained glass. Most of it was executed by Innsbruck Glassmakers in Austrian Tyrol and installed around 1900. Other features include an Italian marble altar, the stations of the cross (which were imported from Munich), and the coat of arms of Pope John XXIII. Depending on the timing of your visit, you may not see much of the cathedral. The building just underwent a massive restoration, indoors and out, and is now fully open in its restored glory.

The Andrew Low House
329 Abercorn Street
Savannah, GA
(912) 233–6854

On the northwest corner of Lafayette Square is the Andrew Low House, built in 1848 by Low, a wealthy cotton merchant. Low's son, William McKay Low, married Juliette Gordon, founder of the Girl Scouts. In fact, the carriage house in back of the home is the first official headquarters of the Girl Scouts of the U.S.A. Juliette Low left the building to the organization following her death.

The stunning home, with its elegant front gardens and beautiful ironwork, is built of stuccoed brick. It is owned by the National Society of the Colonial Dames of America in the State of Georgia, whose members also donated its furnishings. Even the three-tiered fountain in the center of the square was donated by the organization. Some of the home's most noted guests have included Robert E. Lee and William Makepeace Thackeray. The home is open for tours on Monday and on Wednesday through Saturday from 10:30 A.M. to 4 P.M., and on Sunday from noon to 4 P.M. It is closed on Tuesday. Cost to tour the house is $7 for adults and $4.50 for students, Girl Scouts, and Girl Scout leaders.

The Hamilton-Turner House
330 Abercorn Street
Savannah, GA

The Hamilton-Turner house is a Second Empire chateau built in the 1870s by a former mayor of Savannah. The Lafayette Square home was the first house in the city to get electricity and has many distinctive features, including a mansard roof and cast-iron balconies. In 1969, it was scheduled for demolition, but those plans were abandoned after the Historic Savannah Foundation stepped in. It has changed hands several times since then. (Read more about its current incarnation in our Bed-and-Breakfast Inns chapter.)

Flannery O'Connor House
207 East Charlton Street
Savannah, GA
(912) 233–6014

Noted Southern author Flannery O'Connor was born in this high-stoop, nineteenth-century home on the outskirts of Lafayette Square. She lived here as a child until 1938. The parlor floor has been restored to its original appearance and houses a small museum dedicated to the author. The home is open from 1 to 4 P.M. on Saturday and Sundays, and there is no admission charge.

Continuing north on Abercorn Street, cross Liberty Street. On the east side of Abercorn Street is Colonial Park Cemetery.

Colonial Park Cemetery

Button Gwinnett, who signed the Declaration of Independence, and miniature painter Edward Green Malbone are two of the notable Georgians buried in this cemetery, the second public burial ground in Savannah. The cemetery, which takes up several blocks in the Historic Downtown, opened in 1750; it closed to burials one hundred years later. Visitors are welcome to tour the cemetery and glimpse the old tombstones and inscriptions.

After exploring the cemetery, continue north on Abercorn Street, crossing Oglethorpe Avenue. As you cross Oglethorpe, you will pass the city's fire department headquarters, then the Jack Leigh Gallery—the studio of photographer Jack Leigh, who gained national fame for his picture of the "Bird Girl" on the cover of Midnight in the Garden of Good and Evil. *Leigh has captured Southern life in many of his photos, some of which have been published in a variety of books. Next is Oglethorpe Square.*

Oglethorpe Square
Abercorn Street, between State and York Streets

Oglethorpe Square was named for Georgia's founder, James Edward Oglethorpe. It was laid out in 1742. On the northeast corner of the square is one of Savannah's most famous museum houses, the Owens-Thomas House.

Owens-Thomas House
124 Abercorn Street
Savannah, GA
(912) 233–9743

Taking up an entire block on the eastern edge of the square is the Owens-Thomas House, considered to be one of the finest examples of English Regency architecture in the country. The home, with its columned entrance portico, brass inlaid staircase, and more, was designed by architect William Jay from 1816 to 1819 for cotton merchant Richard Richardson.

The home is made largely of tabby—an indigenous, concretelike material made of lime, oyster shells, and sand. The exterior is English stucco. The interior, which includes three rare built-in marble-top tables that belonged to the Richardsons, has many stunning features, including an entryway with a brass inlaid staircase and a drawing room with an unusual ceiling that makes the room appear to be round. The carriage house, also open for tours, is one of the earliest intact urban slave quarters in the South and opens into an English-inspired parterre garden.

In 1830, after the home had been used as a boardinghouse, George Welchman Owens, a congressman and former mayor of Savannah, purchased it for $10,000. The property remained in the Owens family until it was bequeathed to what is now the Telfair Museum of Art. The home is open from noon to 5 P.M. Monday, 10 A.M. to 5 P.M. Tuesday through Saturday, and from 2 to 5 P.M. on Sunday. The cost to tour the house is $7 for adults, $2 for children. Children younger than six are free. (A combined ticket to this attraction and the Telfair Museum of Art is $10.)

One of Savannah's other noted museum houses is just around the corner from the Owens-Thomas house on E. State Street. If you would like to detour to this house, head east on State Street and cross Lincoln. One block on your left will be the Davenport House.

Isaiah Davenport House
324 E. State Street
Savannah, GA
(912) 236–8097

As you walk around today in the Historic Downtown enjoying the beautifully restored homes and other sights, know that it was the Davenport House that was largely responsible for the preservation of the national treasure that is the Historic District. In the 1950s, when developers came up with a plan to demolish the house, sell the brick, and put in a parking lot, seven local women banded together to stop it. That group, which later became the Historic Savannah Foundation, raised $22,500 to purchase the home; such were the beginnings of restoration efforts in Savannah.

At the time of the rescue purchase, the home was a tenement, divided into small apartments and full of people. The Federal-style home was originally built in 1820 by master builder Isaiah Davenport, who used the home as a kind of showcase for his work. One of the incredible features of the house is the delicate and ornate molding and plaster work found throughout. The detail is so incredible that in some cases it looks almost like a wedding cake border has been placed around the edge of the ceilings. There is also a lovely house garden and museum shop that sells period items, note cards, Savannah specialty items, and more. The Davenport House is open from 10 A.M. to 4 P.M. Monday through Saturday, and 1 to 4 P.M. Sunday. Cost is $5.

After viewing the Davenport House, head west on State Street to Abercorn Street. Again, travel north on Abercorn. As you cross Broughton Street, you'll notice a large building on your right. Savannah College of Art and Design has transformed this former department store into a library. Continuing along Abercorn Street, you will come to the Lucas Theatre.

Lucas Theatre
22 Abercorn Street
Savannah, GA
(912) 232–1696

This Savannah landmark, built in 1921, served not only as a theater, but also as a general center of entertainment for the city. It had floors of imported marble, a dome ceiling surrounded by 600 incandescent lights, and thirty-six ornate boxes. However, it deteriorated with the rest of downtown after World War II. A group of citizens—Lucas Theatre for the Arts Inc.—banded together to reopen the theater and has been raising the millions of dollars needed to complete the project. As part of their fund-raising efforts, when the crew filming *Midnight in the Garden of Good and Evil* was in town in 1997, it participated in a fund-raiser for the theater. Among those in attendance were director Clint Eastwood and actor Kevin Spacey. The theater is now in full operation (see our Arts and Culture chapter for more information).

After passing the Lucas Theatre you will enter Reynolds Square, the last square on our trip.

Reynolds Square
Abercorn Street, between Bryan and Congress Streets

Reynolds Square was named for Capt. John Reynolds, who served as governor of Georgia in 1754. In the center is a statue of John Wesley, the founder of Methodism. On the northwestern corner of the square is The Olde Pink House, a popular eatery.

Continuing north on Abercorn Street, you will reach Bay Street. Look to the west and you will once again see the dome on City Hall, where the tour began. Directly across Bay Street is Factors' Walk and River Street.

Factors' Walk and River Street

Bay Street Factors' Walk is named for the cotton brokers (or "factors") who brought, sold, and shipped their wares along the banks of the Savannah River. This unique row of buildings, built on the bluff overlooking the water, rise two or three stories on the street side and three or more stories over the riverfront.

The focal point is the old Cotton Exchange, a redbrick building with the name "Cotton Exchange" etched along the top of the facade. It was built in 1886 by William G. Preston and was one of the first buildings in the United States to be erected entirely over a public street. At one time this building was where the world price for cotton was set. While the brokers set the price of cotton, the lower floors served as cotton and naval warehouses with entrances at several levels including on River Street.

Today, both River Street and Factors' Walk are full of shops, restaurants, and galleries, all housed in the restored warehouses. It is a favorite spot for visitors. Take a stroll on the river for a fitting end to our tour.

Guided Tours

Savannah abounds with guided tour companies. Their offerings are varied—general history, ghosts and hauntings, African American history, you name it. Modes as well as subjects vary: travel by air-conditioned minibus, open-sided pseudo-trolley, horse-drawn carriage, riverboat, or plain old shank's mare (walking, in other words).

This is a very fluid industry. New tours are added constantly, schedules and itineraries change, etc. Although the following is not a comprehensive listing, it will get you started. We have avoided naming any one set of tours "the best." The quality of a given tour, we believe, really varies based on the guide more than the tour company. The city of Savannah requires guides to earn licenses by passing a test on local history and attractions every two years, so you can expect reasonable competence from any guide.

When you are making those required reservations, it's a good time to take advantage of the competitive nature of the industry. Ask specifically which sites are entered (most tours don't actually go inside buildings) and what perks are included. We've found that a constantly changing array of extras—discount coupons, refreshments, etc., are put into play in an attempt to stand out in an industry where everyone is selling essentially the same thing. Remember, all prices are subject to change and are likely to increase slightly when the tourists return in large numbers each spring. The city also

This hour-long cruise takes you up and down the Savannah River on a replica riverboat, either the *Savannah River Queen* or the *Georgia Queen*. It's really the only good way for a tourist to get a firsthand look at the industrial and shipping side of the city—the bread-and-butter for many of us who live here. You can also get a waterfront perspective on historic structures. River Street from the water lends itself to good panoramic photos. Depending on river traffic, you may get to see some of the massive ships that make the Port of Savannah among the busiest in the nation.

The daytime sight-seeing cruise is narrated. Wear sunscreen! This company also offers a variety of other cruises, keyed around dinner and dancing, Sunday brunch, or even gospel music with a buffet dinner.

The sight-seeing cruise is $14.96 for adults and $8.50 for those younger than twelve, plus tax. The meal cruises range from $23 to $34.95. A "murder afloat" mystery cruise with actors staging a "whodunit" is staged once a week (currently on Thursday nights) at a fare of $22.50 for adults and $16 for children. Prepaid reservations are required for most tours, except the daytime sight-seeing. Note that schedules vary seasonally and can be affected by the weather.

frequently revises the rules under which these tour companies operate, because the areas they tour through are also fully operational residential and business districts. They've also recently added a dollar-a-head fee as a tax.

We can't overemphasize what we touched on in the last paragraph: *Reservations are required*. Call ahead. It's easy. We've usually managed to make same-day arrangements except at peak tourism times, but don't push it if a particular tour is central to your plans.

Boats

Savannah Riverboat Company
9 E. River Street
Savannah, GA
(912) 232–6404, (800) 786–6404

Buses

In this category, we've grouped together big buses, minibuses, vans, and trolleylike vehicles—the whole motorized land travel thing. Reservations (again) are required and easily made by phone. Most tours make pickups at the visitors center at 301 Martin Luther King Boulevard, which has reasonably ample parking if you are vacationing with a car. (The first hour of parking is free.) The tour companies use the large parking slots near the front entrance, and each space is marked with a posted sign identifying and advertising the company that leases that space. Convenient pickup is also available at most downtown

This trolley-style bus is one of many vehicles used for guided tours. PHOTO: KYLE CASON

hotels and bed-and-breakfasts. In fact, you can probably make arrangements for most tours to pick you up anywhere you like downtown—this is a competitive business.

Although most tours will take credit cards, some drivers do not have the means of processing them. If you plan on paying by plastic, mention that while making your reservations, because it may impact your selection of pickup locations. Also, prices don't include tips for the guide/ driver, which most of the brochures and onboard signs shamelessly hustle for; they are strictly optional.

Gray Line Red Trolley Tours
215 W. Boundary Street
Savannah, GA
(912) 234–8687, (804) 426–2318

This national tour firm offers a variety of different tours via red trolleylike vehicles and air-conditioned minibuses from its headquarters near the Georgia foot of the Talmadge Bridge, which crosses into South Carolina. One trolley version is the "Explorer" tour, where you'll have unlimited on and off privileges at eleven stops in the Historic District from 9 A.M. to 4:30 P.M. daily. The cost is $22 for adults and $9 for children and includes admission to one attraction. Or you might try their overview tour of ninety minutes, which costs $17 for adults and $7 for children. Or, if you like mystery, you might want to know they offer a haunted trolley tour, too; it lasts just over an hour, with departures times that vary with dusk. It departs from various hotels and the price is $17 for adults and $7 for children.

Bus tours include a grand tour of over two hours, which includes admission to an attraction and is priced at $20 for adults and $10 for children. A Low Country tour will take you to the Wormsloe Historic Site, Isle of Hope, Bethesda Orphanage, Bonaventure Cemetery, Victory Drive, and Ardsley Park. It concludes with a drink at Rivers End Restaurant in Thunderbolt and costs $25 for adults and $10 for children. Finally, you might be

Paddle wheel boats give tourists a unique view of River Street. PHOTO: COURTESY OF SAVANNAH AREA CHAMBER OF COMMERCE

interested in the "Book" tour, which you'll find described in our special chapter on Savannah and Hollywood.

Hospitality Tours
135 Bull Street
Savannah, GA
(912) 233–0119, (888) 869–0119

Owner Pat Tuttle originated the "Book" tours in Savannah, and so probably had a role in the multitude of specialty tours that followed in the footsteps of that one. Meanwhile, the Hospitality Tours menu includes six standard tours on air-conditioned minibuses. The "Talk of the Town" costs $15 for adults and $6 for children, covering the Historic District in about an hour. The "Julep & Jasmine" tour lasts twice as long and includes admission into one of the city's historic sites, varying with availability. Prices for this version are $19 for adults and $8 for children. Other options exist for groups and there's even a group of walking tours that includes an evening ghost tour ($15 for adults and $5 for children).

Negro Heritage Trail Tour
502 E. Harris Street
Savannah, GA
(912) 234–8000

This tour offers an African American perspective of Savannah's history. Stops include the Ralph Mark Gilbert Civil Rights Museum, First African Baptist Church, the King-Tisdell Cottage, and Beach Institute. It runs ninety minutes to two hours, and the admission cost is $15 for adults and $7 for children younger than twelve. The tour is sponsored by the nonprofit King-Tisdell Cottage Foundation (800–517–9007).

Old Savannah Tours
514 Berrien Street
Savannah, GA
(912) 234–8128

White, trolley-style vehicles offer on-off privileges throughout the Historic District for self-paced tours. Tickets are $23 for adults and teens and $9 for children. There are also more conventional tours: a

Historic Downtown overview (90 minutes; $18 for adults and $8 for children), and a "hauntings" tour ($19 for adults, $8 for children).

Less-conventional offerings that take you outside the Historic Downtown can be arranged with Old Savannah Tours, as can a dual riverboat-trolley tour. Rates vary.

Old Town Trolley Tours of Savannah
234 Martin Luther King Jr. Boulevard
Savannah, GA
(912) 233–0083

This ninety-minute tour offers reboarding options throughout the Historic Downtown on orange and green trolley-style vehicles. Tickets cost $22 for adults and $9 for children. There's even an evening "Ghosts and Gravestones" option. The tour company also operates a gift shop downtown.

Victorian Lady Tours
(912) 236–1886

Ardis Wood dons Victorian costume to lead groups on customized tours. You can choose either walking tours or those conducted via various other transport, from your own car to a limo. The standard walking version lasts about two hours and costs for $15 for adults and $7 for those under eighteen. Rates for custom tours start at $45 per hour and go up. Options include downtown, the Colonial Coast, and the Low Country. The phone number reaches a recording; leave your number for a call-back on specifics.

Horse-Drawn Carriages

Although children generally don't jump up and down at the prospect of a guided tour of historic sites, we've found horse-drawn carriages up the appeal significantly. Who knows? You may be lucky enough to see a chartered and decorated carriage ferrying a bride and groom from a wedding at one of the Historic Downtown churches. During rain or extreme heat, tours are not given.

Carriage Tours of Savannah
10 Warner Street
Savannah, GA
(912) 236–6756

Narrated tours are about an hour in length. Options include a daytime historic tour ($17 for adults, $8 for those ages 4 to 11), evening historic or ghost story tours ($17 for adults, $8 for children), and private carriage tours for couples, starting at $65.

Historic Savannah Carriage Tours
305 W. Harris Street
Savannah, GA
(912) 443–9333

Pickup service can be arranged at hotels or at City Market. Fees are $18 for adults and $8 for children.

Magnolia Carriage Company
8 Warner Street
Savannah, GA
(912) 232–7727

Prices for wedding or other private charters begin at $65. Prices hinge on size of the party, carriage, and time of day.

Plantation Carriage Company
P.O. Box 1301
Savannah, GA
(912) 201–0001

These horse-drawn tours run close to an hour and cover the historic district, departing at roughly twenty-minute intervals from the middle of City Market. Fees are $17 for adults and $8 for children.

Walking

Walking tours have really taken off in recent years and small wonder—all that's required is expertise and the ability to walk and talk at the same time. It seems to us there are new entries in this category constantly, so here's a sampling. Note, too, that many of the tour bus companies offer a walking version as well. These tours generally depart from a specific downtown square so check when you make your

A carriage ride offers leisurely sight-seeing. PHOTO: BETTY DARBY

reservations. Remember, all such tours are offered weather permitting.

Ghost Talk, Ghost Walk
127 E. Congress Street
Savannah, GA
(912) 233–3896

The ghost tour is the mainstay (there are actually two different versions). They depart from Reynolds Square, beside the statue of John Wesley (one wonders what the famous preacher would have thought of it). Tours depart at dusk, varying according to the time of year, so call for info. Fees are $10 for adults and $5 for those under twelve. Other tours available include a Civil War version, a botanical tour, a historic architecture walk, and a literary walking tour. Rates vary; check when you make reservations.

The Savannah Walks
123 E. Congress Street
Savannah, GA
(912) 238–9255

This walking tour firm offers a varied menu with different meeting points. Be sure to check on these things when you make your reservations. Fees are $13 for adults and $6.50 for children ages 6 to 16. Options include general tours, a book tour, a ghost tour, a pub walk, a Civil War walk, a walk featuring churches and graveyards, and one featuring gardens. The historic homes walk is slightly higher ($20 adult, $13 children) because it includes admission to one of the city's house museums.

See Savannah
133 Drayton Street
Savannah, GA
(912) 234–3571

Daytime options here include a romance version that keys in on Eugenia Price's Savannah books, a general history tour, and an architecture and ironwork tour. Prices are $10 per person with children five and under free. The evening version is the hauntings tour ($12 per person, $10 for students and seniors, and children five and under free).

Tootsy Tours
12½ W. State Street
(912) 232–0032

Offerings here include a ghost tour, a *Midnight in the Garden of Good and Evil* tour combined with a pub crawl, and a history tour. Other options, varying seasonally, include gardens, the Civil War, Colonial and maritime Savannah, natural history, and a tour based on the best-selling historical romance novelist Eugenia Price. Tours last about ninety minutes. Prices vary but start at $15 for adults.

Other Savannah Attractions

What follows are listings of several other terrific Savannah attractions. Some are in the Historic Downtown but weren't covered by our walking tour; others are in the city's outlying areas.

Historic Downtown

Beach Institute
502 E. Harris Street
Savannah, GA
(912) 234–8000

The Beach Institute was established in 1865 by the American Missionary Association to educate newly freed slaves. It was the first school in Savannah for African Americans and became a public school in 1919. The institute is an African American cultural center and houses art, sculpture, and artifacts relating to the cultural contributions of black Americans. Lectures and other programs are frequently held. It is open from noon to 5 P.M. Tuesday through Saturday. There is no admission charge.

First African Baptist Church
23 Montgomery Street
Savannah, GA
(912) 233–6597

Overlooking Franklin Square is First African Baptist Church. This church, which is still active, is descended from the oldest African American congregation in the United States. George Leile, a slave, began making missionary visits to plantations up and down the Savannah River as early as 1774. A permanent congregation was formed at Brampton Plantation in 1788—the first black missionary Baptist church in Savannah.

Eventually, the congregation constructed the present building. It is the first brick building erected in Georgia by African Americans for African Americans; it was built by slaves who worked on it at night after being in the fields all day. The sanctuary has beautiful stained-glass windows framing the back of the altar, which displays pictures of the founding pastors. In the balcony are original pews with markings left by the slaves who built the church.

Ralph Mark Gilbert Civil Rights Museum
460 Martin Luther King Jr. Boulevard
Savannah, GA
(912) 231–8900

More than 40,000 people toured Ralph Mark Gilbert Civil Rights Museum during its inaugural year of 1996. The museum chronicles the story of Savannah's civil rights struggles during the 1940s, '50s, and '60s. Along with traveling exhibits and special programming, it spotlights how Martin Luther King Jr. Boulevard, formerly known as West Broad Street, was once the center of the city's thriving black business community. Besides educating the community, the museum also serves as an educational resource for southeastern coastal Georgia.

Development of the museum took place over several years. More than $1.7 million went into the museum, which included the renovation of the Wage Earners Savings Bank building where the museum is housed. The Wage Earners Bank is believed to be the second bank for African Americans in the nation. The museum is the brainchild of local historian and activist W. W. Law. It is named after the Rev. Ralph Mark Gilbert, a pastor at First African Baptist Church, who pioneered Savannah's modern civil rights movement. Admission is $4 for adults, $3 for seniors, and $2 for students. (For information on the museum's annual anniversary celebration, look under September in our Annual Events and Festivals chapter.)

Historic Railroad Shops
601 W. Harris Street
Savannah, GA
(912) 651–6823

The Historic Railroad Shops are the oldest and most complete antebellum railroad manufacturing and repair facilities still in existence in the United States. Thirteen of the original structures, which were built beginning in 1859, are still standing. Included are the roundhouse and turntable (where the engines were turned around) and the 125-foot brick smokestack. The site is a National Historic Landmark. It is open from 10 A.M. to 4 P.M. Monday through Saturday and from noon to 4 P.M. on Sunday. Cost is $2.50 for adults and $2 for students. Children younger than five are free.

King-Tisdell Cottage
514 E. Huntingdon Street
Savannah, GA
(912) 234–8000

Built in 1869 by W. W. Aimar, this cottage, with its original gingerbread ornamentation, is in the Beach Institute neighborhood of the Historic Downtown and serves as a museum dedicated to preserving the African American history of Savannah and the sea islands. Inside the small home you will find art objects, documents, and furniture of the 1890s. It is open by appointment only; cost is $3.

Savannah History Museum
Savannah Visitors Center
303 Martin Luther King Jr. Boulevard
Savannah, GA
(912) 238–1779

Delve into Savannah's colorful past at the Savannah History Museum, located in the old passenger station of the Central of Georgia Railroad that also houses the Savannah Visitors Center. The structure, a National Historic Landmark, features a variety of exhibits, including an 1890 steam locomotive that is still sitting on the original Central of Georgia tracks. A genuine antique cotton gin is on display, along with artifacts from the Civil War and other eras. A small theater shows a film that provides an overview of the city's history. The museum is open from 9 A.M. to 5 P.M. seven days a week. It costs $3 for adults and teens, $1.75 for children 6 to 12. Kids younger than six are free.

Ships of the Sea Museum
41 Martin Luther King Jr. Boulevard
Savannah, GA
(912) 232–1511

Scarbrough House and its related garden (a true undiscovered treasure) have added a lot of tone to this museum, previously

Insiders' Tip

Want to see all of Savannah's museums for free? Plan your trip to Savannah around Super Museum Sunday. Every year the museums open up their doors free of charge to anyone who wants to stop by. You even get free transportation provided by the county's bus system. Not a bad deal. (See our Annual Events and Festivals chapter for more information.)

housed on River Street. The exhibits are more formal now, showcasing paintings and intricate models. The collection also includes scrimshaw, ancient navigational tools, and a china cat figurine with its own risque story to tell. Learn about Savannah's maritime history while exploring this museum. The home, built in 1819 for the principal owner of the *Savannah,* the first steamship to cross the Atlantic Ocean, was designated a National Historic Landmark in 1974. Cost is $5 for adults, $4 for children seven and older (if you have a college ID you can get the discounted rate). Children younger than seven get in free. The museum is open from 10 A.M. to 5 P.M. Tuesday through Sunday. It is closed Mondays.

Telfair Mansion and Art Museum
121 Barnard Street
Savannah, GA
(912) 232–1177

The Telfair is the oldest art museum in the South. Its permanent collection of paintings, prints, sculpture, and decorative arts is housed in a mansion designed by English architect William Jay for Alexander Telfair, son of Georgia governor Edward Telfair. The family lived here until 1875.

Among the museum's holdings are paintings by Childe Hassam, Frederick Frieseke, and Gari Melchers, along with Robert Henri, George Bellows, and George Luks. The museum also has a decorative arts collection that includes American and European objects from 1790 to 1840, including a rare Philadelphia suite of maple furniture, a secretary-bookcase commissioned from Duncan Phyfe of New York, and a dining table ordered from Thomas Cook of Philadelphia.

The Telfair is open from 10 A.M. to 5 P.M. Tuesday through Saturday, 2 to 5 P.M. on Sunday, and noon to 5 P.M. Monday. Cost is $8 for adults, $7 for seniors, $2 for students twelve and older, and $1 for children six to twelve. Children younger than six are admitted free. Chatham County residents are admitted free on Sunday, but the regular rates apply to all others.

Islands

Oatland Island Education Center
711 Sandtown Road
Oatland Island, GA
(912) 898–3980
www.oatlandisland.org

A visit to Oatland gives you a good idea of what Georgia's first European settlers might have seen when they landed in 1733. Walk the 1.75-mile trail through the center's seventy-five-acre forest of oaks, pines, and magnolias, and you'll encounter enclosures providing natural settings for animals native to the state: shorebirds, alligators, panthers, birds of prey, white-tailed deer, black bears, timber wolves, and bison. The enclosures are large and wooded and the inhabitants are often hard to spot, but getting a look at them in their environment is worth the effort. The trail leads you to the Heritage Homesite area, where two log cabins (built in 1835, moved to Oatland and restored there) convey a feeling for life on the farm during pioneer days. Another Oatland feature is a barnyard where youngsters can see and feed farm animals.

Oatland, once cleared farmland where cotton was grown in the eighteenth and nineteenth centuries, was the site of a retirement home built in 1927 for railroad conductors. The home was in the center's main building, which later was used by the federal government as a test lab for the Centers for Disease Control until it was declared surplus in 1973. The Savannah-Chatham County School System (see our Education and Child Care chapter) took possession of the site for use as an environmental education center, and the main building now houses classrooms, offices, and a conference center. Although Oatland's main focus is on teaching students from local and out-of-county public and private schools, it is open to the public from 8:30 A.M. to 5 P.M. Monday through Friday and 10 A.M. to 5 P.M. on Saturdays, except those following national holidays.

Temple Mickve Israel is the only Gothic synagogue in the country. PHOTO: KYLE CASON

On the second Saturday of several months, Oatland hosts special events such as its annual cane grinding and crafts festival, sheepshearing and crafts festival, and cultural history celebration (see our Annual Events and Festivals chapter). Admission to Oatland is $2 for persons four years old and older and free to those three and younger. Sandtown Road runs south off Islands Expressway 4 miles east of Historic Downtown. The tour of the center's animal habitats is self-guided and takes about ninety minutes.

The center was closed for about a year starting in November 1998 when traces of the banned pesticide DDT, a remnant from Oatland's days as the site of a government test lab, were found on the grounds. During 2000, the public was restricted from taking self-guided tours of the forest, and no festivals were held. In the interim, a DDT cleanup was accomplished, and a grand reopening of the center was held in March 2001.

Old Fort Jackson
1 Fort Jackson Road
Savannah, GA
(912) 232-3945
www.chsgeorgia.org

Georgia's oldest standing brick fortification is an intriguing place. The fort perches right on the banks of the Savannah River—built there so its guns could fire on any vessel coming into Savannah—and chances are good you'll get an up-close view of an oceangoing ship during your visit.

Walk on the parapet of the fort and then investigate the structure's many nooks and crannies. Two powder magazines and most of the casemates are open to the public, and they contain displays of weaponry and tools used at the fort and artifacts from the CSS *Georgia,* a Confederate ironclad whose remains lay on the river bottom a few hundred feet away. Inspect nine cannon, six of which are authentic, and three of which are reproductions. The nine-inch Dahlgren cannon is the largest functional piece of Civil War–era heavy artillery in the United States. Cannon-firing programs are presented during the summer; call for more information.

Construction of Fort Jackson was begun in 1808 on the site of what had been an earthwork battery during the Revolutionary War. It was manned during the War of 1812 and expanded between 1845 and 1860. Confederate forces used it as headquarters of the Savannah River defenses during most of the Civil War, and it was garrisoned by Union troops after the city's surrender in December 1864. The only time it was fired upon was on October 1, 1862, when two Union steamers shelled it for about an hour during a reconnaissance mission. For a thorough rundown on the history of the fort, watch the fifteen-minute film that's shown in one of the powder magazines.

The fort is not on an island, but we've placed it in this section because it's a couple of miles from the Historic Downtown on the way to the eastside islands. To get there, take President Street Extension (also known as Islands Expressway) east to the red, white, and blue Fort Jackson sign; then turn left onto Woodcock Road and follow the brown signs to the fort. The nonprofit Coastal Heritage Society operates the fort under a lease with the state of Georgia. Admission is $3.50 for adults and $2.50 for students, senior citizens, and members of the military. There's no charge for children five and younger. The fort is open from 9 A.M. to 5 P.M. seven days a week, but it is closed on Thanksgiving, Christmas, and New Year's Day. There are a variety of special programs available for groups and gatherings for a variety of fees; these include some after-hours events that the society will cater. The fort is also the site of special events including the Scottish Games and Highland Gathering in May and the Coastal Heritage Society's auction and crab boil on Labor Day weekend (see our Annual Events and Festivals chapter).

Wormsloe Historic Site
7601 Skidaway Road
Isle of Hope, GA
(912) 353-3023

You'll find the last architectural remnant of the Oglethorpe era in Savannah at Wormsloe Historic Site, which is at the end of Skidaway Road on the doorstep of the Isle of Hope, about 10 miles south of the Historic Downtown. After driving under a large masonry arch at the entrance to Wormsloe, you'll travel down an "avenue of oaks," a wide, crushed-stone road lined with majestic live-oak trees. After 1.25 miles, the road narrows to a walking trail. At this point, you'll find a parking lot and the Wormsloe museum.

Continue on foot down the trail about a quarter mile, and you'll be looking at the remains of a fortified house where construction was started in 1739 during the ten-year span James Edward Oglethorpe spent founding and nurturing the colony of Georgia (see our History chapter). The builder and owner of the house—a physician, carpenter, and surveyor named Noble Jones—came to the new colony in

The entryway to Wormsloe Historic Site, where visitors can view the remains of a house dating to 1739.
PHOTO: WORMSLOE HISTORIC SITE

1733 with Oglethorpe and the first boat-load of settlers. Three years later, Jones leased 500 acres from the Trustees of Georgia, land that would be part of a plantation he called Wormslow. The name was changed to Wormsloe in the mid-1800s by his great-grandson, and the plantation eventually grew to cover nearly 900 acres. Jones's descendants donated 822 of those acres to the Nature Conservancy in 1972, and the property was transferred to the state of Georgia, which manages the site via the Parks and Historic Sites Division of the Department of Natural Resources.

The house Jones completed in the mid-1740s was a five-room, one-and-one-half-story dwelling built into a fortlike, rectangular wall intended to protect its inhabitants from attack by the Spanish. The house and wall were made of tabby, a concoction of oyster shells, lime, and sand mixed with water. You can see parts of the foundation of the house and large portions of the wall. Other points of interest at Wormsloe are the museum and theater,

where you can learn more about the site and the early days of the colony; a stone monument marking the first Jones family burial plot; nature trails; and the Colonial Life Area, which contains re-creations of outbuildings characteristic of Wormsloe's early period. This area is also the site of living history demonstrations and programs presented during special events (see our Annual Events and Festivals chapter).

During your drive down the avenue of oaks, you may notice an elegant, two-story frame house on the eastern side of the road. This structure was built in 1828 and is home to the ninth generation of Jones's descendants; it is closed to the public. Wormsloe is open from 9 A.M. to 5 P.M. Tuesday through Saturday and from 2 to 5:30 P.M. on Sunday. It's closed on Mondays that are not legal holidays, Thanksgiving, Christmas, and New Year's Day. Admission is $2.50 for adults, $2 for senior citizens, and $1.50 for those 6 to 18 years old; children younger than six are admitted free.

After you visit Wormsloe, take a few minutes to drive through nearby Isle of Hope, a community of narrow streets and beautifully preserved houses. Turn right after leaving Wormsloe, and you'll be on Parkersburg Road, which meanders through Isle of Hope until it reaches Bluff Drive, one of the prettiest streets in the Savannah area. A jaunt down Bluff Drive, which runs alongside the picturesque Ski-daway River, is worth the time it will take to make this short detour. (For more on Isle of Hope, see our Neighborhoods and Real Estate chapter.)

Southside/Midtown

Bethesda Home for Boys
9520 Ferguson Avenue
Savannah, GA
(912) 351–2040
www.bethesdahomeforboys.org

Bethesda, America's oldest children's home, reposes on 600 oak-filled acres overlooking the Moon River (yes, that Moon River, the one made famous in the song by Henry Mancini and Savannahian Johnny Mercer). You can stroll or ride around the well-kept grounds of the main campus and visit the Bethesda museum and chapel, but the home's administrators ask that you report to the office after you arrive so that they know you're there. The museum—located in what was once the dining room of Burroughs Cottage, which was built in 1883 and is the oldest standing building at Bethesda—contains documents and artifacts pertaining to the history of the home and of coastal Georgia. Whitefield Chapel was completed in 1925 and is named for George Whitefield, one of the home's founders. It's a reproduction of Whitefield's church in England, and with its straight-back wooden pews, brick floor, and airy interior, the chapel is a spartan but beautiful place in which to spend a few moments in meditation. The chapel is open year-round; museum hours are from 9 A.M. to 5 P.M. Monday through Friday, and there's no admission, but donations are accepted.

Whitefield and his friend James Haber-sham started Bethesda in 1740 as a home for the orphaned boys of the fledgling colony of Georgia. The home has served more than 9,000 children and nowadays offers a residency program for fifty boys who are housed in five cottages staffed by house parents. These days, few of the boys at Bethesda are orphans; most come from broken homes or from at-risk situations. They attend school at Bethesda through eighth grade and go to high school at public or private schools in Chatham County. Through the years, according to Assistant Director Bill McIlrath, the mission of Bethesda has remained the same: "To teach the boys a good work ethic, to give them a good education, and to raise them in the nurture and admonition of the Lord."

Chatham County Garden Center and Botanical Gardens
1388 Eisenhower Drive
Savannah, GA
(912) 355–3883

See more than 900 varieties of trees, shrubs, and flowering plants when you visit this Savannah Area Council of Garden Clubs project on the Southside. The clubs maintain ten acres of gardens featuring roses, perennials, herbs, and vegetables and separate gardens devoted to flowering plants that bloom during the different seasons of the year. There's also a garden for plants such as ferns that grow best in spots that don't get much sunshine. Most of the plants are labeled, so neophyte gardeners will be able to tell what they're looking at. A tabby walkway meanders through the gardens, and a small pond and a nature walk add to the ambience of this spot, which is nestled in a fairly well-developed part of town. The garden center is headquartered in an 1840s-era farmhouse that was moved to the Southside from a downtown location in 1991. The Council presents lectures and courses on horticulture at the two-story house, which boasts features such as two fireplaces, heart-of-pine floors, and clam molding on the doors that's more than 150 years old. The center and gardens are on Eisenhower Drive at its intersection with Sallie Mood Drive; hours are from 10 A.M. to 2 P.M. Monday through Friday, and admission is $2 for the gardens and $3 for the house and gardens.

West Chatham

Bamboo Farm and Coastal Gardens
2 Canebrake Road
Savannah, GA
(912) 921–5460

If you like digging in the dirt and growing things, you should love this spot in southwest Chatham County that was once an experimental station where the federal government introduced plants from throughout the world.

Called the Bamboo Farm through the years by Savannahians because of the groves of the tropical plant grown there, the facility has a large collection of daylilies, a Xeriscape garden, a cottage garden, and bamboo, of course—more than 200 varieties of it. The bamboo collection is the largest in the United States open for viewing by the public, and there's also a grove of giant timber bamboo—the reason the farm was purchased for the U.S. Department of Agriculture in 1918. The bamboo grove, where stalks can reach a height of more than seventy feet and a diameter of six inches, originated with three seedlings planted on the site in 1890; twenty-five years later, it attracted the attention of plant explorer David Fairchild, who bought the forty-six-acre farm where the bamboo grew and donated it to the government.

The plant introduction station was closed in 1978, and the property was deeded four years later to the University of Georgia, whose Cooperative Extension Service operates it today as a center for research and education. The farm offers a self-guided walking tour that will take you to (among other botanical treasures) the bamboo collection and grove, beds of ornamental and turf grasses, a collection of crape myrtle trees that's probably the largest in coastal Georgia, and a variety of other interesting trees, including one whose fruit resembles popcorn.

The Bamboo Farm and Coastal Gardens holds a number of special events throughout the year, most of which require reservations, and makes available a 500-seat, open-air pavilion and a 100-seat conference hall. The farm is open from 8 A.M. to 5 P.M. Monday through Friday and from 8 A.M. to 3 P.M. on Saturday; it's closed on Sunday, Thanksgiving, Christmas, New Year's Day, the Fourth of July, and Labor Day. Admission is free, and donations are accepted. The facility is on U.S. Highway 17, about 13 miles south of the Historic Downtown.

Mighty Eighth Air Force
Heritage Museum
175 Bourne Avenue
Pooler, GA
(912) 748–8888
www.mighty8thmuseum.com

It's not unusual for veterans of World War II aerial combat to leave this museum's Mission Experience exhibit with tears in their eyes. This re-creation of an Eighth Air Force bombing mission brings back vivid memories to those who flew over Europe—recollections of heavily defended targets, stricken aircraft, and fallen comrades. The panoramic, eight-screen theater and its B-17 flight are a featured part of the 90,000-square-foot museum in Pooler near the intersection of Interstate 95 and U.S. Highway 80 (exit 102 from I–95). In addition to the Mission Experience and other displays, the museum has a research library stocked with books pertaining to aviation and air warfare, an art gallery, Memorial Gardens, store, and restaurant.

The museum opened in May 1996. It honors the more than one million men and women who have served in the Eighth since its creation in Savannah on January 28, 1942, at the Chatham Artillery Armory on Bull Street at Park Avenue. A small command force worked there for a few

The Mighty Eighth Air Force Heritage Museum commemorates the exploits of World War II heroes.
PHOTO: KYLE CASON

months before moving to England, where the organization manned bases from August 1942 until May 1945 and grew to have more than 350,000 members during World War II. The Eighth flew more than 600,000 sorties against Nazi Germany and dropped more than 700,000 tons of bombs on enemy targets. Today, the building where the Eighth was born is the home of American Legion Post 135.

Besides the Mission Experience, the museum's exhibit area contains presentations featuring more than fifteen units that were part of the Eighth; a scale model depicting a World War II bomber base in England; areas dealing with escape and evasion, prisoners of war, and the contributions of African American airmen; a diorama portraying the raids on the Ploesti oil fields; a PT-17 Stearman trainer, and a Messerschmitt Komet rocket plane on static display; and several other theaters. The newest major additions to the complex are an F-4 Phantom jet fighter and a B-47 Stratojet bomber on display outdoors. The six-engine B-47 was a mainstay of the U.S. Air Force's Strategic Air Com-

mand during the early stages of the Cold War, and was a sight familiar to Savannahians in the 1950s, when Hunter Air Force Base (now Hunter Army Airfield) was the home of a B-47 wing. The museum is open from 9 A.M. until 5 P.M. daily except for New Year's Day, Easter, Thanksgiving, and Christmas. Admission to the exhibit area is $7.50 for adults and teens and $5.50 for children 6 to 12, with those younger than six admitted free; tickets are not sold after 5:30 P.M. There are discounts for members of the military, senior citizens, and groups of twenty or more. There is no charge to visit the library and Memorial Gardens. The library is open from 10 A.M. to 5 P.M. Monday through Saturday and from noon to 5 P.M. on Sunday.

Savannah-Ogeechee Canal Museum and Nature Center
681 Fort Argyle Road
Savannah, GA
(912) 748–8068
www.co.chatham.ga.us

The Savannah-Ogeechee Canal, which played a role in the commercial development of Savannah during the 1800s, lay virtually forgotten for a century until a group of Chatham Countians reclaimed a third of it from the tangle of foliage that had grown over it. These volunteers started their work in 1992 and now, organized as the Savannah-Ogeechee Canal Society, oversee the continued development of the waterway as a historic and recreational area.

The 16.5-mile canal, which once was fifty-eight feet wide at water level, was completed in 1830 and links the Savannah and Ogeechee Rivers. It accommodated horse- and mule-drawn barges as much as seventy feet long, and also boats poled by their occupants. These barges and boats carried lumber, cotton, rice, naval stores, and other goods. Six 18-foot-wide locks, some originally made of wood and later replaced with brick, controlled the hydraulics of the canal, which faded from usage in the early 1890s because of the destructive effects of a hurricane, and because it could not compete with the region's railroads and road system.

You can get a splendid idea of what the southern portion of the canal was like by visiting the society's museum and 184-acre nature center, which is on Fort Argyle Road (better known as Georgia Highway 204), a little more than 2 miles west of exit 94 of Interstate 95. The museum, a converted bungalow, has two exhibit rooms, one depicting the history of the canal and another displaying reptiles and amphibians that inhabit the area the waterway runs through.

Within view of the museum is Lock 5, which is on a trail you can follow for 0.4 mile along the canal south to Lock 6 and the Ogeechee River; this trail is the towpath that horses and mules trod while pulling barges more than one hundred years ago. The Tow Path is one of several trails you can walk while at the nature center (see our Parks and Recreation chapter for more details). The museum and nature center are open from 9 A.M. to 5 P.M. each day of the year. Admission is $2 for adults and $1 for students; children five and younger are admitted free.

Savannah: Hollywood of the South

Lights! Camera! Action!

We've got all three, and then some. Savannah's place in history is well assured, and with Pulitzer Prize-winning poet Conrad Aiken and the famous lyricist Johnny Mercer, the city can stake out a solid claim to high culture.

But what about the more transitory forms of fame? What about best-sellers and box-office draws? What about celebrity citizenry? What about catchphrases and similar claims to fleeting fame?

Oh, yes, Savannah can do all that.

It didn't all start with John Berendt's best-selling book, *Midnight in the Garden of Good and Evil*. Hollywood was a factor before Berendt made the city's naughtier foibles into entertainment fodder for others. Savannah has been a movie set ever since Hollywood first stepped outside its own city limits, and things have accelerated in recent years.

Savannah has hosted at least forty film or television projects since 1975, and it formalized the whole process by establishing a film liaison office at City Hall in 1995.

Some of those productions have been among the most critically acclaimed movies of our day. Some have starred the biggest names on the Silver Screen. Some have launched catchphrases into the lexicon of popular culture ("Life is like a box of chocolates..."). And some of them... well, some of them were *Return of Swamp Thing* and the like.

Examples of the outstanding include *Glory*, the historically based account of African American soldiers in the Civil War that won three Oscars; *Forrest Gump*, which claimed six Oscars and solidified Tom Hanks's superstar status; and *Roots*, filmed here in part, which became the standard against which all miniseries are still measured. Going back even further, to 1962, when location shoots were rarer, the original *Cape Fear* was filmed here in part. City Hall and the downtown business district were on display. This original movie, since remade, featured Robert Mitchum at his creepiest.

If you want to experience some of Savannah's movie past in person, there's some interesting spots. Go to Chippewa Square, for example, where Bull Street flows around a statue of General Oglethorpe. Here is the filming site of the waiting-for-the-bus scene that was so crucial in *Forrest Gump*. Don't waste time looking for the bench—although Savannah's squares have plenty of real benches, that one was a movie prop. It was situated on the square's northern face, looking down Bull Street. Back in the movie's heyday, you could spot the occasional fan positioned there, hovering with his or her backside perched on empty

Insiders' Tip

The late John Rousakis, longtime mayor of Savannah and the man credited with much of the renaissance of the city's Historic District, has a cameo appearance in *Gator*, filmed in 1975.

This popular pub's sign had to be shelved (temporarily) during filming of The Legend of Bagger Vance, *which is set during the Depression and before Churchill's political career.* PHOTO: BETTY DARBY

air, "sitting" on the nonexistent bench for a Kodak moment.

The Legend of Bagger Vance had all the right ingredients for a megahit: star director (Robert Redford), star stars (Will Smith, Matt Damon, etc.), and lovely sets and costumes from its Depression-era setting. As is so often the way with Hollywood, the film was only a moderate success. Still, if you are a fan, you can recapture a touch of the film. Most of the period storefronts are gone with the movie, but in the most northern two blocks of Drayton Street, where it empties out into Bay Street, you can find some vestiges. That pub sign over Churchill's, complete with Winston's famous face had to be mothballed while the period piece was filmed. And the Realty Building, that ten-story office building at Bryan and Drayton Streets, shows signs of movie sprucing-up—the awnings were installed by the movie crew (a major improvement) and the pair of golf-lettered signs reading CAFETERIA on the first floor window are also left over from the movie. Look inside the finance company that is the current ground-floor tenant, and you'll see the massive painting that covers the rear wall and was left by the movie crew. Funny thing, however, we've diligently looked at the movie several times and we've never seen any of the scenes filmed there.

Some of Savannah's film legacy moves around. In the summer of 2001, the town was agog that movie star Sandra Bullock had bought a mansion at Tybee Island. There's a regular rumor circuit that runs from some of the high-dollar real estate offices on which celebrity will next join local ranks.

Although Savannah's *Midnight* phenomenon is not as all-consuming as it once was, it is still a viable tourism force. You would probably have to look long and hard to find a parallel for the financial windfall this book brought this city. Berendt says his next book will be set in Venice—are gondola tours of scandal sites in that city's future?

With *Midnight*'s curiously appealing set of character sketches loosely held together by a lurid murder trial, the New York author created a phenomenon in the tourist world. His work gave rise to a plethora of themed guided tours and silly souvenirs, and over the course of its first six years *Midnight in the Garden of Good and Evil*—known locally as The Book—created enough of a furor to drive a statue out of a graveyard and make a drag queen into a local celeb.

The Book deals with homosexuality, murder, voodoo, weird social customs, and charismatic con men—not necessarily the most flattering portrayal imaginable. However, it was eagerly embraced by the local populace as well as the reading public.

Perhaps, the locals just want that promised fifteen minutes of fame, which *Midnight in the Garden of Good and Evil* certainly gives to Savannah and its residents. It seems that normally reticent people are willing to put up with the public airing of any amount of dirty laundry as long as it brings Clint Eastwood to town to film a movie about it.

The real answer, however, probably lies deep within a cash register. The city has discovered that the coattails of a best-seller with a fan following are a comfortable and profitable place to ride.

There's still plenty of opportunities for Book fans to sample in person what they've experienced in print. One sure sign that the phenomenon is well past its peak, however, is this—the prices on the guided tours have not gone up. The whole phenomenon might have had longer legs if the movie version had been more successful.

For the duration, we'll follow local practice and continue to call Berendt's best-seller The Book—shorthand we have all adopted in self-defense, since an eight-word title takes a while to say in a Southern drawl, and locals have trouble pronouncing Berendt's name.

CLOSE-UP

Savannah Filmography: 1975–2000

Note that accompanying dates are filming dates, not necessarily release dates.

2000: *The Gift*

1999: *The Legend of Bagger Vance*

1998: *Forces of Nature, The General's Daughter*

1997: *The Gingerbread Man, Midnight in the Garden of Good and Evil, Claudine's Return*

1996: *Wild America*

1995: *Something to Talk About*

1994: *Now and Then*

1993: *Forrest Gump, Camilla*

1990: *Goldenboy, Love Crimes*

1989: *The Rose and the Jackal, Flight of the Intruder, Glory*

1988: *The Return of Swamp Thing, The Judas Project*

1987: *My Father, My Son, 1969, War Stories*

1986: *Pals*

1983: *Solomon Northup's Odyssey*

1981: *All My Children, Tales of Ordinary Madness*

1980: *The Slayer, White Death, Scared to Death, When the Circus Came to Town, Fea, East of Eden, Mother Seton*

1979: *Gold Bug, The Ordeal of Dr. Mudd, Orphan Train, Hopscotch, Carny*

1978: *The Double McGuffin*

1977: *The Lincoln Conspiracy*

1976: *Roots*

1975: *Gator*

This side of Chippewa Square is where the movie-prop bench for Forrest Gump *sat.* PHOTO: COURTESY OF SAVANNAH AREA CONVENTION AND VISITORS BUREAU

A Little Background

Midnight in the Garden of Good and Evil was published in January 1994. Berendt, a columnist and former editor at *Esquire,* had spent several years living off and on in Savannah, collecting the stories that make up the book. The unifying thread of the book is the four murder trials that followed the fatal shooting of a young man by self-made millionaire antiques dealer Jim Williams. Mingled in are the stories of a flamboyant drag queen, a tax lawyer who excels as a bad-check artist and a piano player, white socialites who play cards and black debutantes who dance the minuet, an oddball genius with a penchant for poisons, and so on.

Random House quickly had a hit on its hands. The Book hit the *New York Times* best-seller list in March 1994 and pretty much stayed there for the ensuing four years.

Ah, but is The Book as true as it claims? That brings to mind what the character Huck Finn had to say about the Tom Sawyer story, that it was "mostly true

but with some stretchers." The timelines, for example, are a little out of sync, and the slant of the stories can still spark debate among locals. Several of the names of central figures are pseudonyms, and that told-as-true tale about the dead cat, the dinner party, and the stomach pump is a classic urban legend—consider it modern folklore.

With book sales so brisk and a larger-than-life cast of characters on the page, it was inevitable that Hollywood would go Gardening. In May 1996, director Clint Eastwood began filming the screen version with Kevin Spacey in the Williams role, John Cusack as Berendt, and the Lady Chablis (the aforementioned drag queen) as the Lady Chablis. The story got a revision for the screen, and the city got an out-of-season facelift, as the squares involved in the shooting were decked out in Christmas greenery in a month that already qualifies as full summer in Savannah.

So now fans of The Book have had a refresher course, and those who haven't read it at least have an idea of what we are talking about. Let's move on to how visitors

Bonaventure Cemetery: Good Fortune for Lovers of The Book

"Bonaventure" means "good fortune," which may strike you as a strange name for a graveyard. But once you visit this serenely beautiful place, chances are the name will seem more appropriate. Bonaventure Cemetery plays a prominent role in John Berendt's *Midnight in the Garden of Good and Evil*. It is here in this lush Victorian graveyard that the book's narrator drinks martinis and gets his introductory course on Savannah society. The massive cemetery stands under the moss-draped shade of towering live oaks, is peopled by row upon row of elegant statuary and headstones, and commands a waterfront view that would make a condo developer drool.

The graves made famous in the book include the Aiken family plot. Here, the parents of Pulitzer Prize–winning poet Conrad Aiken—killed in a murder-suicide—are buried. Conrad Aiken's own grave, marked by a bench engraved with poetry, stands alongside. Not too far away, you'll spot the graves of famed Savannah lyricist Johnny Mercer and wife, Ginger.

This is the culminating point for the guided tours of Book sites. If you happen to be a nonfan of The Book, and you were swept along by a fervent spouse or group, hang in there. The 160-acre graveyard was well worth seeing in its own right well before *Midnight* was published, and it will be well worth seeing when all the hubbub dies down (assuming, of course, that it ever will). Fame carries with it drawbacks, for places as well as people. On our last visit to Bonaventure, we encountered an unseemly traffic jam of competing tour bus groups, with some guides quietly leading their charges to alternate sites until the crowd cleared; another guide brashly interrupted a national gourmet magazine's efforts to photograph two models posing with martinis on Aiken's grave-marker bench.

The tour companies have been cooperative in efforts to minimize impact on the cemetery, according to Terry Shaw, who heads up the Bonaventure Historical Society, which was founded in 1994. One result is that the largest tour buses aren't allowed within the gates—instead, only Book tours using smaller minibuses can enter. In fact, the cemetery is even cashing in on The Book to some extent. Berendt named Bonaventure as one of three local nonprofits to receive his share of royalties from the sale of Byrd's cookies in the commemorative Book tin. The cash will come in handy for cemetery preservation and research efforts, Shaw said.

Bonaventure was once an elegant plantation, but the grand home burned down more than once. Local folklore has it that the roof caught fire during a dinner party, and the guests finished the meal outdoors by the light of the burning house. If you are looking for ghost stories, there's a tale that you can still hear the revelry and breaking glass of that party at certain times. You'll find these tales repeated in The Book. The property became a cemetery in the 1800s and was put into city hands in 1907. It is still an active cemetery with an occasional burial, but the few remaining spaces are taken—don't get attached to the place.

Many important figures from the history of Georgia and the nation are buried here. There's Noble Jones, who arrived with James Oglethorpe at the beginning of the colony; several members of Georgia's Liberty Boys; and a number of prominent physicians, including Brodie Herndon, chief surgeon of hospitals for the Confederacy and the first doctor to perform a Caesarean operation in the United States. John Walz, sculptor of many of the impressive funerary statues in Bonaventure and other local cemeteries, is buried here. Ironically, there is no headstone at his grave.

You can get these and other interesting details in a brochure put out by the Historical Society and available at the front office just inside the cemetery gates. Shaw can provide more information about the Bonaventure Historical Society. Write to him at 1317 E. 55th Street, Savannah, GA 31404. If you are interested in joining the society, the $15 annual membership fee includes a subscription to a monthly newsletter with stories on Bonaventure's significant residents. Shaw said the group has more than one hundred members, including thirty who live out of state. The membership even includes folks from Canada and Hungary.

Little Gracie *marks the grave of a young girl in Bonaventure Cemetery.* PHOTO: KYLE CASON

If you want to visit Bonaventure Cemetery without a tour, here are some fairly detailed instructions. How you get there depends, of course, on where you start. Because we reasoned most visitors would be starting from the Historic Downtown, we launch our trek at the intersection of Bull and Liberty Streets, right beside the Hilton Savannah DeSoto Hotel. Set your trip odometer there; you have about 3.5 miles to go. Liberty Street is a major east-west thoroughfare downtown. Follow it east. You'll quickly leave the Historic District and pass through areas that include low-income housing and small industry. Don't be distracted by the large cemetery to your left shortly after you leave downtown—that's Hillcrest. The road forks just beyond that, so bear right. It will be fairly obvious in doing so that you are staying on the same road. The road assumes different names as you travel—from Liberty to Wheaton to Skidaway.

Immediately past a complex five-way intersection, you'll see the only real turn you'll make, a left onto 36th Street. It's identified by a street sign hanging between double traffic lights, and there's a turn arrow to help you make the turn in the increasingly heavy traffic you'll encounter. A McDonald's stands on the right just past this intersection; if you go past it, you've gone too far. Just after you get on it, 36th Street merges into Bonaventure Road so seamlessly you probably won't even notice. Bonaventure Road is a narrow, two-lane road that winds through neat, modest housing and is lined by massive trees that are literally on the edge of the road. Pay attention!

In just under a mile, where the road curves away to the right, you'll see the cemetery gates. Don't be distracted if a Forest Lawn Cemetery billboard is still in place in the vicinity. The sign on the gate identifies Bonaventure. There's a large, framed map just inside the entrance, but it gives locations by grave site number, not name. Instead, depend on the small wooden signposts stationed along the lanes between the plots. Book fans are looking for the sign marked AIKEN and the nearby MERCER. The wooden marker signs are easy to follow.

Park with care, as there is a lot of tour bus traffic. There's a small lot behind the office building just inside the gates if you are the hiking kind; there's also a grassy parking area for a few cars that's near the water and not far from the Aiken plot. Although we haven't heard of any trouble, it's an isolated spot between tours, so it's probably a good idea to lock your car and bring a friend.

Meanwhile, let's clear up some misconceptions in parting. Jim Williams, The Book's central figure, isn't buried at Bonaventure—or anywhere else in Savannah, for that matter. Instead, he was put to rest in his hometown of Gordon, Georgia. And Bonaventure is not the graveyard from which the Minerva character dug up the dirt for her voodoo spells, so leave the soil where you found it. It's history, not dirt.

to Savannah can walk inside Berendt's pages.

Tours

If you want to cover a lot of Book territory relatively quickly, the tour buses are your best bet. We're describing them in plural here because they offer essentially the same thing: a two- to two-and-one-half-hour tour that is mainly a drive-by of important sites from The Book, capped off with a cemetery visit. Be aware that tours have a tendency to run longer than advertised, so allow plenty of time. All tours require reservations, which can be made by phone. If this is an important event for you, call well in advance—tours are often full or nearly full. The various tour companies take the major credit cards, but because tour drivers usually don't handle anything other than cash transactions, ask where you'll pay if you plan to use a credit card—it might affect which of the pickup locations you specify.

Tours pick up at the Savannah Visitors Center, 301 Martin Luther King Jr. Boulevard, which has reasonably ample parking. Stash your car and look for the large parking slots near the center's front door, marked with signs identifying the tour

company that uses that spot—that's where you'll board. Major downtown hotels and some bed-and-breakfasts in the Historic Downtown also serve as pickup locations. Get details when you make your reservations.

Remember that Book-related tours are just part of a wider tour menu offered by each company. Others include ghost tours, walking tours, Civil War–themed tours, carriage tours, Savannah history tours, and the like. (See our Attractions chapter for more on other types of guided tours.) The city of Savannah requires that tour guides pass a test and hold a license. On a typical tour, you'll drive by Mercer House, the mansion that was the site of The Book's fatal shooting; Club One, performance venue for the Lady Chablis (see our Nightlife chapter for details); various homes where lawyer and professional partier Joe Odom stayed, often without the owners' knowledge; the jail where Williams was incarcerated (now replaced by a structure outside town); the modern county courthouse where the first three trials were held; the ornate old federal courthouse that stands in for it in the movie version; and so on. The walking versions can't range far enough to include Bonaventure Cemetery, so choose another walking tour and opt for wheels if you are a Book fan—it just isn't the same without the graveyard.

Along the way, you'll get a chance to see the city's more conventional attractions as well, and chances are the tour guide will throw in a few comments about those. The highlight of all the tours is a visit to Bonaventure Cemetery, which you can read about elsewhere in this chapter. But while you are welcome to visit the dead, don't expect to get inside any of the homes of the living. The tours don't go inside the buildings involved in The Book, most of which are private homes. Mercer House, especially, is private territory: Don't expect to see its fabled luxurious interior except in the movie scenes that were filmed there.

Gray Line Red Trolley Tours
215 W. Boundary Street
Savannah, GA
(912) 234-8687
This long tour includes a visit to Bonaventure and tends to spill over its advertised two-hour length. Tickets are $15, and transportation is via minibus.

Hospitality Tours of Savannah
2610 Jefferson Street
Savannah, GA
(912) 233-0119
This two-and-a-half-hour tour bills itself as the first of the bunch. Parts of this tour were featured in the "Midnight in Savannah" two-hour special that ran on the Arts & Entertainment cable channel in late 1997. Tickets are $16.

Tootsy Tours
12 W. State Street
Savannah, GA
(912) 232-0032, (888) 736-3828
The long menu of tours at this walking-tour company includes two with Book connections. For $15 ($6 for those eleven and younger), you can "Walk Savannah's Midnight." This tour departs Wright Square at 1 P.M. "The Book Pub Crawl" sets out at 7 P.M. for the same sites, plus bars.

Seeing It On Your Own

If you want to see some of The Book sites but don't fancy tours, you can get to many of them on your own. After all, the Historic Downtown itself is a character in the book. The following are some tips on what you can see solo. There's no shortage of maps in Savannah (hardly surprising in a city with a thriving tourism industry), and there's a good one in this very book. With a copy of The Book in hand and the map of the Historic Downtown you'll find at the front of our guide, you can find major Book sites such as Monterey Square.

Easily Accessed Sites

Now that you have a map, we'll list a few of the most easily found sites. We'll start with two general outdoor sites, where you can stand on the sidewalk and gaze, then move on to places you can actually get into.

Monterey Square

400 block of Bull Street, bounded by Taylor and Gordon Streets

This square is home to many of the central events in The Book, but it's worth a good look on its own merits. The massive central monument to Polish Count Casimir Pulaski, a hero of the American Revolution, has finally been returned to its pedestal, after a seemingly endless delay during its restoration. The absence was so long that when the movie of *Midnight* was filming on location, prop makers had to fake a version of the monument.

Mercer House

429 Bull Street

Savannah, GA

The famous house looks out on the square from Bull Street. This is where Williams lived and threw his famous parties, and where he shot his companion to death. It remains a private residence, although it went on the market in June 1999 for more than $8 million (a price safely inflated enough to keep the manse in family hands awhile). Mercer House had claims to fame well before Williams's misfortunes. While lyricist Johnny Mercer ("Moon River," "That Old Black Magic," etc.) never lived there, he had close family ties to it.

Jackie Kennedy Onassis once showed up to tour it, and The Book claims she concluded that tour with a request for directions to the nearest Burger King. (It's a cute story, true or not, and if you believe it and want to follow in the footsteps of the rich and famous, the nearest Burger King is in the 600 block of Martin Luther King Jr. Boulevard.)

Next to Mercer House, across narrow Wayne Street, stands the home of the neighbors Williams feuded with. He gets in some sharp digs on them from beyond the grave, thanks to The Book. Again, this is a private house—no tours. Directly across the square from Mercer House stands the historic Temple Mickve Israel synagogue, whose congregation, along with many other Savannahians, was affronted when Williams hung a Nazi flag from his balcony in an attempt to disrupt filming of a period movie.

Intersection of Bull and Gaston Streets

Remember, The Book maintains nothing counts unless it's North of Gaston Street (NOGS, for short). This is where Bull Street hits that great divide. The sweeping white brick building on the western side of Bull is Armstrong House, which crops up in the book several times, most prominently as the offices of the lawyer who handled Williams's defense. On the eastern side you'll see the Oglethorpe Club, which also turns up in said Book. This is the city's most exclusive private club, with rigid membership requirements that include white skin, blue blood, and money that's yellowed with age.

Clary's Cafe

404 Abercorn Street

Savannah, GA

(912) 233–0402

Clary's was the setting where Berendt first encountered the Luther Driggers character who tried to make goldfish glow and enjoyed toting about a bottle of poison. At the time, Clary's was a drugstore with a lunch counter. The drugstore is long gone, but the restaurant has grown. (Read more about it in our Restaurants chapter.) Clary's has opened a second location farther south in Midtown, but there's no book connection.

Club One Jefferson
1 Jefferson Street
Savannah, GA
(912) 232–0200

The Lady Chablis performs in the drag show here periodically. For more details, check out the Close-Up in our Nightlife chapter.

The Jack Leigh Gallery
132 E. Oglethorpe Avenue
Savannah, GA
(912) 234–6449

The black-and-white work of photographer Jack Leigh is displayed in this gallery, and his range goes well beyond The Book's oddly hypnotic cover shot. You'll see other examples of his published work here. You can buy a *Bird Girl* poster (economy version about $35; embossed and signed specialty print just over $80) or pick up a Windows screen saver ($16) featuring Leigh's work, including the *Bird Girl*.

Telfair Museum of Art
121 Barnard Street
Savannah, GA
(912) 232–1177

> ### Insiders' Tip
>
> Savannah's Paula Deen's cooking skills have made her restaurant, The Lady and Sons, very popular. That success has led to two cookbooks. Even if you aren't a cookbook collector, however, she may be a familiar face—she's a regular guest on the cable shopping network QVC, hawking her books and a line of signature seasonings.

This local art museum is the new home for the *Bird Girl* statue pictured on the cover of The Book. The figure once stood guard over the Trosdal family plot in Bonaventure Cemetery, and neither the statue nor the Trosdals are in the print version of the story. Family members had the statue removed when Book tourists overran the family plot to pose for photos beside it. (By the way, photography is not allowed inside the Telfair, a common enough prohibition by museums.) The Telfair is worth a visit in its own right (see our Arts and Culture chapter). Admission costs are $8 for adults, $7 for seniors, $2 for older children, and $1 for elementary school students.

Souvenirs

The variety of Book souvenirs is impressive. Here's a very partial list: a woven afghan featuring book scenes, bookmarks picturing one of Joe Odom's rubber checks, paintings of Mercer House, a video "tour" with interviews of some of the real-life characters, coffee mugs and jewelry featuring the Bird Girl figure, a limited-edition candle shaped like the cover statue, postcards depicting the Lady Chablis, and miniature cookies in a tin patterned after the book cover. Several T-shirts are on the market.

The ultimate souvenir is, clearly, The Book itself. Of course, you'll find it in local bookstores, but you'll also spot it in local stores that have never sold any other book before. You'll find a huge supply of books that have been autographed by the author. Early in the phenomenon, there was a scandal about fake autographs at one supplier, and Berendt himself came forward to get that stopped. The book lists for $25, $10 in paperback. Some of the downtown souvenir places jack the price for an autographed copy. All the local independent booksellers and chains also carry the book, and we encourage you to keep your copy close at hand. The Lady Chablis holds an autograph session after her nightclub set. You'll never get a complete set of character

Great Savannah Books on the Other Side of Midnight

John Berendt's *Midnight in the Garden of Good and Evil* is not the first book to be set in Savannah, although you might get that impression the way some folks carry on. If you want to read more Savannah-as-a-setting books, we have some suggestions.

Savannah bookstores tend to have their regional sections prominently displayed near the front. There you'll find predictable stuff like cookbooks from area restaurants (some of which are quite good) and coffee-table books displaying beautiful homes. But look closer: The collections usually include plenty of unexpected things as well. Here's a sample, starting with three books that have a *Midnight* connection, then moving on to more general topics.

More Than Mercer House: Savannah's Jim Williams and His Southern Houses, by Dr. Dorothy Kingery (Williams' sister, an academician), reviews Williams role in the preservation of many Savannah and surrounding areas and tells tales of his outstanding antiques-finding adventures. For the most part, it is an attractive coffee-table book, featuring essays penned by Williams and family photos, as well as before-and-after restoration shots. It's a pretty book and a nice display copy, but only a genuine fan would find it absorbing. It does display that Southern touch of neatly omitting awkward topics: There's no reference to the series of shooting trials and jail time that marked the 1980s for Williams. You can buy the book in the author's store or order it by mail or phone (see store listings elsewhere in this chapter).

Hiding My Candy: The Autobiography of the Grand Empress of Savannah, by the Lady Chablis and Theodore Bouloukos ($22 hardback, $14 trade paperback), tells the story of the drag queen Berendt made famous. It includes pictures of the performer.

To Live and Die in Dixie, by Kathy Hogan Trocheck ($4.99 paperback), is an installment in her mystery series about a housekeeper/sleuth. Trocheck was a newspaper reporter in Savannah before moving on to Atlanta, where most of her books are set. This 1993 mystery (published a year before The Book) features a rich antiques dealer implicated in the murder of an employee-house guest. He's known for disrupting movie filming with a Nazi flag and feuding with his Jewish neighbor over gentrification versus rehabilitating housing for the poor. The plot diverges from there, but Book fans will still catch the allusions.

Savannah Lore and More, by Tom Coffey ($24 hardback), is a second compilation of the veteran newsman's pithy essays on Savannah. The first is *Only in Savannah.* Instead of Berendt's social/sexual tales, you'll read about the political side of the city, which can be similarly outrageous. Look for these volumes in local bookstores.

Savannah Spectres and Other Strange Tales, by Margaret DeBolt ($9.95 trade paperback), is a collection of local ghost stories that has become sort of the standard reference work on the topic hereabouts. Williams, of *Midnight* fame, crops up as the restorer of one of the more vigorously haunted structures in this collection.

Hooligans, by William Diehl (paperback), was published in 1984. It never attracted as much attention as Diehl's more successful works such as *Sharkey's*

Mercer House was the home of Jim Williams, a major player in The Book. PHOTO: KYLE CASON

Machine and *Primal Fear,* which became movies. This tale of political corruption is set in a thinly veiled Savannah: "Oceanby" for Tybee, "Isle of Sighs" for Isle of Hope, and so on. Diehl is part of a productive writers' colony on St. Simons Island, about 90 miles south of Savannah as you near the Florida border.

Savannah, by Eugenia Price ($6.99 paperback), is a historical romance distinguished by Price's research and a literary approach that stands far above the genre's norm. If you like what you read, you're in luck: This is the first of a four-volume saga set in Savannah. Price, who died in 1997, was another St. Simons Island author.

Direct Hits and Cheap Shots, by Mark Streeter ($11.95 trade paperback), is a compilation of editorial cartoons by the *Savannah Morning News* cartoonist. The city-specific portion of this compendium will be lost on nonlocals, who won't understand the digs at the foibles of local politicians, but Streeter takes plenty of shots on the national and international fronts. One of our favorites features King of Pop Michael Jackson gripping his newborn son and saying, "He doesn't look a thing like me. . . . But then again, neither do I!" There are even a couple of Book cartoons (there's just no escaping that topic lately).

autographs, however; many of the central characters have died.

An example of the hold The Book still has on local affections was clear when pianist and singer Emma Kelly died after a long illness. She was a well-known figure in Savannah and nearby Statesboro well before The Book came out, but The Book amplified that dramatically. Her funeral was front page news in both cities.

Random House has produced audio versions of The Book, both abridged and unabridged. If you haven't gotten around to reading it, these might be good options for car listening if you are driving into Savannah from some distance. Beware, however: The unabridged version runs more than eleven hours.

Basically, the same items are available at all stores that carry Book souvenirs. We've listed two stores that devote a large percentage of their stock to Book items, but you can find the same stuff in any number of general gift shops along River Street and even in scattered suburban and mall stores. We've also included Dr. Kingery's new store, a small but essential point for die-hard book fans. The only specific recommendation we make on these things concerns the cookies. If you

While this monument to Revolutionary War hero Casimir Pulaski was undergoing renovations, movie crews used a prop to fill in during the filming of Midnight in the Garden of Good and Evil.

PHOTO: BETTY DARBY

want Byrd Cookie's Key Lime Coolers in the Byrd Girl commemorative tin, check out our Shopping chapter. Byrd Cookie operates a gift shop as part of its bakery, and it stands to reason this would be the cheapest place to get the cookies. We've seen them as expensive as $3 per box higher elsewhere. Besides, at Byrd's you can sample the Key Lime Cooler and the other flavors available.

"The Book" Gift Shop
127 E. Gordon Street
Savannah, GA
(912) 233–3867

This shop occupies the garden floor (which is what we in Savannah call the ground floor of a building, topped by the parlor floor, followed by a second floor, which is really the third floor, and so on) of a building at Abercorn and Gordon Streets. Wander through several rooms to see a mix of Book souvenirs and general gifts. Stock includes shot glasses bearing the name of the married women's card club ($5.25), which aptly illustrate the southern idea of tackiness.

You'll find elements of a Book shrine along with the merchandise. The back room boasts some not-for-sale items such as a painting by Williams, a chair he once owned, a large collection of clippings about the phenomenon, and so on. Deborah Sullivan is the owner.

Hospitality Tours and Gifts
135 Bull Street
Savannah, GA
(912) 233–0119

The Book has been very, very good to these people. The tour company operator realized her patrons needed something cold to drink, courtesy of Savannah's climate, and of course a bathroom. She provides both in a shop that also sells souvenirs. It has grown from its original small location to a better corner spot on Wright Square. The shop is open to the general public as well, not just tour patrons. The stock has grown well beyond Book souvenirs to include general gift merchandise.

Mercer House Carriage Shop
430 Whitaker Street
Savannah, GA
(912) 236–6352

A small room in the rear of Mercer House's carriage house fronts Whitaker Street and it is here that Williams's sister has opened a small shop in what was once part of her brother's antique shop. There's a small selection of nice, higher-priced gift items, along with such pedestrian fare as mugs with sketches of Mercer House ($5.50) and tins of Byrd's Cookies (but not the ones featuring *Midnight* on the cover). The chief item in trade here is the owner's book about Williams (see the Close-Up on Savannah books in this chapter).

St. Patrick's Day

Kermit the Frog of Muppets fame occasionally croaks out a melancholy little ditty, "It's Not Easy Being Green." Obviously, Kermit has never hopped into the midst of St. Patrick's Day in Savannah, where it's not only easy being green, it's darn near mandatory.

On St. Patrick's Day in Savannah, people clothe themselves in outfits featuring every shade of green imaginable. They decorate themselves with green accessories, such as green beads, green-and-white-striped Cat in the Hat headgear, and green-and-white buttons conveying a variety of messages, the most prevalent being "Kiss Me, I'm Irish." The revelers color their hair, beards, and mustaches green and affix little green shamrock appliques to their faces. They even dye their dogs and the water of the city's fountains green.

On St. Patrick's Day in Savannah, people eat green grits and drink green beer, which tends to make some of them feel a wee bit green at the gills. On St. Patrick's Day in Savannah, people give themselves over to a wonderful green giddiness that permeates the atmosphere. Is this the work of the mischievous leprechauns—the little people of Irish lore? We're not sure, but we know it's there, wafting through the soft air of springtime, transforming human beings into creatures of whimsy.

Why St. Patrick's Day?

You might be wondering why St. Patrick's Day has evolved as the most festive day of the year in Savannah, and why a city of fewer than 150,000 people has ended up playing host to some 500,000 celebrators on that day.

These are good questions—ones on which we can only speculate. It's not enough to say that a large segment of Savannah's population is, or has been, Irish or of Irish descent. That's true of lots of cities that don't make anywhere near the fuss over St. Patrick's Day as does Savannah.

Part of the reason for the popularity of the day might stem from the fact that it's been celebrated here for a long time, longer than in most American cities. According to the late William L. Fogarty, who wrote a history of the local observance entitled *The Days We've Celebrated*, the first celebration here was in 1813 when the Hibernian Society, formed by Irish Protestants seeking to help their impoverished countrymen, held a private procession. The city's first public procession, which is recognized as Savannah's first St. Patrick's Day parade, was also held by the society and took place in 1824.

"Why and how this celebration could possibly have carried on these many years is perhaps one of the most fantastic mysteries of all," wrote Fogarty in 1980 as he attempted to answer questions regarding the parade's origin. "I don't know of anyone who could really give the actual reason.... Perhaps the answer would be the 'Pride of the Irish' has sustained it."

The observance was, for many years, mainly an Irish Catholic religious celebra-

During St. Patrick's Day festivities, Savannah's fountains flow green. PHOTO: PHYL M. GATLIN

tion aimed at honoring Patrick, the priest who brought Christianity to the Emerald Isle in the fifth century. Although the celebration remains religious in nature (many Savannahians begin the day by attending morning Mass at the Cathedral of St. John the Baptist on Lafayette Square), the observance has become more secular over the years and has been adopted by other segments of the population, leading to the saying that "everyone's Irish on St. Patrick's Day."

Another reason for celebrating the day in a big way might have to do with its occurring at a time of year when Savannah is blessed with some of its best weather. The normal high temperature on St. Patrick's Day is 70, and the normal low is 49. There is a saying around here to the effect that "it never rains on St. Patrick's Day in Savannah." This is usually the case, although it doesn't always hold true: We recall one year when we stood and watched the parade with ice-cold rain running down our green-shirted necks, with only a jugful of mimosas (that's champagne mixed with orange juice) to keep us from deserting our posts.

On most St. Patrick's days, however, the often dreary days of winter are over, and folks are just itching to get outside and cut loose. What better way to do so than with a citywide party?

It's More Than Just a Day

The celebrating that is part of St. Patrick's Day festivities in Savannah occurs over a span of three or four days. St. Patrick's Day is observed on March 17, and the annual parade is held on that day except when it falls on Sunday—in that case, the parade is on Saturday, March 16. Some people celebrate by holding parties and get-togethers in their homes or by attending the invitation-only functions of Savannah's Irish societies. The latter range from the early morning shenanigans of the Sinn Fein Society—which features green grits, Irish whiskey, and a master of ceremonies who continually announces "The bar is open"—to the comparatively staid, black-tie banquet held by the Hibernian Society.

The Hibernians pride themselves on their ability to attract banquet speakers of considerable note. In 1978, the Hibernian banquet speech was delivered by former Georgia governor Jimmy Carter, who at the time happened to be working as president of the United States. Another, shorter speech Carter gave that day is the basis for one of Savannah's better St. Patrick's Day stories. In the mid-1960s, Carter developed a friendship with local character and bar owner Pinkie Masters. Pinkie—who reveled in telephoning local newspaper reporters and impersonating another character, onetime Georgia governor Lester Maddox—was fascinated with politics, and he became a fervent Carter booster. Carter didn't drink alcoholic beverages, but when he visited Savannah, he would invariably stop and see Pinkie at his lounge on Drayton Street near what was then known as the DeSoto Hilton Hotel (see our Nightlife chapter for more about this well-known bar). Masters died in the latter part of 1977, and Carter was unable to attend the funeral, which drew a huge number of political dignitaries. When Carter came to Savannah on St. Patrick's Day 1978 for the 8 P.M. Hibernian banquet, he arrived in late afternoon at the Hilton, where a large crowd waited to greet him.

According to author William Fogarty, Carter's "first act" upon his arrival "was to sneak out through the [hotel's] underground parking garage, cross Drayton Street and enter Pinkie Master's bar unannounced. Needless to say, Pinkie's family and friends who were operating the bar were flabbergasted, as were the customers in the bar." Carter "climbed upon the bar, where they have since added a plaque, and spoke to the crowd, then returned to the hotel. He had paid his respects to Pinkie."

The public partying on St. Patrick's Day occurs at Pinkie's and other watering holes throughout the city, but the bulk of the celebrating takes place on River Street, in City Market, and along Bay Street.

Most of the merrymaking happens on the day of the parade and the weekend closest to it. When the parade is on a Monday, Tuesday, or Wednesday, the partying will be on that day, the weekend before, and the day or days before. When the parade is on a Thursday or Friday, the celebrating will be on that day, the day before, and the weekend following. On parade days and weekends, River Street and City Market are packed with celebrators. Bands pump out the rock and roll, and the beer flows from an endless array of taps (see our Annual Events and Festivals chapter for more details).

In 1999, there began an effort to curb underage drinking and reduce the size of the overflowing crowds on River Street. Based on a proposal from a Savannah Area Convention and Visitors Bureau task force, the Savannah City Council approved the gating of entry points to the riverfront area during the six-day "St. Patrick's Day on the River" festival and required people desiring to drink outdoors to buy $4 wristbands. The decision brought howls of opposition from some River Street merchants and many dyed-in-the-wool (green, no doubt) party-goers. The plan was implemented, and officials of the city and the Savannah Waterfront Association said it worked well enough and used it again in the year 2000. The wristbands have become a fact of life,

with the cost of purchasing one rising to $5 in 2001.

The St. Patrick's Day holidays are also a time of traditional events such as the investiture of the parade grand marshal on the first Sunday in March, the gathering of Irish descendants at the Celtic Cross on the following Sunday, and the laying of a wreath at the Sgt. William Jasper Monument on the afternoon before the parade. There are also family-oriented events emphasizing Irish heritage and culture such as the Savannah Irish Festival at the National Guard Armory in mid-February and the Tara Feis festival in Emmet Park on Bay Street on the Saturday before the parade. For the athletically inclined, there's the St. Patrick's Day Rugby Tournament, held in Daffin Park on the weekend closest to the big day. (For more about all these events, see our Annual Events and Festivals chapter.) The focal point of the festivities, however, is the St. Patrick's Day parade.

A tip of the hat and a big smile will make you feel welcome at the St. Patrick's Day festivities.
PHOTO: PHYL M. GATLIN

The Parade

Savannah's St. Patrick's Day parade is the third oldest and one of the largest in the United States. It dates back to 1824, and only New York City's (1762) and Philadelphia's (1780) have been in existence longer. There are more entries—usually about 250—in Savannah's parade than those in Chicago (200), Philadelphia (101), Boston (100), or New York (75). With 10,000 marchers, Savannah had fewer than New York (150,000) and Chicago (20,000) but as many as Boston and more than Philly (9,700).

Savannah's parade covers a lot of pavement: specifically, 2 miles, making it almost as long in distance as the parades in Boston and Philadelphia (2.6 miles) and longer than New York's (1.5) and Chicago's (1). As you can imagine, given the number of people who march and how far they have to walk, the local parade takes quite a while to unfold—almost four hours. That being the case, it's a good idea to bring lawn chairs or stadium cushions so you can be as comfortable as possible while you watch, particularly if you arrive early and stake out a viewing spot closer to where the parade ends than where it begins. The farther you are from the starting point, the longer you'll have to wait for the first marchers to reach you, maybe as long as an hour.

Speaking of beginnings and endings, the parade starts at 10:15 A.M. at Abercorn and Gwinnett Streets and ends at Bull and Harris Streets. The route of march is north on Abercorn to Broughton Street, east on Broughton to East Broad Street, north on East Broad to Bay Street, west on Bay to Bull, to the finish line. We think you'll find this event to be as enjoyable and festive as you can imagine, but don't go expecting to see something akin to the Tournament of Roses parade or Macy's Thanksgiving Day bash. There are floats in Savannah's parade, and they seem to be more numerous and elaborate each year, but you won't see anything that remotely resembles what you'd watch in Pasadena,

> ## Insiders' Tip
> The water of the Forsyth Park fountain is traditionally dyed green each year for St. Patrick's Day, but don't expect the Savannah River to be treated in similar fashion. The last and only attempt at turning the river green occurred in 1961 with less than desirable results. A thousand pounds of the chemical Uranine was used, and the outcome was a striped effect.

California, on New Year's Day or on the streets of New York during the pre-Christmas holidays.

What you'll see in Savannah on St. Patrick's Day is more like a small-town parade that has grown to the point that it has burst clean out of its Kelly green britches. The down-home flavor of the parade is a big part of its appeal; one of the reasons we Savannahians keep going back year after year is to watch our relatives, neighbors, and co-workers as they march or ride by and wave and yell at each other. You'll see a lot of folks stepping out of or into the line of march as they shake hands and hug necks. And you're likely to see a woman or two dash from the sidelines to plant kisses on the cheeks of marchers, particularly those in uniform and especially members of the U.S. Army Ranger and Benedictine Military School aggregations.

What you'll see are lots of high school marching bands, numerous glad-handing politicians riding in convertibles, some

Kids and adults go a little crazy over St. Patrick's Day in Savannah. PHOTO: PHYL M. GATLIN

beauty queens, several military color guards, the parade grand marshal, a gaggle of past grand marshals, and a multitude of men, women, and children of Irish descent, all dressed up in their best greenery and marching in family groups or as members of Savannah's many Irish societies. Keep your eyes peeled for one of our favorite entries, the "Irishman at Large." You'll see college cheerleaders and dance teams, officials of the Catholic church, bagpipers, and detachments of soldiers, sailors, marines, and veterans groups. People will be waving at you from more than twenty floats representing a variety of organizations and businesses.

Among our favorite parade units are those of the Shriners of Savannah's Alee Temple. The most outlandish of the Shriner groups is the Oriental Band, which consists of a group of pillars of the community clad in colorful burnooses, jackets, and pantaloons and wearing shoes that have been spray-painted gold, turned up at the tips, and decorated with tiny bells. As the band members tootle and bang away

on their recorders, cymbals, and drums, they are led by the least inhibited of all the outgoing St. Patrick's Day parade marchers. He wears a turban, pantaloons, and a vest, an outfit exposing to spectators a belly that appears to have seen more than a few beers pass its way. In his navel is a huge "gem," reputed to be a ruby. Swinging a scimitar over his head, the leader of the band pauses periodically to perform a bump-and-grind routine that would put most Bourbon Street strippers to shame. Female onlookers unable to resist the temptation to dance in the middle of the city's main streets often join him.

Other crowd pleasers from the Shrine are its Dunecat Unit, whose members zip around in souped-up go-carts, and the Keystone Kops, who hand out tickets to spectators amid much frenzied whistle blowing and scurrying around. In short, what you'll see at Savannah's St. Patrick's Day parade are lots of enthusiasm, a world of pride in being Irish, and the smiles of thousands of people having one heck of a good time.

Prime Parade-Watching Spots

One of the best places from which to view the parade is Lafayette Square, which is on Abercorn Street between Charlton and Harris Streets. This is where the folks who judge the marching bands sit, so you'll see the bands performing at their best if you hang out here. Another good spot is the steps of the U.S. Custom House on Bay Street at Bull Street. The steps here are like bleachers, perfect for sitting and watching the festivities.

Here are some other good places for parade watching, as detailed by the *Savannah Morning News*:

The 600 block of Abercorn Street, where "the parade's performers aren't tired yet. The bands step higher; the people waving from their floats aren't yet suffering from arm fatigue."

East Broad Street between Broughton and Bay Streets—"A good place to see the picturesque variety of parade spectators....SCAD (Savannah College of Art and Design) students tend to be in full bloom around here. Green dogs abound. So do green people."

Bay Street between East Broad and Bull Streets—"The closest convenient spot for those who've been cavorting down by the river."

Insiders' Tip

Be sure to make a note of where you park your car. There will be vehicles parked all over the place, and it will be easier to lose track of yours than you might think.

We would also like to make this suggestion: To obtain a unique view of the parade, try getting a spot on the southern side of Calhoun Square (Abercorn and Gordon Streets), Lafayette Square (Abercorn and Charlton Streets), or Oglethorpe Square (Abercorn and York Streets) or on the northern side of Wright Square (Bull and State Streets) or Chippewa Square (Bull and Hull Streets). You'll be watching the parade come straight at you rather than viewing it from the side, and it's a perspective that can be quite enjoyable.

Parking on St. Patrick's Day

If there is a downside to St. Patrick's Day, it might be locating a place to park. Metered spaces are free on this holiday, but vacant ones won't be easy to find unless you get to town real early. Another option is to park in one of the city's garages or lots, which you can do all day for $10; here, too, an early arrival will be mandatory. The garages are at State and Abercorn Streets, at Montgomery and York Streets, and at Bryan and Abercorn Streets, and the lot is at Liberty and Montgomery Streets.

An alternative to parking downtown is to park away from the area and take a Chatham Area Transit bus into the city. There are regular bus routes to and from downtown (see our Getting Here, Getting Around chapter), and there will be an express St. Patrick's Day shuttle from a staging area on the Southside—in recent years, it's been at Oglethorpe Mall—that will offer continuous service starting early in the morning and running into the early evening. You can call (912) 233-5767 for more information on this shuttle service.

Whatever you do, don't park in a lot or space that's designated for use by a business or private individual. If there's a sign saying your car will be towed, that's probably what will happen, and you'll have to pay a minimum of $90 to get your vehicle back.

Annual Events and Festivals

Savannahians love to party. They love their history. They also love getting outdoors and taking advantage of coastal Georgia's congenial climate. Is it any wonder, then, there's almost always something going on in Savannah? The something might be a festival attracting thousands of people or the commemoration of a historic event drawing a few hundred, but a week seldom passes in which there's nothing to do in Savannah.

We admit things slow down a tad during the summer months because of the heat, but that doesn't mean you can't get out and enjoy yourself. Grab your suntan lotion, cooler, and lounge chair and head for a day at the beach on nearby Tybee Island, just as Savannahians have been doing for more than a century.

Savannah's biggest party is its celebration of St. Patrick's Day, a green-hued blast bringing up to a half-million visitors to the city in mid-March. It's such a big deal we've devoted an entire chapter to it. But because we want to be sure you don't miss any of the fun, we've included in this chapter brief looks at significant happenings on that great day for the Irish and the days leading up to it.

As we indicated earlier, finding a parking space in Savannah can be a hassle, and the problem intensifies when a festival is held in the downtown area. It's a good idea—particularly if you're attending an event on River Street, where parking is extremely limited—to arrive early, find a spot on a street or in a lot a few blocks from the festival, then hoof it to your destination. Savannah is a city that's ideal for walking, and your stroll to and from the festival could be one of the most enjoyable parts of your day.

We need to mention one other thing before taking you through our month-by-month rundown of events and festivals: Dates, times, and admission fees can change, so it's best to call ahead for the most current information. The telephone numbers included with the following writeups are the numbers of the individuals, organizations, or agencies sponsoring or coordinating the events.

January

Historic Downtown

Emancipation Day Service
Location varies
Savannah, GA
(912) 234–6293, (912) 232–8507

By holding a special church service on New Year's Day, Savannah's Emancipation Association commemorates the signing of the proclamation that ordered the freeing of slaves in the Confederate states. During the 11 A.M. gathering, held at a different church each year, a student reads the Emancipation Proclamation, a mass choir sings hymns, and a speaker delivers an address concerning the significance of that historic day.

Martin Luther King Jr.
Observance Day Activities
Various locations
Savannah, GA
(912) 234–5502

This month-long tribute to civil rights leader Martin Luther King Jr. features a parade through downtown on the third Monday in January, the national day of observance for King Day. The parade, starting at 10 A.M., follows a busy weekend featuring a breakfast for the business community at the Savannah Marriott Riverfront hotel on Saturday morning, an educational program and career fair at a local school from noon until 2 P.M. on Saturday, and a citywide memorial worship service at the Savannah Civic Center on Sunday. On the second weekend of the month, the Dr. Martin Luther King Jr. Observance Day Association presents the Unity Luncheon at the Marriott at noon on Saturday, and an interfaith service at a local church is held during the week. The observances wind up with the Freedom Ball at the Savannah Civic Center on the Friday night following the parade. Tickets to the Freedom Ball are $15, and you can reserve a seat at the Unity Luncheon for $25 to $30.

Schoolchildren celebrate the state's founding during the annual Georgia Day celebration.
PHOTO: KYLE CASON

Heart and Stroke Ball
Savannah Marriott Riverfront
100 Gen. McIntosh Boulevard
Savannah, GA
(912) 355–0233

The American Heart Association's premier fundraiser has a different theme every year and is held in late January or in early February, which is Heart Month. Tickets are $175 per person, and they entitle guests to a cocktail party with open bar at 6:30 P.M. and dinner with wine and beer at 8 P.M. A band plays popular dance music until midnight, and live and silent auctions add to the festivities.

February

Historic Downtown

Georgia Heritage Celebration
Various locations
Savannah, GA
(912) 651–2125

This observance celebrating Georgia's founding and heritage unfolds during the first two weeks of February and usually focuses on the twelfth of the month—the day on which the first colonists landed in 1733. Georgia Week opens on the first day of February with a ceremony in a downtown square featuring a portrayal of a significant figure in the history of the state. There are town assemblies in local schools and a lecture and a dignitaries' coffee at the Georgia Historical Society, which hosts the celebration in partnership with the Chatham-Savannah Board of Education. Programs at historic sites also are offered. On the morning of Georgia Day, February 12, schoolchildren dressed as colonists and the Native Americans who welcomed them walk in a procession from Forsyth Park up Bull Street to City Hall on Bay Street. The Georgia Day Luncheon follows, and wreaths are laid at monuments throughout the city. Tickets to the Georgia Day Luncheon run $18; the other events are free.

Black Heritage Festival
Savannah Civic Center and other locations
Savannah, GA
(912) 651–6417
www.ci.savannah.ga.us

Various musical groups entertain with performances of gospel, reggae, blues, and jazz music, and craftspeople at a marketplace sell items related to African culture during this festival, which is held throughout February. Funded by Savannah's Department of Cultural Affairs, this event highlights the multifaceted contributions of African Americans in the areas of music, the performing arts, and cuisine. Many of the activities take place at the Savannah Civic Center and the Savannah International Trade and Convention Center, and admission is free.

Super Museum Sunday
Various locations
Savannah, GA

More than twenty of the area's museums, educational institutions, and historic homes open their doors and invite the public in at no charge during this event, which serves as the last activity of the Georgia Heritage Celebration and occurs on a Sunday in mid-February. Hours are from noon until 5 P.M. To determine if a specific museum participates in this program, contact the museum ahead of time. (You can find museums and their telephone numbers in the Attractions chapter.)

Savannah Onstage
International Arts Festival
Various locations
Savannah, GA
(912) 236–5745
www.savannahonstage.org

Savannah Onstage enhances the beauty of the city with ten days of classical music and cultural arts in late February and early March. The cornerstones of this steadily growing festival are the Jepson Classical Concert Series and the American Traditions Competition. Each year additional major events are incorporated into the festival. In 2001, Savannah Onstage presented special events such as a performance by Sweet Honey in the Rock, the Grammy Award–winning female a capella vocal ensemble; "An Evening With Celeste," starring film star Celeste Holm;

and a series of festive weekend jazz brunches and free outdoor jazz concerts.

The Concert Series presents the winners of many of the world's most prestigious music competitions performing at Savannah's historic churches and synagogues. The American Traditions Competition, with the finals taking place at the Lucas Theatre for the Arts, features solo vocalists singing music that has played a significant role in forming the cultural heritage of the United States. Ticket prices range from $10 to $40, with discounts for students. Several events sell out quickly, so you'd do well to call early to reserve seats and obtain details about performers and venues.

Islands

Colonial Faire & Muster at Wormsloe
Wormsloe Historic Site
7601 Skidaway Road
Savannah, GA
(912) 353–3023

Historical reenactors clad in the garb of Georgia's colonists demonstrate craft skills, such as making candles and musket balls, at this program, held in an open area near the marsh overlooking the Skidaway River. At the visitors center, you can view artifacts excavated from Wormsloe's tabby ruins and watch an audiovisual show

Insiders' Tip

Get a unique view of activities on River Street and stay out of the crowds by renting a hotel room facing the Savannah River, but be prepared for some late-night noise from musicians and merrymakers.

about the founding of the thirteenth colony. The program takes place from 10 A.M. until 4 P.M. on the first Saturday and Sunday in February. Admission is $2.50 for adults, $2 for senior citizens, and $1.50 for those 6 to 18 years old. Children younger than six are admitted free.

Southside/Midtown

Savannah Irish Festival
Savannah Civic Center,
Liberty and Montgomery Streets
Savannah, GA
(912) 234-8444, (800) 436-3746
www.savannahirish.org

This family-oriented event uses song, dance, and recitation to emphasize the heritage of the Irish and the contributions of Irish immigrants here and throughout the United States. In addition to the main stage, where much of this activity takes place, there are stages for children's entertainment and workshops in Celtic art, poetry, and music. Vendors market Irish clothing, jewelry, and artifacts, and members of twelve local Irish organizations prepare and sell food, including shepherd's pie, Irish stew, and other ethnic dishes. The festival is on the third weekend in February from 6 to 10 P.M. on Friday, noon to 7 P.M. on Saturday, and from noon until 7 P.M. on Sunday. Admission to the festival is $10 per day or $20 for a three-day ticket. Children twelve and younger are admitted free.

March

Historic Downtown

Grand Marshal Investiture Ceremony
DeSoto Hilton Hotel
15 E. Liberty Street
Savannah, GA
(912) 233-4804

The St. Patrick's Day Parade Committee presents the parade grand marshal with his sash and recognizes civic dignitaries at this ceremony in the ballroom of the DeSoto Hilton Hotel. The event takes place at 2:45 P.M. on the first Sunday in March, one week after the committee elects the leader of the parade. There is no charge for admission.

Celtic Cross Ceremony
Emmet Park
Bay and Price Streets
Savannah, GA
(912) 233-4804

Members of the city's Irish organizations gather at the Cathedral of St. John the Baptist for Mass at 11:30 A.M. on the second Sunday of the month, then march in procession to Emmet Park, where they lay a wreath at the Celtic Cross and listen to a speech about their heritage. The cross, officially named the Irish Monument, was carved from a single piece of Irish limestone in County Roscommon, Ireland. The Savannah Irish Monument Committee erected the Celtic Cross in 1983, the 250th anniversary of the founding of Savannah and Georgia, to commemorate Georgians of Irish ancestry. The ceremony starts about 1 P.M., and it's open to the public.

Tara Feis
Emmet Park
Bay and Price Streets
Savannah, GA
(912) 651-6417
www.ci.savannah.ga.us

The City of Savannah's Department of Cultural Affairs puts the emphasis on family-oriented activities at this Irish festival on the Saturday before St. Patrick's Day. Irish music and dancing, crafts demonstrations, storytelling, and poetry recitations fill the spotlight. Youngsters can participate in hands-on activities with a Celtic touch and enjoy carnival rides. Alcoholic beverages are prohibited in an effort to enhance the family-day atmosphere. The event, in sun-dappled Emmet Park, runs from 11 A.M. until 5 P.M., and admission is as free as the Irish mist on a day in Killarney. In case you're wondering, *feis* is pronounced "fesh."

Sgt. William Jasper Memorial Ceremony
Madison Square
Bull Street, between Harris and Charlton Streets
Savannah, GA
(912) 233-4804

On the eve of the St. Patrick's Day Parade, the parade grand marshal and his aides recognize the contributions of the military by walking from Johnson Square down Bull Street to Madison Square, where they lay a wreath at the monument honoring Revolutionary War hero William Jasper. A band or two that will be participating in the parade usually accompanies them. A twenty-one-gun salute is fired during the ceremony, which occurs about 4:30 P.M.

St. Patrick's Day Parade
Various downtown streets
Savannah, GA
(912) 233-4804

Savannah's biggest annual event lasts upwards of four hours and involves thousands of participants. Some 250 units take to the streets for the parade, including marching bands, floats, and the city's numerous Irish organizations. The parade starts about 10:15 A.M. at Forsyth Park and winds its way around several of Savannah's squares and down its main thoroughfares. (For more information, see our St. Patrick's Day chapter.)

St. Patrick's at City Market
City Market
Jefferson and St. Julian Streets
Savannah, GA
(912) 232-4903

City Market celebrates the big day with live music and dancing in the courtyard. This laid-back party occurs over a span of time that includes St. Patrick's Day and can last as long as five days, depending on when the holiday falls. On St. Patrick's Day, the bands crank up as soon as the parade passes nearby. It's free.

Music fills the air as marching bands parade down Savannah's streets during St. Patrick's Day activities.
PHOTO: PHYL M. GATLIN

St. Patrick's Day on the River
Rousakis Plaza,
River Street
Savannah, GA
(912) 234-0295

The Savannah Waterfront Association sets up food booths on the plaza and brings in nationally known entertainers to perform on three stages, but the biggest attraction of St. Patrick's Day on the River isn't eating or listening to music—it's being part of the crowd that jams River Street. This 9-block party is free for nondrinkers, and it's the place to be during St. Patrick's Day festivities if you like to rub elbows with people—literally. Those wishing to drink beer outdoors will have to purchase $5 wristbands. The merrymaking is at its peak on St. Patrick's Day and the weekend closest to the holiday; the party cranks up about 10 A.M., and food sales and scheduled entertainment end at midnight.

The Savannah Tour of Homes and Gardens
Parish House of Christ Church
18 Abercorn Street
Savannah, GA
(912) 234-8054
www.savannahtourofhomes.org

This granddaddy of Savannah's seasonal tours offers a different tour of private homes and/or gardens on each day of its four-day run. Each three-hour, self-guided walking tour takes you to six to eight sites in the Historic District. The homes and gardens on the tours are open from 10 A.M. until 5 P.M., and participants are encouraged to stroll from site to site at their own pace and in any order they choose. There are tours on Friday of an area outside the district (check with tour headquarters for the hours on these). Special events such as luncheons, seminars, and teas are also presented, and they vary from year to year. The event is held on a Thursday through Sunday in late March. Begun in 1935, the event is sponsored by the Episcopal Church Women of Christ Church, along with Historic Savannah Foundation, and proceeds benefit outreach ministries of the churchwomen and the foundation's preservation efforts. The fee for each walking tour is $35, and it's essential to order tickets for the tours and other activities ahead of time. You pick up your tickets at tour headquarters, the Parish House of Christ Church.

Islands

Sheep to Shawl Festival
Oatland Island Education Center
711 Sandtown Road
Savannah, GA
(912) 898-3980
www.oatlandisland.org

While musicians of the Savannah Folk Music Society fiddle and strum up a storm on the porch of a log cabin built in 1835, visitors watch an old-fashioned sheepshearing. This activity on the second Saturday in March takes place at the education center's Heritage Homesite.

The main events occur about 11:30 A.M. and 2 P.M. when workers clip the sheep with hand-operated shears. Members of the Fiber Guild of the Savannahs card wool from the previous year's shearing, spin it into yarn and, using a 150-year-old

> ## Insiders' Tip
> Although city officials are reconsidering this, you can still walk around in public in Savannah with an alcoholic beverage in your hand without fear of being arrested as long as the drink is in a plastic cup or mug. However, drinking beer, wine, or other spirits from bottles, cans, and glasses is prohibited.

loom, weave yarn spun beforehand into a shawl. The shawl is raffled off, and the winner is announced near the end of the festival, which runs from 10 A.M. until 5 P.M. The center invites youngsters to try their hands at carding and spinning wool. Folks interested in viewing Oatland's wild and domesticated animals can walk the facility's 1.75-mile nature trail and visit the barnyard. Admission is $2 for persons four and older, free for those three and younger.

Southside/Midtown

St. Patrick's Day Rugby Tournament
Daffin Park
Victory Drive and Bee Road
Savannah, GA
(912) 234-5999
Billed as the largest tournament of its kind in the United States, this event is staged by the Savannah Shamrocks rugby club on the weekend closest to St. Patrick's Day. About seventy teams participate. There's no charge for roaming the sidelines and learning about this sport that's akin to American football and has been called "a ruffians' game played by gentlemen." The action starts about 9 A.M. on both days of the tourney, which was first held in 1978.

Spring Gardening Festival
Bamboo Farm and Coastal Gardens
2 Canebrake Road
Savannah, GA
(912) 921-5460
Swing into the planting season at the Bamboo Farm (see our Attractions chapter) by attending this program, which features garden exhibits and talks on horticulture. Also on the agenda are a container gardening competition and a silent auction, and plant vendors will be on hand, perhaps offering that hard-to-find plant you've been looking for. There's no charge for attending this festival, which is held on a Saturday in late March, but admission to the main horticultural lecture is $5.

April

Historic Downtown

First Saturday
Rousakis Plaza
River Street
Savannah, GA
(912) 234-0295
Browse through the wares of artisans and craftspeople from throughout the Southeast and listen to light jazz or folk music

Insiders' Tip
Pick up some bargains at the Junior League Thrift Sale or the Landlovers Flea Market. The Landlovers, residents of The Landings residential community on Skidaway Island, load up about ninety tables with sale items on a Saturday in mid-March. The event at The Village shopping center on Skidaway runs from 11:00 A.M. to 2:00 P.M. The Junior Leaguers fill the arena of the Savannah Civic Center with good deals on the first Friday and Saturday in October. There's a $4 admission fee to the thrift sale on Friday and a $2 charge on Saturday, when all items are sold at half-price. Hours are from 10 A.M. until 2 P.M. on Friday and from 10 A.M. until 3 P.M. on Saturday.

Savannah's many festivals pay homage to the city's multicultural heritage. PHOTO: RICK LOFT

during First Saturday on the plaza on River Street. While enjoying the breeze blowing off the Savannah River, you might find yourself staring at a large cargo ship as it glides along the waterway, so close you'd swear you could reach out and touch it. The forty to sixty open-air arts and crafts booths on the plaza offer a variety of treasures, everything from original oil paintings and watercolors to rocking horses fashioned from wood scraps. If you can't turn up something that catches your fancy among the artists' booths, visit the shops in the renovated cotton warehouses lining River Street.

Hungry? You have your choice of restaurants dishing up a variety of cuisine. The Savannah Waterfront Association presents First Saturday festivals from 9 A.M. to 6 P.M. on—what else?—the first Saturday of each month, with the exception of January, February, and March. First Saturdays in May, October, and December are part of expanded, more distinctive festivals: the Great Atlantic Seafood Festival in

May, Oktoberfest in October, and Christmas on the River in December (see subsequent listings for more details on these festivals). Admission is free.

Roundhouse Blues and Barbecue Festival (A Night in Old Savannah)
Historic Roundhouse/Railroad Museum
601 W. Harris Street
Savannah, GA
(912) 651–6840

The Girl Scout Council of Savannah presented the first A Night in Old Savannah festival as a bicentennial project in 1976. The celebration of music and ethnic foods was held in Johnson Square and attracted national attention and huge crowds. After several years, the Shriners of the Alee Temple became sponsors of the festival and staged it in the parking lot of the Savannah Visitors Center on Martin Luther King Jr. Boulevard. The event is now presented by the Coastal Heritage Society at the Historic Roundhouse/Railroad Museum 1 block south of the visitors center.

The Friday night and Saturday night celebration in April continues to provide festival-goers with an opportunity to hear distinctive music and enjoy local cuisine. But the change in the name of the festival reflects a recent emphasis on blues and barbecue. Intended as a "gathering of neighbors and visitors," the festival offers performances by nationally known artists such as C. J. Chenier, who holds the title of Crown Prince of Zydeco music; Pinetop Perkins; and Bob Margolin. The music is played and the food is served rain or shine, because there is cover for 2,000 people at the roundhouse. Parking is available in nearby lots at the visitors center and the Savannah Civic Center (at Montgomery and Liberty Streets). The festival runs from 6 P.M. until 11 P.M. both nights, and admission is free. The event is sponsored by the city's Department of Cultural Affairs and others.

Savannah Garden Exposition
Broughton Street between Habersham and Lincoln Streets
Savannah, GA
(912) 233–7787
www.davenportsavga.com

Historic Savannah Foundation presents a tour of "secret gardens" in the downtown area and seminars by renowned landscape and garden professionals during this event on the first weekend in April. There's also a market offering hard-to-find plants, antique garden ornaments, and furniture and fine gardening tools. The seminars are held at various locations in the Historic District. Admission in 2001 was $8 in advance and $10 at the site, with tours and seminars running $15 to $25 extra.

NOGS Hidden Gardens of Savannah Tour
Telfair Museum
121 Barnard Street
Savannah, GA
(912) 238–0248

For more than twenty years, the members of the Garden Club of Savannah have, via this tour, enabled folks to glimpse a part of the city they would not otherwise see. As its name implies, this self-guided walking tour is your chance to get a look at some of the elegant gardens hidden behind the walls and gates of downtown homes. Chosen because of their beauty and unusual arrangement, six to eight gardens are opened to the public by their owners for only the two days of the tour.

You buy your tickets at the Savannah Visitors Center at 301 Martin Luther King Jr. Boulevard or at the Telfair Museum at 121 Barnard Street, and then off you go at your own pace. A splendid way to end your walk is by finishing at the Telfair and attending the tea served there, a treat included in the $20 ticket price ($18 for members of groups of twenty or more, free for children younger than ten). A visit to the Massey Heritage Center and its garden is included on the tour, which is presented on a Friday and Saturday in mid-April, about the time Savannah is in full bloom. The gardens are open from 10 A.M. until 5 P.M., and light refreshments are served at the tea from 2 to 5 P.M. By the way, NOGS stands for North of Gaston Street, the locale of all the gardens on the tour.

Sidewalk Arts Festival
Forsyth Park
Savannah, GA
(912) 525–5868

The normally sedate slabs of the sidewalks leading through Forsyth Park pulsate with color in late April, when the Savannah College of Art and Design stages its Sidewalk Arts Festival. SCAD students, alumni, prospective students, children, and preteens cover the concrete with chalk drawings, creating an immense art exhibit on the ground. You'll see everything from reproductions of famous masterpieces to the flights of fancy of five-year-olds as you stroll through the park. More than 800 artists participate. Other attractions include the music of various bands and art projects for young children and preteens. The festival starts at 11 A.M. and ends at 5 P.M.

Confederate Memorial Day
Forsyth Park
Savannah, GA
(912) 651–6840

An observance that began in 1866 with women decorating the graves of husbands, sons, and brothers who fell while wearing the gray and butternut of the Confederacy continues in Savannah with a gathering at the Confederate Memorial monument in Forsyth Park on the Sunday closest to April 26, the day Gen. Joseph E. Johnston surrendered the last Confederate army at Greensboro, North Carolina. Civil War reenactors fire a twenty-one-gun artillery salute, and there is a performance by a fife and drum corps consisting of students from Old Fort Jackson's spring Field Music School. The solemn ceremony takes place in early afternoon.

Savannah Shakespeare Festival
Forsyth Park
Savannah, GA
(912) 234–9860
www.ci.savannah.ga.us

"The play's the thing" at the Savannah Shakespeare Festival in Forsyth Park on a Friday, Saturday, and Sunday in late April or early May. A different work of William Shakespeare is presented outdoors each year by the City Lights Theatre Company (see our Arts and Culture chapter), with the curtain rising at 8 P.M. There is folk singing and Renaissance dancing beforehand, starting at 7 P.M. It's a free event funded by the city's Department of Cultural Affairs, and many playgoers use the festival as an opportunity to have a picnic in the park. Recent productions have included *The Merry Wives of Windsor*, *Othello*, *The Tempest*, and *Twelfth Night*.

West Chatham

Sunday Supper in the Strawberry Patch
Bamboo Farm and Coastal Gardens
2 Canebrake Road
Savannah, GA
(912) 921–5460

Held on a weekend in mid- or late April at the peak of strawberry-growing season, this Bamboo Farm fund-raiser gives folks

The Talmadge Memorial Bridge is the setting for the most grueling—and rewarding—portion of the Savannah Bridge Run, which is held in May. PHOTO: BETTY DARBY

a chance to get outdoors and enjoy a good ol' Southern supper—fried chicken, rice and gravy, fresh squash, field peas, Vidalia onions, sliced tomatoes, cornbread, iced tea, and strawberry shortcake, of course. The meal is served at the lakeside pavilion at the Bamboo Farm (see our Attractions chapter), but the berries are fresh from the farm's strawberry patch; the shortcake is provided by Mrs. Wilkes' (see our Restaurants chapter). It's a dessert combination that's tough to beat.

Those attending also enjoy self-guided tours of the gardens, and there's live entertainment and a silent auction. You need to make reservations for this get-together, which starts at 4 P.M.; cost of the meal is $15 per person.

Stand Up for America Day
Various locations
Port Wentworth, GA
(912) 964–4379
Residents of the west Chatham County town of Port Wentworth show their red, white, and blue colors from early morning until midnight on a Saturday in late April devoted to patriotism and fun. A parade featuring go-carts and bicycles decorated by youngsters starts at 10 A.M. near the city's elementary school, winds its way through town and ends next to the fire station on Cantyre Street. That's also the site of a late morning rally, craft sales, activities for children, and a nighttime street dance that goes on until midnight and includes a fireworks show about 9 P.M. Festivities start at 7:45 A.M. with a 5-kilometer run and a 1-mile fun walk.

May

Historic Downtown

Great Atlantic Seafood Festival
Rousakis Plaza
River Street
Savannah, GA
(912) 234–0295

Fresh seafood prepared at booths on River Street's Rousakis Plaza is the main attraction of this event on the first weekend in May. Menus feature shrimp, crab, and crayfish—much of it caught in local waters. Festivalgoers munch away as they check out sales of arts and crafts and boogie to the beach and Cajun music provided by bands playing on the plaza's main stage. Hours are 9 A.M. to midnight on Friday and Saturday and 9 A.M. to 6 P.M. on Sunday. Admission is free.

Savannah Duck Race
Rousakis Plaza
River Street
Savannah, GA
(912) 236–9536
If horse racing is the sport of kings, rubber duck racing could be the pastime of... you, maybe. You'll spend a fortune to buy a racehorse but a mere $5 for a little yellow entrant in the Savannah Duck Race on the second Sunday of May. OK, OK, if your synthetic fowl triumphs in this race, you won't wind up in the winner's circle at Churchill Downs, but a win, place, or show will earn you a nifty prize. First prize in 2001 was a five-night, six-day stay in the Virgin Islands, plus $1,000 in cash.

The Savannah Symphony Women's Guild presents this fund-raising event. The ducks—usually about 3,500 of them—bob their way to the finish line of a one-quarter-mile course in the Savannah River alongside the plaza on River Street. Starters dump the ducks in the water during mid-afternoon, depending on when the tide is right for racing.

If you wanna buy a duck, call the listed number or purchase a ticket on the day of the race. If you just want to watch, you can do that for free.

Savannah Bridge Run
Various downtown streets
Savannah, GA
(912) 644–6414
Participating in this 10-kilometer race and 2-kilometer health walk will give you a

unique view of Savannah—on foot from the Eugene Talmadge Memorial Bridge, a 1.4-mile span that rises 196 feet above the Savannah River. The race—which is for runners or walkers—takes entrants from the starting line in the Historic District, over the bridge and onto Hutchinson Island, then back over the bridge and into downtown. You can register ahead of time for $15 or enter for $25 on the first Saturday in May, the day of the race. A total of 993 competitors finished the race in 2001.

Kids Day
Savannah Civic Center
Liberty and Montgomery Streets
Savannah, GA
(912) 355–8111

One of the organizers of Kids Day is fond of saying the event gives children an opportunity to receive some education with a little *e* while having fun with a capital *F*. Kids Day shows children and their families the services available to them in the community and exposes youngsters to the arts and sciences via hands-on activities such as decorating pottery, delivering mock television weather reports, and listening to storytellers. Staffed by volunteers of the Jewish Educational Alliance and other members of the community, the event is free for adults and $1 for kids (or 50 cents with coupons distributed to schools and printed in the *Savannah Morning News*). Kids Day occurs on a Sunday in early May from noon to 4 P.M.

Kirkin' O' the Tartan
Independent Presbyterian Church
25 W. Oglethorpe Avenue
Savannah, GA
(912) 236–3346

The Kirkin' O' the Tartan service begins with a procession of bagpipers and Scottish descendents bearing tartan banners representing their clans. After their entry into the church, the reading of scripture, the presentation of the banners, and a special sermon, there is more piping on the green outside the church. The service is at 11 A.M. on the second Sunday of May,

and it's an occasion when many worshipers, Scottish and otherwise, rededicate themselves and their families to God.

Scottish Games and Highland Gathering
Old Fort Jackson
1 Fort Jackson Road
Savannah, GA
(912) 898–8593
www.savannahscottishgames.org

Although tests of strength and dexterity are the focal point of the Scottish Games, there's more to the event than brawny laddies tossing long poles ("cabers") and heaving sheaves of hay into the air. Aye, there are winsome lassies performing the dances of the Highlands and stout-hearted bagpipers playing their melancholy tunes. Also, members of more than fifty Scottish clans bring a touch of plaid to the green fields of Old Fort Jackson (see Attractions) as they gather to parade, socialize, and celebrate their heritage during this festival on the second Saturday in May. Gates open at 8 A.M. and opening ceremonies are at noon. The entry fee to the games is $10 for adults and teens; $5 for children younger than twelve.

Arts on the River
River Street and other locations
Savannah, GA
(912) 651–6417
www.ci.savannah.ga.us

Presented on Mother's Day weekend, Savannah's celebration of fine arts features an artists' street market on Rousakis Plaza and free performances by the Savannah Symphony Orchestra in Morrell Park. The street market on the plaza along River Street runs from 10 A.M. until 6 P.M. on Saturday and Sunday. Ceramics, hand-blown glass, fine crafts, jewelry, and yard sculptures fill more than sixty booths beside the Savannah River. Bands and dance troupes perform on the Arbor Stage of the plaza during both days of the festival. The symphony entertains in the evening in the park at the east end of River Street, and fireworks fill the air during the finale on Sunday night. Admission to the festival, a project of the city's Department of Cultural Affairs, is free.

Islands

Birds of Prey Program
Oatland Island Education Center
711 Sandtown Road
Oatland Island, GA
(912) 898–3980
www.oatlandisland.org

Conservationist Doris Mager presents two 45-minute talks about eagles, owls, and other birds of prey during this educational event on the second Saturday of May. Mager, known nationwide as "The Eagle Lady," brings four to five birds with her to liven up her lectures at 11:30 A.M. and 1:30 P.M. in the conference room of the center. The event runs from 10 A.M. until 5 P.M. and offers activities for children. The center's nature trail is made available to visitors. The 1.75-mile trail takes you through Oatland's maritime forest and saltmarsh to large, fenced-in enclosures housing animals native to coastal Georgia: alligators, panthers, bobcats, foxes, deer, bears, wolves, bison, eagles, owls, and hawks. The center's barnyard gives children the opportunity to touch and feed cows, sheep, goats, rabbits, pigs, and fowl. Admission is $2 for persons four and older, free for those three and younger.

War of Jenkins' Ear Observance
Wormsloe Historic Site
7601 Skidaway Road
Savannah, GA
(912) 353–3023

Wormsloe emphasizes the military aspect of life in the Georgia of the 1740s with living history demonstrations on the last Saturday in May. In a program running from 11 A.M. to 4 P.M., members of the Wormsloe militia depict the lives of soldiers who fought in the War of Jenkins' Ear—England's struggle with the Spanish for possession of the southeastern portion of North America between 1739 and

1742. Admission is $2.50 for adults, $2 for senior citizens, and $1.50 for children ages 6 to 18. Those six and younger are admitted free.

June

Historic Downtown

First Saturday
Rousakis Plaza
River Street
Savannah, GA
(912) 234–0295

See our April listing for more information on this monthly event.

Savannah Asian Festival
Savannah Civic Center
Montgomery and Liberty Streets
Savannah, GA
(912) 651–6417
www.ci.savannah.ga.us

A response to the contributions of Savannah's growing Asian community, this one-day event on a Saturday in June features displays and entertainment reflecting the heritage of people of Chinese, Filipino, Indian, Japanese, Korean, Thai, and Vietnamese descent. A Chinese dragon dance ceremony, an Asian fashion show, martial arts demonstrations, and Vietnamese fan dancing are highlights. Representatives of the Asian cultures, some of them clad in native dress, display and sell arts and crafts at tables set up in the Civic Center lobby and host workshops. You can purchase samples of Asian cuisine at booths lining an outdoor concourse. Among the offerings are Chinese egg rolls, Indian curry, Thai beef, Filipino rice cakes, Vietnamese shish kebob, Japanese sushi, and Korean cucumber salad. The festival runs from noon until 7:30 P.M. It's sponsored by Savannah's Department of Cultural Affairs, which means admission is free.

West Chatham

Catch 'em and Cook 'em
Bamboo Farm and Coastal Gardens
2 Canebrake Road
Savannah, GA
(912) 921–5460

Come out and eat the fixings prepared at this family fish fry or catch your own and have the Bamboo Farm clean 'em and cook 'em for you. It's an opportunity for family members to do some fishing together in the four acres of ponds at the Bamboo Farm and Coastal Gardens on a Saturday in mid-June. For $10, you can take your catch home and clean it and cook it yourself or enjoy the fish dinner prepared by the staff.

July

Historic Downtown

First Saturday
Rousakis Plaza
River Street
Savannah, GA
(912) 234–0295

See our April listing for more information on this monthly event.

The Great American Fourth of July
Rousakis Plaza
River Street
Savannah, GA
(912) 234–0295

The sky above the Savannah River explodes in fireworks as folks gather on the plaza to celebrate the nation's birthday on July 4. Technicians shoot off shells three to six inches in diameter from nearby Hutchinson Island or a barge in the river during a twenty-two-minute, computer-synchronized "pyro-musical." Come early to stake out a good spot for viewing the show and bring lawn chairs and a picnic supper to participate in what resembles a gigantic tailgate party. While you're waiting

for the fireworks, you can listen to live music and people-watch. The free event opens about 5 P.M., and the rockets start bursting in air about 9:30 P.M.

August

Historic Downtown

First Saturday
Rousakis Plaza
River Street
Savannah, GA
(912) 234–0295

See our April listing for more information on this monthly event.

Old Fort Jackson
Auction and Crab Boil
Old Fort Jackson
1 Fort Jackson Road
Savannah, GA
(912) 232–3945

If you're going, you need to call ahead for tickets to this evening of fun, history, and food at the oldest standing fort in Geor-

A young angler admires his catch during the Catch 'em and Cook 'em event at the Bamboo Farm and Coastal Gardens. PHOTO: COURTESY OF THE BAMBOO FARM AND COASTAL GARDENS

gia. The easygoing event on the Saturday of Labor Day weekend takes place within the brick walls of the structure, which was manned during the War of 1812 and used during the Civil War as a headquarters for the Confederacy's defense of the Savannah River (see our Attractions chapter). After visitors chow down on boiled crabs and all the trimmings, a live auction is held. The youngsters enjoy themselves scampering around in what amounts to a walled playground, and there's a cannon firing to further liven things up. Admission is approximately $8 for adults and teens and $5 for children 6 to 12. Children younger than five are admitted free. Proceeds are used for the preservation of the fort.

Islands

Tools and Skills That Built the Colony
Wormsloe Historic Site
7601 Skidaway Road
Savannah, GA
(912) 353-3023

Wormsloe staff members in Colonial attire demonstrate carpentry, blacksmithing, and other skills essential to the development of Georgia. This living history program is offered from 11 A.M. until 4 P.M. on the Saturday of Labor Day weekend. Admission is $2.50 for adults, $2 for senior citizens, and $1.50 for children 6 to 18. Those six and younger are admitted free.

September

Historic Downtown

Ralph Mark Gilbert Civil Rights Museum Anniversary Celebration
Ralph Mark Gilbert Civil Rights Museum
460 Martin Luther King Jr. Boulevard
Savannah, GA
(912) 231–8900

Workshops and lectures inside the museum and activities held outside the building emphasize its founding in 1996. Workshops, lectures, and traveling exhibits deal with aspects of African American heritage and so do the activities, which include entertainment by dancers and musicians. Another major part of the celebration, which takes place the first weekend of September, is a benefit dinner at a local hotel. Admission to the museum is $4 for adults, $3 for senior citizens, and $2 for students. Tickets to the dinner are $50.

First Saturday
Rousakis Plaza
River Street
Savannah, GA
(912) 234–0295

See our April listing for more information on this monthly event.

Savannah Jazz Festival
Forsyth Park
Savannah, GA
(912) 232–2222

Forsyth Park heats up with the sounds of jazz on the last weekend in September when nationally and internationally famous musicians come to Savannah. These entertainers, along with local and regional talents, play their special brand of American music in the park from 6 to 11 P.M. on Thursday and Friday and 2 to 11 P.M. on Saturday. The festival continues on Sunday with an event for children at Rousakis Plaza on River Street at 2 P.M. Among the jazz greats who've performed at past festivals are singer Nancy Wilson,

organist Jimmy Smith, and vibraphonist Lionel Hampton. The festival is funded by the city's Department of Cultural Affairs and organized by the Coastal Jazz Association, a nonprofit, community organization that depends on volunteers to run the event. Sessions are free.

Southside/Midtown

Bethesda Labor Day Festival
Bethesda Home for Boys
9520 Ferguson Avenue
Savannah, GA
(912) 351–2040

Held on Labor Day under the large, shady oaks at the Bethesda Home for Boys (see our Attractions chapter), this gathering for families offers live entertainment, kiddie rides, games, craft sales, and hot dogs and hamburgers, the last being made from Bethesda's home-grown beef. Special features have included antique automobile shows and a petting zoo. Admission is free, but there is a $1 fee for parking. You buy tickets for games and food, and the prices won't set you back much. The festival runs from 10 A.M. until 4 P.M.

October

Historic Downtown

Oktoberfest
Rousakis Plaza
River Street
Savannah, GA
(912) 234–0295

If you happen to have a dachshund handy, you might want to enter it in the Wiener Dog Race, a comical competition that's become a featured part of the Savannah Waterfront Association's Oktoberfest event. Some 200 low-slung pooches "sprint" down the 50-foot racecourse as they seek to win prizes for their masters. The race—run in heats of four to six dogs until an overall winner prevails—benefits the local Friends of the Animals organization, and costs $5 to enter. Watching is fun even if you don't have a dog running: Some pups never get out of the starting gate, and others wander around instead of heading for the finish line. The race is staged on the Saturday morning of the festival, which occurs during the first weekend of the month.

There will also be German food and music and plenty of beer. Booths manned by employees of River Street restaurants sell Wiener schnitzel, sauerbraten, bratwurst, and German chocolate cake, but there is also food for those whose tastes aren't Teutonic. Oompah band members decked out in lederhosen and Tyrolean hats provide much of the music, and festivalgoers are invited to join them in doing the arm-flapping, head-bobbing "Chicken Dance." Also, a headline entertainer usually performs at Oktoberfest. Admission is free, but the food is not. Hours of operation are noon to midnight on Friday and Saturday and 9 A.M. until 6 P.M. on Sunday.

Revolutionary War Memorial Celebration
Savannah History Museum
303 Martin Luther King Jr. Boulevard
Savannah, GA
(912) 651–6840

The Coastal Heritage Society uses this celebration to commemorate the climactic battle of the Siege of Savannah (see History), which was fought on the site of the Savannah History Museum and the nearby Historic Roundhouse/Railroad Museum. The ceremony is held about 2 P.M. on a Sunday in early October. Admission is free.

River Street plays host to numerous seasonal events including Oktoberfest. PHOTO: RICK LOFT

Kids and parents get a look at turkeys and geese during the Bamboo Farm's Fall Festival in October.

Historic Savannah Foundation Gala
Location varies
Savannah, GA
(912) 233-7787

One of Historic Savannah Foundation's major fund-raisers starts with cocktails in private homes and moves to a site in one of the city's historic neighborhoods for a black-tie dinner party. The event is held in late October or early November, but the date and location vary. Tickets are $175.

Picnic in the Park
Forsyth Park
Savannah, GA
(912) 236-9536

Sip wine under the stars and enjoy the music of the Savannah Symphony Orchestra at Picnic in the Park on a Sunday in mid-October. The more elaborate your picnic meal, the better. Judges select the best table settings, with awards for the most elegant and most creative. One year, some enthusiastic picnickers rigged up a chandelier to add some sophistication to their dinner, and the sight of fully set tables complete with candelabra is not uncommon. If you prefer to simply sit on a blanket and nibble on a sandwich, that's OK too. The concert and your seats on the grass are free of charge; you provide the food and drink.

The event is funded in part by the Georgia Council for the Arts and Savannah's Department of Cultural Affairs.

Hard Lox Cafe Jewish Food Festival
Forsyth Park
Savannah, GA
(912) 233-1547

Congregation Mickve Israel presents this opportunity to sample Jewish foods such as blintzes, potato latkes, matzo ball soup, knishes, kosher hot dogs, pastrami sandwiches, bread called challah, and, of course, bagels with cream cheese and lox. These delectable items are sold from booths set up in Forsyth Park.

While you're strolling the square, be on the lookout for a booth manned by Arnold Belzer, the rabbi of the temple, who'll be dishing up portions of his own specialty, a type of stir-fry he calls "Ahmein Lo Mein." Live entertainment and activities for children add to the event, which runs from 11 A.M. until 4 P.M. on a Sunday in late October. Admission is free, and you purchase food and beverages by buying tickets at the square.

Savannah Film and Video Festival
Various locations
Savannah, GA
(912) 525-5051

Hosted by the Savannah College of Art and Design, this presentation of film and video productions takes place during a week's time in late October and/or early November. The latest in feature-length films, shorts, animations, documentaries, and student work are screened at the City Lights and Trustees Theaters in downtown Savannah.

Southside/Midtown

Savannah Folk Music Festival
Daffin Park
Savannah, GA
(912) 927-1376

The focal point of this three-day musical jamboree is a concert in Daffin Park in Savannah's midtown area. The concert consists of four to five acts featuring nationally recognized musicians. In recent years, folks such as singer-musicians Mike Seeger, John Jackson, and Dave Van Ronk have graced the stage. The free concert, funded by Savannah's Department of Cultural Affairs, lasts from 1 to 6 P.M. on the Sunday of the festival, and it's held under the oaks just west of the park's lake. Don't let the threat of rain scare you away; festival organizers erect a large tent on the site, so inclement weather won't stop the singing, picking, and grinning. The festival starts on Friday evening of the second weekend in October with performances of local musicians at City Market in downtown Savannah and continues Saturday night with an old-time country dance, usually at the

Oatland Island Education Center. Admission is free. The whole shebang is presented by the Savannah Folk Music Society.

Savannah Greek Festival
Hellenic Center
14 W. Anderson Street
Savannah, GA
(912) 236–8256
When we think of the Savannah Greek Festival, we can taste the baklava and loukoumades melting in our mouths. Those scrumptious pastries are two of the tasty concoctions offered for sale at the Hellenic Center adjacent to St. Paul's Greek Orthodox Church in midtown Savannah during the third Thursday, Friday, and Saturday in October. Among other favorites of the patrons of the festival are the Greek salad, baked chicken seasoned with oregano and lemon juice, and a spinach pie called spanakopita. While you're enjoying the food, sit back and watch the Hellenic Center's dance group perform. You can also tour the church. Festival hours are 11 A.M. until 9 P.M. A $2 admission fee is charged on Saturday and after 4 P.M. on Thursday and Friday.

Coastal Empire Fair
520 W. 63rd Street
Savannah, GA
(912) 354–3542
During eleven days in late October and early November when the weather turns chilly, the Coastal Empire Fair comes to town. The fairgrounds off Montgomery Street glow and throb with the lights and sounds of thrill rides, sideshows, and game booths. The sixty-odd rides include about a dozen for children. This Exchange Club Fair Association extravaganza also features livestock shows, flower shows, and home demonstrations in skills such as canning and quilt making. The $12 admission fee allows you to hop on as many rides and attend as many shows as you wish, and the price is reduced to $10 for special occasions such as days dedicated to students.

Bamboo Farm Annual Fall Festival
Bamboo Farm and Coastal Gardens
2 Canebrake Road
Savannah, GA
(912) 921–5460
Paint a pumpkin, buy some plants (perennials and fall annuals), or purchase fine

Thrills are plentiful at the annual Coastal Empire Fair. PHOTO: PHYL M. GATLIN

art at this celebration of autumn at the Bamboo Farm (see our Attractions chapter). For those seeking a bite to eat, there's a snack bar; the turnip green luncheon, featuring greens, barbecue, sweet potatoes, cornbread, and iced tea; and a hot-dog lunch. The kids will enjoy hayrides and a wildlife show presented by naturalist Okefenokee Joe. Adults might opt for the garden lecture and plant vendors.

This event takes place from 9 A.M. to 3 P.M. on a Saturday in late October. Admission is free, but there are charges for activities: $1 for a hayride, $2 for the wildlife show, $5 for the lecture, $2 for the hot-dog lunch, and $8 for the turnip green luncheon, for which reservations are required.

November

Historic Downtown

First Saturday
Rousakis Plaza
River Street
Savannah, GA
(912) 234-0295

See our April listing for more information on this monthly event.

Telfair Art Fair
Telfair Square
121 Barnard Street
Savannah, GA
(912) 232-1177

The Telfair Museum's annual fair attracts about sixty-five artists from throughout the United States. They compete for cash awards and sell their creations to the public from displays under tents set up around Telfair Square. You can find paintings, sculpture, photographs, fabric, jewelry, and other fine arts at this exhibition, which takes place on the first weekend in November. Hours are 10 A.M. until 5 P.M. on Saturday and 12:30 to 4:30 P.M. on Sunday. The fair is free.

Islands

Cane Grinding and Crafts Festival
Oatland Island Education Center
711 Sandtown Road
Oatland Island, GA
(912) 898-3980
www.oatlandisland.org

Get a glimpse of pioneer life in the Georgia of the 1830s and do some early Christmas shopping by ambling through the Oatland forest and visiting the Heritage Homesite on the second Saturday in November. At the end of your walk through a wood thick with oak, magnolia, pine, and vines of the muscadine grape, you'll find yourself in a small clearing where sugar cane is being processed and an arts and crafts fair is in progress. Farmers grind the cane into juice at a mill powered by a horse, then boil it into syrup. You can watch the entire operation, then buy a bottle of the sweet-smelling nectar to pour on your Sunday morning pancakes.

As many as seventy-five artists and craftspeople will have their handmade creations on sale, and you can pick and choose while strolling amid the displays and snacking on a chunk of cane, a funnel cake, or a chocolate-covered apple on a stick. You might also want to poke your head into the cozy interiors of the two log cabins at the site and watch weavers at work and costumed women preparing corn bread, or you might hunker down on a bench and listen to members of the Savannah Folk Music Society as they perform songs from Georgia's past. Complete your day at Oatland by walking the nature trail to the wild animal habitats and visiting the center's barnyard. If you need to get off your feet for a while, take a ride through the forest in a horse-drawn hay wagon. The festival opens at 10 A.M. and closes at 5 P.M. Admission is $2 for persons four and older; those three and younger are admitted free.

Historic Downtown

Christmas Open House
City Market
Jefferson and St. Julian Streets
(912) 232–4903

On the first Friday evening of December, the courtyard at City Market glows with the soft light of luminarias as shop owners open their doors and offer complimentary refreshments to visitors. Strolling carolers sing Yuletide classics while Father Christmas—resplendent in his green velvet robe and red velvet cape and hat—talks with children about the spirit of the season and their plans for the holidays. This festive atmosphere takes place at City Market's Christmas Open House, which starts at sundown with the lighting of the luminarias and ends about 9 P.M.

Christmas for Kids
City Market
Jefferson and St. Julian Streets
(912) 232–4903

It's been said that Christmas is for children, and City Market takes that to heart by offering a program for young people from 11 A.M. until 2 P.M. on the first Saturday of the month. This event gives youngsters the opportunity to decorate cookies, visit with Father Christmas, and make ornaments representative of Christmas, Hanukkah, and Kwanzaa. The entertainment varies from year to year, with puppet shows, a petting zoo, and performances by cloggers in the mix. It's all free.

Christmas on the River
River Street
Savannah, GA
(912) 234–0295

Usher in the Christmas season on the first Saturday in December by shopping for gifts created by artists and craftspeople and watching a parade starring Santa Claus. The arts and crafts vendors start selling at 9 A.M. on the riverfront plaza, and the parade begins at 2 P.M. on the western end of River Street. A highlight of the parade is the "Newfies," fifty to sixty Newfoundland dogs from throughout the United States. Newfoundlands are huge canines used in rescue operations in cold climes, and the large gathering of these animals is quite a sight. The parade lasts from an hour to ninety minutes and also includes high school bands, color guards, floats, dance troupes, antique cars, and last, but most important, St. Nick riding in a carriage.

After the parade, Santa sits on the main stage of the plaza and listens to children recite their Christmas wish lists. Enjoy the parade but keep an eye out for flying candy flung from the floats to youngsters lining the route. Arts and crafts booths remain open until 6 P.M. In keeping with the spirit of the season, there is no charge for admission to this holiday festival.

Downtown Neighborhood Association
Holiday Tour of Homes
DeSoto Hilton Hotel
15 E. Liberty Street
Savannah, GA
(912) 231–1494
www.dnaholidaytour.net

Many of the homes on the tours offered during this mid-December event are decorated for Christmas in ways reflecting the lifestyles of their owners. The self-guided walking tours are on Saturday afternoon and evening and Sunday afternoon, with a different set of eight to ten homes featured on each day. The sponsoring Downtown Neighborhood Association selects homes in the Historic District that present a diversity in architectural design and decor. The Saturday evening tour runs from 5 to 8 P.M., and candles light the interiors and exteriors of many of the residences visited. The Saturday afternoon tour is from 1 to 5 P.M., and the Sunday tour is from 1 to 5 P.M. Tickets are $25 per tour, and they can be picked up on the days of the event in the lobby of the DeSoto Hilton Hotel.

Tour organizers schedule special events for out-of-town tour-goers, including lectures pertaining to Savannah's architecture and history. Call ahead to find out more about what's available. The association, which has offered the tour for more than twenty years, returns revenues from the event to the community in the form of projects aimed at maintaining and improving the quality of life downtown.

Historic Inns of Savannah
Annual Holiday Tour
Various locations
Savannah, GA
(800) 379–0638

The owners of fifteen festively decorated inns open their doors to tour-goers, serve refreshments, and discuss the histories and furnishings of their establishments during the third weekend in December. The inns are available for self-guided visits from 1 to 4:30 P.M. on the Saturday and Sunday of the tour. Tickets, which are $15, are good for both days and can be purchased at any participating inn (call the toll-free number for a rundown). The sponsoring Historic Inns of Savannah Association donates the proceeds to charity.

Festival of Trees and Lights
Savannah Civic Center
Liberty and Montgomery Streets
Savannah, GA
(912) 238–2777

This event features more than seventy-five trees and wreaths decorated for the holidays by professional designers, florists, and community groups. There's also a display of menorahs, and special events such as a tea for senior citizens, mini-choral concerts by school children, and a black-tie gala dinner are held during the first week of the festival. Parent and Child Development Services, a private, non-profit agency, sponsors the festival, which begins early in December and continues through Christmas Eve.

Hours are from 10 A.M. until 7 P.M. Monday through Saturday and noon until 7 P.M. on Sundays; admission to the display of trees is free. The special events, with the exception of the gala dinner, are also free; tickets to the black-tie affair are $150 each.

Holiday Family Sunday
Telfair Museum of Art
121 Barnard Street
Savannah, GA
(912) 232–1177

The Telfair gets into the holiday spirit by offering demonstrations by local artists, musical performances, storytelling, and activities for children, such as making holiday cards and spice balls. Performances and activities shine the spotlight on diverse holiday traditions. To top all this off, Santa Claus pays a visit, and admission is free. The Sunday on which the festival is held varies from year to year, but the hours are set at 2 to 5 P.M.

New Year's Eve at City Market
City Market
Jefferson and St. Julian Streets
Savannah, GA
(912) 232–4903

Bands or a band and a disc jockey create a party atmosphere at City Market during the hours leading up to midnight on New Year's Eve. When the clock strikes midnight, hundreds of balloons strung across the courtyard are dropped amid the merrymakers. For Savannahians, this is as close as it gets to being in Times Square. The event is free, and the partying starts about 7 P.M. and lasts until 1 or 2 A.M.

Islands

Colonial Christmas at Wormsloe
Wormsloe Historic Site
7601 Skidaway Road
Savannah, GA
(912) 353–3023

While a Yule log is burned, carolers sing to the accompaniment of musicians playing a zither and flutes at this Colonial Christmas celebration. Sip some hot cider and munch on cookies as you enjoy the festivities. This holiday program on the second

Sunday in December runs from 2 to 5:30 P.M., and admission is $2.50 for adults, $2 for senior citizens, and $1.50 for those 6 to 18. Children younger than six are admitted free.

Southside/Midtown

Christmas at Bethesda
Bethesda Home for Boys
9250 Ferguson Avenue
Savannah, GA
(912) 351–2040
The boys of Bethesda (see our Attractions chapter) present a reenactment of the Magi's visit to the baby Jesus and sing Christmas carols during a program at their chapel. The boys and their guests then move to the gymnasium for an Old English Christmas celebration featuring the bringing in of a Yule log and visits from the Switch Man, who gives switches to kids who've been bad; the Cookie Lady, who gives cookies to kids who've been good; and Santa Claus, who has gifts for all the residents of the home. This observance occurs on the Friday two weeks before Christmas and gets started about 6 P.M. The event is free and open to the public; donations are accepted.

Kidstuff

The time has come for a little brutal honesty. Savannah is a wonderful place. You can stay in romantic bed-and-breakfasts, stroll through history, shop for antiques, tour museums showcasing the treasures of gracious living in the past, dine in elegant restaurants on sophisticated dishes. In other words, Savannah's greatest attractions require a little, well, maturity, for full appreciation.

That's wonderful news for many travelers, but if your party includes kids, you're going to need a little help getting them to enjoy the wonders of this city. That's what this chapter is all about. The kids who have the privilege of growing up here have it made—a beach within easy striking distance, a water-oriented outdoor lifestyle that puts crab traps and fishing poles in the youngest of hands, a fanatically organized system of youth sports that covers all the major games (well, not ice hockey—this is the South, you know), a local theater scene that makes room for kids, you name it. Savannah also offers that increasingly rare opportunity of growing up in a place that has a sense of identity and uniqueness.

Chances are, though, that you are just passing through and hooking your kid or kids up to these home-grown attractions isn't really easy in the course of a few days.

With that in mind, we've compiled some suggestions for helping your kids enjoy their Savannah visit. We are not the home of any giant planned theme parks or prefab attractions, for which we should all be grateful. But we are the home of many wonderful things for kids to see and do with their parents while they enjoy themselves and learn something along the way. For organizational purposes, we grouped this chapter loosely along these lines. First of all, we wanted to cover the things that are unique to this city. With that in mind, we open with tips on how to help younger visitors enjoy the historical aspects of the city. Next, still focusing on Savannah flavors, we touch on ways to enjoy some of the unique wildlife of the region. Finally, we cover additional children's activities ranging from playgrounds to laser tag, stuff that is not unique to or even related to Savannah, but which could prove invaluable in keeping young vacationers busy.

Before we begin, though, let's touch on the issue of accommodations. If you are traveling with children, we recommend spending at least part of your stay at Tybee Island, the local beach. We've got a whole chapter on options there. Any child who tags along dutifully on historic site tours and antique shopping rounds deserves a chance to dig in the sand and splash around in the ocean.

Some bed-and-breakfasts in Savannah welcome children, although many have age restrictions. Check beforehand. Personally, we recommend the selection of a hotel or motel with a swimming pool instead of a bed-and-breakfast with a Jacuzzi.

History for Kids

Parents won't be able to resist the Historic District, no matter how much their children complain. Don't worry though: With a little preparation, you can make your trip through time more of an adventure and less like a field trip with a required school report afterwards.

Most people choose at least one guided tour of the Historic District while they are in Savannah. It gets rid of a lot of orientation quickly, and you can go back later on foot to examine what really interested you. This option even works with kids, if you choose your tour carefully. You'll find the full menu of available tour options described in our Attractions chapter, so we won't review them here. Based on our experience with younger guests, however, take these things into consideration when choosing a tour: The purely historical versions won't really hold a child's interest, unless the entire tour group is made up of children on a planned trip and the guide can pitch his or her delivery solely to that age group. Also, find something else to do with the children if you are just dying to do one of the tours based on the best-seller *Midnight in the Garden of Good and Evil.* The guide's patter isn't going to be too explicit, but there's no getting around the fact the book is about murder, homosexuality, transvestites, and larceny.

What does that leave in the tour category? Two really good options: carriage tours and ghost tours. Many city and suburban children have never had a close encounter with a horse, and the novelty of a carriage ride will appeal strongly (and make good family photos). If your children are old enough—say, at least second or third grade—you should check out the ghost tours, especially the walking or carriage versions. The stories are tame enough that they are unlikely to inspire screaming nightmares. (You know your own child best: Don't submit the timid to what the rest of us would consider a friendly chill.) The tours don't actually go inside any buildings, and the whole motif appeals to the adolescent sensibility.

With younger children, you can add interest to historic sight-seeing with the help of a locally produced little book, which exists in two versions. *Savannah Safari* and its updated version, *Savannah Safari II,* are the work of locals Polly Wylly Cooper and Emmeline King Cooper. They are slim paperback volumes, designed to serve as coloring books if you so desire, that send kids on a scavenger-style hunt for "animals" while touring the Historic District. The "animals" are the iron downspouts shaped like dolphins, the sculptured herons in the Forsyth Park fountains, and so on. Stretch the interest for older children by chipping in one of those disposable cameras so they can photograph their "animal" finds.

The *Savannah Safari* books are $5 and available in local bookstores, which you'll find listed in our Shopping chapter.

Juliette Gordon Low Center
142 Bull Street
Savannah, GA
(912) 233–4501

If your children are, have been, or aspire to be Girl Scouts, don't miss this wonderful house museum. In fact, it's your best bet among the museums for entertaining children. The birthplace and childhood home of Juliette "Daisy" Gordon Low is a virtual mecca for Girl Scouts from throughout the country, and you'll spot field trips full of them trooping around Savannah all the time. As a result, the staff at the center is experienced in the art of entertaining children without boring their adult escorts.

The elegant and beautifully preserved home of the wealthy Gordon family, which includes a masterpiece of a garden, works well for both age groups. Hours are 10 A.M. to 4 P.M. Monday through Saturday (closed Wednesday), and 12:30 to 4:30 P.M. Sundays. Cost is $8 for adults and $7 for children. (Read more about it in our Attractions chapter.)

Ships of the Sea Museum
41 Martin Luther King Jr. Boulevard
Savannah, GA
(912) 232–1511

The kids can learn all about Savannah's maritime history at this museum, which recently relocated to one of Savannah's historic old residences. The more upscale setting probably lowered the kid appeal here, but it should still work for kids. If you have a lovestruck Leonardo DiCaprio fan in your group, take note: The collection includes a *Titanic* exhibit. Cost is $5 for adults, $4 for children seven and older (if you have a college ID, you can get the discounted rate). Children younger than seven are free. The museum is open from 10 A.M. to 5 P.M. Tuesday through Sunday and is closed on Mondays.

> ## Insiders' Tip
> You wouldn't normally think of shopping for a child in a cigar store, but hear us out: The shops sell their empty cigar boxes, starting at $2. Even adamant nonsmokers will admit there's nothing better for storing those shells from the beach than a cigar box. (Check out the listings for tobacco in our Shopping chapter. You'll find a shop near River Street and another in the Historic District.)

River Street

River Street, especially by day, can appeal mightily to the young tourist. All along the river are lots of shops, and while they are stocked with expensive gift items with the usual tourist-area markup, there are also plenty of wares geared toward kid tastes and kid pocketbooks. Follow them from shop to shop here and watch them buy candy and trinkets. There's even one real toy store, Toy Smart (2 N. Lincoln Street, which is really just a side entrance a few steps off River Street). (Read more about your choices here in our Shopping chapter.)

If luck is with you, your young entourage will get to spot one or more of the giant container ships, escorted by a team of tugboats, on its way upriver to the Georgia Ports Authority. These ships are such an imposing presence that even jaded teenagers will stop in their tracks to stare.

Wildlife

It's a shame for an inland kid to visit the coastal South and leave without seeing at least one alligator (from a safe distance, of course). Fortunately, that sighting can be arranged, along with such exotic fare as possible glimpses of dolphins. Read on!

The Aquarium at Skidaway Island
30 Ocean Science Circle
Savannah, GA
(912) 598–3474, (912) 598–2496

Scout out Georgia's marine life at The Aquarium at Skidaway Island. This small facility, operated by the University of Georgia Marine Extension Service, also includes a picnic area (which you may appreciate, because it is quite a drive out to Skidaway) and a walking trail. See 200 live animals—including fish of all shapes and sizes, turtles, and maybe even a small shark in the many wall tanks lining the

exhibit hall. You owe this one to your kids if they have never seen a live flounder, our candidate for weirdest looking fish in the world. Then go outside for a stroll along the Jay Wolfe Nature Trail, which passes by scenic marshes. The aquarium is open from 9 A.M. to 4 P.M. on weekdays and noon to 5 P.M. on Saturdays. It is closed on Sundays and holidays. The cost is $2 for adults, $1 for children and seniors; children ages three and under enter free.

Bull River Yacht Club Marina
8005 Old Tybee Road
(U.S. Highway 80 E.)
Tybee Island, GA
(912) 897–7300

This marina offers a ninety-minute dolphin cruise and a longer, three-hour eco-exploration cruise. The shorter version is $15 for adults and $10 for children; the longer version is by charter arrangement only. Call for reservations. They're essen-

Oatland Island Education Center features native animals in natural habitats. PHOTO: KYLE CASON

tial, because these trips are keenly affected by the weather. No one can guarantee you a dolphin sighting, but it is highly likely. The real challenge is to make the trips long enough to justify the price and short enough to remain interesting if the local wildlife choose not to perform. Winter visitors are less likely to find these trips an option, although the marina will arrange custom trips, birthday parties, fishing charters, and other boating recreation excursions.

Lazaretto Creek Marina
U.S. Highway 80 E.
just across Lazaretto Creek Bridge
Tybee Island, GA
(912) 786–5848, (800) 242–0166
While enjoying the scenery of Fort Pulaski and the North Beach of Tybee Island, see friendly bottle-nosed dolphins playing in their natural habitat. The ninety-minute tours cost $12 for adults and teens and $5 for children twelve and younger. Diving and deep-sea/inshore fishing charters are available.

Oatland Island Education Center
711 Sandtown Road
Savannah, GA
(912) 898–3980
You are virtually guaranteed to spot your alligator here at a natural habitat facility operated by the local school system as an educational center. Other once native animals—buffalo, wolves, birds of prey—and an authentic Colonial farm setting, complete with livestock, can also be seen. A self-guided outdoor hike takes you through marshes and around to the different animal and plant exhibits. Admission is $2 and free for those three and younger. The center, which hosts many popular annual events and festivals (see our Annual Events and Festivals chapter), is open from 8:30 A.M. to 5 P.M. Monday through Friday and 10 A.M. to 5 P.M. on Saturdays (holidays impact Saturday hours). As teachers, the staff members are good with kids, so don't miss this attraction. Bring your own bug repellent,

> ## Insiders' Tip
> Let the kids try their luck at fishing. At Tybee's pier, you can rent gear and buy bait. We've seen some interesting catches there.

though—you'll need it. (For more on the center, see our Attractions chapter.)

Savannah National Wildlife Refuge
S.C. Highway 170
Savannah, GA
(912) 652–4415
Take a coastal safari through the 26,349-acre Savannah National Wildlife Refuge. It's full of freshwater marsh, tidal rivers, creeks, and bottomland hardwood swamps. While driving through the refuge, see if you can spot alligators, owls, hawks, turtles, snakes, or maybe even a bald eagle. The refuge is managed by the U.S. Fish and Wildlife Service. It is open seven days a week during daylight hours (except federal holidays), and visiting is free. The refuge is about 9 miles from downtown. (For more information and directions—which are a bit complex—see our Parks and Recreation chapter.)

Tybee Island Marine Science Center
14th Street parking lot
Tybee Island, GA
(912) 786–5917
Stroll the beach, toss a net into the ocean, then learn about what you find during a beach discovery walk held daily at the center. A tour guide leads the way and explains about Tybee's marine life. Don't forget to check out the stuff inside the center too—you'll find a touch tank, aquariums, and shark displays. Admission is $1. (See our chapter on Tybee Island for more information.)

Nature walks over Savannah's well-known marshes are popular with kids. PHOTO: KYLE CASON

Outdoor Adventure

Forsyth Park
Bull Street
between Gaston Street and Park Avenue
Savannah, GA

Thirty acres perfect for letting off some steam are set aside in the Historic Downtown. There are swing sets, slides, and other contraptions for youngsters needing to get rid of some energy, along with plenty of open space to just plain run around in. There are lots of benches, beautiful magnolia trees, and scenery for Mom and Dad to enjoy too. May we suggest a picnic?

Lake Mayer
Montgomery Crossroad and Sallie Mood Drive
Savannah, GA
(912) 652–6786

Bring your bike and take a spin around the 1.5-mile trail at Lake Mayer, located in the seventy-five-acre community park of the same name. While there, you can also play tennis or basketball or feed the ducks swimming in the lake.

Skidaway Island State Park
52 Diamond Causeway
Skidaway Island, GA
(912) 598–2300

Camping sites, picnic areas, trails, playgrounds, and a swimming pool can be found at 533-acre Skidaway Island State Park, the only state park in Chatham County. Maps of the park and trails are available at the park office. If you don't want to tackle the trails alone, free guided hikes are available with advance reservations. The pool is open Memorial Day to Labor Day and costs $2 per swimmer. Cost to enter the park is $2 per car. (For more information, see our Parks and Recreation chapter.)

The Ol' Ball Game

Savannah Sand Gnats
Grayson Stadium
Daffin Park
1401 E. Victory Drive
Savannah, GA
(912) 351–9150

If you happen to be in town during the Sand Gnats season (early April through the end of August), round up the kids and take them to a ball game. Besides being entertained by the Gnats, the single-A affiliate for the Texas Rangers, kids and parents will have fun watching the dueling mascots and between-inning contests (including the classic one in which two people spin around dozens of times with their heads on the ends of bats, then try to make it to first base), munching on barbecue and boiled peanuts, and getting caught up in the atmosphere of this old-time ballpark. Games start at 7:15 P.M. on weekdays and Saturdays and at 2 P.M. on Sundays until mid-June, when Sunday games begin at 4 P.M. General admission is only $5 for adults and $3 for students and children. Cheaper seats offer the best chance of catching foul balls. Parking is free around the stadium. (For much more on the Sand Gnats, see our Spectator Sports chapter.)

Enjoying the Arts

Midnight Star Pottery
32 Barnard Street
Savannah, GA
(912) 236–3473

Paint a bowl for your grandmother or a water dish for your favorite kitty at Midnight Star Pottery, a unique and enjoyable pottery painting studio in City Market.

A corner of ToySmart on River Street is set up as a museum for baby boomer (and earlier) playthings.
PHOTO: BETTY DARBY

Kids can spend hours choosing among the dozens of pottery pieces—included are plates, picture frames, pasta sets, tiles, napkin rings, even dog and cat dishes—and creating masterpieces. It's a lot of fun for Mom and Dad, too. Costs include the pottery items, which start at $2 for a tile and go up from there, and an hourly studio fee. Children ten and younger pay $5 per hour for studio use; adults pay $6 per hour. The fee includes all creative materials (paints, brushes, glazes), firing, and instruction. The clock doesn't start ticking on the studio fee until you've picked out your piece of pottery, colors, and designs and have sat down to paint. In other words, if your child takes an hour trying to figure out just the right present to create for his or her teacher, it won't cost you anything extra.

Saturday Art Colony
Tybee Arts Association
P.O. Box 2344
Tybee Island, GA
(912) 786–5920

Make a puppet, create art out of sand, or just paint and draw during this class offered by the Tybee Arts Association. The association offers Saturday Art Colony year-round. It runs from 10:30 A.M. to noon and costs $6 per session for Tybee residents and $8 for nonresidents. A different medium is featured each Saturday, with kids involved in activities such as working with clay, painting, or creating sand sculptures.

The Light at the End of the Tunnel

Tybee Island Lighthouse
30 Meddin Drive
Savannah, GA
(912) 786–5801

Hike 154 feet to the top of Tybee Lighthouse for a great view of Tybee and Savannah. You'll also be learning a few things

about one of America's historic light stations. From April 1 to Labor Day, the lighthouse is open daily (except Tuesdays) from 9 A.M. to 6 P.M. After Labor Day it is open from 9 A.M. to 4 P.M. on weekdays and is closed on Tuesdays. Cost, which includes admission to the Tybee Museum, is $4 for adults, $3 for seniors and children.

Options of Last Resort

Did it rain after you rashly promised a day at the beach? Has too much walking left your feet too blistered to keep up with the kids? Then you might consider these options. They aren't unique to Savannah. In fact, they're the franchise-ish type thing that this book purposely doesn't include in most instances. But as any parent knows, when it comes to kids, it never hurts to have a fallback plan. All four of these places cater to visiting birthday parties. All feature high noise and hyperactivity levels. Adults who bring children here must summon up lots of fortitude. With that warning, here goes:

Insiders' Tip

If you visit in the summer, the various branch libraries are in full swing with summer programs for kids. Call (912) 652-3600 to find the branch nearest you. Visitors are always welcome, and with a temporary card (cost $2.50), you can even check out books, videos, and tapes.

Surf's up at Tybee Island! PHOTO: PHYL M. GATLIN

Chuck E. Cheese
6700 Abercorn Street
Savannah, GA
(912) 355–6420

The Flying Frogs
1100 Eisenhower Drive
Savannah, GA
(912) 356–0075

We lumped these two together because to us they are pretty much indistinguishable, despite the fact they are business rivals. Essentially, each is an indoor playground where kids are not only allowed to run wild, but are encouraged to do so. Pizza is the menu mainstay. There are also games that pay off in points that kids can amass for prizes. At Chuck E. Cheese, there are giant animated figures that sing and perform skits. Chuck E. Cheese is open from 10 A.M. to 10 P.M. weekdays and Sundays and 10 A.M. to 11 P.M. Friday and Saturday. Flying Frogs features a kiddy

train. Admission is free at Chuck E. Cheese, although you pay for the food and games. At Flying Frogs, admission is $3.95 for ages 1 to 3 and $6.95 for ages 4 to 13 (although the average 13-year-old isn't going to be interested). Although the frog place costs more, desperate parents can buy beer there. The Flying Frog hours are 10 A.M. to 9 P.M. weekdays, 10 A.M. to 11 P.M. Friday and Saturday, and 11 A.M. to 8 P.M. Sundays.

Galaxy Laser Games
1800 E. Victory Drive
Savannah, GA
(912) 234–3666

OK, if you can't get enough out of a computer war game, take it to the next level. Don a vest and stalk fellow players with a light gun. We don't get it, but older kids and teens do, along with some adults. Prices are $10 a person but change frequently with various specials. Children have to be big enough to wear the vest, usually around age six or so. Recreational warfare, anyone?

The Playground
1127 Fulton Road
Savannah, GA
(912) 925-7529
Save your quarters, then head to The Playground, a giant playland for kids, filled with video games, tunnels for crawling in, special prizes, and much more. It's roughly across the street from the Savannah Mall and sort of behind the parking lot of a currently vacant building that used to house a Wal-Mart. The Playground could keep kids busy and happy (provided the quarter-provider's pockets don't empty out too soon) for hours. Admission is $3.99 for children ages 1 to 3 and $5.99 for kids four and older. It is open 10 A.M. to 7 P.M. Monday through Thursday, 10 A.M. to 9 P.M. Friday and Saturday, and noon to 8 P.M. on Sunday.

Insiders' Tip

Looking for kid-friendly restaurants that aren't fast-food franchises? Lots of restaurants cater to families, but if you're looking for a vacation dinner that will offer something for both adult and child appetites, try The Pirates' House downtown. The decor, along with tales of pirates and ghosts, will keep the kiddies entertained while you wait. (See our Restaurants chapter for more details.)

Arts and Culture

Savannah prides itself on its arts and culture scene, and justifiably so. The city is not only a consumer of the arts, but with the advent of a Savannah-based art college of growing repute, it is also a producer of the arts. Music, drama, and the visual arts are all well represented here, both in the form of outlets for local talent and in venues for touring artists of greater renown.

You can take your arts and culture on various levels in Savannah. You can don your designer duds and shop in ultrachic art galleries, picking up pieces by artists who never set foot on these shores; you can dress in jeans and pick up a sketch from a sidewalk artist on River Street; or you can rent a garret, buy a backpack, and enroll in art classes yourself. You can also work through the same type of strata musically as a symphony concertgoer, a jazz follower in smoky nightclubs, or as a community band or civic orchestra performer bent on honing your talents. As for theater, you'll find several active local theater groups, thriving secular performance venues in some local churches, and for those who prefer the role of spectator, the occasional national touring troupe.

In this chapter, we outline Savannah's major cultural organizations and venues for you. We provide plenty of telephone numbers and instructions on how to tap into specific schedules. You might also want to check out our Annual Events and Festivals chapter for further suggestions for an artsy afternoon or evening. Keeping abreast of the local cultural scene is fairly easy. The *Savannah Morning News* (see our Media chapter) offers its most comprehensive arts coverage in a Sunday *Accent* section. The *Morning News*'s Friday *Diversions* section also contains event listings, but the coverage there tends to be more club and concert oriented. *Diversions* can be picked up free at various downtown and Southside shopping centers and restaurants after it appears as part of Friday's edition, but if you want to get your hands on a Sunday section during the week, you either have to pay full face value at the newspaper's offices (111 W. Bay Street in the heart of the Historic Downtown) or swing by a library.

CONNECT Savannah/Creative Loafing, the result of the recent combining of a pair of weekly papers, is a good resource on entertainment and the club scene, with the ads as informative as the articles and the listings among the city's most complete. Again, check our Media chapter for suggestions on where to find this publication.

Venues

Lucas Theatre for the Arts
32 Abercorn Street
Savannah, GA
(912) 234-3200
www.lucastheatre.com

The restoration of the Lucas Theatre for the Arts seemed to take forever, but it has been worth the wait. The facility had a soft opening in 2000 but really got into the swing of things with a full 2001–2002 performance schedule that had something for everyone.

The theater was built in 1921 and rode the popularity of the Silver Screen for decades. Alas, it fell into disrepair as the 1970s came on, and after some ill-fated attempts to keep it running (such as a short stint as a dinner theater and period

The Lucas, a restored movie palace from the 1920s, offers everything from touring Broadway shows to vintage movies. PHOTO: BETTY DARBY

when the lobby was a restaurant), the magnificent building went into mothballs.

But the Italian Renaissance–style building with its ornate interior was just too fantastic to let go, and a lengthy fundraising campaign was started to get this grand dame back on her feet. Restoration, however, is expensive, especially when you do things like bring in an Italian artisan to recreate the plaster moldings. Look for the forty-foot-wide ceiling dome, lots of gold leaf, and—a welcome sight to Savannah eyes—the bars upstairs and down. It took thirteen years to pull it off, but the end result is beautiful. The marquee, with its chasing lights, adds an exciting touch to Savannah's nightlife, and the proximity of the theater has probably been a factor in the restoration of a set of nearby fire-damaged buildings that now host cafes.

Still, the plushest of surroundings don't amount to much if there isn't something to see. The first year's schedule struck a promising note, and chances are you can expect subsequent ones to do the same. The "dance card" is chosen to find something to appeal to everyone. For example, the premiere season (September 2001–March 2002) includes touring shows of *My Fair Lady, Buddy: The Buddy Holly Musical, Ragtime,* and *Titanic,* not to mention the performers Penn and Teller. The Grand Night Out series included the Hong Kong Ballet, Boys Choir of Harlem, the London City Opera's presentation of *The Merry Widow,* and the Vienna Choir Boys.

That's just the formal portion of the calendar, however. The Lucas is also in use as a concert venue, with performers such as bluegrass crossover sensation Alison Krause. It even returns periodically to its movie heyday, showing offbeat but trendy fare or even a made-in-Savannah movie.

The box office is on the premises.

The Roundhouse Complex
601 W. Harris Street
Savannah, GA
(912) 651-6823
Adjacent to the old Central of Georgia Railroad Station that now serves as the Savannah Visitors Center, this old railroad yard where trains used to turn around has been developed as a rustic outdoor performance venue. We caught a blues-and-barbecue festival there in 1999. It's also hosted a variety of outdoor concerts, although there is no set schedule. Check the sources we've mentioned above for info on upcoming acts. The bill of fare tends to run to aging heavy rock acts.

Savannah Civic Center
Montgomery and Liberty Streets
Savannah, GA
(912) 651-6556
This is a place, not an entity like a symphony or a drama group, but we list it here because it is the major performance venue in the city. The city of Savannah owns and operates this major facility, but groups, including private ventures and touring companies, stage the shows here.

The Savannah Civic Center has two main components, not including various meeting rooms and a ballroom. The arena, named for the late Dr. Martin Luther King Jr., can seat up to 9,000, depending on the event configuration. The theater, which seats about 2,500, is named in honor of Johnny Mercer, the famed Savannah-born lyricist ("Moon River," etc.). By and large, the more formal events, such as dramatic presentations or one-person shows, play in the theater, with the arena going for large-scale, pack-'em-in audiences for such events as rock or country music concerts, wrestling matches, and monster truck shows. But that isn't a hard-and-fast rule: When Mikhail Baryshnikov danced in Savannah with the touring experimental White Oak Dance Troupe, they filled the arena.

The offerings at the Civic Center vary, depending on the tastes and daring of various promoters. The concert scene has become more lively with the continued growth of the Savannah College of Art and Design and its built-in audience potential. To keep up with what might be available during your visit, check the media sources mentioned at the opening

Savannah: Style Central for Architecture Buffs

Stroll along the streets of Savannah's Historic Downtown, and you'll be looking at a blend of buildings reflecting architectural styles prevalent in America during the late-eighteenth and nineteenth centuries. Among these types were Federal, which was in vogue from 1790 to 1838; English Regency, 1811 to 1830; Greek Revival, 1820 to 1875; Gothic Revival, 1830 to 1885; Italianate, 1830 to 1900; Romanesque Revival, 1850 to 1890; and Victorian, 1860 to 1915.

Probably the city's most outstanding example of the Federal style is the Isaiah Davenport House, with its central hallway and arched fanlight doorway. This brick and brownstone house at 324 E. State Street "reflects the balance and symmetry" of the Federal style, says Roulhac Toledano in *The National Trust Guide to Savannah*, and its double-entry stairway "must have set the standard for future graceful curving entry staircases leading to high stoops that dot the city in houses of all styles." The Davenport House, one of Savannah's many museum houses, was built in 1820; a successful effort to save it from demolition in the mid-1950s brought about the creation of the Historic Savannah Foundation preservation group. (Read more about the house in the walking tour section of our Attractions chapter.)

The Regency style is best typified by the work of English architect William Jay and two of his designs, the Owens-Thomas House at 124 Abercorn Street and the Scarbrough House at 41 Martin Luther King Jr. Boulevard, both of which are open to the public. The porches and columns of these buildings are prime examples of the Regency style. A commission to build the former house for cotton merchant Richard Richardson is what brought Jay to Georgia, and he "went on to create a series of buildings that qualify as the state's first architectural masterpieces," says Tom Spector

The Isaiah Davenport House, built on East State Street in 1820, is a fine example of the Federal style. PHOTO: COURTESY OF SAVANNAH AREA CONVENTION AND VISITORS BUREAU

in his book, *The Guide to the Architecture of Georgia*. These two houses "rank among the best works produced in America" during the early 1800s. The Owens-Thomas House, which Toledano deems "probably the finest example of English Regency architecture in America," was constructed in 1819 and the Scarbrough House was completed in the same year.

Greek Revival–style buildings are reminiscent of the temples of Greece with their long front porches supported by towering columns. To see two fine models of this style, take a look at the Aaron Champion House at 230 Barnard Street and the Sorrel-Weed House at 6 W. Harris Street. Both houses were designed by Charles Cluskey, the Champion House in 1844 and the Sorrel-Weed House in 1841. Cluskey was Georgia's premier architect during the 1830s and '40s.

Walk over to Madison Square for a look at what Toledano calls Savannah's "foremost Gothic-style house." The Green-Meldrim House at 1 W. Macon Street, which can be toured by visitors, was designed by John S. Norris and built in 1853. Exterior features are the crenelated parapet, oriel windows, and the heavily detailed iron porch. (See our Attractions chapter for more on the Green-Meldrim House.)

The Mercer House at 429 Bull Street is another Norris design, but it is an example of the Italianate style, which has the look of Italian villas—low-pitched roofs, wide eaves, long porches, and cast-iron balconies. The house was designed before the outbreak of the Civil War but was completed in 1871 by two former assistants of Norris. (For more on the Mercer House, see our chapters on Attractions and Popular Culture.) Another Italianate-style residence (and another of the city's house museums) is the Andrew Low House at 329 Abercorn Street (see our Attractions chapter).

The Romanesque Revival style is embodied by two Savannah landmarks, the Cotton Exchange at 100 E. Bay Street and the Chatham County Courthouse at 124 Bull Street. Both were designed by William G. Preston. The Cotton Exchange, with its brick and terra cotta facade and turned wooden posts, was constructed in 1886. Preston came to Savannah to build the courthouse three years later.

An interesting example of the gingerbread style of the Victorian period is the King-Tisdell Cottage at 514 E. Huntingdon Street, which now serves as a black cultural museum. It dates to 1896.

of this chapter, or simply check the large billboard on the Liberty Street side of the building. The number listed here is for the box office, and tickets generally are on sale well in advance of performances.

The Civic Center consumes an entire block between Oglethorpe and Liberty Streets, with entrances on Montgomery Street and facing the parking lot. A word of warning about parking is in order: Popular events at the Civic Center put parking at a premium. The closest lots associated with the center fill quickly. Because it is easier to get out of a street side parking space, many patrons prefer to park along the surrounding streets. You don't have to feed the meters at night, but be sure not to block the crosswalks leading to the squares or make up any imaginative parking spaces—lots of parking tickets get handed out on the evenings of big performances. Also, avoid the temptation to whip into the vacant parking lots of obviously closed businesses: Many businesses choose to defend those spaces at night and will have after-hours parkers towed. There is ample parking in the city's parking tower a few blocks away at 132 Montgomery Street, and it is usually scheduled to be open on nights when the Civic Center is in action.

Savannah College of Art and Design
Various addresses and numbers

You may wonder what an art college is doing under the "Venues" heading. Actually, SCAD (as it is referred to locally; see our Education chapter for additional information) is a major player in the local arts and culture scene, not just for its own students, but for the general public. Check out the SCAD art galleries listed later in this chapter, but first, two of the newest (including the most attractive and

Savannah College of Art and Design has adapted many historic structures, including this old armory, for its scattered urban campus. PHOTO: KYLE CASON

unique) theater entries are from SCAD. Trustees Theater, 206 E. Broughton Street (912-239-1447), is a circa-1946 movie theater that has been refurbished and reopened as a 1,100-seat performance venue capable of handling both stage productions and movie screenings. Its basic purpose is to house performances and classes for SCAD's performing arts majors, but it also offers performances to the public. Crooner Tony Bennett was the debut act in a real put-on-the-dog evening of glamour and glitz in May 1998, and a year later he was followed by the Neville Brothers. This is also the home of SCAD's annual film festival.

Pei Ling Chan Garden for the Arts, 324 Martin Luther King Jr. Boulevard (912-239-1447) is a small and beautiful garden billed primarily as an outdoor sculpture gallery, but it includes a small roofed, open-sided amphitheater that is home to occasional performances. We caught a performance of *Godspell* there that was remarkable for several reasons: the setting, a SCAD cast that brought great energy to a play that was popular before the cast was born, and—it was free! Don't count on the free part to always be the case, though.

Music

Savannah Symphony Orchestra
225 Abercorn Street
Savannah, GA
(912) 236-9536, (800) 537-7894

The Savannah Symphony Orchestra is the crown jewel of Savannah's cultural collection. Before turning up your nose at smaller city orchestras, consider this—the Savannah Symphony was rated the best in the state in 1995 by the Georgia Council for the Arts. That field included Augusta, Columbus ... and Atlanta.

The orchestra has a core of about thirty permanent performers, supplemented by additional musicians who come in from around the Southeast when their services are needed for the Masterworks Series, Pops, and other large-scale programs. The symphony gives more than 300 performances in a season that begins in September and runs through May. Many feature smaller subdivisions of the group, say, a string quartet or a brass ensemble. Others are in-school performances as part of an exceptionally active outreach program to young people.

The real mainstays of the schedule, however, are the Masterworks and Pops series, regularly scheduled performances held in the Savannah Civic Center's Johnny Mercer Theatre on Saturday nights. The Masterworks series describes itself with its title. The program runs to Beethoven, Verdi, Brahms, Mozart, and their peers. Nationally and internationally known guest performers join the symphony for these performances. The Pops series is also pretty self-descriptive—lighter fare and a slate of guest artists who will be recognized outside the circle of classical music aficionados.

The symphony derives about 60 percent of its $2.5 million operating budget from ticket sales, so it's hardly surprising that guests will find an efficient and professional ticketing operation. The symphony handles its own ticket sales at its offices up to the day of performance, only then shifting it to the box office at the Civic Center. The easiest way to get tickets is to order by phone, pay by credit card, and pick them up at the "will call" window at the Civic Center (just give yourself a few extra minutes before curtain to do so).

The best ticket deals come in series and packages, but visitors will hardly need those. Single tickets run $10 to $40 for Masterworks performances and $15 to $35 for the Pops. What to wear? Business attire is sufficient. People tend to dress more formally for the Masterworks than the Pops, but you really don't have to. As long as guys wear a jacket and tie, they're dressy enough. (In other words, shelve the tux unless you are just dying to wear it.) Women can stop at the semiformal level, and they certainly don't have to go that far unless after-concert plans dictate it.

The symphony also stages a number of free admission concerts in other settings, predominantly outdoors. Foremost among these are the Picnic in the Park in Forsyth Park, held on a Sunday evening each October, and the Arts on the River weekend, which culminates in an outdoor concert on River Street in May. Definitely build your weekend around these events if you are lucky enough to be in town when they are staged. They show Savannah at its best, with large crowds turning out for good-natured enjoyment of a light classical program in two of the city's most attractive settings. (For more on both of these happenings, refer to our Annual Events and Festivals chapter.) The symphony maintains the listed toll-free line for information and ticket orders.

Theater

Savannah has two full-time drama groups, but the theater scene is larger than that infers. Several churches have recently launched highly successful productions of secular works such as Gilbert and Sullivan offerings, and there are also collegiate theatrical groups. Check the event pages of the newspapers cited earlier for schedules and further information.

Asbury Memorial United Methodist Church
1008 E. Henry Street
Savannah, GA
(912) 233-4351

This venerable church was dying out as its congregation aged and the neighborhood changed, but it got a shot in the arm when a performance-minded pastor and the congregation opened their arms to the arts community. The church social hall serves as a performance arena. Don't mistake these productions for Sunday school projects. They're at least on a par with the other local offerings (actually, all the local theater efforts involve different arrangements of essentially the same theater performers).

Although the offerings often have a religious theme (*Godspell* and *Jesus Christ Superstar*), this group has also tackled Gilbert and Sullivan. Ticket prices vary, usually around $12. Other local churches occasionally dip into secular drama, mainly to keep their youth groups involved, but this one definitely strives for and achieves a higher level.

City Lights Theater
125 E. Broughton Street
Savannah, GA
(912) 234-9860

Offerings here tend to be a little heavier, though City Lights will do the occasional musical or comedy as well. The theater setting is more intimate (once more, the setting is a renovated movie theater—we're well stocked with those), and the approach involves a little more risk taking. City Lights, for example, hosts a local playwrights' festival. They also join forces with the city to present the Savannah Shakespeare Festival (see Annual Events) in Forsyth Park. The spring 1998 offering was a modern-dress *Macbeth* complete with handguns and golf carts—they've stuck to comedies since then. Again, performances are generally reviewed by the daily paper after the opening night performance.

Savannah Theatre
222 Bull Street
Savannah, GA
(912) 233-7764

The home base for this group is billed as the oldest continuously active theater in

the country. Of course, the building burned down a few times over the years, but the location and foundation are the same. Before its conversion to serve the local theater group, this was the last of the once-plentiful downtown movie theaters.

Look here for a varied schedule of community theater productions: light musicals, mysteries, dramas, and what have you. You want examples? How about *The Almost Ed Sullivan Show, Nunsense* and its sequels, *Plaid,* and others. Heavier fare included the winter 2000 staging of *To Kill a Mockingbird.* The quality of the productions will vary from show to show, but these are generally fun evenings that tap into local talent. The *Savannah Morning News* usually reviews the opening night performance if you are looking for guidance. Ticket prices are $15 for musicals and $12 for dramas, with reduced rates for students and seniors.

Things are often in flux for community groups such as this, and Savannah Theatre has had a few growing pains—with the real estate up for sale, for example. Local theater buffs, however, have proven to be a hardy lot.

The City Lights Theatre showcases local talent. PHOTO: BETTY DARBY

Museums and Galleries

Savannah College of Art and Design
345 Bull Street
Savannah, GA
(912) 238–2480, (912) 239–1486,
(800) 869–SCAD

This growing art college's campus is scattered throughout Savannah's Historic Downtown and Victorian District. Among its holdings are multiple on-campus galleries featuring rotating displays in a variety of media. Some feature the work of students, both graduate and undergraduate, or the college's faculty. Frequently, however, these galleries host works of internationally known artists such as Jasper Johns, Robert Rauschenberg, and Dale Chihuly.

The flagship galleries, most likely to feature professional work, are Exhibit A and West Bank. These exhibits are free and open to the public. Times vary, particularly in keeping with the academic year, so call one of the listed numbers for hours and information on what is currently on exhibit. Also, check out the media outlets discussed earlier in this chapter for exhibit details. Following is a rundown of SCAD's galleries. Consider this list fluid. As the college grows, the roles of its various galleries are subject to change—not to mention that it keeps acquiring new real estate.

Exhibit A Gallery

This gallery, housed in an old armory building in the center of the Historic Downtown at 340 Bull Street, was among the first of the college's now-significant real estate holdings. This gallery concentrates on visiting national and international exhibits and is among the easiest of the SCAD galleries for a visitor to find. If you are only doing one SCAD gallery, and the details on current exhibits don't give you a reason to pick one over another, do this one. A look at the Rococo building is worth the trip by itself.

Bergen Hall Galleries

This gallery, located at 101 Martin Luther King Jr. Boulevard, concentrates primarily on exhibiting photographic work.

Eichberg Hall Gallery

This is another general gallery that will feature the work of students and professionals on rotating schedules. It is located at 229 Martin Luther King Jr. Boulevard.

Ex Libris Third Floor Gallery

Atop the college-operated book and supply store at 228 Martin Luther King Jr. Boulevard, this gallery sells the work of SCAD faculty, students, and alumni. (See more on Ex Libris in the Bookstores section of our Shopping chapter.)

Hamilton Hall Gallery

This building at 522 Indian Street houses the college's video department. The gallery hosts both student and faculty work and traveling exhibits.

Henry Hall Gallery

This gallery at 115 W. Henry Street showcases painting and fiber arts works.

Pinnacle Gallery

The college describes this gallery (located at 320 E. Liberty Street) as "dedicated to celebrating multiculturalism through the arts." Most of the featured artists are from outside the states.

Rapid Transit Gallery

This dark, basement, Bohemian-style gallery at 342 Bull Street exhibits graduate student thesis shows. It's right alongside the Exhibit A Gallery.

The Red Gallery

This gallery is located inside SCAD's Jin Library, which was once a major department store and fills the entire block on Broughton Street between Abercorn and Lincoln Streets.

West Bank Gallery

SCAD devotes this gallery to contemporary cutting-edge art. When you are finished inside at 322 Martin Luther King Jr. Boulevard, check alongside the building for one of the more interesting entries in the SCAD gallery collection, the Garden for the Arts. This outdoor sculpture garden has four sections: the African-American Garden, Asian Garden, English Garden, and French Garden.

Telfair Museum of Art
121 Barnard Street
Savannah, GA
(912) 232–1177

It's billed as the oldest museum in the south, but the Telfair Museum of Art is shaking off some of its staid image and stepping up to the plate with new programs and a controversial new building. Granted, its heart will remain an ancestral mansion, but a separate building on the same square is being built in a decidedly modern fashion.

Programs are modernizing as well. The Telfair branched out in 2001 by putting together a major traveling exhibition that played to record crowds here and then moved on to Memphis and San Diego. The exhibition, "Frederick Carl Frieseke: The Evolution of an American Impressionist," was definitely the most ambitious project of the museum's current history, and it demonstrated well the wisdom of the museum's leadership early in the last century: The museum's collection includes two prime Friesekes.

The touring schedule has also gotten more ambitious. The museum closed out 2001 by hosting "Close Friends" by Andrew Wyeth, a collection of paintings focusing on the African American neighbors of the Pennsylvania artist.

Savannah boasts many museums, but most are either theme museums (like the Ralph Mark Gilbert Civil Rights Museum) or house museums—interesting homes whose main attraction is the historical significance of the building itself, backed up by the re-creation of a bygone lifestyle through period furnishing. (You can find out more details about these places in our Attractions chapter.)

The Telfair, however, is a true art museum, although the house museum description certainly applies to a portion of the Telfair mansion. Housed in the Neoclassical Regency mansion designed by English architect William Jay for the prominent Telfair family (a Georgia governor was among the family members), this is the oldest art museum in the South. Think of it as having three elements: It's part house museum, part permanent collection, part gallery for visiting exhibitions and programs.

The permanent collection includes paintings, sculpture, prints, and decorative arts. The collection includes examples of American impressionism, Ash Can Realists, and classical sculpture casts. Included are works by Childe Hassam, Gari Melchers, Robert Henri, George Bellows, and George Luks.

The museum also holds the largest existing collection of the works of Lebanese mystical poet and artist Kahlil Gibran, best known for *The Prophet*. His patroness, Mary Haskell, made her home in her later years on Gaston Street in Savannah. Because of the fragile nature of the artwork (it was done predominantly in pencil), it is only on display occasionally. On a more contemporary note, the Telfair is the new home for the *Bird Girl* sculpture featured on the cover of John Berendt's *Midnight in the Garden of Good and Evil*. Fans of the book hounded it out of its original setting in a family plot at Bonaventure.

Admission to the Telfair is $8 for adults, $7 for seniors, $2 for students ages twelve and older, and $1 for children 6 to 12. Younger children are admitted free. Chatham County residents are admitted free on Sundays, but, citing budget cuts, the museum has discontinued the practice of blanket free admission on Sundays. Hours are 10 A.M. to 5 P.M. Tuesday through Saturday, 2 to 5 P.M. Sunday, and noon to 5 P.M. Monday.

Statues stand in front of the Telfair Museum of Art. PHOTO: BETTY DARBY

Other Galleries

Savannah has a large stock of art galleries. We listed those with collegiate connections separately. The following list consists of independent galleries. This is only a very small sample to get you started. The Sunday arts section of the *Savannah Morning News* usually offers a current listing of shows. And you'll stumble on others by accident: Lately half the coffee shops and little restaurants in town have turned their walls into impromptu galleries. For examples of this trend, check out Soho South (in our Restaurants chapter) and the Angel House Café and Gallery, on the corner of Broughton and Montgomery Streets.

A. T. Hun
302 W. St. Julian Street (City Market)
Savannah, GA
(912) 233–2060

Three artist friends who say they got tired of having their work censored at more conventional galleries launched this colorful gallery. It's all contemporary, and includes many larger pieces. The nudes that sparked the birth of the gallery aren't shocking, just a good reflection of how conservative Savannah can be. Potters, jewelers, and photographers are represented as well, and there is an affiliation with an English gallery so there is a regular exchange of international work.

Don't look here for soft watercolors or memento landscapes of Savannah. It's young, funky, and even sells T-shirts sporting a Latin phrase that translates (roughly) as "We don't do snobby." Don't be misled, however; there's good stuff here.

Gallery 209
209 E. River Street
Savannah, GA
(912) 236–4583

This River Street gallery is the place to start your search for local artwork. Stuff here varies in quality, from some wannabe artists to the real thing. We especially like the enamel jewelry, such as a jewel tone seahorse. In addition to paintings that run the gamut from very good to not very, you'll find fiber art and interesting and affordable ceramics.

Jack Leigh Gallery
132 E. Oglethorpe Avenue
Savannah, GA
(912) 234–6449

Leigh was the cover artist for the book *Midnight in the Garden of Good and Evil*. His small gallery has copies of that print of the *Bird Girl* statue, but the gallery mainly is the showcase for his black-and-white artistry. Leigh does series on vanishing Southern ways of life: oystering, farming, and so on. The works on display can be both haunting and appealing.

Off the Wall
206 W. Broughton Street
Savannah, GA
(912) 233–8840

This colorful, cheerful gallery features a mix of work by area artists and others and includes some very reasonably priced pieces. Paintings account for most of the art, but there are a few other pieces as well, such as jewelry and, when we last went by, some whimsical sculpture. Since owner Gail Levites moved to Broughton Street, Savannah's revitalized "main street," she amended her stock to include some interesting pieces priced more for the gift market, but the real stuff is still well represented. Since setting up shop in what would once have been an unlikely location, she has acquired some interesting gallery neighbors.

Library Resources

Chatham-Effingham-Liberty Regional Library
2002 Bull Street
Savannah, GA
(912) 652–3600

Don't be put off by the bureaucratic name, which comes from the three counties the library system serves. The recent opening of an $8.3 million expansion and addition to the circa-1916 main branch on Bull Street has revitalized the entire library system. The building's addition is clad in marble and features park views from massive clerestory windows. The collection had drifted off into inadequacy and obsolescence until the renovation project gave it a shot in the arm—and a $3 million injection of public and private monies to stock the new shelves. (One anonymous couple chipped in $1 million.) While you may not think of libraries as places to visit while vacationing, there are resources here of interest to the traveler. Foremost among them is the local history and genealogy collection. Those in search of the dirt on their ancestors have been known to make the trip just to get into those records. Visitors can use the resources of the library without charge and can even check items out if they pay the $2.50 nonrefundable card fee for out-of-towners. (It's free if you live here.) A video collection that circulates free and a "Stellar Sellers" program (where you can "rent" best-sellers for a nominal fee if you

don't want to wait for them to turn up on the request list) are among the features that might be of particular interest to those passing through.

Insiders' Tip

Are you a fan of sculpture in iron? You're in luck. Ironwork artist Ivan Bailey now lives in Atlanta, but he was formerly a Savannahian. You'll find his work on several decorative gates in the Historic Downtown as well as the courtyard fountain at the Eliza Thompson House (a bed-and-breakfast).

Parks and Recreation

From time to time we hear local residents say, "There's nothing to do in Savannah." A look through this chapter will prove those folks don't know what they're talking about, at least as far as outdoor activities are concerned. Chatham County has more water than you can shake a shillelagh at, so opportunities for boating, sailing, and fishing abound. We're blessed with parks and parklike areas of every description and in every jurisdiction—national, state, regional, county, and city—and these provide settings for picnics and play and trails for hiking, biking, and jogging. Golfers and tennis players will find numerous venues that are open to the public.

Those who like their recreation organized can participate in a variety of team sports offered for adults and youngsters by the county, city, YMCA, and the recreation departments of the smaller municipalities; athletes eighteen and younger can keep busy playing practically year-round, and many do. Much of this organized activity takes place at facilities comprising Bacon Regional Park, a 500-acre complex in Southside/Midtown. This is the site of Memorial Stadium, where many of the area's high school football games are played; Lake Mayer Community Park; and public facilities for golf (Bacon Park Golf Course), tennis (Bacon Park Tennis Complex), youth baseball and softball (Ambuc Park and Guy Minick Youth Complex), adult softball (Allen E. Paulson Softball Complex), soccer (Chatham County Soccer Complex), swimming (Chatham County Aquatic Center), and weightlifting (Paul Anderson-Howard Cohen Weightlifting Center). All of these venues are included in individual write-ups in this chapter.

On the following pages, you'll also find information concerning the parks and activities we've mentioned. While you're reading, keep in mind that a big part of the beauty of the area's recreational offerings is that, because of Savannah's mild climate, they're available to you just about every day of the year.

Parks and Nature Trails

Historic Downtown

Forsyth Park
Drayton and Gaston Streets
Savannah, GA
(912) 351-3841

This downtown park on the southern boundary of the Historic District has sort of a split personality, but it's a delightful one. The northern portion consists of eleven acres filled with trees and shrubs and has an ornate fountain as its focal point. Splashing waters and shady sidewalks make this part of the park, which was laid out in 1851, a wonderful spot for strolling, relaxing on benches, and just plain goofing off.

The southern portion has a more active persona. Here you'll find a large playground, basketball and tennis courts, and wide open spaces often used by folks engaged in softball, team Frisbee, and other athletic pursuits. The southern portion, a drill field for local military units before it was made part of the park in 1867, is also the site of monuments commemorating the Confederacy and honoring Georgians who served in the

Spanish-American War. The city's Bureau of Leisure Services maintains the nineteen acres of the southern part of the park, and the Park and Tree Commission looks after the northern portion.

Two dummy forts, structures built in 1909 and used for military exercises before World War I, straddle the line dividing the two areas. The fort on the western side of the park was renovated in 1963 as the Fragrant Garden for the Blind; the eastern fort is used as a storage shed.

The park was laid out on the site of a pine forest that was at the southern reaches of the city, a wood that made "sad and sea-like music, when stirred by the breeze," according to a historian of the late 1800s. Over time, the pines were removed, died out, or were uprooted by storms. Of the park's numerous existing trees—forty-four per acre in the northern portion—a few are pines, but you'll see many more oaks, sycamores, and magnolias when you visit. Particularly impressive are the live oaks that line the central walkway stretching from the park's northern end at Gaston Street to its southern end at Park Avenue.

Chatham County's many parks offer treats to kids and birds alike. PHOTO: PHYL M. GATLIN

The monuments are on this wide promenade, as is the much-photographed fountain, which features a female figure surrounded by water-spouting swans and tritons (men with the lower bodies of fish). The fountain, said to be the largest in the United States when it was unveiled in 1858, is modeled after one in the place de la Concorde of Paris. A lighted sidewalk that's much favored by walkers and joggers who live or work downtown borders Forsyth. According to the city, the distance around the park is 1.5 miles. The park is also the site of several major annual events, including the Sidewalk Arts Festival, the Savannah Shakespeare Festival, and Picnic in the Park (see our Annual Events and Festivals chapter).

Islands

Old Savannah-Tybee Railroad Historic and Scenic Trail
U.S. Highway 80 E.
Savannah, GA
(912) 652–6780

When you walk, jog, or bicycle on this 6.5-mile trail, you're traversing the roadbed of a railroad that took passengers from eastern Savannah to Tybee Island for nearly fifty years starting in the late 1800s. Chatham County maintains the palm-lined, limestone trail on McQueen's Island and created it beginning in 1991 as part of the Rails Into Trails program, an effort to transform abandoned railroad rights of way into recreational areas. A trip along the entire length of the trail takes you past eighteen fitness stations, past thirty wooden picnic tables, and across ten wooden footbridges. Besides what it offers in the way of exercise, the trail presents visitors with vistas of marshland and the south channel of the Savannah River, opportunities for fishing and crabbing, and glimpses of wildlife indigenous to the marsh. Keep your eyes peeled for creatures such as the Eastern box turtle, the diamondback terrapin, the American alligator, the red-tailed hawk, the brown pelican, and the great blue heron, and don't be surprised if you walk up on a rattlesnake or two. We haven't seen any on our trips here, but we understand they enjoy sunning themselves on the trail.

The railroad was built over 17.7 miles of salt marsh, rivers, and tidal creeks by a group of investors led by Savannahian D. G. Purse, who in 1885 owned a good portion of Tybee Island and was trying to find a way to transport people there that was faster than the two-hour ride by steamboat. His solution was to build a railroad, and the idea was considered a harebrained scheme by local folks; they were convinced it was an engineering feat that couldn't be accomplished. But Purse persisted, and his Savannah and Tybee Railway began making regularly scheduled runs in July 1887.

A few years later, the line became part of the Central of Georgia Railway system and was operated from then on as the Savannah and Atlantic Railroad. The last passenger excursion was in July 1933; by then, the advent of the automobile and the construction of a road to Tybee (now U.S. Highway 80) had made the railway obsolete. But in its heyday, the little railroad carried thousands of Savannahians and out-of-towners to Tybee for days of sunning and swimming at the beach and nights of dancing at the Tybrisa Pavilion. The entrance to the trail places you at its midpoint and is on U.S. 80 just east of the Bull River Bridge. The highway is well traveled, and there is not much space at the

trail entrance, so be careful when you pull off the road to park. The trail is off limits after darkness falls. (For much more on Tybee's interesting past and present, see our Tybee Island chapter.)

Skidaway Island State Park
52 Diamond Causeway
Savannah, GA
(912) 598–2300

Get back to nature on the Big Ferry or Sandpiper Trails at Skidaway State Park. Walking either will give you a good look at a maritime forest and the salt marsh, their plants, and possibly some of their animals, including fiddler crabs, egrets, deer, and alligators. The trails also take you to earthwork fortifications built as Confederate defenses during the Civil War and the remains of a moonshine still. Big Ferry can be hiked in either a 2- or 3-mile loop, with the latter taking about ninety minutes to walk. Sandpiper is a mile long, takes about twenty minutes and can be traversed by people using wheelchairs (with a little help) and parents pushing baby strollers. A path connects the trails, enabling hikers to get in as much as a 5.5 mile walk.

The 533-acre park, created during the early 1970s and opened in 1975, is in the western portion of Skidaway Island and borders a stretch of the Intracoastal Waterway called the Skidaway Narrows. Other features of the park are a pool, picnic sites, interpretive nature programs, and campsites (see the Camping section of this chapter). The seventy-five-by-forty-foot pool is open from Memorial Day to Labor Day, and the entry fee is $2. In addition to the picnic sites, there are five covered shelters available on a first-come, first-served basis. If you don't want to take a chance, you can rent one at $35 a day; a group shelter accommodates 150 people and rents for $150 per day.

The park is open from 7 A.M. to 10 P.M. seven days a week. There's a $2 parking fee on all days except Wednesday, when admission is free. If you're planning to come here often or visit other state parks and historic sites in Georgia, you might consider purchasing an annual Georgia Park Pass for $25 ($12.50 for those 62 and older). That will get you unlimited admission to all state parks.

Southside/Midtown

Daffin Park
1301 E. Victory Drive
Savannah, GA
(912) 351–3841

When Savannah's Park and Tree Commission members conceived plans for Daffin Park in 1908, the recreational area was on the outskirts of the city. Now, Daffin is in the middle of Midtown, and it's a drawing card for residents of that area. The park, which is maintained by the city of Savannah's Leisure Services Bureau, covers seventy-seven acres bounded by Victory Drive, Waters Avenue, Washington Avenue, and Bee Road.

Opportunities for enjoying the outdoors in a residential setting abound at Daffin, which has a large playground; grassy fields that accommodate softball, baseball, football, soccer, rugby, and, on occasion, cricket; basketball courts; nine tennis courts; a pool; a four-acre lake where you can fish for bass, bream, and catfish; and a pavilion on the lake that can be rented for six hours for $55 to $65 for a variety of gatherings. Call (912) 351–3837 for reservations.

The eastern portion of the park is the site of Grayson Stadium, home of the city's minor-league baseball team (see our Spectator Sports chapter), and a picnic area shaded by towering pine trees. The playing fields on the southern side of the park—once the site of polo matches and a landing strip for airplanes before the city built its first airport in 1929—are also fine for flying kites, driving golf balls, and exercising Rover, when the fields are not otherwise occupied. If you're into walking or jogging, you'll find room to roam on the eight-foot-wide, 1.5-mile long sidewalk surrounding the park. For a shorter jaunt, try the lighted sidewalk around Daffin Lake, which is a third of a mile long.

Insiders' Tip

While you're at Skidaway Island State Park, consider visiting the University of Georgia Marine Extension Service aquarium on the north end of Skidaway. The aquarium has fourteen tanks ranging in size from 30 to 1,600 gallons and containing fish and other animals indigenous to Georgia's coastal and offshore waters. Admission is $2 for visitors thirteen years old and older and $1 for senior citizens and children 3 to 12; children younger than three are admitted free. The aquarium is open from 9 A.M. to 4 P.M. Monday through Friday and from noon to 5 P.M. on Saturday. To get there after leaving the park, take Diamond Causeway east to McWhorter Drive, turn left on McWhorter, and stay on it until you reach the Skidaway Marine Science complex, the site of the aquarium.

Lake Mayer serves as a training site for the Savannah Sailing Center. PHOTO: RICH WITTISH

Lake Mayer Community Park
Montgomery Crossroad
Savannah, GA
(912) 652–6786
www.co.chatham.ga.us

As the name implies, the centerpiece of this seventy-five-acre park on the Southside is the lake, but there's more here than recreational offerings involving water. Lake Mayer is surrounded by a 1.5-mile walking and jogging track dotted with eighteen fitness stations. The park grounds provide space for eight lighted tennis courts, two lighted basketball courts, an unlighted ball diamond, a conditioning course and a basketball court for people using wheelchairs, a playground, a remote-control auto racetrack, and an outdoor skating rink designed to accommodate in-line hockey games. Picnic tables are sprinkled throughout the park, and two covered areas accommodate large groups: a pavilion with space for as many as 500 people and a shelter with room for 80 to 100. These can be reserved

at fees of $125 for five hours of usage and $150 for more; otherwise, they are available on a first-come, first-served basis. Nighttime rental of the pavilion is $200.

Getting back to the thirty-five-acre lake: Swimming is prohibited, but you can fish for bass, bream, catfish, and crappie if you have a freshwater license. The possibilities for boating abound; the lake is the site of the Savannah Sailing Center (see this chapter's Sailing section), which offers instruction to young people and adults, and of Red Cross classes in kayaking and canoeing. Windsurfing is permitted on the lake, which is also where remote-control-boat racing enthusiasts come to compete.

Staff members at Lake Mayer present numerous special events throughout the year, including the Make a Kite workshop and contest and three on three and four on four basketball competitions in March; Easter festivities in April; fishing rodeos in May, June, and July; the Bacon Park Sizzler Footrace in June; a Halloween festival in

October; and a Christmas tree lighting in December. For details on special events, call (912) 652–6791.

Lest we forget, numerous ducks and geese call the park home, and they are more than happy to take stale bread off (and out of) your hands. The park—created in 1972 and operated by Chatham County's Department of Parks, Recreation and Cultural Affairs—is on Montgomery Crossroad at Sallie Mood Drive. It's open from 8 A.M. to 11 P.M. in the spring and summer and 8 A.M. to 10 P.M. in fall and winter.

Southside Community Park
Science Drive
Savannah, GA
(912) 351–3841

Developed by the city of Savannah in cooperation with Armstrong Atlantic State University (see our Education and Child Care chapter), this twenty-eight-acre wooded area on Scenic Drive across from the ASSU field house features a nature walk that's two-thirds of a mile long. A playground and picnic tables round out the facility. The park opens at dawn and closes at dusk.

William E. Honey Waterfront Memorial Park
Mechanics Avenue
Thunderbolt, GA
(912) 447–1900

The drawing card of this recently opened park in the east Chatham town of Thunderbolt is the T-shaped fishing pier, a facility that gives anglers and crabbers access to the Wilmington River and its aquatic bounty. The pier extends eighty-two feet from high ground out over the water, and the crossbar of the T paralleling the riverbank is ninety-six feet long and sixteen feet wide. If you're here to picnic and not to fish, you'll find tables and a pavilion where you can enjoy a meal alongside the river. The park, opened on Labor Day 1997, is named for a Thunderbolt resident who

donated funds for its creation. It's at the eastern end of Mechanics Avenue, which runs off U.S. 80. The park and pier open at sunrise and close at sunset, and there's no charge for using them.

West Chatham

L. Scott Stell Community Park
383 Bush Road
Savannah, GA
(912) 925–8694
www.co.chatham.ga.us

Helicopter pilots once prepared for war on the site of this 108-acre park southwest of Savannah. Now Chatham Countians come here to play ball on the four lighted diamonds of the Jim Golden Sports Complex, shoot hoops on the four lighted basketball courts, jog and walk on the 1-mile fitness trail, and picnic under the pines. There are also a BMX bicycle track, a tree farm, and a dog exercise area. During the early 1970s, the park site was Cu Chi Stage Field, a training area for South Vietnamese helicopter pilots stationed at nearby Hunter Army Airfield. Later in the decade, the county planted the seeds, literally, for the park by making garden plots at the site available to local residents free of charge.

You can still farm one of these thirty-by-sixty-foot plots (there's no cost involved; participants simply sign an agreement stating they will be responsible for their plot) in addition to taking advantage of the other recreational opportunities offered here since the park's completion in 1984. The fun includes fishing for bream, catfish, bass, and crappie in the pond. The park is open all year long, from 8 A.M. to 10 P.M. during fall and winter and from 8 A.M. to 11 P.M. during spring and summer. Special events include garden workshops, basketball tournaments, fishing contests, Easter festivities, and a Halloween festival.

Savannah National Wildlife Refuge
S.C. Highway 170
Savannah, GA
(912) 652–4415
www.savannah.fws.gov

By traveling the Laurel Hill Wildlife Drive, you can see some of the refuge's 27,771 acres of freshwater marshes and hardwood islands, which are known locally as "hammocks." This 4-mile gravel road is open to hikers, bicyclists, and motorists, and it takes you along dikes built during the late-eighteenth and early-nineteenth centuries by rice planters. The U.S. Fish and Wildlife Service, which manages the refuge, maintains 3,000 acres of freshwater pools created by the dikes, areas that serve as feeding grounds for wading birds and waterfowl. Unless posted as closed, all the dikes are open to foot travel, as is the Cistern Trail, a winding path that runs off the Wildlife Drive; however, if you're planning on leaving the drive to hike or bike, call ahead to ascertain the condition of the dike system.

The Wildlife Drive is open from sunrise to sunset throughout the year, except for two days during the fall, usually in October, when it's closed to the general public to allow a deer hunt by people using wheelchairs; you should check to see if this event falls at a time when you intend to visit the refuge. The drive and the dikes are great places from which to observe wildlife, in particular birds and alligators. A marvelous time for bird-watching is late December and early January, when the refuge is visited by thirteen different types of ducks in concentrations of up to 20,000 birds. The best times for viewing gators are in March and April and in October, when the big reptiles crawl onto the banks of the refuge's canals to bask in the sun.

Laurel Hill Wildlife Drive and about half of the refuge are in South Carolina but right across the Savannah River from Chatham County; the entrance to the drive is only a couple of miles from the West Chatham town of Port Wentworth on S.C. Highway 170, which is Georgia Highway 25 south of the river. The drive is not far from downtown Savannah. To get to it from downtown, about a fifteen-minute trip, take U.S. Highway 17 north across the river to its intersection with SC 170, then turn south on SC 170.

You can fish from the banks of the Wildlife Drive and in the Kingfisher Pond year-round and in the remainder of the refuge's freshwater pools from March 1 to November 30, but the angling at these spots isn't anything to write home about, and you'll need a South Carolina license. You'll get better results fishing in the Savannah River along the refuge's boundaries, and a Georgia license will suffice if you stay in the main channels. The refuge manages hunts for deer, feral hogs, squirrels, waterfowl, and turkeys during the fall and winter. Permits to hunt there are required and can be obtained by mailing requests or applications to Savannah Coastal Refuge Hunts, Parkway Business Center, 1000 Business Center Drive, Suite 10, Savannah, GA 31405.

Savannah-Ogeechee Canal Museum and Nature Center
681 Fort Argyle Road
Savannah, GA
(912) 748–8068
www.co.chatham.ga.us

The 184-acre nature center and its several trails will give you a look at three environments: pine woods, hardwood tidal river swamp, and sand hills. Two of the trails start in the pines at the museum and follow the southern portion of the canal, which dates to 1830, faded from usage near the end of the nineteenth century and has recently been cleared of brush and other growth. These trails—the Tow Path and the Heel Path—are each 0.4 mile long and lead you past Locks 5 and 6 of the canal to the Ogeechee River. The only bridge across the canal is at Lock 5 near the start of the paths, so don't expect to walk to the end of one and back on the other. However, a trail recently created as an Eagle Scout project allows you to walk from the end of the Tow Path (on the eastern side of the canal) to the 0.5-mile-long Jenkes Road Trail.

Jenkes Road, once a thoroughfare for wagon traffic, will also take you from the museum to the river. The road and the paths take you through the swamp; you can see the sand hills by walking the 1-mile Holly Trail. The nature center is open from 9 A.M. to 5 P.M. daily. Admission is $2 for adults and $1 for children older than 5. (For more on this site and the history of the canal, see our Attractions chapter.)

Tom Triplett Community Park
U.S. Highway 80 W.
Savannah, GA
(912) 652–6780
www.co.chatham.ga.us.

The first phase of this 200-acre park along U.S. 80 just west of Dean Forest Road was opened to the public in October 1998. Visitors will find a nineteen-acre lake that's stocked with fish and circled by a paved path intended for walking, running, and bicycling. Plans call for the eventual construction of a boathouse and docks and the creation of campsites, hiking trails, picnic areas, and a playground. When it's completed, this 200-acre, county-owned park will be the largest in Chatham. The park is open from sunup to sundown.

Recreation

Recreation Programs

What follows are listings for three entities that help organize a wide variety of sports activities for youth and adults in Savannah and Chatham County. Note also that most of the smaller municipalities in the county have recreation departments, some of which are extremely active. To register to play on teams sponsored by these agencies, or to find out about their programs, call their representatives in Bloomingdale at (912) 748-7400, in Garden City at (912) 966-7788, in Pooler at (912) 748-5776, in Port Wentworth at (912) 966-7428, in

Thunderbolt at (912) 447-1900, and on Tybee Island at (912) 786-9622.

Chatham County Department of Parks, Recreation and Cultural Affairs
Montgomery Crossroad
(912) 652–6780
www.co.chatham.ga.us

Operating out of offices at Lake Mayer Community Park on Montgomery Crossroad at Sallie Mood Drive, the department's Sports Division provides league play for youngsters in a variety of sports. These include basketball (January through March for boys ages 8 through 14 and girls ages 9 through 14), soccer (March through May for boys and girls 6 through 19), baseball (April through July for boys 6 through 14), slow- and fast-pitch softball (March through July for girls 6 through 18), and football (October through December for boys 6 through 10). The division also sponsors swimming and weightlifting complexes near Lake Mayer and holds a cheerleading competition for youngsters at Memorial Stadium in December and fast-pitch softball clinics in the fall. Entry fees are $50 per team for participation in basketball and $125 per team for participation in soccer, baseball, softball, and football.

City of Savannah Department of Recreation Services
7171 Skidaway Road
Savannah, GA
(912) 351–3852
www.ci.savannah.ga.us

The city provides team athletic competition for youngsters and adults throughout the year. Youth sports include basketball (January through March for kids ages 8 to 18), baseball (April through July for boys 6 to 18), football and cheerleading (September through November for kids 6 to 12), and soccer (September through November for girls and boys 6 to 19). For adults, there are leagues in softball in the fall and in spring/summer, basketball from January through March, baseball from April through July, and soccer from September through November.

Chatham County is a boater's paradise. PHOTO: KYLE CASON

Entry fees for youth sports are $100 per team, with no fees charged for youth basketball. Fees for adult teams can run anywhere from $265 to $460, depending on how many games are played in the sport involved and the expenses incurred by the city in providing the program.

YMCA of Coastal Georgia
6400 Habersham Street
Savannah, GA
(912) 354–5480
ymca@coastalga.org

Besides the programs you'd expect to find at the Y (such as those involving swimming and other types of physical fitness for individuals), the YMCA of Coastal Georgia, through its five branches in Chatham County, offers youngsters opportunities to participate in youth basketball, baseball, softball, soccer, and in-line hockey. Participants are registered and teams are formed at the branches, while leagues are set up and scheduled through each branch office. For the most part, games are played at facilities owned or leased by the Y.

Programs are open to nonmembers at fees slightly higher than those charged to members, and scholarships are available. Basic fees for individuals participating in under-six-year-old divisions in all sports are $30 for members of the Y and $45 for nonmembers. For all other age divisions, fees are $45 for members and $68 for nonmembers. To enroll your child in a program, contact the Y branch nearest you. The facilities are the Habersham Branch in Southside/Midtown at 6400 Habersham Street (912–354–6223), the Southside Branch at 11702 Mercy Boulevard (912–961–9622), the Tybee Island Branch at 204 5th Street (912–786–9622), and branches on the eastside islands (912–897–1192) and in West Chatham in Pooler (912–748–9622).

The last two branches recently occupied new quarters, with the new West Chatham Branch opening in the spring of 2001 in a 32,000-square-foot facility that's more than two and a half times as large as its predecessor. The new branch features an outdoor pool, a day-camp facility, and two large gymnasiums. The new Islands Branch on Johnny Mercer Boulevard on Whitemarsh Island is built on fifty acres and has much more room for parking than the old Islands Y, where finding a space was often a problem. The new Islands Branch, which opened in January 2002, has new additions such as racquetball courts and a Sprayground—a fully equipped playground that incorporates the use of water. Both branches also are sites of a St. Joseph's/Candler Health Systems Children's Place to Be Fit, where children of elementary school age are offered activities while their parents work out. Total cost of the two new facilities was $12 million.

All the Y branches provide health screening services free to members via the Health Connection, which is staffed by St. Joseph's/Candler personnel.

Basketball

The county offers basketball for boys ages 8 through 14 and girls ages 8 to 14 at a variety of sites between January and March. The city runs basketball programs for adults 18 and older and for youngsters 8 to 18 during January, February, and March. Teams play at gyms in community centers and public schools, and the youth program puts eighty to ninety squads on the floor.

The YMCA hoops program attracts about 1,600 youngsters, making it bigger than both the county's and city's. Teams of boys and girls play in leagues starting at under six and progressing to under eighteen, and they do their dribbling and shooting at gyms at the Y's branches, previously listed.

Baseball/Girls' Softball

In April, the fancy of many a youngster in the Savannah area apparently turns to...baseball and softball. The city's youth baseball program involves from 140 to 150 teams in 6-and-under, 8-and-under, 10-

and-under, 12-and-under, 14-and-under, 16-and-under, and 18-and-under leagues. The county fields in the neighborhood of sixty-five teams in 8-and-under, 10-and-under, 12-and-under, and 14-and-under competition, and the YMCA's program accounts for seventy-five teams in those age groups, plus an under-6 category. Some city and county teams play into July, while the Y program ends in May. City teams play at numerous locations including the Guy Minick Youth Complex and on diamonds in parks and at public schools. The city also conducts an adult baseball program, with games being played from April through July at fields in Daffin Park, at Savannah State University, and at Jenkins and Windsor Forest High Schools. Fees are $460 per team.

Diamonds are also the best friends to many local young women: The county's softball program for girls ages 6 to 18 will field close to one hundred teams between March and July, and the Y has leagues for under-10 and under-12 teams during April and May. The county schedules its baseball and girls' softball games at the Charles C. Brooks Sports Complex on the Islands, Ambuc Park in Southside/Midtown, and the Jim Golden Sports Complex in West Chatham, all of which have rest rooms and offer sales of snacks and beverages. Y teams play at the Y branches, at the Brooks complex, and on local school fields.

Ambuc Park
Sallie Mood Drive
Savannah, GA
(912) 351–6754

This twenty-five-acre sports complex in Southside/Midtown has four lighted diamonds for baseball and girls' softball. Maintained by Chatham County, it's also the site of youth football games and soccer matches.

Charles C. Brooks Sports Complex
Johnny Mercer Boulevard
Savannah, GA
(912) 898–7430

If you hear locals talk about this twenty-acre county facility on Wilmington Island, they'll probably refer to it as "the landfill" because that's what it's built on. The complex has four lighted fields for baseball and softball and a football field that can be used for soccer matches. The road leading to the complex is on Johnny Mercer near that street's intersection with Quarterman Drive.

Guy Minick Youth Complex
Eisenhower Drive and Sallie Mood Drive
Savannah, GA
(912) 351–3858

This Savannah-owned facility is the site of many of the baseball games played by teams in city leagues. Four lighted fields are also used for soccer games played by teams in the younger age groups in the city's fall program.

Jim Golden Sports Complex
383 Bush Road
Savannah, GA
(912) 925–8694

The twenty-five-acre Golden complex has four lighted fields for baseball and girls' softball and an unlighted T-ball field. It's part of L. Scott Stell Community Park in West Chatham.

Bicycling

We mention in several places in this book that the Historic Downtown, with its quaint streets and squares and its laid-back attitude, is an ideal place for walking. It follows that this area is also a wonderful place to see from the seat of a bicycle. But if you opt to ride a bike rather than stroll around the downtown, be aware that you'll be competing with traffic that seems to become increasingly heavier as Savannah grows in popularity as a tourist destination. To avoid the worst of the traffic, consider taking your ride on a weekend morning before the sight-seeing starts in earnest. Also, be sure to observe the same traffic laws as you would when driving your car and give serious thought to wearing a helmet. Georgia law requires kids younger than sixteen to use protective headgear; if you're older than the age limit, you can set a good example by wearing a helmet, and you might even save yourself a bump on the noggin. Keep in mind that adults are prohibited from riding bikes through Historic District squares.

Dedicated cyclists who delight in long rides will find that the city and county haven't done a great deal to accommodate them; however, there is a governmental committee on bikeways and greenways that's working to come up with facilities that will make bike riding more enjoyable. Until the committee devises some plans and officials implement them, however, bike riders will have to make do with the existing designated bike paths and bike trails at their disposal.

The city has two bike paths, each of which use streets that are often heavily traveled by motorists:

The West to East Corridor runs along 52nd Street to Ward Street to LaRoche Avenue to the entrance to Savannah State University.

The North to South Corridor follows Habersham Street to Stephenson Avenue to Hodgson Memorial Drive to Edgewater Drive to Hillyer Drive to Dyches Drive to Lorwood Drive to Tibet Avenue to Largo Drive to Windsor Road to Science Drive at Armstrong State University.

The county offers a couple of trails for bicyclists:

The McCorkle Bike Trail ambles for 4 miles over ten acres on Wilmington Island. The eastern end of this trail is at Walthour Road near Concord Road, and the western end is on Cromwell Road just past its intersection with Wilmington Island Road.

The McQueens Island Trail runs between Bull River and Fort Pulaski and is part of the Old Savannah-Tybee Railroad Historic and Scenic Trail (see entry in the Parks section of this chapter). This crushed-stone trail is best suited to mountain bikes.

Coastal Bicycle Touring Club
Savannah, GA
(912) 351–7797
www.cbtc.com

This group of biking enthusiasts holds organized rides just about every weekend and special rides throughout the year. The club has about 150 members who meet monthly and receive a newsletter ten times during the year. Annual membership fees are $15 for individuals and $20 for families. Members meet on the first Monday of the month at 6:30 P.M. at various restaurants.

Bird-Watching

Its location on the air route of migratory birds known as the Atlantic flyway makes Savannah a splendid place for watching birds. The premier spot for this activity is the Savannah National Wildlife Refuge (see entry in the "Parks" section of this chapter), a haven for thousands of mallards, pintails, teal, and as many as ten other species of ducks that migrate here during the winter months. Transient songbirds and shorebirds stop by briefly during the spring and fall. The peak time for viewing ducks at the refuge occurs in late December and in January. According to Pat Metz of the U.S. Fish and Wildlife Service, you might also do some worthwhile bird-watching on the beach on the north end of Tybee Island during the spring, fall, and winter and on Skidaway Island during the spring and fall. Tybee's north beach is a good place for spotting gannets and purple sandpipers during the winter, and you might find migratory shorebirds and neotropical songbirds at Skidaway Island State Park and along the 4-mile trail on the northern end of the island running from the Georgia Marine Extension Service aquarium to Priest's Landing.

Reworking the Concept of the Ideal Vacation: The Caretta Project

If your concept of the ideal vacation involves lazing on a sandy beach with accommodations that include air-conditioning and a hot tub, then you probably won't want to spend a week during the summer serving as a volunteer for the Savannah Science Museum's Caretta Research Project.

On the other hand, if you don't mind paying $525 for seven days and nights of no A/C, no hot water, no privacy, and lots of bugs, then working with the environmentalists who run this sea turtle monitoring program might be right up your alley.

About now you're probably wondering why anyone would want to fork out all that money to endure what sounds like the original Vacation from Hell. Well, it's simple. For your hard-earned dough, your time, and your sweat, you get the satisfaction of helping save a threatened species—the loggerhead sea turtle. Depending on when you devote a week of your life to the Caretta Project, you have the opportunity to either see loggerheads crawl up the beaches at Wassaw Island and lay their eggs, or watch hatchlings scramble down the beaches to take up residence in the Atlantic Ocean. It's a mystical experience that a 1998 volunteer from Albuquerque, New Mexico, described as "like a door opening on another world."

"People say the project changes their lives," said biologist Kris Williams, who serves as director of the undertaking. After their weeks on Wassaw, "many students have changed their majors to biology to work with sea turtles," she said.

The Caretta Project—*Caretta caretta* is the scientific name of the loggerhead—was in its twenty-ninth year in 2001, and more than 2,000 volunteers from nearly every state and about a half-dozen foreign countries had participated during its lifetime. It's one of the oldest sea turtle monitoring programs anywhere and the only one in the United States whose volunteer sessions last an entire week and are thoroughly hands-on. Hands-on means that you'd better be ready to work if you volunteer. "We don't want people wanting to spend a vacation," said Williams.

Volunteers who participate in the sessions running from mid-May through early August spend their nights—we're talking from dusk to dawn—patrolling 7 miles of Wassaw's practically pristine beaches looking for turtles intent on digging a nest and laying eggs. Once a turtle is found, she is checked for an identification tag; tagged, if necessary; and measured. The turtle-monitoring team—which consists of six volunteers, a member of the Caretta Project staff, and an assistant—then either marks the nest and covers it with a screen to protect it from marauding raccoons or digs up the eggs and relocates them to a spot farther from the water's edge. Relocating the eggs is often necessary because erosion has caused a shelf to form along much of the beach at Wassaw; unable to climb up the shelf, the turtles sometimes dig their nests where the tide can wash their eggs out to sea.

"The eggs probably wouldn't hatch if we didn't move them," said Williams, noting that a major aim of the project is to maximize the survival of hatchlings. Seeing the hatchlings dash for the ocean is the lure for the volunteers who take part in sessions running from late July through mid-September.

"We watch the nests and try to make sure we're there to ensure the hatchlings make it to the water," said Williams, explaining how volunteers ward off predators such as coons and ghost crabs. "We usually stay up until midnight, then get up at dawn to make sure no hatchlings are stuck."

While on Wassaw, a sea island southeast of Savannah that's accessible only by boat, volunteers sleep in a one-room, rustic cabin that's not air-conditioned; there's no hot water, and the shower is outside. Team members share housekeeping duties, including the preparation and cleanup of supper, the only organized meal of the day. "We eat well," said Williams, noting that suppers revolve around hearty dishes such as beef Stroganoff, pizza, spaghetti, and vegetable lasagna.

The $525 fee covers a volunteer's food, lodging, and transportation by boat from Skidaway Island to Wassaw and back.

Volunteers should be eighteen years old or older, but Williams said the program will accept those sixteen or even younger, provided they are highly motivated and independent types. "This is not a summer camp," said Williams. "This is a working vacation—it's not fun and games."

There's no maximum age limit, but participants in the program must be in good health and have reasonably good night vision and the ability to handle a moderate amount of walking. "Perhaps most important is your mental attitude," states the program's informational literature. "The project requires upbeat, adaptable folks who can cheerfully endure close quarters, insects, rainstorms and the heat and humidity of a week in the subtropics without air-conditioning."

If you fit that bill and you're interested in participating, you can start the process of volunteering by calling (912) 447–8655 or writing to Caretta Research Project, P.O. Box 9841, Savannah GA 31412-9841. Project staffers start accepting applications in January, and it's a good idea to get yours in early—the 96 slots available in 2001 filled up fast.

"It's a very rewarding experience," Williams said of the volunteer program. "We've had people coming back for their tenth and eleventh years."

Even with no A/C, no hot water, no privacy, and lots of bugs.

Boating

Chatham County has about 86,700 acres of tidal marshlands laced by approximately 420 miles of navigable tidal waters. In other words, the area is a paradise for boaters.

Three of the most accessible scenic waterways are the Wilmington, Bull, and Skidaway Rivers, and they'll lead you to Wassaw Sound and the beaches of Wassaw, Williamson, and Beach Hammock Islands, where you can picnic, swim, sunbathe, and look for shells. The 7 miles of beach at Wassaw, a barrier island that's part of a national wildlife refuge and accessible only by water, are most inviting, particularly the "boneyard" on the northeast end where the bleached remains of toppled trees present opportunities for taking intriguing photographs. The southernmost and northernmost ends and the ocean beachfront of Williamson Island are open to boaters, but the middle of the island is a Critical Wildlife Area closed to humans; this area is reserved for birds such as the American oystercatcher. The basically pristine beaches of these islands are about a twenty-five-minute trip from the marinas in Thunderbolt.

When you make a landing, you shouldn't have to worry about rocks, but be aware of what the tide is doing—if it's running out, you could get stranded for several hours if you're not careful. Also, be sure you're wearing shoes when you jump out of your boat into the water so oyster shells, broken glass, or the occasional stingray won't injure you.

The county maintains boat ramps at several locations that will provide you with access to local waterways. In the Islands area, there are two double ramps at Skidaway Narrows on the Diamond Causeway, and double ramps at Lazaretto Creek on U.S. 80 E. at Tybee Island and at Frank W. Spencer Park on the Islands Expressway just east of the bridge over the Wilmington River. In West Chatham, there are two double ramps at the Houlihan Bridge on GA 25 at the Savannah River and at Kings Ferry on U.S. 17 S. at the Ogeechee River; and there is a single ramp at Salt Creek on U.S. 17 S. All of the ramp facilities have rest rooms, and all but Skidaway Narrows have wooden docks. You'll find picnic areas at all the ramps (with the exception of Lazaretto Creek), and Kings Ferry has a swimming area and a playground.

Downtown via Boat

You can reach River Street and its shops, restaurants, and other attractions by boat via the Savannah River, but make sure to stay well clear of the commercial vessels using the shipping channel. These are huge ships, and they throw huge wakes. You can tie up alongside River Street at a pier of vertical pilings at the western end of Rousakis Riverfront Plaza or at vertical pilings on the eastern end. The pier and pilings accommodate vessels from 35 to 450 feet long.

Rates for using these city-owned facilities are 75 cents per foot. Limited services (water and refuse collection) at the pier and at the pilings are available on request. If you plan to stay more than three hours at these facilities, you must register with the city's Revenue Department, which can be contacted by calling (912) 651-6451. If you're tying up for less than a couple hours,

there's no docking fee. You'll also find a dock at the Hyatt Regency hotel that's 460 feet long and available for boats 25 feet or longer. The fee for using the hotel dock overnight is $3 per foot, and electricity, water, and cable television hookups are provided, as is use of the hotel's indoor pool and fitness center.

Marinas

If you're traveling to Savannah by boat and are looking for a place to dock during your visit, or if you need somewhere to store your boat, you can choose from several marinas.

Bull River Marina
8005 Old Tybee Road
Savannah, GA
(912) 897-7300

As the name implies, this relatively small marina sits on the Bull River some 9 miles from the mouth of Wassaw Sound, making it about halfway between Tybee Island and Savannah. The marina provides sixty deepwater slips, a ship's store, bathrooms, showers, and gasoline and diesel fuel. It's home to the Savannah Light Tackle Fishing Co., Bull River Adventure Cruises, and Lowcountry River Excursions, which offers ninety-minute dolphin and nature cruises from March 1 through November 30—call (912) 898-9222 for departure times. The marina is off U.S. 80 at the western end of the bridge over the Bull River.

Fountain Marina
2812 River Drive
Thunderbolt, GA
(912) 354-2283

Tie up at Fountain Marina and you're within walking distance of the restaurants on the bluff at Thunderbolt. This facility, on the Wilmington River near Intracoastal Waterway mile marker 583, offers 30 wet slips and 148 dry racks, plus a bait house, store, bathrooms, and showers. The marina has served local boaters since 1980.

are seventy wet slips and a ship's store. Gas and diesel fuel are available, as are showers, and you can rent kayaks and powerboats. It's at Intracoastal Waterway mile marker 590.

Palmer Johnson Marina
3124 River Drive
Thunderbolt, GA
(912) 356–3875

Yacht owners docked at this marina, next to the Palmer Johnson boat works in Thunderbolt, get donuts delivered to them in the morning. Palmer Johnson has more than 1,100 feet of dock space available for transient boaters. The marina offers a convenience store and gift shop, has gas and diesel fuel, will perform maintenance service, and provides a laundry and showers. Rivers End Restaurant is on the premises. Palmer Johnson is on the Wilmington River at Intracoastal Waterway mile marker 583.

Sail Harbor Marina
618 Wilmington Island Road
Savannah, GA
(912) 897–2896

As the name implies, Sail Harbor caters mainly to owners of sailboats, but this marina on Turner Creek near the Wilmington River will also accommodate powerboats. (For more on this facility, see this chapter's Sailing section.)

Savannah Bend Marina
Old Tybee Road
Thunderbolt, GA
(912) 897–DOCK

This marina on the Wilmington River at Intracoastal Waterway mile marker 582 has transient dockage at 45 wet slips and a dry storage building containing 262 racks for boats up to 32 feet long. The ship's store carries nautical gifts and apparel, and the Wheelhouse Cafe serves deli-style sandwiches and beverages. After you've eaten, you can relax and get a fine view of the river from one of the rocking chairs lining the porch of the restaurant/store. Savannah Bend offers fuel

Hogan's Marina
36 Wilmington Island Road
Savannah, GA
(912) 897–FISH
www.hogansmarina.com

Situated on Turner Creek about three-fourths of a mile from the Wilmington River—the Intracoastal Waterway—Hogan's has more than 1,100 linear feet of dock space and 272 dry-rack spaces. Name it and they've got it at this marina on Wilmington Island, which opened in the spring of 1991. You'll find a store with nautical gear and fishing tackle, a boat hoist, gasoline, rest rooms and showers, live and frozen bait, a fish-cleaning facility, and ice and beverages. Hogan's also repairs engines.

Isle of Hope Marina
50 Bluff Drive
Savannah, GA
(912) 354–8187

On a picturesque bend of the Skidaway River sits the Isle of Hope Marina, which was established here in 1926. The marina was the first dealer of Cris Craft boats in the nation and was the site of the dock scenes in the original production of the movie *Cape Fear*, the first in a long line of films made in the Savannah area. There

service and has showers and rest rooms. The marina is in Thunderbolt near the eastern end of the bridge over the Wilmington River.

Bowling

If you've got a yen to knock down some pins, you can go bowling at a couple of places in Savannah.

AMF Savannah Lanes
115 Tibet Avenue
Savannah, GA
(912) 925–0320

Bowlers will find fifty lanes, a pro shop, a snack bar, and a full-service sports lounge at Savannah Lanes. This establishment in the Southside is the home of about fifty bowling leagues and two special promotions: Moonlight Bowling from 9:30 to 11:30 P.M. on Saturdays and Extreme Bowling, which starts at midnight on Fridays and Saturdays and runs until 3 A.M. and from 9:30 P.M. to midnight on Sundays. Prizes are awarded during Moonlight Bowling; when it's time for Extreme Bowling, the regular lighting is turned off, disco lights are turned on, and a DJ plays Top 40 dance music. Daytime rates are $3.49 per game for adults and $2.99 per game for children, students, and senior citizens. After 6 P.M., all age groups bowl for $3.99 a game. Savannah Lanes is open year-round.

AMF Victory Lanes
2055 E. Victory Drive
Savannah, GA
(912) 354–5710

A well-received promotion at this establishment—which has forty lanes, a pro shop, a full-service snack bar, and a lounge that opens nightly at 5 P.M.—is Saturday Night Extreme Bowling, which features psychedelic lighting effects from 11 P.M. to 2 A.M. Rates as of the summer of 2000 were $3 per game before 5 P.M. and $3.50 a game afterward. Victory Lanes is the home of fifteen leagues, plays host to

bowlers seven days a week, and is closed only on Christmas Eve.

Camping

Skidaway Island State Park
52 Diamond Causeway
Savannah, GA
(912) 598–2300

The park has eighty-eight pull-through campsites set amid the serenity of a maritime forest on Skidaway Island. Each has water and electrical hookups and elevated tent pads; grills and tables are provided. You can build campfires in the fire rings found at each campsite, but please don't build them on the tent pads. The park is a popular spot because of its natural beauty and also because it's only about thirty-five minutes from the Historic Downtown (see the state park's listing in the Parks and Nature Trails section of this chapter). Many campers use the park as a "bedroom" while they visit the city, so the sites tend to fill up on major holidays and the weekend closest to St. Patrick's Day. If you're planning to stay at the park during those times, make a reservation by calling (800) 864-7275. Fees per night for campsites between March 1 and November 1 are $18 for motor homes and most pull trailers and $16 for tent campers. They're $2 less the rest of the year.

Fishing

If you like to fish, you've come to the right place. Year-round, there's somewhere in Chatham County or offshore in the Atlantic Ocean where you can wet a line and catch something. Basically, we're talking about three types of fishing: inshore and offshore, which involve fish that live in saltwater, and freshwater.

The inshore area stretches from the beachfronts into the tidal rivers and creeks and includes Wassaw Sound. This is where you'll find spotted trout, red drum (also known as spot-tail bass), flounder, sheepshead, tarpon, croaker, and spots in the summer and whiting in the spring and summer. If you're visiting or new to the area and want to do some inshore fishing, hire a guide to show you some good fishing holes, which local folks call "drops." There are countless drops in Chatham's inshore waters, and it pays to know where they are; if you don't, you might find yourself sitting in a boat doing nothing while anglers in a vessel less than fifty feet away are hauling them in.

It's also a good idea to consult the local tide charts before you go fishing inshore; Chatham County has a high tidal range and when the tides are "springing" (i.e., rising to eight to ten feet), the fishing isn't good because the bottom is churned up and the water is muddy. Go fishing when the tides are in the six- to seven-foot range and the water is clear. You can find tide charts on the weather pages of the *Savannah Morning News*.

When you fish offshore, you'll either be bottom fishing or trolling for sport fish. Bottom fishing will net you black sea bass, grouper, and a variety of snapper. The sport fishing is seasonal, starting in spring with bluefish, followed by cobia, king mackerel, bonito, wahoo, marlin, sailfish, amberjack, tuna, and Spanish mackerel. The sport fishing is good into November, and some veteran anglers say the optimum time to venture out is after Labor Day. Offshore angling is best in the Gulf Stream and at a particularly fishy live bottom called the Snapper Banks. The Snapper Banks are about 40 miles out, and a trip there from Wilmington Island will take about two hours; the Gulf Stream, the warm ocean current that flows from the Gulf of Mexico along the U.S. coast to New England, is about an hour farther.

If you're after freshwater fish in Chatham County, head for the Ogeechee River above Kings Ferry and the Savannah River above Port Wentworth. You'll encounter largemouth bass, shad, bluegill bream, redbreast bream, shellcracker bream, and crappie.

Insiders' Tip

Crabbing is a favorite pastime of many Savannahians. It's a recreational pursuit that's relatively inexpensive, and you don't need a boat to do it. All you do need is a basket net, some bait (chicken parts, such as the necks, will do fine), and a tidal creek in which to crab. If you don't want to buy the basket net, you can affix your bait to a line with a lead weight attached, but you'll probably need a dip net for getting the crabs you catch out of the water. You can buy the items you'll need at bait shops or most hardware stores.

Make sure you have a Georgia fishing license, which will cover both salt- and freshwater angling; you'll be fined if you get caught without one. Note that the licensing requirement involving saltwater fishing is a relatively new one, having gone into effect in July 1998. Licenses can be purchased just about anywhere you can buy fishing tackle, including discount department stores. A one-day license costs $3.50. Licenses that are good throughout the year are $9 for residents and $24 for nonresidents. Seven-day licenses for nonresidents run $7.

OK, now gather up your gear and bait and go fishing. To help you get started, we've listed a few charter services and marinas that cater to anglers. Also, the marinas included in our section on Boating can hook you up with charter boat captains and fishing guides.

Amick's Deep Sea Fishing
8010 Tybee Road
Savannah, GA
(912) 897–6759

Amick's offers mostly offshore fishing trips and can accommodate from six to twenty people on its 41-foot, custom-built Morgan, the *Scat II*. Full- and half-day trips are available for private parties or individuals, and the company also has a 31-foot Morgan, the *Scamp*, for offshore fishing. A third boat, a 17-footer, can be chartered on weekends for inshore fishing. Amick's is based at the Williams Seafood docks, which are just off U.S. 80 E., at the western end of the Bull River Bridge. Open-boat trips to the Snapper Banks (approximately eleven hours) aboard the *Scat II* are $85 per person. Private charters on the *Scat II* (also eleven hours) are $745 for six passengers.

Bona Bella Marina
2740 Livingston Avenue
Savannah, GA
(912) 355–9601

Bona Bella Marina rents out 14- and 16-foot johnboats to anglers and offers guide service for inshore fishing. Boat storage and 400 feet of dockage are available at this facility, which is on Country Club Creek about one hundred yards from the Herb River. Anglers can buy live and dead bait here, purchase snacks from the store, and gas up their boats. The marina also offers a rod and reel repair service and sells a full line of inshore and offshore fishing tackle. Boats rent for $60 a day, which includes gas and oil, and you can hire a guide for $350 for a full day and $225 for a half day. On weekends from 6:30 to 10 P.M., the back deck is the site of

> ## Insiders' Tip
> You won't find Sallie Mood Lake Park listed in Chatham County's guide to its major facilities and activities, but a handful of avid anglers know it for its fifteen-acre pond, a body of water that's stocked with fish by the Georgia Department of Natural Resources. To get to this off-the-beaten-path spot in the Southside, park your vehicle just south of the county Public Works Department facility on Sallie Mood Drive and hike a couple hundred yards up the nearby dirt road. You can also reach the pond via a dirt road running alongside the Chatham County Soccer Complex. You'll have to park and hoof it up this road, too.

Lowcountry boils featuring shrimp and crabs. The marina is closed on Tuesdays.

Chimney Creek Fish Camp
40 Estill Hammock Road
Tybee Island, GA
(912) 786–9857

Located adjacent to the Crab Shack restaurant and operated by the restaurant's owners, this fish camp sells live and dead bait and launches boats up to 24 feet long.

Chimney Creek leads to Tybee Creek and the Atlantic Ocean, which is only ten minutes away. The camp also has a dock for fishing and offers boat storage in the water.

Coffee Bluff Marina
14915 White Bluff Road
Savannah, GA
(912) 925–9030
Even if you didn't take advantage of the services offered by Coffee Bluff Marina, the ride out to the end of White Bluff Road would be worth making just to get the panoramic view of the Forest River and the wide expanse of adjacent marsh. Anglers who make the trip will also find the marina's large convenience store with a supply of fishing tackle and equipment, a boat hoist, gas, oil, bait, and ice. The marina also offers boat storage in the water and in sheds, but there are no rentals. This facility is closed on Tuesdays.

Miss Judy Charters
124 Palmetto Drive
Savannah, GA
(912) 897–4921
Go fishing and have fun doing it with Miss Judy Charters. Why is it fun? Owner Judy Helmey, who started skippering boats in the mid-1960s at the age of fourteen, says it's because her company caters to customers by making them aware of their surroundings during trips, answering their questions, showing them rod and reel operations, and swapping a fish story or two. "They get to do everything that's fun and we take care of the hard stuff," she says. The Wilmington Island–based company—started in 1947 by Judy's father, the late Sherman I. Helmey—provides inshore and offshore fishing via the *Miss Judy Too*, a customized 33-foot Sportfisher, and from a variety of other boats. Trips leave from the company's dock on Turner Creek; the entrance to the road leading to the dock is on Wilmington Island Road about a mile south of Johnny Mercer Boulevard. Weekday rates for fishing parties of up to six people are $380 for

a four-hour trip, $469 for a six-hour trip, and $599 for an eight-hour trip; on weekends and Fridays, rates are $420 for four hours, $500 for six hours, and $650 for eight hours.

Youth Football

The county provides facilities and support for 8-and-younger and 10-and-younger football teams that play games September through November at Ambuc Park, the Jim Golden complex, the Charles C. Brooks Sports Complex (see previous listings for these venues), and Memorial Stadium. The city's youth football program is for 8-and-younger, 10-and-younger, and 12-and-younger teams. From thirty to forty squads participate, playing games at Daffin Park (see previous listing) starting in mid-September and finishing just before Thanksgiving.

Golf

If golf is your game, you have several public and semiprivate courses in Chatham County from which to choose—one on the islands, four in Southside/Midtown, and three in West Chatham. We've also included write-ups on a couple of courses in nearby Bryan and Effingham Counties for those golfers who don't mind taking about a thirty-minute ride to the links. The following listings will give you an idea of what's available; greens fees include cart rentals, and yardage is from men's tees.

Islands

Wilmington Island Club
612 Wilmington Island Road
Savannah, GA
(912) 897–1615
Set amid the oaks, pines, and palms of southwestern Wilmington Island, this par 72 course rambles over 6,528 yards. Raised, undulating greens are planted in Tifton and Bermuda grass, and there's

Savannah's municipal golf complex in Bacon Park provides three nine-hole courses on which to play, plus a clubhouse, practice green, and driving range. PHOTO: RICH WITTISH

water on ten holes, including no. 7 and no. 14, two of the course's four well-bunkered par 3s. The signature hole is 14, a 148-yard par 3 with a pond in front of the green and bunkers on the right.

Donald Ross designed the course, which opened in 1927 as part of a resort, the centerpiece of which was the eight-story General Oglethorpe Hotel on the Wilmington River. In the mid-1960s, the hotel was refurbished and renamed the Savannah Inn and Country Club, and the golf course was rebuilt and improved by Willard Byrd. The resort was later purchased by the Sheraton corporation, which gave the property a new name. The hotel closed in 1994, but the semiprivate golf club remained open under the name of the Sheraton Savannah Resort & Country Club. In May 1998, a family-run development company based in Macon bought the hotel and golf course and changed the

name of the golfing facility to the Wilmington Island Club.

The developers have built a $1.5 million clubhouse near the eighteenth fairway—a two-story, 25,000-square-foot building featuring gym and locker rooms, a card room, a lounge-grill area, a full-service kitchen, and a banquet room capable of seating 300 people. The course was upgraded with new cart paths and a new irrigation system, and a pro shop, lighted driving range, and a practice green are also part of the layout.

Only club members are allowed to walk the course, and only after 4 P.M. Greens fees are $56 Tuesday through Sunday, and the course is closed on Monday. Although the course was to remain semiprivate for a time, the owners will eventually close it to nonmembers, so it would be wise to call ahead to ascertain the status of the Wilmington Island Club before driving from town to play a round there.

Southside/Midtown

Bacon Park Golf Course
Shorty Cooper Drive
Savannah, GA
(912) 354-2625

Bacon Park's twenty-seven-hole layout presents golfers with three nine-hole courses—Cypress, Live Oak, and Magnolia—featuring narrow, tree-lined Bermuda grass fairways and elevated greens. Each course carries a par 36, and the combined length of any pair of the courses is more than 5,900 yards. Donald Ross designed the original layout, which is in the midst of suburban Savannah; it's owned by the city and operated by EDR Management Inc. The clubhouse contains a pro shop and full-service snack bar, and a driving range and practice green are available. You can walk the course on weekdays and after 4 P.M. on Saturdays and Sundays. Playing eighteen holes runs from $22 to $30, depending on the time of the week.

Cypress Course

The shortest of Bacon Park's three courses at 2,956 yards, Cypress has water on seven holes, including no. 8, the signature hole. This 135-yard par 3 has a narrow green with bunkers on both sides; the water is on the left side of the green.

Live Oak Course

The first hole is long and narrow, a 384-yard par 4 with a green that's well bunkered. The ninth hole is the longest at Bacon Park, a 528-yard par 5 with a fairway that is crossed by a canal past midpoint; there's plenty more water along the remainder of the fairway and in front of the green. The course runs 3,215 yards.

Magnolia Course

This course starts with a long hole, a 463-yard par 5 whose green has lots of water on the right. Another interesting hole is no. 8, which is crossed near midpoint by a canal that runs down the left-hand side of the latter half of the fairway. Total length of Magnolia is 2,960 yards.

Henderson Golf Club
1 Al Henderson Drive
Savannah, GA
(912) 920-4653
www.hendersongolfclub.com

Henderson, opened in March 1995 and owned by Chatham County, offers a good mix of lengths among its eighteen holes, ranging from just 127 yards on the fifteenth to 522 yards on the first hole. The course was built on farmland in southwest Chatham that contained 240 acres of wetlands, so there's plenty of water to look at. In most cases, however, the water is an intimidation factor rather than a sheer hazard.

In laying out the 6,273-yard, par 71 course, designer Mike Young took advantage of the wetlands and an abundant number of native trees by weaving them in with fairways and greens. Some of the holes eventually will be overlooked by homes; a private investment group is developing the area as a golf community where 350 residences in the $135,000 to $200,000 range are planned.

Rapidly gaining a reputation as Henderson's signature hole is the eighteenth, a par 4 that's 416 yards long. Accuracy is paramount here because there's water on the entire left-hand side of the hole and to the right of the green. The sixth hole also presents a worthy challenge; it's a long (437 yards) par 4 that plays more like a par 5 because of the usual prevailing winds from the southwest. This is the hole where the ability to hit long counts most. Henderson has a pro shop, driving range, practice green, and a grill serving hot food and sandwiches. It's the home of the Savannah Golf School, which offers a variety of lesson packages and hosts golf camps for youngsters.

Walking at Henderson is permitted anytime on weekdays and after 1 P.M. on weekends and holidays. Fees for residents of the local area are $32 on weekdays and $37.75 on weekends and holidays; for non-residents, $37 on weekdays and $44 on weekends and holidays; and for senior citizens, $27 Monday through Thursday.

The course is off Georgia Highway 204 just east of the Interstate 95/GA 204 interchange.

West Chatham

Crosswinds Golf Club
232 James B. Blackburn Drive
Savannah, GA
(912) 466–1909

This recently opened semiprivate club boasts the area's only par 3 course, a 1,126-yard layout that's illuminated for nighttime play. The par 3 is suitable for families, people new to golf, and the occasional player, but it's challenging enough to allow veteran golfers to sharpen up their iron play. "It's not a pitch-and-putt course," says Crosswinds head pro Drew DeBrito, noting that water comes into play on five holes and that the par 3 has undulating greens similar to the club's eighteen-hole course.

The larger course at Crosswinds, which derives its name from its location—less than 2 miles from Savannah International Airport—covers 2,910 yards and is different from most layouts in that it has five par 5s and five par 3s and is devoid of residential development. The front nine features tree-lined fairways, while the last nine holes offer, in DeBrito's words, "a wide-open, Scottish links feel." Water is in play on eight of the eighteen holes, and no. 3, a par 5, 514-yarder, might give you fits because of a small green with lots of slope that provides the potential for putting balls in the drink.

Crosswinds, which opened for play in October 2000, has a spacious clubhouse featuring a full-service restaurant that's open for breakfast, lunch, and dinner seven days a week and a banquet room that seats 126 people. Also on the premises are a pro shop, a driving range, and putting and chipping greens. Walking is permitted on both courses. Greens fees for the eighteen-hole course are $39 on weekdays and $46 on weekends; fees for the par 3, which is open at night Wednesday through Saturday, are $27 during the day on weekdays and $31 at night, and $29 during the day on weekends and $33 at night.

The club is just off Airways Avenue near that boulevard's exit (104) from Interstate 95.

Mary Calder Golf Club
West Lathrop Avenue
Savannah, GA
(912) 238–7100

Owned by International Paper Company and located on the grounds of the company's kraft paper-manufacturing plant just east of Garden City, this par 35, nine-hole course exists mainly for the enjoyment of employees but is open to the public. Play eighteen holes, and you'll cover 5,799 yards on a course that's not difficult but does present some challenges because of its tight, elevated greens. On the par 4, 393-yard fourth hole, for example, you're faced with a green that's narrow in front and has a slight swale in the middle that can keep your ball from getting to the back. The course's three par 3s are well bunkered and can be tough, particularly the finishing hole, a 179-yarder with a small green.

The course, opened in 1937 on the site of Hermitage Plantation, has a pro shop, snack bar, and two putting greens. You can walk the course anytime. Because of its semiprivate nature, the club does not schedule tee times for nonmembers. Fees for eighteen holes are $20 on weekdays and $22 on weekends. You reach Mary Calder from downtown Savannah by driving west on Bay Street, turning north on West Lathrop Avenue, and entering the manufacturing complex at Blue Gate 1.

Southbridge Golf Club
415 Southbridge Boulevard
Savannah, GA
(912) 651–5455

Rees Jones designed this 6,458-yard, par 72 course, blending in the tall pines, graceful oaks, and wetlands of the West Chatham woodlands. Water comes into play on eleven holes on the course, opened in 1988 as part of the South-bridge residential community. The signature hole is no. 4, a par 3, 179-yarder involving a shot over water to an elevated green cut into three sections. The thirteenth hole is also challenging; it's a long par 5 typical of holes on the back nine. This hole was carved out of a thick forest. Water on the left side is involved in every shot on this 492-yarder, and bunkers guard the right side.

Southbridge is off Dean Forest Road at Interstate 16, making it about five minutes from downtown Savannah. An antebellum-style clubhouse adorns the semiprivate course, and the building houses a pro shop and the Southbridge Grill, a full-service dining room. The course rents clubs, has a driving range and putting green, and is the home of the Georgia School of Golf, a facility that provides instruction to players of all skill levels. Use the same phone number for information on the school. Greens fees at Southbridge, which has cohosted the Georgia Open several times, are $38 on weekdays and $44 on weekends and holidays. Walking is allowed after 1 P.M. daily at the discretion of club officials.

Outlying Courses

Black Creek Golf Club
Bill Futch Road
Black Creek, GA
(912) 858–4653

Playing the eighteen-hole layout at Black Creek is a bit like competing on two different courses. The front nine has an open-links feel with its rolling hills and greens; the back nine, with its extensive wetlands, will remind you that you're not far from the coast (you're about 26 miles from downtown Savannah). Water comes into play on eleven holes on the 5,701-yard, par 72 course, which was designed by Jim Bivins of Atlanta and opened in September 1994. The signature hole, no. 15, was cut right out of a swamp and features an island-type green with a large pond in front of it and wetlands on the right and left. You want to make sure you use enough club on this par 3, 140-yarder,

because anything short of the green is in the water. All four of Black Creek's par 3s will test you, as will the green at no. 7, a par 4, 354-yard hole that presents a dogleg to the right. The green is well bunkered and two tiered, with the right and left sides sloping away from you, so your shot to the pin has to hit in just the right spot.

Semiprivate Black Creek—which is part of a golf community featuring eighty-six large lots priced from $22,500 to $34,500—features a Lowcountry-style clubhouse accommodating a spacious pro shop and a grill and full-service bar. There's also a driving range and practice green. Walking is allowed on weekdays. Fees are $27 on Monday, Wednesday, and Friday before 1 P.M. and $23 afterward; $23 on Tuesday and Thursday; and $34 on weekends and holidays.

To get to Black Creek, take I-16 to exit 143 and head west on U.S. Highway 280 toward the Bryan County town of Pembroke. Drive about 2 miles from the interstate to Wilma Edwards Road and turn right; the entrance to the club is less than a half mile on your right.

Lost Plantation Golf Club
1 Clubhouse Drive
Rincon, GA
(912) 826–2092

This semiprivate course near the Effingham County town of Rincon is a long one—7.5 miles from first tee to eighteenth green, so spread out that you'll never see another hole from the one you're playing. Narrow, tree-lined Bermuda grass fairways set on rolling hills offer an abundance of hazards. There are ponds, lakes, or wetlands on fourteen holes, and the greens are big and protected by large bunkers. The signature hole of the 6,445-yard, par 72 course is no. 18, a 390-yard par 4 featuring a dogleg to the left and a lake that shields 70 percent of the green—on the front, left-hand side, and back.

Lost Plantation's rustic-looking clubhouse provides golfers with a well-stocked pro shop and a snack bar. The course, which was built in 1988 and designed by Ward Northrop, has a driving range and practice green. You can walk the course after noon; fees are $27 on weekdays and $32 on weekends.

Lost Plantation is 21 miles from downtown Savannah. You can get there from the city by taking Bay Street and Georgia Highway 21 to Fort Howard Road in Rincon and turning right. The road leading to the golf course is about a mile down Fort Howard Road on the right.

Ice Skating

Savannah Civic Center
Liberty and Montgomery Streets
Savannah, GA
(912) 651–6550

Believe it or not, you can enjoy this winter sport in Savannah, even at a time when it's liable to be downright warm. During December, the arena of the Civic Center is transformed into an ice rink where intrepid Southerners try their luck—and ankles—at skating. The rink fee of $6 entitles you to the use of a pair of skates. Skating times vary, so call ahead for information on when the rink is available.

In-Line Hockey

YMCA of Coastal Georgia
6400 Habersham Street
Savannah, GA
(912) 354–5480

This sport—hockey played on in-line roller skates—is new to the area but growing in popularity. The Y started its first leagues in the fall of 1995 and offers the sport from mid-September through mid-November. From twenty to twenty-five teams are formed, and they play in leagues for under-8, under-10, under-12, and under-16 age groups. The majority of participants are boys, but girls are welcome to take part. The Y stages its games at parking lots at its Habersham Branch, on the south end of Tybee Island at the end of 16th Street and at the Savannah Festival outlet mall at I–95 and GA 204.

Running

You'll see lots of people running and jogging in Savannah, particularly during the more temperate months of autumn, winter, and spring. Good spots for running—places where you won't have to worry about colliding with motorists—are the sidewalks around Daffin Park and Forsyth Park and the jogging track at Lake Mayer Community Park (see listings in the beginning of this chapter). Each of these facilities covers 1.5 miles, so you can get a good workout by making a circuit or two. Some of the more experienced local runners drive out to the north end of Skidaway Island, park at the marine science center, and take to the roads there. These thoroughfares are fine for running because they are in good condition and sparsely traveled by drivers.

Savannah is the site of several major races, principally the Savannah Bridge Run, a 10K race held in May (see our Annual Events and Festivals chapter), and the Tybee Marathon in February. If you're a competitive runner, you can probably find a race most weekends (except during the hot and humid summer months) within a two-hour radius of Savannah.

Savannah Striders
(912) 921–IRUN
www.savystrider.com

The Striders meet monthly, and many members get together for runs during the week. The club, whose membership numbers about 180, sponsors the Tybee Marathon, Half-Marathon, and 5K in February and the Women's Wellness Walk/Run 5K in September. Annual dues are $15 for individuals and $20 for families, and membership forms can be picked up at the Habersham Branch YMCA on Habersham Street. The listed telephone number is the Striders' information line, and calling it will provide you with data on club meetings and upcoming races. Members meet on the first Thursday of each month at 7 P.M. at the Red, Hot & Blue restaurant at 11108 Abercorn Street.

Sailing

Sailing is smooth in Savannah, as you might expect from the venue for the yachting events of the 1996 Summer Olympics. The best sailing is in Wassaw Sound, which is where the Olympic competition was staged. The sound has lots of deep water and few hazards, and you can bank on getting a tradewind breeze in the afternoon. Another good place for sailing is the Wilmington River, which is the site of several local regattas. The following are great places to get started.

Geechee Sailing Club
Savannah, GA
(912) 897–5597

The club sponsors two major sailboat races, the St. Patrick's Day Regatta on the weekend after the holiday and the Oktoberfest Regatta in early October, and organizes eight to ten extensive cruises for members each year.

Members meet at Snapper's restaurant on Whitemarsh Island on the first Monday of each month at 7 P.M. Upwards of 120 people actively participate in club functions. Membership fees are $75 a year.

Sail Harbor Marina
618 Wilmington Island Road
Savannah, GA
(912) 897–2896

Sail Harbor is on Turner Creek, right around the corner from the Wilmington River and about 7 miles from Wassaw Sound. This marina has 130 wet slips, 5 of them for transients; a ship's store offering a variety of sailing merchandise; and a laundry, showers, and recently remodeled rest rooms.

Sail Harbor offers sailing charters, either skippered or bare boat, and is the site of a sailing school providing instruction in the basics of the sport and in coastal piloting. Contact the school, Sail Harbor Academy, by calling the marina. Sail Harbor was the 1996 Olympic yachting marina, meaning it served as a shore base for officials

coordinating the sailing events. The actual sailing was done from a floating marina in Wassaw Sound that was dismantled after the Olympics. Bare-boat charter fees range from $140 to $300 for the first day of sailing, depending on the size of the boat rented. Hiring a skipper will cost about $125 more. The basic sailing course is $250 for four five-hour lessons.

Sail Harbor is also the site of The Lightship, a lounge that serves food and offers splendid views of Turner Creek and its marsh.

Savannah Sailing Center
Lake Mayer, Montgomery Crossroad
at Sallie Mood Drive
Savannah, GA
(912) 231–9996
www.savannahsailingcenter.org

Youngsters and adults can learn to sail and sharpen their skills by participating in the programs offered by this community-based, nonprofit organization. The center began operations in 1993 and trained all of the volunteers who served on the water for Olympic yachting in Savannah in 1996. Courses are taught at the boathouse at Lake Mayer. The center will accept children as young as seven if they know how to swim. The center offers instruction on Saturdays during the summer and every other Saturday during the spring and fall, with rates set at $25 per session. During the summer, there are half-day, weeklong sessions for junior sailors, with each session costing $80. Scholarships are available, as are discounts for multiple sessions and multiple family members.

Soccer

Youth soccer is huge here, so big that there are spring and fall seasons. The county handles the spring program from March through May and typically has sixty teams in leagues for youngsters 6 to 19. The city coordinates play for a total of about 160 teams in those age groups during September, October, and November.

The water's fine for swimming under the Chatham County Aquatic Center dome, which is supported by air pressure. PHOTO: RICH WITTISH

Most matches are played at the county's soccer fields on Sallie Mood Drive, but the city also stages matches at Guy Minick Sports Complex on Sallie Mood at Eisenhower Drive and in Daffin Park. In 1998, the city started an autumn adult soccer program, with fees set at $460 per team.

Teams participating in city and county youth leagues are members of either the Coastal Georgia Soccer Association, which can be reached by calling (912) 691–2472, or the Savannah Magic Soccer Club at (912) 232–2791. Register your child to play by contacting these groups. The YMCA of Coastal Georgia runs its own fall soccer program, fielding about seventy teams in the under-6, under-8, under-10, under-12, and under-14 age groups. Matches are played at the Y branches in the county between September and November.

Chatham County Soccer Complex
7221 Sallie Mood Drive
Savannah, GA
(912) 356–2503

Local youngsters get their kicks on eight lighted fields at this fifty-acre complex on Sallie Mood Drive near Eisenhower Drive.

There are three fields that are 64 by 110 yards, three that are 60 by 105 yards, and two that are 75 by 115 yards. On occasion, the larger fields are divided into smaller fields to accommodate matches being played by the youngest participants.

Adult Softball

Allen E. Paulson Softball Complex
7171 Skidaway Road
Savannah, GA
(912) 351–3852

Winter is the only time you won't find softballs flying at the city's Allen E. Paulson Complex, one of the finest facilities of its kind in the Southeast. Other times, the place is jumping with slow-pitch activity. From 125 to 130 teams compete in Savannah's open, church, and co-ed leagues during the spring and summer season, which ends around Labor Day. In September, the fall leagues crank up, and from seventy-five to eighty teams hit the five lighted, 300-foot fields; play ends around Thanksgiving. Paulson hosted two national tournaments in 1999, and there are tourneys of some description scheduled on most weekends during softball-playing months. Fees for teams playing in spring leagues are $460; teams that play in the fall leagues pay fees of $370.

Swimming

Chatham County Aquatic Center
7240 Sallie Mood Drive
Savannah, GA
(912) 351–6556
www.co.chatham.ga.us

Chatham County opened this state-of-the-art, $4.3 million facility in February 1998. A dome supported by air covers a 40,000-square-foot area containing an eight-lane, 50-meter pool and a six-lane, 25-yard warm-up and instructional pool, both of which are accessible to the handicapped. In addition to accommodating recreational swimming, the large pool is used for district, regional, state, and national swim meets; there's seating for 976 spectators. The building also has men's and women's changing rooms, a pro shop, a snack vending area, several offices, and the privately owned and operated LifeTime Fitness health club.

The 50-meter pool keeps things calm with a water-motion stabilizer that minimizes swimmers' wakes, and a ventilation duct running around the inside of the center keeps the air temperature at 88 to 90 degrees and the humidity at 50 percent. Swimmers enter the pool area through an airlock that maintains the air pressure inside at the level needed to support the dome.

The center offers a variety of programs for swimmers of all ages, those who want to develop their strokes and train for competition, and those interested in aquatic fitness. Swimming lessons are $45 for eight sessions; fees for aquatic fitness and coached swimming programs range from $30 to $50 per month. Recreational and lap swim times during the fall, winter, and spring and lap swim times during the summer run from 6 A.M. to 8 P.M. Monday through Friday, from 11 A.M. to 6 P.M. on Saturday, and

from noon to 6 P.M. on Sunday. Recreational swimming during the summer is offered from noon to 9 P.M. Monday through Friday, from 11 A.M. to 6 P.M. on Saturday, and from noon to 6 P.M. on Sunday. Daily admission passes for Chatham County residents cost $4 for adults and $2 for children ages ten and younger and $3 for senior citizens, college students, and active-duty military personnel, with kids two and younger admitted free. Rates for noncounty residents are $1 more.

Tennis

About 1,500 tennis players participate in the United States Tennis Association league program here, making it the second-largest program in the state next to Atlanta's. A total of 150 of the teams in the program, more than a third of those involved, play at public courts. That number has grown from fifty teams in 1987. There are courts at city and county parks throughout the area, but the biggest public tennis complexes are at Bacon and Daffin Parks.

Insiders' Tip

One of the nicest of the numerous small parks and sixty playgrounds scattered throughout the city of Savannah is Hull Park at 54th Street and Atlantic Avenue in Midtown. Hull Park—with its picnic tables, shade trees, playground equipment, and ball diamond—is a splendid place to spend a weekend afternoon.

Bacon Park Tennis Complex
6262 Skidaway Road
Savannah, GA
(912) 351–3850

Tucked into a wooded area on Skidaway Road, this complex has sixteen lighted hard courts open from 9 A.M. to 9 P.M. Monday through Thursday and from 9 A.M. to 5 P.M. on Friday, Saturday, and Sunday. A pro shop sells tennis merchandise and beverages. Fees are $2.50 per hour.

Daffin Park Tennis Courts
1001 E. Victory Drive
Savannah, GA
(912) 351–3851

Daffin's six clay courts and three hard courts sit near the park's lake, so you can occasionally catch a breeze off the water. You can play for free on the lighted hard courts (available from 7:30 A.M. to 10 P.M.); there's a fee of $2.50 an hour for using the soft courts, which don't have lights and are open from 8:30 A.M. until 5 P.M. seven days a week.

Savannah Area Tennis Association
(912) 598–8824

The Savannah Area Tennis Association organizes and oversees the operation of the majority of United States Tennis Association leagues here. The board of directors of SATA meets at 6 P.M. on the third Monday of each month at Barnes Restaurant at 10201 Abercorn Street, and the meetings are open to the public. The association, which has about 1,200 active members, publishes a newsletter twice a year. To join, contact the pros at public or private tennis facilities in the area. You'll pay a $25 USTA membership fee and a league fee of from $5 to $7.

Weightlifting

Paul Anderson-Howard Cohen Weightlifting Center
7232 Varnedoe Drive
Savannah, GA
(912) 351–3500
www.co.chatham.ga.us

Work out for free at the Weightlifting Center, which is adjacent to Memorial Stadium in the Southside and is part of Chatham County's recreational setup. The 15,000-square-foot center is geared toward Olympic-style weightlifting and strength training for local sports teams, but it's open to the public from 8 A.M. to 8 P.M. Monday through Saturday.

At the center, you can lift free weights or train on weight machines. Coaches are on hand to answer questions and there are separate showers and saunas for men and women. The facility opened in February 1995 and is home to Team Savannah, the largest Olympic-style weightlifting team of its kind in the U.S.

Team Savannah
Paul Anderson-Howard Cohen
Weightlifting Center
7232 Varnedoe Drive
Savannah, GA
(912) 351–3500

There are bigger regional weightlifting organizations in the nation, but Team Savannah is the largest one representing a specific locality. Team Savannah has 150 registered weightlifters and twelve coaches, including head coach Henry Myers III. The team was founded by Michael Cohen, a former Olympian who started the organization in 1987 while serving as the strength coach for the Jenkins High School football team. Since then, Cohen's pupils have set numerous records and claimed a passel of championships. In 2000, five members of Team Savannah were part of the U.S. weightlifting squad that participated in the Summer Olympics in Sydney, Australia, and Cohen served as the women's coach. Cheryl Haworth of Team Savannah won a Bronze medal. Membership is free and open to anyone who wants to join, according to weightlifting center director Henry Myers.

Spectator Sports

Because there are so many opportunities to participate in recreational activities throughout the year in Savannah, most spectator sports tend to take a back seat. Even so, fan interest in minor-league baseball and automobile racing remains strong.

Minor-league baseball has been a part of the Savannah sports scene since the turn of the century (the twentieth century, that is), with the most recent in the city's long line of diamond organizations being the Savannah Sand Gnats of the Class A South Atlantic League. The Sand Gnats are affiliated with the Texas Rangers, and they play their games in Grayson Stadium, the city's gem of an old-time ballpark.

Like baseball, automobile racing in Savannah has a long history, and operations in stock car racing and drag racing have been around quite a while.

In 1997, another type of racing exploded onto the scene, albeit briefly. The staging of the first Savannah Grand Prix that year marked the return of road-course auto racing to the city after an eighty-six-year hiatus. Back in 1908, 1910, and 1911, famed drivers such as Ralph DePalma and Louis Chevrolet zoomed over the roads of Chatham County at speeds of up to 85 MPH as Savannah stepped to the fore of the racing world with its Grand Prize and Vanderbilt Cup competitions. In 1997, Helio Castro Neves, Clint Mears, and other up-and-coming drivers hit 165 MPH as they gunned their open-wheel racers around a newly built track on Hutchinson Island.

Unfortunately, the road-racing return has been sidetracked, at least for the time being. The Hutchinson Island circuit remains in place; only time will tell if big-time racing will ultimately get the green light in Savannah.

If you're hankering for some big-league sporting action, you can find it within reasonable driving distance of Savannah. Atlanta, with its Falcons of the National Football League, Braves of Major League Baseball, Thrashers of the National Hockey League, and Hawks of the National Basketball Association, is five hours to the northwest. The NFL's Jaguars of Jacksonville, Florida, are even closer—about two and a half hours south on Interstate 95. Nearer still is Hilton Head Island, the site of a major sporting event in the spring: the World-Com Classic PGA golf tournament (for more on this event, see our Hilton Head chapter).

If you're into intercollegiate sports, you'll find a lot to choose from close to home at the city schools, or you can hit the road for Georgia Southern University in Statesboro (about an hour away), the University of Georgia in Athens (four and a half hours), or Georgia Tech in Atlanta.

Baseball

Savannah Sand Gnats
Grayson Stadium
1401 E. Victory Drive
Savannah, GA
(912) 351-9150
www.sandgnats.com

If you believe there's nothing as American as spending an evening or Sunday afternoon at the old ballpark, a visit to Grayson Stadium to watch the Savannah Sand Gnats is for you. The city's Class A minor-league baseball team plays seventy regular season games at Grayson, where the brick grandstand was built in 1941.

SCAD's baseball team is one of several organizations participating in intercollegiate competition locally. PHOTO: COURTESY OF SAVANNAH COLLEGE OF ART AND DESIGN

Located at the eastern end of Daffin Park, the stadium stands amid tall pines and oaks dripping with Spanish moss, and it's a great place to sit back, relax, and enjoy the national pastime while sipping a cold beer and devouring some peanuts—the boiled variety being the most popular in this part of the world.

Savannah began fielding a professional baseball team in 1904 and is a charter member of the South Atlantic League. Following lengthy affiliations with the Atlanta Braves and St. Louis Cardinals, the local club became part of the Los Angeles Dodgers organization in 1996, adopting the name Sand Gnats (see the Close-Up on these pesky critters in our Area Overviews chapter) and the unique team colors of burgundy, forest green, and tan. In November 1997, the team again changed its big-league organizational affiliation, becoming a part of the American League's Texas Rangers. The local team has in recent years developed a winning tradition: Savannah clubs captured Class A Sally League championships in 1993, '94, and '96. A big part of the fun of following the Sand Gnats, regardless of their affiliation, is knowing that you might very well be watching a future big-

league star. Three members of the '96 team—third baseman Adrian Beltre, pitcher Mike Judd, and catcher Angel Peña—made it to the big leagues in 1998 as members of the Dodgers.

Grayson's covered grandstand seats 5,000 people, and there's room for 2,500 in the bleachers. Most of the viewing area is screened from foul balls. If you can't resist eating while watching the old ball game, you can find plenty to munch on—in addition to the usual ballpark fare, Grayson in past years has offered Philly cheesesteaks, chicken fingers, and beef kabobs.

The Sand Gnats organization schedules numerous special events and promotions. In 2001, there were fifteen game-night fireworks shows, a Turn Back the Clock Night and a Negro League Night when players wore uniforms from the past, a wrestling extravaganza, and giveaways of items such as posters, baseballs, caps, T-shirts, tote bags, beach towels, and jerseys.

Games start at 7:05 P.M. on weekdays and Saturdays and 2 P.M. on Sundays. General admission is $5 for adults and $4 for ages 3 to 15, senior citizens, and military personnel; kids younger than three

Insiders' Tip

Members of the Savannah Sand Gnats baseball team sign autographs for fans before home games on Friday and Saturday nights. Three or four of the players gather at a booth below the Grayson Stadium grandstand to sign programs and other paraphernalia from about 6:45 to 7:05 P.M.

A batter waits to hit during a Savannah State University baseball game, one of many college sporting events that take place in the area. PHOTO: DANIEL J. GRANTHAM JR.

Baseball fans flock to see minor-league action at Grayson Stadium, the city's grand old gem of a ballpark.
PHOTO: RICH WITTISH

get in free. Reserved seats are $7.50, and box seats run $9.50, if you can get them. You can reserve tickets by calling the number listed, or you can pick them up ahead of time at the team's offices at Grayson from 9 A.M. until 4 P.M. on game days and from 9 A.M. until 5 P.M. when the team is out of town. Parking is free in the mostly unpaved areas under the oaks of Daffin Park.

Auto Racing

Oglethorpe Speedway
Jesup Road off U.S. Highway 80
Savannah, GA
(912) 964–RACE
www.ospracing.net

This speedway gives the green flag to stock car drivers competing in the NASCAR Weekly Racing Series every Friday night from April through September. Special racing events are held on Saturday nights.

You'll see more than 115 entries competing each week on the half-mile dirt track in Weekly Series ministock, street stock, pure stock, and late-model division events.

The racing is handled by NASCAR officials, who keep things moving at a brisk pace. Oglethorpe Speedway is on Jesup Road off U.S. 80 in West Chatham County. The 5,000-seat aluminum grandstand was built in 1995 and is wheelchair accessible. Tickets for Weekly Racing Series events are sold at the gate and are $9 for adults and teens and $7 for senior citizens and persons in the military. Children twelve and younger are admitted free. Parking is also free, and camping is available at no charge. The gates open at 6 P.M., and racing starts at 8 P.M.

Savannah Dragway
U.S. Highway 17
Savannah, GA
(912) 234–1965
www.savannahdragway.com

The drag racing is legal at this 0.8-mile track in West Chatham. The dragway owners hold "grudge" night competitions on Wednesdays starting at 6 P.M. for racers who want to challenge each other, and there are National Hot Rod Association-sanctioned races on Saturdays. On NHRA race days, the gates open at 1 P.M., qualifying starts at 3:30 P.M., and the races get underway at 7 P.M. Admission is $7 on Wednesdays and $12 on Saturdays, with tickets purchased at the gate. Children younger than twelve are admitted free on both days.

The grandstands seat about 2,500 people. Concessions are open, but you can bring your own grill and food and cook out if you want. The racing takes place year-round. The dragway entrance is on the north side of U.S. 17, about 1 mile west of Chatham Parkway.

Big-League Sports

For years sports fans in Savannah have been making pilgrimages to Atlanta to watch the Braves, Falcons, and Hawks in action and enjoy the big-league surroundings. However, Savannahians no longer have to drive five hours to Georgia's capital to witness sports at a top level—at least not during football season. Florida's Jacksonville Jaguars play eight home games in a recently refurbished stadium that's half the traveling time of the Savannah-to-Atlanta junket. The Jags, in existence since only 1996 but a contender since their second year of play, have become a hot ticket here and have put a decided dent in the Falcons' local fan base. To order tickets to Braves, Thrashers, Falcons, and Hawks games, call Ticketmaster in Atlanta at (800) 326–4000. You can obtain Jaguars' tickets by calling (800) 618–8005.

Intercollegiate Sports

You can witness competition on various intercollegiate levels in football, baseball, men's and women's basketball, and women's volleyball and stay in town while doing so. Armstrong Atlantic State University, Savannah State University, and the Savannah College of Art and Design all compete in basketball; Savannah State plays football; and Armstrong, Savannah State, and SCAD field baseball and volleyball teams.

You'll have to do some driving to see the big-time college athletes compete. Georgia Southern University in Statesboro (a one-hour drive west) plays Division I-AA football and has won six national championships since 1985, the last in 2000. The GSU men's basketball team has been to the NCAA Division I playoffs twice since 1987, and the women's team has gone two times since 1993.

But the really big shows are in Athens at the University of Georgia, where the Lady Bulldogs and Bulldogs compete in the Southeastern Conference, and in Atlanta, where Georgia Tech's Rambling Wreck participates in Atlantic Coast Conference play.

Insiders' Tip

If you attend a football game at the University of Georgia in Athens, you'll get a chance to see UGA VI (that's "UGH-uh Six"), one of the premier mascots in the nation. This white English bulldog, who lives at the home of Savannah attorney Sonney Seiler, is the offspring of the late UGA V, the mascot whom *Sports Illustrated* magazine called the best in the country. UGA V, who protrayed his sire, UGA IV, in the movie *Midnight in the Garden of Good and Evil*, appeared on the *SI* cover for April 28, 1997, promoting a feature story titled, "America's Top 50 Jock Schools."

Daytrips

You obviously will find plenty to occupy your time in Savannah, but if you want to go roaming a bit, you'll discover lots to see and do in the rest of coastal Georgia. To get you started on your explorations of the territory to the south of Savannah, we've mapped out trips to Richmond Hill-Liberty County and to Jekyll Island. The spotlighted sites in the Richmond Hill-Liberty County area are within an hour's drive of Savannah. It will take a little longer to reach Jekyll, which is about a ninety-minute jaunt from Savannah. For those inclined to head north into the South Carolina Lowcountry, we've included a trip to Beaufort, a charming, history-filled town located 50 miles from downtown Savannah. Happy wandering!

Richmond Hill-Liberty County

Lovers of history and nature will enjoy a tour of Richmond Hill and Liberty County, an area of extensive marshlands, lush forests, and meandering rivers, where the past is rich in significant people and events. To adequately visit all the spots we'll be sending you to, you'll probably need more than a day. That said, you might want to split this tour into a couple of daytrips or pick a few places that sound the most appealing and spend a day visiting those.

Begin your tour of the area by driving to the Bryan County municipality of Richmond Hill, a fast-growing town that's become a bedroom community of Savannah during the past twenty years. This one-time stomping ground of industrialist Henry Ford is 19 miles southwest of downtown Savannah and can be reached by heading west on Interstate 16 to Interstate 516. Then head south on I–516 to the Southwest Bypass (Veterans Parkway), south on the Southwest Bypass to Georgia Highway 204, west on GA 204 to U.S. Highway 17 and south on U.S. 17 to the highway's intersection with Georgia Highway 144. Turn left from U.S. 17 onto GA 144 and head east through the heart of Richmond Hill; it's 1 mile to your first stop, the Richmond Hill Historical Society and Museum. The museum building, which once housed a kindergarten that was a project of Ford and his wife, is on the right on the corner of GA 144 and Timber Trail Road.

Richmond Hill Historical Society and Museum
Ga. Highway 144
Richmond Hill, GA
(912) 756–3697
www.richmondhillga.com

You'll learn the fascinating story of Richmond Hill's Henry Ford era (1925–1951) when you visit this museum. The billionaire Ford purchased 85,000 acres in Bryan County in the mid-1920s, in effect buying the town of Richmond Hill, which was then known as Ways Station. Ford spent his winters there, living on a plantation that accommodated a laboratory where chemists attempted to transform agricultural products into goods that could be used by the automobile industry.

Ford revitalized an area where moonshining was one of the major occupations; he put people to work on his plantation and at a sawmill that he refurbished, and he built medical clinics, houses, chapels, and the town's Community House. Ford also improved existing schools and built a trade school for boys and a grammar and high school for African American youths. A museum staffer will tell you about Ford's accomplishments and their impact on the community while you look at photographs and artifacts from the period. You'll also learn about sites from the Ford era that you can visit, such as the Community House, which is now a funeral home, and one of the chapels, now a Catholic church.

Other sections of the museum depict the area's plantation era and offer displays of photos and some of the furniture used in the county's one-room schoolhouses. One room is devoted to the re-creation of a country store whose shelves are filled with authentic tins and boxes that held products popular during the early 1900s, and if you're interested in the really distant past, be sure to check out the timeline mural depicting the history of the area from prehistoric times to the present. An admission fee is not charged, but donations are accepted. The museum is open from 10 A.M. to 4 P.M. daily.

After you've looked at the displays at the Richmond Hill Museum, hop in your vehicle and head east on GA 144 to Fort McAllister State Historic Park. To reach the park, you'll drive 4 miles into the countryside on GA 144 to Ga. Spur 144, then turn left onto Ga. Spur 144; the entrance to the park is 4 miles ahead, and the drive to it will take you past upscale Lowcountry-style and ranch-style homes, some of them with backyard boat docks on the beautiful and fast-flowing Great Ogeechee River, which can be seen on your left.

Fort McAllister State Historic Park
3894 Fort McAllister Road
Richmond Hill, GA
(912) 727–2339
www.gastateparks.org

This 1,700-acre park between the Ogeechee and Red Bird Creek has two alluring identities: It's a recreational area featuring amenities for campers and picnickers, and it's also the site of an earthen fort where much of the Savannah area's

Insiders' Tip

Some of the attractions on our Richmond Hill-Liberty County daytrip are in somewhat remote areas that aren't near restaurants, so you might consider packing a lunch for the day. You can dine in relative comfort at picnic areas at several stops on this tour, including Fort McAllister State Historic Park, Fort Morris State Historic Site, the Midway Museum, and the Fort Stewart Museum. Each of these picnic areas has tables and pleasant surroundings.

most significant Civil War action took place.

Prior to 1980, these two attractions existed as Richmond Hill State Park and Fort McAllister Historic Site. That year, they were combined to form Fort McAllister State Historic Park, which today is operated by the Georgia Department of Natural Resources. There's a $2 parking fee to enter the park, which is open daily from 7 A.M. to 10 P.M.; admittance is free on Wednesdays. To keep things as simple as possible, we'll discuss the recreational area and the historic site separately.

The Recreational Area

For daytrippers, the main attraction here is the tree-filled picnic ground running along a high bluff overlooking the Ogeechee River. Tall pines and hardwoods make this a shady, serene spot for walking or sitting in a glider-type swing and watching the river flow by. You'll find fifty sites with picnic tables and grills, a fishing pier that extends out over the river, and plenty of rustic-looking playground equipment for the kids in this area, which borders the main road leading to the fort. Across the road from this area is the start of a 3.5-mile nature trail complete with a primitive campsite that can be rented for $5 a night.

If you plan on making your visit to Richmond Hill-Liberty County last longer than a day and you like roughing it, consider staying at the park's Savage Island Campground, which has sixty-five campsites—fifty for recreational vehicles and fifteen with tent pads, and all with water and electrical hookups, grills, and tables. Two comfort stations provide campers with toilets, heated showers, and washer/dryers, and the campground also has a playground, nature trail, and dock and boat ramp on Red Bird Creek. The RV sites rent for $15 a night, and the tent pads are $13 a night, with rates for senior citizens dropping to $12 and $10.40 respectively.

The Historic Site

Fort McAllister is one of the best-preserved earthwork fortifications built by the Confederacy during the Civil War. The southernmost of the defenses ringing Savannah, the fort withstood several attacks by Union warships before being overpowered by Federal forces on December 13, 1864, at the end of Gen. William T. Sherman's March to the Sea. The site was once owned by Henry Ford, who began an extensive restoration in the late 1930s, and the fort eventually fell into the hands of the state of Georgia, which restored it to its 1863–64 appearance.

You can wander around the walls and through the interior of the fort and look inside its central bombproof, but be careful not to climb on these earthen structures, which are extremely susceptible to erosion from foot traffic. Take the self-guided tour of the fort and check out a

thirty-two-pounder smoothbore gun that fired red-hot cannonballs and the furnace where these projectiles were heated; the reconstructed service magazine, which held shells, powder, and fuses for the rebels' thirty-two-pounder rifled gun; and the fort's northwest angle, where the attackers placed the first U.S. flag planted on the parapets.

The fort site has a museum that's part of a new visitor center that opened on September 1, 2001. The museum contains Civil War shells and weapons; implements such as those used in the construction of the fort; artifacts from the Confederate blockade runner *Nashville*, which was sunk in the Ogeechee by the Union ironclad *Montauk*; a diorama of the assault on the fort; a display depicting life at the fort as experienced by its 230 defenders; and exhibits involving the Guale Indians, who once inhabited the area, and Henry Ford's efforts to preserve the site. The fort is open from 9 A.M. to 5 P.M. Monday through Saturday and from 2 P.M. to 5 P.M. on Sunday. Admission is $2.50 for adults, $2 for senior citizens, and $1.50 for youngsters 5 to 18; children younger than five are admitted free.

After visiting Fort McAllister State Historic Park, head back to Richmond Hill on GA 144 and then south to Liberty County and the Historic Liberty Trail. The first attraction on this tour of the trail is Fort Morris State Historic Site, and you can get there from Richmond Hill by turning left onto U.S. 17 from GA 144 and driving 2 miles to I-95, heading south on I-95 for 11 miles, and leaving the interstate at exit 76. Next, turn left onto U.S. 84/GA 38 (Fort Morris Road) and stay on it for 7 miles until you come to the entrance to the site.

Fort Morris State Historic Site
2559 Fort Morris Road
Richmond Hill, GA
(912) 884–5999
www.gastateparks.org

This peaceful little spot on a low bluff on the Medway River was the scene of one of

force and the exact knowledge of the strength of the troops at Fort Morris, the Redcoats did not follow McIntosh's suggestion; instead, they retreated. Fort Morris, however, eventually fell to the British and was dismantled.

A smaller earthen fort, called Defiance in honor of McIntosh's reply, was built during the War of 1812 from the remains of Fort Morris, and you can explore it by visiting this site. Strolling around the walls of the fort under the majestic oaks towering over it, you have a wonderful view of the Medway and its marshes, and you might even get a glimpse of a shrimp boat trawling in the river. The interpretive center/museum at the site tells the saga of the fort and of Sunbury, the town it was built to protect, and there's also a 1-mile nature trail through marsh and scrub oak forest.

The Georgia Department of Natural Resources, which maintains the seventy-acre site, offers several special events during the year, including the Independence Day Colonial Faire in July and the "Come and Take It!" reenactment in October. Admission to the site is $2.50 for adults and $1.50 for youths 6 to 18; entry for children younger than six is free. Fort Morris is open from 9 A.M. to 5 P.M. Tuesday through Saturday and from 9:30 A.M. to 5:30 P.M. on Sunday. It's closed on Monday.

While you're at the interpretive center at Fort Morris State Historic Site, be sure to view the award-winning, twelve-minute video, "Sunbury Sleeps: The Forgotten Town of Sunbury, Ga." This hauntingly beautiful tribute to one of Georgia's "lost towns" serves as the perfect introduction to the next stop on our daytrip, the Sunbury Cemetery. The cemetery is a little more than a mile from the entrance to Fort Morris. After leaving the fort, turn right onto Fort Morris Road and keep to your left until you reach Sunbury Road. Turn left onto this dirt road and drive to Dutchmans Cove Road, then take a right and follow this unpaved lane a short distance to the cemetery.

the classic rejoinders in American history. During the Revolutionary War, the British besieged the American earthworks of Fort Morris and the nearby town of Sunbury, and the Redcoat commander demanded a surrender. The fort's commander, Col. John McIntosh, answered the demand in this defiant manner: "We, sir, are fighting the battles of America, and therefore disdain to remain neutral till its fate is determined. As to surrendering the fort, receive this laconic reply, 'Come and take it!'" Lacking some expected support from another British

Sunbury Cemetery
Dutchmans Cove Road
Richmond Hill, GA

This small cemetery is all that remains of the once bustling town of Sunbury, which in 1764 had eighty dwellings, three stores, several wharves, and a trio of town squares. By 1773, Sunbury was a seaport beginning to rival Savannah as a place of commerce. That year, the town saw 56 vessels clear port as compared with Savannah's 160. Sunbury also had another claim to fame: All three of Georgia's signers of the Declaration of Independence had a connection to the town—Lyman Hall lived there, Button Gwinnett resided on nearby St. Catherines Island, and George Walton was confined there when Sunbury was made a military prison after its capture by the British during the Revolutionary War.

By the end of the war, most of Sunbury had been destroyed, and the town never recovered. There were fewer than eight families living there by 1855, and all evidence of the town eventually disappeared— everything but the cemetery and the thirty-four grave markers that remain standing. When we visited Fort Morris, we knew when we left there wouldn't be a great deal to see at the cemetery. But after viewing the Department of Natural Resources video about Sunbury, we felt compelled to take a look and pay our respects, so to speak. Maybe you will, too.

Now it's time to get back on the Historic Liberty Trail and head to the town of Midway. We recommend, though, that while you're on the way, you visit Seabrook Village, which you can find by turning right off Fort Morris Road onto Trade Hill Road.

Seabrook Village
660 Trade Hill Road
Richmond Hill, GA
(912) 884–7008
www.seabrookvillage.org

This 104-acre site portrays the history and culture of African Americans living in coastal Georgia during 1865 to 1930. Using authentic buildings and displays of artifacts, Seabrook brings that period to life. Among stops on guided and self-guided tours of the village are Bowen's Farm, with its rice fields and a barn containing tools used in farming, gathering oysters, and making turpentine; the Ripley Corn Crib, where corn is ground into grits and meal; the Seabrook School, with its original wooden blackboard and desks made by former student John Stevens; the Gibbons-Woodward House, in which you can see a rural kitchen, a featherbed, and a replica of the original clay chimney; a mill and boiler house where stalks of sugar cane are ground by horse power and cooked into syrup; the Delegal-Williams House, with its family photographs and local furnishings; and a train depot that was moved to the site from nearby Riceboro.

While you're visiting Seabrook, be sure to see the unusual artwork of Cyrus Bowen, with which he adorned local gravesites. Seabrook is open from 10 A.M. to 4 P.M. Tuesday through Saturday. Group tours lasting three hours and conducted by costumed guides are available, as are one-hour guided tours in the afternoon. Fees for group tours are $7 for adults, $6 for youths 10 to 18 years old, and $5 for children from 5 to 10; fees for the one-hour tours are $5.

The next stop on the tour is Midway, which was established in 1754 by a group of Congregationalists from Dorchester, South Carolina. Their Midway Society produced governors, cabinet members, U.S. senators and congressmen, numerous ministers, and foreign missionaries. The parish they settled, St. John's, was a hotbed of patriotic fervor during the years leading up to the American Revolution, and two of its residents, Lyman Hall and Button Gwinnett, were among Georgia's three signers of the Declaration of Independence. To get to Midway, head west on U.S. 84 back to I-95 and stay on U.S. 84 until you reach U.S. 17. Turn right onto U.S. 17. Clustered just up the road are the

Midway Museum, Midway Congregational Church, and the Midway Cemetery.

Midway Museum
U.S. Highway 17
Richmond Hill, GA
(912) 884–5837

This museum gives visitors an idea of what life was like for landowners in coastal Georgia during the late eighteenth century and early nineteenth century. The museum building is an elegant, raised cottage-style house erected in 1957 and based on a sketch made in 1828 of a home in nearby Riceboro. The rooms of the house are filled with original eighteenth-century furnishings; among the more unique items are a walking cane-gun that fired a .45 caliber slug and a set of musical glasses that are played by rubbing vinegar around the rims. A museum staff member will tell you about many of the items in the three first-floor rooms of the house and will play a tune on the glasses; you're free to look at the upper-floor bedrooms and displays in the ground-floor rooms on your own.

This attraction, which is operated by the Midway Museum Board of Governors, is open from 10 A.M. to 4 P.M. Tuesday through Saturday and from 2 to 4 P.M. on Sunday; it's closed on Monday. Admission, which includes access to nearby Midway Congregational Church, is $3 for adults and $1 for youngsters 6 through 14; children younger than six are admitted free.

Midway Congregational Church
U.S. Highway 17
Richmond Hill, GA

Built in 1792, this stately church reflects a style reminiscent of Colonial New England (some of the founders of Midway were descendants of Puritans from Massachusetts who had settled in South Carolina). The existing building replaced a church that was burned by the British in 1778. The church is a short walk from the Midway Museum, and you can obtain a key from a museum staff member and take a look inside. If you visit at a time when the museum is closed, you can get a key at White's Auto Care, a service station located next to the church. The church has no heating system or artificial lights, but services are conducted there each April by the Midway Society.

Midway Cemetery
U.S. Highway 17
Richmond Hill, GA

Researchers believe Midway Cemetery was laid out in the late 1750s and that it contains about 1,200 graves. Among those buried there are James Screven, a brigadier general in the American army who was killed in November 1778 in a skirmish with the British about a mile south of his resting place, and Daniel Stewart, who attained the rank of brigadier after fighting in the Revolution and Indian Wars and was the great-grandfather of President Theodore Roosevelt; Fort Stewart, the U.S. Army's military reservation at nearby Hinesville, is named after him. The cemetery is open to the public, and a brochure featuring a map and self-guided tour of the site is available at the Midway Museum for 25 cents.

Midway Cemetery is also the burial site of Louis LeConte, who owned a rice plantation south of Midway where he created a botanical garden of great renown. You can reach the plantation by driving south on U.S. 17 for 3 miles to the Barrington Ferry Road. Turn right onto Barrington Ferry and follow it for 5.5 miles to the entrance to the plantation site.

LeConte-Woodmanston Rice Plantation and Botanical Gardens
Barrington Ferry Road
Richmond Hill, GA
(912) 884–6500
www.geocities.com/RainForest/Vines/3365/

In its heyday during the early 1800s, Woodmanston Plantation covered more than 3,300 acres and was the largest inland rice plantation in Georgia. Louis LeConte came into possession of Woodmanston in 1810, and the garden he planted there gained fame throughout the United States and Europe.

The plantation was abandoned in 1869, but a restoration of a 63.8-acre site was begun in the late 1970s as a project of The Garden Club of Georgia. The project, being carried on now by the LeConte-Woodmanston Foundation, is a work in progress that so far has resulted in the creation of a 1.5-acre botanical garden featuring plants that LeConte might have grown and a 2.5-mile nature trail along a network of rice dams. The garden contains more than one hundred different plants, including beds of older varieties of camellias and roses. Several structures that were part of the plantation—a chicken coop, a garden shed, a smokehouse, and a slave cabin—have been re-created on the site. Visitors can also stroll along a path through a 3-acre bog containing flowering plants native to the area and observe rice being grown on 2 acres of wetlands.

The plantation is open to the public from 9 A.M. to 5 P.M. Tuesday through Saturday, and admission is $2 per person. The site is closed from December through mid-February, when the area is prone to flooding. Because LeConte-Woodmanston is in a somewhat remote spot, you might want to call ahead to the listed number before you visit, and you definitely should call to make arrangements for group tours. Also, be aware that the last 1.6 miles of the drive to the plantation is on dirt roads.

The last attraction on this tour is the Fort Stewart Museum, a military museum just inside the main entrance to Fort Stewart, the huge U.S. Army post at Hinesville. From LeConte-Woodmanston, drive back to the intersection of U.S. 17 and U.S. 84 and head west on U.S. 84 about 7 miles to Hinesville. Turn right onto General Stewart Way, which will take you to the entrance to Fort Stewart. The museum is on the post at the corner of Wilson Boulevard and Frank Cochran Drive.

Fort Stewart Museum
2022 Frank Cochran Drive
Richmond Hill, GA
(912) 767–7885
www.stewart_army.mil

Displays at the museum focus on the history of Fort Stewart and its current occupant, the Third Infantry Division (Mechanized). Fort Stewart, now the largest Army installation east of the Mississippi River, was established in the summer of 1940 as Camp Stewart and served as an antiaircraft artillery training center during World War II and the Korean War. During the early 1960s, the post was the site of a variety of tests and training by military units, and in the latter half of the decade it served as a training area for Army helicopter pilots.

In the mid-1970s, the Twenty-fourth Infantry Division (Mechanized) was activated at Fort Stewart, and the unit was based there until April 1996, when the post became the home of the Third Infantry. The story of the Third's service in the two world wars and Korea is related at the museum, portions of which are also devoted to the Twenty-fourth Infantry and the military history of coastal Georgia. Uniforms, weapons, and other items used by the Third Infantry and their opponents are on display in the museum, as is a T-72M-1 tank abandoned by Iraqi Republican Guard crewmen in an engagement with the Twenty-fourth Infantry during the war in the Persian Gulf. There's also an exhibit featuring Audie Murphy, a Third Infantry hero in World War II whose exploits won him the title of "America's Most Decorated Soldier." Outside the museum, you'll find static displays of equipment used in warfare, including an M4A3 Sherman tank, a UH-1 Huey helicopter gunship, and numerous Iraqi artillery pieces and vehicles captured by U.S. forces during the Gulf War. Entry to Fort Stewart is open to civilians, and admission to the museum is free. Hours of operation are from 10 A.M. to 4 P.M. Tuesday through Saturday.

Jekyll Island

Georgia's coastline is a fascinating and varied one. Savannah, which snugs up to

The Jekyll Island Club Hotel, now a full-service resort, was once a private club for the very rich.

PHOTO: COURTESY OF THE JEKYLL ISLAND CLUB HOTEL

South Carolina, marks its northernmost point. At the southern extremity, up against the Florida line, you'll find St. Mary's, with its access to Cumberland Island National Seashore. And in between you'll find the Golden Isles.

Four islands make up this cluster, accessible from Brunswick, a port and industrial city that retains a small historic district. It is the jumping-off point for the Golden Isles, reachable by causeway with one exception. St. Simons Island is the biggest and most developed of the Isles, with beaches, motels, restaurants, and historic sites. Little St. Simons is accessible only by boat and is open to a limited number of guests (by arrangement). Consisting of largely undeveloped beaches and marshlands, this island is a real treat for environment-minded tourists. Sea Island, largely residential and from a geographical point of view part of St. Simons, is home to the extremely toney resort known as The Cloister.

Jekyll Island is the southernmost of the four Golden Isles. We think it is likely to appeal to the same type of traveler who is attracted to Savannah. You'll find places to eat and sleep there, but development has not run wild. In fact, the state of Georgia owns the place, and the business and residential ventures there are really long-term leases. Enjoy the beaches (which are all public) and consider a trip along the extensive network of bike paths a must-do (bike rental places abound; check the lobby of larger motels). Jekyll, like the rest of the Golden Isles, is also covered with golf courses, most of which are accessible to the public at large.

The Brunswick & The Golden Isles Visitors Bureau, 4 Glynn Avenue, Brunswick (912–265–0620); and the Jekyll Island Welcome Center, P.O. Box 13186, Jekyll Island (912–635–3636, 877–453–5955) are two general sources that can provide additional information, including lodging details and how to get onto the golf courses. Expect to pay a $3 "parking fee" as you drive onto Jekyll.

To get there, head south on I-95. It takes about ninety minutes. While it's not that long a trip (we know people who commute there from Savannah for work daily, in fact), it can be harrowing. This is the corridor that runs between the Northeast population centers and Florida, and it is always heavily traveled by time-conscious vacationers. Exits are clearly marked.

Jekyll Island Historic District Museum
Visitors Center
Stable Road
Jekyll Island, GA
(912) 635–2119

Georgia was originally founded as a refuge for debtors, but the richest and most powerful men in America originally developed Jekyll Island. They bought the island in 1886 and made it into a private resort where you need not apply unless your annual income included at least seven figures, all to the left of the decimal point. Names that are synonymous with Ameri-

can fortunes were among the Jekyll Island Club's members: Rockefeller, Gould, Morgan. And they didn't stay in rented quarters, although the club was (and now is again) a fine hotel. Instead, they built "cottages"—mansions that took advantage of beautiful views, cooling breezes, and balmy weather. This was, indeed, the playground of the rich and famous.

That era lasted for fifty-five years of Jekyll's history, and you can still see its vestiges. The cottages personify a lifestyle most of us have trouble imagining. They've been fixed up (coastal climate and humidity require diligent upkeep) and are now open to the public. Tours are available via open trams (which look like golf carts linked together) at a cost of $10 for adults and $6 for those ages 6 to 18. Children younger than six are free. Tours depart on the hour from 10 A.M. to 3 P.M. from the visitors center on Stable Road. (Later tours are often available during the summer.) There's bad news for independent-minded travelers: Only the guided tours get inside the choice buildings. The

The dining room at the Jekyll Island Club Hotel has been restored to its late-nineteenth-century splendor.
PHOTO: COURTESY OF THE JEKYLL ISLAND CLUB HOTEL

Horse-drawn carriages provide a leisurely and entertaining way to tour Beaufort's historic streets.
PHOTO: COURTESY OF GREATER BEAUFORT CHAMBER OF COMMERCE

Beaufort's riverfront marinas provide moorings for a picturesque array of watercraft.
PHOTO: COURTESY OF GREATER BEAUFORT CHAMBER OF COMMERCE

The Old Point neighborhood in Beaufort boasts lovely antebellum homes. PHOTO: COURTESY OF GREATER BEAUFORT CHAMBER OF COMMERCE

A ride along the beach at Jekyll Island is a perfect way to spend a summer afternoon. PHOTO: COURTESY OF JEKYLL ISLAND AUTHORITY

Visitors enjoy viewing Jekyll Island's historic district from a horse-drawn carriage. PHOTO: COURTESY OF JEKYLL ISLAND AUTHORITY

Jekyll Island has been attracting golf enthusiasts for more than 100 years. PHOTO: COURTESY OF JEKYLL ISLAND AUTHORITY

Jekyll Island's Summer Waves Waterpark attracts visitors with rides like the Slow Motion Ocean and the Frantic Atlantic. PHOTO: COURTESY OF JEKYLL ISLAND AUTHORITY

Take a tour and see what "cottage" living meant to the rich and famous who once vacationed on Jekyll Island. PHOTO: COURTESY OF JEKYLL ISLAND AUTHORITY

Goodyear Cottage, which houses the offerings of the Jekyll Island Arts Association, is the only house open to the non-paying public, but there is a good selection of shops.

Jekyll and St. Simons Islands are not accessible from one another—you have to make the trip back to the mainland on the causeway and then take the other causeway to the next island. It's a pleasant drive through the marshes, watching herons and marsh rabbits, but it does take a little time.

St. Simons is a more developed beach community than Jekyll Island, but it has still retained its charm and individual character. There's a large year-round population, and they clearly cherish the winter months when the tourists aren't as prevalent. That doesn't mean visitors aren't welcome; it does mean a quieter pace of life in the winter. There's even a "downtown," a short strip of shops leading to the water and including the usual tourist stuff, an interesting toy store, a bookshop, etc. St. Simons has large, legible signs posted at key intersections, and the names of specific destinations are clearly listed. We get lost a lot elsewhere, but we get around just fine on St. Simons. The King and Prince Hotel is a good lodging choice (the selection is rather limited). It's by no means as tony as the Cloisters, the region's four-star resort, but they've got the amenities you'd expect in a beachside resort. The island offers multiple restaurant options, predictably leaning toward seafood. We always seek out Blanche's Courtyard, a dressy-to-casual dinner spot where we have never been disappointed in the food or drink.

Beaufort, South Carolina

Beaufort is situated between Savannah and Charleston, S.C., and it exudes much of the charm of those two cities, but on a smaller scale. This town of about 9,500 residents has a historic district filled with elegant homes built in the 1700s and 1800s and a quaint but bustling waterfront shopping district that's brimming with intriguing stores and unique eating places.

The Beaufort area is rich in history. The Spaniards unsuccessfully attempted to found the colony of Santa Elena here in 1559, and French Protestants, led by explorer Jean Ribaut in 1562, tried to start a settlement called Charlesfort on what is now Parris Island. It failed, and the Spanish returned to the area in 1566, building a fort, San Phillipe, and the Mission of Santa Elena at Port Royal. According to the Historic Beaufort Foundation, this settlement was, by 1580, one of the largest Spanish towns north of Mexico. It was abandoned in 1586 following attacks on Spanish Florida by the English privateer, Sir Francis Drake.

The English laid claim to the area in the 1600s and by the turn of the next century had established a foothold at Port Royal. Beaufort was founded in 1711, and, in the years leading up to the American Revolution, local planters turned profits by growing rice and indigo. During the Revolutionary War, residents of the area were sharply divided over the issue of independence from Britain and allegiance to the crown. British forces occupied Beaufort in July 1779 but evacuated later in the year. Cotton planting was introduced to the area after the Revolution. Subsequent crops made rich men and women of many of Beaufort's citizens in the years leading up to the Civil War. Early in the conflict, in November 1861, South Carolina's Sea Islands were invaded by Union forces and Beaufort and the Port Royal area fell into Federal hands. Beaufort became the main base of Union squadrons blockading the South Atlantic. During the Union occupation, the first school for black freedmen, which eventually became Penn School, was established east of Beaufort on St. Helena Island.

Beaufort is about fifty-five minutes from downtown Savannah by car. To get there, take Oglethorpe Avenue west and drive across the Eugene Talmadge Memorial Bridge on U.S. Highway 17 into South Carolina. It's 5 miles from the bridge to the intersection of U.S. 17 and Alternate S.C. Highway 170; turn right onto Alt. SC 170 and stay on it for 6 miles until you reach its intersection with SC 170 (also S.C. Highway 46). Turn right at the stop sign and drive 3 miles to where SC 170 leaves SC 46. Turn left onto SC 170 and enjoy the scenery—a narrow, two-lane road shrouded by the moss-covered branches of gnarled oaks. Take a good look, because this area might not be heavily forested for much longer; civilization and the developers of subdivisions and shopping centers appear to be taking over.

You'll be on SC 170 for about 8 miles until it bears to the right; stay on it for another 15 miles, which will take you into the outskirts of Beaufort. While on SC 170, you'll pass country roads with fascinating-sounding names such as Bulltomb, Bufflehead, Heffalump, Old Bailey's, Crippled Oak, Bellinger Bluff, and Mudbar, and you'll catch glimpses of marshland and open water. You'll cross the picturesque Chechessee River, drive through relatively pristine Lemon Island, and then find yourself marveling at the majestic expanse of the aptly named Broad River, which is spanned by a bridge that's 1.4 miles long.

SC 170 will lead you to U.S. Highway 21 S. (also known in these parts as Boundary Street); turn right onto U.S. 21 and stay on it for about 2 miles until you reach the traffic light at Ribaut Road. Turn right onto Ribaut Road and drive to the third stoplight, then turn left onto Bay Street, which will take you about a mile past stately homes and a bay dotted with sailboats and into Beaufort's waterfront district.

The focal points of this area are Bay Street, which is lined on either side with shops and restaurants, and Henry C. Chambers Waterfront Park, a pleasant, tree-filled swath of greenery lying south of Bay Street between the street and the bay formed by the Beaufort River. The park, with its wide walkways, swinging benches, and elaborate children's playground, is a

Insiders' Tip

While visiting Beaufort, consider taking a side trip to nearby Penn Center, a fifty-acre National Historic Landmark District on St. Helena Island. Penn Center is the site of Penn School, one of the most significant African American institutions in the United States, and an active community center. The mission of the center is to preserve the history, culture, and environment of the Sea Islands. You can get there by taking U.S. 21 east from Beaufort to St. Helena Island and turning right onto Martin Luther King Jr. Drive.

wonderful place for strolling or for sitting and catching a breeze off the nearby water. Several of the restaurants that dot the south side of Bay Street open onto patios and porches that offer outdoor dining on the fringes of the park. Among these eating places are Ollie's By The Bay at 822 Bay Street, which specializes in seafood; Plum's Cafe, at 904½ Bay Street, which is known for its gourmet soups, salads, and sandwiches and homemade ice cream; and The Bank Waterfront Grill & Bar at 926 Bay Street, which was built in the mid-1920s as the Beaufort Bank and now has waitresses who refer to themselves as "tellers" and who serve beverages they call "liquid assets."

The stores along Bay Street and on the narrow lanes running to the north off Bay provide a plethora of shopping opportunities. There are several galleries, one of the more unique of which is the Rhett Gallery at 901 Bay Street. In addition to selling prints and paintings, this gallery offers antique maps and nautical charts and Civil War art and artifacts, including pages from *Harper's Weekly* and *Frank Leslie's Illustrated Newspaper*—bits of history that make interesting artwork when matted and framed. Antique stores abound, among them The Consignor's Antique Mall at 913 Port Republic Street, where a wide variety of items are on sale; Heritage House Antiques and Gardens at 1013 Charles Street; and Legacy and Whimsy at 812 Port Republic Street. Specialty shops you might want to visit include The Craftseller at 818 Bay Street, which deals in local and regional arts and crafts; Boombears, a store at 501 Carteret Street that is stocked with "timeless toys"; The Cat's Meow Shoppe, a gift shop on Bay Street that caters to collectors of all things feline; and Blackstone's Deli Cafe, at 915 Bay Street, where you can eat breakfast and lunch and purchase gourmet groceries. If you're looking for books, stop in at The Book Shop at 808 Bay Street, McIntosh Book Shoppe in the recently refurbished Old Bay Market Place at 917 Bay Street, or Firehouse Books & Expresso Bar at 706 Craven Street. Each has a good inventory that features books related to the region, and McIntosh has a large selection of rare, out-of-print editions.

Those in search of history will find it throughout town in general and in two locations in particular:

Beaufort Museum
713 Craven Street
Beaufort, SC
(843) 525–7077

Housed in an arsenal that was completed in 1798, the museum tells the story of Beaufort's history through its exhibits and displays of artifacts. Among the exhibits are those involving the Native Americans who lived in the area, the European colonization of the region, the development of the town in the era prior to the Civil War, the Union occupation during that conflict, and early twentieth century industries.

The museum has been situated in the arsenal since 1939 as the result of a WPA project to add a wing for a museum and relic room. The building was the site of National Guard musters until 1966, and it was acquired by the city of Beaufort in 1990 for the continued purpose of preserving the town's heritage and that of the surrounding Sea Islands. The museum is closed on Sundays and city holidays but is open the rest of the time from 11 A.M. until 4 P.M. Admission for adults is $2, and children six years old and younger are admitted free.

John Mark Verdier House Museum
801 Bay Street
Beaufort, SC
(843) 524–6334

Beaufort can boast of many historic and beautiful residences, but the John Mark Verdier House is the only one that's open to the public on a regular basis. Revolutionary War hero the Marquis de Lafayette was entertained at the house during a visit to Beaufort in 1825, and the Union Army used it as a headquarters during the Civil War. Built in the late 1790s by one of the town's leading merchants, the two-story frame house rests on a tabby foundation and is an example of the Federal style of architecture. Interior features are the paneled reception parlor, first-floor dining room, graceful staircase, and spacious second-floor drawing room. The décor and furnishings reflect those of the period from 1790 until Lafayette's visit in 1825.

The house was condemned in 1942, but public-spirited citizens spearheaded a drive to save the structure, and a restoration effort was begun in the fall of 1975. It was completed a year later. The house is open to viewing Monday through Saturday with the first tour at 11 A.M. and the final tour at 3:30 P.M. Admission is $4 for adults and $2 for students.

You can see more of Beaufort's elegant old houses—their exteriors, at least—by visiting an area called The Point, which is east of Bay Street. This oak-filled section of town is not large and doesn't take long to drive through, but it's abundantly graced with what the local historic foundation calls "Beaufort-style" homes. According to the Historic Beaufort Foundation, these homes were "designed for airiness and coolness" and "incorporated elements of Georgian and Colonial architecture as well as those of Greek Revival and semi-tropical Spanish." The foundation's guidebook states that the Beaufort-style home "differs from the more urban designs of Charleston and Savannah in that the Beaufort house is free standing on a large lot, frequently with a formal garden, and is oriented to take full advantage of the prevailing southwesterly breezes. It more nearly resembles the plantation house, brought to town, as some indeed were, and adapted to the summer heat and the dampness of the Lowcountry." Many of these homes have fascinating histories, and some bear enchanting names, such as The Castle, Tidewater, Marshlands, The Oaks, Tidalholm, Riverview, and The Little Taj.

A wonderful way to view these homes and the rest of Beaufort's Historic District is on foot on your own; you can pick up free maps of the area at many of the downtown shops and at the visitors center, which is at the intersection of Congress and Carteret Streets. If you're looking for something that's a little more structured, there are numerous tours available, including those provided by appointment by The Point Tours at 1002-B Bay Street (843-522-3576); by Carolina Buggy Tours (843-525-1300); Southurn Buggy Tours (843-271-2130), whose carriages leave from the marina area of the Waterfront; and by The Spirit of Old Beaufort, which conducts walking tours from its gift shop at 103 West Street Extension (843-525-0459). Ghosts of the South (843-252-2586) provides a spookier look at Beaufort, with candlelight walking tours leaving nightly at 8 P.M. from West Street at the Waterfront Park. For those who are nautically inclined, there are cruises aboard the *Islander*, which sails from the Waterfront Park and can be contacted for reservations by calling (843) 524-4000.

Neighborhoods and Real Estate

Savannah Neighborhoods
Real Estate Companies
Apartments

Savannah was a well-kept secret for many years, according to local real estate experts. While places like Charleston and New Orleans garnered national attention as the "in" Southern hotspots, Savannah stayed quietly out of the spotlight, content in restoring its Historic Downtown, developing its suburbs, and going about its daily business.

How things change! Since the late 1980s and early 1990s, factors ranging from media attention generated by *Midnight in the Garden of Good and Evil* to low interest rates have helped fuel a relatively solid market, resulting in steady sales and in some areas—especially the Historic Downtown and Tybee Island—significant jumps in housing prices, according to several local real estate experts. "It used to be that Savannah was the best-kept secret in the Southeast," said Realtor David Byck, who has been selling real estate in Savannah for forty years. "Now we aren't that way."

Take the Historic Downtown for example. In the mid-1970s, Realtor Celia Dunn remembers selling a four-story home with a carriage house, off street parking, and side garden for $150,000. In 1997, the selling price for the same home, since restored, was $850,000. Another home she sold for $60,000 around 1976 was selling for $475,000 a little more than twenty years later. "When you have a finite commodity, once they are gone, they are gone," said Dunn.

Helping fuel all this interest has been Savannah's success as a movie location. That's an interesting novelty, but it's not unusual to find a star passing through a local real estate office looking for a lease or a sale. The latest celeb to join local ranks? Sandra Bullock at Tybee Island.

It is hard to believe, but there was a time when it seemed as if you couldn't give property away in the Historic Downtown. In the late 1950s, this area was full of dilapidated, abandoned, and neglected buildings. Like many places around the country, residents had slowly left the city core for the suburbs. Restoration didn't become a priority until 1955, when a historically significant building (the Isaiah Davenport House; see our Attractions chapter) was going to be demolished to make room for a parking lot. This prompted the formation of the Historic Savannah Foundation and the beginning of Savannah's resurrection.

By the mid-1970s, the restoration effort had received a boost when a couple from Atlanta decided to move to Savannah and start an art school. In 1979, Paula Rowan (now Paula Wallace) and Richard Rowan launched the Savannah College of Art and Design in a massive old building, once an old National Guard armory. The college continued acquiring and restoring buildings, many of them the "extra" schools that the end of segregation left sprinkled through and around downtown. As the college grew, it attracted more students needing places to live, which in turn fueled more restoration efforts as investors saw potential profits. Prices started creeping upward, while the number of available houses to restore began to decline throughout the '80s. As a matter of fact, one subset of the local real estate market is made up of parents who buy a residence for their college student sons and daughters to live in while pursuing a degree, and then have it as investment property once the offspring leave this second "nest."

Helping fuel all of this was a best-selling book, *Midnight in the Garden of Good and Evil* by John Berendt, which spawned its own cottage industry. Just exactly what impact the phenomenon had on the real estate market is a subject of debate. Do people who are interested in the segment of the real estate market that begins at $250,000 and goes up quickly (the Historic District) really base their decisions on the best-seller list? Still, there's no denying that The Book (as it is known locally) brought lots of attention to the city, and Savannah is one of those places that you don't forget after you notice it.

But *Midnight* wasn't the only attention Savannah was getting in the mid-1990s. In 1996, Savannah was in the limelight hosting Olympic yachting during the Summer Olympic Games in Atlanta. The ballyhooed hordes of Olympic spectators never showed up, but the event did give the city an international panache.

That same year Savannah's historic beauty was spotlighted when PBS's popular series *This Old House* came to town to capture the renovation of a Monterey Square home. "The Olympics and *This Old House* made a lot of people aware of Savannah as a comfortable place to live," said Dunn, who has been selling homes in the Historic District for several decades. "Until then, many people had never heard of Savannah."

The secret is definitely out. On Tybee, prices in some cases have risen as much as 50 percent in the last few years, according to Judy O'Neill of Tybee Island Realty. People were finding an all-too-scarce commodity—affordable beachfront property; it was just a matter of time before the laws of economics kicked in. "If you are looking for a bargain you are about five years too late," said O'Neill. "Tybee used to be a vacation spot where people had second homes. More and more people want to live here year-round now."

A two-bedroom, two-bath condo with a view will cost around $150,000, while a newer home with three bedrooms and no view will cost around $175,000. Classic old beach houses and oceanfront homes are becoming harder to find, as more people realize their value and sit on them, O'Neill said. If you do find one, it could cost $500,000 or more. (For more on Tybee Island neighborhoods and real estate, including realty company listings, see our Tybee Island chapter.)

As the redevelopable property downtown dwindles and the restored properties literally soar in price, there is a new trend in the Historic Downtown housing market. New construction is putting pseudohistoric town home condos—designed to blend in with the authentic surroundings—in dense concentrations, particularly on the fringes of the district.

Even Broughton Street, the once-booming retail "main drag" downtown, is getting in on the residential act. Revitalization is bringing restaurants and trendy shops back to the first-floor retail storefronts, and now developers are reconfiguring the upper stories of these buildings into luxury condos for the well-heeled urbanite. Initial asking prices for condos with a complete luxe finish were over $200,000 on Broughton Street. Cooler heads seem to have prevailed among buyers, however, and the prices have broken a little—or, in the case of those who prefer to do their own work, a lot. This is one downtown residential market where buyers have a little more room to maneuver.

Elsewhere in the county, especially the other islands and outlying suburbs, development has been on the rise, and with it, prices in many cases have also steadily increased. "I think we are seeing areas going up in value throughout the county," said Gary Udinsky, chief appraiser for Chatham County. "We live in a very desirable part of the country. The force of supply and demand drove prices up."

However, prices haven't outpaced people's wallets. First-time home buyers can still find a home in most areas of the city, while those with significantly more money have some of the world's most attractive and unique residences to choose from. "We can take care of people who want a $60,000 home up to a $600,000 home," said Realtor Charles Lamas, who has been selling real estate on Savannah's eastern islands for several decades. "We have got the hardworking blue-collar workers up to the very rich, which makes it a neat community."

This beautiful home overlooks downtown Savannah's Forsyth Park. PHOTO: COURTESY OF SAVANNAH AREA CHAMBER OF COMMERCE

Savannah Neighborhoods

There are stories about people coming to Savannah for a visit, only to return a few months later in a U-Haul. One couple, after a weekend getaway, went back to New York, quit their jobs, and were back in town in a few months. They fell in love with the romance of the city, they said. That was more than twenty years ago.

Soon after arriving, our newcomers face a very difficult decision—where to live. Savannah offers many choices—there is the beach, tree-lined suburbia, and, of course, the Historic Downtown. Each neighborhood is as distinctive as those who call it home. As one Realtor said of living in the Historic Downtown, it is as much a way of life as a place to live. Outside your doorstep are coffee shops, art galleries, and history. And it's the same story no matter where you are in the city. Each neighborhood provides a glimpse into people's lives and lifestyles. Travel through Midtown's Ardsley Park, and you will see kids playing in front of wonderfully colorful craftsman bungalows:

wood-frame homes, typically with front porches and interesting architectural touches like archways and wood floors.

On the Islands, new homes sprawl out next to pristine golf courses, while special garages are tacked on just to make room for golf carts. Young professionals a few years out of college can often be found in new developments on the Southside, near the hustle and hurry of shopping malls, restaurants, and everything commercial.

People are very proud of their neighborhoods in Savannah and don't mind bragging about what makes their choice of location clearly the only place to live in the city. There are literally hundreds of neighborhoods in Savannah. To show their loyalty, in the Historic Downtown area alone there are more than forty neighborhood associations.

We can't list every Savannah neighborhood, but we have attempted to spotlight a few. It should provide a starting point as you consider a very important decision.

Begin downtown, with the Historic District and the Victorian District, which currently is the Historic District's poor relation but which clearly has ambitions. From there, you have three options for suburban stretching: south, which was the area's first suburban direction; east, toward the series of residential islands; and west, toward the newest land opening to development.

About the Basics

Every area has its peculiarities on which newcomers should be briefed when they enter the home market. Your real estate dealer should touch on these with you, but we'll review a few.

Buy flood insurance. It is not part of the standard homeowner policy. The whole of Chatham County is in a hurricane zone, and although we've been lucky for decades, well, if luck were enough, there would be no insurance industry. Also, find out whether any house you are considering has been subject to storm-related flooding. A solid downpour on a high tide, coupled with recent development and increased runoff in an area, can mean street flooding that occasionally invades homes, a short-lived but damaging phenomenon. The city of Savannah is in the midst of a drainage improvement program. Check the drainage factor out thoroughly when you are considering property.

If you go to some of the outlying areas of the county or some of the smaller municipalities, you will run across volunteer fire departments or subscription fire departments. Some of these have very good ratings, which you will find affects your fire insurance rating. A handful of private water systems remain in the county, for-profit companies instead of municipal operations. Not all homes are on community sewerage systems, and long rainy spells can make life with an older septic tank difficult. Again, these situations are not unique to our area, just something you want to include in your evaluation of a property.

School zones often influence a family choice of a home. Remember, though, that school zones can be changed and the

Available houses in the Historic Downtown area are becoming increasingly difficult to find.
PHOTO: KYLE CASON

Detailed ironwork distinguishes many downtown homes, such as these on Monterey Square.
PHOTO: BETTY DARBY

local public school system offers magnet school and other options not based on where a child lives. Check these matters out directly with the school system by calling (912) 651-7000 and asking for the placement office.

Looking at waterfront property? Remember, almost all the waterfront property in the area—not just the beaches, but also riverfront and creekfront—is tidally influenced, so check the place out at low tide.

With those tips out of the way, let's look at some neighborhoods.

The Historic Downtown

The Historic Downtown is a miniature city within a city. Inside the 2.5-square-mile area you will find restaurants, churches, antique shops, museums, banks, government buildings, art galleries, and even some wildlife—that is, if you count the hundreds of squirrels who call the many squares and parks home. (See the maps at

the front of the guide for a close-up look at the Historic Downtown.)

Of course, there are also the houses. Hundreds of homes painstakingly restored to their original nineteenth-century splendor fill the area. Within a few steps in the Historic Downtown, you are apt to encounter wrought-iron balconies, bricked courtyards, and other architectural delights such as historic downspouts shaped like dolphins that empty water into the street.

In addition to being a neighborhood, this is also a tourist attraction. That carries some drawbacks: slow-moving and loud tour buses that the city has not yet regulated heavily, on-street parking that's at a premium, and so on. The charms outweigh the drawbacks, though.

The Historic Downtown is also an area of great diversity. Some of Savannah's wealthiest and oldest families live a door or two away from art students who came to town from California or Ohio or someplace overseas. In the Beach Institute area on the eastern edge of the district, many longstanding African American families raise their children in homes that have been in the family for generations.

Home prices vary in the area, but because of the interest in living in the Historic Downtown, it is becoming increasingly difficult to find a home for less than $250,000. First-time buyers will find duplexes starting around $150,000, while a few condos are available for less than that. Glance through a local real estate book, and you will see listings in the Historic District ranging from as much as $499,000 for a renovated two-bedroom town house with a garden apartment, carriage house, and courtyard to $112,000 for a small, frame, two-bedroom town house on the outskirts of the district.

The Victorian District

Just south of the Historic Downtown, the Victorian District is several blocks roughly bounded by Victory Drive, Gwinnett Street, Martin Luther King Jr. Boulevard, and East Broad Street. There you will find two- and three-story Victorian frame houses, many in various stages of disrepair. Urban pioneers with a taste for hammers and paintbrushes will find this an exciting area.

Despite appearances, this residential area is increasingly becoming a popular spot for those interested in renovation work, especially as the number of houses needing work in the Historic Downtown continues to decline. It isn't unusual to find a very large Victorian home dating back to the 1800s, with porches, fireplaces, three or four bedrooms, and other unique features for well under $100,000. It will, however, need a lot of work, if not a complete overhaul. Restoration in the area is sporadic. On one block you may find two or three houses that have been restored, while a block away the entire area may be filled with abandoned homes.

Gentrification is a real issue in the Victorian District, just as it once was in the Historic District.

Southside/Midtown

Ardsley Park

Ardsley Park is Savannah's original suburb. Laid out in 1911, the development is south of the Historic Downtown and the Victorian District in Savannah's Midtown. Although it was designed as a single residential subdivision, over the years it has grown to include a large area loosely bounded by Victory Drive on the north, 55th Street on the south, Bull Street on the west, and Waters Avenue on the east.

Ardsley Park offers wide, tree-filled streets with many sizes and styles of older homes. Drive around and you will see large four- or five-bedroom mansions with elegant entrances, sunporches, and several fireplaces selling for well over $400,000. In other blocks, first-time home buyers with small children live in very nice craftsman-style bungalows with big backyards that they purchased for under $100,000. Because the area appeals to such a wide section of the community—from professionals to young families—it is a popular place to buy. In fact, this area has the curse of being trendy and real estate prices are inflated at present. Another major selling point is its Midtown location, which puts residents about ten minutes away from either the Historic Downtown or the edge of the Southside. This desirability means it isn't unusual for homes in Ardsley Park, especially the good deals, to be snapped up the first day they hit the market. Potential homeowners should watch for localized flooding, and note that blocks where homes don't have driveways often become clogged with street-side parking—a big nuisance if you have to deal with it on a daily basis.

Gordonston

Gordonston is a small neighborhood nestled into Savannah's eastside. It is made up of both longtime residents and newcomers and, according to local Realtors, is a popular spot for many local professionals including professors and others working in education.

Bordered by Skidaway Road, Gwinnett Street, and Pennsylvania Avenue, it was developed in the 1920s by the brother of Juliette Gordon Low, the founder of the Girl Scouts, on property that was once part of the family farm. In some ways, it is like a miniature Ardsley Park. Similar to its bigger cousin, throughout the development you will find tree-lined streets filled with a variety of older homes on large properties with front yards and backyards. Home styles include bungalows, cottages, and large mansions, and they tend to be less expensive than those in Ardsley Park. First-time home buyers might be able to find a two- or three-bedroom bungalow for around $80,000, while someone needing more space could find a large three- or four-bedroom home for $150,000. A friend even got a fixer-upper on the borders of this area for $46,000 (although it required a fortune in "elbow grease").

Windsor Forest

When the city began suburban sprawl in earnest during the 1960s, south was the

direction and Windsor Forest was the place. Windsor Forest is now a sprawl of neighborhoods between Savannah's malls. This is classic American suburbs—ranch-style homes, split-levels, two-car garages, backyard barbecues, and so on. You can find virtually any price range here, even tony marshfront property, but it's a decidedly middle-class enclave. Here, you'll find your biggest, most elaborate grocery stores, your movie theaters, and on the nearby commercial arteries, the car dealerships and the fast-food franchises.

Georgetown

Although Georgetown debuted in 1974 on open land most Savannahians consider south of the Southside, you will still find homes going up there. More than 1,600 homes have been built throughout the development, located off the far southern reaches of Abercorn Street on King George Boulevard. There are nine subdivisions in total in the community offering a variety of home styles and prices. First-time home buyers should be able to find a two-bedroom home in Georgetown for around $80,000. Others wanting to move up to a larger house with many amenities like gourmet kitchens, Corian countertops, and hardwood floors, will be able to find what they are looking for in Georgetown for $250,000 and up.

Islands

The Islands area covers a lot of ground. Places like Dutch Island and Skidaway Island, home of The Landings, are high end and exclusive (we mean that literally: they have gates). Islands like Wilmington, Whitemarsh, and Talahi are more standard suburbia, and people who don't live there can't tell where one island ends and another begins. Tybee Island, the only one of the islands that actually feels like an island, covers a wide range of incomes and is sort of a world unto itself.

Dutch Island

Dutch Island, an exclusive, gated enclave twenty minutes from downtown Savannah, is a popular choice for young professionals or those looking to move up to a larger home. The first neighborhoods on the island opened up seventeen years ago. Today, it is home to about 300 families and is expected to reach its maximum capacity of 500 homes within the next few years. Spacious homes with pristine lawns and traditional architecture can be found throughout Dutch Island. Home sizes range from 2,400 square feet up to 12,000 square feet, while prices reach up to $600,000.

Providence Plantation is the island's newest neighborhood. Half-acre lots start at $39,000, and homes begin at $225,000. Gourmet kitchens, hardwood floors, screened porches, and fireplaces are just some of the many amenities available. There is also a pool, playground, and lagoons stocked with fish for anglers. There are no recreation fees charged to use these facilities.

Isle of Hope

This peninsula in southeast Chatham County was an early summer resort for tourists. Situated with the Herb River on the west and the Skidaway River on the east, the community is one of Savannah's most picturesque. Beautiful old cottages with white picket fences and massive oak trees in the front yards overlook the waterways, while newer homes scatter throughout

Tree-lined Jones Street offers some of the prime Historic District real estate. PHOTO: BETTY DARBY

In the Historic District, stairs lead to the main entrance on the "parlor floor," while the ground floor of the building is known as the "garden level." PHOTO: BETTY DARBY

other neighborhoods. The very old and very new mix together nicely.

There is a small-town feel even though large developments and the hustle of Savannah are just twenty minutes away. Longtime residents live on Isle of Hope as well as young families and professionals. Home prices vary from modest, older two-bedroom bungalows around $100,000 to new three- and four-bedroom homes with all the amenities for $250,000 or more. The sky's the limit for the really beautiful waterfront mansions on Bluff Drive.

Long Point

More than 130 new homes have been built since 1992 at this popular Whitemarsh Island development. Conveniently located on Johnny Mercer Boulevard, it comfortably puts homeowners a short, fifteen-minute drive away from downtown or the Southside. Homes range in price from $229,000 to $450,000 and include many amenities like hardwood floors, cathedral ceilings, gourmet kitchens, and more. Styles differ throughout the development from sprawling single-story brick homes with circular drives to two-story stuccos with large front porches. Wide streets circulate through the community, and there is a guard gate that is typically occupied during the evening hours. According to local real estate agents, when the most recent section of interior and lagoon lots opened at Long Point, twenty-five were sold within the first sixty days.

The Landings on Skidaway Island

Spend any time in Savannah and no doubt you will hear someone refer to "The Landings." This massive, gated community takes up approximately 4,450 acres on Skidaway Island and is considered among Savannah's premier developments. Started in 1972, The Landings is currently home to 6,500 residents from forty-five states and fifteen foreign countries.

Since debuting more than twenty years ago, four phases have been built at The Landings, providing a diversity of architectural styles in a variety of prices

ranging from $200,000 to $900,000. In Midpoint, one area of the development, you will find Colonial, Federal, and Southern Lowcountry homes, while traditional, ranch-style wooden homes can be found elsewhere. Corian countertops, custom cabinets, hardwood floors, cathedral ceilings, terraces, and bay windows are just some of the many amenities available in homes at The Landings.

All the homes are on nicely landscaped lots that are often filled with trees, giving the feeling that you're living in the country, not a development with thousands of homes. The Landings' other main selling points include six golf courses, designed by such golfing luminaries as Arnold Palmer and Tom Fazio; thirty-four tennis courts; two marinas; and a yacht club. At the Oakridge Fitness Center there is a pool, plus fitness and exercise rooms. At the Franklin Creek Activity Center, there is a pro shop, clubhouse, twenty-five-meter pool with hydrospa and a snack bar. Membership fees are required to use the various facilities.

Although all the original lots have been sold, there are usually about one hundred listings, including resale homes and homesites, available at any one time, according to The Landings. Many interested people purchase a lot a few years before retirement in anticipation of eventually building a home. A more recent trend for a community made up so heavily of out-of-state retirees is the interest of affluent families already living in the area. All development at The Landings is closely monitored and must be approved by the Architectural Review Board. A number of restrictive covenants apply.

West Chatham

Southbridge

Southbridge is a 1,100-acre planned community 8 miles west of the Historic Downtown. Developed by Hall Development of Myrtle Beach, South Carolina, it is the first community of its size to open in West Chatham.

More than 350 families, including a mix of retired residents, young families, and professionals, have moved to South-bridge since its opening in 1987. As its literature explains, Southbridge is "a residential golf community blending Southern tradition with the amenities of a country club." Traditional Southern architecture is the development's hallmark. Drive around the neatly landscaped neighborhoods and you will see classic Georgian- and Federal-style wooden, brick, and stucco homes nestled among trees or along fairways on the golf course. Inside are many extras including modern kitchens, high ceilings, parquet floors, formal dining rooms, fireplaces, and breakfast nooks.

Two-, three-, or four-bedroom home options are available from roughly 1,600 to 2,400 square feet; prices range from $140,000 to $500,000. One of the newest additions to the development is Steeple Run, offering three-bedroom town houses of roughly 2,000 square feet. These run $165,000 to $185,000 and include such features as vaulted ceilings, hardwood floors, and skylights. If you prefer, you can purchase a lot for $30,000 to $100,000 and have a home built to your specifications. You pick the home style, wallpaper, where you want it on the lot, and the builders do the rest. The developers added golf course condos and large duplexes they call "villas" in 1999.

Golf architect Rees Jones designed Southbridge's eighteen-hole course, which is rated one of Georgia's twenty-five best courses by *Golfweek Magazine*. The semiprivate Southbridge Golf Club includes a 6,000-square-foot clubhouse with a pro shop, dining room, and lounge. Besides golf, there is the Southbridge Racquet and Swim Club, featuring twelve clay tennis courts, two hard courts, a swimming pool, and spa. Membership dues are required to use these facilities.

Godley Station

In the spring of 1999, construction began on the first homes in this planned unit, mixed-use development. It turned into an almost "instant community," with a growing population and adjacent "big box" retail all well established by 2001. This massive tract is near the Savannah International Airport and just off Interstate 95. As predicted, this has been the major new direction for suburban expansion in Chatham County. The neighborhoods here are heavily pitched to families and have a strong sense of traditional community. The residential section, which lies partly in Savannah and partly in the West Chatham municipality of Pooler, has protective covenants, sidewalks, and community amenities such as a pool and clubhouse.

Westbrook

This new gated community in western Chatham County began home construction in mid-2001. If all goes according to plan, it will ultimately include 625 home-sites averaging half an acre in size—each of them offering a view of the lake, golf course, or woods. Robert Cupp designed the golf course, and Troon Golf is managing it. Also on the agenda are golf, tennis, and clubhouse facilities, all on previously undeveloped land just reached by a utility infrastructure and a new off-ramp from Interstate 95.

This will be Savannah's newest country club community (although it actually isn't in Savannah but in the municipality of Pooler). As of this writing, no home stands there, but several lots have been presold. Lot prices are $67,900 to $225,000, and restrictive covenants govern what type of homes may be built.

Other Westside

New residential development is booming around the West Chatham municipalities of Pooler and Bloomingdale. These tend to be smaller subdivisions, not the massive planned developments like those outlined earlier—solid, middle-class homes for folks who are willing to drive a bit to get out of the city. Many of these include starter homes in the $70,000 range.

But don't get the idea that these municipalities began with these neighbor-

Development has begun
on The Ford Plantation,
a massive estate in
neighboring Bryan
County near Richmond
Hill that was once the
Southern retreat of auto
magnate Henry Ford.
The target market is
essentially those
seeking second or, more
likely, third homes.
Amenities include a
golf course, spa, and
trap shooting.

Although Savannah doesn't approach the metropolitan gridlock of larger cities during commuting hours, it still takes time to cover distance. We've heard radio ads cheerfully tout these out-of-county addresses as "twenty minutes from Savannah." Remember, Savannah is a big place, and perhaps whoever timed that trip was in a helicopter. Still, many families find the open spaces, near rural quiet, and a lightning bug population that hasn't succumbed to mosquito spraying to be well worth a daily drive.

It's hard to leave this topic without at least mentioning the Ford Plantation in Bryan County. This literally was the Fords' plantation, as in Henry Ford. The land is being developed into ultraluxury homes designed as second or third homes for the jet set. There's a club, spa, marina, shooting, and other outdoor sports—you name it. Prices are predictably stratospheric.

hoods. These fiercely independent little communities have been around for years, housing the blue-collar workforce for the industries of Chatham County (which are clustered toward the west) and the remnants of the county's agricultural population. If you are looking to buy acreage, this is about your only remaining option in Chatham County.

Outside the County

Savannah has developed its own commuter culture as well, with people driving into Savannah from bedroom communities in adjacent Richmond Hill (Bryan County) to the south, and Rincon, Guyton, and Springfield to the west in neighboring Effingham County. These bedroom communities have thrived, depending on your viewpoint, because of lower taxes, nonurban school systems, and "white flight." Here, you'll find typical suburbia, with its typical advantages and disadvantages. A word of caution: Don't trust anyone's estimate of commuting time. Drive it yourself during peak morning and afternoon traffic times.

Real Estate Companies

Regardless of the area or price range you are considering, there are hundreds of local Realtors ready to help you with your real estate needs. What follows is a rundown of some of the best in the area, but remember that this is a small sample. Companies are listed in alphabetical order.

You might also want to touch base with the Savannah Area Board of Realtors. They won't recommend one member over another, of course, but they can provide information about a member's credentials. Their number is (912) 354-1513.

Barroll and Barroll Realty Company
101 W. Liberty Street
Savannah, GA
(912) 235-5665

Since returning to Savannah from Philadelphia in 1981, Margery and Larry Barroll have formed a family real estate business that includes their two sons. Together, the husband and wife team have been in the real estate business since 1975.

Although the Barrolls live in Ardsley Park and, in fact, have purchased many homes there themselves, they don't limit their business to that area—but it is one of their areas of expertise. Their listings are throughout Savannah and include Tybee.

David Byck Realty Company
13 E. York Street
Savannah, GA
(912) 233–1276

Commercial and residential sales and property management are what this twenty-five-year-old company concentrates on. Although its commercial and residential departments often specialize in the Historic Downtown, its rental apartments and homes are located throughout the city, including the Southside. The company's commercial department is affiliated with a national network specializing in commercial and industrial leasing. They also work with a national relocation group with more than 900 agents throughout the country. According to owner David Byck, who has been selling real estate for forty years, the company's ten agents strive to meet all the needs of someone relocating to Savannah, whether the person requires rental property or wants to buy a home.

Celia Dunn Realty Company
9-13 W. Charlton Street
Savannah, GA
(912) 234–3323

Celia Dunn has been selling real estate in the Historic Downtown for twenty years. In fact, her offices take up the bottom floor of a beautifully restored three-story home overlooking Madison Square. Besides specializing in the historic area, she and her six licensed agents sell in several other areas of Savannah including Ardsley Park, Habersham Woods, Tybee, and Thunderbolt.

Konter Realty
5801 Abercorn Street
Savannah, GA
(912) 354–9314

Konter Realty is one of Savannah's largest real estate companies, with thirty to fifty agents selling throughout the city and surrounding counties. It is also one of the oldest. Husband and wife team Lawrence and Harriet Konter founded the company thirty-six years ago in a small, two-room office in the Historic Downtown. Today, the family-run company occupies a 9,300-square-foot office building on Savannah's Southside.

There are six individual divisions under the corporate umbrella of Konter Realty, including real estate, construction, and property management. The company also manages more than 500 residential units, along with 600,000 square feet of commercial/office space. Konter builds between fifty and sixty homes each year and is also involved in light commercial development including apartments, offices, and retail buildings.

The Landings Company
1 Landings Way
Savannah, GA
(912) 598–0500, (800) 841–7011

This real estate company is part of The Landings on Skidaway Island—Savannah's largest development and one of its most exclusive. Up to twenty agents are in the office, which, of course, specializes in selling homes, lots, and condos at The Landings.

Mopper-Stapen Realtors
31 West Congress Street
Savannah, GA
(912) 238–0874

Mopper-Stapen has been in downtown Savannah for fifteen years. During this time, the company has been involved with many properties requiring renovation—sometimes entire neighborhoods with dozens of vacant houses. Besides specializing in historic properties, the company also concentrates on commercial real estate and property management. There are six agents in the company, which is located in the Historic Downtown.

Judy Nease Realty
7505-F Waters Avenue
Savannah, GA
(912) 354–9966

Judy Nease's specialty is her own backyard: She has called Savannah's eastern islands home for the past thirty years. This is also where she sells the majority of her real estate. Nease has been in the business since 1978 and started her own company around the beginning of 1996. There are seven agents in the office, all of whom have been selling real estate for many years and have built up their own areas of expertise. The company also offers relocation services for people moving to the area.

The Prudential S. East
Coastal Properties
1 Diamond Causeway
Savannah, GA
(912) 355–4171

There are twenty-eight agents in this office, which is the only Prudential affiliate in Savannah. Reva and Bob Laramy started the company in 1982 and offer many services including relocation, property management, short- and long-term rentals, and commercial sales. The company sells real estate throughout the city from West Chatham to the Southside. However, one of their main areas of expertise is The Landings on Skidaway Island.

RE/MAX Professionals
6813 Johnny Mercer Boulevard
Savannah, GA
(912) 897–1955

RE/MAX Professionals has ten agents specializing in Wilmington, Tybee, and other islands. Owner Lynda Werntz has been in real estate since 1978. The office is one of three RE/MAX offices in Savannah, each with its own area of expertise and services.

Shore, Bell and Seyles Realty
401 Mall Boulevard, Suite 102B
Savannah, GA
(912) 356–1653

Relocation is the specialty of Shore, Bell and Seyles Realty. As part of their relocation efforts, owners Carey Shore, Nick Bell, and Charles Seyles, who each have twenty-five years of real estate experience, will send you a relocation packet, give you a tour of Savannah, and even pick you up at the airport if you need a lift. They handle individual and corporate moves involving several employees. The company's main areas of concentration are Dutch Island and Long Point, two high-end island developments with properties ranging in price from $200,000 to $750,000.

Cora Bett Thomas Realty
24 East Oglethorpe Avenue
Savannah, GA
(912) 233–6000

Drive around the Historic Downtown and more likely than not, you will see several

Insiders' Tip

Shopping for a home? Try the grocery store. A wide range of free real estate publications, complete with photos and often in color, is distributed in Chatham County. Grocery stores are popular distribution points. There are at least five competing publications. Also, check the real estate section of Sunday's *Morning News*. It includes, by zip code, listings of recent sale prices of properties. It's a good idea to check what stuff is really selling for, not just what is being asked for it.

Cora Bett Thomas Realty signs. This office specializes in prestige and historic properties, and the clientele includes discretely unconfirmed celebrities. In April 1999, this firm affiliated with the real estate arm of Sotheby's, the London-based auction house, for the marketing of unusual and high-end properties.

Apartments

Several apartment complexes complete with pools, recreation rooms, and clubhouses are available in Savannah. Most have been built within the last ten to fifteen years, if not more recently, and will be found on the Islands and Southside/Midtown. They are clustered in the Islands area because of the local reputation of the schools there, and on the Southside, in large part, because that is where off-base housing for Hunter Army Airfield tends to concentrate, close to base. The complexes are listed in several free publications offered in racks at area grocery stores.

The Historic Downtown also has a healthy market. Many residents have converted part of their private homes into apartments, and there are also a few apartment buildings to choose from. With the influx of students wanting to live downtown, finding an apartment in this area has become more of a challenge. Prices have been on the rise. Typically, you can find a one-bedroom apartment starting around $700 a month, and a two-bedroom will rent for around $800. However, depending on the apartment's size, quality, and amenities, monthly rents can go for more than $1,000 in some cases.

One of the best ways to find apartments in the Historic Downtown is to check local newspapers including the *Savannah Morning News* and the *Georgia Guardian* (see our Media chapter). However, many owners don't bother advertising and simply post a FOR RENT sign on their apartment—a walk or drive around town is a good way to get leads.

You will also find houses for rent in several areas of Savannah including Southside, Midtown, and the Islands. The homes vary from area to area and can include everything from older bungalows to new homes in gated developments. Like apartment rentals, many of the owners simply post a FOR RENT sign or advertise in a local newspaper. Some list their homes with local Realtors. Prices range anywhere from $500 (not many of those to be had) to $2,000 a month.

Education and Child Care

Education

Savannah and Chatham County offer a wide spectrum of educational opportunities. In addition to the forward-looking public school system, there are a variety of private high schools, a technical school, two state universities, and the largest art school in the United States. This chapter presents overviews of all these plus a broad look at what's available in the area of child care.

Public Schools

Savannah-Chatham County
Public Schools
208 Bull Street
Savannah, GA
(912) 651-7000

The public school system of Savannah-Chatham County is in the latter stages of an aggressive $221 million building program that began in the mid-1990s and is scheduled to be completed in the fall of 2003. By then thirteen new schools will have been added to the system. Garden City Elementary School in west Chatham County was completed in August 1996. Coastal Middle School opened on Whitemarsh Island in August 1997; it's the first middle school built in the county in forty years and one of six being constructed as part of the program. The adjacent Marshpoint Elementary School opened at the same time.

The new Savannah High School, built on the city's east side and opened in time for the 1998-99 school year, replaces its

namesake in Midtown on Washington Avenue. The old Savannah High, which was built in 1937, now houses the Savannah Arts Academy, a magnet school dedicated to the visual and performing arts. Two new middle schools, Southwest Middle near the Georgetown residential community in the Southside and West Chatham Middle in Pooler, also opened for business in August 1998. Three new schools were completed in August 1999: Southwest Area Elementary, West Area Elementary, and Tomkins Middle. Scheduled to be ready for classes between 2001 and August 2003 are a new Myers Middle School, a new DeRenne Middle School, and a new Ellis Elementary School, all being built on or near the sites of existing buildings that have outlived their usefulness. In January 2000, a new Johnson High School opened adjacent to the site of its predecessor.

In another development involving a new school, a charter public middle school—Oglethorpe Academy—opened in August 1999 in west Savannah on the site of a one-time elementary school. The academy's charter is based on providing students with a rigorous curriculum and an environment—that is, a student body—that's smaller than those of other schools. Another feature calls for parents or guardians of students being asked to sign contracts obligating them to accept responsibility for their children's behavior and compelling them to participate in the educational process.

The Savannah-Chatham school system serves 36,000-plus students in prekindergarten (four-year-olds) through

299

Children from Savannah's public schools celebrate the arrival of spring with the traditional Maypole dance. PHOTO: KYLE CASON

twelfth grade. They are enrolled at 48 schools and participate in several alternative programs. Students in the system attend 31 elementary schools, 10 middle schools, and 7 high schools.

Among the school system's alternative programs are the Savannah Corporate Academy, which promotes the academic and social development of at-risk students by means of a nontraditional program, and the Adult Education Center, which offers basic skills and secondary education for persons seeking to pass the General Educational Development Test or enhance their personal growth through education. The system also operates the Coastal Georgia Comprehensive Academy for students with severe emotional and/or behavioral disorders and autism.

The system has an extensive Magnet Academy program that enables students to concentrate on special talents and interests. Magnet programs are available at nine elementary schools, three middle schools, and three high schools. Academies for the arts are available at each level of instruction. Among the other magnets are Butler Elementary School's Core Knowledge and

Microcommunity Academy, which features Bearsville, USA, a program in which students hold jobs, earn wages, and practice citizenship in a free-market society they design; and Groves High School's School-to-Career Academy, at which students are introduced to the technical nature of today's world in an effort to prepare them for their future careers.

The average class size at schools in the system is twenty-five students. There is an emphasis on computer technology, and the system has more than 6,000 computers in its classrooms and access to the Internet at each school. The system has 160 partnerships with the business community through which business people voluntarily assist individual schools in areas such as mentoring, accomplishing building projects, cleaning up campuses, and raising funds.

Two unique features of the local system are the Massie Heritage Interpretation Center and the Oatland Island Education Center (see our Attractions chapter). Massie, which is at 207 E. Gordon Street, is the oldest standing school in Georgia. The school does not hold regular classes, but programs on the history of Georgia are offered. Teachers arrange for their classes to attend programs at Massie. Oatland, at 711 Sandtown Road, covers seventy-five acres, and its 1.75-mile Discovery Trail takes visitors through woodlands, past marshes, and to specially constructed habitats of endangered and protected animals of the state—wolves, bison, panthers, and birds of prey among them. There's a re-creation of a Colonial settlement and a barnyard where youngsters can get a feel for life on the farm, past and present. The Oatland staff holds several special events throughout the year, including a festival featuring sheepshearing in March and a crafts festival in November (see our Annual Events and Festivals chapter).

Private Schools

Savannah's private high schools provide teenagers and their parents with alternatives to what's offered by the public school system. Most of the private schools are Christian based, and all are focused on preparing their students for college.

These schools are predominantly co-ed, but there is a school for girls and one that admits only male students. There's at least one private high school in each section of the city, with the majority being centrally located in the Midtown area.

Benedictine Military School
6502 Seawright Drive
Savannah, GA
(912) 356–3500
www.bccadets.org
This Catholic high school for boys dates back to 1902, when it was founded on Bull and 33rd Streets as Benedictine College. Having sons become "BC boys" is a tradition in many Savannah families, a circumstance that has led this military school for ninth through twelfth graders to have an extremely faithful and active group of alumni. Sixty percent of those who attend the school are Catholic, but the remainder of the student body is as

Insiders' Tip

The Savannah-Chatham County public school system allows individual schools to adopt a policy enabling students to wear uniforms on a voluntary basis. Three-quarters of the faculty and three-quarters of the parents of students at a school must vote in favor of uniforms for the policy to be placed in effect. Students at these schools are not required to wear uniforms, but they have opted to do so in most cases. Private high schools where uniforms are worn are Benedictine, Calvary, St. Vincent's, and Savannah Christian.

diverse as the faculty, which is composed of Benedictine priests and monks, laymen and laywomen, and military retirees. Enrollment is about 450, and the ratio of students to faculty members is sixteen to one.

Benedictine is a college prep school, and 94 percent of graduates attend college. The school is housed in large, contemporary-style buildings on ninety acres in the Southside. It was moved there in the early 1960s; until that time, students received military training during all four years of school. Since then, however, Junior ROTC classes have been mandatory only for freshmen and sophomores and optional for juniors and seniors. Sixty-two percent

Benedictine Military School, a parochial high school for boys, stages a Pearl Harbor commemoration.
PHOTO: KYLE CASON

of upperclassmen continue to participate in JROTC, training that can give them an advantage should they elect to attend a military college or enter the armed forces out of high school.

The school's mission calls on its faculty to "value all individuals as children of God with emphasis on the Benedictine principles of prayer, work, and hospitality." The school offers opportunities for students to compete in a full range of sports, including one not normally encountered in this part of the universe: wrestling. There are also rifle and drill teams. Extracurricular activities at Benedictine start an hour after the end of school so that participants can avail themselves of the after-school tutoring program.

Bible Baptist School
4700 Skidaway Road
Savannah, GA
(912) 352–3067
www.bbsav.org

The administration and faculty of Bible Baptist seek to educate the whole child while emphasizing the spiritual side of students' development. Bible is taught in every class of this traditional Christian school, which has an enrollment of 370 students in four-year-old kindergarten through high school. The co-ed, college-prep school is a mission of Bible Baptist Church, and it's located on a nineteen-acre church-school complex that includes a football stadium and a gymnasium with two full basketball courts. Although the school is open to students of all faiths, the teaching of Christian values is stressed.

Spacious classrooms give teachers plenty of room for learning centers and computer corners, and the average class size is sixteen or seventeen students. Ninety percent of graduates attend college. Among school traditions are the ceremony at which juniors are presented their senior class rings by parents or friends and attend a social gathering afterward, and the Thanksgiving feasts held in each classroom on the Wednesday before the holiday, with parents, grandparents, and siblings invited to join in. Bible Baptist, which was founded in the mid-1960s in reaction to the ban on prayer in public schools and what was seen as a lack of discipline there, has a full program of varsity athletics supplemented by the church's recreational program, which provides opportunities to participate in sports to students ages fourteen and younger. The school is a member of the Georgia Christian Athletic Association and Georgia Association of Christian Schools.

Calvary Baptist Day School
4625 Waters Avenue
Savannah, GA
(912) 351–2299
www.calvarydayschool.com

This co-ed school in Savannah's Midtown is a ministry of Calvary Baptist Temple and is open to students of all faiths and creeds. The school and church occupy twenty-two acres at Waters Avenue and 63rd Street. The school started downtown with a kindergarten class in 1961 under the leadership of the Rev. John T. Tippitt Jr., and a grade was added each year. Calvary, which moved south to Midtown in 1964, now provides Christian-based education to some 850 students in prekindergarten through twelfth grade.

According to school officials, academics are blended with a strong program of athletics and other activities to help students evolve into well-rounded citizens. The student-teacher ratio is seventeen to one. The curriculum is designed to prepare students for college, and 98 percent of Calvary's graduates attend institutions of higher learning. Among the tools used in accomplishing the goal of readying students for life after high school are five computer labs, a high school medical profession program, a middle-school technology lab, and a Resource Center. The teachers of the Resource Center help students who might be struggling academically to build the skills they need to progress in their classes.

The school offers a full program of athletics and has its own football stadium and track, a complex named M. C. Ander-

son Field. In addition to providing day care for young children through the second grade and an after-school program for students in grades three through six, the school has an early-morning program that starts at 6:45 A.M.

Memorial Day School
6500 Habersham Street
Savannah, GA
(912) 352–4535
www.memday.org

Memorial, a nonsectarian, Christian co-ed school, was founded in 1971 by Memorial Baptist Church and had its first graduating class five years later. Although the school shares its Midtown location at the corner of Habersham Street and Stephenson Avenue with the church, the school is independent and has its own board of directors. Memorial is a college prep school for students in prekindergarten (age 4) through high school and also provides care for children as young as six weeks.

Memorial aspires to prepare students for college and adult life by tending to their spiritual, social, emotional, and physical growth. There are about 275 students in prekindergarten through twelfth grade, and average class sizes are 15 students in the lower school, 20 in the middle school and 18 to 22 in high school. About 90 percent of graduates continue their education by attending college. As a member of the Georgia Independent Schools Association, Memorial provides its students with a full range of athletic and extracurricular activities. There are before- and after-school programs for children up through the sixth grade.

Providence Christian School
11111 Rio Road
Savannah, GA
(912) 927–0185
www.pcslions.org

This small but growing reformed Christian school in the Southside prides itself on offering its 180 students a familylike atmosphere. All subjects are taught from a Christian perspective as the staff seeks to "support home and church in developing children academically and spiritually so they will be able to accept the responsibilities of life as strong, Godly leaders."

The co-ed school, a mission of Providence Presbyterian Church, was started as a prekindergarten class in 1987. A grade or two was added in each of the ensuing years, and Providence Christian held its first high school graduation in 1999.

Maximum class sizes are eighteen in the lower school and twenty-one in the middle and upper schools. The curriculum is aimed at preparing students for college, but a limited joint enrollment program with Savannah Technical College offers an alternative. The school also has a one-on-one therapeutic program for children with diagnosed learning disabilities.

Providence Christian, situated on tree-filled acreage at the intersection of Rio Road and Shawnee Street just north of Savannah Mall, competes in middle school and high school sports by fielding teams in soccer, track and field, boys' and girls' basketball, girls' volleyball, and girls' softball.

St. Andrew's School
601 Penn Waller Road
Savannah, GA
(912) 897–4941
www.saintschool.com

The upper school at St. Andrew's is the only high school on the eastside islands. St. Andrew's includes classes for prekindergarten and up. About 400 students are enrolled at the co-ed, college prep school, which is on twenty-five tree-filled acres on Wilmington Island.

According to Headmaster E. C. Hubbard, St. Andrew's seeks to "inspire passion for learning," prepare students to be leaders in the community, and develop their personal integrity. The student-teacher ratio is nine to one, and all graduates attend college. A series of scholarship seminars, an on-line counseling office, and school-arranged tours of various colleges assist students in making their post-

secondary decisions. Limited need-based financial aid is available for qualifying families. St. Andrew's offers a broad range of extracurricular activities, including participation in nine varsity sports, with St. Andrew's competing in the South Carolina Independent School Association because of its proximity to similar-size schools in the Palmetto State. The school's fine arts programs are extensive.

St. Andrew's has its roots in a day school that was begun downtown in 1947 by Independent Presbyterian Church. During the 1970s, the church formulated plans for a larger institution, and the result was St. Andrew's, which was founded on Wilmington Island in late 1978. Although the school is no longer affiliated with Independent Presbyterian, St. Andrew's retains aspects of its Scottish heritage, including a field day in the fall when the school holds its own Scottish games.

St. Vincent's Academy
207 E. Liberty Street
Savannah, GA
(912) 236–5508

St. Vincent's—a Catholic, college preparatory school for girls—has been owned by the Sisters of Mercy since 1845 and is the only private high school in the Historic District. The three main buildings of the school cover a city block on the south side of Liberty Street between Abercorn and Lincoln Streets, and St. Vincent's also includes the Walsh Hall gymnasium on Harris Street and the Peg F. Dressel Library at Liberty and Lincoln. Although the Sisters of Mercy still operate the school, the majority of the faculty consists of professional lay teachers.

St. Vincent's teaches grades nine through twelve. About two-thirds of the school's 400 students are Catholic, but St. Vincent's is open to all young women regardless of creed, race, or socioeconomic status. Classes average about twenty students, with 95 to 100 percent of graduates attending college. The school administration believes the downtown location is an asset because it enables students to experience an urban environment and brings them into direct contact with Savannah's history and culture. St. Vincent's places an emphasis on Christian values and "the acceptance of individuals as God's gift to the world," says the principal, Sister Helen Marie Buttimer. This philosophy has led to a long tradition of graduates sending their daughters and granddaughters to their alma mater, up to the fourth and fifth generations. At the same time, St. Vincent's cherishes the diversity of its student body and makes its services available to all of Savannah's young women.

St. Vincent's offers an extensive program in visual arts, and the school's chorus is known throughout Savannah. St. Vincent's competes in eight varsity sports: volleyball, softball, basketball, tennis, track, soccer, riflery, and swimming.

Savannah Christian Preparatory School
1599 Chatham Parkway
(912) 233–9607

Savannah Christian offers a college preparatory curriculum in a nondenominational, Christian atmosphere at two campuses. The heavily wooded, 300-acre campus on Chatham Parkway in West Chatham is the site of the upper school (grades nine through twelve), a lower school (prekindergarten through fifth grade), and a preschool and day-care center (for children six weeks to three years old). New facilities on this campus include the Week Science and Media Center and the Atkins Learning Center. A twenty-five-acre campus at 2415 DeRenne Avenue accommodates a smaller lower school and a middle school (grades six through eight). Each campus has dining facilities, a gymnasium, and computer labs. The Chatham Parkway campus is also the site of EDEN (Ecological Diversity for Educational Networking), a 125-acre outdoor education center that provides a wetlands laboratory for science students.

The emphasis at Savannah Christian is on preparing students for college and for life. A vigorous academic curriculum produces above-average SAT scores and a college placement rate of 100 percent. The ratio of students to teachers ranges from 20 to 25 to 1. A wide variety of extracurricular activities and athletics is available. The co-ed school has its roots in the Evangelical Bible School, which was started in 1951 on the West Chatham site by the Rev. George Akins, a Presbyterian minister who founded Savannah's Union Mission. In its early days, the school served the children of the city's homeless; it became Savannah Christian School in the 1960s, when ties with Union Mission were severed, and assumed its current name in the late '70s. The DeRenne campus, former site of Hancock Day School, was acquired in the 1980s. Savannah Christian's enrollment for the 2000–2001 school year was 1,500.

Insiders' Tip

Several of Savannah's private schools compete athletically as members of the Georgia High School Association, which means they play against public schools as well as other private institutions. Calvary and Country Day participate in Class A, the division for the association's small schools. Savannah Christian competes in class AAA, while Benedictine and St. Vincent's are in Class AAAA, along with the largest schools in the state.

Savannah Country Day School
824 Stillwood Drive
Savannah, GA
(912) 925–8800
www.savcds.org

Country Day strives to fulfill its motto—"Searching for the excellence in each of us"—through a college prep program that emphasizes top-flight performance in academics, the arts, and athletics.

The student-teacher ratio is ten to one, with class sizes averaging 21 students in the lower school, 16 in the middle school, and 15 in the upper school. The average SAT scores of students at Country Day are among the highest in Georgia, and the eighty-seven graduates of the Class of 2000 were accepted to one hundred different colleges. The co-ed school offers fifteen Advanced Placement courses.

Country Day has 980 students. A broad range of athletics and extracurricular activities is offered, with the middle and upper schools fielding more than forty sports teams. The school has two libraries with more than 25,000 volumes and eighty-five on-line services, four computer labs with 300 networked computers, four music and art studios, a fine arts center, three gymnasiums, and a football stadium.

The Country Day campus is on sixty-five wooded acres tucked away in the Windsor Forest subdivision on the Southside. The school moved there in 1957 from a building on Forsyth Park that had been the home of the Pape School for Girls from 1905 until 1955, the year Country Day was chartered.

Technical Schools

Savannah Technical College
5717 White Bluff Road
Savannah, GA
(912) 351–6362
www.savannah.tec.ga.us

Savannah Tech seeks to provide the local business and industrial community with highly trained workers—a service it has rendered since its founding by the Savannah Chamber of Commerce as the Opportunity School in 1929. Back then, the school turned out mainly stenographers and clerks; these days, the emphasis is on providing students with the opportunity to acquire quality technical education and training that will allow them to be productive members of a global workforce.

From the mid-1940s until the summer of 1997, the school was governed mainly by the Savannah-Chatham County Board of Education. Savannah Tech is now governed solely by the Georgia Department of Technical and Adult Education and is part of a statewide network of thirty-three postsecondary schools. The school offers credit, noncredit, and specialized industry services and training. Credit offerings include technical certificates of credit, diploma programs, and two associate of applied technology degrees. The school has more than forty different credit programs, ranging from one-quarter programs in areas such as aircraft structural assembly and commercial truck driving; to four- to five-quarter programs involving fields such as practical nursing, accounting, industrial/mechanical control technology, and welding; to two-year associate degree programs in marketing and management, automotive technology, and electronics/computer engineering technology. Some 3,000 students in credit programs attend Savannah Tech.

The school serves four counties—Chatham, Bryan, Effingham, and Liberty—from its main campus on the Southside and a satellite center in Liberty County at Hinesville and in Pooler at the West Chatham Technology Center. Savannah Tech began offering classes in Effingham County in fall quarter 1999. The main campus consists of four separate buildings on thirty-seven well-manicured acres that were once part of Hunter Army Airfield. There are sixty full-time and sixty part-time instructors, and the average class size is eighteen students.

Colleges and Universities

Armstrong Atlantic State University
11935 Abercorn Street
Savannah, GA
(912) 927–5277, (800) 633–2349
www.armstrong.edu

Armstrong Atlantic provides seventy-five fields of study through its College of Arts and Sciences, College of Education, College of Health Professions, and School of Graduate Studies. The university's teacher education program has gained state and national recognition, and its economics, computer science, and chemistry programs are also particularly strong. The College of Health Professions is the regional health professions education center for southeast Georgia. Among master's degrees are those offered in history, criminal justice, nursing, education, public health, services administration, sports medicine, and physical therapy. Armstrong has an abundance of evening and weekend classes.

A total of 5,500 students, including almost 500 graduate students, attend the school. They are taught by 250 professors, among them Dr. Richard Cebula, who holds the Shirley and Philip Solomons Eminent Scholar Chair in Economics. The great majority of students are commuters, and most hold full-time or part-time jobs. Armstrong has a somewhat mature student body: The average age is 27. The school is situated in the Southside on 250 acres dotted with pine trees and azalea bushes, and the campus has been graced with the addition of University Hall, an 85,000-square-foot classroom and office building that opened in fall 1997. A 128,000-square-foot, $20 million science building is expected to open during the spring semester of 2002, and work continues on the renovation of other campus facilities. A new 300-bed dormitory will add to the ever-expanding campus.

Armstrong moved to the Southside in 1966 from Bull and Gaston Streets in the Historic Downtown, where it was founded in 1935 as Armstrong Junior College,

A double-decker bus helps SCAD students get around campus. PHOTO: COURTESY OF SAVANNAH COLLEGE OF ART AND DESIGN

which was then a city-supported school. It became a part of the University System of Georgia in 1959, gained college status in 1964, and achieved university status in 1996, when its name was changed from Armstrong State College to Armstrong Atlantic State University. The school fields NCAA Division II teams in men's basketball, baseball, tennis, and golf and in women's basketball, fast-pitch softball, volleyball, and tennis (the 1995 and '96 teams were national champions). Armstrong hosts more than 200 cultural events each year, including a faculty lecture series, concerts, and dramatic presentations, all of them open to the public and most of them free. The university is also the site of a criminal justice training center providing instruction to law enforcement officers from nineteen surrounding Georgia counties.

Savannah College of Art and Design
342 Bull Street
Savannah, GA
(912) 525–5100, (800) 869–7223
www.scad.edu

The Savannah College of Art and Design has grown tremendously since its founding in 1979 by Richard and Paula Rowan, who came from Atlanta and started the private, co-ed school with one building and seventy-one students. Today, SCAD is the largest art school in the country with its enrollment of almost 5,000 students. The college has forty buildings spread throughout the Historic and Victorian Districts, many of them of historic significance and beautifully renovated by the school. The college's restoration efforts have been so striking that the National Trust for Historic Preservation awarded SCAD the National Honor Award for Historic Preservation in 1994.

The college offers bachelor's degrees in fine arts and architecture and master's degrees in arts, fine arts, and architecture through its Schools of Building Arts, Fine Arts, Design, and Media Arts. Among its eighteen fields of study are historic preservation, interior design, painting, photog-

Insiders' Tip

There's hope for Georgia residents entering their freshmen years at the state's colleges and universities. The Hope Scholarship pays tuition, some fees, and up to $150 per semester for books to students who have earned a B average in high school. B students attending eligible private colleges in Georgia can receive Hope in the amount of $3,000 per academic year for tuition. Students can renew these scholarships in their sophomore, junior, and senior years by maintaining 3.0 grade point averages in college. Hope is funded by the Georgia Lottery for Education. For more information on the Hope program, call (800) 546-HOPE.

raphy, furniture design, and product design. Programs involving computer art and graphic design attract scads of students, if you'll pardon the expression. The student-teacher ratio is eighteen to one.

The median age of students is twenty, and they come from throughout the United States and from eighty-three foreign countries; only about 12 percent of the student body hails from Georgia. Thirty percent live in the school's six resi-

An old National Guard armory provides the setting for a gallery and other facilities of the Savannah College of Art and Design. PHOTO: BETTY DARBY

dence halls, several of which are former hotels, inns, or apartment buildings. SCAD has more than forty student organizations and an intercollegiate athletic program fielding teams in basketball, golf, tennis, volleyball, crew, baseball, softball, and soccer. The school competes in NCAA Division III.

Savannah State University
B. J. James Drive
Thunderbolt, GA
(912) 356–2186
www.savstate.edu

Savannah State University has three colleges—Sciences and Technology, Business Administration, and Liberal Arts and Social Sciences—offering a total of twenty-four undergraduate degrees and three master's degree programs (social work, urban studies, and public administration). The campus, located adjacent to the town of Thunderbolt, covers 165 acres, many of them shaded by large oak trees festooned with Spanish moss. The eastern portion of the campus is bordered by salt marsh and

the Wilmington River; that and the school's proximity to the Atlantic Ocean (about 8 air miles) led to its sobriquet of "College by the Sea," which it was called for many years before its upgrade to university status by the Georgia Board of Regents in 1996. Now it's known, not surprisingly, as the "University by the Sea." The school's location also lends a uniqueness to the university's marine sciences program; the program is the only one of its kind in the state situated in a natural setting. Among features of the program is the *Sea Otter,* a 35-foot cabin cruiser that's used for exposing students to marine science research.

The school was founded in 1890 as Georgia State Industrial College for Colored Youth and retained that name until 1950, when the regents dubbed it Savannah State College. It is the oldest public, historically black college in Georgia, and Savannah State has a student body that is 90 percent African American, but university officials say the student population and faculty become more diverse each year. There are approximately 2,200 students

University Village, a $22 million residency complex that opened in January 2001, has brought apartment-style living to students at Savannah State University. PHOTO: DANIEL J. GRANTHAM JR./ GRAPHIC COMMUNICATION

and 145 instructors, about 70 percent of whom hold doctorates.

Savannah State has a full-scale athletic program and competes intercollegiately in football, baseball, men's and women's track and field, men's and women's basketball, and women's tennis, volleyball, and cross-country. The school achieved Division I status in 2001. There are seventy-five student organizations, including honor societies for high-ranking students in every major field of study, a theater group, concert choir, gospel choir, and marching band. Savannah State's Naval ROTC program sends more graduates to naval postgraduate school than all other small colleges in the country, according to university officials. The school also has its own FM radio station, WHCJ (90.3 FM), which broadcasts sixteen hours a day.

South College
709 Mall Boulevard
Savannah, GA
(912) 691–6000
www.southcollege.edu

This small, four-year commuter college provides a variety of courses of study in its School of Business Administration and School of Health Professions. Within the School of Business Administration, the college offers a bachelor of business administration degree with five areas of concentration: legal studies, finance, hospitality management, management information systems, and organizational communications. Associate of science degrees are available in accounting, business administration, computer information systems, and paralegal studies. The School of Health Professions offers a bachelor of science degree in the physician assistant program and associate of science degrees in medical assisting and physical therapist assistant.

The school is attended by about 520 students, 75 percent of whom are women. The average age of students is twenty-eight, but the student population has been getting younger since the college attained four-year status in 1996. The average class size is twelve.

Students in Savannah State University's marine biology program inspect a fish during a laboratory session. PHOTO: COURTESY OF SAVANNAH STATE UNIVERSITY

The school dates to 1899, when it was founded as Draughon's Practical Business College. The college was situated in various downtown locations prior to 1980, when it was relocated to Mall Boulevard in the Southside. The school recently completed a $4.5 million expansion project that brought all classrooms, labs, an expanded library and technology center, and administrative offices together on the main campus. The campus covers almost nine acres and features a new forty-seven-foot-high clock and bell tower.

The college was purchased by the South family in 1975, renamed Draughons Junior College two years later, and became South College in 1986. There is no athletic program, but the college does have a student government organization and several field-specific clubs.

Child Care

The state of Georgia regulates the businesses of people who provide care for more than two children at a time. To comply with state law, a person who provides care for up to six children in his or her home—officially called a family day-care home—must obtain a certificate from the Child Care Licensing Section of the Georgia Department of Human Resources.

Persons operating businesses caring for more than six children must obtain licenses. Such businesses fall within two categories: group day-care homes, which provide supervision and care for seven to twelve children either in a home or another location, and day-care centers, which provide care and supervision for thirteen or more children. To be certified or licensed, the operator of a child-care business must be at least twenty-one years old, have a high school or general equivalency diploma, and pass criminal background and fingerprinting checks. They must have completed training in first aid and in infant and child cardiopulmonary resuscitation, and must annually undergo ten hours of continuing education in health and safety and child development.

When you're shopping for child care, make sure the provider you're dealing with is registered with or licensed by the state. Take a good look at the facility you're visiting: Ascertain that the inspection data on the fire extinguisher is current, that the smoke alarm and telephone operate properly, and that rooms are in good repair, well lit, and spacious. Check to see if instructions involving fire drills and other emergency procedures are posted. Ask about the program offered—it should provide age-appropriate toys and activities that encourage children to use their five senses.

As of January 1999, there were 534 family day-care homes and a total of 90 group day-care homes and day-care centers operating in Chatham County. They offer a wide variety of care—everything from the legal minimum to operations featuring state-funded and private prekindergarten programs, field trips, and other extracurricular activities, plus food programs that serve balanced meals.

Childcare Information Center
6349 Abercorn Street
Savannah, GA
(912) 355–0771, (800) 281–9343

A great way to start your quest for the child care that meets your needs is by calling the Childcare Information Center, a child-care resource and referral service of Lutheran Ministries of Georgia. This child placement agency is licensed by the Department of Human Resources and serves six counties in coastal Georgia including Chatham. Tell the parent counselor about your requirements involving child care; you will be given five or six referrals to check out at no cost to you.

Parent counseling is also available from Lutheran Ministries, which administers the A+ Parenting program. This program provides support for people striving to be good parents and is a collaborative effort involving Lutheran Ministries, the University of Georgia Cooperative Extension Service, Memorial Health University Medical Center's Community Health Education Program, the Housing Authority of Savannah, and the Georgia Council on Child Abuse. For more information on the program, call (912) 652–7981 or (912) 355–2083.

Babysitting Services

Vacationers in need of babysitting or drop-in child-care services should speak to the concierge or desk clerk at their hotel, motel, or inn. Most establishments have lists of child-care providers who offer short-term services. Among these are Angel's and Imp's Babysitting Agency (912–355–1068).

Healthcare

Savannah has experienced the good fortune of being a magnet for medical care almost since its founding in 1733. According to historians Preston Russell and Barbara Hines, the city's "first civic hero" was a physician, Dr. Samuel Nunes Ribeiro, who was among a boatload of Portuguese Jews who came to the town about five months after Savannah was settled. Georgia's founder, James Oglethorpe, credited Nunez, as he became known, with saving the colonists from the fevers that had killed several of them, including the only other doctor, William Cox.

The city was the site of Georgia's first hospital, a facility incorporated in 1808, and since the mid-1950s Savannah has been served by three large hospitals, two of which merged into a single healthcare system in the spring of 1997. The other hospital, Memorial Health University Medical Center, is the regional tertiary medical center, a circumstance that draws many medical specialists to the area.

The latest available statistics involving healthcare indicate that Chatham County is the home of 540 physicians, giving the area a ratio of one medical doctor for every 422 residents. Georgia's first public health agencies were established in Savannah more than one hundred years ago to combat yellow fever and improve the health of poor children. Since then, public health services have been expanded to offer preventive health services to all residents of the area and to provide primary care to those who do not have private physicians.

Hospitals

Memorial Health University Medical Center
4700 Waters Avenue
Savannah, GA
(912) 350-8000
www.memorialcare.com

This 530-bed hospital in Savannah's Midtown offers tertiary care to residents of thirty-five counties in southeast Georgia and southern South Carolina. In this role, Memorial provides the region with several one-of-a-kind facilities and services including the area's only pediatric intensive care unit (part of The Backus Children's Hospital), the only perinatal testing center, the only emergency helicopter service (LifeStarOne), the only ambulance specially equipped for sick newborns (Angel 3), and the only Level I trauma center, meaning the medical center offers extensive, immediate, round-the-clock services for emergency, life-threatening needs.

Memorial's Women & Infants Center is one of only six perinatal centers in Georgia, and the Neonatal Intensive Care Nursery is among only five in the state. The hospital's Center for Cancer Care is southeast Georgia's referral source for cancer treatment, and its Heart Institute is the regional coordinator of comprehensive cardiovascular services. Memorial's fifty-acre campus is also the site of the Georgia Eye Institute, the Georgia Ear Institute, the Georgia Neurological Institute, and the Rehabilitation Center, which provides a comprehensive regimen of services for people recovering from illnesses and injuries.

Memorial opened in 1955 as a 300-bed general hospital. As a regional referral center, it now ranks in size among the top 5

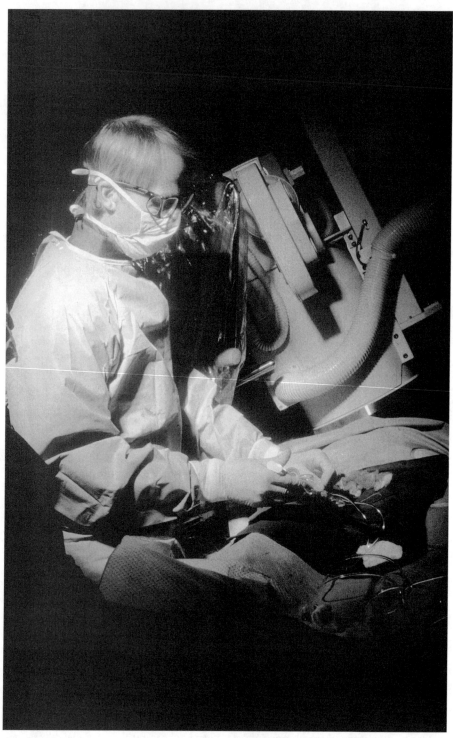

A cardiologist performs a catherization procedure at St. Joseph's Hospital, one of three major medical facilities in Savannah. PHOTO: COURTESY OF ST. JOSEPH'S/CANDLER

percent of hospitals in the United States and employs approximately 4,000 people, with about 1,000 of those working for CareOne, Memorial's home care organization. CareOne brings home care to patients in thirty-seven counties throughout southeastern Georgia and southern South Carolina, with its nurses providing services ranging from giving simple medications to highly technical care. Memorial is also a teaching hospital, and its name was changed in 1999 from Memorial Medical Center to reflect a beefed-up connection with Mercer University School of Medicine in Macon, Georgia. Under an agreement with Mercer, with which Memorial has been affiliated since 1985, the school will supply the hospital with more third- and fourth-year medical students, appoint faculty members in Savannah, and oversee the hospital's residency program, which had been operated independently by Memorial. Another feature of the medical center is its physician network of thirty-six practices for family doctors, internists, and other specialists.

St. Joseph's/Candler Health System

This healthcare system was created in April 1997 as the result of the merger of Savannah's two oldest hospitals, 305-bed St. Joseph's on the Southside and 335-bed Candler in Midtown. The system has four Centers of Excellence—The Birthplace at Telfair, the Center of Orthopaedic Excellence, the Neurosensory Center, and the HeartCare Center—and also offers services involving gastroenterology, women's health, sports medicine, geriatrics, wellness, cancer care, diabetes treatment and management, and outpatient surgery.

In 1998, St. Joseph's/Candler opened The Children's Place on the campus of Candler Hospital. This pediatric acute-care program serves the special needs of sick children and their concerned parents. The Children's Place utilizes a "kid-friendly" decorative theme in which each unit is adorned in primary colors from

floor to ceiling. Also in 1998, the health system introduced its Care Call Center, which enables you to obtain a physician referral and information about treating minor health problems by dialing (912) 921-3360.

Beyond these hospital services, the system maintains a presence in almost every community in southeast Georgia via its network of primary-care physicians.

St. Joseph's Hospital
11705 Mercy Boulevard
Savannah, GA
(912) 925–4100
www.stjosephs-candler.org

This general acute-care hospital dates to 1875 when the Sisters of Mercy of the Roman Catholic Church took over operation of the Forest City Marine Hospital, a facility in downtown Savannah that specialized in the treatment of sick seamen. A year later, the operation was moved to more spacious facilities at Taylor and Habersham Streets and was renamed St. Joseph's Infirmary. It was named St. Joseph's Hospital in 1901 and expanded several times before a new facility was built on the Southside in 1970.

Memorial Health University Medical Center is Chatham County's largest hospital. PHOTO: KYLE CASON

In the years between the move south and the merger with Candler, St. Joseph's accomplished a $7 million expansion of its Emergency and Outpatient Building and opened its Sports Medicine Center, Multiple Sclerosis Clinic, and Diabetes Management Center. The hospital is situated on twenty-eight acres and is affiliated with the Mayo Clinic Jacksonville and Neumors Children's Hospital in north Florida.

Candler Hospital
5353 Reynolds Street
Savannah, GA
(912) 692–6000
www.stjosephs-candler.org

One of the longest continually operating hospitals in the United States and the first in Georgia, Candler was founded in 1805 and chartered in 1808 as the Savannah Poor House and Hospital. A new facility of the same name was built on

Gaston Street in 1819, used as a Confederate hospital during the Civil War, and renamed Savannah Hospital in 1872. The first school of nursing in Savannah was established there in 1902, and twenty-eight years later the Methodist Episcopal Church purchased the hospital from the city and renamed it Warren A. Candler Hospital in honor of one of its bishops.

During the 1960s, the hospital was renamed Candler General Hospital and expanded through the purchase of the Telfair Hospital (which became its obstetrical unit) and the Central of Georgia Railway Hospital. Construction of a new hospital at DeRenne Avenue and Reynolds Street began in fall 1978, and it was opened in late 1980. Its name was changed to Candler Hospital in 1992, with the word *General* being dropped to reflect the hospital's growth in specialized healthcare services. Candler is affiliated with the Emory University System of Health Care.

Physician Referral Services

Savannah has two services you can contact for help in finding doctors and obtaining free information about hospital services and your health. They are the Care Call Center at (912) 921-3360 and NurseOne at (912) 350-9355.

Walk-In Clinics

If you find yourself in need of medical care during your visit to Savannah, there are clinics where you can obtain treatment without having an appointment. These facilities are in addition to the emergency rooms at the three local hospitals.

Immediate Med
2014 E. Victory Road
Savannah, GA
(912) 234-8466
10410 Abercorn Street
Savannah, GA
(912) 927-6832

Immediate Med handles minor emergencies and comprehensive family medical care at its two offices: one in Midtown on Victory Drive and the other in the Southside on Abercorn Street. These clinics are open from 9 A.M. to 9 P.M. seven days a week. Major credit cards are honored, but Medicare and Medicaid are not accepted.

Hospice Care

Several organizations in Savannah offer specialized care for the terminally ill and

---

Emergency Services

If you have an emergency or need general information about community resources, here are agencies you can contact. For emergencies requiring ambulance, police, or fire departments, call 911.

ALANON	(912) 354-0993
Alcoholics Anonymous	(912) 354-0993
First Call for Help	(912) 651-7730
Crime Stoppers	(912) 234-2020
Georgia Medical Society	(912) 355-6607
Helpline Georgia (crisis line)	(800) 338-6745
Narcotics Anonymous	(800) 334-3322
Poison Control Center	(800) 282-5846
Rape Crisis Center	(912) 233-7273
Safe Shelter	(912) 234-9999
Savannah Runaway Home	(912) 234-4048

assistance to members of their families, such as respite care and bereavement counseling. One of them, Hospice Savannah, which introduced this type of care to the area in 1980, provides living quarters for patients who cannot be cared for at home. The three local options for hospice care provide essentially the same services. They are Hospice Savannah Inc., 1352 Eisenhower Drive (912-355-2289), Spanish Oaks Hospice, 8510 Whitefield Avenue (912-356-3300), and VistaCare Hospice, 105 Wheeler Court (912-691-1476).

Complementary Medicine

Although it's nowhere near a hotbed of complementary medicine, Savannah shows signs of beginning to catch on to this style of healing. As far back as two decades ago, at least one physician in town was practicing nutritional medicine, but an awareness of and growth in complementary medicine took shape about five years ago. Now, there are a handful of full-fledged acupuncturists available and several medical doctors learning acupuncture techniques. You can avail yourself of the services of a slew of chiropractors, and there are also practitioners of herbal medicine, massage therapy, aromatherapy, Rolfing, and shiatsu (Japanese pressure point massage).

If you're looking for practitioners of complementary medicine, a good place to start is the Brighter Day natural foods and organic produce store at Bull and Park Streets. Owners Peter and Janie Brodhead don't make recommendations pertaining to practitioners, but they do maintain a "community bulletin board" that might steer you in the right direction.

Media

Newspapers

Magazines

Television

Radio

National Publications

Need to know something? Well, you're in luck. Savannah is well equipped in the media department. We've got a TV affiliate for each of the major networks, cable access everywhere except a few remaining spots in the boondocks, radio stations in formats from country to classical (although nothing really experimental), a daily newspaper, and several weeklies, monthlies, and specialty publications, even a city magazine.

To go along with this, Savannah has a solid journalism tradition. In the early 1980s, a now-defunct weekly even won the Pulitzer Prize in editorial writing. In the days when such things were economically possible, there were competing daily newspapers in Savannah, and desktop publishing and niche markets periodically keep some variety moving in the print world.

As for TV, when you add all the morning, midday, evening, and night local newscasts up, they total an impressive nine and a half hours each weekday. Savannah has joined national media trends with absentee corporate ownership. The last locally owned television station was sold in 1998, meaning that all the major daily print and television media outlets now are owned by companies headquartered elsewhere. Radio has joined the trend. With a handful of exceptions—one independent holdout, a college station, a public radio affiliate—three corporations own all local FM radio stations.

Newspapers

Dailies

In addition to the *Savannah Morning News*, you can also get daily delivery of the *Wall Street Journal* and the *New York Times* (depending on which neighborhood you live in). Ironically, however, you can't get home delivery of the *Atlanta Constitution*, the major paper from the state capital, in most neighborhoods, but you can buy it at convenience stores, newsstands, and vending boxes. (Check our Shopping chapter for info on where to get really out-of-town newspapers.)

Savannah Morning News
111 W. Bay Street
Savannah, GA
(912) 236–9511

Savannah's daily newspaper is the *Savannah Morning News*. It's part of Morris Communications, which owns several other Georgia papers (in Athens and Augusta, where the company is headquartered) as well as Jacksonville's *Florida Times-Union* and a host of other newspapers and publications.

Don't be confused if you hear the paper called the *News-Press*. Until 1996, the same company put out the *Savannah Evening Press*, and the combined weekend editions were known as the *News-Press*. The *Press* may be several years dead, but habit dies hard in Savannah and we still use the name from time to time.

The paper is a mix of conservative editorial stances and increasingly liberal news coverage. Recent years have seen an emphasis on modern design and less focus on breaking hard news. Regular readers know where to find the regular features— an automotive section on Saturdays, food coverage on Wednesdays, a pull-out entertainment tabloid called *Diversions* on Fridays, and lots of special sections on Sundays. The newest Sunday offering is *The Exchange,* a business section launched in 1998. Cost is 50 cents for single copies daily ($1.25 Sundays) and $11.50 monthly for home delivery.

The editorial pages feature a mix of local and nationally syndicated columns by the likes of Molly Ivins and David Broder. The real star of these pages, though, is editorial cartoonist Mark Streeter, who takes on local, national, and international topics with razor-sharp points, humor, and humanity.

In the news columns, a popular feature is "Vox Populi," consisting of a selection of anonymous phoned-in comments that are alternately rants and raves, reasoned commentary, whimsical observations, or frightening evidence of social disintegration.

Diversions, a tabloid that runs every Friday, includes listings on everything from what movies are playing in local theaters to concerts, gallery exhibits, and more. A favorable review of a restaurant in *Diversions* will pack the place for a while. *Diversions* is also available at selected eating-and-drinking establishments and some vending boxes around town.

The *Closeups* are a selection of weekly neighborhood newspapers published as sections in the regular paper (*The Islands Closeup, The Intown Closeup,* etc.) You can pick them up free from the vending boxes in front of the newspaper offices at 111 W. Bay Street.

Business Newspapers

The Savannah Business Report and Journal
P.O. Box 9591
Savannah, GA
(912) 231–1110

This business niche newspaper was launched in May 1998 and publishes every other Monday in tabloid format.

Subscriptions are $44 a year. Single copies are $1 and are available at the newspaper office, a scattering of vending boxes, and restaurants and newsstands in the business district.

The publication is regional, covering eleven coastal Georgia counties and Hilton Head Island and Beaufort in South Carolina. It is a mixture of staff and freelance written, and it includes listings of property transfers, business licenses, etc. Local nonprofits are covered as well as business news.

Ethnic Newspapers

Savannah has two weekly newspapers devoted to covering the African American community. These papers had their roots in the days of segregation, when mainstream papers did not cover the black community. As that has changed, these papers have evolved. Although they still have news content—often of social events, achievement, or coverage of the historically black Savannah State University—they also devote a large portion of their pages to political commentary and opinion columns. Of the two papers, the *Herald* is the dominant.

Savannah Herald
1803 Barnard Street
Savannah, GA
(912) 232–4505

Savannah Mayor Floyd Adams Jr. is the editor and publisher of this weekly newspaper, which was founded in 1945 by Adams's father. The *Herald's* motto is, "Publishing Positive News for and about Savannah's African-American Community." Inside you will find local news stories, church news, sports, and editorials.

In "Around Town," columnist Jettie Adams fills people in on a variety of subjects like who is having a birthday and the accomplishments of local children. The *Savannah Herald* is published on Wednesday, when 8,500 copies are distributed. Subscriptions are by mail, and the paper sells in vending boxes throughout town. Copies are also distributed at the larger African American churches.

The Savannah Tribune
916 Montgomery Street
Savannah, GA
(912) 233–6128

The *Tribune,* as it is known, is Savannah's other weekly newspaper devoted to the black community. Publisher and Editor Shirley B. James includes local, state, and sometimes national items pertaining to African Americans. The *Tribune* is published on Wednesdays. Subscriptions are predominantly by mail.

Other Newspapers

Coastal Antiques and Art
111 W. Bay Street
(912) 236–9511

This monthly tabloid, distributed free throughout town, was purchased by the *Savannah Morning News's* parent company in 1999. The ads are more useful than the editorial content if you are antiquing in Savannah.

Coastal Family
7 Drayton Street
Suite 310
Savannah, GA
(912) 232–0312

In 1998, the same folks who put out the *Business Report* acquired this monthly devoted to family-friendly content like parenting advice, coverage of schools, lessons and programs for children, and the like. It has evolved from essentially a press release bulletin board to a monthly niche publication that's distributed free at area restaurants, various schools, and stores that handle lots of kids' merchandise. It's also mailed to 5,000 target households.

Coastal Senior
111 W. Bay Street
(912) 236–9511

This monthly publication, distributed free at racks throughout town, subtitles itself "Lifestyles of the 50+." Like its sister publication, *Coastal Antiques and Arts,* it was acquired by the *Morning News's* parent company in 1999. Content is all geared toward older readers and includes advice columns from local physicians, schedules of senior-oriented events, and the like.

Insiders' Tip

Looking for work? The serious job ads are in Sunday's *Morning News*—the weekday stuff is pretty run-of-the-mill. You might also want to track down one of the city's two African American newspapers. Companies that are meeting corporate affirmative action commitments often make a special effort to advertise in those publications.

CONNECT Savannah/Creative Loafing
1800 E. Victory Drive
Savannah, GA
(912) 238–2040

Two weekly newspapers—one a generic and one devoted largely to the entertainment and cultural scene, along with alternative news—became one in late 2001 with Morris Newspapers' purchase of *Creative Loafing*. Morris combined the publication with the *CONNECT Savannah* it was already producing. At this point, it is too early to say what the hybrid publication will look like in the long run, but the first of the early editions looked like only slightly retooled versions of *Creative Loafing* (itself a lone offshoot of better-known former sister papers in Atlanta). At this point, it looks like the new publication will stick with free distribution in racks and go to mailed subscription options at $1.50 a week.

Magazines

Savannah Magazine
111 W. Bay Street
Savannah, GA
(912) 652–0291

Savannah Magazine is owned by Morris Communications, which also owns the city's daily paper, but it has its own staff. This slick, good-looking city magazine is published every two months and targets upper-middle-class and professional residents. The magazine was launched in the early 1990s, which means it has been around long enough to get all those tiresome stories about the ten most eligible bachelors out of its system. Content is all local and ranges from pithy pieces such as the best lawyers in town (can't you imagine what those who were left out had to say?) to soft decorating features. It also covers the city's charity festivals and other annual events—sort of like the old-time society pages with better production values—and carries a regular listing of city events of all types.

Television

Remember those nine and a half daily hours of television news programming we mentioned earlier? They can lead to some strange newscasts, since many days, well, there isn't that much happening. As a result, sometimes the evening news looks like a televised version of a weekly newspaper, complete with stories about unusually large vegetables and congratulations to couples celebrating their golden wedding anniversaries. But let's not sell local efforts short—they also have mobile vans for live broadcasts off-site, generally good production values, and a willingness to cut into regular programming when real news breaks.

Weather coverage is particularly strong here—and a good thing, too, since the local National Weather Service office fell victim to federal budget cuts a couple of years ago, and the nearest NWS location is now in Charleston. Stations give their meteorologists good equipment and ample air time. After all, outdoor lifestyles are the norm here, and we do live in a region of "active" weather. Want to see a news team drool with excitement? Just pick a station—any station—and tune in when the area is under a hurricane watch.

The newscast personalities are local celebrities, and they are generous with their time, visiting schools, taping public service announcements, and the like.

Notice that in the following listings the channel numbers are broadcast channels. If you are on a cable system—and most people here are—the channel numbers are different, but we've included the broadcast numbers so you'll know what people mean when they say "22 was at our wreck today" or "Was 11 there?". Two cable companies serve the Savannah area: Comcast, 5515 Abercorn Street (912-354-7531), and U.S. Cable Coastal Properties, 203 Second Avenue, Tybee Island (912-786-5277). There's also a separate private system to serve residents at The Landings, a gated community on Skidaway Island.

Morning News *columnist Tim Guidera interviews Davis Love III at the MCI press tent at the Hilton Head Island golf tournament.* PHOTO: COURTESY OF CAROLINA MORNING NEWS

WJCL–ABC (Channel 22)
WTGS–Fox (Channel 28)
10001 Abercorn Street
Savannah, GA
(912) 925–0022

These stations are jointly managed. Meanwhile, however, they share personalities, addresses, etc. In the past, the news coverage here has been usually weak. WJCL was the last of the locally owned stations, and it had its share of programming quirks. For example, it was one of the last national holdouts refusing to air the successful *NYPD Blue* because of its content, yet it has begun to run *The Jerry Springer Show* during after-school hours. Go figure.

WSAV–NBC (Channel 3)
1430 E. Victory Drive
Savannah, GA
(912) 651–0300

WSAV is the city's major runner-up in the news race and has spent quite a bit of time and money tinkering with its program. WSAV hired an up-and-coming anchor

away from their chief competitor—despite having to put him on ice for a year while waiting out his noncompete contract clause. The newscast tends to be younger, and the content played more dramatically. The early morning newscast is a particularly good example of folksy without being overly cutesy.

WTOC–CBS (Channel 11)
11 The News Place
Savannah, GA
(912) 234–1111

This station has been the news ratings leader so long it calls its 6 P.M. broadcast—both arrogantly and accurately—"THE News." While the demographics may be aging slightly, the station still holds a solid lead. Longtime anchor Doug Weathers retired in the spring of 2001 amidst a virtual orgy of congratulations to arguably the most recognizable face in town. Will his departure spell the end of the station's long-term and lucrative domination of the local news scene? Film at 11…

WVAN–PBS (Channel 9)
260 14th Street NW
Atlanta, GA
(800) 222–6006

While airing the more familiar offerings, such as *Sesame Street* and *NOVA*, this PBS station also runs some very interesting local programming (on Georgia history, B&Bs, and such) in cooperation with its Georgia affiliate, Peach State Public Television.

Radio

Radio isn't a serious player in the news game in Savannah. Where once the local media pack included radio reporters, they are all now either rip-'n'-reads out of the daily paper or making use of clearly promotional guest appearances from one of the television news teams.

But if you are looking for entertainment, not news, the radio dial here can meet your needs. The formatting is conventional. One exception would be Savannah State University, which offers the only local college radio station (90.3 FM) and provides an interesting mix of jazz, hip-hop, alternative, and more eclectic stuff if you get tired of the tried-and-tested radio out there. Note that it is a low-power station and can be hard to tune in, so be patient. Another exception is Jerry Rogers' WRHQ, the only remaining locally owned

Insiders' Tip
Jerry Rogers operates the only locally owned FM radio station in town, WRHQ, where he regularly works a shift as DJ on the classic rock format station.

station. Its playlist is sort of light rock/occasional oldies/a light touch of local groups/some new stuff—all perhaps best characterized by the format "stuff Jerry likes." By the way, radio stations tend to shift formats without notice after rocky ratings periods, so just hit the scan button on your radio if you suddenly find country music where you expected talk radio.

Adult Contemporary
WAEV 97.3 FM
WYKZ 98.7 FM
WHBZ 99.7 FM
WRHQ 105.3 FM
WJOY 108 FM

Big Band/Swing
WLOW 107.9 FM

College Radio
WHCJ 90.3 FM
(Savannah State College)

Country
WCHY 94.1 FM
WJCL 96.5 FM
WCHY 1290 AM

Gospel
WSOK 1230 AM

News/Sports/Talk
WBMQ 630 AM
WEAS 900 AM

Oldies
WGCO 98.3 FM

Public Radio
WSVH 91.1 FM

Rock
WIXV 95.5 FM
WZAT 102.1 FM

Urban Contemporary
WXLQ 92.1 FM
WEAS 93.1 FM
WLVH 101.1 FM
WSGF 103.9 FM

National Publications

These publications aren't Savannah oriented—they're just produced here. We thought you might be interested to know Savannah was in on the national publishing scene, so here goes.

Contents
14 E. Jones Street
(912) 447–0200

This nationally acclaimed and distributed magazine covers Southern art, literature, design, and music. Publisher and creative director Joseph Alfieris returned to his native Savannah in 1987 after spending time in New York and France. A National Endowment for the Arts fellow, Alfieris studied at the School of Visual Arts in New York City and designed book covers for Random House and other major publishers. He also created record sleeves for A&M Records before returning to launch *Contents*, which is produced in a town house in the city's Historic Downtown. In 1994, *Vanity Fair* magazine called *Contents* "one of the most striking new independent magazines in America." Recent contributors have included author Laren Stover and photographer Shelby Lee Adams.

Rodale's Scuba Diving
6600 Abercorn Street
Savannah, GA
(912) 351–0855

Savannah's other nationally distributed magazine is *Rodale's Scuba Diving*. Published ten times a year, it covers anything and everything about scuba diving. There are articles about such topics as diving health and fitness, adventure travel, and marine environment.

Insiders' Tip

The *Savannah Pennysaver* is a "shopper"—an ad-oriented publication with little or no editorial content. It gets tossed on just about every lawn in town Wednesday night and is especially valued for its garage sale ads and lists of miscellaneous merchandise for sale: exercise machines, collector's dolls, used appliances, whatever. We aren't making this up: We really did once spot an ad in there offering to sell a parrot or trade it for a boat motor.

Retirement

Senior Citizens Inc.

Other Senior Services

Golden Age and Other
Senior Centers

Savannah's moderate climate, recreational resources, and the other charms that make the city attractive to visitors are particularly important to retirees. Savannah is home to a large population of senior citizens—some with families that have been here for generations, others who have chosen this area specifically as their retirement getaway.

Recreational opportunities for the active retiree abound, from the opportunity to play golf virtually year-round on a variety of courses to sailing opportunities that are attractive, plentiful, and challenging enough to have landed the city Olympic venue status. Social opportunities are plentiful also, with a variety of organizations tailoring their offerings strictly to older members. Those who are eager to explore new educational horizons have the resources of area universities and their related programs.

Services for the changing needs of an elderly population are in place in Savannah, and they are growing in scope as the demand increases. If you have family members who are likely to need assistance with household chores or daily supervision because of Alzheimer's disease, programs are available to help both them and you. Expanded transportation, meal, and utility programs have been established to serve the elderly who need additional help.

Senior Citizens Inc.

Think of this nonprofit organization, located at 3025 Bull Street (912-236-0363) as a clearinghouse for senior services. It opens its membership rolls at $15 per year to anyone age 55 or older. (Note that dues were under consideration at the time this was written and may have gone up.) Social and educational opportunities, as well as discounts provided by various merchants, are the primary benefits available to the younger segment of members. The range of services (some on a fee basis, others free or on sliding scales) runs all the way to home-delivered meals and utility assistance—whatever it takes to keep even frail and very low-income seniors independent as long as possible.

Senior Citizens derives much of its funding from federal grants, foundation donations, and personal bequests. It is also a participating member in the United Way of the Coastal Empire.

The next several listings provide information on Senior Citizens' offerings for active members of the retirement community. We follow those up with Senior Citizens' options that address social service needs.

Club 55
3025 Bull Street
Savannah, GA
(912) 236–0363

This separate suite within the Senior Citizens complex is designed as a social and educational center for all Senior Citizens' members. It includes meeting facilities, rooms for scheduled bridge games and other recreation, exercise facilities that include treadmills and other machines, computers for classes and Internet access, and a gathering place for health screenings, courses, and seminars on topics of interest to seniors.

Merchants' Discounts

More than 170 participating merchants and service providers offer discounts to Senior Citizens' members (and many give price reductions to any senior citizen, member or not). Maintaining a current inventory of the very fluid list of participants and the terms of their discount offers has proven to be a pretty overwhelming challenge for the Senior Citizens' staff. Participating merchants are asked to display the Senior Citizens' logo where customers are likely to see it. If a freshly updated list isn't available when you join, and if you don't see a logo displayed by a merchant, the organization encourages you to show your membership card and ask if they participate in the program. After all, even if you don't have fixed-income problems, it's nice to pay less if you have the opportunity.

Ruth F. Byck Social Center
64 Jasper Street
Savannah, GA
(912) 234–6666

The Social Center's adult day-care program provides an option for families facing the hardships of caring for a loved one with Alzheimer's disease or similar chronic disorders. Residents receive social interaction, exercise, and meals while family members are freed to go to work or take a break from constant care. The center is located at the rear of the Senior Citizen's complex.

Other Senior Citizens Inc. Services

Other services available to senior citizens in need include Meals on Wheels, which delivers hot lunches on weekdays; a transportation program; a Senior Companion program that offers a stipend to low-income seniors for assisting frail elderly persons they are paired with; social work assessment and advocacy; and the loan of fans and medical equipment. Senior Citizens Inc. programs make heavy use of volunteer labor, and active retirees are well represented among that corps of volun-

Insiders' Tip
Savannah's movie theaters offer discount ticket prices to senior citizens.

teers. To inquire about services or volunteer opportunities, call (912) 236–0363.

Other Senior Services

Elderhostel
75 Federal Street
Boston, MA 02110
(617) 426–8056
Armstrong Atlantic State University
11935 Abercorn Street
Savannah, GA
(912) 921–5439
Congregation Mickve Israel
20 E. Gordon Street
Savannah, GA
(912) 233–1547
Savannah State University
P.O. Box 20523
Savannah, GA
(912) 356–2253

Elderhostel is a resource everyone 55 or older who travels should become familiar with. It offers noncredit educational opportunities on a wide range of topics (and we do mean wide, from phonics to history to literature). Tuition is moderate, and arrangements are made for you to stay near the class site, usually in area motels. The program is generally arranged to allot time for classes, socializing, and taking in the various sights around the host location.

Elderhostel is a particularly thriving program in Savannah, where Armstrong Atlantic State University, Savannah State University, and Temple Mickve Israel/Jewish Educational Alliance all have course offerings that take particular advantage of the Savannah area setting. Other nearby units of Georgia's university system, such as Coastal Georgia Community College in Brunswick and Georgia Southern University in Statesboro, also participate.

Costs are moderate when you consider prices include motels, meals and, in most cases, local transportation. The offerings we scanned ranged from $431 to $741, with more in the lower end of that range than the higher. Preregistration is absolutely essential. Local residents can get discounts because they won't need the meals and lodging. They can register through the local addresses, but we really recommend you get the catalog and handle registration through the Massachusetts office. If you call Savannah State, note that the director of that Elderhostel program has other duties, so don't assume you have the wrong number when another office answers.

Courses will vary from quarter to quarter.

Armstrong Atlantic's courses are based in two locations: at the university's Southside Savannah campus and on Tybee Island, Chatham County's beach municipality. Offerings are varied but recent ones included "Moon River Music Magic," focusing on the work of Savannah native son Johnny Mercer.

Savannah State University has equally diverse offerings. The university's marshfront setting comes into play in a course on marine life of the Southeast, and other recent courses include Savannah history, phonics, and Gullah culture, which examines the language and African culture retained by a community of Lowcountry slave descendants. Among Savannah State's most popular Elderhostel offerings are its various jazz courses, taught by members of Savannah's thriving community of jazz musicians and scholars, and Savannah history as taught by W. W. Law, a veteran of the Savannah civil rights struggle and specialist in Savannah's African American history.

The courses sponsored by Mickve Israel/Jewish Educational Alliance tend to focus heavily on Jewish culture and history. The Mickve Israel congregation itself, as the oldest Jewish congregation in the South, is the focus of one course. Not all courses are centered on local topics, however. For example, check out "The Jewish Heritage of the American Musical."

Elderhostel offers a continually changing cycle of courses available both to travelers coming into the area and local residents.

Retirement Services Office
Third Infantry Division (Mech.),
368 Hase Road
Ft. Stewart, GA
(912) 767-3326

We've found that military retirees are well versed on the benefits they carry into retirement. They probably don't need a reminder that they retain shopping privileges at post exchanges and commissaries, and that there are active posts in Savannah for all the various military organizations. But those moving into or passing through the area might be pleased to know the extent of services available in the region, thanks to the major military presence here.

Insiders' Tip

The Chatham-Effingham-Liberty Regional Library offers records and cassettes of print items to those with vision problems and can also arrange to deliver items to homebound patrons. Call (912) 652-3600 for more information.

Hunter Army Air Field in Savannah is a subinstallation of Fort Stewart, which is about 40 miles southeast of the city. Some 4,300 soldiers are assigned to Hunter, and 16,000 are based at 279,000-acre Fort Stewart, the largest military installation east of the Mississippi. With that many personnel, you've got recreation facilities, and retirees have access to the Morale, Welfare, and Recreation programs at these installations. Although it is unlikely that many retirees are interested in the concerts staged for young soldiers, they may well want to know about the golf courses, skeet shooting, movie theaters, and other activities and facilities at the two military reservations. Because it is far larger, many of these will be found at Fort Stewart in Hinesville, which is an accessible commute.

On the more serious side of things, Tuttle Army Health Clinic serves Hunter for primary and ambulatory care, and the larger, full-service Wynn Army Community Hospital is at Fort Stewart. The office listed at the head of this entry is largely concerned with such major tasks as straightening out retirement check problems or arranging veteran burials at sea, but personnel there can also provide information on other retiree services.

Hunter's main gate in Savannah is at White Bluff Road and Stephenson Avenue.

Hospital-Sponsored Clubs

Both of Savannah's two hospital systems offer special clubs to senior citizens, focusing not only on healthcare and wellness activities but also on education and social opportunities.

Care65
No. 8 Medical Arts Center
Savannah, GA
(912) 352–4405

This program of St. Joseph's/Candler Health System provides health seminars, educational programs, medical screenings, and visits to members hospitalized at either St. Joseph's Hospital or Candler Hospital. That may sound a bit stodgy, but it isn't— much of this group's activity is geared toward active retirees. There's a travel club that has gone from the Bahamas to Canada and points in between, ranging from two-week excursions to overnighters to catch an Atlanta Braves game. The holiday party is an enormous dine-and-dance bash. Activities scheduled throughout the year include tours of local industry, arts and crafts classes, and line dance lessons, for example. One of the unexpected annoyances that accompanies retirement is the loss of access to such office conveniences as a copier, and Care65 addresses that by providing free faxing, photocopying, notary services, and Internet access. In addition, the group provides member discounts at participating merchants. Annual dues are $12.

GenerationOne
P.O. Box 23089
Savannah, GA
(912) 350–7587

This club, sponsored by Memorial Health University Medical Center, offers health fairs and screenings, a member discount program, and visits to members hospitalized at Memorial. Classes in such areas as arts and crafts, line dancing, and bridge are scheduled, along with Senior Net computer classes and Internet access. Seminars are offered on health and retirement issues, healthy aging, and driver's safety. Membership eligibility here begins at the age of fifty-five, as opposed to the rival group's sixty-five (which you probably figured out from looking at the names of the groups, eh?). Membership is free.

Golden Age and Other Senior Centers

Golden Age Centers and Community Centers are daily gathering places that provide active senior citizens with an opportunity to participate in classes and other events.

Lunches are served. The centers operated by the city of Savannah are known as Golden Age Centers. Senior Citizens Inc. operates three additional centers in arrangements with the municipalities of Garden City, Port Wentworth, and Thunderbolt. Pooler has its own center. All offer very similar programs.

The following is an alphabetical listing of The Golden Age Centers (all of them are area code 912): Cunningham Center, 121 E. 36th Street (651-6779); Cuyler Center, 812 W. 36th Street (651-6780); Frazier Center, 805 May Street (233-4796); Grant Center, 1310 Richard Street (651-6785); Savannah Gardens Center, 2500 Elgin Street (651-6775); Stillwell Towers Center, 5100 Waters Avenue (351-3855); Stubbs Towers Center, 1301 Bee Road (651-6776); Wimberly Center, 121 W. 37th Street (651-6778); and Windsor Forest Center (921-2104).

The three nearby community centers operated by Senior Citizens Inc. include the Garden City Center, 100 Main Street, Garden City (966-7791); the Port Wentworth Center, 100 Aberfeldy Street, Port Wentworth (964-5411); and the Thunderbolt Center, 3236 Russell Street, Thunderbolt (352-4846). The Pooler Center is at 100 W. Collins Street, Pooler (964-5411).

Insiders' Tip

State and local regulations give older property owners special exemptions on property taxes. Most, but not all, of the exemptions are keyed to income. If you are interested in purchasing a retirement home in Chatham County, learn more about your property tax status by calling the Tax Assessor's Office at (912) 652-7271.

Worship

Where to Worship?

Sacred Music

Ecumenical Services
and Projects

You won't have to look very far in Savannah for evidence that you are at least on the fringe of the Bible Belt—simply turn on a radio or television Sunday morning or stroll downtown, where you'll find normally stringently enforced parking regulations abandoned as suburbanites return to the downtown churches.

But don't let the label delude you into thinking you've wandered into a world of one-size-fits-all religion. Savannah is a city of great religious diversity, with more than 260 houses of worship that range from the splendor of a historic cathedral to the simple outreach of humble storefronts. You'll find the major denominations represented, along with other faiths that reflect the growing international community that comes to Savannah via the ports, local colleges, or seasonal agricultural needs for the nearby Vidalia onion harvest. You'll find out that religion in Savannah assumes a highly visible position in local life. Elsewhere, it might be unusual for a public meeting to begin with a brief prayer, but the practice still surfaces here from time to time and draws little, if any, public comment when it does.

Churches and synagogues are also active players in private education in Savannah. Not only is there a kindergarten through grade twelve Catholic school system—certainly not uncommon in any city with a significant Catholic population—but Baptist, Jewish, and Pentecostal congregations also sponsor private schools, along with other nondenominational Christian groups. (For information on many of these schools, see our Education and Child Care chapter.)

According to statistics compiled in the University of Georgia's *Georgia County Guide,* a third of Chatham County's population identifies itself with the Baptist faith. That identity covers a lot of ground, however, ranging from churches affiliated with the conservative Southern Baptist Convention to independent Baptist churches to those affiliated with historically African American branches of the faith. The same survey shows roughly equal numbers of Catholics and United Methodists, each accounting for just more than 8 percent of the population. Smaller percentages are identified as belonging to other denominations or faiths, but the list contains no startling omissions. Local houses of worship include three synagogues (one each for Reform, Conservative, and Orthodox Jews) and a mosque.

Unlike several other of the original British colonies, Georgia cannot claim a religious motive for its founding. Instead, economic and social conditions were the driving force behind the settling of this, the thirteenth of the storied thirteen original colonies. Still, religion was a major part of Colonial life from the day Oglethorpe and his original settlers arrived (see our History chapter). The group was largely Anglican in its faith (no surprise there), but its charter provided for religious freedom—for the most part. Catholics were

Insiders' Tip

The Gothic synagogue that serves Temple Mickve Israel was built on Monterey Square in 1876.

prohibited from settling in the colony in its early days, reflective of Georgia's early role as a military buffer between other English settlements to the north and the Catholic Spanish settlements in Florida.

Insiders' Tip

John Wesley, a founding figure in the history of Methodism, is honored with a statue in Reynolds Square.

That proviso about religious freedom got its first major test five months after the colony began. A shipload of mainly Spanish and Portuguese Jews, fleeing religious persecution in Spain, arrived in 1733. Whether the promised religious tolerance in the Georgia colony would have held up under normal circumstances is unclear, but this ship was made welcome—probably due, in no small part, to its showing up in the midst of a deadly fever epidemic with a doctor on board. Thus, a Jewish community has roots that date back practically to the founding days of the colony. Temple Mickve Israel became the oldest congregation in the state of Georgia and is believed to be the third oldest in the nation (see our Attractions chapter for more on the temple).

Methodism, too, has deep historical roots in Savannah. John Wesley preached here in his Anglican days; he went on to become a founding father of the Methodist denomination.

The churches along the downtown Savannah squares house some of the oldest congregations in the country. Some members trace their membership back for generations; others have just moved to town. The buildings themselves are often historic, quite apart from their religious significance, but for the most part the congregations predate the current buildings. The earliest churches were destroyed by the fires that were a constant threat to the city in its earliest centuries.

Savannah's strongest claim to historical religious fame is in African American history. Savannah is the founding point of the oldest black congregations in the country, and the two churches that sprang from slave roots—First Bryan Baptist Church and First African Baptist Church—are still active and influential participants in the city's spiritual and social life.

Where to Worship?

Finding a spiritual match in an unfamiliar city is an important task that can be time consuming when you are relocating. If you are vacationing or staying for a short time, however, chances are you are more interested in simply continuing your usual religious observance while away from home. So, how does a spiritually observant traveler go about choosing a congregation to visit? Print media outlets provide several options in Savannah. The *Savannah Morning News* publishes a religion section every Saturday, and you'll find there a collection of religious news items, schedules of special events, and advertisements by various churches. The *Herald*, a weekly newspaper, provides detailed coverage of religious news in Savannah's African-American community. The *Morning News* (see our Media chapter) can be found in vending boxes all over town, especially around hotels and motels. You may have to look harder to find the *Herald*. It's in vending boxes in the downtown area, hospital lobbies, and major shopping centers, and you can call (912) 232–4505 to find out other locations. The *Savannah Jewish News* is a monthly publication serving Savannah's approximately 3,000 Jewish families. It is normally available by subscription only, but there's a good chance you can pick up a current copy at the Jewish Educational Alliance, 5111 Abercorn Street (912–355–8111).

New Age interests and other less-conventional spiritual paths are harder to

The steeple of St. John's Episcopal Church has towered over the historic area for generations.
PHOTO: KYLE CASON

The twin steeples of the Cathedral of St. John the Baptist mark Savannah's skyline. PHOTO: KYLE CASON

track. You might check out the event columns of the Savannah edition of *CONNECT SAVANNAH/Creative Loafing,* available free at a wide range of locations but especially copious at downtown restaurants and nightclubs.

Other good sources of info are the windows and bulletin boards of shops in the downtown area that sell New Age and nontraditional spiritual products (see our Shopping chapter). This might seem a little hit or miss to you, but we've discovered that organizers of such less-than-mainstream events are usually extremely diligent about getting flyers posted and word of events circulated.

Sacred Music

Maybe you are not trying, while traveling, to find a church you believe you would be compatible with for a lifetime. Instead, maybe you are more interested in continuing long-standing habits of worship without attention to specific denominational issues. If that's the case, we can heartily suggest the sacred music options available in Savannah's wide range of churches. A visit to a different church often offers a chance to hear the uplifting vocal talents of local choirs while viewing the architectural grandeur of Savannah's churches.

We asked our musical friends which churches they felt offered the most outstanding and uplifting sacred music. We had them focus on the geographic areas where visitors are likely to be staying and able to find their way around; that's why you'll note the predominance of downtown churches here. The list that follows is by no means comprehensive. Almost every church has music of some kind, and many play host to visiting singing groups. No doubt we've left some outstanding examples off, but this brief list should give you a starting point.

A full carillon of bells can be heard beginning around 10 A.M. each Sunday morning, pealing out hymns from atop St. John's Episcopal Church, 1 W. Macon

Street, just off Bull Street. The church also has a good organ and choir. The Lutheran Church of the Ascension, 120 Bull Street, has what may be the largest organ in town, along with a fine choir. Wesley Monumental United Methodist Church, 429 Abercorn Street, boasts outstanding organ, choral, and even occasional handbell performances.

First Baptist Church at 223 Bull Street is known for its organ and choir. Bull Street Baptist Church, at the corner of Bull and Anderson Streets, has a wonderful pipe organ and choir. Farther south, another notable choir (accompanied by an electronic organ) sings at the White Bluff United Methodist Church at 11911 White Bluff Road. A performance by the Savannah Community Choir is an event that shouldn't be missed. Consider this group an "all-star team" from Savannah's African American churches. Their performances are infrequent but well publicized, and their recording has even won a Grammy.

Ecumenical Services and Projects

Ecumenical services among churches are common during the holiday seasons. Downtown churches, for example, often come together to jointly sponsor Holy Week services at midday. At Christmas, one or more churches may stage a living nativity scene, always a popular attraction, and cantatas showcase the best efforts of local choirs. At Easter, a group sunrise service on the beach at Tybee Island greets the day.

Savannah's churches work as well as worship. You'll find them intensely involved in the support of the Inner City Night Shelter, which feeds the homeless and provides shelter, and in other projects addressing the needs of the homeless. Coastal Empire Habitat for Humanity, the local chapter of the international home-building project that counts Georgian and former president Jimmy Carter among its carpenters, thrives with help from about twenty different churches. To volunteer with Habitat, either through a church or as an individual, call (912) 234–6112.

Insiders' Tip
Bull Street Baptist Church, at the corner of Anderson and Bull streets, offers a Spanish language service. Call the church at (912) 236-1511 for a schedule.

Hilton Head, S.C.

Introduction/History

Something that strikes us when we're on Hilton Head Island—aside from the natural beauty of the place—is the relative newness of what has been built there. This becomes even more evident when the island is compared with the Historic Downtown of Savannah some 35 miles to the southwest, an area where much of what you see dates to the 1800s and early 1900s.

In contrast, most of the structures on Hilton Head are less than fifty years old, the products of two momentous events in the island's history that occurred in the mid-1950s. One was the opening of a set of two bridges connecting the 41-square-mile sea island with the South Carolina mainland. The other was the start of the Sea Pines residential/resort community by a southeast Georgian named Charles Fraser.

"The opening of the bridge had a major impact on development," states Porter M. Thompson in the book *Hilton Head Island Images.* "Suddenly building materials, equipment and people were able to come and go freely—Hilton Head had lost its isolation and a new era had begun."

Sea Pines, in its basic form a residential area built around a golf course, set the tone for the other planned communities that would be created on Hilton Head and spurred the development of the island as a mecca for retirees and vacationers. Back in the early 1950s, Hilton Head was home to about one hundred families, "little more than a quiet community of farmers and shrimpers," as author Richard Rutt put it in *Hilton Head Island: A Perspective.* Now the island—with its natural assets of marshes, wide creeks, hardwood forests and 12 miles of beach—is the site of eleven planned communities harboring a multitude of stylish homes and upscale condominiums known locally as villas. Hilton Head boasts 23 beautifully manicured golf courses, more than 300 tennis courts, 8 marinas, 4 large hotels, a bevy of villa-style resorts and midsize hotels and motels, some 230 restaurants, and 36 shopping areas and more than 200 shops. Permanent residents now number nearly 29,000, many of them engaged in satisfying the needs of visitors, of whom there are 2.38 million annually, according to the island's chamber of commerce.

All this growth has occurred in a manner that places an emphasis on preserving Hilton Head's natural surroundings: live oaks, magnolias, pines, palmettos, and other flora. Following ideas originally credited to Fraser, most islanders continue to adhere to the concept that buildings must blend in with the environment and that development be as unobtrusive as possible.

Although Hilton Head's modern era begins in the '50s, the island's recorded

Among Hilton Head's many attractions are 12 miles of beautiful beach. PHOTO: RICH WITTISH

history goes back considerably further—to the 1500s, when Spaniards and Frenchmen visited while exploring the area bordering Port Royal Sound, the large bay on Hilton Head's north shore that's one of the world's finest natural harbors. The Spanish and French fought over the sound for almost fifty years, with the Spaniards triumphing but never settling the area. That was left to the British, who in 1717 were responsible for the island's first English-speaking settler, John Barnwell.

Englishmen had been in the area well before that, however. In 1663, sea captain William Hilton sailed into the sound and came upon the island. He spotted a headland on the northeastern end and named it after himself. As time went on, the entire island came to be called by the name of this promontory, Hilton Head.

The settlers who came to Hilton Head in the 1700s eventually planted the land in cotton, indigo, sugar cane, rice, and other crops. They purchased slaves brought to America from Africa and used them to create large plantations. According to Richard

Rutt, there were twenty-four plantations on the island by 1860, most of them producing cotton. Also by that time, South Carolina was on the verge of seceding from the Union and leading the South into the Civil War, a conflict in which Hilton Head would play an interesting part.

The island was invaded by Union troops on November 7, 1861, seven months after the war began, in an effort to control Port Royal Sound and establish a portion of the blockade of the Confederacy's Atlantic coast. In the Battle of Port Royal, a Union fleet of fifteen warships and thirty-one transports and supply ships exchanged shots with four Confederate gunboats and two forts, one of them on Hilton Head. The Confederate guns were silenced, the forts were evacuated, and Union forces took possession of the island and held it until the end of the war.

The area near the fort on Hilton Head—called Fort Walker by the Southerners and renamed Fort Welles by its Federal conquerors—became a town during the Union occupation, when the population of Hilton Head mushroomed to 40,000. "Enlisted personnel—both soldiers and sailors—constituted the bulk of that population, or, 23–30,000 men," Rutt stated in his book. "The balance of Hilton Head's wartime population consisted primarily of freedmen who sought refuge on the island, civilian dependents, and Yankee tradesmen. The latter opened and operated a variety of business establishments, ranging from hotels, blacksmith shops, and theatres to photography studios, tattoo parlors and bordellos."

The main street of the town, which was located in what is now Port Royal Plantation, was named Sutler's Row after the merchants who lined it. The military men who paid exorbitant prices for the sutlers' goods called it Robber's Row, the name now borne by one of the plantation's golf courses. Another settlement sprang up in what is now Hilton Head Plantation. It was called Mitchelville and consisted mostly of tents and barracks housing freed slaves who had fled to the island. When the war ended, the military and the sutlers left and, said Rutt, "the shops and houses of Robber's Row and Mitchelville rapidly disappeared from the island, no doubt torn down by freedmen seeking to build homes of their own."

From the end of the Civil War until the middle of the twentieth century, Hilton Head was a sleepy sea island largely bypassed and forgotten by the rest of the world. All that began to change in 1950, when Fred Hack, C. C. Stebbins, and Lt. Gen. Joseph B. Fraser bought 8,000 acres of pine forest and formed the Hilton Head Company for the purpose of selectively cutting the pines. In 1956, the company's holdings were divided, with Fraser acquiring 4,000 acres on the southern end of the island. A year later Fraser's son Charles, a University of Georgia and Yale Law School graduate in his twenties, bought his family's holdings and another 1,200 acres and started planning and developing Sea Pines.

Meanwhile, Hack and O. T. McIntosh, who had purchased 12,000 acres on the northern end of the island in the early

'50s, began work on their own developments: Spanish Wells Plantation and Port Royal Plantation. (Sea Pines also used the term *plantation* in its name in its early years, as have many of the planned communities on the island; it refers to the antebellum plantations once located on the sites of the communities.)

"These few men," wrote Porter Thompson in referring to Fraser, Hack, McIntosh, and other developers, "began with the idea that large holdings of land could be subdivided into lots and sold for residential purposes. There was a twist to this. Hilton Head is ideally suited by climate and location for resort activity so the communities developed would have to accommodate both resort and residential activities. It is Charles Fraser who is largely credited with first developing the concept that a resort/residential community could be successful, if a few considerations were made. He embodied two excellent and highly compatible interests: the understanding of development and a love of nature and of the natural beauty of the island."

Among the concepts advocated and practiced by Fraser were blending development with the environment, creating green spaces, keeping the density of housing as low as possible, cutting as few trees as necessary, and restricting the height of buildings so they were no taller than the tallest surrounding trees.

Under Fraser's direction, Sea Pines became, in the words of the Associated Press, "a big-time leisure landmark, a model for resort playgrounds and planned communities from Virginia to the Philippines." Other developers followed his lead, creating their own planned communities and, in the process, transforming Hilton Head into the world-renowned resort that it is today.

Getting There

Some people arrive at Hilton Head Island by boat or fly directly onto the island, but if you're like most visitors, you'll be coming by car, either from home in your own vehicle or from the Savannah International Airport in a rental. Whatever the case, here's how to get to the island.

By Car

Getting to Hilton Head by car is fairly simple because there's only one road onto the island, U.S. Highway 278, a four-lane that runs west to east through the South Carolina Lowcountry. Finding U.S. 278 is no big deal, particularly if you're arriving at Savannah International Airport and renting a car for the forty-minute drive to the island (you can find information on flights to Savannah and car rentals in our main Getting Here, Getting Around chapter). U.S. 278 is also easy to get to if you're coming from the south or north on Interstate 95, or if you're arriving from the west via Interstate 16 and I-95.

U.S. 278 intersects I-95 just north of Hardeeville, South Carolina, so once you're on the interstate, all you have to do is watch for the exit for U.S. 278 (exit 8). Take that exit and head east; it's an 18-mile straight shot to Hilton Head. You'll be on the island in twenty minutes and at the middle of it in about a half hour. To get to I-95 from Savannah International Airport, take Airways Avenue west for a little more than a mile to the interstate. Get on I-95 and head north into South Carolina. The U.S. 278 exit is 16.5 miles up the interstate from where you left Airways Avenue.

If you're not renting a car, you can get to Hilton Head from the airport via the Low Country Adventures Ltd. shuttle service. Low County Adventures meets all incoming flights before midnight with either a nine-passenger van or a twenty-one-passenger bus. Fares from the airport to the island are $27 per person one way and $46 round-trip. You can reach Low Country Adventures at (843) 681-8212 or (800) 845-5582.

If you're visiting Savannah and want to pop over to Hilton Head for the day or spend a night on the island, you can drive there by following the I-95/U.S. 278 route

just discussed, or you can go the "back way." If you take the I-95/U.S. 278 route, you'll be on multilane highways, and it will take about an hour and five minutes for you to get from Savannah City Hall to the Hilton Head Island Chamber of Commerce building at the middle of the island. (To get to I-95 from city hall, drive west on Bay Street through three traffic lights to Martin Luther King Jr. Boulevard, turn left on MLK and head south three traffic lights to the entrance ramp to I-16, then take I-16 west for 8.5 miles to I-95.)

The back way is shorter (about fifty-five minutes from city hall to the middle of Hilton Head), more scenic and a little more complicated. It involves traveling on two-lane roads. If you want to try it, take Oglethorpe Avenue west to the Eugene Talmadge Memorial Bridge and drive north across the Savannah River into South Carolina. You'll be on U.S. Highway 17 for 5 miles from the South Carolina side of the bridge to the intersection of U.S. 17 and Alternate S.C. Highway 170. Turn right on Alt. SC 170 and stay on it for 6 miles until you reach its intersection with S.C. Highway 46 (also labeled for a short distance as S.C. Highway 170). Turn right at the stop sign and drive east on SC 46 for 12 miles to U.S. 278. Turn right on U.S. 278 and head east—you'll be on the island in about five minutes. Along your way on SC 46 to U.S. 278, you'll pass through piney woods, hardwood swamps, and the laid-back, offbeat little town of Bluffton with its Squat & Gobble restaurant and 30 MPH speed limit (be sure to observe it). While in Bluffton, you'll come to a four-way stop; turn left to stay on SC 46.

By Boat

If you're going to Hilton Head by boat, you can get there via the Intracoastal Waterway, which runs along the west side of the island. There are several public marinas and harbors where you can tie up and enjoy your stay while aboard your vessel. These include Harbour Town Yacht Basin at Sea Pines (843-671-2704), Outdoor Resorts Yacht Basin at Intracoastal Waterway Marker 20 (843-681-3256), Palmetto Bay Marina at 164 Palmetto Bay Road (843-785-3910, 800-448-3875), Shelter Cove Marina at Shelter Cove (843-842-7001), Skull Creek Marina at Hilton Head Plantation (843-681-4234), and Windmill Harbour (843-681-9235). The maximum length of the slips at these marinas ranges from 60 to 200 feet and the cost per night for docking runs from $1 per foot to $2 per foot, depending, in some cases, on the size of the vessel involved. Call ahead for specific details.

By Airplane

Hilton Head has its own airport on the north end of the island. The Hilton Head Airport is on Beach City Road, which runs north off U.S. 278, the island's main drag. Beach City Road is at mile marker 4 on U.S. 278, and the entrance to the airport is about a mile from U.S. 278. There are two fixed-base operators across the runway from the airport terminal that can accommodate private planes. The FBOs are on Gateway Circle off Dillon Road less than a mile north of U.S. 278.

Hilton Head Airport
120 Beach City Road
Hilton Head, SC
(843) 689–5400
www.hiltonheadairport.com

Hilton Head's airport has an up-to-date, spacious terminal that was served in summer 2001 by one commercial carrier, U.S.Airways Express (800-428-4322). U.S.Airways Express airline offers flights each day to and from Charlotte, North Carolina.

Five rental-car agencies maintain desks at the airport: Avis Rent A Car (843-681-4216, 888-897-8448), Budget Rent A Car (843-689-4040, 800-527-0700), Hertz Rent A Car (843-681-7604, 800-654-3131), National Car Rental (843-681-7368, 800-CAR-RENT), and Thrifty Car Rental (843-689-9990, 800-364-2277). Taxicab and shuttle services operating from the airport are Diamond Taxi (843-785-2888), Ferguson Transportation & Taxi (843-681-5883), Low Country Adventures Ltd. (843-681-8212), and Yellow Taxi Cab Service (843-686-6666). Rates to and from the airport are set by the cab companies and monitored by Beaufort County: Fees are $10 to the Hampton Inn; $13 to Hilton Head Plantation; $14 to $15 to the Marriott/Palmetto Dunes; $17 to Shipyard; $18 to the Holiday Inn Oceanfront; $20 to Sea Pines; $35 to Del Webb Sun City near Bluffton, South Carolina; and $65 to Savannah, with the lower rate to the Marriott being charged by Yellow Cab. Gray Line of Hilton Head (843-341-6868) also has a shuttle to the Marriott, and the fee is $12.

The airport has short- and long-term parking lots: Short-term rates are 50 cents for the first fifteen to thirty minutes and 50 cents for each additional half hour, with a maximum charge of $6 for each twenty-four-hour period; long-term rates are 75 cents for the first hour and 50 cents for each additional half hour, with a maximum charge of $4.50 for each twenty-four-hour period and a weekly charge of $22.50. The first fifteen minutes in the short-term lot are free.

Carolina Air Center Inc.
52 Gateway Circle
Hilton Head, SC
(843) 689–3200

In addition to the usual services you'd expect from a fixed-base operator, Carolina Air Center offers an exercise room with a shower, a nine-hole putting green, and courtesy crew cars on request. The ramp charge is $5 per night, and 100 LL and Jet A fuel service is available twenty-four hours a day if you call ahead after normal business hours, which run from 6 A.M. to 10 P.M.

Hilton Head Air Service Inc.
38 Gateway Circle
Hilton Head, SC
(843) 681–6386
www.hhairservice.com

The ramp charge at this fixed-base operation is $7.50 per night. The facility provides catering and has on-site car rentals through Enterprise Rent A Car. Hilton Head Air is open from 6:30 A.M. to 10 P.M. April through October and from 6:30 A.M. to 8 P.M. in the off-season.

Getting Around

The best way to get around on Hilton Head is by car. Walking isn't much of an option because things are pretty spread out. Bike riding is popular, but if you take to the splendid network of bike trails, be prepared to do some pedaling to far-flung destinations. If you haven't driven your own car or rented one, there are numerous taxi companies and limousine services to help you arrange transportation.

Driving on the Island

Finding your way around Hilton Head is fairly easy, but actually finding the places you're looking for can be a challenge. At first glance that statement might not make much sense, but consider this: Most of what a visitor would be looking for can be found on or very near three main roads (U.S. 278, Pope Avenue, and South Forest Beach Drive), but spotting a specific restaurant, shop, or motel can be difficult because of town regulations limiting signage and promoting natural beauty. Businesses are not allowed to have signs off the premises, and the signs they do have must conform to strict rules involving size and lighting. These regulations, combined with the emphasis on preserving trees and foliage and having buildings blend in, can make it easy for you to drive right past your intended destination. This is particularly true when it comes to the island's main thoroughfare, U.S. 278, a busy four-lane divided highway also known as the William Hilton Parkway. Most everything is set back off the road on tree-lined side streets that often resemble driveways.

William Hilton Parkway

Once you cross the Karl S. Bowers and J. Wilton Graves Bridges to Hilton Head on U.S. 278, you're on William Hilton Parkway, which runs east for 5 miles to the northern end of the island, then bends south and continues 6 miles to Sea Pines Circle. This 11-mile stretch passes numerous restaurants, motels, shopping centers, and other businesses and the entrances to resort communities such as Hilton Head Plantation, Port Royal, Palmetto Dunes, and Shipyard.

To aid motorists, the town has placed mile markers along the parkway, with the lower-numbered markers closer to the bridges and the higher-numbered ones closer to the traffic circle. In many of our individual write-ups on businesses on the parkway, we've included a mention of the mile marker nearest the business being discussed.

Sea Pines Circle

When you enter this traffic circle from William Hilton Parkway, you'll encounter exits to the Cross Island Parkway one-quarter of the way around, Greenwood Drive halfway around, and Pope Avenue three-quarters of the way around. Greenwood Drive is the main road leading into the Sea Pines resort community. The stretch of the Cross Island Parkway directly west of the circle, also known as Palmetto Bay Road, was widened into a four-lane highway in 1997.

Pope Avenue

Pope Avenue runs east a tad more than a mile from Sea Pines Circle to Coligny Circle. On Pope, you'll find a variety of restaurants, stores, shopping plazas, another entrance to Shipyard, and the entrance to the public parking lot at Forest Beach.

Coligny Circle

The Coligny traffic circle is practically on Forest Beach, and it routes motorists from Pope Avenue to South Forest Beach Drive

Sea Pines' premier marina features Hilton Head's most celebrated landmark, the Harbour Town Lighthouse (center of photo). PHOTO: COURTESY OF HILTON HEAD ISLAND CHAMBER OF COMMERCE

(one-quarter of the way around the circle) and North Forest Beach Drive (three-quarters of the way around). North Forest Beach Drive is residential and leads to many of the older vacation homes and permanent residences on the island; short side streets run east to the beach, but access is private and public parking is a no-no.

South Forest Beach Drive

There are several resorts and restaurants along South Forest Beach Drive, which leads to another entrance to Sea Pines. Access to the beach via the side streets is private unless marked otherwise.

Cross Island Parkway

The Cross Island Parkway, a four-lane toll road that bypasses the southern portion of William Hilton Parkway and alleviates traffic congestion on that heavily traveled thoroughfare, was opened in January 1998. The 6-mile, limited-access highway stretches from near the intersection of William Hilton Parkway and Spanish Wells Road, at mile marker 2 in the north-western portion of the island, to Sea Pines Circle. Part of the Cross Island Parkway is

a sixty-five-foot-high bridge that crosses Broad Creek at Palmetto Bay. The toll for riding the length of the parkway (one way) in a car has been set at $1; it's $1.75 for three-axle trucks and $3.25 for five-axle trucks. Planners say the new road saves motorists anywhere from eight to ten minutes in travel time.

Biking on the Island

Hilton Head has some 20 miles of paved public bicycle paths, and there are many more miles of paths within the island's resort communities. The public paths run along William Hilton Parkway from Gumtree Road (just past mile marker 2) to Sea Pines Circle for 9 miles, along both sides of Pope Avenue from Sea Pines Circle to Coligny Circle for a total of 2 miles, along North Forest Beach Drive from Coligny Circle to the end of North Forest for 1.3 miles, along South Forest Beach Drive from Coligny Circle to Sea Pines' Ocean Gate for 1.4 miles, along the Cordillo Parkway from South Forest Beach Drive to Pope Avenue for 1.1 miles, and to the Folly Field Beach Park (see Public Beach Access in this chapter) from William

Hilton Parkway for 0.8 mile. A 3.5-mile path along Gumtree and Squire Pope Roads in the northwestern part of the island was completed in 1998, as were a 1-mile stretch on Point Comfort Road and 1.1 miles of pathway on Arrow Road in the southern portion of the island. Also open for riding are a 2.2-mile path along Beach City Road and the wider paths along North and South Beach Drives.

You can make arrangements to rent a bike through the resort where you're staying or by calling one of the more than twenty bike rental outlets that can be found in the Yellow Pages of the local telephone directory. In season, expect to pay $25 to rent a bike for a week and $9.50 to $12 for a day.

Taxis and Limousines

In addition to the taxicab and limousine companies that serve the Hilton Head Airport, there are several other limo operators on the island. Limousine services include At Your Service Transportation Inc. (843–837–3783), Camelot Limousine & Tours (843–842–7777), and Resort Limousine (843–671–5466).

Taxi rates are not regulated by the city of Hilton Head and vary from company to company and point to point. To find out how much a trip will cost, tell the dispatcher where you are and where you're going and ask what the fee will be. Rates for limousines run from $65 to $75 per hour with a two-hour minimum.

Bus Service

The island is served by the buses of Beaufort County's Lowcountry Regional Transportation Authority (LRTA), but this public transportation service is mainly a means of getting working people from towns on the mainland on and off Hilton Head. These buses serve Hilton Head in the early morning and in the late afternoon, meaning the LRTA is not a means

> ### Insiders' Tip
> The man for whom the Coligny traffic circle and the Coligny Plaza shopping center is named was Gaspard de Coligny, who sponsored two exploratory expeditions by French Protestants to the Port Royal Sound area in the mid-1500s.

of conveniently getting around the island throughout the day. However, there is a limited-demand response system through which riders can schedule transportation by calling (843) 757-5782 (a round-trip to Bluffton using this system is $12). Also, the LRTA is working on establishing a fixed-route system for the island.

Public Beach Access and Parking

The only public parking lots and metered parking spaces on the island are at Hilton Head's public beach access points. As far as parking on the rest of the island goes, there is an abundance of free spaces in the lots of restaurants, shopping centers, motels, and other commercial establishments, much of it shaded by trees, which can be a blessing in the summer months.

Coligny Beach Park

The access at Coligny Circle offers about 30 metered spaces and a parking lot with about 350 spaces. The meters allow you to park fifteen minutes for a quarter. Rates when the lot is manned by an attendant—usually on Fridays, weekends, and holidays—are $4 per day.

Collier Water Sports Park

Plans called for this site, which is designed mainly for kayakers and windsurfers, to be ready for use by April 2002. The park will be at the end of Singleton Beach Road, which runs off William Hilton Parkway near mile marker 7. There will be thirty parking spaces accessible to the general public, provided motorists have purchased a $15 annual parking permit.

Driessen Beach Park

Located at the end of Bradley Beach Road, which intersects William Hilton Parkway just past mile marker 6, this access has a lot with 212 spaces where parking is 25 cents per half hour. The lot is about a half mile from the parkway.

Folly Field Beach Park

This access is on Starfish Drive, which runs off Folly Field Road. Parking at the fifty-two spaces here is metered, and the rate is 25 cents for fifteen minutes. Folly Field Road also runs into William Hilton Parkway at mile marker 6; it's a little more than a half mile from the parkway to the access.

Islanders Beach Park

This facility is on Folly Field Road about a mile from William Hilton Parkway. The one hundred spaces here are reserved for persons having annual beach passes (there are also thirty such spaces at Driessen Beach and thirty at Coligny). Passes are available only to Hilton Head residents or property owners; they cost $15 a year and can be obtained at the town's governmental offices near the entrance to Wexford Plantation.

Sources of Information

Hilton Head has visitors centers where you can pick up information that might be helpful to you during your stay.

Hilton Head Chamber of Commerce
1 Chamber of Commerce Drive
Hilton Head, SC
(843) 785-3673

The lobby of the chamber building, which is just off William Hilton Parkway near mile marker 8, is filled with brochures and other publications dealing with the island's accommodations, restaurants, recreational opportunities, and real estate. If you have questions, there are friendly folks at the desk who can provide answers. This information center is open from 8:30 A.M. to 5:30 P.M. Monday through Friday.

Hilton Head Chamber of Commerce Welcome Center
100 William Hilton Parkway
Hilton Head, SC
(843) 785-3673

The chamber of commerce staffs a welcome center at this site just past mile marker 1 on William Hilton Parkway. Stop here and you'll find displays and brochures involving shopping, dining, lodging, long- and short-term rentals, golf, tennis, fishing, and events. There's a video display that will introduce you to the island in several different languages (you make the choice) and a large-scale map of the island, plus smaller maps of Hilton Head and the surrounding areas that you can take with you. The center is open from 9 A.M. to 6 P.M. daily (8:30 A.M. to 5:30 P.M. in the winter).

The welcome center shares a building with The Museum on Hilton Head Island, which offers exhibits involving the area's history, native crafts, and wildlife. Admission is $2. There's also an art gallery exhibit room that features continuous showings of a televised history of the island. Museum hours are from 10 A.M. to 5 P.M. daily, and there's a museum shop featuring books on the Civil War and topics of local interest.

Planned Residential Communities

Hilton Head's eleven planned residential communities cover 65 percent of the island. All of the island's golf courses (see subsequent listings) are located within or associated with the communities, as are the four largest hotels and many of Hilton Head's homes, vacation villas, tennis courts, and marinas.

These communities are, for the most part, private, meaning they have gates staffed by security personnel who check the identities of arriving motorists. Some are more private than others: A few admit only residents and their guests; others are accessible to vacationers staying at hotels and villas within the communities and to golfers playing on courses that allow public participation. Sea Pines, which is the site of several restaurants and two shopping areas, allows the public to visit at a charge of $5 per car.

As we've mentioned before, the buildings in these communities are, in most cases, designed to melt into the landscape; stucco and wood are used extensively as building materials, and painting is in muted colors. The grounds surrounding these structures are often left in as natural a state as possible. In most communities, buildings must be approved by architectural review boards. This section is comprised of sketches of the island's eleven planned communities, listed in alphabetical order. For each we've provided, when possible, an address, telephone number and/or Web site of a source for additional information: either a sales office, an administrative office, or the office of the property owners' association.

Hilton Head Plantation

Hilton Head Plantation is the second-largest planned community on the island, covering 4,000 acres on the northern tip of Hilton Head between Port Royal Sound and Skull Creek, which is part of the Intracoastal Waterway. Within the plantation's borders are 4,400 residential lots, four 18-hole golf courses, a beach fronting on the sound, the Whooping Crane Pond and Cypress Nature Conservancies, the Seabrook Farm garden plots, and tennis courts and swimming pools.

On the Skull Creek side of the plantation are Skull Creek Marina, a deepwater facility with 180 boat slips, the Old Fort Pub restaurant, and Fort Mitchel, a historic site that was a Union gun battery during the Civil War. Two of the golf courses within the plantation (the Country Club of Hilton Head and Oyster Reef) can be played by the public.

Outside the plantation's main gate, which is off William Hilton Parkway near mile marker 3, is Main Street, a development of shops and professional offices. The Hilton Head Plantation Property Owners Association is within the plantation at 7 Surrey Lane, and the telephone number there is (843) 681–8800. The Web site is www.hiltonheadplantation.com.

Indigo Run

Most of the homesites at this 1,775-acre development on the northern portion of Hilton Head border one of two 18-hole golf courses: The Golf Club at Indigo Run, a members-only layout designed by Jack Nicklaus and his son, Jack Nicklaus II, and opened in 1996; and the Golden Bear Golf Club, which was designed by Nicklaus's company and can be played by the public (see listing in this chapter's "Golf" section). All property owners at Indigo Run are entitled to join Golden Bear, and membership includes access to Sunningdale Park, which has six tennis courts, an Olympic-size pool, a kiddie pool, and a large playground for children. Membership in The Golf Club is open to owners of homesites and homes in Indigo Run.

As of spring 2001, there were 482 homes on the 1,517 acres comprising Indigo Run's private residential community and another 43 in the building or design stages. These residences represent a wide range of styles and construction materials and are valued at $350,000 and up. Fifty of Indigo Run's homesites are in the River Club section along the banks of Broad Creek, and many owners of homes there have backyard boat docks. There are no villas at Indigo Run, and the only rentals allowed are long-term arrangements of a year or more.

Indigo Run is also the site of Indigo Park, a 258-acre retail and commercial center bordering William Hilton Parkway. Started in the mid-1980s by the Hilton Head Company, Indigo Run was acquired in 1991 by the Melrose Company, which continues to develop the community. The Indigo Run sales office is at 100 Indigo Run Drive within the main gate, which is off the parkway near mile marker 3. You can reach the sales office by calling (843) 681-3300 or (800) 487-2645.

Long Cove Club

The centerpiece of this community is a 6,900-yard golf course designed by Pete Dye that's been ranked best in South Carolina and as high as nineteenth in the nation. Property owners automatically become members of Long Cove Club, entitling them to use the golf course, the elegant 17,000-square-foot clubhouse, the pool, eight tennis courts, and docks on Broad Creek that have slips for one hundred boats. According to John McKenzie, president of Long Cove Club Realty, some club members live on other parts of Hilton Head but have bought lots at Long Cove just so they can play on the private golf course.

Development of Long Cove began in 1980, and all 570 homesites in the 600-acre community were sold by 1987. Ninety-seven percent of the sites have a view of a lagoon, marsh, or the golf course, and, as of spring 2000, about 365 homes had been built, all of them single-family residences. The median price tag for these homes—one- and two-story structures of stucco and cypress—is around $600,000. Privacy is prized here, and there are no short-term rentals. There's a sales office within the community at 44 Long Cove Drive, where the phone number is (843)

842-2442. The entrance to Long Cove is off William Hilton Parkway near mile marker 10.

Palmetto Dunes

Spread over 2,000 acres on the eastern side of the island, Palmetto Dunes offers 3 miles of beach bordering the Atlantic Ocean; 5,000 homes and villas, more than 500 of which can be rented by vacationers; three 18-hole golf courses; a world-class tennis facility; an 11-mile lagoon system; and two of the island's "big four" hotels—the 505-room Hyatt Regency Hilton Head Resort and the 323-room Hilton Head Island Hilton Resort (see listings under Accommodations). All three of the golf courses—named for designers Arthur Hills, George Fazio, and Robert Trent Jones—are accessible to the public (see listings in this chapter under Golf), as are the twenty-three clay and two hard courts of the Palmetto Dunes Tennis Center. Homes in Palmetto Dunes range from $250,000 to well over $1 million.

Palmetto Dunes was started in the late 1960s and acquired in 1979 by the Greenwood Development Corporation, which since then has created the Shelter Cove Harbour yacht basin and retail complex and the Leamington community. Shelter Cove—a marina surrounded by shops, restaurants, and villas built in the style of a Mediterranean village—opened in 1982 and is directly across William Hilton Parkway from Palmetto Dunes. Leamington, covering 400 acres within Palmetto Dunes, is a private community with security gates that's centered on the Arthur Hills golf course. Development of this area was begun in 1986. You'll find the Palmetto Dunes sales office at the entrance to the community, which is off William Hilton Parkway near mile marker 8. The phone number is (843) 842-1111.

Palmetto Hall Plantation

Palmetto Hall is a golf-oriented community covering 775 acres in the northern portion of the island. Most of the 500 homesites border the fairways of the plantation's two 18-hole golf courses—the Arthur Hills and Robert Cupp Courses—both of which are open to the public (see listings in this chapter under "Golf"). Started by Greenwood Development Corporation in late 1990, Palmetto Hall offers its residents a 16,000-square-foot clubhouse and an activities center with pools, tennis courts, and a children's playground.

The homes here, all of them single-family residences, reflect the style of the Lowcountry with their verandas, dormers, and colorful shutters. Patio homes start at $225,000, and other residences range up to $600,000. Palmetto Hall is also the site of more than one hundred acres of nature preserves. For information on home sales, call (843) 689-3333. Palmetto Hall's main gate is on Beach City Road about a half mile from the road's intersection with William Hilton Parkway at mile marker 4.

Port Royal Plantation

Living on the beach (or having easy access to it) is the main drawing card of this 1,000-acre community in the northeastern corner of the island. There are 2.5 miles of beach stretching along the plantation on the east and southeast—1.5 miles on the Atlantic Ocean and the rest on Port Royal Sound. The eastern side is the site of the actual Hilton Head, the bluff where English sea captain William Hilton looked out on the sound while exploring the region; it's the spot for which the entire island was eventually named.

Port Royal was one of the island's first planned communities, and the 860 homes within its gates reflect a wide variety of sizes and styles. They range in value from $350,000 to $3 million; most are in the $400,000 to $600,000 range, and those on the oceanfront average about $1.5 million.

Another big attraction at Port Royal is golf. There are three 18-hole courses: Planter's Row, Barony, and Robber's Row, which are open to the public on a rotating basis (see listings in this chapter's Golf section). Residents of the plantation can be members at all three courses. Also out-

side the plantation but considered part of Port Royal resort complex are the Port Royal Racquet Club, which has grass, composition, and hard-surface tennis courts; the 412-room Westin Resort Hilton Head hotel (see listing in this chapter's Accommodations section); and the villas at Island Links, Ocean Palms, Port Royal Village, Royal Dunes, The Links and The Lyons, Crown Reef, and the Barony Beach Club. The property owners' association office is at 10 Coggins Point Road just before the main gate, which is off William Hilton Parkway near mile marker 5. The phone number is (843) 681-5114.

Sea Pines

A Hilton Head architect once called Sea Pines the "daddy rabbit" of planned residential/resort communities. It's an apt description of the largest and oldest of the island's major developments—the first community of its kind in the nation.

Sea Pines covers 5,200 acres on the south end of Hilton Head and was started in 1957. It's the site of the island's first golf course, the Ocean Course, one of three courses in the community, all of which can be played by the public (see Golf in this chapter). The most popular of these courses is the Harbour Town Golf Links, which is the site of the island's biggest annual event, the WorldCom Classic—The Heritage of Golf, a tournament that brings many of the world's best golfers to Hilton Head for four days during April. (See this chapter's "Annual Events" section for more on the WorldCom Classic.) The racquet club has twenty-three courts and offers comprehensive programs of tennis instruction under the direction of former Wimbledon champion Stan Smith.

Sea Pines is the site of Hilton Head's best-known landmark, the maroon-and-white striped lighthouse at the Harbour Town Yacht Basin. Villas, shops, and restaurants ring the basin at Harbour Town; it's one of two marinas in Sea Pines, the other being at South Beach, where you'll find a New England–style village with shops, restaurants, and all sorts of watersports. Both marinas provide access to Calibogue Sound. More shops and eating places are available at the Sea Pines Center.

Within the borders of Sea Pines are a 605-acre nature preserve, 5 miles of beach, the ruins of the Baynard-Stoney Plantation, three swimming pools, the Lawton Stables equestrian center, and a beach club that has an open-air grill, an oceanfront bar, a gift shop, and picnic tables. The community offers 10,000 square feet of meeting space at the Plantation Club Conference Center, the Harbour Town Clubhouse, and the new Harbour Town Conference Center.

Sea Pines has nearly 3,500 single-family homes, with an average value of $387,000. A total of 530 villas and homes are available for rent by vacationers, and the new Inn at Harbour Town provides luxurious accommodations for those seeking a hotel-type setting. To learn more about Sea Pines, visit the reception center at 32 Greenwood Drive or the Web site at www.seapines.com, or call (843) 785-3333 or (800)-SEAPINES. The reception center is right outside the community's main gate, which is on Greenwood Drive just south of the Sea Pines traffic circle.

Shipyard Plantation

Shipyard has a mixture of single-family residences, condominiums, timeshare units, and commercial developments within its 834 acres. There are about 250 residences ranging from patio homes starting at $225,000 to larger houses on golf courses that start at $300,000. The plantation, in the southeastern part of the island, is the site of more than 1,400 villas grouped in twenty different villa regimes.

The Shipyard Golf Club consists of twenty-seven holes on three courses open to the public: Brigantine, Clipper, and Galleon (see Golf). Residents and guests have other forms of recreation available, particularly tennis and the beach. The Van der Meer Shipyard Racquet Club boasts twenty championship courts, and the

> **Insiders' Tip**
> The Harbour Town Lighthouse, Hilton Head's most enduring symbol, stands ninety-three feet tall and is visited by a quarter-million people a year. The observation deck perches sixty-six feet above the base floor of the lighthouse on Calibogue Sound, and you reach it by climbing 110 steps. Completed in 1970, the lighthouse was the first one built on the Atlantic coast in more than 150 years. Flashing a white light every 2.5 seconds, it's a navigational aid for the sound and the Intracoastal Waterway, even though it's not operated by the U.S. government. (It's run by the company that owns Harbour Town.) The structure is open daily from 8 A.M. to dusk.

eastern side of the plantation is on the Atlantic Ocean. Shipyard's ocean side is the site of the 340-room Crowne Plaza Resort Hotel (see this chapter's "Accommodations" section) and a beach club for residents. The plantation is also the home of the Hilton Head Health Institute, a resort for folks seeking to change their lifestyles by learning how to control their

Travelers visiting Hilton Head by boat have their choice of several marinas at which to dock, including the yacht basin at Shelter Cove. PHOTO: RICH WITTISH

weight, reduce stress, and become more physically fit.

Ironically, Shipyard has no marina; its name is derived from the cotton plantation that once occupied the site of the community. Administrative offices are at 10 Shipyard Drive, and the phone number is (843) 785-3310. They're just outside the main gate, which is off William Hilton Parkway near mile marker 10. There's a Web site at www.spoa.com.

Spanish Wells

Spanish Wells and a development associated with it, Wells East, are about 80 percent built. There are some 200 single-family lots at this 350-acre community on the western portion of the island; the houses at Spanish Wells are on lots of at least one acre. Residences range in value from the low $300,000s to $2 million-plus.

Spanish Wells is the most secluded of the island's communities; it's at the end of Spanish Wells Road, nearly 3 miles from William Hilton Parkway. The private golf club has a nine-hole course, two tennis courts, and a swimming pool that was opened for use in summer 1999. Many of the homes at Spanish Wells are on Calibogue Sound or Broad Creek, and those on Brahms Point, a narrow finger of land at the southwestern reaches of the community, have views of both bodies of water. The community derives its name from the wells from which Spanish explorers drew fresh water while visiting Hilton Head. Also of historical note is the fact that Spanish Wells is the site of Battery Holbrook, a Civil War gun emplacement. To learn more about Spanish Wells, call the property owners' association at (843) 842-4138.

Wexford Plantation

The emphasis is on privacy at Wexford, where rentals are prohibited and admittance is open only to residents, their guests, and prospective homebuyers. This golf and yachting community covers 525 acres near the middle of the island. All of the 459 lots at Wexford are sold, and about 270 homes had been built as of summer 2001, most of them two-story, British Colonial–style houses valued from $500,000 to $5 million.

About a third of the homes are on the plantation's thirty-five-and-a-half-acre harbor, which winds through the center of the community and is lock controlled to keep the water calm and at a minimum of eight feet deep. The harbor, with slips accommodating yachts up to seventy-five feet long, provides access to Broad Creek. Most of the other homes are on Wexford's eighteen-hole golf course, a layout by Willard Byrd that's reserved solely for members and their guests and was recently restored to its original design. Other amenities take the form of a harborside clubhouse graced with pink Georgian marble and Tiffany glass skylights; a pool with a patio that overlooks the water; six tennis courts, four of them lighted; and a croquet lawn. Sales offices are at 2 Town Center Court and can be reached by calling (843) 686–8800 or (800) 345–2392. Wexford's main entrance is off William Hilton Parkway near mile marker 10.

Windmill Harbour

Designed for boaters and other folks who love being around the water, Windmill Harbour covers 172 acres in the northwestern portion of Hilton Head. Unlike the island's other planned communities, Windmill Harbour has no golf course, but it does have a fifteen-and-a-half-acre yacht basin with 261 boat slips, the largest in the area by more than one hundred slips. The harbor, the site of the South Carolina Yacht Club, has a lock system that keeps tides and currents to a minimum; the lack of movement of water also inhibits the growth of barnacles on the bottom of boats, allowing their owners to save on maintenance costs. The harbor lies on Calibogue Sound, which is part of the Intracoastal Waterway.

Eighty percent of the homesites at Windmill Harbour have views of the water. Among the residences at Windmill Harbour are estates on lots of an acre or more, villas, patio homes, and condomini-ums, all of them reflecting architectural styles seen in the historic district of Charleston and the South Carolina Low-country. Prices for condos start at $139,000; homes run from $275,000 to $1.5 million.

Residents seeking recreation other than boating can find it at the community's sports center, which provides an Olympic-size lap pool, seven clay tennis courts, and extensive workout facilities. The elegant building that serves as headquarters for the yacht club overlooks the harbor and offers a meeting place where members of the club can dine and attend cookouts, oyster roasts, and parties. Although Windmill Harbour is mainly a private community, the yacht basin is open to the boating public, and residents can rent out their dwellings for periods of sixty days or more. Shorter-term rentals are prohibited. The sales office is at 2 Harbour Passage Patio inside the main gate, which is off William Hilton Parkway just after you cross the bridges to the island. You can reach these offices by calling (843) 681–5600. You can also see more about Windmill Harbour at www.richardsongroupllc.com.

Accommodations

When you vacation at Hilton Head, you have the option of staying at hotels, motels, villas, or private homes that are being rented out by their owners. The hotels and motels range from modern, well-maintained establishments on the island's main thoroughfares to full-blown resorts situated in or adjacent to Hilton Head's luxurious golf communities. The villas are fully furnished condominiums set in apartment buildings and town houses, many of them with pools and locations close to beaches, golf clubs, and tennis courts.

There's plenty to choose from—Hilton Head has more than 3,000 hotel and motel rooms, 6,000 villa units, 1,000 time-share units, and an array of rental homes ranging from oceanfront mansions to laid-back cottages. We've provided a run-down of hotels and motels—places that offer nightly accommodations; for information on villas, time-shares, and private homes, which usually rent for longer-term stays (anywhere from three nights to two weeks), we suggest calling one of the island's numerous central reservations services. Among these are the Hilton Head Condo Hotline (843-785-2939, 800-258-5852), Hilton Head Accommodations and Golf Hotline (843-686-6662, 800-444-4772; vacation@hiltonheadusa.com), and Hilton Head Island Villa & Hotel Reservations (843-842-6212, 800-845-8602).

In general, rates for accommodations are higher from the end of April through September, although some places raise their prices starting in February, and others lower them after Labor Day. Call ahead to see what's available (well ahead if you're planning on staying during the summer, especially on weekends) and ask about special deals—many of the larger establishments have a variety of vacation packages from which to choose. Be aware that some motels and hotels will give you a lower rate if you stay with them early in the week when they might be struggling to fill up their rooms.

Most of the hotels and motels we surveyed don't allow pets and have nonsmoking and wheelchair-accessible rooms; we've noted exceptions and have also included a symbol with each entry denoting a price range for the average one-night stay, in season, for two adults. These prices do not include tax, gratuities, and add-on amenities such as room service.

Price-Code Key

$	$95 or lower
$$	$96 to $125
$$$	$126 to $150
$$$$	$151 to $215
$$$$$	$216 or more

Unless we've indicated otherwise, you'll have to pay to play golf or tennis at the resort where you're staying. Most places have packages or special deals involving these sports, and you should inquire about these if you intend to play. The following properties are listed alphabetically.

Adventure Inn Beach Resort and Rentals
41 S. Forest Beach Drive
Hilton Head, SC
(843) 785-5151, (800) 845-9500
www.hihislandsc.com
$$

Relax poolside under the graceful branches of the spreading live oak tree, take an early morning, guided walking tour of the beach, or play tennis for free at the Adventure Inn. This oceanfront establishment—which has been creating pleasant dreams for vacationers since 1963—offers a full slate of activities geared to youngsters from 9 A.M. to 5 P.M. Monday through Friday during the summer months. Some of the programs (such as scavenger hunts) are free, and there are fees for others (such as poolside bingo and beach-bag designing).

Tennis is complimentary on two courts across South Forest Beach Drive from the inn, health club privileges for all guests older than fourteen are provided, and discounted golf packages for nineteen courses on and off the island are offered. Although there is a five-night minimum stay in the majority of the units during summer, daily rentals are available. Some oceanfront efficiency rooms are well suited to families—each has a queen-size bed, a queen sleeper sofa, and a kitchenette.

Fitzgerald's, a restaurant serving dinner seven days a week during summer and every day except Sunday in the off-season, is on the premises. Because the units here are individually owned time-shares, there are no nonsmoking or wheelchair-accessible accommodations.

Best Western Hilton Head Ocean Resort and Spa
36 S. Forest Beach Drive
Hilton Head, SC
(843) 842-3100, (800) 535-3248
$$$

You'll be directly across the street from the beach when you stay at this 140-room, full-service hotel, and less than half a mile south of the Coligny traffic circle and the shops and restaurants of Coligny Plaza. Guests are entitled to complimentary visits to a nearby property to use the indoor pool, the hot tub, the racquetball courts, and fitness center.

The Ocean Resort features two outdoor swimming pools, a fitness center, rooms with minirefrigerators and microwave ovens, and Mulligan's, an onsite restaurant that sports a golf motif.

Comfort Inn & Suites
2 Tanglewood Drive
Hilton Head, SC
(843) 842–6662, (800) 228–5150
www.comfortinnhiltonhead.com
$$

You can walk to the beach in five minutes from the five-story Comfort Inn, but if you'd rather not hoof it, you can hitch a ride on the hotel's beach buggy, which runs continuously from 10 A.M. to 4 P.M. during the warm months. If freshwater activities are more your style, take a dip in the hotel pool, where the surroundings have a Hawaiian flair, or zip down the water slides at the adjacent Water Fun Park, where hotel guests are given a discount.

The 153-room Comfort Inn, situated on six acres graced by three lagoons, sits well back from South Forest Beach Drive, a few blocks from the Coligny traffic circle. The hotel began as a Days Inn in 1987, was reborn as a Comfort Inn in the early '90s, and was totally renovated in 1999. Guests can partake of deluxe continental breakfasts from 7 to 10 A.M. in the registration building, which also houses 900 square feet of meeting space. Some of the rooms have refrigerators, coffeemakers, and microwave ovens, and there's a store nearby where you can purchase groceries. Golf packages are available. The hotel accepts pets for a fee of $25.

Crowne Plaza Resort
130 Shipyard Drive
Hilton Head, SC
(843) 842–2400, (800) 334–1881
www.crowneplazaresort.com
$$$$$

Built in a U-shape on the ocean in Shipyard, the Crowne Plaza opens onto a courtyard filled with subtropical gardens, extensive green spaces, and lagoons crossed by graceful wooden bridges. One bridge is a favorite spot for couples saying their wedding vows, and if you plan to get hitched there, you might consider enlisting the services of Crowne Plaza's notary public. The large courtyard is also the location of a pool, outdoor hot tub, toddler's pool, and Dockers, which serves light fare and drinks.

Amble down to the beach, and you'll pass by the beach snack bar, which specializes in snow cones and hot dogs. Nearby is the hotel's 7,000-square-foot outdoor pavilion, which is popular for meetings, dinners, and those weddings we referred to. The Crowne Plaza has 340 rooms, including twenty-five suites, with views of either the island, the courtyard, or the ocean. Portz restaurant offers fine dining in the evening, and you can get breakfast and lunch indoors or outdoors at Brellas.

The hotel's leisure activities department operates Camp Castaway, a structured and supervised program for children 3 to 12. Among the many activities provided are shell hunts and turtle feedings for the youngest kids, games on the beach and in the pool for those 6 to 12, as well as bike tours. Fees for a full day of fun are $50 per child; children 3 to 5 are restricted to morning sessions, which are $35 per child. Afternoon sessions are $30. Adults seeking opportunities to exercise can find them at the Crowne Plaza's fully equipped fitness center and adjacent indoor pool and at Shipyard's golf courses and tennis courts.

Disney's Hilton Head Island Resort
22 Harbourside Lane
Hilton Head, SC
(843) 341–4100, (407) 939–7540
www.dvc.disney.go.com
$$$$$

The Disney folks are famous for creating atmosphere, and they've done it again at their Hilton Head Island Resort, where the Live Oak Lodge and 102 villas have the look of Lowcountry hunting and fishing cabins of the 1950s. These are cabins with style, though, rustic but rich with natural-wood accents and first-class reproductions of country-style furniture. There are interesting touches such as pine-log headboards and a reminder or two that you're staying at a Disney property—we found the initials "W. D." carved in one end of a wooden bench in an alcove of a villa, and there were two hearts bearing the names "Mickey" and "Minnie" scratched into the other end.

Accommodations take the form of studios and one-, two-, and three-bedroom villas. The villas have whirlpool tubs and full kitchens. The rustic theme is carried throughout the resort, which was built in 1996 and covers wooded Longview Island, a sixteen-acre tract between Shelter Cove Harbour and Broad Creek. Guests splash and sun at a pool called the Big Dipper Swimming Hole, buy groceries at the Broad Creek Mercantile general store, and gather for activities at Community Hall.

There's no restaurant on the premises, but there are several at nearby Shelter Cove, and there's Tide Me Over, which is near the swimming hole and has a quick-service pickup window where you can get hamburgers, hot dogs, and chicken sandwiches. Disney provides oceanside enjoyment for its guests via its 13,000-square-foot private beach house at Palmetto Dunes, a facility that has an Olympic-size pool, a snack bar, and children's play area, plus the beach. The beach house is 1.5 miles from the resort, and daily shuttle service is provided. The resort also offers the Disney Discovery Club, a special program for children ages 6 to 12 that places emphasis on learning about the environment through activities such as bicycling and crabbing. There's a version of the club for kids 3 to 5, too. Adult activities include the Longview Cooking Club. Program fees vary.

Fairfield Inn by Marriott
9 Marina Side Drive
Hilton Head, SC
(843) 842–4800, (800) TEE–OFF4
$

Each of the fourteen suites at the Fairfield Inn has a nice touch—French doors separating the bedroom from the large sitting room. The other 105 rooms at the three-story motel off U.S. 278 just past mile marker 9 have king-size and double beds, and there is a pool. Guests in quest of another form of recreation might opt to play the Pirates Island miniature golf course, which is adjacent to the Fairfield. The motel's complimentary continental breakfast awaits guests in a dining room off the lobby from 6 to 9:30 A.M. The Fairfield Inn is centrally located and near a slew of restaurants and shops.

Hampton Inn
1 Dillon Road
Hilton Head, SC
(843) 681–7900, (800) HAMPTON
http://hampton-inn.net
$

If you're not particularly interested in going to the beach, the Hampton Inn might be for you. This two-story, 125-room motel just off U.S. 278 at mile marker 5 caters to business travelers and people visiting the island for the golf of it. And, heck, if you do desire to take a dip in the ocean, the Atlantic is only a little more than a mile away at the Folly Field Beach access. There's an outdoor pool for those who want to stay close by to do their swimming, a putting green, and a well-equipped exercise room for the fitness-minded. The Hampton—which was completely renovated in 1997–1998—offers deluxe, complimentary continental breakfasts from 6 to 10 A.M., and free copies of *USA Today*. Some of the rooms have kitchenettes with microwave ovens and small refrigerators, and some have whirlpool baths. A special feature of the Hampton is the " afternoon snack" of fresh-baked cookies and lemonade.

Hilton Head Island Hilton Resort
23 Ocean Lane
Hilton Head, SC
(843) 842–8000, (800) 845–8001
www.hiltonheadhilton.com
$$$$$

Open hallways catching ocean breezes and lagoons winding their way through lush foliage give this beachfront Hilton Hotel at Palmetto Dunes a semitropical aura. All guest rooms and many of the common spaces were redecorated during a $5 million renovation completed in mid-April 1999. The extralarge rooms have equally spacious balconies, each with at least a partial view of the beach and sea. All 323 rooms have kitchenettes and amenities such as ceiling fans in dining areas and separate vanities in bathrooms. The five-story hotel is built in a horseshoe shape that opens onto the beach, and the nooks and crannies of the spacious garden within the horseshoe harbor small courtyards and rambling wooden decks.

The ground-floor Activity Center houses three eating places—the Palmetto Cafe, the Deli Pizza, and Mostly Seafood—and the Regatta Lounge, which serves as a sports bar in the afternoons and early evenings and a nightclub after 9 P.M. Monday through Saturday. Guests can also eat lunch at the Buoy Bar and Grill at the main pool. There's also an adults-only pool for those seeking a quieter atmosphere. For more relaxation, try one of the two oceanfront whirlpool baths or the saunas in the men's and women's locker rooms of the fitness center.

The hotel offers special rates for golf and tennis at the courses and courts at Palmetto Dunes and special activities for children via Vacation Station. This day and evening camp program is for kids ages 4 through 11 and is priced at $35 per child for a full-day session, $20 per child for a half-day session, and $30 per child for an evening session. The Hilton has 14,000 square feet of meeting space and a full-scale conference center, and there's a shuttle from the hotel to all the activities Palmetto Dunes and nearby Shelter Cove Harbour have to offer.

Hilton Head Marriott Beach & Golf Resort
1 Hotel Circle
Hilton Head, SC
(843) 686–8400, (800) 228–9290
$$$$$

With its 505 rooms and 41,000 square feet of meeting space, this Marriott is billed as the largest luxury oceanfront resort between Atlantic City, New Jersey, and Palm Beach, Florida. Even so, this ten-story hotel at Palmetto Dunes has the comfortable feel of a place where guests are kicking back and going on vacation. It's not unusual to see youngsters padding through the spacious lobby in their flip-flops on their way to a day at the pool or to take part in the activities provided by the Adventure Club, which is for kids ages 6 to 12. The camp provides fun (including nature walks and sand sculpting) via half-day and full-day programs available from Memorial Day to Labor Day. Rates are $30 for morning sessions; $40 for afternoon sessions, which usually include an off-site activity such as kayaking; and $60 for the entire day.

The pool is Olympic size, and there's also a one-foot-deep pool for toddlers. Poolside, guests will find Quinn's II restaurant, which serves salads and sandwiches, and the Point Comfort bar, specializing in frozen drinks. For indoor dining, there's The Cafe for breakfast, lunch, and dinner, and Conroy's for dinner and Sunday brunch. Conroy's Lounge overlooks the ocean and offers nightly entertainment. If you're in need of snacks, try The Grocery, an offbeat little convenience store on the hotel's lower level. Other shopping opportunities take the form of a large W. H. Smith gift shop and a swimwear shop. If you crave exercise, you can work out in the Marriott's well-equipped fitness center, play a round of golf at one of five courses within walking or shuttle distance, or hit the courts at the Palmetto Dunes Tennis Center.

Holiday Inn Express
40 Waterside Drive
Hilton Head, SC
(843) 842–8888, (888) 813–2560
www.hiexpress.com/exhiltonheadsc
$$$

Although the Holiday Inn Express sits only a block off busy Pope Avenue, the three-story hotel affords its guests peace and quiet because of the wooded areas surrounding it. Rooms on the rear side of the inn overlook a large lagoon.

Another drawing card for the ninety-one-room hotel is its proximity to Forest Beach, which is a five-minute walk; for those wishing to take a dip and stay closer to home, there's an inviting pool at the inn. The hotel also provides guests with free continental breakfasts each morning from 6:30 to 9:30 A.M. Rooms at this inn, whose stuccoed exterior gives it a Spanish look, offer three different arrangements: with a king-size bed, with two queens or two doubles, and some of the rooms with kings have recliners.

Holiday Inn Oceanfront
1 S. Forest Beach Drive
Hilton Head, SC
(843) 785–5126, (800) HOLIDAY
www.hihiltonhead.com
$$$$

Life's just beachy at the Holiday Inn Oceanfront, where the meandering, free-form pool is only steps away from the white sand of the Hilton Head strand. The contemporary decor of the inn's 202 rooms (all of which have refrigerators and all of which open onto interior hallways) carry out the beach motif, as do the five-story motel's eating and drinking places— Grouper's restaurant, which has plenty of windows and great views of the ocean; the Island Eatery, which stands on a concrete peninsula jutting into the pool and serves lunch fare from 11 A.M. to 6 P.M.; and the

poolside Tiki Hut beach bar, which offers live entertainment. Large-scale renovations were expected to be completed in 2002, and additions include an oceanview banquet room that caters to receptions and meetings of up to 400 guests.

The inn offers numerous recreational activities, some of them free and many intended for the younger set. A children's program that runs from Memorial Day to Labor Day provides kids with activities such as relays on the beach, sand dollar painting, and underwater treasure hunts. The inn also has a children's pool, kids' playground and Dolly the Dolphin, a mascot who greets guests and interacts with youngsters.

The Inn at Harbour Town
7 Lighthouse Lane
Hilton Head, SC
(843) 785–3333, (800) 732–7463
www.seapines.com
$$$$

You won't find any soft drink machines at this luxurious sixty-room hotel in Sea Pines; butlers do the vending instead. Each floor of this new inn has a butler who'll perform a multitude of tasks for guests, from bringing drinks and sandwiches to seeing that business papers are typed, shoes are shined, and pants are pressed. The butlers, some of them wearing Scottish attire in keeping with Harbour Town's Highlands heritage, are a big part of the concept of patterning The Inn at Harbour Town after small, fine European hotels. That concept extends to the rich furnishings of the common areas and guest rooms and the trappings of the bathrooms, which feature soaking tubs, walk-in showers, and lots of marble.

The inn, which opened in late November 2000, also has much to offer in the way of recreation. The hotel overlooks the first tee of the famed Harbour Town Golf Links, and the Sea Pines Racquet Club is a short stroll from the front door. Guests have access to the pool next to the Racquet Club and can take advantage of a complimentary shuttle service that will take them anywhere in Sea Pines at any time of day.

The inn serves a continental breakfast from 7 to 10 each morning at a cost of $8 per person, and there are lots of restaurants nearby, including the Heritage Grill and the eateries at the Harbour Town yacht basin.

Main Street Inn
2200 Main Street
Hilton Head, SC
(843) 681–3001, (800) 471–3001
www.mainstreet.com
$$$$

A couple seeking a spot for a romantic getaway will find it at the elegant Main Street Inn off U.S. 278 between mile markers 3 and 4. The thirty-three rooms are luxuriously appointed with classic furnishings: wooden armoires handmade on Hilton Head, beds adorned with Italian linens and goose-down pillows and comforters, and baths featuring pedestal sinks and Italian marble floors and shower walls. The Deluxe Queen rooms have fireplaces and balconies large enough for a wrought iron table that's a perfect spot for breakfast.

The inn's crowning glories are the four Courtyard King rooms with their bay windows, window seats, whirlpool tubs, glassed-in showers, and pine floors fashioned from the 150-year-old beams of a Lowcountry mill. In each King, French doors in the bathroom open onto an intimate courtyard abounding with fig vines, fruit trees, and jasmine. Guests staying in rooms on the upper two floors can step outside onto wide verandas complete with rocking chairs. From there, you'll see the Charleston-style gardens of the courtyard and a pool designed for swimming laps; the view beyond is of the lush fifteenth green and sixteenth fairway of Hilton Head Plantation's Bear Creek Golf Course and of the forested wetlands of a nature preserve.

Your stay includes European-style buffet breakfasts served in the dining room/library, the dining room/lounge, or the courtyard. Much of the fare is prepared by the inn's own baker. If all this isn't relaxing enough, try a massage, which is available on-site.

The Quality Inn & Suites
200 Museum Street
Hilton Head, SC
(843) 681–3655, (800) 995–3928
www.qualityinn.com/hotel/sc208
$$

Located on the rapidly developing north end of the island, The Quality Inn boasts many of the features you might expect to find at a full-service hotel. Among them are the Coconuts Comedy Club, which is available for private parties; a putting green; 2,000 square feet of meeting space; and same-day valet, laundry, and dry cleaning service. Also, there's a restaurant adjacent to the motel, a Shoney's serving breakfast, lunch, and dinner. The 127-room motel, which is on U.S. 278 at mile marker 3, was completely renovated in 1999–2000.

Red Roof Inn Hilton Head
5 Regency Parkway
Hilton Head, SC
(843) 686–6808, (800) THE–ROOF
$

This 111-room motel just off U.S. 278 at mile marker 9 was thoroughly renovated between September 1997 and March 1998. The two-story inn offers rooms with king-size beds and California kings (they're a little smaller than standard kings), along with four spacious suites complete with minirefrigerators and wet bars. According to the management, the emphasis here is on making guests "feel good and giving them value for their dollar." The inn is adjacent to Crabby Nick's restaurant, which serves dinner. The motel provides complimentary continental breakfasts from 6 to 9:30 A.M. in a room off the lobby. A heated pool in an enclosed shaded area provides a spot where guests can relax or get some exercise.

Residence Inn by Marriott
12 Park Lane
Hilton Head, SC
(843) 686–5700
www.residenceinnhhi.com
$$$

The only all-suite hotel on the island rambles over a quiet wooded area in the Central Park office complex just off U.S. 278 between mile markers 9 and 10. The centrally located Residence Inn provides full-scale continental breakfasts in the lobby from 7 to 9:30 A.M. Each of the 156 suites has a balcony and fully equipped kitchen including a full-size refrigerator, and the King- and bilevel loft suites have wood-burning fireplaces.

Loft suites are designed for entertaining, family gatherings, and romantic getaways—each has an enlarged dining area, a sleeper sofa, and a loft-type bedroom with its own bathroom. Complimentary social hours are offered starting at 5 P.M. Monday through Thursday. Golf packages are available, and there's a putting green near the pool. Guests can play tennis for free (using the hotel's rackets and balls, if needed) on two lighted courts on the backside of the property, which is also the site of a tree-shaded playground and picnic area.

South Beach Marina Inn
232 S. Sea Pines Drive
Hilton Head, SC
(843) 671–6498, (800) 367–3909
www.southbeachvillage.com
$$$

Were it not for the distinctly Southern foliage and marshlands within view, you might think you're in New England when you stay at the South Beach Marina Inn. This charming, seventeen-room hotel is part of a small complex of shops and restaurants patterned after a fishing village on Nantucket Island, Massachusetts. The rooms of the inn, a nightly rental property at Sea Pines, reflect the Yankee atmosphere via the highly polished heart-of-pine floors, brass beds, and colorful rag rugs.

All of the one- and two-bedroom accommodations have kitchenettes, and most have separate, cozy living rooms that will make you feel as if you've found a second home. Although the inn is deep within Sea Pines, the village and marina offer just about everything a vacationer would need. You could park your car and not leave, except to play a round of golf on the nearest course, which is a five-minute drive. At your front door is the marina on Braddock's Cove, which offers various recreational opportunities for hire—Jet Skiing, boat rentals, charter fishing, parasailing, instruction in windsurfing, and sailing lessons. Also, just outside your doorstep, you will find a pool, a dozen tennis courts, and 15 miles of paved trails for hiking, bicycling, jogging, and in-line skating. You can walk to the beach in three to four minutes, and there are six eating places within the village. All rooms are on the second floor, and there are no non-smoking or handicapped accommodations. Pets are allowed in some units, but there is a $50 cleanup fee.

Westin Resort Hilton Head
2 Grasslawn Avenue
Hilton Head, SC
(843) 681–4000, (800) WESTIN1
www.westinhiltonhead.com
$$$$$

The architecture of the Westin radiates the charm of a classic, turn-of-the-century seaside hotel and is designed to complement the historic cities of Savannah and Charleston. A feeling of Southern hospitality carries throughout the five-story oceanfront hotel at Port Royal Plantation. The lobby features polished woods, palms, elaborate chandeliers, and Asian porcelains, and a mix of comfortable seating offers an ambience characteristic of the homes of the Old South. The Gazebo Lounge looks out on the hotel's spacious courtyard, where swans swim in a pond set amid lush foliage. In the cooler months, the lounge and its comfy drawing-room furniture and wood-burning fireplace beckon to guests. When the weather's warm, the courtyard is the place to be. You'll find two pools (a round pool and a lap pool) and extensive wooden decks where you can sunbathe, have a bite to eat at Turtles Beach Bar & Grill, and relax in rocking chairs and enjoy the scenery. A band often provides entertainment by the pool during summer afternoons, and you can get a massage at the water's edge if you're so inclined. There is also an indoor pool with a hydraulic lift for the physically impaired. Take advantage of the Westin Resort Health Club with its aerobics room, sauna, steam room, and exercise rooms filled with state-of-the-art strength-training equipment.

Those seeking outdoor recreation can find it at the nearby Port Royal Golf Club, which has three championship courses (see the Golf section of this chapter), or at the Port Royal Racquet Club, which offers grass, clay, and hard-surface courts. A shuttle service is provided from the hotel to both sites. For youngsters ages 4 to 12,

Camp Wackatoo provides activities such as Looney Lawn Games and crabbing and shrimping. Awesome Jim and his Awesome Adventures beach camp offers juniors 9 to 16 the opportunity to learn kayaking and sailing among other beach activities. Both camps operate from Memorial Day weekend through Labor Day weekend, and fees for a day are $55 for the first child in a family and $35 for succeeding kids; a half-day at Camp Wackatoo is $40.

There's fine dining during the evening at Westin's Barony Grill; casual dining and cocktails in the late afternoon and evening at Turtles, which overlooks the ocean; and family dining throughout the day at the Carolina Cafe, which features a nightly seafood buffet, an eighteen-foot-long dessert table and Sunday brunch. The Westin recently completed a $10 million renovation of its 412 guest rooms (including the resort's thirty suites), meeting space, lobby, and fitness center.

Poolside is where you'll find many of the guests at island hotels, such as the Westin Resort Hilton Head.
PHOTO: RICH WITTISH

Restaurants

The Yellow Pages of the Hilton Head telephone book contain nearly thirty pages of listings and advertisements for restaurants—make no mistake, there's a lot to choose from here in terms of eateries and cuisine. In this section, we look at some of the island's more popular restaurants in an attempt to provide you with selections offering a variety of foods in a variety of atmospheres at a variety of prices.

All the restaurants discussed here serve alcoholic beverages, and most have areas where smoking is allowed; we've noted the exceptions. Many of these eating places either recommend or require that you make reservations, and we've pointed out the ones that do. All take most major credit cards. Listings are in alphabetical order.

Price-Code Key

To give you an idea of the prices at these restaurants, we've provided a dollar-sign code showing what you can expect to pay for a dinner for two minus alcoholic beverages, appetizers, desserts, taxes, and tip.

$	$30 and lower
$$	$31 to $35
$$$	$36 to $40
$$$$	$41 to $50
$$$$$	$51 and higher

Alexander's
76 Queens Folly Road
Hilton Head, SC
(843) 785-4999
$$$$

Located on a lagoon at Palmetto Dunes, Alexander's provides casual but dressy dining in three settings: an enclosed porch, a wine bar adorned with a fireplace, and a cozy dining room. Established in 1977, the restaurant serves dinner daily and specializes in seafood, including salmon Oscar and the Island Seafood Collection—a combination of fresh broiled fish, oysters Rockefeller and

Insiders' Tip

A good source of information concerning the island's eating places is *Hilton Head Island* Restaurants magazine, which you should be able to find at rental villas, hotels and motels, shops, grocery stores, and other locations, including the chamber of commerce building off William Hilton Parkway near mile marker 8. This free booklet of some 150 pages has listings for more than one hundred restaurants and reprints of menus. The centerfold of this guide is a map that will help you locate these eateries.

Savannah, shrimp, stuffed crab Daufuskie, and scallops. If you enjoy wine, you have your choice of one hundred different bottles. Reservations are suggested.

The Barony Grill
2 Grasslawn Avenue
Hilton Head, SC
(843) 681-4000
$$$$$

With its cozy hunt club atmosphere, The Barony Grill provides an ideal setting in which to celebrate special occasions. High ceilings, brick archways, comfortable chairs, and elegant table settings create an ambience that's refined yet relaxed.

A special feature is the wine-tasting room, where diners can find assistance in selecting the wines that will best complement their meals. The room—with its sand-colored stucco walls, polished wood floors, and wrought iron wine racks—is also a spot where patrons can simply enjoy the experience of tasting various wines. To further aid in choosing wines, the Barony's menu lists a recommended wine with each of its entrees.

The Barony specializes in chops and pasta, and among the favorite dishes of diners are the beef Wellington, the double-cut pork chop, the sea bass and pasta, and the grilled veal chop, which is accompanied by baby green lentils and Vidalia onion rings. For starters, there are appetizers such as lobster bisque, grilled portobello mushrooms, and the onion soup, which features a three-cheese melt. Desserts, including the chocolate-covered, banana-rum cream cheese cake, are hard to miss—they're displayed on a large marble and iron table situated at the entrance.

The Barony—located on the first floor of the Westin Resort Hilton Head at Port Royal Plantation—serves dinner Tuesday through Saturday and is closed during December, January, and February. This restaurant is completely nonsmoking.

The Big Bamboo Cafe
Coligny Plaza
Hilton Head, SC
(843) 686–3443
$

According to the legend of The Big Bamboo that appears on the front of the cafe's menu, this restaurant on the ocean side of Coligny Plaza shopping center has been constructed as closely as possible to the configurations of the original Big Bamboo, a bar and grill opened on the Pacific island of Tarawa in 1944 by ex-fighter pilot Jimmy Phipps. From the bamboo of the bar to the thatched palm fronds and camouflage netting of the ceiling to the World War II regalia tacked on the walls, Hilton Head's version of The Big Bamboo reflects the feel of the real thing....If

there had been a real thing, that is; for, you see, The Big Bamboo of the Pacific is a figment of the imagination of a former owner, albeit one that has been brought vividly to life on Hilton Head.

What is real about this eighty-five-seat dining room and bar is the atmosphere of fun that has been created; that and the interesting mix of dishes available, ranging from the roasted turkey sandwiches to the barbecue ribs, Greek pasta, and seafood fettucine. Harder to believe is an item called the "war dog"—a hot dog stuffed with cheddar cheese, wrapped with bacon, dipped in beer batter and fried, then tucked in a toasted roll and smothered with chili, cheddar cheese, and onions. Wow! Or as Jimmy Phipps would have put it, "Whew!" The Big Bamboo—where you can gaze on a mix of authentic memorabilia and reproductions from the 1940s while listening to the Big Band music of that era—puts out the welcome mat daily for fighter jocks and other customers seeking dinner.

The Brick Oven Cafe
25 Park Plaza
Office Park Road
Hilton Head, SC
(843) 686–2233
$

Gourmet pizzas from the brick oven and "Things to be Shared" give this restaurant in Park Plaza on Office Park Road an identity all its own. Among the pizzas on the menu are scampi, five cheese, and mesquite grilled chicken varieties, but you can also create your own. Dining parties are encouraged to share two or three dishes designed for that experience, including sesame-crusted tuna, calamari, and tempura chicken fingers. The cafe, in existence since December 1996, serves dinner in two areas accommodating a total of eighty people, including the Velvet Room, where live entertainment is provided on Saturday and Sunday nights. The wine list is extensive and offers numerous good values.

Cafe at Wexford
Village at Wexford
1000 William Hilton Parkway
Hilton Head, SC
(843) 686–5969
$$$

The food and atmosphere of a cafe in the French countryside await you at this restaurant in the Village at Wexford near mile marker 10 on William Hilton Parkway. Wood floors and lots of brickwork give the sixty-seat cafe an intimate aura. The menu offers a wide selection of country French cuisine; among the most popular entrees are the veal sweetbreads, which are sautéed in cream sauce with mushrooms and strips of ham; the cherry-glazed roast duckling; and the potato-onion crusted fillet of grouper. For an appetizer, try the pâté de foie gras. The cafe serves lunch Monday through Friday, dinner Tuesday through Sunday, and brunch on Saturday and Sunday. Reservations for dinner are required.

Cafe Europa
160 Lighthouse Road
Hilton Head, SC
(843) 671–3399
$$$$

Excellent views of Calibogue Sound are available from just about all of the 140 seats at this restaurant. It's at the boaters' entrance to the Harbour Town Yacht Basin at Sea Pines, meaning the Cafe Europa is a wonderful place to watch a sunset. Linen-covered tables adorned with candles, the awning-covered ceiling, and large picture windows give the restaurant an ambience that's airy and upscale. The cuisine is continental with an emphasis on seafood. Customer favorites are the baked shrimp Daufuskie; the salmon Southern style, which comes with stone-ground grits and simmered greens; the Cuban fire-roasted tenderloin of pork, which features a mango barbecue sauce and smashed sweet potatoes; and the strip sirloin, which is accompanied by Lulu's smashed potatoes. Cafe Europa also has outdoor dining in an area at the base of the Harbour Town Lighthouse and overlooking the marina.

The cafe serves breakfast, lunch, and dinner seven days a week but is closed from November through mid-February. It's completely nonsmoking, and reservations are recommended.

Charleston's
8 New Orleans Road
Hilton Head, SC
(843) 785–5008
$$$$

The food is continental with a Southern slant at this elegant restaurant near the Sea Pines traffic circle. Among the seafood selections are the pecan-crusted shrimp, the pan-fried flounder, and the benne wafer-crusted sea bass, which comes with country-ham grits. Filet mignon, prime rib, and rotisserie roasted chicken are among the other entrees, and there are a host of intriguing appetizers, including Isle of Palms eggrolls, Sullivan Island crab cakes, and oysters Florentine. Approximately sixty wines are available by the glass.

As you might expect from its name, the restaurant reflects the charm of the captivating city to the north of Hilton Head; once seated, it's not hard to convince yourself that you're dining in one of the stately homes of Charleston. The marble flooring of the entryway and the granite bar add to the ambience. Charleston's serves dinner on a daily basis and offers brunch on Sunday.

Charlie's L'Etoile Verte
1000 Plantation Center
Hilton Head, SC
(843) 785–9277
$$$

Ask an islander where to eat on Hilton Head, and the first word out of his or her mouth is liable to be "Charlie's." This busy little bistro in Plantation Center off William Hilton Parkway near mile marker 8 serves lunch and dinner Tuesday through Saturday, specializing in more than a dozen types of fish cooked in many ways.

Charlie's is not a French restaurant, despite the name (*L'Etoile Verte* means "green star" in French); this eclectic-looking cafe serves, as its affable owner Charlie Golson puts it, "whatever we feel like cooking," "we" being Golson, his entree chef, and his dessert and appetizer chef. The three of them put their heads together and brainstorm during the day, a process that creates a menu that's different each night, written in longhand, and copied for distribution to diners.

Among the most popular selections are the chicken salad, Cobb salad, rack of lamb, pompano with mango sauce, and triggerfish in Parmesan crust.

Golson grew up in Savannah, apprenticed himself to a French chef for a year in 1970, and eventually moved to Hilton Head to serve as the chef at the now-defunct Hilton Head Inn. He opened Charlie's in 1984 and has been enthralling islanders with his culinary artistry ever since. His eighty-seat restaurant is completely nonsmoking.

CQ's Restaurant
140 Lighthouse Road
Hilton Head, SC
(843) 671–2779
$$$$

Housed in the first structure built at Harbour Town in Sea Pines, this restaurant is filled with memorabilia reflecting the history of the South Carolina Lowcountry, Hilton Head, and Sea Pines, in particular. Modeled after a Lowcountry rice barn, the two-story building was originally an artist's studio, and many of its features are authentic—the flooring was part of a church in nearby Jasper County, roof beams were taken from an old Savannah warehouse, and the spindles on the staircase reportedly once graced the interior of a house of ill repute in Savannah.

Seeing as how the restaurant exudes all this local history, it's appropriate that the food served here tends to be regional in nature. Many of the dishes are American Southern, and among the featured entrees are the venison, sea bass, and lobster-stuffed flounder. The mouth-watering appetizers include seafood bisque and baked brie. There's also an extensive wine menu. Q's has outdoor seating on a deck. Reservations are highly recommended at this well-known establishment, which serves dinner seven days a week.

The Crazy Crab
104 William Hilton Parkway
Hilton Head, SC
(843) 681–5021
$$
Lighthouse Road
Hilton Head, SC
(843) 363–2722
$$$

The island's two Crazy Crab restaurants serve fresh seafood and steaks in rustic wharfside surroundings offering splendid views of the water. At the Crazy Crab on the William Hilton Parkway near mile marker 1, the view is of picturesque Jarvis Creek and its marsh. The other Crazy Crab is among the shops alongside the Harbour Town Yacht Basin in Sea Pines. The menus at both restaurants are the same, with the mainstays being the fried shrimp and the steamed seafood pot, which consists of half a Maine lobster, Alaskan crab legs, mussels, shrimp, and oysters. The Crazy Crab at Harbour Town, which has been in business since 1986, is open for lunch and dinner seven days a week. The Crazy Crab on the parkway, which is two years older than its sister establishment, was severely damaged by a fire in February 1998 but was rebuilt and opened in June 1999.

The Gaslight 2000
Park Plaza
Hilton Head, SC
(843) 785–5814
$$$$$

Serge Prat, formerly of the Rainbow Room in New York City, has prepared classic French cuisine for islanders and visitors to Hilton Head since 1977, when he opened The Gaslight restaurant in The Market Place off the Sea Pines traffic circle. Prat moved from that site in 1998, opening the doors of his newly named restaurant in Park Plaza off Office Park Road in May. Among Prat's specialties are his beef Wellington, salmon wrapped in puff pastry, and Caesar salad. The lobster ravioli is one of several tempting appetizers available at this dressy casual restaurant, which is open for dinner Monday through Saturday. Reservations at The Gaslight 2000 are preferred but not required.

Hilton Head Brewing Company
7-C Greenwood Drive
Hilton Head, SC
(843) 785–2739
$

Billed as South Carolina's first brewpub since Prohibition and the only one on the island, this establishment in Hilton Head Plaza just off the Sea Pines traffic circle always has five handcrafted beers ready for drinking: South Atlantic Pale Ale, Calibogue Amber, Old Duck Dark, Raspberry Wheat, and a seasonal brew. Although the pub takes on the atmosphere of a bar late at night, the restaurant offers casual dining for families at lunch and during the evening. Watching the turtles, ducks, and geese in the pond outside the pub's enclosed porch will keep the kids entertained, and you can feed the fish and fowl from an outdoor deck with food purchased at the restaurant for 25 cents a pop. The menu yields a large variety of choices, including hand-tossed pizzas, burgers, steaks, and huge sandwiches. And then there are the chicken wings, named the best at the island's Wingfest event in 2000 and 2001 (see the "Annual Events" section).

The pub, which opened in December 1994, serves brunch on Saturday and Sunday and has room for about 155 customers, including seats for 60 on the porch. On Wednesday evenings, the staff removes the tables and chairs from the area around the large bar and a DJ presides over Disco Night dancing. On Saturday nights, the karaoke machine gets a workout. On Sundays from mid-June to Labor Day, the pub hosts Summerfest, a celebration featuring arts and crafts, a balloon artist, a face painter, and a juggler.

Hofbrauhaus
Pope Avenue
Executive Park
(843) 785–3663
$$

This cozy, Bavarian-style restaurant off Pope Avenue offers old standbys of German cuisine such as sauerbraten and wiener schnitzel, plus a variety of seafood, steaks, and fowl, including baked salmon, prime strip sirloin, and roast duckling. The Hofbrauhaus, in business since 1973 and featuring an accordion player squeezing out Bavarian music most evenings, serves dinner daily but is closed during the first part of December. Reservations are suggested at the restaurant, which pours up to a dozen different German beers.

Hudson's Seafood House
1 Hudson Road
Hilton Head, SC
(843) 681–2772
$$

The emphasis at Hudson's—a fixture on the Hilton Head restaurant scene since 1967—is on fresh seafood, much of it caught locally, including shrimp hauled in on the boats you might see tied at the docks just outside. The vessels and Skull Creek can be viewed from the main dining room, one of three at the 335-seat restaurant, which also has an oyster bar. Forty percent of Hudson's business involves shrimp—fried, steamed, or boiled—but the steamed oysters, scallops, and crab cakes (made with 100 percent lump backfin meat) are also big sellers. As you might expect, the dining rooms at Hudson's have a nautical look, and the tables and bar of the oyster bar are made from shrimp boat doors, the wooden pieces of equipment used in trawling.

The Oyster Factory Dining Room occupies the site of an oyster processing plant built in 1912 and bought by J. B. Hudson in the '20s. The Hudson family added shrimp to the processing operation in the mid-1950s and opened the restaurant with ninety-five seats in the latter half of the '60s. Brian and Gloria Carmines purchased Hudson's in 1975 and have expanded it since then.

Hudson's serves lunch and dinner daily. The restaurant is off Squire Pope Road about 1.5 miles from Squire Pope's intersection with the William Hilton Parkway between mile markers 1 and 2.

Juleps Restaurant
14 Greenwood Drive
Hilton Head, SC
(843) 842–5857
$$

The name is Southern and so are the surroundings at Juleps, which has the look of the fine old homes of Charleston. The food is continental, says owner/host Sam Cochran, but prepared with Southern ingredients by his chef and wife, Melissa. This combination produces entrees such as Kentucky bourbon ribeye steak, roasted stuffed quail, jumbo shrimp stuffed with lump crab meat, sautéed trout N'awlins with shrimp and crawfish, and Dixie cornmeal flounder. Among the appetizers are coconut pecan shrimp, which comes with a spicy citrus dipping sauce, and ravioli filled with smoked chicken and topped with crawfish and a sherry cream sauce. Specialty drinks can be ordered from the bar, including—what else?—mint juleps.

This restaurant in the Gallery of Shops near the Sea Pines traffic circle serves dinner seven days a week and is closed during January and on Sundays in December, February, and late November. Reservations are recommended, and the owners request that diners wear shirts with collars.

La Maisonette
20 Pope Avenue
Hilton Head, SC
(843) 785–6000
$$$$$

You might expect to pay high prices at this elegant, well-established restaurant on Pope Avenue, but the cost of a dinner at La Maisonette is comparable to what is charged at other places on Hilton Head that offer fine dining. La Maisonette—in business since 1976 and owned and operated by Adolph Weinberger since '79—serves three-course, French continental dinners, each of them priced at $25.95. A dinner consists of an appetizer such as escargot, smoked salmon, or a seasonal fruit cup topped with yogurt; a Caesar salad; and an entree. Among the entrees are the rack of lamb baked with dijon and fresh rosemary and glazed with a mint sauce; flounder stuffed with blue crab meat and topped with a dill sauce; and marinated duckling served with a caramelized fruit sauce. Desserts, made daily on the premises and priced daily, are extra.

The restaurant has two dining rooms, one designed for private parties. Both are appointed with original art, white linen tablecloths, and fine crystal and china. La Maisonette serves dinner Monday through Saturday. Reservations are recommended, and men are asked to wear jackets. Smoking is prohibited.

Old Fort Pub
65 Skull Creek Drive
Hilton Head, SC
(843) 681–2386
$$$$

If you're looking for a romantic setting for a meal, end your search at the Old Fort Pub. Set on a bluff along Skull Creek amid a tangle of live oaks, this restaurant offers evening-time diners candlelight, classical music, a rustic Lowcountry atmosphere, and spectacular sunsets over a creek and its marsh. There are great views of the water from the first-floor dining room, bar, and outdoor deck that get even better as you ascend to the second-floor Sunset Room and the rooftop widow's walk, a wooden deck reached via a cast-iron spiral staircase. Up there in the treetops, you'll find an ideal place for small cocktail parties, marriage proposals, and wedding ceremonies.

Old Fort Pub serves Lowcountry cuisine for dinner seven days a week and offers brunch on Sunday; reservations are a must in the evenings and should be made three to four days in advance. The dinner menu includes dishes such as seared salmon, sautéed lump crab cakes, and sweet-corn grouper.

While you're at Old Fort Pub, which was built in 1974 in a style inspired by the architecture of the Lowcountry, take time to stroll around the remains of Fort Mitchel, a Civil War gun battery on the site adjacent to the restaurant. Pathways wind through what were once the bunkers and moats of a fortification constructed by the Union Army after it captured the island in November 1861.

The restaurant is in Hilton Head Plantation on the northwestern part of the island (see the "Planned Residential Communities" section of this chapter). To get there, take William Hilton Parkway to Squire Pope Road, which is between mile markers 1 and 2. Turn north on Squire Pope and stay on it until you reach the Hilton Head Plantation gate; the guard there will give you a pass and directions to the restaurant.

The Old Oyster Factory
101 Marshland Road
Hilton Head, SC
(843) 681–6040
$$$

With its floor-to-ceiling windows, this multilevel restaurant offers splendid views of beautiful Broad Creek and the adjacent marsh from its 270 seats. Built of pegged timbers on the site of one of Hilton Head's oyster canneries and opened in 1989, the restaurant serves steaks and seafood, including oysters from surrounding waters prepared six or seven different ways. The shrimp offered by The Old Oyster Factory comes from nearby Calibogue Sound, provided by Capt. Woody Collins and brought to the restaurant's dock aboard his boat. Shrimp is part of one of the restaurant's big sellers—part of the seafood medley, which also consists of scallops, oysters, and choice fish filets. Another popular dish is the salmon en croute (in pastry), but you'll have to ask your server about it—it's not on the menu. The Old Oyster Factory is open for dinner daily and provides live entertainment on the dock from May through September.

The Quarterdeck
149 Lighthouse Road
Hilton Head, SC
(843) 671–2222
$$$

When it comes to Hilton Head, we can't think of a better location for a restaurant than that occupied by The Quarterdeck. From the picture windows of the second-floor dining room and bar of this establishment at Harbour Town in Sea Pines, you can watch sailboats ply the waters of Calibogue Sound against a backdrop of Daufuskie Island or observe golfers finishing up their rounds on Harbour Town Golf Links' renowned eighteenth hole. There's also a ground-floor deck by the sound and a patio overlooking the Harbour Town Yacht Basin, all of this adjacent to the marina's famed lighthouse.

The Quarterdeck serves American fare and seafood. Among its specialties are the Lowcountry shrimp, crab cake sandwiches, and steamed seafood platters. Orders from a raw bar are available outside and in the downstairs lounge, which features live entertainment seven days a week. In the afternoons, the patio is the site of live performances of reggae music. You can get breakfast, lunch, and dinner on a daily basis at The Quarterdeck, which opened in 1975.

Reilley's
7-D Greenwood Drive
Hilton Head, SC
(843) 842–4414
Port Royal Plaza
Mathews Drive
Hilton Head, SC
(843) 681–4153
$

The easygoing atmosphere of the Reilley's in Hilton Head Plaza on Greenwood Drive is what you'd expect from a restaurant that has a deck once called the "Bermuda Triangle" and a sign outside the door that counts down the days remaining until St. Patrick's Day. Reilley's menu, adorned with shamrocks and leprechauns, lists a wide variety of offerings including several variations of Blarney Burgers and Super Sandwiches. If you're in the mood for a dinner, flip to the Longtime Favorites section, where you'll find steaks and a couple of dishes suited to Gaelic tastes—the corned beef and cabbage and the cottage pie, which is ground chuck seasoned with mushrooms and onions and topped with peas, homemade mashed potatoes, and cheddar cheese.

Reilley's takes credit for organizing the island's first St. Patrick's Day parade, a celebration started in 1983, the year after the restaurant opened in the Gallery of Shops. In 1995, the restaurant moved to its existing location in Hilton Head Plaza just south of the Sea Pines traffic circle. Reilley's serves lunch and dinner daily and offers a champagne and eggs brunch on Saturdays and Sundays. The menu and atmosphere are much the same at the Reilley's at Port Royal Plaza on Mathews Drive, but there's no deck.

Rendez-vous Cafe
The Gallery of Shops
Hilton Head, SC
(843) 785–5070
$$$

Operated by chef Serge Prat, who also owns another favorite restaurant of islanders, The Gaslight 2000, this cafe off Greenwood Drive just south of the Sea Pines traffic circle offers the atmosphere of a French bistro and cuisine from the provinces of France. The onion soup, pâté, escargot, and sea scallops man Provençal will have you proclaiming "Vive la France!" The Rendez-vous, which also features a wine bar, was opened in 1996 and serves lunch Monday through Friday and dinner Monday through Saturday.

Santa Fe Cafe
700 Plantation Center
Hilton Head, SC
(843) 785-3838
$$$

Owner and chef Jim Buckingham spent his younger days in the Southwest, and he brings his appreciation for that region to his cooking. The upscale Southwestern cuisine of his Santa Fe Cafe is spicy food based on many types of chiles, resulting in dishes such as grilled pork tenderloin with smoked habañero barbecue sauce, black beans, and sweet potato fries; herb-roasted free range chicken with jalapeño corn bread stuffing and roasted garlic mashed potatoes; and grouper with chipotle (smoked chile) Parmesan au gratin. After several years of operating a limited chain of Mexican restaurants, Buckingham decided to concentrate his efforts on one establishment and in 1993 opened this cafe off William Hilton Parkway near mile marker 8. The stylishly Southwestern Santa Fe serves dinner seven nights a week and lunch on Monday through Friday, and reservations are accepted.

Spartina Grill
70 Marshland Road
Hilton Head, SC
(843) 689-2433
$$$

Owners Leah and Richard Vaughan call the food served at the Spartina Grill cross-cultural, meaning the focus of their efforts is on dishes from coastal regions throughout the world. You might also think of the atmosphere of the Spartina in the same way. It's located in a one-time Mexican restaurant whose decor now has a Mediterranean flair. We get a relaxed feeling just driving up to the Spartina, with its white stucco exterior and red-tile roof resting under the oaks in a secluded spot on Marshland Road.

Among the entrees served here are the rattlesnake chicken with fried southwest ravioli; the China Coast duck, which is stir-fried duckling with straw mushrooms, water chestnuts, snow peas, and carrot threads, all in a wonton basket; and the grilled pork tenderloin on a bed of collard greens with black-eyed pea vinaigrette. All of the restaurant's offerings are available in small and large servings, so, as Richard Vaughan puts it, you can "graze as well as dine." Leading off the list of appetizers is "pazza," a combination of pasta and pizza. The Spartina has a wine room for private parties of up to eight, a bar featuring martinis, and a patio for outdoor dining. Dinner is served nightly. Reservations are suggested.

Steamers Seafood Company
28 Coligny Plaza
Hilton Head, SC
(843) 785-2070
$

Steamers specialies in fresh fish, shrimp, lobster tails, and certified Angus beef, all cooked over a hardwood-burning grill. For shellfish lovers, there's a platter consisting of steamed oysters, clams, shrimp, crawfish, and snow crab. At Steamers, you can eat outside on the decks beside the Coligny Plaza shopping center lagoon or inside in the fish-camp atmosphere of the dining room or raw bar. Buckets are recessed in the middle of the tables of these two rooms, and that's where you toss your oyster shells, shrimp tails, and other scraps; each table also has a roll of paper towels for cleaning up your hands and face. Barn and dock wood on the walls and bars composed of wood and corrugated tin complete the pier-side look.

Steamers, which serves lunch and dinner daily, offers fifty traditional and unique appetizers and more than one hundred beers from around the world. This fun-loving restaurant has served seafood lovers on Hilton Head since 1991.

Stellini Italian Restaurant
15 Pope Avenue
Executive Park
(843) 785-7006
$$

This "little star" of an Italian restaurant shines forth from a wooded nook off Pope Avenue. Owner Joe Pesce and his partners have created the comfortable look of the Little Italy section of New York City at Stellini, which serves dinner Monday through Saturday. Especially inviting is the forty-seat Carolina Room, a porch with views of the surrounding forest. The restaurant also has a main dining room for fifty. The menu provides an extensive selection of northern Italian fare, including chicken pancetta, a chicken breast sautéed in a light cream sauce with pancetta bacon and broccoli over angel hair pasta; veal sorrento, medallions of veal sautéed in white wine topped with eggplant and melted mozzarella cheese in marinara sauce over angel hair; and zuppa di pesce, clams, shrimp, scallops, mussels, calamari, and grouper in marinara over linguine. One item you won't find on the menu is a special that's offered often: the veal chop stuffed with prosciutto and mozzarella. Pesce suggests making reservations to dine at Stellini, which opened in 1988. The restaurant is closed on Sunday and during the first three weeks in January.

Stripes: An American Grill
114 Office Park Road
Hilton Head, SC
(843) 686-4747
$$$$

Coowner and chef Steve Hancotte describes the food served at his restaurant near the Sea Pines traffic circle as "American regional." By that, Hancotte means that in creating his dishes he takes advantage of all the United States has to offer in the way of cuisine. Some examples of his red, white, and blue artistry: jumbo lump crab tossed with diced bacon, shiitake mushrooms, and toasted pine nuts served on a homemade spinach capellini; chargrilled prime beef filet served with horseradish mashed potatoes and a bleu cheese custard; and Louisiana catfish filet, panfried in Cajun spices and served with Smithfield ham on a black pepper cream.

Stripes, which opened in 1991, has seating for seventy-two in a casual atmosphere featuring caned chairs. The full bar offers a long wine list that's constantly changing and growing. The menu at Stripes also changes, with the list of dishes being revised on a seasonal basis. The restaurant is open for dinner seven days a week and is closed during the first three weeks of December. Reservations are recommended.

The Tapas Restaurant
13 Northridge Plaza
Hilton Head, SC
(843) 681-8590
$$$

Ever wanted to try something a companion is eating but felt self-conscious taking it from him or her? When you dine at The Tapas, such behavior is not only acceptable, it's expected. *Tapas* is Spanish for "little bits," and the small dishes served at this cozy, elegant bistro in Northridge Plaza off William Hilton Parkway between mile markers 4 and 5 are perfect for sharing. Say you're dining with three other people and each of you orders three different selections from the restaurant's menu of about forty items, that means you get a taste of twelve different dishes. Each item is served on an individual plate, and diners are provided with sharing plates.

Among the dishes you might try are the veal Anthony (tenderloin of veal sautéed in garlic butter, cream sherry, and mushrooms), escargot spinnochi (snails sautéed with garlic, spinach, and bacon cream sauce, topped with Parmesan cheese, and baked) and shrimp Parthenon (shrimp sautéed with feta cheese, oregano, and tomato bisque and served in a phylo shell). While you're at The Tapas, be sure to look up at the ceiling with its multitude of hanging wicker baskets. The fifty-six-seat restaurant is open for dinner Monday through Saturday, and reservations are suggested. Smoking is prohibited.

Truffles Cafe
71 Lighthouse Road
Hilton Head, SC
(843) 671–6136
www.truffles.com
$$

Islander Price Beall has owned and operated this casually elegant restaurant in Sea Pines Center since its opening in 1983. With seating for 150, Truffles is larger than the typical cafe but retains the atmosphere of a bistro. The food is American in style, with specialties like chicken pot pie made with white wine sauce and chicken New Orleans—a chicken breast served over pasta, tossed in a spicy cream sauce. Other favorites of regular customers are the ribs, grilled fish, pasta dishes, and Monterey and Cajun salads, both of which feature grilled chicken. Lunch and dinner are served daily.

Two Eleven Park Wine Bar & Bistro
211 Park Plaza
Hilton Head, SC
(843) 686–5212
$$

Two Eleven Park owner Bill Cubbage refers to the fare offered at his restaurant as "Southern fusion," meaning it combines the cuisine of many cultures with that of Dixie. Many of the exotic sounding entrees—the grilled filet of eggplant, the cedar planked salmon, and the cornmeal-dusted catfish, for example—are accompanied by down-home side dishes such as mashed potatoes, cheese grits, and/or collard greens. The smothered shrimp is served with country ham, black-eyed peas, and Vidalia onions over creamy grits.

These intriguing combinations are purveyed in an equally intriguing atmosphere—it's another combination: the New York and California bistro scenes. A local hangout of major proportions since it opened in 1994, Two Eleven Park serves dinner and is closed on Sunday.

The wine list includes 200 selections, 75 of them served by the glass. Two Eleven Park is near the cinemas of Park Plaza shopping center, which is off Greenwood Drive near the Sea Pines traffic circle. Reservations are not required but are accepted.

Nightlife

Hilton Head is a resort that caters to families who are on the go throughout the day and to golfers with early-morning tee times, so it's not exactly a hotbed of nightlife activity. There are, however, nightspots at several hotels and motels, including the Regatta Lounge at the Hilton, Signals at the Crowne Plaza, the Playful Pelican at the Westin, and Hemingway's Lounge at the Hyatt Regency. Some of Hilton Head's restaurants also have lounges where you can hang out and catch live entertainment.

There are three movie theaters on the island: Main Street Cinemas in the Main Street retail/office complex off William Hilton Parkway at mile marker 3, Northridge Cinemas at 435 William Hilton Parkway at mile marker 5, and Park Plaza Cinemas in the Park Plaza Shopping Center off Greenwood Drive. Main Street has 3 screens, Northridge has 10, and Park Plaza has 5.

If you've spent your day knocking a tennis ball around, pedaling a few miles on bicycle paths, and frolicking in the surf, and you still haven't pooped out, you might consider these other nighttime entertainment options:

The Lodge
Hilton Head Plaza
Hilton Head, SC
(843) 842–8966

The island's only cigar bar has an interior resembling a hunting lodge. You can satisfy your competitive instincts at four billiards tables, the shuffleboard table, and the pinball machines, or you can relax in front of one of the two fireplaces with a drink from the full bar or a cigar from The Lodge's large stock of smokes. In addition to wine by the glass, single malts, ales, cognacs, and bourbons, the bar serves a specialty drink, the chocolate martini. This establishment in Hilton Head Plaza, off Greenwood Drive near the Sea Pines traffic circle, opens at 4 P.M. daily.

Monkey Business
25 Park Plaza
Hilton Head, SC
(843) 686–3545

The fake bananas and high-impact colors that once adorned this upscale dance club in the Park Plaza shopping center are gone, replaced with a more sophisticated look by new owners who took over in the summer of 1999, and redecorated in January 2000. Bands or a DJ provide the music, and the lighting system uses lasers and robo-scans, flashing a multitude of shapes and colors on the dance floor and walls. Monkey Business has a full bar and capacity of 450, and it's open Tuesday through Sunday. When the house band, Sterlin Colvin, is playing on Thursday, Friday, and Saturday, there's a coverage charge of $5 for off-islanders. On Mondays and Tuesdays from Memorial Day to Labor Day, Monkey Business hosts teen nights for those 13 to 18, with a $10 cover charge.

Napa American Grill
37 New Orleans Road
Hilton Head, SC
(843) 785–6272

With its sophisticated surroundings, the Napa American Grill caters to an older crowd seeking to relax with friends. A computerized grand piano plays classic jazz music, creating a background that encourages conversation rather than inhibiting it. The bar provides a large, eclectic selection of wines—160 different bottles, with 64 wines available by the glass. Steaks, seafood, and other dishes are available in the dining area, and there's a separate living room where you can smoke cigars, have a drink, and otherwise unwind before having dinner. Sofas, wingback chairs, and coffee tables make this room a good place for losing the cares of the day.

Shopping

The shopping is plentiful on Hilton Head, which has stores of every description located in large shopping centers, in strip malls, and along the island's out-of-the-way streets and byways. To get you started, we've provided rundowns on a few of the bigger shopping areas and pointed out some of the stores you can find there. Knock yourself out.

Shopping Centers

Coligny Plaza
124 N. Forest Beach Drive
Hilton Head, SC
(843) 842–6050
www.colignyplaza.com

Coligny Plaza, the island's oldest and largest shopping center, rambles over nearly nine acres at the Coligny traffic circle on the south end of the island. Sixty retail stores and restaurants—some of them tucked into nooks and crannies along the center's covered walkways—offer a wide range of goods and dining experiences.

The Plaza mixes specialty shops with conventional businesses such as a Servistar auto parts and hardware store, a Piggly Wiggly supermarket, and Hilton Head Island Pharmacy. Among the specialty stores are Black Market Minerals, a rock and stone store; The Hammock Company; Jamaican Me Crazy, a clothing store that's Caribbean in character; the Mole Hole, which handles unique gifts and accessories for the home; the Island Fudge Shop, where sweets are made before your eyes; the Coligny Kite and Flag Company; and The Magic Puppet & Toys Too. There are also a plethora of clothing stores, with the emphasis on beach and sportswear.

More than a dozen eating places offer everything from fine dining at the Alligator Grille to the Italian cuisine at the Just Pasta Café to the seafood at Steamers Seafood Company (see listing in Restaurants) to the sandwiches at Grinders Express, Coligny Deli, and The Earle of Sandwich.

The shopping center was called Circle Square when it was started by J. Norris Richardson and his wife, Lois, in 1956. Consisting in its earliest form of the Forest Beach Market grocery store, a laundromat, a real estate office, and a beauty shop, the center has been expanded four times since the mid-'50s and was given its existing name in 1965. Members of the Richardson clan continue to operate the center, which is composed mostly of family-owned businesses.

On summer evenings, Coligny Plaza stages puppet shows and other family-oriented entertainment in the piazza off N. Forest Beach Drive. The shopping center also hosts special events during the year, including an Irish festival held in conjunction with the island's St. Patrick's Day parade; the Chocolate Fair, a springtime celebration featuring desserts concocted by local chefs; a Halloween festival, during which shop owners dress in costume and open their doors to trick-or-treaters; and appearances by the Easter Bunny and Santa Claus, with the latter arriving at the shopping center via fire truck.

Harbour Town
Harbour Town Yacht Basin
(843) 363–5655

More than twenty shops and eating places grace the north side of beautiful Harbour Town Yacht Basin. When you're not busy wandering in and out of shops such as Camp Hilton Head, Nell's Harbour Shop, the Cinnamon Bear County Store, the Planet Hilton Head nature store, and Harbour Town Crafts or dining at restaurants such as The Crazy Crab or The Quarterdeck, you can relax outside by plopping down in one of the many rocking chairs and watching the activity in the boat-filled marina. The Harbour Town shopping complex is in Sea Pines. If you're not staying at the resort, be prepared to pay a $5 entry fee.

The Mall at Shelter Cove
24 Shelter Cove Lane
Hilton Head, SC
(843) 686–3090

Hilton Head's only enclosed shopping mall accommodates more than fifty stores in a tropical setting featuring potted palm trees and other plants. Anchoring the northern end of the mall is a department store you might not expect to find on a Southern sea island—Saks Fifth Avenue, which opened in March 1997. At the southern end of the shopping center is the other anchor, Belk, and scattered in between are several stores offering high-

A lagoon and tropical plants enhance Coligny Plaza, one of the island's shopping centers. PHOTO: RICH WITTISH

quality wearing apparel including Ann Taylor, Banana Republic, Talbots, The Gap, The White House/Black Market, Chico's Express, Swim 'n Sport, and Victoria's Secret.

Shoppers seeking to pamper themselves should find products to their liking at Bath & Body Works and Crabtree & Evelyn, and there's a Waldenbooks store for those in search of reading material. Among specialty shops are Gifts of Joy, Bombay, People's Pottery, and Williams-Sonoma cookware store. The mall has spacious corridors and a large center court that's the site of special events, arts and crafts shows, and prolonged visits by Santa Claus and the Easter Bunny. On the fringes of the center area is a food court with lots of seating and four vendors: Chick-Fil-A, Sbarro, Manchu Wok, and Ice Creams & Coffee Beans. The mall, which opened in 1988, is off William Hilton Parkway near mile marker 9.

Pineland Station
430 William Hilton Parkway
Hilton Head, SC
(843) 681-8907

This upscale shopping center was completely renovated in 1997. The center, which dates back to 1979, wends its way over ten acres on the north end of the island. Covered walkways lush with foliage and potted plants connect the four retail buildings, and there's a special events staging area set among gardens, a fountain, a waterwheel, and the center's well-known duck pond.

Shoppers will find stores offering wearing apparel, including Joan Vass and Tanner; several dealing in home accents and gifts, including "It's a Wonderful Thing," Baskets by Jean, the Butterfly Kingdom Emporium, An Added Touch, The Biltmore Village Company, and Marco Polo Imports; a Stein Mart, a Starbucks Coffee Shop, Vic's Tavern, and five restaurants—

Le Bistro, Philly's Cafe and Deli, Antojito's Restaurante Mexicana, Il Carpaccio Ristorante & Pizzeria, and The French Bakery and Cafe. Pineland Station, which has more than 100,000 square feet of retail space, is between mile markers 4 and 5 on the parkway.

Village at Wexford
1000 William Hilton Parkway
Hilton Head, SC
(843) 842–2240

If you're looking for variety, you'll find it at the Village at Wexford, where the majority of the thirty-five stores and eateries are locally owned. This quaint-looking, stucco retail and office complex sits on nine wooded acres off the parkway near mile marker 10, and houses Creative Kitchens, a Hilton Head Surf Shop, an Audubon Nature Store, Golf & Sports Gallery, Mum's the Word florist and gift shop, Needlepoint Junction, and Smith Galleries, which deals in artwork and jewelry. Several stores offer women's apparel, including Bitsy's, The Honey Vine, and

The Porcupine. Island Child specializes in clothing and shoes for youngsters. The restaurants at the Village at Wexford range from those offering fast food to those devoted to casual and fine dining; at one end of the spectrum are Wendy's and Subway, with Damon's, the British Open Pub, Antonio's, and the Cafe at Wexford (see this chapter's "Restaurants" section) at the other. The center is also the site of the Jazz Corner.

Bookstores

Barnes & Noble
20 Hatton Place
Hilton Head, SC
(843) 342–6690

This branch of the nation's largest bookseller opened in July 1998 and offers islanders and visitors more than 175,000 titles, a mind-boggling selection of magazines, and a cafe where you can sit, read, and drink juice, tea, or coffee and munch on gourmet cookies. Special features of the 20,250-square-foot store are the story-

The stores and boutiques at Coligny Plaza, the island's oldest retail center, offer a variety of shopping opportunities. PHOTO: RICH WITTISH

time sessions for children on Wednesdays and Saturdays at 10 A.M. The store's Special Order Express service will order any book from more than 1.2 million in print, and deliveries usually take place within seven days. This spacious store is just off William Hilton Parkway between mile markers 3 and 4.

The Island Bookseller
71 Lighthouse Road
Hilton Head, SC
(843) 671–3773

Although Joni and Jon Minier's bookstore at Sea Pines Center covers only 1,400 square feet, it offers a full range of fiction and nonfiction categories and includes a comprehensive collection of children's books. Another section of the store is devoted to volumes featuring the Lowcountry, and the Miniers do their utmost to promote local authors.

During the summer months, The Island Bookseller keeps on hand a hefty stock of what Jon Minier calls "beach reads"—paperbacks for the side of the pool or the sands near the ocean's edge. This store, which has been in business in Sea Pines since 1983, does a lot of special ordering of books and also carries greeting cards, journals, calendars, puzzles, and games.

Port Royal Bookstore
11 Palmetto Bay Road
Hilton Head, SC
(843) 842–6996

Owner John Stern refers to his small but well-stocked bookstore near Sea Pines Circle as being old-fashioned—one where you can sit in a comfortable chair and read a book or have the staff special order a hard-to-find volume. Stern constantly peruses catalogs in an effort to maintain an extensive inventory of books covering a wide range of topics including "The War of Northern Aggression," which is what some Southerners still call the Civil War.

Speaking of that conflict, Stern also sells hand-painted pewter miniatures of Civil War soldiers. They make unique gifts. The store rents best-sellers by the day or week, a service designed with vacationers in mind. While you're at the store, take a gander at Stern's collection of miniature lead soldiers, which is displayed near the front of the shop.

Golf

Hilton Head is heaven on earth for golfers. There are 23 courses on the island, many of them world-class and all of them dripping with Lowcountry charm. Seventeen are open to the public, and information on these follows.

The courses we've described have amenities such as pro shops, practice greens, and driving ranges. Many of these courses do not allow walking, but we've pointed out which ones do and to what extent. The greens fees listed include carts, and they reflect rates during the most popular playing times (generally spring and fall).

The rates included are for players not staying at the resorts associated with the courses. You can make arrangements to play these courses by calling directly, through the resort where you're staying or via central golf reservation services such as Last Minute Tee Times (843-681-6681, 800-767-5423) and Hilton Head Accommodations & Golf Hotline (843-686-6662, 800-444-4772).

That said, let's tee it up and take a swing at golfing on Hilton Head Island at . . .

Country Club of Hilton Head
70 Skull Creek Drive
Hilton Head, SC
(843) 681–4653

Many of the greens on this par 72, 6,162-yard course at Hilton Head Plantation run near the Intracoastal Waterway, and the twelfth is right on it. Designed by Rees Jones and built in 1985, the course has two holes longer than 575 yards,

The sixth hole at Oyster Reef—a par 3, 192-yarder—overlooks Port Royal Sound, giving golfers a fine view of that majestic body of water on the northern side of Hilton Head. The par 72 layout, which is the work of Rees Jones, covers 6,463 yards at Hilton Head Plantation. The greens were converted to Tif Eagle Bermuda grass in 2000.There are nine ponds and sixty-six bunkers for players to contend with. At the end of a round, players can relax at the club's bar and restaurant. Greens fees run $105.

Palmetto Dunes Golf Courses
1 Trent Jones Lane
Hilton Head, SC
(843) 785–1138

Palmetto Dunes offers golfers three 18-hole courses from which to choose, each of them named for their heavy-hitting designers: Arthur Hills, George Fazio, and Robert Trent Jones. You can cover them on foot if you want to. Unrestricted walking is allowed at all times of the day. Rates on the Fazio and Jones Courses run $95, while the Hills Course is $148.

Arthur Hills Course

This heavily wooded par 72 was reconditioned during the mid-1990s, with all the greens being rebuilt. One of the most interesting holes is the twelfth, a par 4 that's bordered by water along one side. The course measures 6,122 yards.

George Fazio Course

The Fazio Course covers 6,239 yards and is characterized by rolling fairways and lots of long par 4s—there are only two par 5s and three par 3s. You'll have to shoot 70 to make par on this layout, which ends with a hole where two bunkers provide a significant challenge.

Robert Trent Jones Course

If you like playing by the water, you'll enjoy this 6,148-yard course, which provides a winding lagoon system tied into 11 holes and a great view of the ocean from no. 10. Other hallmarks of this par 72 are open fairways and large greens.

including the uphill, par 5, 579-yard eighteenth. Greens and fairways are Bermuda grass. Greens fees are $95.

Golden Bear Golf Club
72 Golden Bear Way
Hilton Head, SC
(843) 689–2200

What a great name for a golf course! Interestingly enough, the chief architect of this Jack Nicklaus design was not the Golden Bear himself but Bruce Borland. Players of this 6,643-yard layout at Indigo Run will find a real challenge in the eleventh hole—it runs 446 yards and features a long dogleg to the left and water on the left side of the green. This par 72 course has fairways and greens of Bermuda grass set among lagoons and stands of pine and hardwoods. Among the amenities are a bar and grill. You'll spend $98 in greens fees to play this course, on which walking is allowed.

Oyster Reef Golf Club
155 High Bluff Road
Hilton Head, SC
(843) 681–7717
www.hiltonheadgolf.net

Palmetto Hall Plantation
108 Fort Howell Drive
Hilton Head, SC
(843) 689–4138

Palmetto Hall offers golfers the opportunity to enjoy a Lowcountry-style clubhouse and eighteen-hole courses designed by Arthur Hills and Robert Cupp. The 16,000-square-foot clubhouse is a repository of historic artifacts (both Lowcountry- and golfing-related), antiques, and paintings and features a grill room with the aura of a gentlemen's club. Greens fees for the par 72 courses are $95.

Arthur Hills Course

The signature hole here is no. 18, a 434-yarder with water running up the left side of the fairway. It's a challenging par 4. Another hole featuring plenty of water is the fifth, but the water on this beauty is on the right side. The hole runs 490 yards and is a par 5. This 6,582-yard course was opened in 1991. Walking is prohibited.

Robert Cupp Course

Unrestricted walking is allowed on this 6,522-yard course, which was unveiled two years after the Arthur Hills layout. Vistas of marshlands and forests of oak and pine are features of this par 72 course, along with its straight lines and sharp angles.

Port Royal Golf Club
10A Grasslawn Avenue
(843) 689–GOLF
www.hiltonheadgolf.net

This golf club at the Port Royal resort community has three 18-hole courses: Barony, Planters Row, and Robbers Row—plus a bar and restaurant. Greens fees run $93 to $98.

Barony Course

The long drivers will take a back seat to the shot makers on this 6,223-yard course, which has many small greens. The Barony, which was designed by George Cobb, presents players with a test of skill at no. 12, a par 4, 428-yard hole with water on both sides of the fairway.

Planters Row Course

Willard Byrd is the designer responsible for Planters Row, where golfers finish on a par 5, 480-yard hole featuring woods and water. If that's not enough of a challenge, consider no. 12, a narrow, 424-yard hole where you've got to cross water to get to the green. The course measures 6,284 yards, and par is 72.

Robbers Row Course

Robbers Row represents a team effort by designers George Cobb and Pete Dye. The course was built in 1967 and reconfigured recently by Dye, who added several water hazards. This par 72 course runs 6,329 yards.

Shipyard Golf Club
45 Shipyard Drive
Hilton Head, SC
(843) 689–5600, (800) 2–FIND–18

Shipyard offers three interconnecting nine-hole courses appropriately named for three types of sailing vessels: Brigantine, Clipper, and Galleon. There is water involved on twenty-five of the twenty-seven holes, which have Bermuda grass fairways and greens. There's a bar and restaurant on the premises. Greens fees are $98.

Galleon Course

This George Cobb–designed, par 36 course is best known for no. 2, a par 5 with an elevated green fronted by water and with bunkers all around. Total yardage for the course is 3,146.

Clipper Course

The 3,302-yard Clipper has a tough ninth hole with lots of bunkers. Water comes into play on all the holes except no. 6, which is a par 4, 427-yarder. George Cobb also designed this course, which carries a par 36.

Brigantine Course

The work of designer Willard Byrd, the Brigantine is a 3,045-yard, par 36 surrounded by private homes and rental condominiums that blend in with the natural environment. You'll be challenged by no. 6, a long par 4, and no. 9. This last hole is a par 5 that runs 523 yards and has water on one side of the fairway.

Sea Pines Resort

Sea Pines is the home of three of the island's most popular golf courses, including the Harbour Town Golf Links, which is the site of Hilton Head's number one sporting event, the WorldCom Classic—The Heritage of Golf. Walking is allowed on all three courses.

Harbour Town Golf Links
11 Lighthouse Lane
Hilton Head, SC
(843) 363–4485, (800) 955–8337

The signature hole at Harbour Town is the one you've seen countless times on television—the windswept eighteenth, a par 4 on Calibogue Sound where shots to the green often end up among the fiddler crabs in the adjacent marsh. Consistently

ranked among the world's top courses, this one was designed by Pete Dye and Jack Nicklaus and has some outstanding par 3s. The yardage at this par 71 course totals 6,119. Greens fees run $240.

Ocean Course
100 N. Sea Pines Drive
Hilton Head, SC
(843) 363–4475

The fifteenth hole on this oldest and newest of island courses offers a terrific view of the ocean. It's the oldest course because it was designed by George Cobb in 1962 and the newest because it was remodeled by Mark McCumber in 1995. Greens fees for this par 72, 6,493-yard layout run $105.

Sea Marsh Course
100 N. Sea Pines Drive
Hilton Head, SC
(843) 363–4475

You'll encounter wide fairways and lots of lagoons, trees, and marshes when you play this par 72 course, which was also designed by George Cobb. It was remodeled in 1990 by Clyde Johnston, and it measures 6,169 yards. Expect to pay $95 in greens fees at Sea Marsh.

Hilton Head is heaven on earth for the golfer. PHOTO: PHYL M. GATLIN

Tennis

If you'd rather be hitting a fuzzy yellow ball instead of a dimpled white ball, you'll find plenty of opportunities to do so at the numerous tennis facilities on the island. Among those open to the public for play are the following:

Palmetto Dunes Tennis Center
6 Trent Jones Lane
Hilton Head, SC
(843) 785–1152, (800) 972–0257
www.palmettodunes.com

An array of instructional programs and daily round-robin tournaments are featured at the tennis center at Palmetto Dunes. The tournaments are billed as "lively afternoon social competition with the emphasis on fun." There are twenty-three clay and two hard courts, eight of which are lighted.

Reserved rates are $20 for guests and $25 for players not staying at the resort. Walk-on rates are $15 from noon to 4 P.M.

Port Royal Racquet Club
15 Wimbledon Court
Hilton Head, SC
(843) 686–8803

The Port Royal Racquet Club is the only tennis facility on Hilton Head—and in all of South Carolina, for that matter—offering all three Grand Slam–type playing surfaces. There are ten clay courts, four cushioned hard courts (all of which are lighted), and two grass courts. The club, which consistently has been ranked by *Tennis Magazine* as one of the "top 50 greatest tennis resorts," offers a variety of instructional programs and will custom design clinics for individuals and teams.

Located at Port Royal Plantation, the club has a well-stocked pro shop that provides a varied selection of men's and women's tennis wear and the latest in equipment. Reserved rates for clay and hard courts are $20 per hour, with walk-ons accepted from noon to 4 P.M. at a fee

of $14 per hour. You'll need reservations for the grass courts, and you'll pay $45 an hour to play on them.

Sea Pines Racquet Club
5 Lighthouse Lane
Hilton Head, SC
(843) 363–4495, (800) 955–8337
www.seapines.com

Programs and instruction take center court at the Sea Pines Racquet Club, which *Tennis Magazine* rated number one in programming in 1998. The flagship program is the Stan Smith Tennis Academy, named after the former U.S. Open and Wimbledon champion who serves as the club's touring pro and tennis consultant.

There are various programs for every age group, and twenty-three courts are available for play. The club has eleven instructors led by Job de Boer, a genial Dutchman who specializes in teaching groups.

The club dates to the early 1970s and is undergoing a redesign that started in 2000 and involved the creation of new courts and the building of a state-of-the art pro shop. The courts are in use, and the pro shop is expected to be completed by spring 2003. The existing shop offers players the latest in tennis fashions, equipment, and footwear. Court fees are $20 per hour for those with reservations and $16 per hour for walk-ons.

Van der Meer Shipyard Tennis Resort
116 Shipyard Drive
Hilton Head, SC
(843) 686–8804, (800) 845–6138
www.vandermeertennis.com

Twenty courts set amid the lush surroundings of Shipyard Plantation await the tennis buff at this racquet club, which the United States Tennis Association presented with its Outstanding Tennis Facility of the Year Award for 1997. There are eleven clay courts and six hard-surface courts outdoors and three DecoTurf

Players of all ages can refine their tennis games at numerous racket clubs and complexes available on Hilton Head. PHOTO: RICH WITTISH

courts indoors (a total of five courts have lights). The club offers a variety of instructional programs, with sessions involving the stroke of the day, daily drills, and intensive drills available year-round. The intensive drills are geared for players with 4.0-plus ratings and are designed to take skills to the next level.

The club, owned by premier tennis teacher Dennis Van der Meer, holds exhibitions by tennis professionals on Mondays from March through October, with admission and refreshments free. The Shipyard Racquet Club has a large pro shop displaying an extensive variety of items, and it's also the site of the United States Professional Tennis Registry's International Tennis Symposium and $25,000 Championships, which are held annually during the middle of February.

Reserved rates for the club's outdoor courts are $18 per hour, with walk-ons paying $14 per hour from noon to 4 P.M.

Covered courts must be reserved, and fees are $24 per hour.

Van der Meer Tennis Center
19 DeAllyon Road
Hilton Head, SC
(843) 785–8388, (800) 845–6138

This tennis center operated by well-known instructor Dennis Van der Meer provides a multitude of programs for adults and junior players in all stages of development, from beginners to aspiring professionals. Among the programs are tennis getaway weeks and weekends. There are twenty-five hard-surface courts, three clay courts, and four covered hard courts, with fees for an hour of play set at $15. The center has a pro shop and is the headquarters of the Van der Meer Tennis University, which offers training programs for tennis teachers. The center is on DeAllyon Road, which runs off Cordillo Parkway on the south end of the island.

The island's most significant annual events occur during the spring. The biggest one—the WorldCom Classic—shouldn't be missed if you're a golf fan.

WorldCom Classic—The Heritage of Golf
Harbour Town Golf Links
11 Lighthouse Lane
Hilton Head, SC
(843) 671–2448, (800) 234–1107

The WorldCom Classic—The Heritage of Golf brings 120 invited players and 125,000 spectators to famed Harbour Town Golf Links in Sea Pines during four days in April. In 2001, the players competed for a total of $3.5 million in prize money and the right to wear the Tartan plaid jacket awarded to the winner of this prestigious tournament. Jose Coceres captured the jacket and the winner's share of $630,000 in 2001. Coceres shot an 11-under-par 273 over seventy-two holes of play, then won a playoff with Tommy Mayfair. Coceres is on a list of champions that includes Jack Nicklaus, Greg Norman, Davis Love III, Nick Price, Hale Irwin, Tom Watson, and Arnold Palmer, who won the tournament in its inaugural year of 1969 when it was known as the Heritage Classic.

Attending the WorldCom Classic—which some longtime residents of the Savannah-Hilton Head area still call The Heritage—involves more than watching a golf tournament. The event is usually held during the second week in April, when the weather is generally lovely and nature is putting on a springtime show. It's a terrific time to get outdoors, amble around the verdant Harbour Town course, visit the shops and restaurants at the Harbour Town Yacht Basin near the first tee and eighteenth green, gawk at the high-priced boats docked in the marina, and observe the hordes of spectators doing all of these things. Sometime during their day at the course, those attending are invariably drawn to the eighteenth hole, which overlooks Calibogue Sound and has the Harbour Town Lighthouse as part of its backdrop, to see how the players finish up and deal with the wind blowing off the water.

During the three days leading up to the tournament, which starts on Thursday and ends on Sunday, there are two pro-am events, a challenge in which several members of the PGA tour play a select group of Harbour Town's holes, and a youth clinic at which two stars from the tour give youngsters eighteen and under free golf lessons. At 4 P.M. on the Tuesday before Thursday's first round of play, the WorldCom Classic presents opening ceremonies focusing on golf's Scottish heritage and the game's long history in South Carolina (the South Carolina Golf Club of Charleston was founded in 1786 and is reputed to be the oldest membership golf club in America). The defending champion, tournament board members clad in plaid, and bagpipers from The Citadel military college parade along the yacht basin to the eighteenth green, where the defending champ gets the tourney under way by smacking a ball into Calibogue Sound as a Civil War-era cannon is fired. The opening ceremonies and youth clinic are free and open to the public; in 2001, there was a $35 fee for watching the other three days of pretournament events, with admission included in the cost of purchasing a tournament practice round badge.

A season badge, which is good for admission to the tournament grounds for the entire week of WorldCom Classic events, costs $100. A clubhouse badge, which gives you access for the entire week to the grounds, the clubhouse, and the Heritage Pavilion, a hospitality tent, costs $150. As stated earlier, practice round badges enable you to attend all the events leading up to the four-day tournament. Also, there are patron plans available for large groups of spectators; for details on these, contact the WorldCom Classic staff at the phone numbers listed for this entry. Parking for the WorldCom Classic is in lots within Sea Pines, and spectators are shuttled by bus to Harbour Town. The parking and the bus service are complimentary.

Hilton Head's Gone Gator

If you get near a body of fresh or brackish water on Hilton Head, which is hard not to do given the preponderance of the island's lakes and lagoons, there's a good chance you will see a creature that looks as though it has crawled right out of *Jurassic Park*. This is the American alligator, the largest reptile on the North American continent and one of the oldest surviving vertebrates on the planet.

Alligators abound on Hilton Head, where developers have provided ready-made homes for them by creating the waterways that decorate the island's communities and golf courses. "If there's a mud puddle in the Lowcountry, there's an alligator in it," says Dean Harrigal, who coordinates the alligator nuisance program in the area. There have been no formal surveys of the alligator population on Hilton Head, but there are probably from 2,000 to 4,000 gators living on the island, says Walt Rhodes, the alligator project supervisor for the South Carolina Department of Natural Resources.

Alligators, which are protected by state and federal law, can grow to a length of twelve feet, but most of the gators removed from Hilton Head under the nuisance program are from six to eight feet long, according to Harrigal. Even so, if left alone, alligators pose little threat to humans, say Rhodes and Harrigal. "Gators are naturally shy of people," says Rhodes. According to the two alligator experts, humans are more of a threat to gators than vice versa.

If the state receives a complaint about a gator on Hilton Head, and the animal is deemed a nuisance because of its behavior or location, the reptile will be removed. Removed, in this case, means destroyed, not relocated. Relocating a gator doesn't work because of the animal's strong homing instinct: Gators have been known to travel as much as 30 miles to return to their nesting areas, Rhodes and Harrigal say. Fifty to sixty gators are removed from Hilton Head each year because of complaints

One of the alligators that abound on Hilton Head Island suns itself near a pond at an island golf course.

against them, but the two say that wouldn't be the case if people were more tolerant of the animals, who were here first (present-day gators are direct descendants of a creature that lived in what is now Florida during the Miocene epoch, which occurred 25 million years ago).

People don't like gators for a number of reasons. For one thing, the alligator's appearance is not in its favor. The gator looks like a big lizard, only uglier, and it seems to have a malevolent smile permanently plastered on its bumpy face. "It's not Bambi," says Rhodes. "It's not warm and fuzzy, it's cold and scaly." For another, most people don't know much about alligators and their relatively placid temperament. Folks confuse gators with the crocodiles found on other continents, in particular the fourteen-foot crocs seen devouring water buffaloes in sensationalized nature flicks. Gators, says Rhodes, "will let you alone if you let them alone, and they'll see you first."

Humans have a tendency to bring out the aggressiveness in gators by feeding them. If a person feeds a gator enough times, the beast's golf ball–sized brain begins to associate the human with food. This is, if you'll pardon the phrase, a recipe for disaster that can be harmful to the human involved and fatal to the gator. It's also against the law; if you're caught feeding an alligator, you can be fined $200 or sentenced to thirty days in jail. There are cases of humans provoking gators into attacking them. Rhodes tells of a golfer who hit his ball near a gator that was sunning itself on a Hilton Head fairway, then smacked the animal with his golf club in the process of recovering the ball. The gator bit the golfer. "The gator did what you would do if someone hit you with a golf club," says Rhodes. There have been reports of people being pursued by gators, but Rhodes says he's handled in excess of 3,000 of the animals and has never been chased.

Rhodes's rules for coexisting with gators: Don't feed them; they find plenty to eat in the form of insects, crustaceans, fish, and snakes. Don't tease them. For goodness sake, don't try to pet them. Look at them all you want but do so from afar. "Give the animal the respect it deserves," says Rhodes. "It has as much right to be here as the deer, squirrels, and people."

St. Patrick's Day Parade
Pope Avenue
Hilton Head, SC
(843) 842–4319

What started as a march by a few residents of Irish descent in 1983 has matured into the largest free spectator event held on the island. Some 15,000 onlookers gather to watch the two-hour parade, which is held on the Sunday before St. Patrick's Day or on the day itself when the holiday falls on Sunday. If you go, expect to see marching bands, in the neighborhood of thirty floats, dance groups, the Piedmont Pipers bagpipe band from upstate South Carolina, local

dignitaries, and maybe even Budweiser's Clydesdale horses.

The parade starts at 2 P.M. at New Orleans Road and William Hilton Parkway, proceeds south on the parkway a short distance to the Sea Pines traffic circle, and then turns east and travels the length of Pope Avenue to Coligny Plaza. The event is run by the Hilton Head Island St. Patrick's Day Parade Foundation, whose president, Tom Reilley, started the celebration in '83 when he and a few friends decided to march in honor of St. Patrick. Because they didn't have a parade permit, Reilley and his pals ran into some legal troubles with local officials, but they managed to straighten things out and resumed marching in 1985. Since then, the parade has grown into the family-oriented event that it is today.

SpringFest
Various locations
(843) 686–4944, (800) 424–3387
www.hiltonheadhospitalityassociation.com
The Hilton Head Hospitality Association and several local businesses sponsor this celebration of the coming of spring, which takes place throughout March and features three main events: the Chocolate Fair, WineFest, and WingFest. At the Chocolate Fair, held on the first weekend of the month at the Coligny Plaza shopping center on the south end of the island, chefs from local restaurants and amateur cooks cover twenty to thirty tables with their chocolate confections. Judges select the most delectable creations, and fairgoers sample whatever catches their attention for 50 cents a taste.

WineFest—billed as the largest outdoor public wine tasting on the East Coast—is presented at Shelter Cove Harbour on the second Saturday of the month. One hundred wineries make 450 wines available for tasting from 1 to 4 P.M. The $30 admission fee buys you a souvenir wine glass that's your ticket to the tasting; needless to say, WineFest is for persons twenty-one or older. On the Friday night preceding the event, the WineFest Auction is held at the Self Family Arts Center starting at 6 P.M. Live and silent auctions and tasting of gold- and silver-medal winning wines are the highlights of this black-tie event, which costs $250 per person. At Wingfest, on the fourth Saturday of the month, fifteen to twenty island restaurants serve their best offerings of chicken wings for 25 to 50 cents apiece. Music and kids' games accompany the munching, which occurs from noon to 5 P.M. at Shelter Cove Harbour. Proceeds benefit the Island Recreation Center.

The beach is a source of fun for all ages. PHOTO: COURTESY OF HILTON HEAD ISLAND CHAMBER OF COMMERCE

Arts and Culture

Hilton Head has for years radiated a vibrant cultural presence. Some twenty community groups—ranging from the Hilton Head Art League to the Hilton Head Orchestra—foster and promote an appreciation of the visual and performing arts. Recently, the community created a new artistic resource, The Self Family Arts Center, which has become the cultural hub of the island.

Hilton Head Art League
430 William Hilton Parkway
Hilton Head, SC
(843) 681–5060, (800) 995–4068

As part of its mission to provide artists with opportunities to hone their skills and exhibit their works, the Hilton Head Art League presents "minishows" every six weeks at its gallery in the Pineland Station shopping complex. Each of these exhibits features the work of a league member, and each opens with an evening reception. The league sponsors two major art shows annually at the Walter Greer Gallery of The Self Family Arts Center. One of the shows is juried, and the event attracts more than 500 entries from throughout the Southeast. The league also presents workshops and a program called Therapeutic Art that's aimed at bringing the arts to physically and mentally challenged children and adults. The Hilton Head Art League was started in 1972 by a handful of local artists. There are more than 950 members, 250 of whom are artists.

Hilton Head Orchestra
32 Office Park Road
Hilton Head, SC
(843) 842–2055
www.hhorchestra.org

The seventy-five-piece Hilton Head Orchestra presents ten master series concerts a year, four miniseries concerts, and sponsors a youth orchestra and international piano competition. About 40 percent of the musicians are from the local area, with the others traveling from Southern cities such as Savannah, Charleston, South Carolina, and Jacksonville, Florida, to participate in performances. Concerts are held at the First Presbyterian Church at 540 William Hilton Parkway, and the 2001–2002 master series included an appearance by internationally known violinist Eugene Fodor. Mary Woodmansee Green serves as the orchestra's music director/conductor, having assumed that role in July 1998. Prior to coming to Hilton Head, she was the music director and conductor of the Kennett Symphony and Philadelphia Festival Orchestras, the Delaware Valley Chorale, and The Mary Green Singers.

The orchestra was founded in the winter of 1982 by a handful of local musicians who incorporated the organization as the Hilton Head Chamber Orchestra later in the year. The name was changed to Hilton Head Community Orchestra in 1983; six years later, it became the Hilton Head Orchestra. The Hilton Head Youth Orchestra was organized in 1996. The Hilton Head Island International Piano Competition was also started in 1996. The competition is held during the first week in March at the First Presbyterian Church. About seventy-five pianists apply, with twenty selected as finalists.

A season ticket for the ten-concert series is $150; general admission for wing seating at individual performances is $15, but concerts are usually sold out.

The Self Family Arts Center
14 Shelter Cove Lane
Hilton Head, SC
(843) 686–3945, (843) 842–ARTS
www.artscenter-hhi.org

A big-city facility on a resort island, this $10 million visual and performing arts center offers theatrical productions, performances by musicians and dancers, art shows, education programs, and community service programs.

The center opened in March 1996 on 4.4 acres at Shelter Cove donated by the James C. Self family of Greenwood, South

Carolina, owners of the Greenwood Development Corporation of Hilton Head. The result of the Self family gift and a fund-raising effort involving numerous corporations and the community, the center grew out of an idea hatched in 1985 by a group of local arts organizations. The group was incorporated as the Cultural Council of Hilton Head Island and was joined in its efforts by The Hilton Head Playhouse, which has produced more than 200 dramas, comedies, and musicals since its first performance in 1977.

Each year The Self Center's 350-seat Elizabeth Wallace Theatre hosts up to six productions. Among the presentations for the 2000–2001 season were *Corpse!, Some Enchanted Evening,* and *Anything Goes.* The theater complex has dressing and costume rooms and a green room. A rehearsal hall has seating for 150.

The center brings islanders a series featuring local talent and regional and national touring companies. Six to eight art shows are exhibited annually in the center's 2,300-square-foot Walter Greer Gallery, which has twelve-foot-high ceilings and flexible lighting for showcasing art. Through its education program, The Self cosponsors residencies by professional artists in area schools and brings children to the center on field trips to performances. The center also offers services and assistance to artists and art groups from throughout the island, providing technical support and space for a variety of organizations.

The Self further serves the island by presenting free events such as the Community Christmas Tree Lighting, Family Fiesta Latina, Youth ArtsFest, and the Gullah Celebration.

Tybee Island

History/Overview

While other beach communities succumb to high-rises, slick resorts, and gated communities with lawns pristine enough to putt on, Tybee stubbornly resists. Look around downtown during summer and you will see a hot dog stand and souvenir shops hawking seashells and bargain T-shirts for less than $10. The only golf you'll find is the miniature kind, and at the moment, there's grass growing through the Astroturf greens there, waiting for someone to either plow it under or start it back up. Meanwhile over at City Hall, council members busily guard ordinances restricting the height of buildings and giving older residents tax breaks so they don't get pushed out by outsiders with fatter wallets. The destruction of one of the island's oldest hotels (equipped with one of the island's oldest bars) in 1998 to clear the way for condo construction has sparked a drive for historic preservation.

Tybee is a place where folksy eccentricity is celebrated and many things have been practiced. Things like gambling, which took place in back rooms throughout Tybee until being exposed and cleared out in the early 1960s. A decade or so later, nearly every bar in town was shut down for staying open too late on Saturday night. Seems people were having too good a time to remember that selling beer on Sundays was illegal. That's the thing about Tybee islanders—they just sorta do their own thing.

"Once you cross Lazaretto Creek Bridge into Tybee you get a laid-back attitude. Not a don't care attitude, but a laid-back one," said Walter Parker, who has served as Tybee's mayor four times and has lived there most of his life. "When you leave Tybee, you can't wait to get back."

Bluntly put, the place is a little scruffy looking, but if you'll get your nose out of the air, you might appreciate the quirky appeal. You'll find million-dollar beachfront construction next door to cinderblock shacks (and don't necessarily assume the owners of the fancy home are the richer: Tybee knew shabby before it was chic). This is a locals' beach at which tourists are welcome. They're glad to see you come and, good naturedly, glad to see you go when the season is over and they get their oddball little island back to themselves. The Beach Bums Parade, wherein locals on makeshift floats armed with large-scale water guns do battle with spectators spraying garden hoses, marks the beginning of the tourist season—a fun, messy, launch to the crowds of summer. Later, mid-September ushers back in "Tybee time," when the residents have the place to themselves and the particular pleasures of a warm winter beach.

There are flashier, better groomed places to vacation, places with more activities and scheduled events. However, we spent one of the best vacations of our lives in a rented cottage near the foot of the lighthouse, with a nor'easter howling outside as we squinted in inadequate light to work a jigsaw puzzle that probably didn't have all the pieces. If you are at peace with the fact that everything doesn't have to be plastic, maybe Tybee is for you. Bring your own 499-piece jigsaw puzzle and find out.

Tybee's past is as colorful as its present. It served a role in several wars and has been home to Lt. Col. George C. Marshall (creator of the Marshall Plan) and to a quarantine station for people with infectious ailments. In the early 1800s, scientists believed the marshes in and around the island held harmful vapors or miasma that rose from the marsh vegetation and were carried by the wind into Savannah. However, it was also widely theorized that the vapors were counteracted by the healing properties of sea air. That was a notion that eventually played a role in Tybee's foray into tourism in the late 1880s.

Native Americans were the first Tybee islanders. They settled this small island (2.5 miles long and about .60 mile wide) and also are generally credited with giving the island its name, which means salt, though there are other competing theories. Next came the Spanish in the 1500s, followed 200 years later by Georgia's founder, Gen. James Edward Oglethorpe.

Because of its location at the mouth of the Savannah River, Tybee was important strategically. Soon after his arrival, Oglethorpe ordered the construction of a lighthouse, which was completed in 1736. During the War of 1812, the lighthouse (see "Things to Do" in this chapter) was used to warn Savannah of possible attack by the British, but this attack never materialized. A fortress known as a Martello Tower, designed with round walls that supposedly would deflect cannonballs, was built on Tybee Island in 1815 to help guard the Savannah River from attack. It was one of only a few such structures in North America.

On the western end of the island, a quarantine station was set up to house sick passengers coming in off ships. This is how Lazaretto Creek got its name. *Lazaretto* is an Italian word for an institution or hospital for those with contagious diseases. "They kept them in quarantine there for four months," said James Mack Adams, local Tybee historian. "If they got sick and died, they buried them right there."

In 1829, construction began on Fort Pulaski (see "Things to Do"). The fort, now a national park, stands off U.S. Highway 80 as you approach Tybee. It was constructed of 25 million bricks and has walls seven and a half feet thick. Robert E. Lee was one of the engineers who planned and supervised construction. During the Civil War, Union forces attacked the fort using a new weapon called "rifled cannon." It took only thirty hours of bombardment for the fort to fall into Union hands. The attack had such devastating effects on the brick fort that after the surrender, all forts like Pulaski were considered obsolete.

Following the war, Tybee turned its attention toward tourism. Before 1885, the only way to get to the island from Savannah was a two-hour boat ride through the dangerously swift Savannah River. This all changed two years later when a locomotive made its maiden trip to the island, and the era of the railroad began. That same year Tybee was officially incorporated as Ocean City. A year later it was changed to Tybee, only to be changed in 1929 to Savannah Beach. It wasn't until many decades later, in the early '70s, that it became Tybee again. A reference today to Savannah Beach is likely to raise the locals' dander.

Daytrippers, as they were known, would come on the train, rent bathing suits from a local hotel, and spend the day at the beach. Some would arrive later in the day to dance to big band music supplied by outfits playing at one of the islands biggest attractions: the Tybrisa Pier. When the Tybee Road opened in 1923, the stream of people coming to the island continued to grow. In a column that ran in the local newspaper in 1931, E. B. Izlar reflected about the "good old days" on Tybee. "The decline of mosquitoes, of picnickers, of bars and of yardage in women's bathing suits constitute the most radical changes in reviewing the past thirty years on Tybee Island," the column stated. "Today, Mr. Izlar declares that mosquitoes, except in the dense wooded places are rare, and he bears out his statement by remarking that he has only seen three this season."

Reminiscing on the bathing suits of the early years, Mr. Izlar lamented the time when suits were sold for $2.50 to $4 a dozen (except, of course, when special suits for women were as high as $12 a dozen) in the days when women "wrapped up" to cover everything. As for bars, Mr. Izlar said that though they abounded in bygone days, there was little disorder—only friendly fights. "There was not even need for a jail in those days."

While the islanders focused on tourism, the U.S. War Department began construction of Fort Screven on the north end of the island. The fort was made up of seven gun batteries that ended up being fired only for practice, not for war. During World War I, part of the Eighth Infantry Regiment was assigned to Fort Screven. One of its commanders was Lt. Col. George C. Marshall, who after leaving Tybee became a five-star general and served as secretary of state, secretary of defense, and author of the Marshall Plan for rebuilding western Europe after World War II.

In the meantime, Savannahians were beginning to build houses at the beach for the summer months. The ocean breezes would give them relief from the city's sweltering summer heat. Many of these magnificent old beach homes can still be found on the island today. Current resident Walter Parker recalls how empty the island was in those days. "I can remember in the winter you could go for several blocks before you saw a light on," said Parker. "No one lived here year-round."

Eventually, that began to change and Tybee's year-round population slowly grew. However, several factors—beach erosion, pollution, the closing of Fort Screven—resulted in several years of decline on the island beginning in the

Insiders' Tip

Tybee hasn't had a major hit from a hurricane in more than one hundred years. The most damaging hurricane occurred August 27, 1881. It landed with a massive storm surge that covered the island and destroyed nearly every structure in its path.

1940s. Residents cultivated an outlaw attitude during this era by engaging in backroom gambling and illegal drinking, which got the attention of the news media. It also helped fuel the island's reputation in some circles as Georgia's unruly stepchild. Eventually, local and state law enforcement agencies cracked down to curb Tybee's wanton ways. The pollution, gambling, and other sins were eventually cleaned up, and Tybee once again became a popular tourist spot.

Since 1980 or so, the island's year-round population has been on the rise to its current level of around 4,000. Today, locals who have called Tybee home for generations live amongst a thriving community of artists and writers, most of whom migrated during the '80s. There are also many retirees whose hometowns are places far away from Tybee. Every socioeconomic group is represented, from the poor to the very wealthy.

"I think Tybee is an easy place to live," said Parker. "I think it has more than its share of characters. . . . But it has a small-community feeling and most want it to stay that way."

Getting There, Getting Around

Tybee is about 18 miles east of Savannah. There is only one road to get you there: U.S. Highway 80. You can reach it from the Historic Downtown by heading east on Bay Street. In less than a mile, it will run into President Street, then President Street Extension. After about 3 miles, it merges with U.S. 80 East. From Midtown, hop on Victory Drive and head east—you are also on U.S. 80 East.

After entering Tybee, U.S. 80 turns into Butler Avenue, the community's main drag, which will take you past hotels, beach houses, and the small downtown area. You will know U.S. 80 has become Butler Avenue after going around a fairly sharp curve. You can't miss it. Follow Butler a mile or so farther into downtown, and you will be deposited in a city parking lot next to the pier.

Most places you need to visit on Tybee should be accessible from this main strip. Near the beginning of Butler Avenue, streets running east and west are numbered, starting with 1st Street at the northern end of the city and ending with 19th Street at the southern end. These are crossed by north-and-south running streets that are named and numbered, starting with Butler Avenue closest to the beach and ending with 6th Avenue.

If you are going to spend the day at the beach on Tybee, you will have to pay for parking. The streets closest to the beach are metered, usually at a dollar an hour, and most require quarters. The city operates three parking lots, all accessible from Butler Avenue: at the end of Tybrisa (which used to be 16th Street), 14th Street, and at North Beach. It costs $7 all day to park in one of these lots. Officially parking is patrolled every day year-round from 8 A.M. until 8 P.M. In reality, and in typical Tybee fashion, it's a more practical system: starting up about 8-ish or 9-ish and depending on the weather or crowds. If it's raining or the crowds are light, the parking enforcers may knock off early, but be aware that you

are gambling if you assume they have. Like the Savannah authorities, the parking enforcers are very generous when doling out tickets and are fairly vigilant. So if you don't want an $8 expired meter ticket, don't leave your meter expired. It usually isn't any trouble finding parking on Tybee, except for a few very busy weekends. Even then, if you drive around long enough, you will almost certainly get a spot. Planning a longer stay? Parking stickers that allow you to park in all lots and at all meters without further payment are available. Property owners get them free; other nearby residents who are frequent visitors buy them from Tybee City Hall at $55 a year.

Accommodations

Affordable hotel rooms, sprawling beach houses, and oceanview condos are some of the choices you will find when searching for accommodations on Tybee Island. Tybee is known as a family beach, so a lot of what is available is geared toward those lugging not only beach chairs but high chairs as well. Regardless of where you land, more likely than not you will be within comfortable walking distance of the beach.

Tybee's season runs typically from the middle of April through the middle of September. After that, the streets become less crowded and rates go down. Stay during the peak season, especially on weekends, and the rates are going to be higher.

A few weekends, including July 4, are especially busy.

While we list some Realtors who can help land you in a beach house and condo, some owners handle property rental on their own. Most simply post a FOR RENT sign in the front yard—when you're in town, pick one of these places that you like and jot down the number for future reference. Some private owners also put listings in the *Savannah Morning News* (see our Media chapter for more information), so check there as well. Our listings begin with hotels and motels, we throw in one bed-and-breakfast, then move on to rentals. Note that Tybee's rental market for houses and condos, just like its real estate market, is booming—so rates are volatile and could well climb between this writing and your reading.

Hotels and Motels

There are only a handful of hotels and motels to choose from on the island. Most are chains with names you will recognize and offer standard, sometimes modest accommodations. The ones we list have nonsmoking and wheelchair-accessible rooms and come with ample free parking. Although Tybee is outside Savannah, it shares area code 912.

Price-Code Key

Our price code is designed to make it easier for you to gauge the cost of staying at one of Tybee's hotels or motels. The dollar sign indicates the average cost for a one-night stay for two adults during peak season, typically mid-April through mid-September.

$	$50 and less
$$	$51 to $100
$$$	$101 to $150
$$$$	$151 and more

Best Western Dunes Inn
1409 Butler Avenue
Tybee Island, GA
(912) 786–4591, (800) 528–1234
$$–$$$$

The Best Western Dunes Inn is across the street from the beach and a block or so away from Tybee's small shopping

This community park on Tybee Island is typical of public playgrounds scattered throughout Savannah, Chatham County, and the county's municipalities. PHOTO: BETTY DARBY

district, where you can find everything from a new swimsuit to suntan lotion. This motel offers spacious rooms comfortably furnished with two double beds or one king bed. Some have balconies overlooking the pool, and a few kitchenettes are also available. Complimentary coffee is served every morning.

Days Inn
1402 Butler Avenue
Tybee Island, GA
(912) 786–4576
$$–$$$$

The Days Inn is within walking distance to Tybee's "downtown." It is on the beach side of Butler Avenue—Tybee's main thoroughfare. The motel offers a pool and free continental breakfast each morning. The rooms are fresh, with bright-colored bedspreads and white walls. Although just a short stroll to the beach, none of the rooms have ocean views.

Savannah Beach Beachside Colony
404 Butler Avenue
Tybee Island, GA
(912) 786–4535, (800) 786–0770
$$$

The Beachside Colony recently underwent a renovation resulting in attractive and neatly styled rooms in light pastel colors. Located on the ocean, there is a pool, sundeck, and cabana, along with a casual but elegant restaurant known as the Beachside Grill. (See "Restaurants" listing later in this chapter.) The hotel juts onto the beach sideways. For the best view, request a room on the second floor on the end closest to the ocean. King and double beds are available, and all rooms have balconies. Fax and copy service are also available.

Howard Johnson Admiral's Inn
1501 Butler Avenue
Tybee Island, GA
(912) 786–0700, (800) 446–4656
$$$–$$$$

A nice, two-story hotel, Admiral's Inn has forty-one spacious rooms, a swimming pool, and is across the street from the ocean. The standard room comes with two queen beds, but if you need a little more space, deluxe king rooms with sitting areas are available. For those coming to Tybee after tying the knot, there is also a bridal suite. The hotel's meeting room holds up to seventy-five people.

Computer, phone/fax, and copy service are available for those unfortunate souls who have to work while at the beach. The hotel is within comfortable walking distance to downtown Tybee and is adjacent to Cap'n Chris' Restaurant, where you can get breakfast, lunch, and dinner at reasonable prices. Seafood and Southern fare like fried chicken and Key lime pie are among the menu selections.

Ocean Plaza Beach Resort
15th Street and Ocean Front
Tybee Island, GA
(912) 786–7664, (800) 215–6370
www.oceanplaza.com
$$–$$$$

This is Tybee's largest hotel, with 240 rooms and suites and two swimming pools. It is also one of the few properties that offers direct room views of the ocean. Head out your door, walk through a parking lot, and within a few steps you are on the sand. Located on the southern end of the island, there are actually three buildings at Ocean Plaza, including two four-story structures facing the ocean. The rooms are spacious and decorated in bright pastel colors. All oceanfront rooms have balconies overlooking the Atlantic.

Many room options are available including a single room with a king bed, one-room suites with queen beds, and two-room suites with one king and one double bed. Kitchenettes are also available. Regardless of the room type, all come with a choice of poolside or oceanview location. Rollaway beds can be rented for $10, and cribs cost $5. The Ocean Plaza offers free HBO and a conference center. The recently opened Dolphin Reef Restaurant, bridging two of the motel buildings, serves breakfast, lunch, and dinner seven days a week.

Bed-and-Breakfasts

Hunter House
1701 Butler Avenue
Tybee Island, GA
(912) 786–7515
$$$

When John Hunter purchased a beach house on the southern end of Butler Avenue with hopes of converting it into a bed-and-breakfast, he had his work cut out for him. It was 1988, and the fourteen-unit apartment house he bought was nicknamed "Animal House." Since then, Hunter has successfully converted the three-story, 1910 beach house into a four-room bed-and-breakfast, and one of Tybee's finer restaurants is also on the premises (see subsequent listing).

All rooms include queen beds and private baths with separate entrances and range in size from a single to a large, four-room suite complete with living room and small kitchenette. In one smaller room, you will find bright pink walls and a white wicker settee and matching headboard, while another includes a four-poster queen bed with a massive fireplace in the living area. There is a wonderful wrap-around porch perfect for relaxing and taking in the ocean breezes. It's a good place to enjoy your continental breakfast, which includes coffee, cereal, and other goodies. Hunter describes his establishment as having "Southern Charm with a Beach Atmosphere."

The Lighthouse Inn
16 Meddin Drive
Tybee Island, GA
(912) 786–0901
$$$

Susie Morris and her husband, Stuart Liles, opened this charming B&B in the fall of 2000 in a circa-1910 home they have restored. It features three fully decorated guest rooms and baths, as well as a front porch for relaxing. The couple lives on the ground floor. The location is close to the north beach (a less-developed segment of

A walk in the sand provides a close-up look at whitecaps. PHOTO: COURTESY OF SAVANNAH CONVENTION AND VISITORS BUREAU

Tybee's beaches) and the lighthouse (as the name no doubt cued you). The North Beach Grill is also close by.

Rentals

Tybee Beach Rentals, Inc.
Solomon Properties
211 Butler Avenue
Tybee Island, GA
(912) 786–8805, (800) 755–8562
Solomon Properties is a local company of Realtors with several private condos and homes for rent. Their offices are on the right after you round the bend (U.S. 80/Butler Avenue) heading toward downtown Tybee. Like all the rental agencies listed here, inside the offices are lists of properties, pictures, rates, and other valuable information. The rental rates seem outrageous compared with what they were a few years ago—$1,700 a week for a two-bedroom house that is near but not on the beach was a landlord's dream in, say, 1997. It's a reality today.

Tybee Island Realty
1016 1st Street
Tybee Island, GA
(912) 786–7070, (800) 379–2298
John and Judy O'Neill, a husband and wife team, own this real estate company, which also deals with several private rentals. You can stop in at the offices, located on your right a mile or so after crossing Lazaretto Creek Bridge into town, and pick up one of their rental brochures. Again, these give all the information you need: pictures of available properties, price ranges, and lists of amenities. When we stopped by, they had many listings—everything from ocean-front condos for $1,175 per week to beachfront homes that sleep fourteen for $2,500-plus a week. Many rentals were also available nightly.

Tybee Island Rentals, Inc.
U.S. Highway 80 and 2nd Avenue
Savannah, GA
(912) 786–4034, (800) 476–0807

Beach homes, condos, and cottages of all shapes and sizes can be rented from Tybee Island Rentals. Check out the varied selection at their offices, located about 2 miles past the bridge onto Tybee. Whether you are looking for a romantic getaway for two or a place to bring the whole family for a week at the beach, you should be able to find something that suits your needs. Choices include everything from a five-bedroom, six-bath home overlooking the ocean for $2,200 a week to a one-bedroom efficiency for $375. Remember that rates are seasonal.

Tybee Real Estate

Like the Historic Downtown in Savannah, Tybee has been one of the most popular places to buy real estate in the last few years. Prices have been on the rise and in many cases have jumped significantly—up to 50 percent in some cases. The small-town atmosphere, along with its proximity to Savannah, has made this island community attractive as a year-round residence for many.

This interest has led to some development and a few growing pains. After a large hotel went up on the beach, a movement was started to restrict the height of all development on Tybee to avoid a resort full of high-rises. Many residents want to keep the beach community what it is—a small town by the sea.

It is hard to identify distinct neighborhoods on Tybee. In some neighborhoods, you might find older beach houses next door to modest, one-story homes. A few doors down there could be two or three new homes or a set of two or three new town houses. Near Fort Screven or North Beach, you will find a few new housing developments that can offer large two- and sometimes three-story homes with ocean views and wraparound porches on fairly large lots. A few streets away there could be a modest home needing quite a lot of work. It's worth noting that streets often don't follow a particular pattern on Tybee; many are dirt roads that zig, zag, and in some cases just stop.

Tybee's older beach homes are usually found along Butler Avenue, the city's main thoroughfare, which goes to the southern end of the island. Here the streets follow a grid pattern with the numbered streets increasing the closer you get to downtown. Again, in many blocks, there is a smattering of new homes followed by several older ones. During the last few years, many older homes have been torn down to make room for condos, town homes, and the like. Single-family homes on the island range from around $100,000 for an older two- or three-bedroom home up to more than $500,000 for a large home with an ocean view. All new homes must be built several feet off the ground to prevent flooding. The realty companies listed earlier are ready to assist you with inquiries concerning the Tybee Island real estate scene. Call for more details.

Restaurants

Tybee's restaurant scene is evolving. Locals don't have to be that old to remember when most eateries were burger and ice-cream joints where you could come in

your bathing suit, and where you were likely to find the door locked shortly after Labor Day. Those places are still there, but they have been joined by a sprinkling of reasonable family restaurants. Latest on the scene: upscale dining that draws a dinner crowd of Savannahians willing to make a moonlight drive through the marshes for dishes with Caribbean flair or seafood with a sophisticated sauce. It personifies Tybee, in a way—white linen tablecloths and a lengthy wine list in a restaurant next to a trailer park, and no one thinking anything strange about it. One thing you won't find (and another personification of Tybee's individuality) is much in the way of fast-food franchises—with the exception of an Arby's—a burger joint on Tybee is going to be named something like Earl's instead of McDonald's.

Price-Code Key

Each listing contains a pricing code representing the amount two adults can expect to pay for a standard meal, not including alcoholic beverages, appetizers, tax, or tip. Of course, what you pay can vary widely, so use this as a general guide. Unless otherwise noted, all these establishments take major credit cards.

$	$10 or less
$$	$11 to $20
$$$	$21 to $30
$$$$	$31 or more

The Breakfast Club
1500 Butler Avenue
Tybee Island, GA
(912) 786–5984
$–$$

If you want to get a table at The Breakfast Club without waiting in line, you may have to get up a little early, especially during the summer months. Lines start forming outside this very popular eatery about 7 A.M. on weekends. During the week, sleep in much past 8:30 A.M., and you will most likely find yourself waiting outside with a handful of other people. Regardless, it is worth the wait. As the line (which

Enjoy the beauty of the sea with a meal along the water. PHOTO: COURTESY OF SAVANNAH CONVENTION AND VISITORS BUREAU

moves fast) attests, this diner on the southern end of the island near downtown is one of Tybee's best. For more than twenty years, members of the Farrow family have been serving up breakfast specialties like chorizo con huevos (flour tortillas, sausage, sharp cheese, salsa, and sour cream) and pecan waffles. For $8.95 you can get the surf and turf omelette, complete with fresh rib eye and local shrimp with garlic butter. While omelettes are a menu favorite, you will also find many other choices, from grits to burgers. Chef Jodee Sadowsky, who purchased the diner from his mother, Helen Farrow, was named one of North America's 101 best cooks in *Cooking Across America*. After the season, when the locals reclaim the island, you'll find them sitting here, sharing the gossip.

The Crab Shack
40 Estill Hammock Road
Tybee Island, GA
(912) 786–9857
$$

Going to the Crab Shack is as much about atmosphere as it is about great seafood. Located in Chimney Creek, a hamlet off U.S. 80 just past the Lazaretto Creek Bridge (you can't miss the signs), the Crab Shack's motto is, "Where the Elite Eat in Their Bare Feet." What started as a small, rustic restaurant on the marsh has grown into a tourist and local favorite. While munching on giant servings of seafood delicacies like Georgia blue crab, snow crab, golden crab, Alaskan king crab, shrimp, and oysters, you can sit out on the huge porch overlooking the marsh. Oak trees decorated with white lights give The Crab Shack a casual, relaxed, fun flair. If you want to try a local specialty, try the Lowcountry boil, which includes boiled shrimp, corn, potatoes, and sausage. As for drinks, the frozen margarita is a good choice along with the pina coladas and daiquiris. Dress is casual. The restaurant can handle parties of up to 150 people and recently added a separate gift shop, dubbed (what else?) The Gift Shack. Some scenes from the movie *The General's Daughter*, starring John Travolta, were shot here in the summer of 1998, which is appropriate—the place has a movie set feel anyway.

Fannie's on the Beach
1613 Strand
Tybee Island, GA
(912) 786–6109
$$

This restaurant and bar, which commands an ocean view across a parking lot, recently added an upstairs outdoor deck for dining and a band on the weekend. It's open lunch, dinner, and late night. Specialties include a shrimp burger—a concoction made of ground shrimp, sautéed onions, and celery. Quesadillas are meals, not appetizers, and include shrimp and scallop varieties. They also offer sandwiches, salads, and burgers, but the staff considers the pizzas to be the signature dish. You can get everything from the standard version to one sporting smoked salmon, capers, cream cheese, scallion, black olives, and sun-dried tomatoes. After dark, the club atmosphere comes to the fore and the band cranks up in summer, playing for a crowd of diverse couples.

Georges' on Tybee
1105 U.S. Highway 80 E.
Tybee Island, GA
(912) 786–9730
$$$$

This is one of Tybee's priciest restaurants, but it's worth that price. The proprietors of the North Beach Grill, George Spriggs and George Jackson (see listing), staked out a spot a couple of rungs up the socioeconomic ladder for their second restaurant, where a talented team of chefs produces what they dub American fusion cuisine. Look here for such creations as grilled grouper on a bed of corn vinaigrette and limas with Tasso ham and a puree of Vidalia onion ($20). Or there's grilled beef tenderloin with oven-roasted purple potatoes, sautéed cauliflower,

grilled asparagus, local lump crab, and mustard-cream sauce ($27). The menu is intentionally small—say, eight entrees covering seafood, beef, chicken, and even a vegetarian offering—but widened by a large selection of generous appetizers. There is an extensive wine list and a full bar, along with a dessert menu that most diners would find a challenge after the large portions. This is definitely an upscale restaurant, and not a place to wear your beach duds, but because it is in a beach community, the dress code is a little more relaxed than the menu and atmosphere would otherwise imply. (Translation: Guys can get by without a jacket and tie, but they won't feel odd with one, either.) The restaurant launched in the summer of 1998, and so far the clientele is largely Savannahians looking for an event dinner. Reservations strongly recommended.

The Grill Beachside
404 Butler Avenue
Tybee Island, GA
(912) 786–4745
$$–$$$

One of the nice things about Tybee is its unpredictability. Where else, we figure, could you walk into what you assume is a typical restaurant linked to the adjoining family-style motel and find a casual but sophisticated restaurant with an islands flair? The decor is bright and chic, but don't let that deter you if you're casually dressed—proprietor George Hammer knows it's the beach. (Hey, it's right outside the back door.) Choose from an array of seating options: the indoor restaurant, the shaded patio, and a large deck overlooking the beach itself, complete with outdoor kitchen. The lunch menu runs to grilled sandwiches, burgers, and salads, while dinner dresses up with such entrees as pan-seared scallops with champagne buere blanc sauce or rack of lamb. There's a full bar and occasional live musical entertainment. They also have a kid's menu.

Hunter House
1701 Butler Avenue
Tybee Island, GA
(912) 786–7515
$$$$

Hunter House was the first of Tybee's current crop of formal restaurants. Housed in a 1910 bed-and-breakfast at the southern tip of the city's main thoroughfare, it features three intimate dining rooms that seat only a few people at a time. Wooden walls line the entryway, and each room is decorated in simple and sophisticated decor. Owner John Hunter says he likes the small size of his restaurant and would rather concentrate on serving forty quality meals instead of sixty or more mediocre ones. Offerings include seafood Patrick, which is jumbo shrimp broiled in olive oil, wine, and garlic and served with buttered pasta, fresh basil, tomato bits, and Asiago cheese. There's also chicken, steaks, and a wide range of appetizers. Because of the restaurant's small size and popularity, reservations are recommended.

MacElwees
101 Lovell Avenue
Tybee Island, GA
(912) 786–4259
$$

Here's a good basic seafood restaurant, nothing fancy, but a nice place for a family to chow down on the likes of deviled crab, raw and steamed oysters, and fried seafood of all types. Steaks, hamburgers, and fried chicken fingers are available for those who haven't mastered seafood yet. The most adventurous dish is a shrimp scampi with a red sauce that includes Southern Comfort—a dish we can't personally vouch for (we prefer the fried shrimp), but it does sound interesting. MacElwees has been a Tybee staple for sixteen years and while haute cuisine it ain't, it is fresh, simply prepared, and ample. Open for lunch and dinner but closed Sundays. Don't let the address fool you: It says Lovell Avenue but its faces Butler

right as it sweeps around the curve and the ocean comes into view.

The North Beach Grill
41-A Meddin Drive
Tybee Island, GA
(912) 786–9003
$$$

The North Beach Grill is one of those places you have to go looking for but are glad once you find it (it's sorta beside the Tybee Museum, across the parking lot from the lighthouse). Located steps from the sand on Tybee's North Beach, it specializes in long, relaxing dinners with a Caribbean flair. If you are in a hurry, you might want to try someplace else. Sit out on the patio or inside the small, inviting dining room to enjoy the many menu choices—there is a constantly evolving set of entrees and appetizers. You will find things like plantain, jerk chicken, jerk salmon, crab cakes, flounder, and much more from which to pick.

The restaurant is one of those entrepreneur dream stories where two friends tired of working for others in the restaurant business and launched their own effort in what was little more than a shack at the time. (They've since launched Georges', described in a previous listing.) It has become a place Savannahians have added to their repertoire for entertaining visiting guests.

Tango Restaurant and Tropical Bar
1106 Highway 80 E.
Tybee Island, GA
(912) 786–8264
$$$$

This is Tybee's newest hip eatery, and the locals who have discovered it are keeping it plenty busy. The restaurant, decorated in bright tropical colors, overlooks a beautiful marsh view that isn't even hinted at from the front. The drinks run to the sweet, the frozen, and the decorated with plastic trinkets—but the kitsch is done tongue in cheek. The food is the real star, and it plays off an international tropical theme. The Tango Pu-Pu Platter includes fritters, calamari, empanades, spring rolls, and Chinese satay ($15.95 for two). From entrees, consider Voo Doo Mahi Mahi ($16.95), blackened with corn and tomato salsa. There are beef, chicken, and pork selections to accompany the broad seafood range, and even a vegetarian plate. Reservations are a good idea during spring and summer.

Keeping Up

If you want to keep up with the changing schedule of events at Tybee, here's a couple of sources.

The Tybee News
P.O. Box 785
Tybee Island, GA
(912) 786–8689

Maybe you find it hard to think of a publication that comes out once a month as a newspaper, but it works fine for Tybee. You can pick this little publication up free at several locations—we always go by the Tybee branch of the public library when we want one. Granted, large chunks of it aren't going to appeal to visitors. If you are from out of town and you really *want* to read the verbatim minutes of the Tybee City Council meeting, you have been in the sun too long. On the other hand, it includes lots of useful information: a tide table, the hours of operation for the dump, the local cable TV lineup, church schedules, and so on. The ads are skewed toward visitors, too.

Tybee Visitors Center
Corner of Campbell and Butler
Tybee Island, GA
(800) 868–2322

You'll spot the Savannah Area Chamber of Commerce's Tybee Visitors Center as you approach the main drag. It's part of a complex of shops but impossible to miss. Inside, you'll find the usual collection of brochures and maps, plus someone to answer questions. Hours are 9 A.M. to 5

P.M. in the summer, varying considerably in the winter.

Things to Do

The Beach. OK, if you came to Tybee, it stands to reason you wanted to go to the beach. Actually, you have two options: South Beach, where the most development (restaurants, shops, entertainment, etc.) and largest crowds are, and North Beach, which is more residential in nature, although hardly what you'd call deserted. Go south for people watching, north for shelling. You're at South Beach when you park in Tybee's downtown, main-drag Strand area. North Beach parking is across from the lighthouse and behind the museum. At low tide, you can walk from one to the other, but if you miscalculate the incoming tide it can be a long walk around.

During the season, Tybee's beaches have lifeguards. Hours and days depend on the weather and crowds. The lifeguard stands are clustered near the public parking. Early on, they're only staffed on weekends. Don't take it for granted that there's a lifeguard on duty, and even if there is, they call it a day when the crowd starts to thin. Be careful! Ocean swimming can be tricky, even for the strong swimmer.

Beach regulations prohibit glass containers or cans. Dogs aren't allowed on the beach, either, and you'll get a ticket if you bring one. The beach is patrolled by officers in shorts and T-shirts, either walking or on all-terrain vehicles.

A quaint cottage houses the Tybee Island Visitors Center and a gift/antique shop. PHOTO: BETTY DARBY

Vendors on the beach rent canvas rafts, umbrellas, boogie boards, and the like.

The Tybee Arts Association
P.O. Box 2344
Tybee Island, GA
(912) 786–5920

This nonprofit group is dedicated to developing and promoting arts throughout the area. Besides operating the Lighthouse Gallery near Tybee Lighthouse, the organization holds exhibits and gives art classes for adults and children. Adult classes can include pottery, stained-glass making, and painting, while children's classes include wearable art, make-your-own puppet, sand and beach art, and painting and drawing, among others. Weekly classes are $60; times vary.

Tybee Island Marine
Science Center
14th Street Parking Lot
Tybee Island, GA
(912) 786–5917

Learn about Tybee's marine life at the Tybee Island Marine Science Center. Located just steps from the sand in the 14th Street Parking Lot, the center has aquariums with species indigenous to the area, such as starfish and jellyfish. There is a small library, a touch tank, and displays featuring such things as sharks and shells—always favorites with the kids. Don't expect anything polished or Sea Worldish, but it is informative. Beach walks are one of the most popular programs offered. Folks are invited to stroll the beach to learn about the things that inhabit it. The center staff also throws a seine net into the ocean to see what they might catch. The center is open Monday through Saturday from 9 A.M. to 4 P.M. and from 1 to 4 P.M. on Sunday. Admission? A modest $1.

Tybee Museum
30 Meddin Drive
Tybee Island, GA
(912) 786–4077

Besides learning about Tybee's history, visitors to the Tybee Museum get to walk around one of the few remaining structures at the former Fort Screven. Inside Battery Garland, one of the original seven gun batteries built at the fort, you can learn about hundreds of years of Tybee lore—from the arrival of Native Americans to Tybee's role in the Civil War to the beginning of tourism on the island. From April 1 to Labor Day, the museum is open 10 A.M. to 6 P.M. every day but Tuesday. After Labor Day, it is open from noon to 4 P.M. on weekdays (except Tuesdays), and from 10 A.M. to 4 P.M. on weekends. Admission is $4 for adults, $3 for seniors and children ages 6 to 14; children five and younger get in free. The fee includes admission to the Tybee Island Lighthouse just across the street (see listing).

Tybee Pier and Pavilion
16th Street

The $2.5-million wooden pier was unveiled in time for the 1996 Summer Olympics, when the yachting events were held in the area. It was built in almost the exact location of the Tybrisa, Tybee's former pier and pavilion that was known for its big band concerts before it burned several years ago. Wander out to the end of the pier, and you will witness anglers casting into the ocean to see what they might catch. You can rent fishing poles and bait on the pier, and you can pick up a snack, too. The pier's pavilion, a large wooden platform you cross before heading out over the ocean, is also a popular spot for concerts. While in town, check the *Tybee News* to see if a concert is taking place while you are here. Concerts are often free. It's also a good place for a romantic evening stroll without getting your feet wet.

Hitting the Beach with "Crawfish" Crawford

There is good news for swimmers diving into the ocean off Tybee, according to John "Crawfish" Crawford, a University of Georgia educator and expert on Tybee and its marine life. The thirty to forty species of sharks lurking in the waters offshore probably aren't that hungry.

"We have well-fed sharks here," said Crawford. "The water is full of plenty of food which they would rather eat instead of fooling with something the size of a human being."

Words to live by. Although shark attacks are so rare they are nearly unheard of on Tybee, Crawford says to reduce your risk even further by avoiding swimming during twilight hours when sharks typically feed. Also, don't use a flutter kick—to a shark it could sound like a wounded fish.

Besides sharks, beachgoers might encounter an abundance of other marine life on Tybee, according to Crawford. Some of the more common things you might come across during your day at the beach include:

Sandpipers—These tiny, fleet-footed birds seen running up and down the beach are born and nest in the Arctic tundra. They fly all the way to Tybee just to engage in a little 50-yard beach dash for food.

Ghost Crabs—Look near the dune line, and you might see whitish-colored crabs scurrying then disappearing into a hole. Besides spending their time digging their hole homes, these crabs serve as beach garbage collectors, picking up parts of dead fish and others things cluttering their front yards.

Jellyfish—Several different species of jellyfish live in our waters. The cannonball variety has a brown rim around the edge, and you can't be stung by them. The sea nettle, which comes out typically in the late summer and has long wispy tentacles, is responsible for the most stings off Tybee. If you get stung, putting meat tenderizer on the sting helps ease the pain, according to Crawford.

Tybee Island offers picture-perfect landscapes, but its waters are filled with surprises—from ghost shrimp to jellyfish. PHOTO: COURTESY OF TYBEE ISLAND CHAMBER OF COMMERCE

Ghost Shrimp—If you run across tiny holes just above the low-tide line, you most likely have encountered a ghost shrimp. These tiny shrimp live in a network of burrows that twist and turn in the sand and are only three-fourths of an inch in diameter. Those little brown things you see near the entrance of the hole are their droppings.

Sand Dollars—These small disks are actually live animals. Many people mistakenly take them home while they are still alive, Crawford said. If you find a sand dollar on the beach and it is a greenish color on top and reddish on the bottom, it is still alive, so leave it on the beach. A white color indicates that the sand dollar has died.

Sting Rays—If you happen to see a sting ray while swimming in the surf, don't panic—they aren't aggressive and won't bother you a bit. If you happen to be unfortunate enough to step on a sting ray, however, they do consider this an attack and will sting. To avoid such a confrontation, shuffle your feet back and forth while walking in the surf. This gives them enough time to realize you are coming and head in a different direction.

Sea Turtle Nests—Sea turtles regularly nest on Tybee Island. The city's public works department patrols the beaches for the nests to mark them with wire so people don't run over them. If you do run across a nest, don't disturb it.

Tybee Island Lighthouse
30 Meddin Drive
Tybee Island, GA
(912) 786–5801

Throughout history there have actually been four Tybee Island Lighthouses. The original was completed in 1736, but it sat too close to the shore and was washed away during a storm. Hurricanes, fires, and even an attack by Union forces during the Civil War led to partial or complete destruction of two other stations. In 1866, the fourth Tybee Lighthouse was authorized and was a combination of old and new. It used the lower sixty-five feet of the 1773 Tybee Light as the base, then ninety-four more feet were stacked on top. The light, a first-order Fresnel lens, was displayed for the first time October 1, 1867, and it has been there ever since. It is one of only two of the fifteen original light stations built in Georgia that is still functioning.

Learn about the history of the lighthouse and take a 154-foot climb to the top for a wonderful view of the area. From April 1 to Labor Day the lighthouse is open 9 A.M. to 6 P.M. every day except Tues-days. After Labor Day, it is open from 9 A.M. to 4 P.M. on weekdays (except Tuesdays). During weekends after Labor Day and before April, it is open from 10 A.M. to 4 P.M. Cost is $4 for adults, $3 for seniors and children 6 to 14; children younger than six get in free. The price includes admission to the Tybee Museum (see listing). A major restoration project spruced things up in 1998 and 1999.

Fort Pulaski National Monument
U.S. 80 E.
Tybee Island, GA
(912) 786–5787

Explore a nineteenth-century fort from top to bottom at Fort Pulaski. Located about 15 miles outside Savannah on the way to Tybee, the fort is remarkably preserved and gives a fascinating glimpse into coastal warfare. The fort was completed in 1847 and considered the ultimate defense system of its day. Audio stations provide information on the fort's pivotal role in the Civil War and how it changed defense strategy worldwide after an attack by Union forces. The 5,600-acre monument also provides picnic areas, a

The Tybee Island Lighthouse is open to visitors. PHOTO: BETTY DARBY

boat ramp, and nature trails, along with panoramic views of the Atlantic Ocean and scenic salt marshes. Bring your camera—this is one of the area's most photogenic spots. The fort is open from 8:30 A.M. to 5:15 P.M. Cost is $2. Children sixteen and under enter free.

Lazaretto Creek Marina
U.S. 80 E., just across Lazaretto Creek Bridge
Tybee Island, GA
(912) 786–5848, (800) 242–0166
Dolphin tours, fishing, diving, and sunset cruises are offered at Lazaretto Creek Marina. Rates for dolphin tours are $5 to $12; offshore fishing ranges from $250 to $850, depending on the length of the trip.

Atlantic Star Casino Cruises
Lazaretto Creek Marina
Tybee Island, GA
(912) 786–7827
Floating casinos that cruise outside the territorial waters and then open up the slot machines and blackjack tables have become fixtures in seaside towns, and Tybee has its own. Cruises are held nightly except Tuesday throughout the week, with matinees on weekends. Tickets are $9.95 per person. Reservations are requested. Food and drink are available.

Tybee Island Branch,
CEL Regional Library
405 Butler Avenue
Tybee Island, GA
(912) 786–7733
Chances are there aren't too many public libraries around with an ocean view. Granted, you have to have pretty good eyes to see it, but the view is there, along with an impressive entryway sculpture by ironwork artist Ivan Bailey. (Look up, it's in the ceiling.)

Local library regulations are very kind to guests. Here, as elsewhere in Chatham County, nonresidents can buy a temporary library card with full privileges for only $2.50 (nonrefundable) and it's good for a year. (Library cards are free to residents.)

The collection includes books, magazines, audiobooks, and videotapes. The branch is not large, but it has access to the library system's full collection, if you can wait for delivery.

Shopping

Tybee isn't exactly a shopper's paradise, but you can buy what you need. Beach essentials and tacky souvenirs are easy to come by in a variety of stores clustered around the action. Some places merit more attention, however, and we mention a few of them here.

T.A.G.
Corner of Butler and Campbell
Tybee Island, GA
(912) 786–9244
The name stands for Tybee Antiques and Gifts. Owner Robert Mack has collected about twenty-five dealers under the roof of a renovated house for a unique consignment shop that includes local arts and crafts, collectibles, and a smattering of antiques. A recent visit turned up some conventional seascapes, seashell wreaths, antique dolls, used paperbacks, trinkets, and knickknacks. Good browsing grounds for the dedicated junk afficianado, and good refuge when a shower drives you off the beach.

Tybee Market
1111 Butler Avenue
Tybee Island, GA
(912) 786–4601
The mark of a dedicated Tybee Islander is a refusal to leave the island unless he absolutely has to. That makes Tybee's only grocery store (aside from numerous convenience stores) a godsend for some. It's small and the selection is limited, but it serves the purpose. If you are whipping up a complex recipe in your vacation digs, you might have better luck in the conventional supermarkets you drove past on the suburban islands on your way out to Tybee.

T. S. Chu Co.
6 Tybrisa Street
Tybee Island, GA
(912) 786–4561

T. S. Chu immigrated from China early last century and slept in the dunes until he got things going financially. And get them going he did. His early enterprise has grown to a prosperous local retail empire. For the most part, it's convenience stores and gas stations. But the original store remains on Tybee, a sprawling, dimly lit and unconventional place that sells tourist junk and beach supplies near the door and lightbulbs, hammers, dishpans, and other housewares and hardware farther inside.

Reenactors stage a cannon firing at Fort Pulaski National Monument.

PHOTO : PHYL M. GATLIN

Index

About the Authors

Rich Wittish

When Rich Wittish took a job with the daily newspaper in Savannah in 1974, he intended to stay for a short while, then move on to a larger media market. The charm and leisurely lifestyle of the region won him over, and more than twenty years later, he continues to enjoy the city and its surrounding areas. He and his wife, Linda, often spend parts of their weekends rediscovering the pleasures of meandering through the squares of Savannah's Historic Downtown or strolling on the beach at nearby Tybee Island.

Rich feels that one of Savannah's most attractive qualities is its size—it's large enough to be interesting and small enough to make you feel at home. That atmosphere reminds him of the city where he grew up, Jacksonville, Florida, and the way it was in the late 1950s and '60s before it boomed and became the "Bold New City of the South."

Although Rich was born in New Jersey, he considers himself a Southerner. He spent his boyhood in north Florida, attended college at Auburn University in Alabama, was stationed in rural North Carolina during much of his time in military service, and is married to a lady who's a Georgia country girl at heart. Rich came to Savannah after serving almost five years in the U.S. Air Force, a stint he began immediately after graduating from Auburn with a degree in journalism. He was a navigator and attained the rank of captain while employed by Uncle Sam.

After fulfilling his military obligation, Rich left the Air Force to see if he could put into practice what he had learned in college. He got plenty of opportunities at the *Savannah Morning News* while covering a variety of beats as a reporter—including police, politics, and business—and serving as an editor on the city desk and in the state news department. During his last seven years at the *Morning News*, Rich headed up the company's community newspapers department.

After working at the paper for twenty-two years, Rich decided in May 1996 to go in a somewhat different direction and try his hand at freelance writing. Since then, he's coauthored a book on the aviation history of Savannah, done some public relations work, and written numerous articles for *Savannah Magazine* and *The Savannah Business Report and Journal*, a newspaper that focuses on the local business community.

Rich and Linda are the parents of a daughter, Erica Wittish Parker, who works as a teacher and coach. In addition to staying in touch with what Erica and her husband, Josh, are doing, the Wittishes keep busy with activities at their church, First Presbyterian, where they are involved with the congregation's community outreach ministries.

Betty Darby

Betty Darby is a journalist who has made Savannah her home since 1980.

She is a 1977 graduate of the University of Georgia, where she majored in journalism and minored in political science. She even studied Russian, with some vague idea of covering the 1980 Olympics in the Soviet Union. The subsequent American decision not to participate in those games was a bit of a relief, since she hadn't mastered much of the language.

Betty got her first newspaper assignment in the summer following her freshman year at college, working for the *Rome* (Ga.) *News-Tribune* in her hometown. She returned to the paper for summer and holiday breaks throughout her college years, then joined the reporting staff full-time. She later took a reporting position with the *Savannah Morning News,* where she covered various hard-news beats along with writing movie reviews and serving a stint as a copy editor. Over the course of her newspaper years, Betty covered politics, crime, and education; wrote features; and interviewed subjects ranging from John Wayne on his final movie promotion junket to George Bush in his vice presidential years.

After nine years with the Savannah newspapers, she moved into public relations and marketing work with public schools for several years. Later, she wrote and edited a quarterly magazine for a Savannah hospital. Betty currently is the managing editor of *The Savannah Business Report and Journal,* a niche publication covering business news along the entire Georgia Coast and in Hilton Head Island, South Carolina. She teaches creative writing courses in local continuing education programs. She continues to write for magazines and other outlets and occasionally dusts off a half-finished novel manuscript she's working on.

While in Savannah, Betty has ranged wide over the city's residential real estate. She has lived on some of the grandest squares in the Historic Downtown (albeit in some of the humbler apartments) and in the suburban enclaves of the Islands area. She has now settled in the city's Midtown section in a circa-1930s bungalow.